Foundations of Cognitive Grammar

VOLUME I
Theoretical Prerequisites

FOUNDATIONS

OF COGNITIVE

GRAMMAR

◻ **VOLUME I** ◻

Theoretical Prerequisites

Ronald W. Langacker

Stanford University Press   Stanford, California   1987

Stanford University Press
Stanford, California
© 1987 by the Board of Trustees of the
Leland Stanford Junior University
Printed in the United States of America

CIP data appear at the end of the book

Preface

FOR A LINGUIST, these are fascinating and exciting times. In the past quarter century linguistics has emerged as a separate discipline and established its intellectual significance. It has attracted ever increasing numbers of able scholars and fostered the investigation of virtually every aspect of language through a rich variety of techniques and approaches. The period has consequently witnessed an unprecedented expansion in both our factual knowledge of languages and our analytical understanding of linguistic structure.

Still, many linguists are less than satisfied with the current state of the discipline, especially in regard to linguistic theory. An extraordinary amount of time and energy is devoted to theoretical concerns, but whether this investment has paid proportional dividends is subject to legitimate dispute. The absence of any kind of theoretical consensus is painfully apparent as we thrash about in an almost impenetrable thicket of conflicting theories, which continue to proliferate. In addition, many scholars are disturbed by both the narrowness of currently popular theories and their lack of naturalness. There is no comprehensive and unified theoretical framework available that successfully accommodates our growing factual and analytical knowledge of language structure in all of its many aspects, treating it naturally and insightfully as an integrated whole. In short, the overall picture is one of fragmentation and confusion.

My own dissatisfaction with the dominant trends in current theory is profound. It reaches to the deepest stratum of organizing principles: notions about what language is like and what linguistic theory should be concerned with. I believe that much of the confusion and inadequacy of mainstream theory flows directly from inappropriate decisions at this level, and from the uncritical acceptance of certain attitudes and assumptions (some of them tacit or unrecognized). Rightly or wrongly, I concluded some time ago that the conceptual foundations of linguistic theory were built on quicksand, and that the only remedy was to start over on firmer ground.

My attempt at finding solid ground, and building something of consequence

v

on it, began in the spring of 1976. Many of the central ideas coalesced within the first few years, but that was only the initial (and easiest) phase in the long process of developing, refining, motivating, and at last presenting a coherent body of proposals. On more than one occasion in the early years I started writing, completing several chapters of what was envisaged to be a massive work requiring many years to complete. These efforts were helpful to me, but premature; in writing the present volume I started again from scratch. Part I was circulated in preliminary form in 1982, Part II in 1983, and Part III in 1984. A comprehensive introduction to the framework I propose requires considerably more, but Parts I–III are capable of standing alone, so I am publishing them now as Volume I to ensure their timeliness and to make the basic ideas more generally accessible. I hope to complete Volume II within the next few years.

I initially called this framework **space grammar**. Why is not important—in fact, there are so many good reasons to so label it that an "official" explanation would only impoverish the expression's value. But despite its obvious appropriateness, a number of people have reacted negatively to the apparent frivolity of the term, perhaps with some reason. A theory called space grammar can obviously not be taken seriously, but one called **cognitive grammar** is potentially of great intellectual significance. So as not to foreclose the possible significance of the model, I have opted for the latter term in this work.

The research that led to this volume was greatly facilitated in its early stages by a Guggenheim Fellowship for the 1978–79 academic year, and by two quarters of sabbatical granted by UCSD in 1983. The UCSD Linguistics Department and Academic Senate kindly made funds available for duplicating and circulating preliminary versions of the manuscript. I gratefully acknowledge this support.

Many people have contributed in one way or another to the completion of this project. Deserving special mention are my wife Peggy for preparing the index and for her long-term, uncomplaining support; George Lakoff for help and encouragement in many forms, most notably in being the first well-known scholar to recognize that space grammar is not totally crazy (or at least the first to admit to this recognition); Larry Gorbet, for assembling the glossary and also for helpful discussion on many points; Jim McCawley, for his detailed and constructive criticism; and Dave Tuggy, who has helped me to wrestle (though not always to his satisfaction) with some fundamental issues that bear on the conceptual foundations of the model and with the specifics of its formulation.

Many others have helped significantly, in a variety of ways: by pertinent discussion; by their comments and criticism; by offering moral support and encouragement; by writing letters of recommendation; by calling relevant work to my attention (or even sending it to me); by their editorial support for my unorthodox positions; or by conducting research in the context of the framework. The alphabetical list that follows is certainly not exhaustive—no slight is intended for those not mentioned, nor in many cases is this brief acknowledgment really sufficient: Noriko Akatsuka, Julie Andresen, Zev Bar-Lev, Liz Bates, Ursula Bellugi-Klima, Dwight Bolinger, Bill Bright, Cecil Brown, Claudia Brugman, Frank Thomas Burke, William Carver, Wallace Chafe, Aaron Cicourel, Herb Clark, Alain Cohen, Bill Croft, Roy D'Andrade, Probal Dasgupta, Scott DeLancey, René Dirven, Pam Downing, Suzette Elgin, Jeff Elman, Gilles Fauconnier, Charles Fillmore, Erica García, Dedre Gentner, Cheng-ming Guo, John Haiman, Ken Hale, Eric Hamp, Heather Hardy, Leanne Hinton, Sue Hoover, Bill Jacobsen, Laura Janda, Mark Johnson, Paul Kay, Bob Kirsner, Ed Klima, Margaret Langdon, John Lawler, Kee-dong Lee, Odo Leys, David McNeill, Dan Morrow, Pam Munro, Geoff Nathan, Leonard Newmark, Elissa Newport, Don Norman, Rachel Reichman, Dave Rood, Brygida Rudzka-Ostyn, Dave Rumelhart, Sanford Schane, Hansjakob Seiler, Eve Sweetser, Len Talmy, Jeanne van Oosten, Chuck Walrad, David Waltz, Don Wayne, Don Wesling.

In addition, I offer special thanks to the many students who have participated in my classes on space grammar over the past decade, and who have been willing to take these ideas seriously despite their basic conflict with the received linguistic wisdom of our era. They include students at the undergraduate, graduate, and postdoctoral levels; from linguistics and from other disciplines; my own dissertation candidates and those of other professors. They are too numerous to mention individually, but their comments, questions, and papers, as well as their interest, encouragement, and tolerance of notions still in their formative stage, have done more than anything else to keep me going through the years. It is to all these students that I dedicate this book.

R.W.L.

Contents

Part III: Grammatical Organization   275

Foundations of Cognitive Grammar

VOLUME I
Theoretical Prerequisites

Introduction and Overview

MY OBJECTIVE in this work is to present and support a particular conception of grammatical structure. It emerges organically from a comprehensive and unified view of linguistic organization characterized in terms of cognitive processing. For this reason I will refer to the framework as **cognitive grammar**.[1]

Cognitive grammar is fundamentally at odds with the dominant trends in current linguistic theory. It speaks of imagery at a time when meaning is generally pursued with apparatus derived from formal logic. It claims the inseparability of syntax and semantics at a time when the status of syntax as an autonomous formal system is accepted by most theorists as established fact. It seeks an integrated account of the various facets of linguistic structure at a time when received wisdom calls for specialized theories dealing with numerous separate domains. Finally, at a time when formalization and rigorous argumentation are increasingly regarded as the sine qua non of viable linguistic inquiry, it suggests that these concerns must cede priority to a far more basic need: the conceptual clarification of fundamental issues.

The vital problems of current linguistic theory are not of a formal nature, but lie instead at the level of conceptual foundations. Let me offer two brief illustrations. One is the problem of figurative language, including idiomaticity, metaphor, and semantic extension. Figurative language is generally ignored in current theories; at best it is handled by special, ad hoc descriptive devices. Yet it would be hard to find anything more pervasive and fundamental in language, even (I maintain) in the domain of grammatical structure; if figurative language were systematically eliminated from our data base, little if any data would remain. We therefore need a way of conceiving and describing grammatical structure that accommodates figurative language as a natural, expected phenomenon rather than a special, problematic one. An adequate conceptual framework for linguistic analysis should view figurative language not as a problem, but as part of the solution.

The second illustration pertains to the definition of basic and traditional

[1] Boldface type is used for technical terms.

grammatical concepts such as **noun**, **verb**, **modifier**, **subject**, and **subordination**. Every linguist relies on these concepts, but few if any are prepared to define them in an adequate, explicit, and revealing way. In explaining such terms to students, we normally provide some examples, list some typical properties, and, perhaps, offer a crude verbal definition that we know to be unsatisfactory. The linguistic community has not yet achieved general, workable, deeply revelatory characterizations of these constructs in terms of more fundamental notions in the context of a coherent overall conceptual framework.

I think it reasonable to expect a linguistic theory to resolve such basic issues in a simple, natural, and intuitively satisfying manner. Resolving them, I contend, is not a matter of simply formalizing current knowledge, extrapolating from existing models, or treading cautiously along well-worn paths. Instead it requires a fresh perspective, an innovative approach permitting us to attack traditional problems in new and productive ways. Because cognitive grammar attempts to respond to this imperative, it demands of linguists a radical conceptual reorientation. It introduces a whole battery of new concepts, terms, and notations, which take some time to get accustomed to. It rejects a considerable number of prevalent theoretical assumptions, including certain tacit assumptions so deeply ingrained that their holders are barely conscious of them and have difficulty conceiving of alternatives. Beyond this, cognitive grammar differs from established theories in its basic organizing principles: what it seeks to accomplish, the data it considers, the questions it asks, what it accepts as persuasive evidence, and so on.

A concise and yet intelligible summary of the model is therefore difficult at best. A clear picture of how it analyzes grammatical structure can be presented only through extensive elucidation of its basic perspective and the introduction of a considerable array of concepts and descriptive devices. Further complicating the task is the fact that cognitive grammar is not a finished or formalized theory; it is more realistically viewed as an evolving conceptual framework. As such it is subject to significant modification and will require extension, elaboration, and more explicit formulation.

Nevertheless, its basic notions have crystallized into a relatively stable, highly integrated conceptual system whose general outlines can be sketched with fair precision. Central to its conception of grammatical structure are three closely related claims, which define the focal concern of this book:

1. Semantic structure is not universal; it is language-specific to a considerable degree. Further, semantic structure is based on conventional imagery and is characterized relative to knowledge structures.

2. Grammar (or syntax) does not constitute an autonomous formal level of representation. Instead, grammar is symbolic in nature, consisting in the conventional symbolization of semantic structure.

3. There is no meaningful distinction between grammar and lexicon. Lexicon, morphology, and syntax form a continuum of symbolic structures, which differ along various parameters but can be divided into separate components only arbitrarily.

The specific import of these claims should gradually become apparent over the course of many chapters. The coherence, adequacy, and insight of the overall model must be judged in similar fashion.

Earlier, more limited publications have offered only fragmentary glimpses of the total framework as I now envisage it. Of my own work, certain publications (1975, 1976) can be regarded as precursors; others (1978, 1979, 1982b) reflect earlier formulations of the model; and still others (1981b, 1981c, 1982a, 1984, 1985) present it in its current form. In a number of papers and dissertations, my students have applied the model—with a great deal of individual creativity and insight—to descriptive problems in a variety of languages: Eugene Casad has written on the Cora locational system (1982; Casad and Langacker 1985); Bruce Hawkins on English prepositions (1981, 1984); Susan Lindner on English verb-particle combinations (1981, 1982); David Tuggy on possessives and datives in Spanish (1980), and on the transitivity and morphology of Tetelcingo Nahuatl verbs (1981); and Claude Vandeloise on spatial terms in French (1984).

Every work is a product of its times, even one that pretends to the status of a radical innovation. Despite my profound disagreement with what can fairly be called the "mainstream" of contemporary theory, I cannot begin to cite or properly credit the vast amount of ongoing linguistic research that I regard as basically compatible with cognitive grammar. The heterogeneity of that research should not be allowed to conceal a shared appreciation of the richness and unified character of language in all its many aspects and manifestations, and a common concern for naturalness in linguistic theory and description. This kindred spirit overshadows any points of conflict, and unites a variety of approaches and outlooks into a loose-knit but synergistic collective enterprise seeking a viable alternative to the prevailing theoretical trends. "Natural grammar" would be a reasonable appellation for this overall enterprise.

Exhaustive enumeration of either scholars or their writings is out of the question, so I must characterize the enterprise by citing representative instances, with all due apologies for the many that are not specifically mentioned. One name that must be included is Dwight Bolinger, for many reasons, but most notably for his long-term commitment to elucidating the subtle detail of linguistic data and explicating the semantic value of grammatical morphemes and constructions (e.g. 1961, 1977). Chafe is noteworthy for his seminal efforts at constructing an alternative to the generative paradigm (1968, 1970), and Fillmore for his multifaceted contributions to semantics, especially in regard to deixis and "frames" (1975, 1977, 1982). Lakoff has long insisted on the need for a cognitively grounded approach to grammatical structure, the importance of naturalness in linguistic theory, the centrality of metaphor to language and our mental life, the critical nature of categorization, and the nonautonomy of grammar (1977, 1982, 1984a, 1984b, 1987; Lakoff and Thompson 1975; Lakoff and Johnson 1980; Lakoff and Kövecses 1983). Recent investigation of locative expressions, very significant in its own terms and convergent with the treatment of locatives in cognitive grammar, includes work by Brugman (1981), Herskovits (1982), and extensive contributions by Talmy (1975, 1977, 1978, 1983). Fauconnier's important research (1985) on the correspondences between "mental spaces" is very much in the spirit of cognitive grammar's projected approach to the problems he considers. I greatly appreciate Moore and Carling's views on the nonautonomy of linguistic structure (1982), Haiman's work on iconicity and his comments on encyclopedic semantics (1980, 1983), Hudson's efforts in developing "word grammar" (1984), and Wierzbicka's subtle and imaginative studies of meaning (1972, 1975, 1985). There is a natural affinity between cognitive grammar and several contemporary schools of research, among them variation theory (Bailey 1973) and the "Columbia school" (Diver 1982; Kirsner 1977, 1980; García 1977; García and Otheguy 1983). Especially significant is the vast program of research conducted by scholars in the "functional" tradition spearheaded by Givón (1979, 1983, 1984), including DeLancey (1981), Kuno (1980), Hopper and Thompson (1980), and numerous others. If cognitive grammar provides a unified way of describing the complete spectrum of linguistic structures, functional studies allow us to determine and explain their relative prototypicality.

Cognitive grammar is offered as an alternative to the generative tradition, and rejects many of its underlying assumptions. There are nevertheless a number of parallels to be noted between this framework and developments in one or another version of generative theory. Cognitive grammar is not in any significant sense an outgrowth of generative semantics, but it does share with that conception a concern for dealing explicitly with meaning, and for providing a unified account of grammar and lexicon (cf. Lakoff 1972; Langacker 1973b; Sadock 1980). Moreover, the trend in all versions of generative grammar has been towards greater emphasis on surface form and lesser reliance on transformational derivations from abstract underlying representations; some versions, for instance generalized phrase-structure grammar (Gazdar, Pullum, and Sag 1982), agree with cognitive grammar in doing away with such derivations altogether. Various people have noticed a similarity between cognitive grammar and Montague grammar (Partee 1975; Cooper 1980), particularly in the latter's association of a semantic rule with each syntactic rule; the two theories differ significantly in how this correlation is explicated, however, and quite drastically in their conception of linguistic semantics. The emphasis on lexicon in cognitive grammar parallels that of certain generative approaches, e.g. lexical-functional grammar (Bresnan 1982), and its treatment is similar in various respects to Jackendoff's full-entry proposal employing lexical redundancy rules (1975). There is some resemblance to X-bar syntax (Jackendoff 1977), including a means (namely schemas) for capturing cross-category generalizations. Cognitive grammar also agrees with Bresnan (1978) in seeking a psychologically realistic account of language structure that relates it directly to cognitive processing, and with Jackendoff (1978, 1983) in equating semantic structure with conceptual structure; it disagrees with both scholars on the existence of an autonomous syntactic component.

In its position on certain fundamental issues, cognitive grammar reflects a growing intellectual trend in the analysis of language and mind, away from a mechanistic conception and towards a conception more appropriate for biological systems. There are in fact a number of respects (e.g. its treatment of composition, discussed in Ch. 12) in which cognitive grammar can properly be regarded as an application to linguistics of general systems theory (cf. Laszlo 1972). Further, it considers discrete categorization based on necessary and sufficient conditions to be cognitively unrealistic, and emphasizes instead a prototype or "central tendencies" model (Rosch 1975, 1978; Hawkins 1984; Lakoff 1982). It also rejects the distinction between literal and figurative language (cf. Lindner 1981; Rumelhart 1979) and the adequacy of formal logic to model either thought in general or semantic structure in particular; more specifically, it holds that imagery and metaphor are not peripheral aspects of our mental life, but are in large measure constitutive of it (cf. Kosslyn 1980; Block 1981; Lakoff and Johnson 1980; Lakoff and Kövecses 1983; Ortony 1979). Finally, its emphasis on language use and its view of lexical meaning show many parallels to the later Wittgenstein (1953).

The most fundamental issue in linguistic theory is the nature of meaning and how to deal with it. I take it as self-evident that meaning is a cognitive phenomenon and must eventually be analyzed as such. Cognitive grammar therefore equates meaning with conceptualization (explicated as cognitive processing). In doing so, it conflicts with major traditions of semantic theory (much of which can be read as an elaborate attempt to avoid this conclusion), in particular with the many varieties of formal semantics based on truth conditions, as well as the newer "situation semantics" (Barwise and Perry 1983). Other approaches that identify meaning with conceptualization or cognitive processing include those of Chafe (1970), Miller and Johnson-Laird (1976), and Jackendoff (1983); but despite this similarity, cognitive grammar resembles these approaches very little at the level of specific detail.

Given its basic orientation, the framework shares many basic concerns with cognitive psychology and artificial intelligence. Quite a number of its ideas and assumptions have analogs in these other disciplines, and even greater convergence can be anticipated for the future. I should emphasize, though, that the origins and motivation of cognitive grammar are primarily linguistic; this reflects both my own background and my conviction that linguistic analysis provides the only solid basis for determining what is needed for a revealing account of language structure. Linguists cannot expect to walk into a psychology shop or an AI emporium and find an adequate model sitting on the shelf. They can, however, expect to find there a great many useful concepts and insights about language behavior and cognitive processes in general, and are well advised to design their own models for maximal compatibility with the findings of cognitive scientists.

Some portions of the present work can be regarded as an exercise in speculative psychology. I speak unabashedly about cognitive events, and sometimes go into considerable detail about their architecture and their relationships. All of this must be accepted in the proper spirit. Since I claim no privileged access to the operation of the human mind, there is obviously a substantial (some might say intolerable) element of speculation in any such proposals concerning the specifics of cognitive activity. Still, a cognitively grounded linguistic analysis must at some point receive a serious cognitive interpretation. My suggestions about specific cognitive events may well be off the mark, but it is not too early to start contemplating what a viable analysis at this level might look like. Two considerations induce me to use the term "speculation" for these proposals (as opposed to "sheer guesswork," "pure fiction," or "utter fantasy"). First, I have adhered rather strictly, in developing my proposals, to the dictates of both psychological plausibility and linguistic necessity; I have relied almost exclusively on seemingly indisputable cognitive abilities (e.g. the ability to compare two events and register a discrepancy between them), and I invoke them for linguistic constructs that must somehow be accommodated in any comprehensive and explicit analysis. Second, the overall system that emerges offers a certain coherence, which encourages me to think that it may be valid in many respects. At the very least we might learn something from its shortcomings.

Relative to more familiar linguistic theories, cognitive grammar is broad in scope and radically divergent in conception. A careful, comprehensive, and intelligible presentation of even its foundations (let alone the entire edifice) has therefore required a work of substantial heft, and a second volume is projected. The two volumes are conceived as mutually dependent components of a single work. Though there is considerable overlap in function, Volume I can be roughly characterized as mapping out the major theoretical proposals of a framework for cognitive grammar, and Volume II as applying them to the description of representative grammatical phenomena. Volume I can certainly be read and understood independently, but the notions advanced derive much of their support from their overall descriptive utility, which Volume II will attempt to demonstrate. I do not expect Volume I alone to provide a detailed understanding of how the model accommodates the many domains and interacting dimensions of language structure (though it does give many limited illustrations). Its function is rather to establish the philosophy of cognitive grammar; to lay out its conception of linguistic organization and the nature of grammatical structure; and to fashion the theoretical and descriptive tools required for the insightful characterization of linguistic structure.

Volume I has three parts. Part I addresses itself to organizing assumptions and basic concepts. The orientation it provides is critical because cognitive grammar runs counter to mainstream theory in many fundamental respects. Part II outlines cognitive grammar's notion of linguistic semantics. Semantic structure is characterized with reference to cognitive processing and considered to be encyclopedic in scope; and specific proposals are made for the semantic definition of basic grammatical categories, nouns and verbs in particular. Part III presents the general approach to grammatical structure, discussing in turn the nature of grammatical constructions, the symbolic elements that participate in these constructions, and questions relating to well-formedness and distribution. As presently conceived, Volume II will also have three parts: nominal structure will be dealt with in Part IV, verbal structure in Part V, and a variety of additional topics in Part VI.

☐ Part I ☐
ORIENTATION

BECAUSE THE OUTLOOK of cognitive grammar diverges so greatly from the current theoretical consensus, it is necessary to begin our exposition at the level of organizing assumptions and basic concepts. These are the topics of Chs. 1 and 2, respectively. Collectively, the notions advanced in these chapters amount to a fundamental revision in our view of language and its mode of description. I believe that such a revision is essential if we hope to achieve a natural and revealing account of linguistic structure.

Presented in Ch. 1 are the underlying assumptions that have guided the evolution of the conceptual framework. Some of them are very general assumptions about the nature of language and the various aspects of naturalness in linguistic description. Other assumptions pertain to linguistic methodology. There is considerable agreement about the general principles of scientific inquiry, but very little concerning the appropriate way of applying these principles to the particular problems of linguistic analysis.

Ch. 2 then outlines some fundamental concepts of cognitive grammar. The chapter first discusses the nature of a grammar; of particular importance are its nongenerative character and the indeterminacy of its scope. Next to be considered are symbolization and the sense in which grammar is said to be inherently symbolic. A variety of other notions are examined in conclusion.

CHAPTER I

Guiding Assumptions

WHAT ONE FINDS in language depends in large measure on what one expects to find. Too often these expectations are taken for granted, becoming so deeply ingrained in certain instances that their status as assumptions is not even recognized. I believe that many of the tacit assumptions underlying contemporary linguistic research are gratuitous at best, and very probably false. In this initial chapter I outline the basis for this belief, and also make as explicit as possible the assumptions that have guided my own work.

1.1. General Assumptions

I begin with some very general remarks concerning the nature of language and the way I propose to think about it. Even at this basic level of discussion, there are many vital issues to consider, some of them quite controversial.

1.1.1. *Symbolization*

Language is symbolic in nature. It makes available to the speaker—for either personal or communicative use—an open-ended set of linguistic **signs** or **expressions**, each of which associates a semantic representation of some kind with a phonological representation. I therefore embrace the spirit of classic

Fig. 1.1

Saussurean diagrams like Fig. 1.1, with the understanding that explicit, substantive characterization is required for the elements they depict.

My thinking, however, departs in certain ways from this classic conception. First, the arbitrary character of linguistic signs is easily overstated, despite the important kernel of truth in the principle of *l'arbitraire du signe*. An obvious but seldom-made observation is that any polymorphemic linguistic sign (this includes the vast majority of expressions) is nonarbitrary to the extent that it is analyzable. For example, given that *staple* means what it does, and that *-er* means what it does, it is anything but arbitrary that *stapler* is the form used in English for a stapling device.[1] The principle is therefore limited largely to individual morphemes, but even here it must be significantly qualified. I refer not only to obvious cases of onomatopoeia, but more broadly to the pervasive influence of analogy and subtle forms of sound symbolism as constant contributory (though seldom determinative) factors in the gradual evolution of our lexical stock (cf. Rhodes and Lawler 1981; Samuels 1972; Haiman 1983). Second, and more important, my conception of language as symbolic in nature extends beyond lexicon to grammar. I will argue that morphological and syntactic structures themselves are inherently symbolic, above and beyond the symbolic relations embodied in the lexical items they employ (see 2.2 and Langacker 1982a).

From the symbolic nature of language follows the centrality of meaning to virtually all linguistic concerns. Meaning is what language is all about; the analyst who ignores it to concentrate solely on matters of form severely impoverishes the natural and necessary subject matter of the discipline and ultimately distorts the character of the phenomena described. But it is not enough to agree that meaning is important if this results, say, merely in positing a separate semantic "component," treating grammar separately as an autonomous entity. I contend that grammar itself, i.e. patterns for grouping morphemes into progressively larger configurations, is inherently symbolic and hence meaningful.[2] Thus it makes no more sense to posit separate grammatical and semantic components than it does to divide a dictionary into two components, one listing lexical forms and the other listing lexical meanings. Grammar is simply the structuring and symbolization of semantic content; for a linguistic theory to be regarded as natural and illuminating, it must handle meaning organically rather than prosthetically.

1.1.2. *Cognition*

Language is an integral part of human cognition. An account of linguistic structure should therefore articulate with what is known about cognitive processing in general, regardless of whether one posits a special language "mod-

---

[1] The form is conventional, inasmuch as another form could perfectly well have been chosen for this concept, but it is not arbitrary in the sense of being unmotivated, given the existence of other signs.

[2] For instance, the phonological integration of *staple* and *-er* to form a single word symbolizes their semantic integration to yield a composite semantic structure.

ule" (Fodor 1983), or an innate *faculté de langage*. If such a faculty exists, it is nevertheless embedded in the general psychological matrix, for it represents the evolution and fixation of structures having a less specialized origin. Even if the blueprints for language are wired genetically into the human organism, their elaboration into a fully specified linguistic system during language acquisition, and their implementation in everyday language use, are clearly dependent on experiential factors and inextricably bound up with psychological phenomena that are not specifically linguistic in character. Thus we have no valid reason to anticipate a sharp dichotomy between linguistic ability and other aspects of cognitive processing. Instead of grasping at any apparent rationale for asserting the uniqueness and insularity of language, we should try more seriously to integrate the findings of linguistics and cognitive psychology.

There is of course no question that people have the capacity to learn a language, and that this involves innate structures and abilities. What is controversial is whether some of these structures and abilities are unique to language, possibly constituting a separate modular package with special properties not reflective or derivative of other, more general cognitive functions. In my opinion a convincing case has not yet been made for a unique linguistic faculty. To put it contentiously, language has appeared special and unassimilable to broader psychological phenomena mainly because linguists have insisted on analyzing it in an inappropriate and highly unnatural fashion; once the many layers of artifact are removed, language starts to look much more natural and learnable in terms of what we know about other facets of human cognitive ability. Certainly cognitive grammar offers a conception of linguistic structure that makes it possible at least to entertain the notion that a special *faculté de langage* can be dispensed with. I hasten to add, though, that I take no position on the matter at present, nor does the question appear to have any overriding significance in assessing the viability of the proposed framework. I have some doubt that either linguistic or cognitive studies have advanced to the point where the issue can be addressed in truly substantive terms.

1.1.3. *Naturalness*

It is common for linguists (myself included) to describe their own analyses as **natural**, reserving the term **unnatural** for the analyses of other investigators. From this one deduces that naturalness is something to be desired in a linguistic description. Yet the term natural is elusive and largely unexplicated, having so little intrinsic content that in practice it easily comes to mean simply "in accordance with my own ideas." Because I take naturalness to be an essential criterion for evaluating linguistic theories and analyses, I feel obliged to give the notion some substance, if only quite informally.

I regard a description as natural to the extent that it deals with data in their own terms, with full regard for the richness, subtlety, and complexity characteristic of linguistic phenomena. I regard a description as unnatural, or **ar-**

tifactual, to the extent that it deals with data in a way that does violence to their intrinsic organization, however convenient this may be for the analyst. Artifactuality can be a sin of omission, done by the linguist when he extracts a phenomenon from its supporting matrix and treats it in isolation as an autonomous entity, or when he focuses on one of its dimensions to the exclusion of all others. It can also be a sin of commission, done by imposing on the data various constructs or boundaries that have no analog in reality. In practice, of course, every linguistic description is a mixture of naturalness and artifactuality, and there is certainly some truth in the view that analysis and description inevitably distort their subject matter, since they cannot *be* their subject matter. But from the fact that nothing is perfect it does not follow that everything is equal. We will do well to resist the prevalent tendency for artifactual devices to be accepted by virtue of familiarity alone.

Being abstract, the foregoing comments are probably uncontroversial. The problem arises in evaluating specific descriptive claims; assessing the naturalness of a description presupposes some preliminary conception of the phenomenon described, and linguists are bound to disagree on this score. I leave to others the philosophical question of whether such disagreements can be resolved. My only concern will be to articulate my own assumptions about what constitutes naturalness in linguistic descriptions. To do this, I will organize the discussion under the general rubrics of **discreteness**, **substance**, and **complexity**.

1.1.4. *Discreteness*

Much in language is a matter of degree. Linguistic relationships are not invariably all-or-nothing affairs, nor are linguistic categories always sharply defined and never fuzzy around the edges. This is perhaps unfortunate from the analytical standpoint—discrete entities are easier to manipulate, require simpler descriptive tools, lend themselves to stronger claims, and yield esthetically more pleasing analyses—but it is true nonetheless. Eventually the predilections of the analyst must give way to the actual complexity of the empirical data. Nondiscrete aspects of language structure must be accommodated organically in the basic design of an adequate linguistic theory.

The issue of discreteness has a number of interrelated dimensions. Four merit a closer look here. The first of these is the adequacy of simple, categorical judgments. The second is whether the **criterial-attribute model** or the **prototype model** offers a better account of linguistic categorization. The third dimension is the appropriateness of imposing a sharply dichotomous organization on gradient phenomena. The final dimension is whether an integrated system is adequately described componentially (as a bundle of features), or whether some type of holistic representation might also be required.

1.1.4.1. *Simple Categorical Judgments.* A simple plus/minus value or yes/no answer is not always sufficient in specifying whether a linguistic structure has a certain property, belongs to a particular category, or participates in a given relationship. These conditions are often matters of degree, and we must devise some means of accommodating the complete range of possibilities. A few examples will suffice at present. A familiar one is the generally recognized inadequacy of the simple grammatical/ungrammatical dichotomy for dealing with the well-formedness of sentences. For the most part linguists merely note this inadequacy through a variety of ad hoc and ill-defined notations, e.g. the following, to indicate progressively greater degrees of deviance: ?, ??, ???, ?*, *, **, ***; I will use such notations myself for expository purposes. More to be desired, however, is a unified conception of linguistic organization that intrinsically accommodates assessments of well-formedness along a continuous scale of values.

A second example pertains to the relatedness of lexical items. Almost everyone would agree that the *drive* of *drive a nail* and *drive a golf ball* are related, but what about *drive a car*? Is the use of *cat* to designate a small, furry domesticated mammal connected in any significant way to its use in referring to a spiteful woman or a type of whip? Is there any relation between *ear*, a body part, and *ear*, a corn cob?[3] What about *ring* as a sound, as a boxing arena, and as a piece of jewelry? Intuition argues strongly that a simple yes/no answer would drastically oversimplify matters. The expressions in each of these sets are related to different degrees and in different ways, with the connections between the various uses of *cat*, for instance, being more tenuous and more metaphorical than those uniting the different uses of *drive*. We need straightforward constructs for dealing with the full spectrum of possibilities.

As a final example, consider the relation between a complex lexical item, e.g. *stapler*, and a productive derivational pattern that it apparently instantiates, in this case the V (verb) + -*er* (suffix) pattern for subject nominalization. The question is simple—is *stapler* derived by the V + -*er* rule?—but certain commonly made assumptions prevent a fully satisfactory answer. *Stapler* cannot be rule-derived, it might be argued, since the meaning of this form is far more specific and elaborate than just 'something that staples'; yet merely listing *stapler* in the lexicon stretches credibility in failing to accord it any relation at all to the V + -*er* pattern. One of the erroneous assumptions leading to this dilemma is that a form either is or is not derived by rule, that it either does or does not instantiate a given pattern. This is simplistic. What we want to say instead is that *stapler* does instantiate the V + -*er* pattern, i.e. that its organization and meaning are determined in large measure by the rule, even though it has properties above and beyond those the rule itself specifies.

---

[3] It is not etymological relationship that is at issue here, but rather the connections established by contemporary speakers.

1.1.4.2. *Models for Categorization.* A related issue is the choice between the standard criterial-attribute model of linguistic categorization and a conception based on prototypes. The criterial-attribute model characterizes a class by means of a list of defining features; in its strict form, it requires that every member of the class fully possess every property on this list, and that no nonmember possess all of the listed properties. Class membership is thus an all-or-nothing affair; a sharp distinction is presumed between those entities that are in the class and those that are not.

This conception leads to a number of well-known problems. It often happens, for example, that certain class members lack a property so fundamental (on intuitive grounds) that it can hardly be denied criterial status: flightless birds and egg-laying mammals are familiar illustrations.[4] Another difficulty is that a set of properties sufficient to pick out all and only the members of a class might still be incomplete and inadequate as a **characterization** of that class. Thus, if the semantic specifications [FEATHERLESS] and [BIPED] were in fact adequate as criterial features for defining the class of humans, we would nevertheless hesitate to accept these two features as a comprehensive or revealing description of our species. Yet another problem is that speakers do not adhere rigidly to criterial attributes in judging class membership. Consider the sentences in (1).

(1)(a)   *I've never seen an orange baseball before!*
   (b)   *Look at that giant baseball!*
   (c)   *This tennis ball is a good baseball.*
   (d)   *Who tore the cover off my baseball?*
   (e)   *My baseball just exploded!*

A speaker will not hesitate to call something a baseball even if it happens to be (a) the wrong color, (b) the wrong size, or (c) wrong in virtually all criterial properties. He will also use the term to designate (d) a baseball that has been drastically deformed, or even (e) a baseball that has ceased to exist. Unless one alters its basic character, the criterial-attribute model is not equipped to handle such expressions. It can do so only if one loosens the defining criteria, but then there is no nonarbitrary stopping point, and the relaxed criteria will hardly serve to distinguish class members from other entities.

The cognitive validity of the criterial-attribute model can therefore be doubted, despite its entrenchment in our intellectual tradition, and the prototype model suggests itself as a viable alternative. Experimental work in cognitive psychology (pioneered by Rosch, e.g. 1973, 1975, 1977, 1978) has

---

[4] For an example from another domain, consider voiceless vowels and syllabic resonants. Both are classed as vowels for many purposes, but an adequate description of this category must surely refer to properties they lack (voicing; absence of a significant obstruction in the oral tract).

demonstrated that categories are often organized around prototypical instances. These are the instances people accept as common, run-of-the-mill, garden-variety members of the category. They generally occur the most frequently in our experience, tend to be learned the earliest, and can be identified experimentally in a variety of ways (e.g. respondents accept them as class members with the shortest response latencies). Nonprototypical instances are assimilated to a class or category to the extent that they can be construed as matching or approximating the prototype. Membership is therefore a matter of degree: prototypical instances are full, central members of the category, whereas other instances form a gradation from central to peripheral depending on how far and in what ways they deviate from the prototype. Moreover, the members are not necessarily a uniquely defined set, since there is no specific degree of departure from the prototype beyond which a person is absolutely incapable of perceiving a similarity. The best we can say, as a general matter, is that substantial dissimilarity to the prototype greatly diminishes the probability that a person will make that categorization.

The prototype model thus avoids the problems inherent in the criterial-attribute model. First, it does not require that every member of a category possess a given feature (or even that there be any salient property shared by all members). Flightless birds, egg-laying mammals, and voiceless vowels are thus unproblematic; the absence of an obviously essential property does not force their removal from a category, but merely renders them nonprototypical. Second, the characterization problem is avoided because the prototype model is not inherently minimalist in spirit; instead it encourages the fullest possible characterization of prototypical instances, if only to specify the basis for assimilating the full range of nonprototypical instances to the category. Finally, the prototype model allows an entity to be assimilated to a category if a person finds any plausible rationale for relating it to prototypical members; the term *baseball* can therefore be applied to a ball that is orange, a tennis ball hit with a bat, a ball that has lost its cover, or even a ball that has ceased to exist.

I conclude, then, that the prototype model has considerable linguistic and cognitive plausibility. Its acceptance permits a revealing account of certain linguistic phenomena and the avoidance of descriptive and conceptual difficulties (cf. Brugman 1981; Lakoff 1982; Hawkins 1984). In adopting it over the more discrete criterial-attribute model, we do not forsake the possibility of either precise description or strong empirical claims.[5] The choice is not an a priori matter of preference or scientific rigor, but a factual one pertaining to the organization and complexity of the linguistic data.

[5] There are, however, consequences for the nature of descriptions and the types of predictions they afford. For instance, the prototype model allows statistical predictions to the effect that a class member is more likely to behave in a particular way the more central it is to the category.

1.1.4.3. *Dichotomous Organization.* A third dimension of the discreteness issue concerns the propriety of positing sharp distinctions between certain broad classes of linguistic phenomena, thereby implying that the classes are fundamentally different in character and in large measure separately describable. The nondiscrete alternative regards these classes as grading into one another along various parameters. They form a continuous spectrum (or field) of possibilities, whose segregation into distinct blocks is necessarily artifactual.

Linguists are particularly fond of positing sharp dichotomies. Sometimes the practice serves well initially, allowing the analyst to differentiate a complex mass of data and fix attention on certain variable features. It may even be descriptively appropriate. Not infrequently, though, it leads to the reification of working distinctions into disjoint categories, which are then taken as "established" and accorded a theoretical status quite unjustified by the facts. Among the many distinctions commonly treated by investigators as rigid dichotomies are the following: synchrony vs. diachrony, competence vs. performance, grammar vs. lexicon, morphology vs. syntax, semantics vs. pragmatics, rule vs. analogy, grammatical vs. ungrammatical sentences, homonymy vs. polysemy, connotation vs. denotation, morphophonemic vs. phonological (or phonological vs. phonetic) rules, derivational vs. inflectional morphology, vagueness vs. ambiguity, and literal vs. figurative language. I regard all of these as false dichotomies (most will be examined later). Strict adherence to them results in conceptual problems and the neglect of transitional examples.

One way to produce a false dichotomy is to focus solely on representative examples from the two extremes of a continuum: by overlooking intermediate cases, one readily observes discrete classes with sharply contrasting properties. A good illustration is the traditional distinction between lexical and grammatical morphemes (or content words vs. function words). If we restrict our attention to forms like *giraffe, encyclopedia, upholster, inquisitive,* and *fastidiously* on the one hand, and on the other hand to forms like *-ing, of, be, it* (e.g. *It's raining*), and *that* (e.g. *I know that she left*), the differences are of course striking. The lexical vs. grammatical distinction seems clear on the basis of concreteness of sense, amount of semantic content, whether the choice of a particular form is free or is determined by the grammatical environment, and whether or not a subclass accepts new members.

All these differences are nevertheless matters of degree, and intermediate examples are easily found. Content words vary enormously in concreteness of meaning (as in the ordered sequence *kick > talk > think > live > exist*) and also in semantic specificity (*giraffe > mammal > animal > organism > thing*). I will argue that most (if not all) grammatical morphemes are meaningful, and some are at least as elaborate semantically as numerous content words. It would be hard to claim that modals, quantifiers, and prepositions have less semantic content than such lexical morphemes as *thing* or *have*, nor are they obviously more abstract than *entity, exist, proximity,* etc. I will further argue that grammatical morphemes contribute semantically to the constructions they appear in, and that their occurrence has a semantic rationale even when conventionally determined (cf. Langacker 1982a). Moreover, the speaker is often free to choose from among grammatical morphemes that structure the conceived situation through alternate images (e.g. *try to complain* vs. *try complaining; surprised at* vs. *surprised by*). At the same time, the choice among lexical morphemes is often highly constrained (consider idioms, standard collocations, and formulaic expressions). Finally, certain classes of function words readily accept new members. Quantifiers, prepositions/postpositions, conjunctions, and subordinators are commonly innovated, and in some languages are essentially open-ended classes. It is doubtful that any class, even personal pronouns, is ever definitively closed.[6]

But to posit a continuum is not to abandon the goal of rigorous description: we must still describe the individual structures in explicit detail, even as we articulate their parameters of gradation. Nor does recognizing a continuum render us impotent to make valid distinctions or interesting claims. It is perfectly reasonable, for instance, to speak of lexical morphemes or grammatical morphemes as a group, so long as we avoid pointless questions deriving from the erroneous presupposition that they constitute disjoint sets (e.g. whether prepositions are lexical or grammatical). Rules and generalizations can perfectly well refer to such categories; we need only realize that predictions inspired by representative instances of a category, found near one pole of a continuum, hold with progressively less force as one moves away from that pole towards the opposite extreme.

1.1.4.4. *Integrated Systems.* Most linguistic units are highly integrated structural complexes, or **systems**, which are more than just the sum of their recognizable parts. It is nevertheless common for linguists to impose a componential analysis on these systems, representing them as unordered bundles of discrete features. The vowel sound [i], for instance, is a phonological structure resolvable into the features [−CONSONANTAL, +VOCALIC, +HIGH, +FRONT, −ROUNDED], and the concept [UNCLE] is resolvable into the semantic components [MALE, COLLATERAL, ASCENDING GENERATION]. We are not concerned here with the choice of features, nor with the nature of their values (binary or multivalued, discrete or continuous, etc.); we will consider instead the implications of the feature conception per se. I suggest that a feature representation is perfectly legitimate (if properly interpreted), but does not in itself fully reconstruct the systemic nature of the ac-

---

[6] Witness the innovation and spread of *youall* as the plural of *you*, which I sometimes find even in my own non-Southern speech.

tual phenomenon. For a description to be complete, the feature representation of a structural complex must be supplemented by a more holistic account that accommodates its integrated nature. Such an account is in fact essential to a substantive characterization of the features themselves.

What do I have in mind in saying that a sound such as [i] constitutes an integrated system not reducible to its parts? After all, we *can* decompose its articulation into a number of components, as reflected in a typical feature analysis: vibration of the vocal cords, raising of the tongue towards the palate (without contact or constriction sufficient to cause turbulence), advancement of the tongue towards the front of the palate, spreading and retraction of the lips, and so on. If [i] were merely the sum of these components, I could pronounce it by carrying out these articulatory gestures sequentially: first vibrating my vocal cords, then raising my tongue, then fronting my tongue, and so on. But of course I cannot. The sound is not the mere sum of these components, but rather a matter of blending them into a smooth, coordinated articulatory routine. A complete description of the sound therefore requires more than a separate account of each individual component. It must additionally—and crucially—specify such matters as their relative timing and how they influence and accommodate one another. These are the specifications of the sound's essential systemic character.

Similar remarks hold for concepts. In its narrowest genealogical construal, [UNCLE] makes internal reference to three conceived persons: ego, a linking relative, and the person referred to by the notion. It also invokes (among others) the sibling and offspring relationships. But if the notion were only the sum of these persons and relationships, there would be no difference between, say, [UNCLE] and [NEPHEW]. We must further specify how these entities are connected to form a coherent, integrated structure. More precisely, particular persons are assigned to particular roles in the relationships: the person identified as the uncle is joined through the sibling relationship to the linking relative, and the latter is joined to ego as the parent in a parent/offspring relationship. Normally, of course, we do not focus our attention on these separate specifications; when employing the concept [UNCLE] we generally manipulate the configuration holistically, as a kind of gestalt.

If it is admitted that a sound or a concept must be characterized as an integrated system at some level of description, what is the function of a feature representation? Its motivation is primarily classificatory: a feature like [+HIGH] is posited to group together a set of sounds on the basis of a systematically exploited property that they share; in the same manner, the feature [MALE] unites a set of concepts. The utility and essential correctness of this type of classification is beyond dispute. We can justify the phonological feature [+HIGH] by showing that the class of sounds function alike in various ways to the exclusion of other sounds. Similarly, we can show that the semantic feature [MALE] is not arbitrary, but rather a property of systematic relevance to the language, by citing the numerous contrastive pairs that depend on it: *uncle/aunt, boy/girl, man/woman, stallion/mare, buck/doe*, etc.

The features used to represent a sound or a concept can therefore be regarded as diacritics specifying class co-membership with other units. However, a list of class memberships is not per se a full characterization of the categorized entities, and is only minimally revealing if the defining properties are left unexplicated. Moreover, few analysts would accept the claim that the phonological or semantic features they postulate have only a diacritic function. For a feature analysis to be truly substantive, the features must be attributed intrinsic phonological or semantic content, described as precisely and explicitly as possible.[7]

If these points are accepted, how do we characterize the intrinsic phonological or semantic content of the features we postulate? I suggest that autonomous descriptions of individual features will generally prove inadequate, precisely because sounds and concepts are systemic in nature. Features correspond to properties discernible within an integrated system, and are properly describable only in the context of that system.

Consider the articulatory feature [+HIGH]. We cannot characterize it with full precision as an isolated entity, for its specific value depends on other properties of the sound it occurs in. For example, a different region of the tongue is raised depending on whether the vowel is front or back. More crucially, the height specification can only be understood relative to the matrix of a vocalic articulation. If, while I am eating, my tongue accidentally assumes the shape and position that would be appropriate for the sound [i], I cannot claim to have thereby implemented the phonological feature [+HIGH] (or [+FRONT]) in the sense that linguists understand the term. I can properly be said to have implemented the [+HIGH] feature only when my tongue achieves the requisite configuration by virtue of specific neuromuscular actions synergistically related to those of other speech organs as an integral part of a coordinated articulatory gesture. The feature exists only in the context of a system providing the conditions for its manifestation, where it serves a specific function.[8]

The same is true for semantic structure. The componential analysis of [UNCLE] into [MALE], [COLLATERAL], and [ASCENDING GENERATION] does not eliminate its systemic character, for these features must themselves be defined configurationally. [COLLATERAL] and [ASCENDING

---

[7] It would be pointless for linguists to abjure responsibility for describing linguistic constructs as integrated systems, or for specifying the content of classificatory features. We will not solve these problems by bequeathing them to other disciplines (e.g. experimental phonetics or cognitive psychology) whose separation from our own is essentially arbitrary. Moreover, the systemic character of linguistic units is fundamental to understanding their behavior.

[8] Relevant here are Sapir's remarks (1925) on the difference between the speech sound [W] and the sound made in blowing out a candle.

GENERATION] indicate relative position within a kinship network, hence presuppose the conception of such an entity. The feature [MALE] perhaps does not, but its value must nevertheless be construed in systemic terms: the collection of properties subsumed by [MALE] do not float about unattached within the confines of the [UNCLE] concept; instead they are understood as pertaining to a specific person, who occupies a particular place within the system of relationships. The unstructured feature bundle [MALE, COLLATERAL, ASCENDING GENERATION] therefore conceals behind its digital facade a highly integrated conceptualization providing a necessary context for the interpretation of each component.

The program I advocate is not reductionist. In arguing for the necessity and priority of a systemic view of semantic and phonological units I am not thereby denying either the descriptive utility or the cognitive reality of classificatory features. I contend that speakers extract these features to embody the commonality they perceive in arrays of fully specified, integrated units, and that these features consequently make intrinsic (though schematic) reference to the overall systemic units relative to which they are characterized. But the features do not obviate the need for a systemic representation; they coexist with it as an additional dimension of linguistic organization.

1.1.5. *Substance*

Because language is abstract and complicated, its characterization demands a multitude of abstract notions. A proliferation of theoretical constructs thus accompanies our growing knowledge of language and reflects our ever greater sophistication in grappling with its subtleties and intricacies. Obviously, though, we would like some assurance that the constructs we propose actually contribute to linguistic understanding. There are two facets to this problem. First, a construct has little value unless the investigator's conception of it is sufficiently clear to permit its elucidation with a certain amount of precision and detail.[9] Second, positing a construct will likely prove counterproductive unless it corresponds to something "real," i.e. some actual feature of linguistic organization. To qualify as **substantive**, a construct must be satisfactory on both counts. Substance is an important aspect of naturalness in linguistic description.

Unfortunately there is no reliable, recognized authority to appeal to in determining whether a linguistic construct is substantive. A notion that seems perfectly clear and straightforward to its proponents strikes other observers as vague and mysterious; what is self-evidently real in the context of one theory

---

[9] I do not refer to a completely formal, mathematically precise definition; few if any linguistic constructs (among those that prove valid) are ever blessed with such rigorous formulation. We are perfectly capable of grasping and articulating concepts at a preformal level and wielding them to good effect in linguistic analysis (cf. 1.2.4).

is pure fiction from the standpoint of another. When even the most basic questions about the nature and structure of language are subject to wildly divergent opinions, we have no basis for achieving a consensus on the substantivity of particular constructs. The best I can do, then, is to offer some personal observations concerning the problem.

We are destined by our station in life (as investigators of language rather than its designers) to refer to entities that are not rigorously defined or fully understood. For instance, all linguists employ traditional concepts (e.g. noun, subject, modifier, subordination) that few if any can rigorously define. This is inevitable and not in itself a matter of great concern; the broad utility of these notions makes it reasonably evident that they correspond to something real, and there is little point in decreeing a priori formal definitions that are precise but arbitrary. It goes without saying that serious investigators continually seek to deepen their understanding of linguistic phenomena and sharpen their characterizations of descriptive constructs. The analyst is nevertheless forced to wrestle with phenomena that are only dimly comprehended, and to do so with constructs requiring substantial elaboration. This circumstance is perhaps regrettable, but it is certainly inevitable.

My one exhortation in this regard is to minimize crucial reliance on unexplicated notions. If our understanding of a notion is only preliminary and superficial, we must be wary of strong conclusions that ultimately depend on highly specific assumptions about that notion. This is no idle admonition. The linguistic literature is replete with claims, analyses, and controversies hinging crucially on specific assumptions (often implicit) concerning entities that no one really knows very much about. I will offer just two examples.

One example is the use of idioms by generative linguists to justify movement rules. Sentences like (2)(a) and (3)(a), for instance, are commonly cited as evidence for the transformations Passive and Subject-to-Subject Raising.

(2)(a) *Headway seems to have been steadily made.*
  (b) [△ PAST *steadily make headway*] PRES *seem*
  (c) **Headway is always desirable.*

(3)(a) *Umbrage is likely to be taken at those remarks.*
  (b) [△ *will take umbrage at those remarks*] PRES *be likely*
  (c) **Umbrage depresses me.*

Headway and *umbrage* cannot be the respective deep-structure subjects of *seem* and *be likely*, it is argued, because the two words are generally not permitted in subject position (note the deviance of the (c) examples); they occur instead only as part of the idioms *make headway* and *take umbrage at*, which are listed in the lexicon as fixed, unanalyzable expressions. The deep structures in (b), where △ indicates an unspecified subject, are therefore required to account for the surface forms in (a); only with such a deep structure can the idioms be inserted as integral units. The rules of Passive (in the subordinate clause) and then Subject-to-Subject Raising are thus necessary to derive the surface forms.

The correctness of this analysis is not at issue here (cf. 12.2.3; Langacker 1982a, 1984). What does concern us is the crucial reliance of this classic argument on specific assumptions about the nature of idioms, a phenomenon that transformational grammarians have hardly investigated at all and certainly have not extensively or revealingly characterized. One assumption is that of unanalyzability; the meaning of an idiom is assigned to the expression as a whole, and an "idiom chunk" such as *headway* or *umbrage* does not correspond to any particular facet of this meaning. Under this assumption it would be incoherent to say that *headway* is responsible for a judgment, or that *umbrage* is the basis for an assessment of probability, as would be implied if we posited a relation between the deep-structure subject *headway* and *seem* or between *umbrage* and *be likely*. The second assumption is that idioms have a single, fixed form: that they are stored in the lexicon with their parts arranged in a specific linear order, so that any deviation from this order in surface structure must result from transformational operations subsequent to lexical insertion. These assumptions make the conclusion of a transformational derivation inescapable.[10]

Yet both assumptions are highly questionable. Most speakers would be surprised to be told that, counter to intuition, the *headway* of *make headway* does not mean something akin to *progress*, or that the *umbrage* of *take umbrage at* does not mean roughly the same as *offense* (cf. *make progress, take offense at*). Though some idioms may be fully opaque, I submit that the vast majority are analyzable to some degree, with particular facets of the overall meaning attributed to particular words or morphemes (2.3). Gorbet (1973) has strongly corroborated this view by showing that many idiom chunks participate quite freely in anaphoric relations—involving both pronominalization and ellipsis—provided that the normal conditions for anaphora are fully satisfied.[11] Note the examples in (4):

(4)(a) *Anthony stole her heart and then he broke it.*
   (b) *First he broke her heart and then her spirit.*
   (c) *After making no headway all morning we finally made some in the afternoon.*

---

[10] Both assumptions are made (with virtually no discussion or justification) in Fraser (1970), the best-known transformational treatment of idioms. Considering how central this argument for movement rules is to the whole edifice of transformational grammar, it is strange that this tradition has not made idioms the focus of intensive study.

[11] In particular, the anaphor and its antecedent must be used with approximately the same semantic value; *The surgeon operated on her heart and then he broke it* is peculiar because *heart* is used in its literal sense in the first clause but figuratively in the second. (I make no claim that anaphora is always possible with idiom chunks, since analyzability is a matter of degree and may fall below the threshold required for exploitation in a particular grammatical construction.)

To regard an idiom as opaque or as primarily a fixed phrase is therefore simplistic. It is more accurately seen as a complex of semantic and symbolic relationships that have become conventionalized and have coalesced into an established configuration. We can plausibly suppose that this configuration of relationships might be recognizable even when anaphora disrupts the normal shape of an idiom, or when its component words are split up and used in grammatical constructions such that they do not form a contiguous linear sequence: an idiom may be recognized as a unit that is to some degree independent of a specific overt morphemic arrangement, even if one such arrangement is far more familiar and hence more "usual" than the others. Bresnan and Grimshaw have also concluded, from sentences like those in (5), that an idiom cannot be equated with a particular linear sequence of morphemes: "In short, the assumption that idiomatic verb-object constructions must always be base-generated together is false. The separation of idiom chunks from their verbs cannot be a function of movement transformations alone" (1978, p. 388).

(5)(a)   *We didn't make the amount of headway that was expected of us.*
  (b)   *Unfortunately, we made what the president considered to be insufficient headway on that problem.*

One of the arguments providing crucial support for certain transformations therefore relies quite heavily on unexamined assumptions about a phenomenon that transformationalists have largely ignored; the validity of these assumptions is rendered doubtful by even a very limited amount of open-minded investigation. Clearly such a circumstance has little to recommend it.

In practice, of course, we must often deal with entities that are poorly understood, and make certain assumptions about them if we are to get any investigative enterprise off the ground. But we can reasonably be expected to recognize the limitations of our knowledge, and to refrain in particular from accepting as empirically established fact any properties that we attribute to mysterious phenomena on an a priori basis.

A second instance of reliance on unexplicated notions, considered only briefly, is the distinction in the transformational tradition between **syntax** and **lexicon**, together with the recurrent issue—still regarded as important—of whether a given construction is to be handled "in the syntax" or "in the lexicon." I have never viewed this as a substantive question, since those concerned with it have not thoroughly examined lexicon in its own terms, and since the entire discussion appears to rest on certain dubious assumptions about the necessary character of syntax.

The notion of lexicon as "an appendix of the grammar, a list of basic irregularities" is not a new one (see Bloomfield 1933, p. 274). It is fair to say that this conception was adopted by transformational theorists who were not experienced lexicographers, and who thus lacked an independent, fine-grained, empirically grounded appreciation of the problems posed by lexical phenomena and the devices needed to deal with them. The lexical component was dedicated for use (Chomsky 1965) as a repository for recalcitrant phenomena that were originally considered syntactic but refused to obey certain preconceived ideas about what syntax should be like. Syntax was thought of as the domain of generality and regularity, of productive rules with fully predictable outputs; anything falling short of these standards was relegated to the purgatory of lexicon—the domain of irregularity, idiosyncrasy, and lists. But this deeply ingrained, almost archetypal conception of syntax has very little empirical foundation. I am aware of no a priori or factual grounds for believing that grammatical constructions divide neatly into two groups on the basis of generality, or that the regular aspects of language structure can be segregated in any meaningful way from the irregular ones. Focusing our attention solely on constructions that pass the litmus test of generality and regularity does not promise to leave us with a coherent body of phenomena constituting a natural grouping on any other grounds. Indeed, the history of transformational grammar has seen an ever greater number of constructions exiled from the syntax to be handled by other, rather ill-defined grammatical components.[12] Unfortunately, moving these phenomena from one box to another has singularly failed to illuminate them.

Certain types of constructs automatically raise questions about their substantive character. Since language is symbolic, the reality of semantic and phonological structure is hardly subject to dispute, but the status of constructs having neither semantic nor phonological content is on the face of it less secure, and cognitive grammar claims that such constructs are never valid. Cognitive grammar could not, for instance, follow Perlmutter (1978) in positing a syntactic "dummy"—lacking both semantic value and phonological manifestation—to handle passive and impersonal expressions. Even though this device has internal motivation from the standpoint of driving the formal machinery of relational grammar, considerations of naturalness force the cognitive grammarian to seek an alternative account of the facts.

Intrinsically suspicious in a somewhat different way are the central constructs of transformational grammar, namely the notions of deep structure and syntactic transformations. In essence, these constructs imply that things are not really what they appear to be: that surface structure conceals a more fundamental level of grammatical organization—deep structure—which transformations distort systematically and often drastically. Here I intend neither to review nor to critique the many arguments advanced to support this conception, but simply to raise the question of whether comparable insights

---

[12] Nominalizations were among the first to be consigned to the lexicon (Chomsky 1970), and eventually even classic transformations like Passive were nominated for this fate (Freidin 1975). Today, what may be the sole surviving transformation (the inherently suspicious Move Category) is being eyed for possible elimination (Lightfoot 1980).

might also be achieved in a model that does not rely on constructs with such tenuous claims to reality. Cognitive grammar is not alone in suggesting that they can. It claims that grammatical structure is almost entirely overt: things really are what they appear to be, provided we know how to interpret them properly.

1.1.6. *Complexity*

In any empirical science, the investigator is forced by the complexity of natural systems to make simplifying assumptions about the scope, autonomy, and character of the phenomena he chooses to deal with. It is both necessary and legitimate for linguists to focus selectively on certain problems, extract them from a broader fabric of interrelated concerns, and handle them in an idealized manner. Inherent in this situation is a tendency for the investigator to lose sight of the actual complexity of his subject matter; simplifying assumptions made to facilitate research are sometimes raised without justification to the level of assertions about the actual character of the investigated phenomenon. Idealizations that significantly distort the object of investigation are pernicious, and their avoidance is critical to the goal of naturalness in linguistic analysis.

Certain idealizations commonly made in linguistics seem to me quite reasonable if not pushed too far. It makes sense for generative grammarians to exclude from their data expressions that occur but are recognized by speakers as pure mistakes—slips of the mind or tongue, that is—since speakers clearly do have some conception of what does or does not accord with linguistic convention. Nor am I particularly bothered by the practice of restricting one's attention to a single dialect, provided that its special but unprivileged position in a sea of variation is kept in mind, and that nothing crucial is allowed to hang on its idiosyncrasies.

Quite the opposite is true of certain simplifying assumptions that lie at the core of many theories. One of these is the aforementioned assumption that a sharp and valid distinction can be made between lexical and grammatical morphemes. Because lexical morphemes are clearly meaningful, whereas grammatical morphemes are often less obviously so, this presumed dichotomy encourages the investigator to believe that the meanings of grammatical morphemes—if they are meaningful at all—can safely be ignored for purposes of grammatical analysis. Therefore, since the semantic difference between an active/passive pair like the sentences in (6) is considered slight enough to overlook, it is thought that a passive sentence is adequately described without regard for the possible semantic contribution of *be*, *by*, or the past-participial inflection on the verb.

(6)(a)   *The Chinese invented gunpowder.*

  (b)   *Gunpowder was invented by the Chinese.*

The presumed dichotomy also makes it seem plausible to handle lexical and grammatical morphemes in different components of the grammar (the former listed in the lexicon, the latter introduced by syntactic rules). The classic transformational analysis (Chomsky 1957) therefore inserts the grammatical morphemes of the passive construction as an incidental part of the transformation deriving passives from underlying active structures.[13]

The original assumption thus engenders (or reinforces) a certain conception of syntax: because grammatical morphemes and syntactic relationships are nonsemantic in character, and because sentences can therefore differ in grammatical form without semantic consequences, it follows that syntax is autonomous. My overall objective is to demonstrate that this conception is erroneous on all three counts. If I am correct, then the simplifying assumptions leading to the autonomous-syntax hypothesis are pernicious, inasmuch as they drastically misrepresent the object of investigation and encourage one to ask the wrong questions about it.

One particular simplifying assumption is commonly made that merits special scrutiny; I will call it the **exclusionary fallacy**. The gist of this fallacy is that one analysis, motivation, categorization, cause, function, or explanation for a linguistic phenomenon necessarily precludes another. From a broad, pretheoretical perspective, this assumption is gratuitous and in fact rather dubious, in view of what we know about the multiplicity of interacting synchronic and diachronic factors that determine the shape and import of linguistic expressions. Though pervasive, the assumption is usually tacit; illustrations are thus in order.

Consider a previous example, namely the problem of how to deal with forms like *stapler* in certain versions of the generative framework. There is an apparent dilemma: if the form is derived by rule, one cannot account for its special properties, i.e. the fact that it means more than just 'something that staples'; if it is simply listed in the lexicon, on the other hand, it cannot be assimilated to the productive V + -er derivational pattern, which it certainly seems to instantiate. The mistake is to assume that it has to be one and not the other. There is nothing intrinsically implausible about a position combining the central features of both analyses. That position would allow the claim that *stapler* is in fact an instance—but not solely an instance—of the V + -er derivational rule; beyond its status as an exemplar of this pattern, *stapler* constitutes an established lexical item whose semantic value is specialized in ways the pattern itself does not specify. The source of the apparent problem is the exclusionary fallacy, together with certain artifactual properties of the generative model (e.g. the process metaphor—it is hard to conceptualize an expres-

---

[13] Langacker (1982a) details an alternative analysis. The grammatical morphemes are attributed semantic values compatible with their other uses, and active/passive pairs are seen to differ semantically despite their truth-value equivalence.

sion that is "derived" or "constructed" by a rule being simultaneously listed in the lexicon as a fixed unit).

This example represents an important version of the exclusionary fallacy that I will call the **rule/list fallacy**: the assumption, on grounds of simplicity, that particular statements (i.e. lists) must be excised from the grammar of a language if general statements (i.e. rules) that subsume them can be established. Given the general N + -*s* noun-pluralizing rule of English, for instance, specific plural forms following that rule (*beads, shoes, toes, walls*) would not be listed in an optimal grammar. I have argued (Langacker 1982a) that this is a specious kind of simplicity for anyone taking seriously the goal of "psychological reality" in linguistic description. It is gratuitous to assume that mastery of a rule like N + -*s*, and mastery of forms like *beads* that accord with this rule, are mutually exclusive facets of a speaker's knowledge of his language; it is perfectly plausible that the two might sometimes coexist. We do not lose a generalization by including both the rule and specific plural forms in the grammar of English, since the rule itself expresses the generalization. To claim on an a priori basis that the rule precludes the list, or conversely, is simply to embrace the exclusionary fallacy.

A different type of illustration is provided by a common analysis for certain auxiliary-like verbs, particularly *do* (Chomsky 1957) but also including *be, have*, and their counterparts in other languages (Bach 1967). It is observed that the distribution of these verbs is predictable from their syntactic environment. It is well known that *do*, for instance, occurs in particular constructions where (given certain assumptions) it bears a tense morpheme that would otherwise be stranded, as in (7).

(7)(a) *Do you like children?*
 (b) *They do not sound serious.*
 (c) *I did warn you.*
 (d) *Kittens like pizza, don't they?*

On the basis of this predictability, it is concluded that *do* is transformationally inserted (hence the classic rule of Do Support). It is a prototypical grammatical morpheme, being semantically empty and serving a purely grammatical function.

A number of issues are involved here (cf. 9.2.2; Langacker 1975, 1981c, 1982a), but I want to focus on the tacit role of the exclusionary fallacy in making this analysis seem plausible. The fact that *do* (similarly *be, have*, etc.) has a specifiable grammatical function is taken implicitly as prima facie evidence that it is meaningless. The fact that rules can be given to predict its distribution in grammatical terms is taken as supporting an insertion analysis that sets it apart from other verbal elements. But in neither case does the conclusion actually follow. Linguistic convention might perfectly well adopt a morpheme with limited semantic content for particular grammatical purposes; serving a specifiable grammatical function is not inherently incompatible with being a meaningful element. By the same token, the predictability of its distribution is not inherently inconsistent with the claim that *do* is a true verb and should be treated as such at all levels of structure. It is fallacious to assume that grammatical motivation and lexical status are necessarily mutually exclusive.

Let me mention in passing a few other instances of the exclusionary fallacy.

1. Hankamer (1977, p. 583) correctly observes that "our methodological assumption (and tacitly our underlying theory of the nature of linguistic knowledge) tells us that we *must* choose between two competing analyses" for a grammatical construction. He argues, however, that in some cases no single correct analysis can be found, and that two or more distinct analyses, each of which explains a portion of the facts, can be motivated.

2. Many linguists have been wary of functional explanations for linguistic phenomena. One reason, I believe, is the assumption that a functional account and an explicit description of the facts in nonfunctional terms are somehow competing alternatives rather than complementary facets of an overall characterization. Because functional analyses do not themselves amount to a full description, their value is insufficiently recognized; cf. my review of Givón 1979 (Langacker 1981a).

3. Phonologists have sometimes been troubled by the need to state the same generalization twice, once as a morpheme-structure condition and once as a phonological rule that applies to the output of other rules. However, nothing inherently requires that the two functions be mutually exclusive.

4. Finally, it can be noted that diachronic questions are often posed in dichotomous terms: Should language *X* be grouped with subfamily *Y* or subfamily *Z*? Did sound change *A* precede sound change *B*, or the converse? Did construction *C* arise internally or was it borrowed from a neighboring language? By now most scholars recognize that questions like these are simplistic, for one alternative does not intrinsically exclude the other.

Linguists are driven by esthetic considerations and by the dictates of scientific method to look for simple, elegant solutions to complex problems. This is proper and necessary, but only to the extent that such analyses are consistent with the reality of language. Linguistic phenomena are extraordinarily complex and interdependent. There are limits to the neatness and simplicity of linguistic descriptions that seek to account for these phenomena with any semblance of completeness and accuracy. Whatever our predilections, it is crucial that the conceptual and descriptive tools we fashion for analyzing language be in fact appropriate for the task. More simply put, we must strive for naturalness in linguistic theory and description.

1.2. Methodological Assumptions

In all honesty, I would greatly prefer not having to discuss methodological issues, for a number of reasons. First, I profess little expertise in methodological concerns or the philosophy of science. A second reason is an oft-noted tendency for the amount of attention an author devotes to methodological questions to correlate inversely with the extent of his actual descriptive contribution. A third factor is the consistently inconclusive nature of methodological disputes, which remind me very much of legal disputes. It is not uncommon to find two linguists arguing opposite sides of an issue, each supporting his position on supposedly unimpeachable methodological grounds.[14]

Nevertheless, I feel compelled to discuss the methodological assumptions that have guided me in my work. I fully expect the ideas presented here to be attacked on methodological grounds, not (I like to think) because they lack scientific validity, but because I make very different assumptions from most linguists about the appropriate adaptation of scientific methodology to linguistic investigation. I therefore consider it essential to take an explicit position on methodological issues at the very outset.

1.2.1. *The Role of Methodology*

A scientific discipline evolves through many phases and comprises numerous kinds of interacting activities. One phase is characterized by curiosity, informal observation, and an emerging awareness that a body of phenomena may be susceptible to analytical investigation. Another phase consists in the systematic collection of basic data about these phenomena; even if this enterprise is only taxonomic, it furnishes the empirical basis for theoretical development. Conceptualization follows: the investigator experiments with various metaphors and preliminary theoretical models, searching for revealing formulations and promising lines of attack. He must then elaborate and articulate a theoretical model capable of accounting for the initially available data and enabling further empirical predictions. In the validation phase, a theory's predictions are matched against additional data, and refinements are made to enhance its observational adequacy. A further endeavor is the comparison of alternate models, to determine their points of divergence and the nature of the evidence that will distinguish them empirically. One final endeavor is formalization, in which appropriate mathematical expression is sought for the model.

These phases are not rigidly sequenced, nor are they sharply discrete; in

---

[14] Similarly, no matter how morally reprehensible and blatantly illegal a person's actions may be, he will have no trouble hiring a lawyer to represent these actions as the epitome of virtue and legal rectitude. I need not comment on the parallels between legalese and methodologese.

practice the investigator finds himself engaged in several simultaneously. Moreover, an evolving discipline may cycle through certain phases a number of times before an adequate theoretical formulation is achieved. The concerns of the investigator naturally differ from one phase to another, as does the mode of discourse most appropriate for discussing those concerns. For example, it is unreasonable to demand rigorous formalization for an emergent theory still in the process of conceptualization, and it is pointless—as shown by the sorry history of the controversy between generative and interpretive semantics—to seek definitive evidence for the choice between two competing theories when both remain largely programmatic.

Present-day linguistics would appear to be quite advanced. There are well-articulated theories, whose validation, comparison, and formalization have received considerable attention. However, it must also be admitted that current theories achieve precise formalization only by excluding from their domain many important aspects of linguistic organization; one does not ask, for instance, how Montague grammar handles phonology, or how relational grammar deals with lexicon (or even the syntactic structure of noun phrases). We can also note the striking lack of consensus about the proper characterization of even the simplest or most fundamental linguistic phenomena. Little in the way of established descriptions, basic concepts, analytical techniques, or general theory commands anything even approaching the unanimous assent of serious investigators (compare this with the situation in, say, chemistry).[15] A central reason for these shortcomings, I contend, is that linguistic theory has been built on inadequate conceptual foundations. Surprisingly little effort goes into the critical examination of deeply rooted assumptions, into uncovering the source of apparent dilemmas (which are usually indicative of underlying conceptual confusion), or into cultivating fundamentally new modes of thought. While our factual knowledge of language proliferates, and the scope of linguistic investigation continues to expand, current theoretical attitudes encourage narrowness and fragmentation, offering little hope for a comprehensive synthesis.

My own prescription calls not for theoretical fine-tuning, but for radical conceptual reformulation. The primary need of the discipline, as I see it, is for a comprehensive, integrative, and cognitively realistic conceptual framework—one in which everything fits, and everything fits together. In formulating cognitive grammar, I have therefore concentrated on the conceptualization

---

[15] If the foundations of linguistic theory were really secure, we might expect that by now there would be general agreement about the proper description of something as intensively studied as the English passive or auxiliary system, yet conflicting analyses continue to proliferate. Comparison of the twelve theories of syntax outlined in Moravcsik and Wirth (1980) will leave the reader hard-pressed to find any substantial point of general agreement among the authors, even on the most basic matters (e.g. whether the notion **subject** is an important construct for linguistic theory and, if so, what kind of notion it is).

phase of scientific inquiry, and am now attempting to elaborate and articulate a coherent theoretical model. Rigorous formalization is an unreasonable expectation at this early stage, and systematic comparison with other theories is probably premature. Inasmuch as the model diverges greatly from others at the level of basic concepts and organizing principles, care must be taken not to simply presuppose standard doctrines in evaluating it: the conceptual foundations of linguistic thought are themselves very much at issue.

There are several reasons to avoid becoming obsessed with any particular set of methodological strictures when evaluating alternative theories. First, the philosophy of science is not conspicuous for its unanimity of opinion, and no one body of methodological assumptions can be considered definitive. Second, as Feyerabend (1978) so forcefully observes, every methodology has its limitations; moreover, methodologies tend to reinforce the theoretical status quo—often one must violate generally accepted methodological tenets to uncover the evidence that will call a theory into question.[16] A third reason—quite important here, since I agree with most linguists at the level of abstract principles—is the substantial difficulty of interpreting these general principles in a way that is appropriate for a given discipline at a particular stage of its development.

There is a wide gap between general methodological principles on the one hand, and on the other hand the specific procedural, analytical, descriptive, and theoretical decisions one faces in conducting the daily affairs of a particular field. To pattern linguistic methodology after the model of other disciplines is hazardous at best. For one thing, different subject matter may require different approaches. What is possible in physics (e.g. precise quantitative predictions) may not be possible in linguistics, which deals with aspects of the human mind. Moreover, if two disciplines are at different phases of their evolution, the major methodological concerns of one may be of little immediate relevance to the other. Even if one decides to base the methodology of one discipline on that of another, there is the problem of establishing the proper correspondences between the two fields and drawing the proper conclusions (consider the problems that result from equating sound "laws" with the laws of physics).

Comparable problems arise even if we do not look to other disciplines for instruction. A methodological principle stated abstractly enough to achieve

---

[16] Supposedly neutral methodological principles can be used to insulate a theory from possible challenge. Recall the great concern of many transformational theorists for restricting the generative capacity of a grammar. Innovative theoretical devices, e.g. the use of global rules in syntax, were deemed intrinsically suspect because they supposedly increased a grammar's power. McCawley (1980) correctly points out the spurious nature of this debate: a transformational grammar already had the power of a Turing machine, and those rejecting global rules in syntax simply put equivalent rules in their ill-defined semantic component.

universal agreement does not necessarily translate easily or uncontroversially into guidance on how to approach specific problems. Linguists generally agree, for example, that formalization is a necessary objective in theory and description, but the stage at which formalization becomes possible, useful, or obligatory is subject to continued debate—e.g. Bach (1977, p. 651) criticizes Postal (1974) for his decision not to provide fully explicit rules in his discussion of Subject Raising. Furthermore, different methodological principles are sometimes invoked that lead to conflicting conclusions when applied to linguistic practice. Graphic illustration is furnished by two of the papers in Peters (1972): Postal argues that the principle of generality lends support to a model seeking a unified account of several facets of grammatical organization; by contrast, Chomsky cites the principle of restrictiveness to back up his claim that grammar is best described in terms of separate components, each more highly restricted than would be possible in a "monolithic" framework.

I therefore contend that methodological arguments in linguistics deserve to be used with great caution. An argument that appeals to a general methodological principle commanding universal assent may nevertheless be invalid because it applies the principle to linguistic inquiry in a nonoptimal or even fully inappropriate way. Interpreting methodological canons and applying them to linguistic problems in a revealing and appropriate manner is a difficult but crucial task inextricably bound up with one's conception of the object under investigation. Because my own view of linguistic organization is quite different from the currently predominant one, so is my conception of how methodological principles should be interpreted and applied. In discussing these differences of interpretation and adaptation, I will organize the discussion under the headings of **factuality**, **economy**, **explicitness**, **generality**, and **predictiveness**.

1.2.2. *Factuality*

A fundamental requirement in any empirical science is that a theory be in substantial accordance with known facts. Other things being equal (as if they ever were!), it is considered desirable that a theory account for more data rather than less. It is further required that a theory describe phenomena with some degree of accuracy. A major difficulty of applying these truisms in actual practice stems from the nonautonomy of "facts." Facts are perceived as such only in the context of some theory, if only a very rudimentary one. They are a matter of interpretation and preliminary analysis, inevitably deriving from a set of underlying assumptions and preconceptions about the object of study and the proper way to investigate it.

Contemporary linguistic theory generally views language as being organized into discrete components. In particular, syntax is seen as sharply distinct from both lexicon and semantics, constituting an autonomous set of formal relationships. Cognitive grammar, by contrast, claims that lexicon, morphology, and syntax form a continuum of symbolic units serving to structure conceptual content for expressive purposes. It is incoherent in this view to speak of grammar in isolation from meaning, and the segmentation of grammatical structure into discrete components is rejected. It is hardly surprising that these two positions carry with them very different conceptions of the data to be accounted for, both quantitatively and qualitatively. Let us briefly explore a few of the differences.

A conception of grammatical structure emphasizing discrete components naturally encourages the investigator to focus his attention on phenomena consistent with this type of organization. He concentrates primarily on prototypical instances from each component, where the distinctions seem readily apparent, and tends to overlook any data that do not fit neatly into the preestablished boxes. Thus selected, the data under investigation of course appear to reinforce the original componential arrangement. A case in point is the putative distinction between syntax and lexicon. In the classic conception (now considerably modified), syntax was thought to deal with novel, multiword expressions (phrases, clauses, and sentences) assembled in accordance with general rules. Lexicon was the province of fixed expressions, most no larger than single words; not predictable by rules of any generality, they had to be listed individually. The two classes of phenomena thus stood sharply opposed with respect to novelty, generality, and size.

This dichotomous perspective made it inevitable that a large body of data fitting neither category would be mostly ignored. I refer here to the huge set of stock phrases, familiar collocations, formulaic expressions, and standard usages that can be found in any language and thoroughly permeate its use. Here is a small, random sample from English: *take it for granted that*, *hold . . . responsible for*, *express an interest in*, *great idea*, *tough competitor*, *have a lot of class*, *I don't care*, *kill two birds with one stone*, *good to see you*, *mow the lawn*, *turn the page*, *let the cat out*, *have great respect for*, *ready to go*, *play fair*, *I'll do the best I can*, *answer the phone*, and *never want to see . . . again*. Or consider these examples from the opening paragraph of this section (1.2.2): *fundamental requirement*, *empirical science*, *known facts*, *other things being equal*, *as if*, *theory account for . . . data*, *more . . . rather than less*, *in actual practice*, *as such*, *in the context of*, *if only*, *very rudimentary*, *a matter of interpretation*, *preliminary analysis*, *deriving from*, *a set of*, *underlying assumptions*, and *object of study*.

There are literally thousands of these **conventional expressions** in a given language, and knowing them is essential to speaking it well. This is why a seemingly perfect knowledge of the grammar of a language (in the narrow sense) does not guarantee fluency in it; learning its full complement of conventional expressions is probably by far the largest task involved in mastering it. Yet conventional expressions have received so little attention that I found it necessary to invent this term for the class as a whole.

We can speculate on the reasons for the almost universal neglect of conventional expressions, but one is surely that they do not conform to the stereotype of either lexicon or syntax. They are excluded from the lexicon because they are larger than prototypical lexical items, and also because many are obviously compositional (even fully regular). They are exiled from the syntax because syntacticians are concerned with general rules rather than specific combinations of lexical items. Being neither lexical nor syntactic as these notions are generally understood, the vast inventory of conventional expressions is for the most part simply omitted from the scope of linguistic description.[17]

Cognitive grammar takes a different perspective on this matter. It posits that the grammar of a language represents a speaker's knowledge of linguistic convention, and much of this knowledge resides in his mastery of conventional expressions. Hence these expressions are listed explicitly in the grammar of a language, even those that are regular compositional functions of simpler lexical items and general syntactic rules. Moreover, cognitive grammar posits a gradation uniting lexicon, morphology, and syntax. Any strict dichotomy based on novelty, generality, and size of expressions is rejected; these parameters do tend to correlate in natural ways, but all of them are matters of degree and (with qualifications) are independently variable. There is nothing anomalous about novel words or stems on this view, nor about fixed multiword expressions (though it is prototypical for words and stems to be fixed and for longer expressions to have some element of novelty). Conventional expressions are therefore quite expected, pose no special descriptive problems, and in fact constitute a central and explicitly recognized kind of data to be accounted for.

The selection and interpretation of data prompted by generative theory has had certain striking and well-known consequences. The presumption of generality for syntactic rules has tended to discourage the systematic collection of fine-grained data revealing the actual distribution of grammatical phenomena and the factors that influence them (cf. Gross 1979). The notion of syntax as an autonomous formal system has encouraged the expectation that speakers should be capable of simple categorical judgments (grammatical/ungrammatical) on the well-formedness of sentences, out of context and without regard for semantic considerations: either a sentence meets all the formal specifications or it does not. This is of course not what has been found. Degrees of well-formedness are now generally acknowledged. Typically, moreover, graded judgments correlate with subtle semantic differences. For example,

---

[17] It would obviously be vacuous to treat conventional expressions as a matter of performance rather than competence, or to posit a special "usage component"; these constructs are nonsubstantive.

the acceptability of passive sentences is influenced by various factors, including the degree to which (1) the (surface) subject is definite or individuated; (2) the *by*-phrase object is indefinite or unindividuated; and (3) the process described by the verb approximates a prototypical physical action. These respective factors are illustrated in (8)–(10).[18]

(8)(a) *This view was enjoyed by George Washington.*
 (b) ?*A view was enjoyed by George Washington.*
 (c) ??*Views were enjoyed by George Washington.*

(9)(a) *Dan Fouts is liked by everybody.*
 (b) ?*Dan Fouts is liked by the fan.*
 (c) ??*Dan Fouts is liked by me.*

(10)(a) *Sheila was kicked by her mother.*
 (b) ?*Sheila was wanted by her mother.*
 (c) ??*Sheila was resembled by her mother.*

There is also reason to doubt the context-independent nature of grammaticality judgments. In his analysis of presupposition, Dinsmore (1979) has argued cogently that judgments about sentences are always made relative to real or imagined contexts. Certainly speaker reactions to a string of words— even to a string of words with a particular syntactic analysis—are sometimes influenced by contextual factors. For instance, linguists have normally judged sentences like (11)(a) to be ungrammatical; this assessment has figured in the argument for Equi-NP Deletion, a rule reducing (11)(a) to (11)(b).

(11)(a) **I want me to be elected.*
 (b) *I want to be elected.*

Note, however, that the status of (11)(a) is vastly improved when it is used as an answer to (12):

(12) *Who do you want to be elected?*

In fact, (11)(a) is notably better than (11)(b) in this context, even if it remains somewhat marginal.[19]

Facts like these are no doubt describable in a framework embracing the autonomous-syntax hypothesis. However, they are not really anticipated in such

---

[18] Lakoff (1977) offers a characterization of prototypical actions. Note that English is generous in its tolerance of the passive; most transitives permit it, and the factors mentioned are generally subtle in their effect. Their import is more readily observable in other languages (cf. Givón 1979).

[19] *Me* takes normal focus stress when (11)(a) is used in response to (12): *I want me to be elected* (cf. *I want Ted to be elected* in the same context). There are also contexts where (11)(a) is acceptable even when *me* remains unstressed: *Senator, when you contemplate your future and envisage your life for the next few years should you win the presidency, how would you really like to see yourself fare in the coming election? I want me to be elected.* The sentence becomes felicitous to the extent that the context attributes to the subject of *want* an "external" perspective on his role in the event described by the lower clause. (Observe that coreference is still supposed.)

a theory, and are consequently downplayed, ignored, or left for other components to handle in unspecified ways.[20] Here I offer no detailed analysis of the cases cited, but simply note that the data are quite in line with the expectations engendered by cognitive grammar. It does not assert that syntactic rules are necessarily general; often they are fully established for a class of prototypical examples, and become less firmly entrenched as one deviates from the prototype along various parameters. Because a grammatical construction inherently serves to structure semantic content, it is to be expected that the felicity of a sentence is affected by the degree of compatibility between a construction and other semantic specifications. Finally, it is a premise of cognitive grammar that all linguistic units are defined, and all linguistic expressions assessed, relative to some context.

A theory of autonomous syntax cannot be expected to deal with figurative language as part of the syntactic component, for it is obviously a semantic phenomenon. Generative grammarians have in fact left it to be handled by other components, which means in practice that it has hardly been considered at all. Nor would proponents of autonomous syntax be expected to show much interest in the semantic composition of idioms, or to examine their analyzability in the belief that their grammatical behavior might be determined in part by the degree to which semantic content is imputed to individual morphemes (cf. 1.1; Chafe 1968; Gorbet 1973). It is not surprising, then, that Fraser (1970) falsely and gratuitously assumes that idioms are fully unanalyzable, i.e. that their meaning is associated solely with the sequence as a whole. Cognitive grammarians, on the other hand, regard figurative language to be a prime concern, and assume no clear distinction between literal and figurative language, between idioms and conventional expressions of a nonidiomatic sort, or between lexical and grammatical structure; figurative language is accommodated as an integral facet of linguistic organization, one that can be expected to interact with grammatical processes. The two approaches therefore reflect very different qualitative views of the data used for grammatical analysis.

But cognitive grammar goes even further, and makes a claim that strikes at the very heart of the autonomous-syntax hypothesis: it claims that grammar

---

[20] Perlmutter (1980, p. 203) is singularly explicit on this point: "A particular construction in a given language may be restricted to a particular mood or aspect, governed by particular predicates or classes of predicates, or possible only in certain syntactic environments. Similarly, a particular construction may be linked in individual languages with semantic, pragmatic, or presuppositional effects, with constraints on definiteness or specificity of reference of nominals, with the organization of the sentence into old and new information, and so on. The general strategy of RG [relational grammar] in all such cases is to separate the syntactic nature of a particular construction from the semantic, pragmatic, etc. factors with which it interacts." While this is certainly a coherent research strategy, it drastically impoverishes the domain of the theory. One can argue whether such idealization is justified or pernicious.

itself serves an "imagic" function and that much of it has a figurative character. Grammar (like lexicon) embodies conventional **imagery**. By this I mean that it structures a scene in a particular way for purposes of linguistic expression, emphasizing certain facets of it at the expense of others, viewing it from a certain perspective, or construing it in terms of a certain metaphor. Two roughly synonymous sentences with the same content words but different grammatical structures—including, in particular, sentences generally analyzed as being transformationally related—are claimed instead to be semantically distinct by virtue of their different grammatical organization per se.[21]

Consider the rule of Dative Shift, which supposedly derives sentences like (13)(b) from underlying structures like (13)(a).

(13) (a) *He sent a letter to Susan.*
     (b) *He sent Susan a letter.*

These sentences have the same truth value and can be used interchangeably to describe the same event, but I suggest that they nevertheless differ semantically (cf. Goldsmith 1980). Because (13)(a) employs the preposition *to*, it emphasizes the path traversed by the letter with Susan as goal. By contrast, (13)(b) emphasizes the resulting state in which Susan possesses the letter; I will assume that this possessive relationship is symbolized by the juxtaposition and linear order of *Susan* and *a letter*. I do not claim that the notion of a path is lacking in (13)(b), or the notion of possession in (13)(a): both are present to some degree in each sentence. Instead I claim that the relative **salience** of these notions differs in the two examples owing to their respective symbolization by *to* and by the juxtaposition of nominals. The differences in grammatical structure therefore highlight one facet of the conceived situation at the expense of another; I will say that the two sentences present the scene through different **images** (cf. Langacker 1976, 1979).

I think the contrast between (13)(a) and (13)(b) is apparent on an intuitive basis, but there are also supporting data. If sentences of the form X VERB Y *to* Z emphasize the path Y traverses, while those of the form X VERB Z Y highlight the resulting state where Z controls Y, there should be cases where one construction is preferred over the other on grounds of semantic compatibility. It is of course well known that this is so. For instance, (14)(a) is much more felicitous than (14)(b), since a fence is more easily construed as the endpoint of a path than as the possessor of a ball.

---

[21] Langacker (1982a) explicates the semantic difference between English actives and passives in relatively full detail. Tuggy (1980) shows convincingly that Spanish sentences with datives (e.g. *Le ensuciaron el coche* 'They got his car dirty') are quite different semantically from the corresponding sentences with possessives (*Ensuciaron su coche*) despite their identical translations: the first construes the situation with respect to "affectedness" or "interest," the second with respect to possession. Tuggy argues strongly for an imagic (as opposed to truth-value) conception of linguistic semantics.

(14)(a)   *The shortstop threw a ball to the fence.*
    (b) **The shortstop threw the fence a ball.*
(15)(a) ?*Your cousin gave a new coat of paint to the fence.*
    (b)   *Your cousin gave the fence a new coat of paint.*

The judgments are reversed in (15), for though there is a sense in which a fence possesses a coat of paint (this is akin to a part/whole relation), the notion of a path is inherently far less salient in *paint* than in *throw*. In an analysis based on relative salience, and on the felicity of construing a situation in terms of a particular image, graded judgments such as these are to be expected.

This discussion is only intended to show that cognitive grammar and theories of autonomous syntax have very different qualitative conceptions of the data to be accounted for. To that extent, they are incommensurable. An autonomous syntactician judges (13)(a)–(b) to have the same meaning and thinks nothing of deriving them from the same source. A cognitive grammarian sees the same two sentences as contrasting semantically because of the symbolic import of their grammatical structures; to ignore this imagery (and treat the sentences as simple grammatical variants) would be to overlook an essential aspect of the data.

Theories of autonomous syntax have a natural affinity for truth-value semantics. A truth-value account of meaning and semantic equivalence makes it plausible to derive sentence pairs like (13)(a)–(b) from the same source, ignoring the semantic contribution of grammatical morphemes and syntactic constructions. But for cognitive grammar, meaning resides in hierarchies of conventional imagery. The semantic contribution of a grammatical morpheme like *to* therefore cannot be ignored, even if it represents a figurative extension of the spatial *to* into more abstract domains. A grammatical construction imposes and symbolizes a particular structuring of conceptual content, and in this perspective it makes no sense to speak of autonomous syntax. Consequently it would be a mistake to regard the two approaches as alternate accounts of the same data: they embody substantially different conceptions of what those data are and what has to be said about them.

1.2.3. *Economy*

Let us take as an established methodological principle that economy is to be sought in linguistic description as in any scientific enterprise. Simplicity of description has been an overriding concern of generative theory, and its importance can be acknowledged for cognitive grammar as well. The two frameworks differ substantially, however, in their interpretations of how the principle of economy should be applied in linguistic practice. As illustration, consider two matters touched on previously: conventional expressions and the rule/list fallacy.

Inasmuch as it characterizes a speaker's knowledge of linguistic convention, the grammar of a language is responsible for listing its full set of conventional expressions (such as *go for a walk, absolutely incredible, have a good time, corporate greed, keep an eye out for, mind your own business, rise and shine, cheap imitation, the seconds are ticking away, and so on*, and so on). To furnish such a list would obviously be a vast undertaking, for there are many thousands of such expressions, and new ones are always forming; the question might therefore be raised whether it is actually necessary or desirable to do so.[22] A grammar listing all conventional expressions would be massively complex, and it might be objected that such a list would contribute nothing in the way of insight or general principles.

The reluctance of generative grammarians to concern themselves seriously with conventional expressions is largely inspired by their abhorrence of lists. Obviously their talents are better devoted to the pursuit of general rules and principles, which have broader import than the statement of idiosyncrasies. It would be fallacious, however, to invoke the principle of economy to argue that conventional expressions should not be listed in a grammar—one could just as well argue that phonology should be excluded from a linguistic description because a grammar containing a phonological component is more complex than a grammar without one. The principle of economy must be interpreted in relation to other considerations, in particular the requirement of factuality: true simplicity is not achieved just by omitting relevant facts. Questions of economy are meaningfully raised only with reference to a particular body of data.

The issue of whether conventional expressions should be included in a grammar is factual rather than methodological in a framework taking seriously the goal of psychological reality in linguistic description. If a speaker does in fact learn a large set of conventional expressions as fixed units, it is incumbent on the grammar of a language to represent this fact by providing an inventory of these expressions. The simplest description that accurately accommodates all the data must by definition include such a list.[23]

In generative grammar the goal of economy has often been equated with the goal of capturing significant linguistic generalizations (hence the early emphasis on abbreviatory notational devices and the "evaluation metric"). By capturing such generalizations, particular statements can be eliminated from the grammar in favor of a far smaller number of general statements, i.e. lists

[22] This issue is addressed on the theoretical level, not in terms of what a linguist will actually be expected to do when he gets up tomorrow. No one is presently capable of writing the cognitive grammar of a language, just as no one is about to write a full generative grammar. It is important, however, to reach some understanding of what a grammar would consist of were we really able to write one.

[23] With apologies to Sapir, we can say that not only do all grammars leak, they also list (massively).

can be replaced by rules. To return to a previous'example (1.1.6), specific forms like *beads*, *shoes*, *toes*, and *walls* can be omitted from the grammar of English if one provides a general rule of plural formation that accounts for them. Listing regular forms thus implies lost generalizations and failure to achieve an optimal analysis.

This line of thought illustrates the rule/list fallacy. It is fallacious because it assumes that one is forced to choose between rules and lists: the options are posed as **rules alone** vs. **lists alone**. If these are the only two options, it can be argued that the rules must be chosen, for lists by themselves do not express generalizations. There is in reality a third choice, however, namely **both rules and lists**. It is plausible to suppose that speakers of English master many regular plural forms as fixed units in addition to learning the general rule of plural formation. Similarly, it is clear that speakers learn as fixed units a large number of conventional expressions that are nevertheless fully analyzable and regular in formation (*absolutely incredible*, *cheap imitation*, *great idea*, *turn the page*, *let the cat out*, and so forth). General statements and particular statements can perfectly well coexist in the cognitive representation of linguistic phenomena, just as we learn certain products by rote in addition to mastering general procedures for multiplication.[24] To the extent that this is so, an accurate linguistic description claiming psychological reality must contain both rules expressing generalizations and specific forms learned as fixed units, even if the specific forms accord fully with the rules. When the principle of economy is appropriately applied to linguistics, simplicity cannot be sought at the expense of factuality, nor can brevity be equated with the capturing of significant generalizations.

1.2.4. *Explicitness*

We can agree that a linguist should make his description as precise and explicit as possible at every stage of analysis. We can further agree that at some point in its evolution a linguistic theory must receive appropriate mathematical expression. Recent linguistic history has shown, however, that consensus on these basic methodological principles does not readily translate into agreement on the proper role of formalization in linguistic practice, nor on the nature of an optimal formalism. Let me outline my position on a few of the issues that arise.

Certain truths about formalization are self-evident. The first is that there is no necessary correlation between insight and empirical adequacy on the one hand, and degree of formalization on the other. Ideas concerning the structure of language that are expressed in preliminary, informal terms may neverthe-

---

[24] I have learned that $12 \times 12 = 144$, but I can also use the principles of multiplication to compute this product. Conversely, my ability to compute the product is consistent with my having mastered it as a fixed unit.

less be valuable and essentially correct. Conversely, it is possible to construct a totally rigorous formal system that makes blatantly false claims about language, or that bears no nontrivial relation whatever to linguistic organization. A linguist can never legitimately proclaim the worthiness or superiority of a theory on grounds of mathematical rigor alone. Formalization is not per se a virtue, nor the lack of it a mortal sin.[25]

A second self-evident truth is that formalization is not an end in itself, but rather a means to understanding. From the standpoint of linguistic investigation, a formal system holds no intrinsic interest unless we have reason to believe that it correctly models certain aspects of language. Some would argue that we achieve full and definitive understanding of a linguistic phenomenon only when we represent it explicitly and precisely in the context of a rigorous mathematical system. We will accept this contention for sake of discussion (though it is not beyond dispute), but our acceptance leaves more specific methodological issues unresolved. The question still remains of what constitutes the optimal path towards this goal of complete understanding and formal expression.

One school of thought holds that attempts at formalization are never premature (Dougherty 1973), and emphasizes their heuristic value. Chomsky (1957, p. 5) puts it quite eloquently: "Precisely constructed models for linguistic structure can play an important role, both negative and positive, in the process of discovery itself. By pushing a precise but inadequate formulation to an unacceptable conclusion, we can often expose the exact source of this inadequacy and, consequently, gain a deeper understanding of the linguistic data. More positively, a formalized theory may automatically provide solutions for many problems other than those for which it was explicitly designed." Stated abstractly, this position is unimpeachable. One can, however, question how effective the strategy has actually been in advancing our understanding of language. One might argue, for example, that the basic formalisms of generative linguistics so drastically misrepresent the actual structure of language that the observed shortcomings fail to be truly revelatory; arriving at an adequate theory may not be possible through successive modifications that leave its basic orientation and premises untouched, but only by starting anew from a totally different perspective. Or one might contend that substantial progress in linguistics generally comes about by conceptual breakthroughs that are widely recognized as such irrespective of how precisely they are

---

[25] An analogous point holds for the current emphasis on linguistic argumentation (e.g. Soames and Perlmutter 1979). First it must be realized that argumentation is only a single mode of discourse; it is not the optimal mode for every phase in the evolution of a scientific discipline. Beyond this, it must be admitted that an argument is no stronger than its weakest premise. Contemporary linguistic discourse is permeated by a host of implicit assumptions that fare rather poorly once they are recognized and subjected to critical scrutiny.

stated or how they relate to previous formalisms. I think a case can be made for both these responses, but their validity is a matter of judgment that need not detain us here. The potential heuristic value of formalism can hardly be questioned, and we should exploit it to whatever extent proves feasible.

Our actual concern is with a somewhat stronger position, namely the view that rigorous formalization is *prerequisite* to any substantial achievement in linguistics. On this view, concepts, analyses, hypotheses, preliminary models, and programmatic suggestions count for nothing and fail to advance our knowledge and understanding until they are formulated with great precision in the context of a well-articulated mathematical system. Only by constructing successive generations of formal models can we ever hope to approximate our ultimate goal: a fully adequate, completely formalized grammar. I do not know if any linguist would subscribe to so rigid a position—perhaps we should regard it as a straw man. It will nevertheless serve as a convenient reference point for some brief observations.

Taken to its logical conclusion, this position is obviously extreme and unworkable. Strictly enforced, it would wipe out virtually all of linguistics (and not a few other disciplines). Even the most meticulous linguistic expositions fall short of complete formalization in the strictest mathematical sense, including those that bristle with imposing symbols and complicated formulas. Linguists normally express themselves in a natural rather than mathematical language, and the notations they employ are at most semiformal. Formalization in linguistics is thus not an absolute but a matter of degree. Then how formal is formal enough?

Common sense tells us that there is no fixed answer to this question. All we can reasonably demand is that a linguist be as clear and precise as possible consistent with his objectives and his present understanding of the subject matter. During preliminary phases of investigation, when general organizing principles and optimal ways of conceptualizing central phenomena are not yet apparent, there is virtue in avoiding arbitrary formalizations that tend to limit one's perspectives and freeze one's mode of thought. It may prove helpful at later stages to pursue the course Chomsky suggests, pushing a formal model as far as it will go to see where it leads and where it breaks down. Science comprises many distinct, complementary kinds of activity, and linguists work on different levels with a variety of techniques and approaches; it would be misguided to insist on a single modus operandi or a specific degree of formal precision for all types and phases of investigation. All linguistic constructs evolve from initially vague proposals or sketchily defined concepts that are gradually refined and rendered more precise. Only at the endpoint of the process can they be given revealing, nonarbitrary formal expression.

That brings us to the third and final self-evident truth: it is not impossible for a formal description to be counterproductive by giving a false or drastically distorted account of its subject matter. The demands of formalization tend to impose on the analyst their own constraints and expectations about the nature of the material being described. A particular mathematical device (e.g. truth-value semantics based on formal logic) may be used simply because it is available, not because the facts of language cry out for this approach as opposed to others. Moreover, properties may be falsely ascribed to language just because they facilitate formal description. The analytical convenience of assuming that everything in language is discrete encourages linguists to develop discrete formalizations, resulting in general neglect for the many aspects of linguistic structure not amenable to such treatment. Convenience for the analyst is not a valid criterion in determining whether language manifests certain properties, and we should be aware of the subtle pressures it exerts.[26]

The reader would be mistaken to read into these remarks any antipathy to formalization on my part, or to conclude that the concepts of cognitive grammar are hopelessly vague and incapable of precise formulation; in fact I would argue that quite the opposite is true. I do however believe that the practical virtues of formalization have commonly been overstated and its potential pitfalls overlooked. I further believe it misguided, and wholly gratuitous at our present level of understanding, to use a "more formal than thou" attitude to bludgeon one's opponents into submission. If it is not to be counterproductive, the application of formal methods to linguistic analysis must be thoughtful, judicious, and appropriate.

1.2.5. *Generality*

Generality is a virtue. Linguists properly seek general rules and universal principles. They merit our plaudits in stating obvious regularities, and our encouragement in finding others that are less readily apparent. And counting heavily in favor of a theory or description is its ability to capture nonobvious generalizations or to unify seemingly diverse phenomena.

It must nevertheless be admitted that linguistics is an empirical discipline. We must recognize that language is a mixture of regularity and irregularity, and deal with this fact in a natural, appropriate way. Linguistic practice has sometimes been questionable in this regard. For instance, I find it arbitrary and unrealistic to posit a fundamental distinction between fully general rules on the one hand and statements involving some measure of idiosyncrasy on the other, and to isolate the former in a separate component of the grammar (syntax). Linguists have occasionally invoked suspicious devices to make things appear more regular than they really are. One example is the invention

---

[26] The notion that language constitutes an autonomous formal system is another instance of analytical convenience leading to a priori claims. I will argue that a generative grammar is not a realistic goal, if by this one means a self-contained formal description that enumerates all and only the well-formed sentences of a language (including a full account of their meaning).

of rule features (Lakoff 1970), which preserved the apparent generality of syntactic rules by concealing in the lexicon the actual limitations on their applicability.[27]

Generative grammarians have always operated with an archetypal conception of language as a system of general rules, and have therefore not accommodated irregular and idiosyncratic phenomena in a natural or convincing manner; there has been a tendency to ignore these phenomena in the quest for generalizations. Cognitive grammar, by contrast, is a **usage-based** theory. The grammar lists the full set of particular statements representing a speaker's grasp of linguistic convention, including those subsumed by general statements. Rather than thinking them an embarrassment, cognitive grammarians regard particular statements as the matrix from which general statements (rules) are extracted. For example, the N + -s rule of English plural formation is extracted by speakers from an array of specific plural forms (*toes, beads, walls*, etc.), including some learned previously as fixed units; in fact the rule is viewed simply as a schematic characterization of such units. Speakers do not necessarily forget the forms they already know once the rule is extracted, nor does the rule preclude their learning additional forms as established units. Consequently, particular statements (specific forms) coexist with general statements (rules accounting for those forms) in a speaker's representation of linguistic convention, which incorporates a huge inventory of specific forms learned as units (conventional expressions). Out of this sea of particularity speakers extract whatever generalizations they can. Most of these are of limited scope, and some forms cannot be assimilated to any general patterns at all. Fully general rules are not the expected case in this perspective, but rather a special, limiting case along a continuum that also embraces totally idiosyncratic forms and patterns of all intermediate degrees of generality. The archetypal conception is thus seen as a matter of false expectations.

Linguists have also been known to harbor false expectations at a higher level of generality—that of language universals. An example from an earlier phase of generative theory is the notion that the apparent grammatical diversity of languages is largely superficial: that as we penetrate beneath the surface to more abstract levels of representation, languages begin to appear much more similar, perhaps even identical. According to this view, the underlying syntactic uniformity of languages is obscured at the surface level by the operation of grammatical rules, so it is at the level of underlying structures that we find the most extensive grammatical universals. In contrast, cognitive grammar claims that grammatical structure is almost entirely overt. Surface gram-

---

[27] Another example is the analysis of impersonal sentences presented in Perlmutter (1978); the ostensibly universal passive rule wherein a direct object becomes a subject (i.e. 2 advances to 1) is generalized to impersonals, so that a "dummy" 2 is introduced and advances to 1 even when the verb is intransitive.

matical form does not conceal a "truer," deeper level of grammatical organization; rather, it itself embodies the conventional means a language employs for the structuring and symbolization of semantic content. Grammatical diversity is real instead of only apparent, and although grammatical universals can still be sought and formulated, they must be limited and flexible enough to accommodate the variability actually encountered.

A closely related issue is whether semantic structure is universal. I admit to assuming so in the distant past, but I had not yet taken into account the pervasive importance of imagery, i.e. our ability to construe a conceived situation in many different ways (seeing it from different perspectives, emphasizing certain facets over others, approaching it at different levels of abstraction, and so on). Lexicon and grammar are storehouses of conventional imagery, which differs substantially from language to language. If one language says *I am cold*, a second *I have cold*, and a third *It is cold to me*, these expressions differ semantically even though they refer to the same experience, for they employ different images to structure the same basic conceptual content. It is therefore a central claim of cognitive grammar that meaning is language-specific to a considerable extent. Full universality of semantic structure cannot be presumed even on the assumption that human cognitive ability and experience are quite comparable across cultures.[28]

These remarks do not imply a lack of concern for language universals or the inability of cognitive grammar to reveal universal facets of linguistic organization. To the contrary, certain properties of the model (e.g. the notions of schematicity and prototypes) especially suit it to the statement of both absolute universals and universal tendencies, and I would argue that it clarifies the nature and status of universal constructs. Because it rests on different conceptual foundations, however, cognitive grammar differs from other frameworks in where it looks for universals, how it expresses them, and how extensive they are judged to be.

1.2.6. *Predictiveness*

Linguistic theorists place much emphasis on the importance of making strong empirical claims. Several related factors determine whether a theory or

---

[28] It is thus fallacious to assume that a phenomenon is purely "syntactic" just because it is nonuniversal. For instance, it is a matter of convention (not cognitive necessity) that *scissors*, *pants*, *glasses*, *binoculars*, etc. are plural in form (and largely in behavior), but contra Hudson (1976, p. 6), this does not imply that "syntactic number" is distinct from semantic number or that syntax constitutes an autonomous component of grammar. The plurality of these expressions reflects conventional imagery: they highlight the bipartite character of the objects named, so the assumption that they are semantically singular is incorrect. Contrasting forms like *nostrils* vs. *nose*, *buns/buttocks* vs. *ass/bottom*, *stars* vs. *constellation*, etc. similarly construe the conceived entity by emphasizing either internal multiplicity or overall unity. The existence of an autonomous syntactic component hardly follows from the conventionality of such images.

description satisfies this requirement. For one thing, it should make clear predictions: the nature of supporting or disconfirming evidence should be readily apparent. A theory must also be restrictive, by limiting descriptive options to a narrowly specified range that rules out many conceivable alternatives. It should further provide a principled means of choosing among competing analyses.

It is once again possible to accept these abstract methodological principles while disagreeing about their proper interpretation and application in linguistic practice. The discussion that follows is organized in two parts: we will first consider the level of predictability that can reasonably be expected in linguistic analysis; and then consider the optimal means for achieving restrictiveness in a linguistic theory.

1.2.6.1. *Level of Predictability.* It is common for linguists to demand of a rule, principle, or definition what might be called **absolute predictability**. What this means, roughly, is that a statement pertaining to a certain class must be valid for all and only the members of that class if it is to be accepted as having any predictive value at all. Statements that achieve this level of predictability are obviously desirable, for they make the strongest and most precise empirical claims. Yet it cannot simply be assumed that language invariably or even typically lends itself to statements of this kind. In fact it does not. Expectations of absolute predictability are sometimes unreasonable for natural language and commonly lead to erroneous conclusions, dubious claims, or conceptual confusion. We must scale our expectations down to a level of predictability that is appropriate and realistic for the subject matter.

The expectation of absolute predictability has been prominent in diachronic and typological studies, and has not fared well. The most famous example is the neogrammarian doctrine that valid sound laws have no "true" exceptions: apparent exceptions can always be explained by analogy or by the operation of another sound law yet to be discovered, or in some other manner. Today it is generally agreed that this doctrine is wrong, whatever its heuristic merits; certain types of changes spread by lexical diffusion, typically leaving residues, so at no stage does a sound law necessarily hold true for all eligible forms (see Labov 1981 for a general review). In rather more oblique fashion, language typologists manifest an expectation of absolute predictability when they distinguish between a stable, typologically consistent language and a language that is changing from one consistent type to another.[29] The properties defining a typological class are thus expected to correlate fully, with qualifications

---

[29] "Just as we have determined the typological consistency of a given language from the degree to which it observes the ideal patterns in the proposition, we may begin to do so for the qualifier component of the sentence. When languages show patterns other than those expected, we may assume that they are undergoing change" (Lehmann 1973, p. 55).

made only for languages supposedly caught in transition. Smith (1981) does a good job of exposing the inadequacies of this outlook. Few if any languages can be considered fully consistent, to the extent that we understand what full consistency actually is. Although certain clusters of properties show some tendency to correlate diachronically and cross-linguistically, straightforward interpretation of the empirical evidence runs directly counter to any claim that these correlations are absolute.

The standard criterial-attribute model of categorization also exemplifies an expectation of absolute predictability. If the model is interpreted strictly, all and only the members of a class or category will possess the entire list of criterial properties, which thereby achieves absolute predictability with respect to class membership. We have already questioned the appropriateness of this model for linguistic categorization (1.1.4.2). The prototype model offers a more realistic account in many instances, but adopting it implies that class membership is not predictable in absolute terms: it is a matter of degree, decreasing as an entity deviates from the prototype, with no specific cutoff point beyond which speakers abruptly become incapable of perceiving a similarity and thus assimilating an entity to the category. One would be wrong to claim that the prototype model is nonpredictive—it is founded on the prediction that entities are more readily accepted as members of a category the more closely they approximate the prototype—but its predictions are statistical rather than absolute.

An expectation of absolute predictability is also apparent in the requirement that certain rules (syntactic rules in particular) be fully productive. The validity of a grammatical generalization is often denied unless one can predict exactly which forms it does and does not apply to. For example, Fraser (1976) is amenable to deriving at least some verb-particle combinations by transformation from a more elaborate underlying structure, but he rejects this type of analysis for any set of forms for which the required rule is less than fully productive. Thus the pattern exemplified by *give out, hand out, lend out, pass out, pay out, rent out,* and so on cannot be derived by syntactic rule because not all combinations predicted by such a rule actually occur (*grant out, offer out, show out,* and *proffer out* are ostensibly nonoccurrent and unacceptable); consequently Fraser simply lists them in the lexicon as semantically unanalyzable expressions.[30] Oehrle (1977) makes a similar assumption in his review of Green (1974). Concerned with predicting on semantic grounds the possible occurrence of Dative Shift, Green posits a number of semantically based verb classes that supposedly govern the operation. Among Oehrle's criticisms is the fact that not all verbs meeting her semantic criteria actually undergo the rule: "A significant number of verbs fall into one (or more) of G's

---

[30] See Lindner (1981) for a penetrating critique of Fraser's analysis and theoretical assumptions, as well as for her own highly revealing analysis of verb-particle constructions.

classes, yet do not manifest the syntactic properties which she would require of them. . . . Thus they are all counterexamples . . . to her analysis of the dative alternation" (Oehrle 1977, p. 207). Oehrle suggests that any semantic regularities that might be found can be handled in the lexicon by redundancy rules.

It should be apparent by now that cognitive grammar is at odds with certain assumptions implicit in such arguments. For one thing, it rejects the supposition that full generality is criterial for syntax or that it isolates a natural, coherently describable body of phenomena. Because it rejects the rule/list fallacy, moreover, the ability to predict exactly which forms a rule applies to is not seen as an overriding concern; the grammar specifies a rule's range of applicability directly and explicitly, by listing established expressions (even if regular) together with whatever generalizations they support (i.e. patterns and subpatterns described at different levels of abstraction—cf. Ch. 11). Beyond this, cognitive grammar emphasizes the importance of factors that make it unreasonable to expect rule applicability to be predictable in absolute terms.

One such factor is the relevance of prototypes in determining the conventional range of a construction. I have already noted that the English passive construction, though quite general, is organized around the core of prototypical action verbs. We therefore predict the relative infelicity of passives at the fringes of the conventionally permitted range. A nonaction verb like *want*, for instance, is marginal in the passive, so its acceptability hinges on such matters as the nature of the accompanying nominals:

(16)(a) ?*A bicycle is wanted by me.
    (b) ??That bicycle is wanted by my brother.
    (c) ?That bicycle is wanted by every kid on the block.
    (d)   That bicycle must be wanted by somebody.

We further predict that verbs not passivizing at all should cluster at the opposite extreme from the prototype on the activity scale, as they in fact do.[31] There is, however, no claim to the effect that distance from the prototype allows us to predict exactly which forms will and will not passivize—quite the contrary. To the extent that language employs prototypes rather than criterial attributes for purposes of categorization, such absolute predictability constitutes an unreasonable expectation.

A second factor militating against absolute predictability in rule application

---

[31] *Have, resemble, suit, cost*, etc., are quite far from the prototype of overt physical actions showing a clear agent/patient asymmetry between subject and object. Consider also the non-passivizability of a sentence like *Tuesday saw the arrival of a new set of challenges*. One approach claims that the passive is ungrammatical because *Tuesday* is not the true (underlying) subject of *see*. I would say instead that *see* is used here in an extended sense (something akin to 'be the setting for'), which is much further from the action-verb prototype than its basic sense.

is the importance of conventional imagery, which is inherently variable and nonpredictable. Speakers have the conceptual freedom to construe a given situation in many different ways, and we cannot predict in absolute terms which particular images might be chosen and conventionalized. I suggested previously that the constructions in (17) embody different images: expressions of the form X VERB Y *to* Z highlight the path (with Z as goal) that Y traverses, whereas those of the form X VERB Z Y highlight instead the resulting state where Z possesses Y.

(17)(a) *I sent a book to the library.*
  (b) *I sent the library a book.*

Although (17)(a) is well formed, the status of (17)(b) depends on how one interprets the term *library*. If the speaker construes a library as merely a building or location, (a) is felicitous (for a building or location readily serves as the goal of a path), but (b) is questionable, for it is difficult to conceptualize a location as the possessor of an object. There is no such difficulty if the speaker—emphasizing other facets of this complex notion—construes the library as an institution, since English incorporates the conventional metaphor that institutions are peoplelike and hence conceivable possessors. The existence of this conventional metaphor thus determines the possible well-formedness of (b), and how a speaker views things determines its well-formedness on a given occasion. But nothing dictates in absolute terms either the conventionality of the metaphor or a speaker's momentary intention.

As a third and final factor, we must recognize the role of conventionality per se, reflecting the vicissitudes of language use and change. For instance, if it is accepted that the passive construction extends outwards from prototypical action verbs as its distributional core, precisely how far and in what directions it extends from this core depend on a variety of unpredictable matters: analogical pressures, the existence of competing constructions with comparable function, the exploitation and conventionalization of alternative images, the day-to-day exigencies of language use, and so on. The precise extension of the passive construction can thus be expected to change through time for a given language and to differ from one language to another. English, in extending the construction to the vast majority of transitive verbs, approaches one extreme; in other languages we can expect to find comparable constructions that are considerably more limited in distribution, even restricted to the prototypical core.

Any kind of diachronic perspective should cast severe doubt on expectations of absolute predictability in linguistic structure. It is a matter of general agreement that the path of language change cannot be predicted in absolute terms; at best we can cite general tendencies and common types of innovation. Since a language at any historical stage is the cumulative result of innumerable specific changes, themselves not subject to absolute predictability, it would be strange indeed if such predictability were characteristic of the synchronic system.

1.2.6.2. *Restrictiveness*. Absolute predictability is also relevant to the formulation of a restrictive linguistic theory, i.e. one that specifies universal properties of language as well as its range of possible variation. In discussions of restrictiveness the criterial-attribute model is generally assumed; the class of possible languages is thought to be describable by fully predictive statements, which may be positive ("every language has property X"), negative ("no language has property X"), or implicational ("every language with property X also has property Y"). Checking a putative linguistic system against this list of statements yields a definitive decision about whether it is a possible natural language. A clear yes/no verdict can always be arrived at.

The appropriateness of this scheme cannot be granted a priori. Central concepts of cognitive grammar suggest an alternative, where linguistic theory consists in the substantive characterization of prototypical structures, graded with respect to their degree of prototypicality and cognitive entrenchment; higher degrees of prototypicality and entrenchment translate into greater likelihood that a structure will be implemented among the conventions defining a given language. This conception gives rise to expectations that differ from those suggested by the scheme based on criterial attributes. For one thing, we are led to anticipate not only **absolute universals**, i.e. properties characteristic of every human language without exception, but also **universal tendencies** of varying strength, which are reflected in the cross-linguistic frequency of properties. Secondly, no abrupt transition is expected between what is possible linguistically and what is impossible. The farther something deviates from the prototypical, deeply ingrained structures specified in linguistic theory, the less chance it has of being adopted as part of any particular language; but we cannot necessarily assume any specific cutoff point prior to which a structure is nonproblematic and beyond which it is totally impossible. Finally, absolute predictability may in general be unattainable. For many structural properties, we can only hope to estimate the relative probability of finding them in an arbitrarily chosen language, and should not expect to be able to predict their presence or absence in absolute terms.

Restrictiveness in linguistic theory is commonly thought to demand a battery of explicit prohibitions: for example, that no language can have more than four contrastive nasal consonants; that OVS is never permitted as a basic word order; or that no syntactic rule, in any language, can involve structures X and Y where X is external, and Y internal, to a tensed sentence (cf. Chomsky 1973). Although valid generalizations along these lines are worth noting, the necessity and ultimate legitimacy of fully predictive negative statements is open to question. In the first place, even a very large number of prohibitions would probably not completely delimit the range of linguistic potentiality, and they would certainly not offer a positive characterization of language structure. (Recall the old joke about how to sculpt an elephant: get a huge block of marble; then take your hammer and chisel and knock off everything that doesn't look like an elephant.) Moreover, language has proved itself generally reluctant to adhere to the strictures linguists would impose on it. Not untypical is Pullum's recent experience in having to revoke a previous claim that OVS is impossible as a basic word order (Derbyshire and Pullum 1981).

Stating these restrictions in absolute terms also forces arbitrary limits in what should be matters of degree. If languages can have four contrastive nasal consonants, might there not be a few that have five? (There apparently are some in Australia.) And if five is possible, is it really out of the question that some language might develop six, or even seven? Rather than specify a rigid upper bound, it would seem more reasonable for linguistic theory to identify two-nasal- and possibly three-nasal-consonant systems as prototypical and to rank particular nasal-segment types by prototypicality, reflecting their differential expectation of being found in a given language. A truly impossible linguistic system (e.g. one with two dozen simple nasal consonants in its phonemic inventory) should not be precluded by any specific statement to that effect in linguistic theory, but rather by the extremity of its deviation (including, in this example, its use of many highly marked—i.e. nonprototypical—nasal segments) from anything directly sanctioned.[32]

A substantive characterization of prototypical linguistic structures can therefore in principle be highly restrictive, even without explicit negative statements or the presumption of absolute predictability. A substantive theory of this kind would be easily falsifiable. The widespread occurrence of structures extremely distant from the supposed prototype would constitute evidence against it, as would a totally random cross-linguistic distribution of linguistic traits, or any distribution where structures predicted to be marginal predominate over those nearer the prototype.

Beyond this, cognitive grammar is so defined that it completely rules out arbitrary formal devices. More specifically, I adopt the **content requirement**: the only structures permitted in the grammar of a language (or among the substantive specifications of universal grammar) are (1) phonological, semantic, or symbolic structures that actually occur in linguistic expressions; (2) sche-

---

[32] Morreall (1979) exemplifies this type of approach, arguing convincingly against the generative semantic claim that certain kinds of words are universally impossible because they require prelexical syntactic rules that violate general constraints. Morreall establishes that such words can indeed occur and are unusual only because they stand for concepts that would be useful only under very special circumstances: "There are improbable words, some more improbable than others; but there are no impossible words" (1979, p. 727).

mas for such structures; and (3) categorizing relationships involving the elements in (1) and (2). Hence no descriptive constructs are permitted that lack both phonological and semantic content. Furthermore, overt structures cannot be derived from hypothetical "underlying" structures having a substantially different character. Although the full import of this restriction may not be immediately apparent, I believe it inherently places far more stringent limitations on the descriptive options available to the analyst than are found in any established theory.

It is commonly asserted that a unified account of the various facets of linguistic structure is inconsistent with the overriding goal of restrictiveness, attainable only by dividing language structure into numerous separate components, each characterized individually and specified in exceedingly narrow terms (cf. Chomsky 1972). I believe that precisely the opposite is true. For one thing, positing a continuum—e.g. the continuum of symbolic structures uniting lexicon, morphology, and syntax—does not prevent the recognition of qualitative distinctions between different regions of it (though it does discourage simplistic claims couched in terms of absolute predictability). But more significantly, characterizing one "component" in essential isolation as an autonomous entity frees it from restrictions inherently imposed by other aspects of linguistic structure in the context of an integrated account. Theories of autonomous syntax, for instance, allow the disregard of all semantic constraints in syntactic analysis: syntactic constructs can be invented with no thought for their possible semantic content or implications, and syntactic structures can be related (e.g. by transformational derivation from a common deep structure) despite appreciable differences in meaning; no matter what the analyst does in the syntax, special rules of semantic interpretation can always be invoked to patch things up.[33] Theories that fragment linguistic structure into numerous self-contained components give the investigator enormous freedom to disguise the arbitrariness or shortcomings of an analysis by assigning responsibility for the problems that arise to some other, as yet ill-defined, component, or to the special provisions that must be made for the articulation of the components with one another. Thus it is hard to take seriously any claims of restrictiveness for such theories, at least as they presently stand.

Finally, we can ask whether the type of linguistic theory I have outlined (admittedly in sketchy terms) can furnish a principled means of choosing among competing analyses. I must first deny the assumption that a single analysis is necessarily valid to the exclusion of all others (this assumption is one manifestation of the exclusionary fallacy). Consider the examples in (18).

---

[33] The content requirement rules out many such shenanigans. A cognitive grammar analysis must show how the meaning of an expression results from integrating the semantic values of its overt lexical and grammatical morphemes, each being attributed a meaning that can either be observed in other uses or considered a natural extension from such a meaning.

Analyzing the *out* in (a) as pertaining to the removal of wrinkles from the fabric, parallel to its interpretation in (b), is not considered incompatible with the claim that it also expresses the lengthening of the fabric, as in (c), and possibly even the motion of the girl's hand away from her body, on the model of (d).

(18)(a) *The girl smoothed out the fabric.*
   (b) *The detergent got out all the spots.*
   (c) *We stretched out the carpet.*
   (d) *I reached out my hand.*

Each interpretation represents an established pattern of English grammar, and there is no evident reason for contending that one necessarily holds sway to the total exclusion of the others (cf. Lindner 1981).

Nevertheless, the possibility of multiple analyses does not require that all conceivable analyses be seriously entertained. Suppose we can achieve a substantive linguistic theory, i.e. one that enumerates prototypical linguistic structures with indications of their degree of prototypicality and entrenchment. Because it constitutes a statement of natural linguistic tendencies, a theory of this sort will serve without additional apparatus to indicate the relative likelihood with which speakers will adopt different analyses of a given phenomenon. The general principle is straightforward: unless there is evidence to the contrary, the preferred analysis is that which minimizes the deviation from these natural tendencies. For instance, one substantive universal specified in linguistic theory is the tendency for a consonant to assimilate to an adjacent vowel, and as a special case of this, the tendency for [n] to palatalize before [i], yielding [ñi]. Because [n] is probably the most prototypical of the nasal consonants, the obvious analysis for a language showing this alternation between [n] and [ñ] is to treat [n] as the basic allophone (or category prototype) and [ñ] as a contextually determined variant. The alternative of making [ñ] the basic allophone runs afoul of natural tendencies with respect to both category prototype and assimilatory behavior.

CHAPTER 2

Fundamental Concepts

HOW IS LANGUAGE ORGANIZED? What are the objectives of linguistic description? These are the focal concerns of the present chapter, which begins by discussing the nature of a grammar. It is claimed in particular that a grammar is nongenerative, and that a rigid distinction between linguistic and nonlinguistic elements is arbitrary. A central notion of cognitive grammar, namely the idea that grammatical structure is inherently symbolic, is subsequently explicated. Examined in conclusion are componentiality and correspondence, two basic and pervasive phenomena.

2.1. The Nature of a Grammar

Cognitive grammar takes seriously the goal of psychological reality in linguistic description. The word "goal" must be emphasized. It is not suggested that a strong claim of psychological reality can be made for any particular linguistic analysis as currently constituted. The description of a language is nevertheless a substantive hypothesis about its actual cognitive representation, and linguistic investigation is an empirical enterprise, its claims to be tested against the facts of cognitive structure. Our present inability to observe these facts directly does not render them forever inaccessible in principle.

The **grammar** of a language is a comprehensive description of its structure. There are two broad classes of grammars. The first comprises grammars that are actually written. Subject as they are to the limitations of their authors (including mortality and the lack of omniscience), the grammars in this category are inexplicit in various ways and necessarily selective in coverage, despite their great practical utility. The second class consists of the grammars envisaged by linguistic theorists. These are exhaustive in coverage, fully explicit, and psychologically accurate. In light of their many virtues, it is unfortunate that no such grammars exist. Still, it is useful for theoretical purposes to consider what a grammar of this sort would look like were it possible to formulate one, and in this spirit I speak of the cognitive grammar of a language. The unfeasibility of actually writing such a grammar is not a cause for despair, nor is this shortcoming unique to the present framework.

The psychological representation of a linguistic system is also referred to by linguists as the grammar of a language. The present model identifies this "internal" grammar as its object of description, conceiving it dynamically, as a constantly evolving set of cognitive routines that are shaped, maintained, and modified by language use. A speaker's "knowledge" of his language is therefore procedural rather than declarative, and the grammar of a language is equated with certain linguistic abilities (mental, perceptual, and physical), which do not necessarily constitute an autonomous or well-delimited psychological entity. More specifically, the grammar of a language is defined as those aspects of cognitive organization in which resides a speaker's grasp of established linguistic convention.[1] It can be characterized as a **structured inventory of conventional linguistic units**. The purpose of the present section is to explore the intended import of this definition.

2.1.1. *Units*

A **unit** is a structure that a speaker has mastered quite thoroughly, to the extent that he can employ it in largely automatic fashion, without having to focus his attention specifically on its individual parts or their arrangement. Despite its internal complexity, a unit constitutes for the speaker a "prepackaged" assembly; because he has no need to reflect on how to put it together, he can manipulate it with ease as a unitary entity. It is effectively simple, since it does not demand the **constructive effort** required for the creation of novel structures. Psychologists would speak of a "habit," or say that "automatization" has occurred.

The basic sounds of a language are clearly units for fluent speakers. A native speaker of French, for example, pronounces the *ü* (the vowel of *tu*) quite effortlessly, with no conscious regard for requisite articulatory gestures or their coordination. The situation is quite different for a speaker of English who tries to pronounce this vowel for the very first time. Suppose a French instructor tells him to pronounce a vowel like *i*, but with the lips rounded as for *u*. Following these instructions, our English speaker may pronounce *ü* more or less correctly on the first attempt, but doing so requires a constructive effort on his part. That is, he must focus his attention specifically on positioning the tongue correctly, on rounding the lips, and on integrating these two gestures in a coordinated articulation. With a certain amount of practice, of course, the articulation of *ü* attains the status of a unit even for a speaker of English; once a sound or a segment has **unit status**, and constitutes a well-

---

[1] Except in contexts where the speaker/hearer contrast is clearly at issue, I use **speaker** as a general term for somebody who knows a language, normally capable of acting in either capacity.

rehearsed, thoroughly familiar routine, its articulation no longer requires constructive effort.[2]

Phonological structures much larger than segments also achieve unit status, including syllables, words, familiar phrases, and even longer sequences. We can probably assume that any word in everyday use constitutes an articulatory unit for typical speakers. In addition to phonological units of various sizes, we can posit semantic units, i.e. established concepts. A novel concept requires a constructive effort, just as a novel phonological structure does. In learning what a unicorn is, for example, a person pays explicit attention to its horselike character, to the fact that it has just a single horn, and to the location of this horn on its head. Once the notion has the status of a unit, he evokes these specifications as a familiar gestalt, and need not attend to them individually.

The symbolic association between a semantic and a phonological structure or unit can also gain unit status. The result is a **symbolic unit**, the construct deployed in cognitive grammar for the representation of both lexical and grammatical structure. The simplest kind of symbolic unit is a morpheme, in which a semantic and a phonological structure participate as unanalyzable wholes in a symbolic relationship. Basic symbolic units combine to form progressively larger symbolic structures, which are themselves often mastered as units; the grammar thus contains a large inventory of conventional expressions (not restricted to those traditionally recognized as complex lexical items—cf. 1.2.2). Grammatical patterns are analyzed as **schematic** symbolic units, which differ from other symbolic structures not in kind, but only in degree of specificity.

Symbolic units provide the means for expressing ideas in linguistic form. No substantial constructive effort is required if the idea to be expressed happens to coincide (at least approximately) with the semantic structure of a conventional symbolic unit; the semantic structure automatically calls the phonological structure to mind, and conversely, since the symbolic relation between them has unit status. When no appropriate unit is available, the task of finding a novel expression to do the job demands a kind of linguistic creativity, or problem-solving activity. Typically the speaker assembles the desired expression out of smaller symbolic units; he must then direct specific attention to each of the component units chosen, and must also be sure to combine them correctly. Of course, owing to the vast number of conventional expressions a speaker controls, the actual amount of constructive effort required for a novel sentence is easily overstated. Speech is often so interlarded

[2] These concepts render quite pointless the debate over whether sound segments should be analyzed as unitary phonemes or as bundles of phonological features (cf. Householder 1965; Chomsky and Halle 1965). The assumption that the unitary character of phonemes is inconsistent with their participation in classificatory relationships is an instance of the exclusionary fallacy.

with overlapping conventional expressions of all sizes that even complex sentences are put together with minimal effort and creativity.

When the distinction is pertinent, I use square brackets or polygons (especially squares and rectangles) to enclose structures having unit status; parentheses or closed curves (especially circles and ellipses) are then employed for nonunit structures. The sound *ü*, for example, is given as [ü] in a description of French, where it constitutes a unit for fluent speakers; it is given as (ü) in referring to the linguistic ability of an English speaker unfamiliar with the sound.

Despite their internal complexity, units are effectively simple for purposes of manipulation and combination with other structures. Suppose a speaker has mastered the combination of [A], [B], and [C] to form the higher-order unit [[A]-[B]-[C]], as well as the combination of [D] and [E] to form the higher-order unit [[D]-[E]]. Integrating the complex units [[A]-[B]-[C]] and [[D]-[E]] to yield the larger but novel structure ([[A]-[B]-[C]]-[[D]-[E]]) then demands no more constructive effort from the speaker than does integrating the simple units [F] and [G] to form the novel structure ([F]-[G]): each task involves the combination of just two units, by definition manipulable as pre-assembled wholes. On the other hand, putting together the complex structure (([H]-[I])-([J]-[K])) requires substantial constructive effort, since the speaker must first assemble the nonunit structures ([H]-[I]) and ([J]-[K]) from their components, and then combine the composite structures so obtained. It is important to observe that when a complex structure coalesces into a unit, its subparts do not thereby cease to exist or be identifiable as substructures (the speaker of French, for instance, still rounds his lips and puts his tongue in the high-front position when articulating [ü]). Its components do become less salient, however, precisely because the speaker no longer has to attend to them individually.

It is also important to recognize that automatization is a matter of degree. In distinguishing notationally between units and nonunits, I imply neither a sharp dichotomy nor homogeneity among the structures in either group. Linguistic structures are more realistically conceived as falling along a continuous scale of **entrenchment** in cognitive organization. Every use of a structure has a positive impact on its degree of entrenchment, whereas extended periods of disuse have a negative impact. With repeated use, a novel structure becomes progressively entrenched, to the point of becoming a unit; moreover, units are variably entrenched depending on the frequency of their occurrence (*driven*, for example, is more entrenched than *thriven*). Is there some particular level of entrenchment, with special behavioral significance, that can serve as a nonarbitrary cutoff point in defining units? There are no obvious linguistic grounds for believing so. Provisionally, then, I assume a gradation, with greater entrenchment implying greater centrality and linguistic significance. The absence of a sharp division between units and nonunits has the consequence that the scope of a grammar is not precisely delimited. I find this conclusion both acceptable and realistic.

2.1.2. *Linguistic Units*

As defined, the notion of a unit is so general that it applies to any cognitive or cognitively directed activity. For the grammar of a language we must obviously restrict our attention to units that can be considered **linguistic** in nature. However, it is not at all straightforward to characterize the difference between linguistic and nonlinguistic units. If arbitrary distinctions are to be avoided, we must recognize a core of prototypical linguistic units, and a gradation that leads from this core to structures so distant from it that no practical purpose is served by regarding them as linguistic. This conception has the consequence, once again, that a sharp delimitation fails to emerge between what is to be included in the grammar and what is to be excluded; the linguistic character of a unit is sometimes a matter of degree. I find this conclusion intrinsically plausible and highly natural, despite the problems it raises for the standard, aprioristic conception of a language as an autonomous formal system.

Linguistic units include both semantic and phonological structures, but neither conceptual ability nor the capacity to produce and recognize sounds is specifically or exclusively linguistic in character. Much thought is clearly nonverbal (consider the task of working a jigsaw puzzle), and many established concepts have no conventional linguistic symbolization (an example is the area above the upper lip and below the nose, where a moustache belongs). A conceptual unit becomes a proper candidate for linguistic description only when it functions in a symbolic unit, as either its entire semantic structure or a significant component thereof. By the same token, we recognize and produce many sounds other than the sounds of human speech, and we employ for nonlinguistic objectives many of the same phonetic capabilities used for talking (voicing, rhythm, and pitch control all figure in humming a tune). Sound units fall in the domain of linguistic description only by virtue of symbolizing semantic structures, either individually or in larger combinations.

Evidently, only symbolic units, or parts of such units, qualify as linguistic. But while this condition is necessary, it is hardly sufficient. For example, numerous gestures become conventional in a given culture and convey a definite meaning, but most linguists would balk at including gestures in the grammar of a language, despite their symbolic character. The obvious remedy is to distinguish between a linguistic and a nonlinguistic symbol, specifying that the former has a phonological structure of some kind as its symbolic realization. But what is a phonological structure? Interpreting it broadly enough to include any kind of sound implies that even the ringing of a dinner bell is a linguistic symbol to be described in the grammar of a language. To avoid this anomaly, we can require that the sounds in question be produced by the human vocal apparatus. That still leaves meaningful noises like wolf whistles in the grammar of a language, so we can further specify that the phonological structure of a linguistic symbol has to be segmental in character. But even here our problems do not end: what about the clicks some people use to direct a horse or call a cat?

We can continue adding restrictions, but already we may have gone too far and excluded from consideration certain phenomena that are generally thought of as linguistic. Intonation contours surely fall within the purview of linguistic description despite their nonsegmental character. Sign languages of the deaf are ruled nonlinguistic by the above criteria, and the same is true of language in its written form.[3] Also excluded quite arbitrarily from the linguist's domain are certain phenomena that interact with linguistic structure in conventional (and highly significant) ways, as illustrated in (1):

(1)(a)   *This one is much better than that one.*
  (b)   *When she saw the snake, she went* [SCREAM].

Seldom could (a) be uttered felicitously without some kind of accompanying gestures to clarify the intended referents of the two nominals. One might argue that these gestures are extraneous to the sentence, but this would be harder to maintain in cases like (b), where a directly imitative vocalization or gesture, of any sort whatever, is incorporated as an apparent constituent. Such data suggest that the description of certain linguistic structures is divorced only artifactually from an account of "extralinguistic" matters.[4]

These difficulties suggest the inappropriateness of the strict criterial-attribute model for delimiting the scope of linguistic analysis. The problems largely disappear if we shift to the prototype model. Prototypical linguistic symbols have for their realization a segmentally organized sound sequence produced by the human vocal apparatus, whereas other kinds of symbols and symbolic systems that we would hesitate to call nonlinguistic depart from this prototype in various ways. American Sign Language is thus recognized as linguistic in nature, but as nonprototypical because it occurs in the visual mode.

---

[3] See Householder (1971, ch. 13) for a defense of the autonomy, if not the "primacy," of the written form of language in literate communities.

[4] See the recent work of McNeill (e.g. 1981; McNeill and Levy 1982) for important dependencies between speech and gestures, and that of Bolinger (e.g. 1982a, 1982b) for the close relationship among intonation, gestures, and more central aspects of linguistic structure. Partee (1973) has insightfully discussed sentences like (1)(b). Her conclusion that the incorporated material "is not syntactically or semantically a part of the sentence that contains it" (p. 418) probably represents the optimal "solution" in a highly compartmentalized view of linguistic ability. Shifting responsibility from one compartment to another hardly constitutes an analysis, however.

Intonation contours are nonprototypical both in their nonsegmental character and in the abstractness of the meanings they convey. Jabberwocky deviates from prototypical linguistic symbolization because its content words have no established semantic value.

2.1.3. *Conventional Linguistic Units*

The grammar of a language is a characterization of established linguistic convention. Conventionality implies that something is shared—and further, that it is recognized as being shared—by a substantial number of individuals. If I make up a new word and learn it thoroughly, so that for me it constitutes an entrenched linguistic unit, it does not thereby enter the English lexicon. Only as a unit spreads through the speech community does it become a serious candidate for inclusion in the grammar of a language.

It goes without saying that conventionality is a matter of degree. A linguistic unit may be shared by an entire speech community, by a substantial subgroup (e.g. the speakers within a dialect area, or the members of a profession), or by a mere handful of people. It is further apparent that no two speakers control precisely the same set of units (e.g. the same set of lexical items and conventional expressions), even if their speech patterns appear to be identical. Conceivably, the set of units mastered by all members of a speech community might be a rather small proportion of the units constituting the linguistic ability of any given speaker. In view of all this, just what is a grammar to encompass?

There is no pat answer to this question, for the scope of a grammatical description depends on one's objectives. Theoretically, an exhaustive description of a language in its full structural and social complexity entails a complete characterization of the linguistic system of each and every speaker, but obviously this is neither a realistic nor a terribly interesting goal. If one's concern is the speech of some particular group, taken as a whole, the optimal strategy is to concentrate primarily on those units that all or most members of the group can be presumed to share; the centrality of a given unit and the importance of including it in the description consequently vary depending on the proportion of speakers familiar with it. Alternatively, as a means of investigating language as an aspect of cognitive organization, one can seek a reasonably comprehensive account of the linguistic system of a single, presumably representative speaker.

The objectively given distribution of units across a speech community is, however, only one facet of linguistic conventionality: equally important is the speaker's conception of their sociolinguistic status. It is part of my knowledge of English, for example, that *ain't* is stigmatized, that *sir* indicates the relative social status of speaker and addressee, that *déjà vu* is a borrowing from French, and that the terms *subjacency* and *Move Alpha* are largely restricted to a particular occupational subgroup. To the extent that speakers learn the sociolinguistic status of conventional units, it constitutes an aspect of their linguistic value and is thus a proper concern of linguistic description.[5] To exhaustively characterize a speaker's conventional knowledge of a language, a grammar must not only include the restriction of individual units to particular circumstances (e.g. to a particular register, group, or social setting), but also describe his control of different varieties of speech. A comprehensive grammar therefore provides a polylectal account of linguistic ability (Bailey 1973), and associates with many conventional units (perhaps all) a specification of their sociolinguistic value.

My suggestions along these lines are only programmatic, but cognitive grammar is so conceived and formulated that the sociolinguistic status of linguistic units is readily accommodated. Several basic features of the model combine to offer an integral solution. One is its claim (Ch. 4) that semantic units are characterized relative to cognitive **domains**, and that any concept or knowledge system can function as a domain for this purpose. Included as possible domains, consequently, are the conception of a social relationship, of the speech situation, of the existence of various dialects, and so on. Second, linguistic semantics is held to be **encyclopedic** (4.2). The meaning of an expression typically involves specifications in many cognitive domains, some of which are far more central to its value than others. Third, language is often self-referential. An expression's sociolinguistic status—i.e. its role in various domains pertaining to language use—can therefore be regarded as a peripheral aspect of its semantic value. Finally, units are acquired through a process of **decontextualization** (10.4.1). If a property (e.g. the relative social status of speaker and hearer) is constant to the context whenever an expression is used, the property may survive the decontextualization process and remain a semantic specification of the resultant unit.

2.1.4. *An Inventory of Conventional Linguistic Units*

As conceived in the present framework, the grammar of a language is simply an inventory of linguistic units. A grammar is not a "generative" description, providing a formal enumeration of all and only the well-formed sentences of a language. Nor do I employ the **process metaphor** and speak of the grammar as a device that carries out a series of operations and gives well-formed sentences as its output. These decisions are not arbitrary, but re-

---

[5] Relevant here is the sociolinguistic status that speakers impute to a form, not its actual distribution. If I believe that the plural pronoun *youall* is diagnostic for Southern speech, that characterization—factually correct or not—constitutes for me an aspect of the expression's linguistic value, and is properly included in the description of my idiolect. Observe that conceptions (or misconceptions) such as these are often widespread in a culture and thereby constitute part of linguistic convention for large groups of speakers.

flect a specific, substantive conception of what constitutes linguistic well-formedness, and of the relation between language structure and language use.

2.1.4.1. *Generativity*. The process metaphor is not a neutral mode of thought and description whose appropriateness for language can be taken for granted. Others have pointed out the formal liabilities of descriptions phrased in process terms (cf. McCawley 1968; Stanley 1967); I will simply add that the process metaphor leads to conceptual difficulties that are artifacts of the metaphor itself and vanish when the same phenomena are thought about differently.[6] Nor can one assume without question that generativity is a reasonable requirement to impose on linguistic descriptions, or that explicitness and rigor demand it. For example, if generativity is interpreted to mean that the grammar itself must fully and explicitly enumerate all and only the well-formed expressions of a language, including their semantic structures, then an encyclopedic conception of linguistic semantics will necessarily (but incorrectly) be ruled out, for a grammar of restricted scope cannot be responsible for enumerating an essentially open-ended range of knowledge. Moreover, the requirement of generativity entails the exclusion from the grammar (and hence omission from serious consideration) of both usage and figurative language, which are pivotal to an understanding of linguistic structure. Rather than ensuring explicitness, generativity has had the unfortunate effect of impoverishing the natural domain of linguistic inquiry, leading to maximal inexplicitness (i.e. silence) with respect to fundamental matters.

These problems stem from the erroneous view that language is an autonomous formal system. Cognitive grammar, by contrast, asserts that linguistic structure can only be understood and characterized in the context of a broader account of cognitive functioning. This has the theoretical consequence (which I find neither unnatural nor disturbing) that an exhaustive description of language cannot be achieved without a full description of human cognition. But theoretical consequences are not necessarily practical limitations. Recognizing this dependency of language on cognition does not make linguistic description vague and mysterious, nor does it postpone serious linguistic analysis until cognition is fully understood. The concepts of cognitive grammar make it possible even at present, given minimal and largely uncontroversial claims about cognitive ability, to arrive at precise, explicit, linguistically motivated analyses of grammatical structure.

In a sense, cognitive grammar contrasts with generative theories by placing a lesser descriptive burden on the grammar of a language per se; it does not consider the grammar a **constructive** device—i.e. the grammar is not respon-

---

[6] Recall our discussion of the rule/list fallacy (1.1.6): the process metaphor makes it hard to conceive of a form like *stapler* being simultaneously the product of a derivational rule and a fixed unit listed in the lexicon.

sible for assembling novel expressions out of their component parts and giving them as "output," either in the active sense suggested by the process metaphor or in the mathematical sense of recursive enumeration. Motivating this non-constructive conception of a grammar is the fact that the set of novel expressions available to the speaker of a language is neither predetermined nor well defined given a view of linguistic structure that accommodates both figurative language and usage. Such a view is not only intrinsically desirable but actually necessary for understanding even the more limited range of phenomena that generative models attempt to deal with.

2.1.4.2. *Convention and Usage.*

Putting together novel expressions is something that speakers do, not grammars. It is a problem-solving activity that demands a constructive effort and occurs when linguistic convention is put to use in specific circumstances. Creating a novel expression is not necessarily different in fundamental character from problem-solving activity in general, and the speaker's knowledge of linguistic convention is but one of the many resources he brings to bear in finding a solution; others include memory, the capacity to plan and organize, the ability to compare two structures and judge their degree of similarity, and so forth. We must examine this interface between convention and usage in some detail, for it is the source of language change and the crucible of linguistic structure.

Let us consider abstractly the various factors involved in a particular instance of language use. It is prompted when a speaker, assessing the total context, perceives the need to find linguistic expression for a conceptualization.[7] The need for such expression constitutes a problem to be solved, and the overall situation places a variety of constraints on what counts as an acceptable solution. We need not dwell on these constraints, which include such factors as the following: how much detail the speaker considers relevant; which aspects of the conceptualization he wishes to emphasize; his social relationship to the hearer; his assessment of how much the hearer already knows about the context and the notion to be conveyed; how the expression is to be integrated with previous and anticipated discourse; the effect he wants to have on the hearer; his estimation of the hearer's linguistic ability; and how far he is willing to deviate from linguistic convention.

The task of finding appropriate linguistic expression for a conceptualization can be referred to as the problem of **coding**; its solution is a **target structure**

---

[7] This need is not always communicative, for it also arises in verbal thought. In communicative events, the task of finding appropriate linguistic expressions is faced by both the speaker and the hearer: the speaker puts together a linguistic symbol giving phonological expression to the conceptualization prompting his utterance, and the hearer creates a linguistic symbol constituting his hypothesis about the one employed by the speaker. For expository convenience, I generally discuss usage from the standpoint of the speaker, but adjustments are easily made to accommodate thinkers and listeners.

(the term is used later in a more inclusive sense). The target is therefore a **usage event**, i.e. a symbolic expression assembled by a speaker in a particular set of circumstances for a particular purpose: this symbolic relationship holds between a detailed, context-dependent conceptualization and some type of phonological structure (in the case of speech, it is the actual vocalization). As such, the target structure is not directly given by the grammar of a language. Nevertheless, linguistic convention does afford the speaker a wealth of symbolic resources to choose from in putting it together. Conventional units provide an essentially unlimited range of symbolic potential, but it is left for the speaker to recognize this potential and exploit it in a fashion that responds to all the varied constraints inherent in the situation.

The symbolic resources furnished by the grammar are of two basic kinds: (1) specified symbolic units (including morphemes, polymorphemic lexical items, and larger conventional expressions); and (2) established patterns, represented as schematic symbolic units, for assembling complex symbolic structures out of simpler ones. To the extent that a target structure accords with the conventional units in the grammar, these units are said to **sanction** this usage. It is crucial to realize that sanction is a matter of degree and speaker judgment. It is a measure of an expression's well-formedness, i.e. how closely it conforms to linguistic convention, in all its aspects and dimensions. In preference to the standard term "grammaticality" (which is both narrow and problematic), I will refer to an expression's degree of **conventionality**.

2.1.4.3. *Full Sanction*. In the simplest case, the speaker has only to select a symbolic unit from the inventory of units in the grammar. This is so when a conventionally established unit is judged to be fully adequate as it stands to serve as the target. If an English speaker, engaged in verbal thought, requires a term for the general category of three-sided polygons, the lexical unit *triangle* most likely satisfies all the constraints imposed on the projected target and is thus an optimal solution to the coding problem. The relation between the sanctioning structure and the target structure is one of identity, and the speaker solves the coding problem merely by perceiving this identity. The target accords fully with the conventions of the language, for it is a symbolic unit of the grammar and therefore part of the very definition of linguistic convention.

Typically, however, the speaker is unable to find any symbolic unit that meets the full, detailed specifications laid down for the desired target structure, even in what would be considered straightforward instances of language use. As others have noted (e.g. Lakoff 1977), linguistic expressions almost invariably **underspecify** the conceptualizations they code. Suppose, for example, that I use the term *triangle* not as the name of a general class, but as the complete description of a particular figure; let us say that I point at a drawing in a geometry textbook and declaim *This is a triangle*. The specific conceptualization prompting my vocalization in this situation is obviously more detailed and elaborate than the conventionalized semantic value of the linguistic unit. The triangle I have in mind has an exact size and shape, is drawn with lines having a specific color and thickness, and is found in a particular setting, but nothing about the conventions of English allows a person to deduce, from these conventions alone, that the entity I call a *triangle* has precisely these specifications as opposed to many other conceivable ones. Similarly, my vocalization is far more specific and elaborate in its articulatory and auditory details than is given by the phonological representation of *triangle* in the grammar of English. It is clear, then, that the sanctioning structure (the linguistic unit *triangle*) substantially underspecifies the target structure (the usage event wherein my vocalization symbolizes my conceptualization).

The major elements in this typical instance of language use are summarized in Fig. 2.1. Linguistic convention is embodied in the grammar, which comprises an inventory of conventional units. Among these units is the lexical

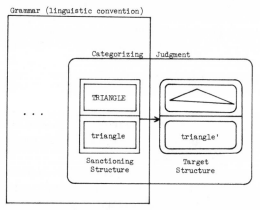

Fig. 2.1

item *triangle*, which we can represent as follows: [[TRIANGLE]/[triangle]]. It consists of the semantic unit [TRIANGLE], the phonological unit [triangle], and the established symbolic relationship between the two. Several points of notation should be observed. (1) I follow standard practice here in using capitalized words as abbreviations for semantic structures, and lower case orthographic representations for phonological structures. (2) In the formula [[TRIANGLE]/[triangle]], the slash indicates a symbolic relationship between the semantic and phonological structures; it corresponds to a horizontal line in the diagram. (3) In this same formula, the inner sets of square brackets mark [TRIANGLE] and [triangle] as units, and the outer set specifies the unit status of their symbolic association. Fig. 2.1 employs rectangles for this purpose.

The target structure in Fig. 2.1 is not a conventional unit. It is created by the speaker as a specific usage event in a particular context, and resides in the symbolic relationship between his detailed conceptualization and his actual vocalization. The semantic, phonological, and symbolic structures are all bounded by closed curves to indicate their nonunit status. Using parentheses for this same purpose, we can represent the target formulaically in this manner: ((TRIANGLE')/(triangle')). Observe that any structure X' is a variant of X; in the present example, (TRIANGLE') and (triangle') are more specific than the corresponding units [TRIANGLE] and [triangle]. The formulaic (TRIANGLE') is replaced in Fig. 2.1 by a mnemonic shape specification.

Sanction reduces to categorization. A conventional unit defines a category, and sanctions a target structure to the extent that the latter is judged by a speaker to be a member of the category. Categorization, in turn, depends on the relation of **schematicity**, which I represent with a solid arrow. The arrow in Fig. 2.1 thus indicates that the sanctioning structure bears a relation of schematicity to the target structure; the target is therefore sanctioned as a well-formed extrapolation from linguistic convention by virtue of this categorizing judgment. The categorizing judgment has the following formulaic representation: ([[TRIANGLE]/[triangle]]→((TRIANGLE')/(triangle'))). The outer parentheses mark its nonunit character.

Schematicity can be equated with the relation between a superordinate node and a subordinate node in a taxonomic hierarchy; the concept [TREE], for instance, is schematic with respect to the concept [OAK]: [[TREE]→[OAK]]. In such relationships I call the superordinate structure a **schema**, and the subordinate structure an **elaboration** or **instantiation** of the schema. The conceptual import of this relationship, I suggest, is that an instantiation is fully compatible with the specifications of its schema, but is characterized in finer detail (cf. 3.3.3). The schema [TREE], for example, defines a category that is instantiated by a variety of more specific concepts, all of them compatible with its specifications ([OAK], [MAPLE], [ELM], and so on). These instantiations elaborate the schema in different ways along various parameters, to yield more precisely articulated notions.

2.1.4.4. *Partial Sanction.* Like categorization in general, sanction is a matter of degree and speaker judgment. The previous examples both involved **full schematicity**, and consequently **full sanction**: the target is compatible with the sanctioning unit, and is therefore judged by a speaker to be an unproblematic instantiation of the category it defines. In one of the examples, the sanctioning and target structures were identical. Identity can be regarded as the limiting case of schematicity, where the degree to which the schema is elaborated by its instantiation happens to be zero. Hence every conventional unit in the grammar is self-sanctioning, being schematic for itself at the minimal possible **elaborative distance**.

But usage is not always so well behaved with respect to the canons of established convention. Often there is some conflict between the specifications of the sanctioning and target structures, so that the former can be construed as schematic for the latter only with a certain amount of **strain**. When this is so the relation between the sanctioning and the target structures is one of only **partial schematicity**, and the relation provides only **partial sanction**. Partial sanction can be equated with deviance or ill-formedness, but it should be emphasized that a considerable amount of nonconventionality is tolerated (and often expected) as a normal feature of language use.

When sanction is based on full schematicity, the specifications of the sanctioning and target structures are fully compatible, and the relation between them is purely elaborative, equivalent to that between superordinate and subordinate nodes in a taxonomic hierarchy. On the other hand, categorization based on partial sanction is the kind described in the prototype model, where a category is defined in terms of prototypical instances. Here a speaker judges class membership through a perception of similarity that permits him to construe a structure as an extension from the prototype. Full compatibility is not required: the more a structure deviates from the specifications of the prototype, the less likely is its assimilation to the category, but there is no specific cutoff point beyond which a categorizing judgment is ruled out in absolute terms.[8]

Consider, then, an instance of usage based on only partial sanction. Suppose I present you with a conical piece of wood; its tip is made of pencil lead, and obviously it is intended as a writing implement. Suppose further that you react by exclaiming *Look at this pencil!* Your choice of the term *pencil* to designate this object implies the categorizing judgment represented in Fig. 2.2. The sanctioning unit is the established lexical item *pencil*, and the target consists of your use of the vocalization (pencil') to symbolize your novel conceptualization (PENCIL'). The sanctioning structure is only partially schematic for the target, because their semantic specifications conflict to a certain degree. In particular, the semantic unit [PENCIL] specifies that the object it designates is roughly cylindrical, whereas the novel conceptualization (PENCIL') specifies a conical shape for the corresponding entity. Despite this strain, the two structures are similar enough that the target structure is easily seen as an extension from the sanctioning unit. This judgment of extension or partial schematicity is indicated by a broken-line arrow.

---

[8] These two types of categorization are intimately connected; a unified account is offered in Ch. 10.

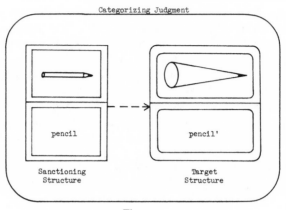

Fig. 2.2

The categorization ([[PENCIL']/[pencil]] --→ ((PENCIL')/(pencil'))) constitutes a semantic extension that is not at all atypical of language use, and is
indicative of our normal flexibility in solving the coding problem. Moreover,
this example differs only in degree from the figurative use of language. Suppose I call someone an *ostrich* (because of his peculiar figure and the funny
way he walks). The lexical unit *ostrich* is used to sanction a novel usage event
where the same phonological sequence symbolizes the conception of a particular type of person: ([[OSTRICH]/[ostrich]] --→ ((PERSON')/(ostrich'))).
The sanctioning unit represents the lexical item in its literal sense, whereas the
target structure corresponds to its novel figurative value. The categorizing
judgment is far more tenuous than in the previous example, for the two semantic structures are incompatible in the great majority of their specifications. But it is precisely this greater amount of strain that renders the categorization nonobvious and leads us to consider the usage figurative.

Apparent now is the reason for referring to the interface between convention and usage as the source of language change and the crucible of linguistic
structure: particular usages, as well as the categorizing judgments that sanction them, often acquire both unit status and some measure of conventionality;
to the extent that this occurs, the structures in question fall by definition
within the confines of a grammar and count as part of the characterization of
linguistic convention. If I use the term *ostrich* to designate a certain type of
person not just once but on repeated occasions, I soon master this figurative expression as a fixed unit: [[[OSTRICH]/[ostrich]] --→ [[PERSON']/
[ostrich']]].[9] Moreover, this usage can readily spread to other speakers and
even become conventional for the entire speech community (note the exten-

[9] Strictly speaking, every usage event is unique. The extension of *ostrich* that achieves unit
status represents a schematization of the targets invoked on different occasions.

sions to people of *pig*, *dog*, *rat*, *fox*, *tiger*, and other animal terms). The conventionalization of what originates as a novel usage thus constitutes a change in the linguistic system, whether the innovative unit simply elaborates preexisting structures or, by violating certain specifications, represents a more substantial departure from the previous definition of conventionality. I have explicitly discussed only the semantic specialization and extension of single morphemes, but the mechanisms are quite general. All of linguistic structure reduces to conventionalized usages, generalizations (schemas) that speakers extract from such usages, and categorizing relationships involving such elements.

2.1.4.5. *Linguistic Creativity*. A fairly sharp distinction is customarily made between two kinds of creativity: (1) rule-governed creativity, consisting in the computation of novel expressions by the correct application of grammatical rules; and (2) creativity in a more general sense of the term, manifested in such phenomena as figurative language, the adaptation of lexical items to new situations, and the willful violation of grammatical rules. The former is considered a proper concern of linguistic description, whereas the latter is generally left to be treated in a theory of performance or an account of overall cognitive ability.

Cognitive grammar sees this distinction as neither clear-cut nor particularly useful. For one thing, the contrast between full and partial sanction, though it is helpful and probably significant for theoretical purposes, proves hard to maintain in practice. Often the relation between a sanctioning and a target structure involves both elaboration and extension. Moreover, whether the structures are incompatible in certain features depends on precisely how the sanctioning structure is construed. Consider the adaptation of *tube* to mean 'subway'. Elaboration is clearly involved, for a subway has very special properties beyond those of tubes in general. But the extent of conflict with the basic meaning depends on a matter of substantial conceptual flexibility, namely the relative salience of certain specifications—in particular, how prominent are the specifications of discreteness and manipulability in the basic sense of *tube*? The difficulty in deciding is not really bothersome, for nothing in the present framework requires a sharp distinction between full and partial schematicity. Suppose we think of conventionality as a measure of how drastically the sanctioning structure must be transformed to make it coincide with the target. In this perspective, elaboration is simply a special (though perhaps privileged) type of transformation: an adjustment in the level of specificity at which a structure is characterized.

The decision not to regard the grammar as a constructive device further erodes the distinction between the two kinds of creativity. Applying grammatical rules to compute novel expressions is something that speakers (not grammars) do in response to a coding problem, and the concepts of cognitive grammar reveal it to have the same basic character as the adaptation of lexical items to novel literal and figurative uses. Let us take just one illustration.

I have observed a child sample a piece of pie and complain that he didn't like it because it was too *apricoty*. The form *apricoty* was a novel polymorphemic expression created in reponse to the demands of usage in accordance with a reasonably productive derivational pattern of English. Like any morphological or syntactic "rule," this pattern is represented in the grammar as a schematic symbolic unit; it embodies the generalization a speaker has extracted from an array of previously encountered instantiations, and coexists in the grammar with those of its instantiations that have unit status (e.g. *salty*, *spicy*, *nutty*, *pepperminty*). Since we are not too concerned at present with the internal structure of these polymorphemic units, the subsuming schema can be abbreviated as follows: [[N/...]-[Y/y]]; [N/...] is to be interpreted here as a schematically characterized noun stem, and [Y/y] is the derivational suffix. The schematic noun stem has no particular phonological shape (hence the three dots), and is specified semantically only as designating something edible. The suffix has both a specific form and a specific meaning (though the latter is fairly abstract). Instantiations of the schema can be given in a comparable notation, e.g. [[SALT/salt]-[Y/y]].[10]

The crucial observation is that relations of schematicity hold not only between simple symbolic structures, but also between complex ones. An illustration for simple structures is the schematic relationship between [N/...] and [SALT/salt], that is, [[N/...]→[SALT/salt]]; this categorizing judgment is presumed to have unit status. But if [N/...] is schematic for [SALT/salt], it follows that [[N/...]-[Y/y]] is schematic for [[SALT/salt]-[Y/y]], since they are assembled in parallel fashion out of their component elements, and each element of one participates in a relationship of either schematicity or identity with the corresponding element of the other. We can therefore posit the complex unit [[[N/...]-[Y/y]]→[[SALT/salt]-[Y/y]]], which represents the established categorization of *salty* as a member of the class defined by the derivational pattern in question.

With the novel expression *apricoty* the situation is quite analogous, except that the composite form and the categorizing judgment lack unit status when the word is first coined. The morphemes [APRICOT/apricot] and [Y/y] are units, but the composite expression is not: ([APRICOT/apricot]-[Y/y]). Spawned by the demands of usage, this symbol can be regarded as a target structure. Its sanction by the [[N/...]-[Y/y]] schema in the categorizing judgment ([[N/...]-[Y/y]]→([APRICOT/apricot]-[Y/y])) amounts to the recog-

---

[10] Internal brackets will often be suppressed for abbreviatory purposes. For example, [SALT/salt] abbreviates [[SALT]/[salt]], where the semantic and phonological structures are individually shown as units.

nition that *apricoty* is a well-formed extrapolation from an established morphological pattern.[11] The potential for this novel form is obvious, given the schema [[N/...]-[Y/y]] and the classificatory unit [[N/...]→ [APRICOT/apricot]], but actually noting and exploiting this potential in a way that responds to immediate communicative objectives amounts to a problem-solving activity on the part of the speaker.

The example is simple, but the approach generalizes to cases of any desired degree of complexity. Cognitive grammar accommodates the projection of grammatical rules to novel expressions through the same basic devices required to handle the specialized use and figurative extension of lexical items. The framework thus offers a unified account of grammatical productivity, lexical extension, usage, and figurative language. This unification would not be achievable if the requirement of generativity were imposed on a grammar. A generative grammar accommodating figurative language and usage would have to enumerate the entire set of target structures potentially receiving full or partial sanction from the conventions of a language. However, this set cannot be algorithmically derived from a list of established rules and lexical items; the set is not well defined, for it depends on the total range of conceivable human experience. Linguistic creativity is best examined not within the confines of a restricted, self-contained grammar, but rather in the overall context of human knowledge, judgment, and problem-solving ability.

2.1.5. *Structured Inventory of Conventional Linguistic Units*

The term **inventory** is meant to convey the nonconstructive nature of a grammar; it should not be interpreted to mean that the units in a grammar are discrete and unrelated entities like a row of boxes on a shelf. The inventory must be seen instead as **structured**, in the sense that some units function as components of others. For example, the phonological units [d], [ɔ], and [g] function as components of the higher-order phonological unit [[d]-[ɔ]-[g]]. This in turn combines with the semantic unit [DOG] to form the symbolic unit [[DOG]/[[d]-[ɔ]-[g]]], to which we can add the plural morpheme to obtain a higher-order symbolic unit, and so on. It should be clear that the same unit typically serves as a component of numerous higher-order structures (consider all the phonological and lexical units containing [d], for instance). The grammar of a language is thus a vast inventory of units structured in hierarchies that overlap and intersect on a massive scale.

Three basic kinds of relations are recognized between the components of a complex structure. The first is **symbolization**, where a correspondence is es-

---

[11] When the schema defining a grammatical pattern is only partially schematic for the target, the resulting strain constitutes what is generally called "ungrammaticality." For instance, ([Y/y]-[APRICOT/apricot]) receives only partial sanction from the schema [[N/...]-[Y/y]] because the linear ordering of its components conflicts with that specified by the schema.

tablished between a semantic structure and a phonological structure. Symbolization is indicated by a slash or a line separating the two components, standing for the boundary between semantic and phonological space, as in [[DOG]/[dɔg]].

The second kind of relation between components is **categorization**, which I analyze in terms of schematicity. As indicated earlier, full schematicity is indicated by a solid arrow; a broken-line arrow is employed for partial schematicity (extension), and also for categorization in general. The elements that participate in a categorizing relationship can be of any sort: semantic, phonological, or symbolic. Fig. 2.3 shows my judgments for a set of semantic

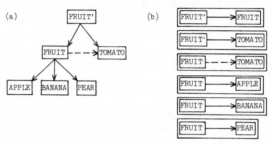

Fig. 2.3

units. [APPLE], [BANANA], and [PEAR] are unproblematic instantiations of the category defined by the schema [FRUIT]. However, [TOMATO] is assimilated to this category only through extension; I have learned that a tomato is "technically" a fruit, but its properties conflict with my informal understanding of the notion (primarily in regard to sweetness). [FRUIT'] is a more abstract conception (a higher-order schema) having both [FRUIT] and [TOMATO] as elaborations. If this unit in fact exists, it represents what tomatoes have in common with prototypical fruits.[12]

I refer to such an assembly of categorizing units as a **schematic network**. Schematic networks are conveniently represented in diagrams like Fig. 2.3(a), which often resemble standard taxonomic hierarchies. However, there are no intrinsic restrictions on the configuration of these networks, and diagrams like Fig. 2.3(a) can be regarded as summary abbreviations for sets of individual categorizing relationships, as shown in Fig. 2.3(b). Categorizations like these define a **schematic plane** of relationships, which are fundamental to lin-

---

[12] These categorizations are in some measure specific to a given culture, and even to a given speaker. They are not determined solely by objective factors, nor are they fully predictable from the properties of two structures. Categorizing relationships are not automatically specified for every pair of units that are potentially subject to comparison; every categorization results from specific acts of judgment (at some level of cognitive processing). Which particular judgments a person makes depends on a host of factors, e.g. imagination, intellectual precision, access to expert opinion, and the accidents of personal experience.

guistic organization. Structures in this plane serve three crucial functions, which are often considered distinct but receive a unified account in cognitive grammar: (1) categorization; (2) the capture of generalizations (expressed by schemas); and (3) the sanction of novel structures (the categorization of nonunits).

Orthogonal to the schematic plane of relationships is the **syntagmatic plane**, where two or more structures in a given domain—semantic, phonological, or symbolic—combine to form a **composite structure** of greater size. For example, the symbolic units [[DOG]/[dɔg]] and [[PL]/[z]] (the plural morpheme) are joined syntagmatically in the plural *dogs*, i.e. [[[DOG]/[dɔg]]-[[PL]/[z]]].The basis for syntagmatic combination is **integration**, the third type of relation between the components in a complex structure. Integration is marked by a dash or line connecting the components.

Structures in the syntagmatic plane can reach any desired size through the successive integration of components to form larger and larger composite structures. We thus encounter componential hierarchies, where the composite structure at one level of organization functions as a component at the next higher level. Fig. 2.4 illustrates two equivalent notations for a componential

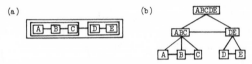

Fig. 2.4

hierarchy. In this abstract example, [*ABC*] and [*DE*] are composite structures at the first (lower) level of organization, whereas at the second level they serve as components integrated to form the higher-order composite structure [*ABCDE*]. Fig. 2.4(a) is a **compacted** representation of the hierarchy; observe that the content of the composite structures is given only implicitly, as a function of their components and the lines of integration connecting them. By contrast, the **exploded** representation in Fig. 2.4(b) shows each composite structure separately from its components.

It must be emphasized that syntagmatic combination involves more than the simple addition of components. A composite structure is an integrated system formed by coordinating its components in a specific, often elaborate manner. In fact it often has properties that go beyond what one might expect from its components alone. Two brief observations should make it clear why this is so. First, composite structures originate as targets in specific usage events. As such they are often characterized relative to particular contexts with properties not predictable from the specifications of their components as manifested in other environments. A related point is that one component may need to be adjusted in certain details when integrated with another to form a composite structure; I refer to this as **accommodation**. For example, the meaning of *run* as applied to humans must be adjusted in certain respects when extended to four-legged animals such as horses, dogs, and cats (since the bodily motion observed in two-legged running is not identical to that in four-legged running); in a technical sense, this extension creates a new **semantic variant** of the lexical item. Accommodation is one of the primary forces driving the growth of schematic networks.

2.2. The Nature of Grammatical Structure

Grammatical structure is claimed to be symbolic in character: it consists in the conventional symbolization of semantic structure and forms a continuum with lexicon. But what does it mean, precisely, to say that grammar is symbolic? Some general discussion of the notion of linguistic symbolization in cognitive grammar will preface our examination of grammatical constructions as symbolic entities.

2.2.1. Semantic and Phonological Space

Cognitive grammar posits just three basic types of structures: **semantic**, **phonological**, and **symbolic**. Symbolic structures are obviously not distinct from the others, but rather combine the two. A symbolic structure is **bipolar**, consisting of a **semantic pole**, a **phonological pole**, and the association between them.

I will assume that one can validly postulate **semantic space** and **phonological space** as two broad aspects of human cognitive organization. We can think of semantic space as the multifaceted field of conceptual potential within which thought and conceptualization unfold; a semantic structure can then be characterized as a location or a configuration in semantic space. Mapping out the various domains of semantic space and their interrelationships, at least in rudimentary terms, is clearly prerequisite to any kind of definitive semantic analysis. Ch. 4 offers some programmatic suggestions along these lines.

Phonological space, similarly, is our range of phonic potential, i.e. our capacity to deal with sounds, and with speech sounds as a special case. Linguists are not at all unaccustomed to thinking about phonic potential in spatial terms. For example, a vowel chart showing the high–low and front–back parameters represents an attempt to map out one domain of phonological space; it characterizes a range of articulatory potential, and a vowel articulation can be defined (at least in part) as a location within this range. A speech spectrogram, plotting energy distribution along the parameters of time and frequency, is a graphic display of sounds from the acoustic standpoint; a sound can be defined acoustically as a configuration (e.g. a particular formant structure) in this spatially conceived domain. Though semantic space is far more complex and harder to elucidate, I see no reason to doubt that it can in principle be handled in similar fashion. The notions of semantic and phonological space may not yet be fully substantive, but neither are they inherently mysterious; it will be more profitable to work towards explicating these notions than to reject them out of hand.

Granted the existence of semantic and phonological space, we can proceed to define a bipolar **symbolic space**, obtained by coordinating the two. A symbolic structure can then be characterized as a configuration in symbolic space. To be more specific, a symbolic structure consists of a semantic structure at one pole, a phonological structure at the other pole, and a **correspondence** linking them together. I have indicated correspondences with dotted lines in Fig. 2.5, which summarizes a number of the concepts presented so far. It is important to distinguish between **symbolization** (*sym*) and **coding** (*cod*), though both depend on correspondences (as does syntagmatic combination). Symbolization is the relation between a structure in semantic space and one in phonological space, whether this relationship constitutes a unit in the grammar of a language or is created on the spot as a specific usage event. Coding, on the other hand, takes place across the boundary between convention and usage. It is a matter of finding an appropriate target structure that "fits" a sanctioning unit within some expected range of tolerance. Note that a tolerably good fit must be achieved at both poles in a typical instance of use: the conceptualization must be plausibly categorized by the semantic unit to which

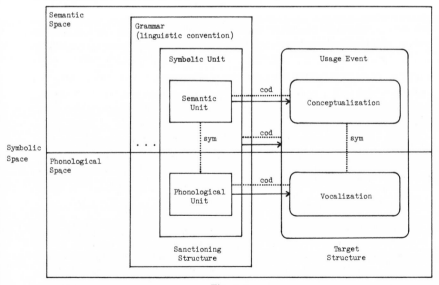

Fig. 2.5

it corresponds, and similarly, the vocalization, by the corresponding phonological unit (which must symbolize the semantic unit). The overall coding
relation between the sanctioning symbolic unit and the target is therefore derivative of the individual coding relations at the semantic and phonological
poles.[13]

At this juncture, some points of clarification are necessary concerning the
nature of phonological structure. They center on the seemingly contradictory
but ultimately rather obvious proposition that sounds (at least for many linguistic purposes) are really concepts. We can begin by noting that usage
events are often purely conceptual, with no overt physical manifestation. This
is so whenever language is used for silent verbal thought: conceptualizations
are coded linguistically and associated with phonetic structures, but though
we mentally "hear" a sequence of vocalizations, no actual sounds are physically emitted. Even when vocalizations are physically realized, the acoustic
signal per se is not the primary concern of linguistic analysis. Because language is a cognitive entity, the speech signal must be regarded not just in
physical but rather in *psychophysical* terms; the cognitive representation of
linguistic expressions derives most directly from auditory impressions, and
only indirectly from the sound waves that give rise to these impressions.

Our knowledge of speech sounds is clearly multifaceted. Because sounds
are perceptual entities, one facet of their cognitive representation consists of
auditory impressions or perceptual routines. We also know sounds from an
articulatory standpoint; cognitively directed motor routines therefore constitute a second dimension of their mental representation. Other dimensions,
which appear to be of less significance, include the kinesthetic sensations that
accompany an articulatory event, as well as the auditory feedback a speaker
receives from his own utterances (this contrasts in both quality and mode of
transmission with auditory impressions from external sources). A complete
linguistic description of phonological units must accommodate all of these dimensions, and thus requires a series of parallel (but coordinated) specifications. In this respect sounds are like other concepts, which normally involve
coordinated specifications in various domains of semantic space (cf. Ch. 4).

Even the articulatory facets of speech sounds are properly regarded as conceptual, in the broad sense in which I understand this term. Consider the segment [i]. From the perceptual standpoint, speakers can deal with this sound in
either of two ways: they can actually hear the sound as a stimulus-driven perceptual event, or they can simply imagine hearing it, i.e. they can activate an

---

[13] The coding relation is neutral with respect to the distinction between speaker and hearer:
both interlocutors must find an adequate bipolar target, whether the conceptualization or the vocalization is taken as the starting point. It would be simplistic to attribute any strict directionality
to the roles of speaking and hearing (e.g. the hearer often has a strong hypothesis about the conceptualization even before the vocalization is emitted).

auditory image of it (as in silent verbal thought). Moreover, the auditory image is plausibly taken as primary, in the sense that it is used to categorize acoustic input as an instance of this particular sound. Exactly analogous observations can be made about the articulatory representation of [i]. A speaker can actually implement the articulatory routine and produce the sound, or he can simply imagine implementing it, i.e. he can mentally run through the motor routine without this mental activity being translated into muscular gestures. Once again the cognitive representation is primary, in the sense that it directs the motor sequence but can also occur autonomously.[14]

If sounds are conceptual entities, our previous characterization of symbolic space was oversimplified in treating semantic and phonological space as disjoint fields of cognitive potential; phonological space should instead be regarded as a subregion of semantic space. Diagrams in the style of Figs. 2.5 and 2.6(a) are thus more accurately given in the format of Fig. 2.6(b). That is, a linguistic symbol is defined by a correspondence between two structures in semantic space (broadly conceived), where one of the two occupies the phonological subregion in particular.[15]

Locating phonological space within semantic space is more than a terminological nicety, for it resolves certain actual or potential conceptual problems. One problem is that of characterizing the meaning of onomatopoetic expressions. If a linguistic symbol implies a correspondence between a phonological structure and another structure in semantic space, we can expect to find—as a special case—symbols that consist of a correspondence between two phonological structures. A word like *clang* is therefore unproblematic as a symbolic unit. The semantic pole of every symbolic unit is a conceptualization situated in one or more domains of semantic space, so there is nothing at all odd about claiming that the meaning of *clang* is the conception (or auditory image) of a particular type of sound, as shown in Fig. 2.6(c). Indeed, it would require special provisions to preclude this kind of symbolic unit.

But we can go even further, for nothing in the definition of a linguistic symbol—a correspondence between two structures in semantic space, one of them phonological—inherently rules out the possibility that the two structures might happen to be identical, i.e. that a phonological structure might symbolize itself, as shown in Fig. 2.6(d). Given the present framework, self-

[14] Observe that a speaker who is temporarily deafened nevertheless retains full knowledge of the sounds of his language and is capable of silent speech. Similarly, a speaker who is temporarily paralyzed, so that nothing happens at the muscular level when he sends the neural commands to produce a speech sound, can still be said to possess the requisite motor routines. See 3.2 for further discussion of imagery and autonomous processing.

[15] Context should make it clear whether the term semantic space is used in the narrow sense (as the region complementary to phonological space) or the broad sense (to include phonological space). Note that Fig. 2.6 and certain later diagrams are simplified by omission of the box surrounding a symbolic unit as a whole.

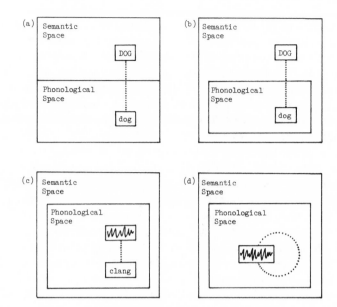

Fig. 2.6

symbolization is an expected limiting case in the spectrum of conceivable symbolic relationships, and I would suggest that it provides at least a partial solution to a previously noted problem (2.1.2). It is posed by sentences like (2), in which [NOISE] stands for any sound the speaker can create, linguistic or otherwise:

(2)   *The boy went* [NOISE].

What is the semantic value of the [NOISE] constituent, and of the sentence as a whole? Does [NOISE] have a meaning at all? If [NOISE] is not attributed a meaning, how can we account for the semantic distinctness of two sentences incorporating different noises?

Sentences like these do have special properties, but the present model handles them straightforwardly. Meanings are conceptual entities, so the conceptualization of a sound can be considered a meaning. In sentences like (2), then, [NOISE] is a meaningful, self-symbolizing constituent; moreover, two sentences of this type differ semantically if they incorporate different noises. Self-symbolization contrasts with onomatopoeia (compare (c) and (d) in Fig. 2.6), but they are not drastically distinct (there is in fact a gradation between them). In an onomatopoetic expression like *clang*, the signifier and signified are similar but not identical, and the signifier is formed from speech sounds conventionally employed in the language. On the other hand, the whole point of sentences like (2) is to allow direct imitation of the signified; hence the signifier symbolizes itself and is not restricted to sounds regularly used in the language. Because the [NOISE] constituent is fully imitative and not limited to conventionally established phonological sequences, these sentences are not prototypical linguistic expressions. They are nevertheless sanctioned by the grammar of English, which has evolved a construction (with *go*) specifically designed to accommodate them.[16]

2.2.2. *Grammar as Symbolization*

A linguistic symbol is bipolar, defined by a semantic structure standing in correspondence to a phonological structure. Most linguists would probably accept this characterization for the great majority of lexical items, which in general have both a form and an obvious meaning. But grammar is another matter. The position that grammar is inherently symbolic is rather unorthodox in contemporary linguistic thought—so much so that it is necessary to elaborate on what this means. Let us consider three kinds of entities in this connection: grammatical morphemes, grammatical classes, and grammatical constructions. It is claimed that all are represented in the grammar as symbolic units.

I will say little about so-called grammatical morphemes at this juncture. Their status as symbolic units hinges on whether they are meaningful, and I have already suggested that they almost invariably are. The only way to demonstrate this is by analyzing a substantial and representative class of examples, including cases generally agreed to be void of semantic content, and showing that a coherent and revealing account of linguistic phenomena emerges just in case they are attributed specific meanings. This is one objective of the present work, and of cognitive-grammar research generally (e.g. Casad and Langacker 1985; Langacker 1981c, 1982a; Lindner 1981, 1982). A number of grammatical morphemes are analyzed in reasonably explicit detail in later chapters.

Basic grammatical classes are defined by schematic symbolic units. The class of nouns, for example, is defined by a schema that we can represent as [[THING]/[...]], where [THING] is a schematic semantic unit (cf. Ch. 5) and [...] a schematic phonological unit. The categorization of a specific form as a noun is then given by a classificatory unit of the sort previously discussed, for example, [[[THING]/[...]] → [[TREE]/[tree]]]; observe that the schematic relation between the two symbolic units overall depends on schematic relations at each pole: [[THING] → [TREE]] at the semantic pole, and [[...] → [tree]]

---

[16] The construction also allows a gesture instead of a noise, or a noise-gesture combination. We must therefore generalize the notion of a symbol to include cases where the signifier belongs to the visual rather than the auditory region of semantic space. This is necessary in any event to handle writing and sign language.

at the phonological pole. Though a number of basic classes are characterized in this manner with reference to their intrinsic semantic properties (cf. Part II), we must also accommodate grammatical classes identified on the basis of distribution (e.g. the class of verb stems that nominalize in a particular fashion). These require a somewhat different (though related) approach, presented in Ch. 11. For now I simply note that only symbolic units figure in the description.

Grammar involves the syntagmatic combination of morphemes and larger expressions to form progressively more elaborate symbolic structures. These structures are called **grammatical constructions**. Constructions are therefore symbolically complex, in the sense of containing two or more symbolic structures as components. There is no fundamental distinction between morphological and syntactic constructions, which are fully parallel in all immediately relevant respects.

When the formation of grammatical constructions is regular to any substantial degree, this regularity is expressed in the grammar by a schematic symbolic unit. This schematic unit is itself symbolically complex in the same way that its instantiations are; i.e. it is a schematic representation of the pattern of integration observed in the formation of particular expressions. The noun *pins*, for example, is a symbolically complex expression formed by integrating the two symbolic units *pin* and *-s*: [[[PIN]/[pɪn]]-[[PL]/[z]]]. This expression instantiates a pattern of plural noun formation embodied in the schematic unit [[[THING]/[...]]-[[PL]/[z]]],[17] where the integration between the two components is exactly analogous to that between the components of *pins* (and of other plural nouns). The schema therefore captures whatever generalization can be made about the nature of the syntagmatic combination defining the grammatical construction.

We must probe more deeply into the complicated set of relationships that are characteristic of a symbolically complex form, be it schematic or specific. Formulaic representations in the fashion of [[[PIN]/[pɪn]]-[[PL]/[z]]] are convenient but highly abbreviatory, for they show directly only a few of the structures and relations required in an explicit, fully articulated account of syntagmatic combination.

Four of the structures that figure in this example are the semantic units [PIN] and [PL] and the phonological units [pɪn] and [z]. These elements combine in various ways to form higher-order units in semantic, phonological, and symbolic space. Most obvious are the component morphemes [[PIN]/[pɪn]] and [[PL]/[z]]. *Pins* results from the syntagmatic combination of these simple symbolic units. What does the integration of two symbolic structures entail? Let us examine the integrative relation at each pole. First, a complete

---

[17] I simplify in various respects, notably by ignoring the distinction between count nouns and mass nouns. Note that **thing** is a technical term, not limited to physical objects.

analysis of *pins* must include a description of how the phonological components [pɪn] and [z] are integrated to give the composite structure [pɪn-z]; it specifies, roughly, that [z] is attached as the outermost consonant in the cluster functioning as coda to the syllable having [ɪ] for its nucleus. Second, a full analysis must similarly describe how the semantic components [PIN] and [PL] integrate to give the composite structure [PIN-PL]; [PL] designates a mass consisting of an indefinite number of replications (in type) of a discrete entity; the entity designated by [PIN] corresponds to each of those implied by [PL], so the composite structure designates a mass consisting of an indefinite number of discrete entities each attributed the specifications of [PIN].

So far we have isolated no fewer than eight units that figure in a simple expression like *pins*. These are the simple semantic units [PIN] and [PL]; the composite semantic unit [PIN-PL]; the simple phonological units [pɪn] and [z]; the composite phonological unit [pɪn-z]; and the simple symbolic units [[PIN]/[pɪn]] and [[PL]/[z]]. It might seem that eight should be sufficient, but in fact they are not. One can demonstrate their insufficiency by observing that a characterization of *pins* consisting of these eight units alone would not preclude a blatantly erroneous analysis for sentences like (3), in which there are two plural nouns:

(3) *The boys lost my pins.*

In the erroneous analysis, sketched in Fig. 2.7, the suffix *-s* on *boy* is taken as symbolizing the plurality of *pin*, and the suffix *-s* on *pin* as symbolizing the

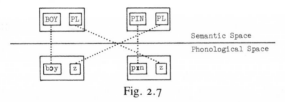

Fig. 2.7

plurality of *boy*. Note that all eight units cited above for *pins* are represented in the diagram. Nothing said so far about *pins* is inconsistent with the analysis.

What is missing, obviously, is a specification that the composite semantic structure [PIN-PL], as a whole, is symbolized by the integrated phonological unit [pɪn-z] specifically, rather than the mere occurrence of [pɪn] and [z] somewhere in the same sentence. This is equivalent to saying that the integration of [pɪn] and [z] has symbolic import: that [z] occurs as a suffix on [pɪn] symbolizes the fact that the notion of plurality conveyed by [z] pertains to [PIN] in particular rather than some other discrete entity. Otherwise phrased, the semantic integration between [PIN] and [PL] is symbolized by the integration of their respective phonological manifestations. We have thus encountered a new kind of symbolic relationship, slightly more abstract than those

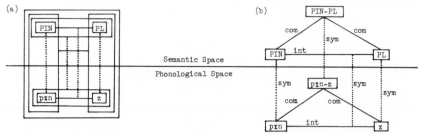

Fig. 2.8

previously considered; instead of holding between a semantic and a pho-nological structure, it holds between two **relations**, one associating two se-mantic structures, and the other two phonological structures.

Fig. 2.8 summarizes the various structures and relations we have found to be necessary for a full and explicit account of the internal structure of *pins*. Diagram (a) is a compacted representation (cf. Fig. 2.4). Integration is marked by horizontal lines of linkage: the overall integration of the symbolic units [[PIN]/[pɪn]] and [[PL]/[z]] implies an integrative relation at each pole—that is, [[PIN]-[PL]] and [[pɪn]-[z]]. Symbolic relations are marked by dotted correspondence lines. Observe that the symbolic correspondence be-tween the composite semantic structure [PIN-PL] and the composite pho-nological structure [pɪn-z] stems from three more-basic symbolic relations: those internal to [[PIN]/[pɪn]] and [[PL]/[z]], and the one between the in-tegrative relations at the two poles. Diagram (b) shows the same structures and relations in the format of an exploded diagram. Certain boxes have been omitted for the sake of clarity, and lines have been labeled to identify the rela-tionships of symbolization (*sym*), integration (*int*), and composition (*com*). The representations in Fig. 2.8 are complex, but only because all the essential elements are made fully explicit (usually they are swept under the proverbial rug, or into other components of the grammar). Every box and line of the figure is there for a specific purpose and indicates one of the structures or relations that are undeniably present in this construction. The sense in which grammatical constructions are symbolic entities should now be quite clear. We have seen that the integrative relation between two morphemes (or larger expressions) is resolvable into separate integrative relations between their se-mantic and their phonological poles; syntagmatic combination is thus bipolar. But it is also symbolic, for the integration of components at the semantic pole corresponds to, and is symbolized by, the integration of components at the phonological pole. This is true of grammatical constructions in general.

Consider now the relation between a particular composite symbolic struc-ture, such as *pins*, and the schema it instantiates. The internal structure of the schema is exactly parallel to that of its instantiations, and specifies how the component morphemes are integrated at the two poles. The schema describing this pattern of plural noun formation is therefore identical to Fig. 2.8, except that the count-noun schema replaces the morpheme *pin* as the first component. The schema for the construction is depicted in compacted form on the left in Fig. 2.9. Recall that a schema coexists in the grammar with those of its instantiations having unit status, which is a reasonable assumption in the case of *pins*. The elaborative relationship between *pins* and the categorizing schema is itself a unit, as Fig. 2.9 shows.

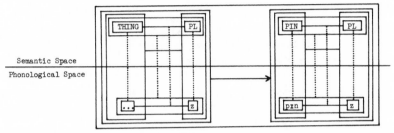

Fig. 2.9

Everything said above about *pins*, a morphological construction, is equally valid (with appropriate adjustments) for a syntactic construction. Consider the syntactic phrase *tall boy*. The symbolic components [[TALL]/[tɔl]] and [[BOY]/[bɔy]] must be integrated at both the semantic and the phonological poles. Semantically, [TALL] designates the relation between a thing and the region beyond the norm on a certain scale, whereas [BOY] designates a type of person; they are integrated through two correspondences: (1) between the thing referred to by [TALL] and the person designated by [BOY], and (2) between the norm on the scale referred to by [TALL] and the category norm in the height specification of [BOY]. The two components are integrated phonologically by being grouped as contiguous words in a phrase arranged in a specific linear order. Most crucially once again, the semantic integration stands in a symbolic relation with the phonological integration: the contiguity and linear ordering of the phonological structures [tɔl] and [bɔy] symbolize the fact that the height specification of [TALL] pertains to [BOY] in particular rather than some other entity. The case of *tall boy* differs from that of *pins* in specifics (e.g. the phonological integration is at the phrase level rather than the word level) but is quite parallel in its overall character.

It is simply incoherent in this perspective to speak of syntax as being "autonomous" from semantics. If the semantic pole is suppressed, then symbolic relationships cease to exist, and what remains is nothing but undifferentiated phonological structure. In that circumstance there can be no basis for even recognizing morphemes (or larger lexical units), let alone assigning them to grammatical classes.

2.3. Componentiality and Correspondence

Componentiality and correspondence are notions that have already figured very prominently in our discussion. The notions are quite general, and are not at all restricted to linguistic phenomena. They are nevertheless fundamental to linguistic structure and ubiquitous in their applicability within this domain.

2.3.1. *Componentiality*

The idea of componentiality is seemingly straightforward: complex structures are assembled out of simpler ones (or have them as components). The linguistic application of this notion nevertheless requires several points of clarification. Some of them relate to its cognitive interpretation. Others pertain to the distinction between "natural" conceptual or phonological units and those established on the basis of symbolic relationships.

2.3.1.1. *Its Cognitive Basis.* The grammar of a language is intended as a set of claims about the cognitive structures constituting a linguistic system, claims that could in principle be proved right or wrong given sufficient independent evidence about human cognition. The notion of componentiality must be understood in this context. Certain conceptions of componentiality and what it entails must be resisted, even though they seem quite natural in a priori terms, because there is reason to think that speakers handle things otherwise.

The concept [CIRCLE] provides a simple example. Anyone who has studied geometry is familiar with its definition as the set of points in a plane that lie at a specified distance from a reference point. The fact that this definition refers to a "specified distance" and a "reference point" might be taken as suggesting that [CIRCLE] has [RADIUS] and [CENTER] as semantic components, i.e. that [RADIUS] and [CENTER] are among the cognitive routines coordinated to form the higher-order routine whose execution constitutes the conceptualization of a circle. But despite the mathematical elegance of this characterization, it is doubtful that it reflects a person's naive or primary understanding of [CIRCLE]. Many people (e.g. young children) acquire [CIRCLE] as a salient and deeply entrenched concept without ever being exposed to the mathematical definition or focusing their attention specifically on the length of line segments from the center to the circumference. [CIRCLE] is probably first learned as a shape gestalt: it is the simplest or minimal closed curve, lacking any dimensional asymmetries or any departures from a smooth trajectory as one traces along its perimeter. [RADIUS] is then learned and characterized with respect to [CIRCLE] (and so is [CENTER], at least as applied to circles); hence [CIRCLE] is a component of [RADIUS] rather than the converse.[18]

The idea of componentiality suggests that structures might be decomposed successively into smaller and smaller subcomponents until no further decomposition is possible, yielding a set of "primitives." Can one posit, for example, a set of semantic primitives in the fashion of generative semantics? Cognitive grammar is essentially neutral on this question. No specific claim is made to the effect that the smallest units of linguistic significance are necessarily primitives. Despite the effective simplicity of a unit (in the sense of requiring no constructive effort), it is explicitly conceived as an integrated system, possibly very complex internally. Semantic units are defined relative to knowledge structures, which can be extremely complicated, even for units that are minimal for most linguistic purposes (e.g. in one of its senses *balk* presupposes extensive knowledge of baseball, but it is a minimal unit from the standpoint of symbolic relationships). Analysis of knowledge structures can be carried out to whatever delicacy is required by linguistic considerations, but the fundamental units uncovered in this way need not be specifically linguistic, nor is it necessary to assume that they ultimately reduce to a specified list of primitives.

The systemic nature of higher-order linguistic structures is a point of some significance. The fact that components can be recognized within a complex structure does not entail that these components exhaust its characterization: it may have properties above and beyond those of its components, which may in turn be manifested in it only imperfectly (cf. Ch. 12). A variety of considerations dictate a **nonreductive** approach to linguistic structure, meaning that a complex structure must be treated as a separate entity in its own right regardless of componentiality. Returning to an earlier example, we certainly want to acknowledge *staple* and *-er* as components of *stapler*, yet this complex lexical unit has semantic properties more specific than those predictable from these components alone. *Stapler*—specified in full detail—therefore coexists in the grammar of English with its components *staple* and *-er* as well as the schema for the V + *-er* derivational pattern. *Stapler* is sanctioned and categorized by this schema, and motivated by its components, but it is nonetheless a distinct unit not algorithmically deducible from these other structures.

In the final analysis, the componentiality we are concerned with pertains to the order in which cognitive routines are coordinated to form progressively more elaborate routines. This type of componentiality must not be confused with part/whole relationships in a conceived entity; the former pertains to the

---

[18] In short, the mathematical definition may be irrelevant to how the concept [CIRCLE] is learned and represented by the geometrically naive. Once a person has been exposed to this characterization, however, it enriches his encyclopedic understanding of the notion.

structure of a conceptualization, and the latter to the structure of what is conceptualized, which is a very different matter. This contrast can be illustrated by how we conceptualize the human body. We know that there are typically five fingers on a hand, one hand on an arm, and two arms on a body. With respect to the conceived entity (the object of conceptualization), there is consequently a part/whole relation between finger and hand, between hand and arm, and between arm and body. It does not follow, however, that the concept [FINGER] is a component of the concept [HAND], that [HAND] is a component of [ARM], or [ARM] a component of [BODY]. It seems rather dubious, in a case like this, that the concept of a whole is derivative of the concepts for its parts; instead, a crucial specification of [ARM] is its position relative to the larger configuration of the overall body, and similarly for the other pairs of concepts. I suggest, then, that [BODY] is a conceptual component of [ARM], [ARM] a conceptual component of [HAND], and [HAND] of [FINGER]: in each case the first conceptualization provides a frame of reference relative to which the second is located and identified.[19]

2.3.1.2. *Unipolar vs. Bipolar Componentiality.* Grammar is the successive combination of symbolic structures to form increasingly elaborate symbolic expressions. The components in a grammatical construction are thus symbolic, with both a semantic pole and a phonological pole. It is essential to realize that the structures most directly relevant to grammar derive their status as semantic or phonological components from the very fact that they participate in symbolic relationships. Components established on the basis of bipolar considerations often fail to coincide with the "natural" components defined by semantic or phonological considerations alone. Both **unipolar** and **bipolar componentiality** must be accommodated in a full linguistic description.

The distinction between the two kinds of componentiality is most easily illustrated in the phonological domain. When symbolic considerations are put aside, we observe a natural, unipolar hierarchy of phonological structures, where segments function as components of syllables, syllables as components of words, words as components of minimal phrases, and so on. If we focus on the organization of syllabic sequences into words, for example, we see that *tables* has two (unipolar) components: [[tey]-[bl̩z]]. (Note that [l̩] stands for an [l] which functions as a syllabic nucleus.) This componential organization is of course quite different from the one required for grammatical purposes, namely [[teybl̩]-[z]]. It is clear that the components [teybl̩] and [z] are established on symbolic rather than purely phonological grounds, i.e. we recognize

---

[19] Explicit knowledge of a part/whole relationship is then seen as a higher-order conceptual structure. For instance, both [BODY] and [ARM] function as components of the more complex notion [BODY-HAS-ARM] (or [ARM-PART-OF-BODY]).

[teybl] and [z] as constituents precisely because they symbolize the respective concepts [TABLE] and [PL]. The description of a morphological construction therefore has to specify how its phonological components—defined in bipolar terms—integrate with respect to the unipolar phonological hierarchy. In the case of the plural morpheme, it is specified that [z] attaches as the last consonant in the coda of the noun stem's final syllable.

The discrepancy between unipolar and bipolar componentiality is equally important in the semantic domain, though perhaps more subtle. A good way to approach it is by examining the contrast between a pair of expressions like *peas* and *corn* (cf. Langacker 1982a). If we consider in purely conceptual terms the notions they convey, leaving aside how these notions are symbolized, we find that they are quite analogous: each involves the conception of a small discrete object (of comparable size in the two instances) replicated to form a mass. We can plausibly suggest that in each case the notion of a replicate mass is a higher-order concept having for (unipolar) components the concept of replication and the concept of a particular type of discrete object.

Despite this conceptual parallelism, the symbolic conventions of English treat these notions differently. They contrast in their **level of initial lexicalization**, i.e. the place in the conceptual hierarchy occupied by the semantic pole of the root morpheme. *Peas* makes its initial lexicalization at the level of the individual discrete object: [[PEA]/[pea]]. It is only by virtue of syntagmatic combination with [PL] that we obtain the composite structure [[PEA]-[PL]] designating the replicate mass, so in this instance the bipolar componentiality mirrors what we have assumed to be the unipolar constituency. *Corn*, however, makes its initial lexicalization at the level of the mass: [[CORN]/[corn]]. The minimal semantic component defined by a symbolic relationship coincides with the whole; the expression is **unanalyzable**, the notions of replication and of a particular kind of discrete object remaining **sublexical** instead of being individually symbolized.[20] Explicit symbolization naturally enhances the salience of a conceptual component, so the notions of replication and of individual discrete objects are more salient within *peas* than in *corn*. This contrast in bipolar semantic constituency has grammatical consequences, for example in verb agreement (*peas are* vs. *corn is*) and quantifier selection (*many peas* vs. *much corn*).

A comprehensive linguistic description necessarily encompasses unipolar structures: phonological and conceptual hierarchies of complexity, each defined in its own terms. The basic units of grammar are nevertheless bipolar, as

---

[20] To designate an individual member of the mass, we resort to periphrastic expressions like *kernel of corn*. This expression is complex in terms of bipolar semantic units (it requires the integration of [KERNEL], [OF], and [CORN]), but the composite semantic structure is analogous to [PEA]. Hence the number of bipolar semantic units in an expression need not reflect its nonlinguistic conceptual complexity; a complex notion can be put succinctly, or a simple notion laid out in laborious, cumbersome fashion.

they are delineated by symbolic considerations. It is the discrepancy between unipolar and bipolar componentiality that makes grammar so variable and gives it the superficial appearance of being autonomous from semantics. The grammatical complexity of an expression, and the specifics of its composition, depend on the symbolic resources a language provides (in particular, its array of bipolar semantic components). Both factors are consequently variable, even for the expression of a specific (unipolar) conceptualization.

2.3.2. *Correspondence*

Essential to cognitive processes is our ability to establish **correspondences** between conceived entities. The entities may be quite distinct or belong to different domains—as exemplified by the correspondences established between seats and guests by the host of a dinner party. But we can also establish correspondences between two representations or occurrences of the same entity, as we do in reading a road map, or recognizing a person as "the same" when seen on different occasions. Whether they are purely mental or are given some physical implementation, correspondences are crucial to the comparison of entities to ascertain their identity or degree of similarity. In working a jigsaw puzzle, for instance, I establish provisional correspondences between particular pieces and vacant spots, and then check the correspondents for identity of shape (and other specifications). I can effect this comparison physically, by moving the piece and putting it down in the vacant spot, but often I can judge the fit by visual inspection alone. When I do the latter I nevertheless carry out a mental act of transportation and superposition, deciding the matter on the basis of the imagined configuration that results.

The comparison of two complex structures requires more than just a global correspondence between them. The global correspondence must be resolved into local correspondences between particular subparts of the structures, with the local correspondents then being assessed for degree of similarity. In the jigsaw-puzzle example, each knob, depression, corner, and side of the piece must be compatible with the corresponding subpart of the vacant spot. Clearly we have the ability to test alternate sets of correspondences between the subparts of two structures (e.g. alternate orientations of a puzzle piece relative to a vacant spot) to find the set that maximizes their compatibility. How finely we analyze complex structures into subparts (the "delicacy" of our analysis) depends on specific objectives. Global correspondences suffice for some purposes, but other cases demand local correspondences between subparts of variable size. At the extreme, two structures may be associated through indefinitely many local correspondences connecting individual points.

These general observations prove relevant in appreciating how correspondences function in grammar. They are significant in all three types of relations between the components in a complex structure: symbolization, categorization, and syntagmatic combination. Let us examine these in turn for their dependence on correspondences.

2.3.2.1. *Symbolic Relations.* Symbolization is dealt with here only by way of summary (cf. 2.2). A linguistic symbol involves a correspondence between two structures in semantic space (broadly construed), one of them in the phonological subdomain. When the two poles of a symbolic structure occupy vastly different regions of semantic space, their comparison for similarity or identity is severely limited; this incommensurability underlies the basic arbitrariness of simple linguistic signs. However, when the semantic pole of a linguistic symbol is itself situated in phonological space, comparison of the corresponding structures is feasible, and we recognize the expression as onomatopoetic when the structures show an appreciable degree of similarity. As a limiting case, moreover, a phonological structure can be put in correspondence with itself and hence be self-symbolizing, as in sentences like (2): *The boy went* [NOISE].

In a grammatical construction, the global correspondence between semantic and phonological structures is resolvable into a number of more specific correspondences. In the lexical unit *pins*, for example, we can note local symbolic relationships between (1) [PIN] and [pɪn]; (2) [PL] and [z]; (3) the composite structures [PIN-PL] and [pɪn-z]; and (4) the integration of [PIN] and [PL] at the semantic pole, and of [pɪn] and [z] at the phonological pole (cf. Fig. 2.8).

2.3.2.2. *Categorizing Relations.* In a relationship of full schematicity, the participating structures are fully compatible in their specifications; hence they must occupy the same general region of semantic space. The schema and its instantiation represent the same entity at contrasting levels of specificity: the schema is a coarse-grained representation showing only gross organizational features, whereas its instantiation delineates the entity in precise, fine-grained detail.

A schematic relationship reflects a categorizing judgment based on comparison. The overall comparison between a schema and its instantiation summarizes over an indefinite number of local comparisons between corresponding substructures. Consider the categorizing unit [[SNAKE]→ [RATTLE-SNAKE]]. Focusing on shape specifications, we observe that [RATTLE-SNAKE] is more specific than [SNAKE] in certain respects: [RATTLESNAKE] characterizes the head more precisely (as being roughly triangular), and it specifies a particular appendage in the tail region ([SNAKE] must be neutral about any such possibility). The overall elaborative relationship is thus derivative of local elaborations. Note, however, that elaborative distance can vary from one pair of correspondents to the next: [RATTLESNAKE] is not sub-

stantially more precise than [SNAKE] in its shape specification for the body
(exclusive of head and tail).

The same basic observations apply to instantiations of grammatical constructions. Recall that the complex symbolic unit *pins* instantiates the schema
describing a pattern of plural noun formation: [[[THING/...]-[PL/z]]→
[[PIN/pɪn]-[PL/z]]] (cf. Fig. 2.9). Clearly this global schematic relationship
reduces to local relations between corresponding subparts. The locus of non-
null elaboration is the noun stem, where *pin* is far more specific than its correspondent in the schema: [[THING/...]→[PIN/pɪn]]; this categorizing relationship can itself be resolved into elaborative relations at each pole, i.e.
[[THING]→[PIN]] and [[...]→[pɪn]]. In addition, [PL/z] occurs in both the
schema and the instantiation, and its bipolar integration with the stem is parallel in the two structures. For each local correspondence, then, there is a relation of full schematicity, including instances of identity (zero elaboration).
The global judgment constitutes a summary over these local relationships.

Full and partial schematicity are treated as aspects of a unified phenomenon. Both reflect categorizing judgments based on the comparison of a sanctioning structure and a target, and in both instances a global categorization
summarizes over the local comparisons of corresponding subparts. The difference lies in whether the sanctioning and target structures are fully compatible;
partial schematicity involves some conflict in specifications. Experientially,
there is a qualitative contrast. The mental operation of shifting from a schema
to its instantiation is analogous to bringing a picture into sharper focus: details
emerge, and uncertainty is confined to a narrower range. When schematicity
is partial, the parallel mental operation amounts to the transformation of one
structure into another whose character may be drastically different.

In view of this qualitative difference, one might question the wisdom of
analyzing extension as a type of categorization. It might be argued that figurative language, which I treat as extension, involves the interplay between a literal sense and a figurative sense, and is therefore intrinsically more complex
than categorization, which appears to involve nothing of the kind. But far
from being problematic, this observation is actually supportive of the analysis, for it is precisely what one expects from the characterization of full and
partial schematicity. Because partial schematicity involves conflicting specifications, the sanctioning and target structures cannot merge into a single, consistent conceptualization; in a categorizing judgment of the form [[SS]--→
[TS]], the discrepancy between SS and TS keeps them at least partially distinct. The result is a bipartite conceptualization including what we recognize
as a literal sense (SS) and a figurative sense (TS). On the other hand, nothing
prevents the sanctioning and target structures from merging into a unified conceptualization when there is full consistency between their specifications. In
the schematic relationship [[SS]→[TS]], SS is in effect "swallowed up" by

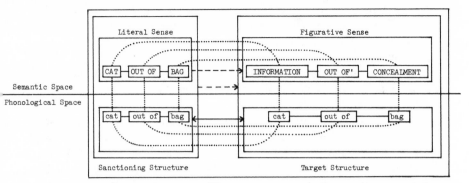

Fig. 2.10

TS, since all of the specifications of the former are implicit in the latter, which simply carries them down to a greater level of precision (cf. 3.3.3). I will refer to this tendency for an instantiation to "absorb" its schema (i.e. the effective equivalence of [[*A*]→[*B*]] and [*B*]) as the **schematic-transparency principle**.

With this background, we can now provide a preliminary account of the many factors at work in a typical idiomatic expression. Let us choose the idiom *the cat . . . out of the bag* (found in both *let the cat out of the bag* and *the cat is out of the bag*). We can simplify by ignoring such matters as the definite articles, the analyzability of *out of* into component morphemes, and the possible discontinuity of the idiom at the phonological pole. The essential components and relations within this idiom are outlined in Fig. 2.10.

Because this idiom is a well-entrenched lexical item, the entire categorizing structure has unit status, as do all of its components. The sanctioning structure, given on the left, represents the expression with its literal semantic value (pertaining to a feline escaped from a sack). It is assembled by the syntagmatic combination of three symbolic units, namely *cat*, *out of*, and *bag*, each defined by a correspondence between a semantic and a phonological structure. This sanctioning structure bears an overall relation of partial schematicity to the target, representing the expression construed in its figurative sense. The target structure is also syntagmatically complex, assembled out of symbolic components; the idiom, in other words, is to some degree **analyzable**, with *cat* attributed a meaning roughly equivalent to 'information', *out of* taken in one of its normal senses, and *bag* conveying some notion akin to 'concealment'.[21]

The overall relationship of partial schematicity between *SS* and *TS* decomposes into a sanctioning relation at each pole. At the phonological pole, the

---

[21] Nothing in the present model requires that *cat* and *bag* have these values outside the context of the idiom.

relationship is one of identity; I have symbolized this with a solid double-headed arrow (since identity is equivalent to bidirectional full schematicity). This identity relation is further resolvable into identity relations between the individual phonological components of SS and TS, as well as identity in their mode of integration. The incompatibility of specifications responsible for making the relation of SS and TS one of only partial schematicity is localized to the semantic pole (the expression illustrates **semantic extension**). This global relationship is also decomposable into local relations, all of partial schematicity, between corresponding semantic components. The extent of the discrepancy is quite variable: the conflict in specifications between [CAT] and [INFORMATION] is blatant—it is hard to perceive any similarities; [BAG], however, bears a natural and salient relation to [CONCEALMENT]; and the difference between [OUT-OF] and [OUT-OF'] is minor (spatial vs. abstract domain). The integration of semantic units is parallel in SS and TS.

Contrast this analysis with the doctrine that an idiom is semantically un-analyzable and constitutes a fixed phonological sequence (cf. Ch. 1). In general idioms are not phonologically invariable (though there may be a proto-typical linear ordering), and the great majority are analyzable to some degree. The essence of an idiom is a complex set of correspondences, both symbolic correspondences and those between components of the literal and figurative senses. This elaborate set of interconnections permits the identification of an idiom despite a considerable amount of phonological variability (cf. 12.2.3).

2.3.2.3. *Syntagmatic Relations.* Syntagmatic combination is the integra-tion of two or more **component structures** in semantic, phonological, or symbolic space to form a **composite structure** of greater size in the same domain. The integration of two symbolic structures involves their integration at both the semantic and the phonological poles. Here we focus on integration at the semantic pole (phonological integration is quite analogous).

Integration depends on correspondences. For two semantic structures to combine syntagmatically, they must have some point of overlap; more pre-cisely, a substructure of one is placed in correspondence with a substructure of the other, and these two substructures are construed as designating the same conceived entity. It is by virtue of having one or more such entities in common that two component structures can be integrated to form a coherent, more elaborate conceptualization.

Consider *The cat is out of the bag*, taken in its literal sense. To simplify matters and avoid tangential issues, we will once again restrict attention to *cat*, *out of*, and *bag*.[22] Fig. 2.11 diagrams the integration of their semantic

---

[22] Constituency is also ignored: *out of* combines with *bag* at the first level of constituency, and *cat* then combines with the composite structure so derived (cf. 8.4).

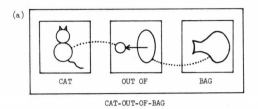

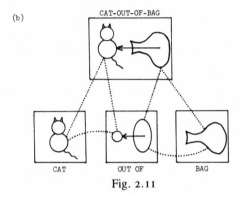

Fig. 2.11

poles in two equivalent notations. Diagram (a) is a compacted representation: the composite structure is given only implicitly, through its components and their specified mode of integration. In diagram (b), an exploded representation, the composite structure is depicted separately, above the components, as an integrated whole.

The semantic units [CAT] and [BAG] designate particular types of physical objects, which for present purposes are adequately represented by mnemonic sketches standing for their shape specifications. [OUT-OF], by contrast, is a relational predication. It describes a spatial configuration involving two objects; the configuration results from one of the objects following a trajectory that leads from an 'in' relation to an 'out' relation with respect to the other. [OUT-OF] thus makes inherent reference to two objects as part of its own characterization, but within this semantic unit itself these objects are specified only in highly schematic terms (one must be able to function as some kind of container, and the other to follow a spatial trajectory). I have used a circle and an ellipse to represent these schematically characterized objects, and an arrow for the presupposed trajectory.

Dotted lines indicate the correspondences that integrate the three semantic units to form a coherent composite structure. [OUT-OF] organizes the conceptual scene, setting up a relation between two schematically characterized objects. The more precisely specified object designated by [CAT] corresponds to one of these schematic entities, and the one designated by [BAG] to the other. Because there is in each case a relation of full schematicity between the corresponding substructures, the superimposition of their specifications produces a fully consistent composite conceptualization, shown at the top in Fig. 2.11(b).

When correspondence lines are used for syntagmatic combination, we can refer to them as **lines of integration**. They can be regarded as instructions for fitting two structures together, in particular as instructions for superimposing the specifications of the corresponding entities.[23] Conversely, the lines can be thought of as a record of the distortion that occurs when a unified conceptualization is fragmented for coding purposes into overlapping components, so that a single conceived entity is represented more than once. In addition to these **horizontal** correspondences, there are **vertical** correspondences equating elements of the composite structure and each of the component structures, as illustrated in Fig. 2.11(b). Vertical correspondence lines will often be omitted here to simplify diagrams, but they are nonetheless essential to grammatical structure.

---

[23] When these specifications conflict (i.e. when the relation between the corresponding substructures is one of partial rather than full schematicity), they engender a discord referred to by linguists as a "violation of selectional restrictions."

☐ Part II ☐
SEMANTIC
STRUCTURE

GRAMMAR CONSISTS in the successive combination of symbolic structures to form progressively larger symbolic expressions. It therefore cannot be adequately described or understood without a reasonably detailed and explicit account of the semantic pole of symbolic structures. Part II outlines the conception of linguistic semantics inherent in cognitive grammar. While programmatic, this conception is sufficiently well articulated to serve as foundation for the later discussion of grammatical organization.

The building blocks of grammar are minimal symbolic units, i.e. morphemes. I refer to the semantic pole of a morpheme as a **predicate**, and to the semantic pole of any linguistic expression as a **predication**. All predicates are therefore predications, but the converse is not so. Moreover, all predicates (but not all predications) have unit status (since morphemes do), and while they may be quite complex internally, they constitute minimal "chunks" of semantic content for symbolic and grammatical purposes. Our primary concern in Part II is limited to the internal structure of individual predicates, but the concepts and descriptive devices required for their characterization prove equally appropriate for describing predications in general.

Meaning is a mental phenomenon that must eventually be described with reference to cognitive processing. I therefore side with Chafe (1970, p. 74–76) by adopting a "conceptual" or "ideational" view of meaning, in opposition to such scholars as Palmer (1976, p. 26–30) and Lyons (1977, p. 113). As Chafe points out, criticisms of this view of meaning are often based on spurious assumptions, e.g. the assumption that a concept is necessarily a "mental picture" (in the most simplistic sense), that cognitive entities are necessarily beyond the pale of empirical inquiry, or that an ideational account would simply posit unanalyzed concepts without saying anything about their internal structure. I assume it is possible at least in theory (if not yet in practice) to describe in a principled, coherent, and explicit manner the internal structure of such phenomena as thoughts, concepts, perceptions, images, and mental experience in general. The term **conceptual structure** will be applied indiscriminately to any such entity, whether linguistic or nonlinguistic. A **semantic structure** is then defined as a conceptual structure that functions as the semantic pole of a linguistic expression. Hence semantic structures are regarded as conceptualizations shaped for symbolic purposes according to the dictates of linguistic convention.

Part II begins with a discussion of certain cognitive abilities and phenomena that I take as self-evident and important to the description of linguistic structures (Ch. 3). All predications are characterized relative to one or more cognitive **domains**, the subject of Ch. 4. The **profile/base** organization they impose on domains is examined in Ch. 5, which also proposes a semantic analysis of **things**. Two classes of relational notions, **atemporal relations** and **processes**, are the respective topics of Chs. 6 and 7.

CHAPTER 3
Cognitive Abilities

SEMANTIC STRUCTURE is conceptualization tailored to the specifications of linguistic convention. Semantic analysis therefore requires the explicit characterization of conceptual structure. Possibly this goal is quixotic. Nevertheless, I believe that mental experience is real, that it is susceptible to empirical investigation and principled description, and that it constitutes the natural subject matter of semantics. If we do not accept the challenge of elucidating our "cognitive map of the universe" (Givón 1979, p. 313), we forfeit any chance of attacking meaning on its home ground, and condemn ourselves to an endless succession of strategically inessential skirmishes.

Omniscience about psychological processes is fortunately not prerequisite to initiating a cognitively grounded investigation of language (helpful though it would be). In particular, linguistic entities generally pertain to higher levels of cognitive organization: the functional and phenomenological characterization of mental experience is consequently more directly relevant to linguistic analysis than descriptions that refer to the firing of specific neurons. For linguistic purposes it is often sufficient merely to establish the existence of a higher-order cognitive entity, regardless of how it might arise from more basic processes (just as for many purposes it is useful to speak of atoms as fundamental units, even if it is known that they are not the ultimate constituents of matter). I should emphasize that the following discussion of cognitive abilities derives from linguistic concerns, and is not tied to any particular psychological theory. The phenomena I call attention to are mostly self-evident, and must somehow be accommodated in any comprehensive model of cognitive processing.

3.1. Mental Experience

Having asserted that conceptualization, mental experience, and cognitive processing are proper concerns of semantic analysis, I must offer some preliminary clarification of these notions. This section also introduces a construct that is fundamental to their proposed characterization, namely an act (or event) of **comparison**. It is suggested that the ability to effect comparisons underlies the detection of regularity and the imposition of structure on cognitive activity.

3.1.1. *The Mind as Process*

Though it is customary—and I think innocuous—to use nominal expressions to designate mental phenomena (e.g. *mind*, *thought*, *concept*, *perception*, etc.), such terms must always be understood as convenient reifications. *Mind* is the same as mental processing; what I call a *thought* is the occurrence of a complex neurological, ultimately electrochemical event; and to say that I have formed a *concept* is merely to note that a particular pattern of neurological activity has become established, so that functionally equivalent events can be evoked and repeated with relative ease.

I will use the term **event** to designate a cognitive occurrence of any degree of complexity, be it the firing of a single neuron or a massive happening of intricate structure and large-scale architecture. We can assume that the occurrence of any such event leaves some kind of neurochemical trace that facilitates recurrence. If the event fails to recur, its trace decays; recurrence has a progressive reinforcing effect, however, so an event (or more properly, **event-type**) becomes more and more deeply **entrenched** through continued repetition.[1] An event-type is said to have **unit status** when it is sufficiently well entrenched that it is easily evoked as an integrated whole, i.e. when it constitutes an established **routine** that can be carried out more or less automatically once it is initiated. I will refer to the execution of such a routine as its **activation**. The activation of a routine is of course itself a cognitive event.

Mental experience is thus a flow of events: it is what the brain does. As recurrent events become entrenched to form established routines, and coactivated routines are coordinated into higher-order routines, the nature of this experience becomes more and more elaborately structured. At any given moment a brain is the locus of countless ongoing events of great complexity and diversity, but typically they are sufficiently patterned and integrated that many facets of this welter of activity constitute a coherent body of interpreted experience rather than a flux of unfamiliar and unrelated sensations. By now it is a

---

[1] It is strictly possible only for event-types to recur, but for convenience I will talk of the recurrence of events. The requisite notion of event-types requires some kind of functional equivalence, but need not specify that different tokens of a type involve the firing of precisely the same neurons across the same synaptic junctions. A coherent notion of functional equivalence is certainly possible in principle. Suppose there are three bundles of neurons, labeled A, B, and C, such that each of the neurons in bundle A has multiple connections to neurons in B, and each of those in B to neurons in C. The event-type A-B-C can then be defined as the coordinated activation of A, B, and C, i.e. the firing of sufficiently many neurons in A to trigger the firing of enough neurons in B to trigger the firing of a certain number of neurons in C. Different tokens of A-B-C might constitute the same mental experience or have the same role in higher-order cognitive phenomena even if no two tokens ever involve the firing of exactly the same set of neurons in the three bundles.

truism that this active, structuring character of mental processing extends even to perception. The quality of our perceptual experience depends only in part on the stimuli that impinge on our sense organs and the signals directly induced by these stimuli. Equally important is the structure imposed on these peripheral events at more central levels of processing in accordance with current expectations and the available inventory of perceptual and interpretive routines. Perception is not a passive phenomenon, but an active process that is reasonably regarded as a kind of problem-solving activity (cf. Arnheim 1969).

3.1.2. *Comparison*

Fundamental to cognitive processing and the structuring of experience is our ability to compare events and register any contrast or discrepancy between them. Such comparison is at work when we perceive a spot of light against a dark background, for example, or when we catch a spelling error. I assume that this ability to compare two events is both generalized and ubiquitous: acts of comparison continually occur in all active cognitive domains, and at various levels of abstraction and complexity; regardless of domain and level, moreover, they are manifestations of the same basic capacity (or at least are functionally parallel). Some nontrivial commonality is thus attributed to the perception of a spot of light against a dark background and the observation that one student in a class is more intelligent than the others, even though the specific processes of comparison must be quite different in the two cases. To account for highly complex experiences, e.g. hearing an orchestra or observing a typical visual scene, we must assume that many acts of comparison are carried out more or less simultaneously within a domain and that these individual acts are coordinated to form progressively more complex events, in ways that I can only hint at here.

Consider the judgment that two pure tones differ in pitch. Presentation of one tone elicits from the perceiver a cognitive event—event A—which constitutes his auditory experience of this sound. Presentation of the second tone induces event B. Now it is conceivable that the perceiver will establish no relation whatever between the two events (especially if the interval between them is quite long, or if he is otherwise occupied); he may treat the two tones as isolated auditory experiences and make no comparison at all. The mere occurrence of events A and B therefore does not constitute a comparison of the two tones or the recognition that they differ in pitch: such comparison implies some cognitive event transcending those induced by the two tones individually as separate experiences. Let the notation $A > B$ symbolize the complex event in which the two tones are perceived in relation to one another and judged to be of different pitch. Clearly this complex event contains events A and B as components. The symbol $>$ then stands for the mental operation—whatever its character—that relates the two and registers the discrepancy between them. This operation is itself a mental event distinct (though not independent) from A and B, and $A > B$ is a higher-order event coordinating these three components.

From this example we can isolate three functional components required for any act of comparison. Such an act has the general schematic form $S > T$, where S can be called the **standard** of comparison and T the **target**.[2] As these terms imply, the relation is asymmetrical: the standard serves as a baseline event or point of reference, relative to which the target is evaluated. The operation connecting them, $>$, will be called **scanning**. The term "scanning" reflects the directionality of the operation: there is in some sense a "movement" from S to T, with the value of T depending on its degree of "departure" from S. One should be careful not to read into the term more than is implied by the characterization just given. In particular, it does not imply a homunculus who sits in a control room observing the operation of the brain and moves his gaze from event S to event T. Nor is scanning equated with shifts in attention (or in the focal area of the visual field). As defined, it is not required that scanning (or an overall act of comparison) be limited to the focus of attention, or even that it be subject to conscious awareness.

A slightly more complicated example will serve to clarify these notions and how they can be invoked to explicate the structuring of experience. Fig. 3.1

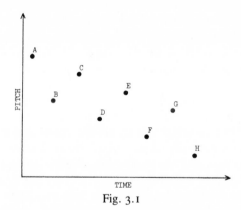

Fig. 3.1

represents a sequence of sounds, perhaps a minute fragment of the great cascade of sounds perceived and processed in listening to an orchestral performance. Suppose the listener succeeds in perceiving this sound sequence as an essentially regular structure, such that each successive pair of sounds, beginning with A and B, differ in pitch by the same amount and are shifted down-

---

[2] Coding requires an act of comparison. The relation between a sanctioning structure and a target structure (Ch. 2) is therefore a special case of the general $S > T$ schema.

ward on the pitch scale by a constant amount from the location of the preceding pair. What are the events that constitute this perception of regularity?[3]

As before, we can assume that each note, taken individually, elicits from the listener a cognitive event constituting an auditory sensation; we will call these events A, B, C, etc. No doubt the listener scans and compares this cluster of events in many ways, but a minimal inventory of the acts of comparison needed for the judgment of regularity must include the following. First, event A provides a standard for evaluating B with respect to the pitch parameter, resulting in the comparison event $A > B$, the perception that B deviates from A along this parameter by a certain amount. We must also posit the analogous comparisons $C > D$, $E > F$, and $G > H$. Observe next that each of these acts of comparison is itself a complex cognitive event and as such is capable of participating as either standard or target in further comparisons. Higher-order comparisons are obviously necessary to account for the attribution of essential regularity to the tone sequence. As a first approximation, we can say that event $A > B$ provides a standard for evaluating the target event $C > D$, resulting in the higher-order comparison $(A > B) > (C > D)$; by assumption, the components $A > B$ and $C > D$ are judged identical; or, otherwise phrased, the magnitude of the discrepancy registered between them is zero (the limiting case). Similar higher-order comparisons are of course needed to complete the string, for example $(C > D) > (E > F)$ and $(E > F) > (G > H)$. Finally, we must posit other first- and second-order comparisons to account for the second facet of perceived regularity, namely the steady downdrift from pair to pair. Needed are first-order comparisons such as $A > C$, $C > E$, and $E > G$ for the higher notes, each with a nonzero value, and the zero-valued second-order comparisons $(A > C) > (C > E)$ and $(C > E) > (E > G)$, together with a parallel set of comparisons for the lower notes. Also pertinent are second-order comparisons such as $(A > C) > (B > D)$, the observation that for each two pairs the difference in pitch between the higher notes is equal to that between the lower notes.

Obviously these brief remarks are not intended as a thorough analysis of the musical experience in question; however, they may indicate the complexity of even minor and commonplace instances of cognitive processing and suggest the possibility of an explicit model of how a structured mental experience emerges from the coordination of more fundamental events. Moreover, by observing the need for certain refinements we can draw some additional conclusions about basic cognitive abilities.

[3] I simplify by ignoring the quality of the sounds as well as the regularity of their time intervals (both of which involve acts of comparison analogous to those discussed). I emphasize once more that the judgments in question need not occupy the center of attention. Even if I concentrate on following the trumpet part, I am capable of experiencing a sequence of notes from the oboe, also, as a structured event.

Note first that even at this low level of processing we must speak of the ability to establish correspondences between distinct entities (the grammatical significance of this ability has already been commented on—cf. 2.3.2). The second-order comparison $(A > B) > (C > D)$, for example, presupposes a correspondence between A and C (both are standards) and between B and D (targets). If correspondences were established instead between, say, A and D as well as B and E, the resulting comparison $(A > B) > (D > E)$ would register a discrepancy and fail to contribute to the perception of regularity. We can plausibly suppose that large numbers of comparisons are continually made, more or less at random, but that structured experience starts to emerge only when comparisons yielding judgments of identity happen to occur.

A second observation is that the comparison of two events need not involve them as unanalyzed wholes; it may instead pertain only to certain facets of them or their manifestation in particular domains. Our discussion has focused on the comparison of sounds with respect to their pitch, but comparisons can also be made with respect to quality, duration, steadiness, location in time, and so on. In large measure these judgments are independent of one another; for example, I can determine that two sounds are quite similar in quality even though they differ markedly in pitch and duration (this allows me to follow the trumpet part in an orchestral performance and distinguish it from other instruments). This capacity for **selection** is also quite important for understanding semantic and grammatical structure.

Related to selection is **abstraction**. Recall that the higher-order comparison $(A > B) > (C > D)$ was taken as yielding a value of zero, i.e. a perception of identity (similarly for other second-order comparisons). But obviously this cannot be so if $A > B$ and $C > D$ are compared with respect to all of their specifications, even limiting our attention to the pitch domain. The complex event $A > B$ has A and B as components, whereas $C > D$ incorporates C and D; therefore, since A is not identical in pitch to C, nor B to D, a comparison of $A > B$ and $C > D$ embracing all of their specifications would necessarily result in the registration of a discrepancy. Clearly the second-order comparisons we rely on in ascertaining the regularity of the tone sequence must abstract away from the absolute location of the individual tones on the pitch scale and pertain only to the direction and the magnitude of scanning operations in the two components. What is actually selected for comparison between $A > B$ and $C > D$, then, are the two **vectors** representing the degree of divergence between A and B on the one hand and C and D on the other. Let us use the notation V_{ST} to indicate the vector value of the comparison $S > T$; that is, the magnitude and direction of the scanning operation relating S and T irrespective of their absolute location in a domain. The actual second-order comparison of concern is thus not $(A > B) > (C > D)$, but rather $V_{AB} > V_{CD}$, and its value is zero.

Yet another refinement is necessary. Even for a basic comparison like $A > B$ it is evident that A and B cannot per se be directly compared, for the simple reason that they occur at different times. Each was defined as the cognitive event immediately elicited by one sound and constituting the perception of that sound; by assumption the sounds are nonsimultaneous, and in fact we can easily judge the relative pitch of two sounds even when they are separated by a very substantial time interval. What is needed, obviously, is some notion of recall (or short-term memory), a well-established phenomenon describable as follows in the present framework. When a cognitive event occurs, it leaves a trace that—prior to its decay—permits its recurrence (i.e. the occurrence of another event of the same event-type). Recall is thus reactivation of a cog-nitive process, and to the extent that the second occurrence is the same as the first it constitutes another instance of the same mental experience. Note, how-ever, that in perceptual events there is a nontrivial difference between the two occurrences. Intuitively, the recall of a perceptual experience is substantially less intense or "vivid" than the original experience; we can reasonably sup-pose that the reactivation involves a lower energy level than the original per-ception owing to the absence of concurrent sensory stimulation. But even in its attenuated form, the recurrence can function as a component of other cog-nitive events, including acts of comparison. Using a capital letter to designate an actual perceptual event, we can employ the corresponding lowercase sym-bol for the attenuated reactivation constituting recall of that event. Returning to our example, then, the comparison previously represented as $A > B$ is now seen to be more properly given as $a > B$, or perhaps even $a > b$. Similarly, the second-order comparison $V_{AB} > V_{CD}$ might be more accurately shown as $V_{ab} > V_{cd}$.[4]

3.1.3. *The Imposition of Structure*

Our mental experience is coherent by virtue of the structure we impose on it. A pivotal aspect of this structuring capacity is the interpretation of novel experience with reference to previous experience, which I relate to the inher-ent asymmetry between standard and target in acts of comparison. The previ-ous experience can be an immediately preceding cognitive event (as in the perception that two nonsimultaneous tones differ in pitch); since the occur-rence of an event leaves a temporary trace that facilitates its repetition, one event naturally tends to be adopted as a standard for evaluating a directly sub-sequent one. The previous experience in question can also take the form of a well-entrenched routine activated for the structuring of current sensations (as in the recognition of a familiar shape).

[4] A great deal of cognitive processing can be carried out on reactivations of a perceptual occur-rence after the original perception is completed. We have all had the experience, for example, of asking someone to repeat a statement we failed to understand, only to figure out what was said before the repetition could be supplied.

An act of comparison has the general form $S > T = V$, where V is a value for the vector of scanning in some domain. **Recognition**, in the present scheme, is simply the limiting case in which no discrepancy is registered between S and T; that is, $S > T = 0$. For perceptual recognition (such as the recognition of a familiar shape or sound) the act of comparison has the form $a > A = 0$: the target A is a stimulus-induced sensation evaluated relative to a standard a that consists of an established routine whose activation constitutes an experience equivalent to the target (apart from its lesser intensity). Recognition thus has the same basic character as the observation of change or contrast; its qualitative distinctness resides in the degenerate nature of the scanning operation relating S and T.

Our proclivity for interpreting new experience by means of previous experience is such that it is very difficult not to observe obvious regularities or to recognize a familiar entity. The reader will find it hard to avoid perceiving a sequence of dots (............) as forming a line, or to see the marks on this page as uninterpreted visual impressions instead of familiar orthographic representations. A well-known consequence of this proclivity is the closure phenomenon, where a degraded input is nevertheless recognized and gaps or minor discrepancies may not even be noticed (note the frequent failure to catch errors while proofreading). Closure is easily described in the present account of recognition. The recognition event involves, as roughly simultaneous components, the activation of an established routine (a) and the occurrence of a stimulus-induced event (A) essentially equivalent to this routine. The act of recognition thus implies the occurrence of an event-token (a) of the event-type in question as the standard of comparison. The full mental experience is thus elicited despite the imperfections of the input, and irrespective of whether they are specifically noted.

Even perception thus depends on previous experience and expectations as well as the actual input. How the input is processed and interpreted is determined by such factors as the entrenchment of applicable routines, facilitation by recent occurrences of the same or related events, or simply random selection from the myriad comparisons possible for any complex stimulus event. Often the same input supports alternate interpretations each constituting a coherent experience. In the example illustrated in Fig. 3.1, we assumed the comparison of A and B, of C and D, and so on, as seen in Fig. 3.2(a). This results in a regular array of four two-note events, within each of which the pitch drops by a certain amount from the first note to the second. However the alternative structuring in Fig. 3.2(b) could also arise should the listener happen instead to effect the comparison of B and C, D and E, and F and G (along with higher-order comparisons of the resulting vectors). Here the listener perceives a regular array of three two-note events, with the pitch rising within each by a constant amount. Either processing pattern constitutes a structured

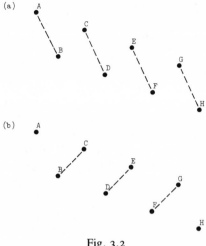

Fig. 3.2

mental experience involving the perception of regularity, but the two experiences are qualitatively different despite being prompted by the same stimulus events.[5]

The broader significance of this observation cannot be overestimated, for it can be extended from perception to conception in general, with direct consequences for the proper understanding of semantic and grammatical structure. Most crucially, it implies that the meaning of an expression is not determined in any unique or mechanical way from the nature of the objective situation it describes. The same situation can be described by a variety of semantically distinct expressions that embody different ways of construing or structuring it. Our ability to impose alternate structurings on a conceived phenomenon is fundamental to lexical and grammatical variability.

3.1.4. *Scanning Chains*

Finally, let us consider how notions of scanning might be extended to accommodate the perception of basic configurations in a field of representation, e.g. patterns defined by contrasts in brightness in the visual field. Suppose, to begin, that the same degree of brightness is registered throughout, so that the field is perceived as a uniform, featureless expanse of white. This is perhaps

---

[5] Hofstadter (1982) describes a more elaborate instance of this type of phenomenon: "After a couple of months of practice my fingers had built up enough stamina to play the piece fairly evenly and softly. This was very satisfying until one day an acquaintance . . . commented . . . that I was stressing every second note rather than every third. Bewildered, I looked at the score, and . . . as she had pointed out, the melody was written in triplets. . . . I tried playing it in threes. It sounded strange and unfamiliar. . . . I went home and took out my parents' old record. . . . I found I could hear it *either* way. . . . All of a sudden I saw that I knew *two* melodies composed of the same sequence of notes!" (p. 22).

not very interesting, but it is a perceptual experience nonetheless, and the observation of uniformity is itself something that requires explication in terms of comparison and scanning. We have been assuming the ubiquity of the comparison process, positing the continued occurrence of countless comparison events in all domains and at all levels of active cognitive functioning. The perception of uniform brightness throughout the visual field can thus be taken as consisting of indefinitely many, essentially random events in which the comparison of brightness between contiguous points yields a value of zero.

Consider next a visual field that is uniformly white with the exception of a single point within it, which is dark.[6] Let us use the letter A to label both this point and the cognitive event that constitutes the brightness sensation associated with it; B through G will similarly represent immediately surrounding points and their associated events. Most of the many comparisons within the largely white field still yield a value of zero (no discrepancy), but all of those involving point A now register a contrast, a uniform nonzero value. Each of the events $B>A$, $C>A$, $D>A$, ..., $G>A$, constitutes the perception that point A contrasts in brightness with one of its immediate neighbors. Because the target is identical in all of these individual acts of comparison, we can treat $(B>A, C>A, ..., G>A)$ as a complex act of comparison that amounts to the observation of A as a contrastive entity sharply delineated from its environment.

How might we handle the perception of a dark line against a white background? Suppose we label the dark points constituting this line (and the associated cognitive events) A, B, C, and so forth. If A_1 and A_2 are the background points immediately adjacent to A, the complex comparison $(A_1>A, A_2>A)$ represents the discrimination in brightness between A and its surroundings on either side; similarly, we can posit $(B_1>B, B_2>B)$, $(C_1>C, C_2>C)$, etc. as complex acts of comparison delineating other points from their background neighbors. These events are certainly necessary, but they hardly amount to the experience of perceiving a line: the integrated nature of this experience requires that these events further be related to one another in some fashion. Clearly, then, we must consider comparisons between adjacent dark points, such as $A>B$. What might be their character?

The overall comparison of two events is resolvable into more fundamental comparisons along different parameters. Two parameters are relevant here, namely brightness and spatial location. The value of $A>B$ thus has two components: a scanning vector for brightness, with a zero value (since A and B are both dark); and a vector registering the positional discrepancy between

---

[6] "Point" is not to be understood in the mathematical sense, which would imply zero extension and infinitely many immediately contiguous points. Instead it is taken as whatever minimal area functions as a quantum of cognitive processing at a given level of organization.

them, including both magnitude (minimal, since A and B are adjacent) and direction. Recall now that a scanning operation is an event in its own right distinguishable from the standard and target (though it cannot occur independently); hence its occurrence leaves a momentary trace that facilitates its recurrence. As a consequence, the comparison $A > B$ facilitates the immediately subsequent occurrence of $B > C$: (1) the standard B of $B > C$ is already activated (as the target of $A > B$); (2) its scanning operation is the same as that of $A > B$ (if we abstract away from absolute location in the visual field); and (3) the trace left by the occurrence of this operation in $A > B$ primes its recurrence as part of $B > C$. In similar fashion $B > C$ facilitates $C > D$, and so on along the extension of the line. The shared components allow us to speak of an integrated event of the form $(A > B, B > C, C > D, ...)$, or in a more revealing notation $(A > B > C > D ...)$, which constitutes the perception of the line as a unitary entity.

We see, then, that the constructs already introduced accommodate a special type of complex scanning event. It consists in a chain of scanning operations, each facilitated by the preceding and equivalent to it in vector value; the chain defines a path through some field of representation that continues so long as this value suffices for the comparison of lower-order events. We can say, in a manner of speaking, that the perceiver scans through a field in a constant direction until a contrast is registered. In the present example, where a single dark line is perceived against an otherwise uniformly white background, the perceiver can be thought of as scanning through this background along multiple and more or less randomly chosen paths, the result being the perception of general homogeneity throughout the visual field in regard to brightness; however, some of these paths terminate with the registration of a contrast in brightness, and an additional scanning path $(A > B > C > D ...)$ then serves to unite those points standing out against the background by virtue of this contrast. It must be reemphasized that this conception of scanning has nothing very directly to do with attention, either in the general sense or in the specialized sense of shifts in focal area within the visual field. Rather it is a type of cognitive processing that occurs both ubiquitously and automatically in a variety of domains, requiring neither the spotlight of attention nor the postulation of an attending homunculus.

3.2. Autonomous Processing

Perceptual examples are convenient and have thus been highlighted in the preceding discussion, but much of our mental life is related only indirectly to perception and objective reality. The linguistic significance of this obvious fact is explored in this section, and relevant constructs are introduced. Attention is also briefly discussed.

3.2.1. *Imagery*

The term **imagery** has been used for several distinct though not unrelated phenomena. All of them figure prominently in the cognitive-grammar conception of semantic structure, but to forestall erroneous notions of what this conception entails it is crucial that we distinguish them clearly. The term imagery is often employed as an equivalent of **metaphor** (or **figurative language**), which I also consider an inherent and fundamental aspect of semantic and grammatical structure. To minimize confusion I will avoid using the terms image and imagery in this sense.

Image and imagery also describe the occurrence of a perceptual sensation in the absence of the corresponding perceptual input. If I close my eyes, I can nevertheless evoke a kind of visual sensation by imagining or visualizing a scene. Similarly, I can evoke a kind of auditory sensation even when surrounded by total silence, for instance by imagining the sound of a barking dog or recalling a certain passage from the performance of a symphony. This type of imagery has attracted considerable interest from cognitive psychologists in recent years, and such scholars as Shepard (1978) and Kosslyn (1980) have demonstrated both its reality as a phenomenon and its status as a valid object of rigorous empirical inquiry. We will return shortly to this kind of imagery, for which I employ such terms as **sensory imagery**, **visual imagery**, **auditory imagery**, etc. when there is any possibility of confusion.

Unless otherwise indicated, I understand the term image and its derivatives in a third (and somewhat idiosyncratic) manner: they describe our ability to construe a conceived situation in alternate ways—by means of alternate images—for purposes of thought or expression. Two images of the same situation may differ as to which features of it are selected for explicit attention, the relative salience of these features, the level of abstractness or specificity at which it is treated, the perspective from which it is viewed, and so on (cf. 3.3). The sentences in (1), for instance, embody substantially different images (and hence are semantically distinct) even though they could all be used to describe the same objective situation.

(1)(a) *The clock is on the table.*
  (b) *The clock is lying on the table.*
  (c) *The clock is resting on the table.*
  (d) *The table is supporting the clock.*

The first sentence is the most neutral. It is essentially schematic for the other three, each of which chooses some facet of the scene for further, individual symbolization, thereby rendering this facet more prominent and characterizing it in finer detail. The verb *lie* in (1)(b) calls attention to the alignment of the clock along the horizontal axis of the table; *rest* in (c), on the other hand, emphasizes the static character of the locative relationship, whereas *support* in (d) highlights the resistance of the table to the gravitational force exerted on the clock. This is a typical example of how the lexical and grammatical conventions of a language provide an array of alternative expressions for coding a conceptualization: expressions that are often functionally equivalent but nonetheless different in meaning by virtue of the contrasting images they convey.

My position that semantic structure is based on conventional imagery pertains primarily to imagery in this third sense. It does not imply any necessary commitment to sensory imagery as an exclusive or essential facet of the meaning of linguistic expressions. Nor should my frequent use of quasipictorial diagrams be construed as an implicit claim that all meaning is based on visual imagery.[7] How and to what extent sensory imagery figures in conceptual and semantic structure is an empirical question, the answer to which is by no means pivotal to the formulation or evaluation of the cognitive-grammar model.

I am nevertheless convinced that sensory imagery is a real phenomenon whose role in conceptual structure is substantial. We can plausibly suppose that a visual image (or a family of such images presupposing different orientations and levels of specificity) figures in our knowledge of the shape of an object; and certainly one aspect of our conception of a trumpet assumes the form of an auditory image representing the sound it makes. The long-standing prejudice against sensory images rests largely on erroneous and gratuitous assumptions about their necessary character (e.g. the notion that a visual image is analogous to a picture and requires the postulation of a homunculus to examine it). Sensory images are in fact nonmysterious, subject to empirical investigation, and straightforwardly accounted for in terms of cognitive processing.[8]

What, then, is a sensory image? Actually we have already dealt with the matter (cf. 3.1). Mental experience is merely the occurrence of cognitive events. A primary sensory experience is a cognitive event evoked directly by the stimulation of a sensory organ. The corresponding sensory image is then nothing but the occurrence of an equivalent cognitive event in the absence of external stimulation. Though a stimulus-induced sensation is typically more intense than the corresponding image, the two constitute mental experiences that are qualitatively similar to the extent that they represent different tokens of the same event-type. Understood in this way, sensory images are in fact an

[7] These diagrams are to be interpreted as informal attempts to graph the relationships among certain entities in a domain, much as a vowel chart diagrams the location of vocalic articulations along the parameters of height and frontness. (Note that a vowel chart is never taken as indicating an implicit claim to the effect that vowel articulations are based on visual imagery.)

[8] Kosslyn (1980, ch. 2) does a good job of exposing the standard misconceptions and countering the usual criticisms. His idea of the basic character of sensory images is quite compatible with my own: "Image representations are like those that underlie the actual experience of seeing something, but in the case of mental imagery these representations are retrieved or formed from memory, not from immediate sensory stimulation" (p. 18). I take no position on the specific features of his model, however.

expected phenomenon granted the general freedom of cognitive processing from direct stimulus control (cf. Chomsky 1959). Though sensory stimulation lays the foundation and provides the raw material for the construction of our conceptual world, often we do not attend to it, and vast portions of our mental experience are connected only tenuously and indirectly at best to specific perceptual input. Cognitive functioning is largely autonomous; it proceeds in the absence of sensory input, follows paths where such input can never take it, and even serves to structure (and in some instances, to override) this input.

I will make a general distinction between **autonomous** and **peripherally connected** cognitive events. The sensation directly induced by stimulating a sense organ is an instance of a peripherally connected event; the corresponding sensory image, evoked in the absence of such stimulation, is an autonomous but equivalent event. For large classes of autonomous events, of course, there are no equivalent events that are peripherally connected (consider emotions or abstract concepts). Moreover, peripherally connected events are not necessarily perceptual, for I include in this class those cognitive events directly responsible for eliciting motor actions (i.e. motor signals). A serious parallel is thus drawn between, on the one hand, the activity of the receptor organs and the cognitive events directly induced by this activity, and on the other hand the activity of the effector organs and the cognitive events that directly induce it. Having made this analogy, we can reasonably speak of a **motor image**, an event equivalent to one that elicits a motor response but which in actuality fails to do so. By virtue of this failure such an event remains peripherally unconnected and is therefore autonomous.

Motor images are real. Often while typing, for example, though I am cognizant of "sending out the signal" to type a certain letter, I fail in fact to implement the motor routine and the letter remains untyped. I can imagine the experience of mentally directing and executing the act of throwing a ball or articulating a certain speech sound, running through each successive phase of the action in my mind without actually translating these autonomous events into motor gestures.[9] I suggest, moreover, that motor images are important for the proper characterization of both semantic and phonological structure. Just as an auditory image is one facet of our conception of a trumpet—and thus part of the meaning of *trumpet* granted the encyclopedic view of linguistic semantics—so the motor images corresponding to walking, kicking, or throwing figure prominently in our conceptions of these activities and are consequently included in the meanings of the verbs *walk*, *kick*, and *throw*. As for

[9] Athletes sometimes rehearse their moves mentally in this way, seeking to further entrench the desired sequence of motor commands and muscular gestures even in the absence of their physical implementation. "Silent speech" (to whatever extent it actually occurs) can also be assimilated to motor imagery. Observe that the "visualization" of a motor activity involves both kinesthetic and motor images; the two are inherently difficult to separate, since motor signals and kinesthetic sensations occur together and form a feedback loop.

phonology, I have already argued (2.2.1) that sounds are best regarded as conceptual entities for purposes of linguistic analysis. An auditory routine is one aspect of a speaker's knowledge of a speech sound, whereas motor and kinesthetic routines constitute his knowledge of a speech sound from the articulatory standpoint. These routines can be activated as either autonomous or peripherally connected events. A speaker who becomes deaf or paralyzed and is no longer able to implement these routines peripherally can nonetheless be said to have auditory or articulatory knowledge of a sound if he can activate them autonomously (as images).

3.2.2. *Imagination and Reality*

A large portion of our mental experience is autonomous. Some of this, for example emotive experience, is inherently autonomous and has no peripherally connected equivalent. Much of it, however, derives from peripherally connected events through some chain of mental processes that may be quite long and complex. The most direct mechanism is recall: a routine established through the recurrence of a peripherally connected event is activated autonomously and thereby constitutes an imagic experience equivalent to this event. Somewhat less direct is the coordination of autonomous events (possibly the imagic equivalents of peripherally connected routines) to form a more complex autonomous event that has never occurred nonautonomously. I have seen golf balls, for instance, and I have seen cubes, so it is easy for me to imagine what a cube-shaped golf ball would look like, though I cannot remember ever seeing one. Yet another mechanism is the extraction from peripherally grounded notions of schemas that are too abstract to be manifested peripherally in unelaborated form. For example, a speaker can grasp the commonality of sounds like [i], [a], and [u], extracting the schema [VOWEL] (unspecified for such properties as frontness, height, and rounding), but our physical makeup is such that the peripheral implementation of this schema per se is impossible: the articulation (and probably even the audition) of an actual vowel must have some specific value with respect to each of these parameters.

Through these mental operations and others, we are capable of constructing conceptual worlds of arbitrary complexity involving entities and phenomena that have no direct counterpart in peripherally connected experience. Such are the worlds of dreams, stories, mythology, mathematics, predictions about the future, flights of the imagination, and linguistic theories. All of us have constructed many conceptual worlds that differ in genre, complexity, conventionality, abstractness, degree of entrenchment, and so on. For many linguistic purposes all of these worlds are on a par with the one we distinguish as "reality." In particular, any conceptualization, regardless of its level of complexity or the indirectness of its relation to peripherally connected experience, can function as the context (or **domain**) for the characterization of a semantic structure. So far as language is concerned, expressions like *unicorn*, *phlogiston*, *Donald Duck*, and *Do Support* are equivalent in status to nouns like *Ronald Reagan*, *dog*, *blood*, and *bicycle*. It seems apparent, then, that any linguistically appropriate notion of reference must resemble the cognitivegrammar notion of **designation** (4.1, 5.1) in being applicable to any of these conceptual worlds.

A person's conception of reality is itself a conceptual world that is built up from peripherally connected experience through complex sequences of mental operations. We construct our conception of the "real world" bit by bit, stage by stage, from myriad and multifarious sensory and motor experiences. It consists of the organization we impose, through the progressive and interactive application of interpretive procedures, on both primary experience and the higher-order cognitive structures that derive from previous processing. The conceptual world we recognize as reality is nevertheless distinguished from others and accorded a privileged status. We can speculate on the grounds for this distinction: likely factors include the greater intensity of peripherally connected events vis-à-vis their autonomous counterparts; the persistence of certain types of sensory experience (in contrast to the freedom of autonomous processing to follow random and highly variegated paths); and the fact that peripherally connected events constitute the ultimate foundation for a substantial portion of our autonomous experience.

It is our conception of reality (not the real world per se) that is relevant to linguistic semantics. When reality is at odds with a speaker's view of it, the latter obviously prevails in determining his use of any grammatical markers serving to indicate the status of a situation as real or unreal. Linguistically it is important that speakers believe in the existence of a "real world" and distinguish it from worlds they regard as purely conceptual, but the validity of this belief is of no direct concern. Reality, of course, is not restricted to the physical. Part of a person's conception of reality is the recognition of his own mental activity, including the fact that he has a conception of reality. Part of this conception as well is the recognition that other people have conceptions of reality that differ in some respects from each other and from one's own. It is further realized that any of these reality conceptions, including one's own, may be inconsistent and in error on many points. Convoluted though they are, considerations of this sort are crucial for the semantic analysis of certain predicates and grammatical constructions (cf. Fauconnier 1985).

3.2.3. *Attention*

Mental experience is the flow of cognitive events. Conscious experience proceeds concurrently in numerous domains. Typically it is a partially integrated blend of perceptual sensations (visual, auditory, tactile, etc.), kinesthetic and motor events, emotive factors, and autonomous processes that may be quite distinct from all of these (i.e. thought directed elsewhere). Obviously we do not attend equally to all of these simultaneous strands of our conscious experience. If I am lost in thought, I may be quite oblivious to all perceptual input, even though such input continues to be registered by my sensory organs and processed cognitively at the margins of my awareness. If I concentrate on one sensory domain, input from the others may similarly be ignored. Within a single domain, moreover, attention can be highly selective, as when I follow the trumpet part while listening to the performance of a symphony.

The reality and importance of attention as a mental phenomenon are beyond dispute. Agreement is also easily reached on certain aspects of a phenomenological account of attention: it shifts quite readily from one domain to another and from one entity to another within a domain; to some extent, it is subject to volitional control (hence we can *direct* our attention or *concentrate* on something); and it lends itself, on introspective grounds, to characterization in terms of a central or focal area fading off into a periphery of indefinite extension (thus we speak of the *center* or *focus* of attention). The neurological and psychological mechanisms responsible for the existence, control, and specific properties of attention are anything but well understood, however (cf. Norman 1976). Fortunately the precise nature of these mechanisms is less important for most of our concerns than the existence of attention and some of its more evident characteristics.

What kind of thing is attention? Clearly we must avoid the image of a homunculus shining a spotlight about or shifting his gaze from one domain to another. We can more realistically assume that the relative level of intensity is a significant (though possibly a concomitant) factor. When attention is focused on auditory input, for example, there may well be an overall rise in the general energy level of processing in the auditory domain, with the effect that the thresholds for auditory events are lowered and their intensity augmented. Similarly, if I concentrate on following the trumpet part in an orchestral performance, I tend to perceive the trumpet sounds as being louder (relative to other instruments) than I do if I am attending to the music holistically. Note further that the sudden intrusion of a highly intense sensation into our conscious experience—e.g. a sharp pain, a loud noise, or a bright flash in the visual field—almost invariably attracts our momentary attention.

I assume, then, that attention is intrinsically associated with the intensity or energy level of cognitive processes, which translates experientially into greater prominence or salience. Out of the many ongoing cognitive processes that constitute the rich diversity of mental experience at a given time, some are of augmented intensity and stand out from the rest as the focus of attention. The higher energy level in the focal area facilitates the activation within it of a more elaborate and richly articulated set of cognitive events; the result is greater **acuity**, i.e. a fuller, finer-grained, more precisely specified mental experience. Clearly, I am far more likely to solve a problem that I focus my attention on than one that remains at the periphery of my awareness. In similar fashion, by attending specifically to the trumpet part in a symphony I perceive and recall this part in finer detail.

I have generally avoided visual examples in this section (3.2) in order to emphasize that the processes in question are not peculiar to the visual domain. As I have characterized them, it is perfectly coherent (and obviously necessary) to speak of scanning, recognition, imagery, attention, focal areas, salience, acuity, etc. as general phenomena whose visual instantiations represent special (though perhaps privileged) cases. Vision of course provides a paradigm example for attention and related notions: the field of vision is centered on a focal area, defining the locus of "visual attention," which has far greater acuity than the periphery. But as we have seen, functional parallels exist even for domains that lack a hard-wired equivalent of the retinal fovea, and the visual domain must compete for overall attention with many others. If I concentrate on looking at something carefully, the focus of my visual attention coincides with my overall focus of attention. However, if I shift my primary attention to another domain (for example if I try to compose a limerick), I may be quite oblivious to whatever happens to occupy the center of my visual field.

Finally, I return to the difference between attention and scanning. The latter was defined as a ubiquitous process of comparison and registration of contrast that occurs continuously throughout the various domains of active cognitive functioning. Highly complex events of comparison and recognition occur, and contribute to the richness of our ongoing mental experience, even in domains to which we are not specifically attending, and at the periphery of those to which we are. When I focus on the trumpet part in a symphony, I nevertheless continue to hear the oboe part and all the others as well, though I process them in less depth and detail. In short, attention is superimposed on the intricately woven fabric of our mental experience and selectively augments its salience; it is not prerequisite for such experience.

3.3. Focal Adjustments

Linguistic expressions pertain to conceived situations, or "scenes." However, the meaning of an expression is not adequately characterized just by identifying or describing the situation in question. For one thing, expressions differ in meaning depending on which entities within the situation they **designate** (cf. Ch. 5). Relative to the same scene, for example, I can form such expressions as *the lamp on the table*, *the table with the lamp on it*, or *The lamp is on the table*, respectively designating the lamp, the table, and the locative relationship between them. Our present concern is with a broader phenomenon of which variable designation is only a special case: the ability of speakers to construe the same basic situation in many different ways, i.e. to structure it by means of alternate images. The contrasting images imposed on a scene amount to qualitatively different mental experiences. Consequently, the image embodied by a linguistic expression—the conventionally established way in which it structures a situation—constitutes a crucial facet of its meaning.

The images employed to structure conceived situations vary with respect to a number of parameters. I will refer to such variation as **focal adjustments** (permitting myself a visual metaphor). The discussion is organized under three broad headings. Focal adjustments of **selection** determine which facets of a scene are being dealt with. **Perspective** relates to the position from which a scene is viewed, with consequences for the relative prominence of its participants. Finally, **abstraction** pertains to the level of specificity at which a situation is portrayed.

3.3.1. *Selection*

Predications are made relative to specific cognitive domains (Ch. 4). Consider, for example, the nominal expression in (2):

(2)   *the big blue plastic cup*

A full semantic characterization of *cup* requires numerous specifications (e.g. shape, function, material, size), which invoke a variety of cognitive domains. Moreover, each modifier in (2) selects a particular domain with respect to which it specifies more precisely the properties of the designated entity: material (*plastic*), color (*blue*), a comparison scale for spatial extension (*big*), and identification by speech-act participants (*the*). An indication of the domain(s) a predicate selects is a fundamental aspect of its description.

Related senses of a lexical item are commonly quite similar apart from their domain specifications, as exemplified by *close* (*to*) in (3) and *near* in (4):

(3)(a)   *The tree is quite close to the garage.*
   (b)   *It's already close to Christmas.*
   (c)   *That paint is close to the blue we want for the dining room.*
   (d)   *Steve and his sister are very close to one another.*

(4)(a)   *The tree is quite near the garage.*
   (b)   *It's already near Christmas.*
   (c)   *?That paint is near the blue we want for the dining room.*
   (d)   **Steve and his sister are very near one another.*

Close pertains to the spatial domain in (3)(a), an abstract temporal domain (involving the calendar year) in (b), the color domain in (c), and an emotive domain in (d). The judgments in (4) show a different distribution for *near*: it is established in the spatial and abstract temporal domains, but its use in the color domain seems marginal, and (4)(d) is ill formed when interpreted emotively parallel to (3)(d). Because *close* and *near* are such close (near?) paraphrases, the data suggest quite strongly that one cannot hope to predict in absolute terms, from its basic semantic value, precisely which set of domains an extendable expression will occupy. This is a conventional matter dependent on the vicissitudes of usage and change.

Predications in a given domain are often quite comparable except that they differ in **scale**:

(5)(a) *The two galaxies are very close to one another.*
  (b) *San Jose is close to Berkeley.*
  (c) *The runner is staying close to first base.*
  (d) *The sulfur and oxygen atoms are quite close to one another in this type of molecule.*

All the instances of *close* in (5) pertain to the spatial domain, and their semantic values are essentially identical if one abstracts away from the absolute distances involved. The spatial *close* permits apparently unlimited focal adjustments with respect to scale. One might suppose that variation in scale is always freely permitted with relational predications and requires no special statements. This is too simple, however, for it is easy to conceive of predicates conventionally restricted to relationships whose scale falls within a certain range. A possible example is *minute*, which seems progressively less felicitous as the scale of predication increases: *minute molecule*, *minute diamond*, ?*minute nation*, ??*minute galaxy* (observe that there is no such infelicity with *tiny*). In the case of nominal predications, restrictions in scale are commonplace. For instance, a difference in scale of predication weighs heavily in the contrast between *cove* and *bay*.

A third aspect of selection is the **scope** of a predication, defined as those portions of a scene that it specifically includes. The entity designated by a predication—what I will later (5.1) call its **profile**—is maximally prominent and can be thought of as a kind of focal point; the scope of a predication (or **base**) is then describable as the context necessary for the characterization of the profile. The scope of predication need not be sharply defined. Instead the salience and relevance of elements within a scene may gradually diminish as one proceeds from the focal point to the periphery. Sometimes this diminution is quantized; i.e. it occurs in discrete steps. In this event we can identify the innermost region within the scope of predication (that with the highest degree of salience and relevance) as the **immediate** scope. The immediate scope of predication always contains the profile.

Consider some examples. The predicate [UNCLE] is defined over an abstract domain consisting of the conception of a network of kinship relations. (This conception is itself based on more-fundamental notions, e.g. gender, mating, and birth, as well as parent/child and sibling relationships.) Starting from ego, this network extends arbitrarily far in any direction, but only a small segment of it figures in any direct or essential way in the characterization of [UNCLE]: this restricted region, which includes at least ego, the linking parent, and the designated person, constitutes the scope of predication. It provides the context relative to which the profiled entity is identified and characterized.

Illustrating a quantized scope of predication are many terms designating parts of the human body. These terms differ in scale as well as immediate scope. The body as a whole functions as the immediate scope of predication for such terms as *head*, *arm*, *leg*, and *torso*, since their position within the overall configuration of the body constitutes an essential aspect of their meaning. On a smaller scale we find such terms as *hand*, *elbow*, *upper arm*, and *forearm*, all of which take the conception of an arm for their immediate scope of predication, as well as *foot*, *knee*, *thigh*, and *calf*, relating to the leg. Certainly a speaker is aware of the location of these entities within the entire body (whose conception is in any case evoked by that of the arm or leg). But there is a clear sense in which, for instance, the concept *elbow* more directly and saliently presupposes the conception of an arm than that of the body as an undifferentiated whole. In similar fashion, the notion *hand* furnishes the immediate scope of predication for *palm*, *finger*, and *thumb*; *finger* for *knuckle* and *fingernail*; and so on.

Linguistic evidence for these constructs is provided by the relative felicity of sentences with *have* (cf. Bever and Rosenbaum 1970; Cruse 1979), as exemplified in (6) and (7):

(6)(a)   *A body has two arms.*
   (b)   *An arm has an elbow and a hand.*
   (c)   *A hand has five fingers.*
   (d)   *A finger has three knuckles and a fingernail.*

(7)(a)   *?A body has two elbows.*
   (b)   *?An arm has five fingers.*
   (c)   *??An arm has five fingernails and fourteen knuckles.*
   (d)   *???A body has twenty-eight knuckles.*

Sentences of this type are most felicitous when the subject designates the region of the body that serves as immediate scope of predication for the direct-object noun, as illustrated in (6). The examples in (7) show that the acceptability of such sentences declines as the distance between the subject and object increases with respect to the conceptual hierarchy described above (if other factors—e.g. the intrinsic cognitive salience of the subject—are held constant). It is not that these sentences are ill formed in any structural sense, only that special effort or motivation is required to focus on the relation between a large region of the body and a small part within it when the latter is more easily or conventionally conceptualized in the context of a region of intermediate size.

3.3.2. Perspective

Numerous scholars (e.g. Talmy 1978; DeLancey 1981) have noted the importance to semantic and grammatical structure of the perspective taken on a scene. The requisite notions are difficult to formulate in rigorous and convincing fashion, but it is crucial that we make a serious effort along these lines. The present section is an initial attempt at erecting a workable conceptual framework to handle the problems of perspective. Considered in turn are **figure/ground alignment**, **viewpoint**, and the related problems of **deixis** and **subjectivity/objectivity**.

3.3.2.1. *Figure and Ground.* I take it as established that figure/ground organization is a valid and fundamental feature of cognitive functioning. By the assumptions of cognitive grammar, the prevalence of figure/ground organization in conceptual structure entails its importance for semantic and grammatical structure as well. Indeed I will make extensive use of this notion. The profile/base, subject/object, and head/modifier distinctions are among those to be analyzed wholly or partially in these terms.

Impressionistically, the **figure** within a scene is a substructure perceived as "standing out" from the remainder (the **ground**) and accorded special prominence as the pivotal entity around which the scene is organized and for which it provides a setting. Figure/ground organization is not in general automatically determined for a given scene; it is normally possible to structure the same scene with alternate choices of figure. However, various factors do contribute to the naturalness and likelihood of a particular choice. A relatively compact region that contrasts sharply with its surroundings shows a strong tendency to be selected as the figure. Therefore, given a white dot in an otherwise black field, the dot is almost invariably chosen as the figure; only with difficulty can one interpret the scene as a black figure (with a hole in it) viewed against a white background. Motion is a highly influential factor. If it is possible to construe one entity in a scene as changing position vis-à-vis the rest (which have constant relationships to one another), that entity is normally chosen as the figure and interpreted as moving against the backdrop provided by the others. These natural tendencies are occasionally overridden, however, and often a scene lacks the striking contrasts or asymmetries that make a particular substructure the obvious choice.

The importance of contrast in determining figure/ground alignment suggests an affinity to the scheme outlined in 3.1 for acts of comparison. It is tempting to relate figure/ground alignment to the inherent asymmetry between target and standard in an act of comparison, and more specifically to analyze the target as a kind of local figure relative to the ground provided by the standard. Or to turn things around, phenomena generally recognized as instances of figure/ground alignment might be regarded as special cases of the more general and pervasive process of comparison. It would then be possible to characterize a figure as the target of scanning at some level of organization. This approach is speculative (and possibly nonsubstantive), but it does afford a unified treatment of some tantalizingly similar kinds of relations and permit us to start fitting various pieces together in a promising way. For the moment a single example will suffice.

If a white dot appears in an otherwise black field, the dot is chosen as a figure unless special circumstances force the opposite alignment. Why should this be so? The answer becomes apparent when we characterize a figure as a target of scanning. Recall from 3.1.4 the notion of a scanning chain, i.e. a comparison-event sequence of the form $(A > B > C > D \ldots)$, where each link $(A > B, B > C$, etc.) involves a scanning operation that is constant in vector value from one to the next; propagating through a uniform field, such a chain defines a path that terminates whenever a contrast is registered with respect to one of the vector components (e.g. brightness). Perceiving a uniformly dark field then consists in the occurrence throughout the field of a large number of essentially random scanning chains of this kind. A white dot is perceived in such a field when a number of such chains all terminate at a single point owing to its contrastive brightness; as the overall target of a considerable number of scanning paths, the dot then constitutes the figure in the scene. For the white dot to be construed as the ground (and the surrounding black area as the figure), a substantial number of scanning operations would have to be executed within the small white region, each defining a path terminating with the registration of a contrast when the black area is reached. This is quite unlikely on statistical grounds given the presumed disparity between the sizes of the black and white regions. Most of the randomly occurring scanning paths originate in the black field, so the white dot is the target of scanning in the great preponderance of instances. Only expectations or special effort will cause the oppositely aligned scanning paths to predominate.[10]

I have treated comparison as a ubiquitous phenomenon that occurs simultaneously in different domains and at different levels of cognitive complexity.

[10] This analysis makes the empirical prediction that the white region should be progressively easier to construe as the ground as it becomes larger and occupies a greater portion of the total field.

We should therefore expect to find simultaneous and hierarchically arranged instances of figure/ground alignment. Video games provide a ready example of concurrent figure/ground organization in multiple domains: while tracking a moving dot (the visual figure) across the screen, I can perfectly well perceive an occasional beep that stands out as a figure in the auditory domain against the background of silence. Hierarchies of figure/ground organization in a single domain are equally commonplace. If I observe a group of trees standing out as a figure against the background of the sky, I can easily focus my attention on one particular tree within the group, and make it the figure, while still perceiving the group as a whole outlined against the sky.

Although an entity receiving the focus of attention is normally perceived as a figure, various factors suggest the need to distinguish these two notions. For one thing, figure/ground contrasts are registered even in domains one is not attending to. While playing a video game, I operate primarily in the visual mode (tracking the moving dots, or whatever), but though the auditory effects are very much at the periphery of my awareness, I nevertheless impose figure/ground alignment on this input and, for example, perceive beeps against a background of silence (as opposed to observing noiseless intervals interrupting a background tone). Figure and focus of attention are sometimes dissociable even within a single domain. If I sit in a dark room and see nothing but blackness throughout my visual field, the lack of contrast eliminates the potentiality for figure/ground alignment, but the center of my visual field nevertheless defines the focus of visual attention (owing to intrinsic properties of the visual apparatus). If someone now turns on a flashlight, so that I see a dot of light at the periphery of my visual field, this dot stands out as the figure against the otherwise dark field even though (by definition) it is not at the center of my visual attention. Probably I will quickly shift my gaze to the flashlight, bringing the figure into the focus of visual attention, but the need for this shift indicates that figure and focus of attention do not inherently coincide.[11]

3.3.2.2. *Viewpoint.* For many types of conception—particularly those grounded in visual experience—the importance of viewpoint is self-evident. We can look at a physical object from different sides (front/back, top/bottom, etc.), and what we actually see varies accordingly. In observing a complex scene with multiple participants, we can assume different positions in relation to them, with direct consequences for their perceived proximity and salience.

[11] If a trumpet solo is performed with piano accompaniment, so that the trumpet part is the figure and the piano part the ground, I can focus attention on the piano part even while recognizing it as an accompaniment (ground). To go beyond this and achieve figure/ground reversal (thereby making figure and focus of attention coincide once more), I would have to construe the performance as a piano solo with trumpet accompaniment.

The effects of variable viewpoint on actual (peripherally connected) visual experience are duplicated in autonomous processing (i.e. visual imagery); thus I can close my eyes and visualize what an object looks like when seen from different angles.

I will understand the general term **viewpoint** as subsuming the two more specific notions **vantage point** and **orientation**. These latter terms are largely self-explanatory. A vantage point is the position from which a scene is viewed: as I walk along the sidewalk looking at a house my vantage point with respect to the house gradually shifts. From a given vantage point, different orientations are possible for the scene observed: I will see a house differently depending on whether I am upright or standing on my head. Orientation thus pertains to alignment with respect to the axes of the visual field (or some comparable coordinate system). I note in passing that linguistic predications relating to orientation can be based on either the actual orientation of a scene in the visual field at the time of speaking or else its canonical orientation. For example, if I stand on my head and look at a kite flying over a house, I can appropriately use either (8)(a) or (8)(b) to describe what I see.

(8)(a)   *The kite is above the house.*
  (b)   *The house is above the kite.*

The first sentence presupposes the normal horizontal/vertical dimensional grid we calculate in relation to the surface of the earth; this in turn reflects the orientation of our visual field when we assume our canonical upright viewing position. The second sentence ignores this conventional coordinate system and locates the house and kite directly in terms of their relative position in the visual field at the moment of speaking.

We are accustomed to seeing most of the objects in our experience from a canonical viewpoint and in a canonical alignment with respect to their surroundings. This is reflected in conventional pictorial representations, like those in Fig. 3.3(a); the corresponding diagrams in (b) are in some cases not even interpretable without explanation, as they presuppose an unorthodox viewpoint or contextual alignment. To the extent that our conception of such objects includes a canonical viewpoint or alignment, this information is necessarily a part of an encyclopedic characterization of the predicates designating them. Note further that a shape specification implies a viewpoint. If snakes were always straight and rigid and we only saw them head on, our conception of their shape would be that of Fig. 3.3(b) instead of diagram (a). It is not claimed, however, that a single shape/viewpoint specification is sufficient to characterize an object. A family of such specifications (and the transformations relating them) is probably necessary.

Specifications of vantage point and orientation are central to the meaning of many relational expressions. Some of these make explicit reference to the

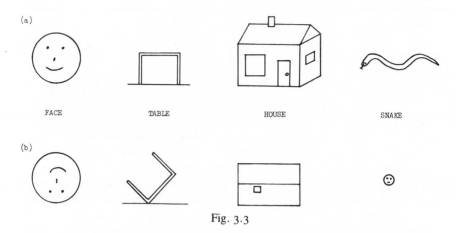

Fig. 3.3

canonical contextual alignment of the objects they situate. For instance, *up-right* and *upside down* presuppose a standard orientation for their subjects along the vertical axis and describe their actual orientation relative to that norm. Other relational expressions, such as those in (9), directly involve a viewer and a vantage point.

(9)(a) *I was about to take a picture of the house when a blimp landed right in front of it.*

   (b) *My father can't take a picture of the house because there's a blimp in front of it.*

   (c) *A blimp just landed in the street in front of the house.*

One sense of *in front of* predicates a tripartite relation involving its subject (blimp), its object (house), and a viewer, such that the subject occupies the path (perceptual or other) that leads from the viewer's vantage point to the object. In (9)(a) the viewer is the speaker, and the sentence is appropriate even if the blimp landed behind the house, provided that the speaker was going to photograph the house from the rear. Though the viewer is often identified as the speaker (especially when left implicit), (b) shows that other entities can play this role; (b) is possible even if the speaker is inside the house. It might appear that (c) requires no viewer or vantage point for *in front of*, but such a conclusion would be imprecise. The reason that one face of a house is conventionally regarded as its front is that this side provides canonical access to the house, either physical or visual. This sense of *in front of* differs from the others only in that the viewer and vantage point it presupposes are generalized and canonical rather than specific.

A scene can generally be viewed from different vantage points. A particular choice of vantage point imposes on the scene an alignment into **foreground** and **background**, where the foreground is an area of indeterminate size extending from the portion of the scene most nearly adjacent to the vantage point. A participant in the foreground is typically more prominent and easily perceived than one in the background, simply because of greater proximity to the viewer. Hence there is a tendency for a foreground object to be perceived as the figure within a scene and to occupy the focus of attention.

Despite these correlations, it is crucial that we maintain the subtle distinctions among closely related notions. For one thing, vantage point cannot be equated with foreground. The vantage point determines which facets of the scene constitute the foreground, but the vantage point itself is part of neither the foreground nor the background of an externally viewed scene. It is also essential not to confuse the notion foreground with either figure or focus of attention. I can perfectly well ignore what is immediately in front of me and focus attention on an object in the background, making it the figure in the scene I am observing. Fig. 3.4 is an interesting case. This ambiguous cube

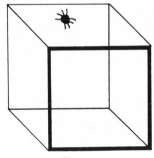

Fig. 3.4

diagram is a paradigm example of figure/ground reversal, but I suggest that it might better be regarded as illustrating reversal of foreground/background alignment. Let us construe the square drawn with heavy lines as the face of the cube closest to the observer, i.e. as the foreground side. Holding this interpretation of the diagram constant, it is quite possible to focus attention on the spider and to see it as crawling along the opposite face of the cube, in the rear. The spider can therefore be the figure, even when construed as located in the background. The notions figure, foreground, and focus of attention do not always coincide, despite the naturalness of their association.[12]

Attention and figure/ground organization are clearly relevant to both spatial (especially visual) and nonspatial domains. To what extent is this true for such notions as viewpoint and foreground/background alignment? Recent work suggests that appropriate generalizations of these constructs are critical for

[12] All three can be dissociated in Fig. 3.4. Keeping the same face of the cube in the foreground, I can focus my visual attention on the upper right-hand corner of the rear panel in the background, while still perceiving the spider, towards the periphery of my visual field, standing out as figure against the ground of the otherwise uniform surface of this panel.

the revealing description of many nonspatial phenomena. DeLancey (1981) has profitably applied his own concept of viewpoint to problems of aspect, voice, and grammatical relations; I will comment no further at this juncture, other than to note that this seminal paper has been important to the evolution of my own ideas about these topics (Part V). Vandeloise (1984) has insightfully discussed the extension of French spatial expressions into other domains. In some instances (notably for *avant/après*), a unified account of their meaning emerges if the vantage point in a perceptual relationship is treated as functionally equivalent to the point of origin for both physical motion through space and also for more abstract, nonspatial motion. We will examine this matter more carefully in 4.3.

3.3.2.3. *Deixis*. I will use the term **ground** to indicate the speech event, its participants, and its setting.[13] A **deictic** expression can then be defined as one that includes some reference to a ground element within its scope of predication. Straightforward though it is, this definition conceals several dimensions of complexity. First, the level of analysis (constituency) must be taken into account. We must next consider various types of deictic expressions, distinguished by the role of the ground element within the overall predication. Finally, deictic expressions differ with respect to how objectively the ground element is viewed.

At the level of individual lexical items, a great many expressions are nondeictic. No intrinsic reference is made to the speech event or its participants by nouns like *pencil*, *mountain*, and *raccoon*, for example, or by verbs like *stand*, *calculate*, and *hear*. Composite expressions are also nondeictic provided that the same is true of all their components; phrases like *broken pencil*, *tall mountain*, *standing*, and *calculate correctly* are thus nondeictic as well. However, most linguistically defined expressions that occur in actual language use are deictic in one way or another. A full nominal (i.e. noun phrase) invariably incorporates an **epistemic predication** (not always phonologically overt) that specifies the relationship of the designated entity to the ground in certain types of domains. Thus, while *pencil* and *broken pencil* are nondeictic, the nominal *this broken pencil* is deictic because *this* contributes predications of definiteness (identification to speaker and hearer) and proximity to the speaker. In similar fashion, *a tall mountain* makes reference to ground elements through the indefiniteness predicated by *a*. Finite verbs (hence finite clauses and sentences) contain epistemic predications that locate the desig-

---

[13] The convenience of ground as a shorthand reference to the speech situation leads me to employ the term in this sense despite its possible confusion with the sense opposed to figure (the two are not unrelated). Langacker 1985 provides more extensive discussion of the topics treated here and in 3.3.2.4.

nated process relative to the ground, typically with reference to the time of speaking. *Stand, standing*, and *be* are thus nondeictic when considered individually, but *is* and *is standing* are **epistemically grounded** (hence deictic). The composite structure of *calculated* is similarly rendered deictic by the past-tense predication.

There are several distinct types of deictic expressions. One type consists of expressions that specifically designate a ground element. Primary examples are *I* and *you*, which designate speech-act participants; others include *here* and *now* (when used as nouns—e.g. *The best place is right here, Now is a good time*), which refer to the place and time of speaking. *Here* and *now* are more commonly used adverbially, in which case the same ground element participates in a relational predication. Third-person pronouns, as well as forms like *then* and *there*, are deictic expressions defined negatively: the entity designated by a third-person pronoun, for example, is specifically characterized as being other than a speech-act participant.

All these expressions—whether the specification is positive or negative—involve the conception of a ground element as the entity designated by a nominal predication or as a major participant in a relational predication. Frequently, however, a ground element figures less prominently in a deictic expression, functioning only as a secondary point of reference. This is true of epistemic predications in particular, and is crucial to understanding their special grammatical properties. For example, the demonstrative *this* does not designate the speech-act participants (hence it is not equivalent to *we*), but it does take these participants as reference points in its predications of definiteness and proximity. The time of speaking has a similar role in the past-tense predication, where it functions as the point of reference for the temporal location of the designated process.

Many expressions other than those I recognize as epistemic predications also take a ground element as the point of reference. In some of these, the deictic construal appears to be primary, i.e. they presuppose a reference point that is equated with some facet of the ground unless there is an indication to the contrary. The basic sense of *come*, for instance, describes motion towards a goal, and one basic sense of *go* describes motion away from a point of origin; the position of the speaker serves as a default-case reference point in both instances, albeit one that is easily overridden (contrast *Come immediately!* with *Sharon asked the repairman to come immediately*). With other expressions a deictic construal appears to be secondary, though sanctioned by established convention. We do not normally think of prepositions like *over* and *across* as being deictic in character, and in many uses they are not. In (10)(a) and (b), for instance, they designate nondeictic relations with two participants:

(10)(a)   *There is a picture over the fireplace.*
   (b)   *An elderly man walked across the field.*
   (c)   *An old church lies just over that hill.*
   (d)   *There is a mailbox across the street.*
   (e)   *There is a mailbox across the street from the drugstore.*

However, both prepositions also exhibit meanings involving tripartite relationships, where one participant is conventionally equated with the position of the speaker unless otherwise indicated. Thus in (c) the church is situated at the end of a potential path that is anchored by the location of the speech event, traverses the hill, and terminates on the other side. In (d), similarly, a potential path leads across the street from the position of the speaker to the mailbox. Neither example mentions the speaker or the speech event; the role of the ground as a point of reference is left implicit. It is possible to make this reference point explicit, however, as in (e), in which case it is normally equated with something other than a ground element. *Over* and *across* are therefore deictic in (c) and (d), by the definition provided above, but not in the other sentences.[14]

3.3.2.4. *Subjectivity/Objectivity.* A final dimension of complexity concerns the degree of objectivity at which the ground element is construed in a deictic predication. The notion of subjectivity/objectivity hinges on the dual role of ground elements in a deictic expression: they serve both as the source of the predication, and as participants within the predication. Deixis is thus a manifestation of the self-referential character of language (cf. Hofstadter 1979), which is of substantial significance for linguistic structure. It is important that we seek to clarify the relevant concepts.

Let us begin by considering the role of the speaker and hearer as the source of a predication. Every linguistic expression, at its semantic pole, structures a conceived situation (or scene) by means of a particular image. In conceptualizing a scene for expressive purposes, the speaker (and secondarily the hearer, in reconstructing the speaker's intent) is obliged to make choices with respect to the various parameters discussed here under the rubric of focal adjustments. I will say that the speaker (or hearer), by choosing appropriate focal "settings" and structuring a scene in a specific manner, establishes a **construal relationship** between himself and the scene so structured. The construal relationship therefore holds between the conceptualizer of a linguistic predication and the conceptualization that constitutes this predication.

With obvious qualifications, the speaker (or hearer) participates in a construal relationship with respect to every linguistic expression. Precisely be-

---

[14] See Hawkins (1984) for discussion of this phenomenon in particular, and for his highly illuminating analysis of English prepositions in general.

cause of this ubiquity, the existence of a construal relationship is irrelevant for classificatory purposes; in particular, it does not establish an expression as deictic in character. To qualify as deictic, an expression must involve some facet of the ground not only as conceptualizer, but also as an object of conceptualization; that is, a ground element must be included within the scope of predication. It is the interplay between these two roles—conceptualizer and object of conceptualization—that is critical to the problem of subjectivity.

The terms subjective and objective are commonly used in a variety of senses, but I will understand them in a particular way. It is convenient to characterize them first in perceptual terms, where their import is easiest to grasp. In order to do this, I will introduce a construct to be called the **optimal viewing arrangement**, sketched in Fig. 3.5(a). *S* stands for the viewer, or SELF,

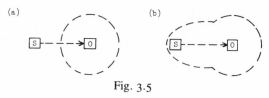

Fig. 3.5

and *O* for the object being observed, or OTHER; the arrow indicates the perceptual relationship between the two. For a viewing arrangement to be optimal, several conditions must be met. First, *S* and *O* must be fully distinct. This condition reflects the obvious limitations on the observation of SELF, which is more restricted than the observation of an OTHER and different in character. Second, *O* must be properly situated relative to *S*: it must be sharply differentiated from its surroundings, and located in a region of maximal perceptual acuity; in general this region is close to the observer, but does not include the observer himself or the area immediately contiguous to him, which shares to some degree the limitations on SELF-observation. I will use the term **objective scene** for the locus of viewing attention. In optimal cases, the objective scene coincides with the region of maximal acuity, as indicated by the broken-line circle in Fig. 3.5(a). Finally, optimal perception requires that the attention of *S* be focused solely on *O*, to the extent that *S* loses all awareness of his own role as perceiver. Otherwise phrased, what *S* observes is *O*, not *S observing O*.

When these conditions are met, the asymmetry in the roles of *S* and *O*—as observer and object of observation respectively—is maximized. The role of *S* in the perceptual relationship is then said to be maximally **subjective**, and that of *O* maximally **objective**. To the extent that these conditions fail to be satisfied, the *S/O* asymmetry is eroded, resulting in a lesser degree of subjectivity for the observer, and a lesser degree of objectivity for the entity being observed. It should be apparent that deictic expressions do not reflect maximal

S/O asymmetry, since ground elements function not only as observers (conceptualizers), but also as objects of observation.

A parallel is thus being drawn between a perceptual relationship on the one hand, and the construal relationship for a linguistic predication on the other. It is by no means claimed that predication is necessarily modeled in any direct way on perception. However, since predication and perception are both special instances of conceptualization, it is not unreasonable to suppose that analogous constructs may prove both useful and appropriate to their description. In terms of the hypothesized analogy, the conceptualizer in the construal relationship is equated with the perceiver; the **maximal** scope of predication in the construal relationship, with the maximal region of perceptual access; the **immediate** scope of predication (3.3.1), with the objective scene (general locus of viewing attention); and the entity designated by a predication, with the primary object of observation (i.e. the focal point within the objective scene).

Let us simplify matters by concentrating on the speaker. If all linguistic predications were structured in the fashion suggested by the optimal viewing arrangement of Fig. 3.5(a), the role of the speaker would always be maximally subjective: he would function solely as conceptualizer and not at all as an object of conceptualization, remaining external to both the immediate scope of predication (objective scene) and the maximal scope of predication. It follows that no linguistic expression would ever designate the speaker (since the designatum [profile] defines the focal point within the objective scene) or even take the speaker as an implicit point of reference. Obviously, though, the speaker is commonly an object of predication as well as its source, so his role is not purely a subjective one. **Objectification** of the speaker (and other facets of the ground) occurs in various ways and to various degrees. Two classes of instances can be noted: those that simply depart from the optimal viewing arrangement, and those that invoke a special mechanism.

In the optimal viewing arrangement, the objective scene—which might also be called the "onstage" region—coincides with the area of maximal perceptual acuity; the coincidence of the two is largely responsible for the optimality of the arrangement. However, not every perceptual or construal relationship can be expected to attain this sort of optimality. Quite commonly, in fact, the viewer's attention is centered on the viewer himself. Because people are often concerned with themselves and with their own situations, it is unsurprising to find that a ground element is often put onstage, or at least included within the scope of predication as an offstage point of reference.

Fig. 3.5(b) depicts what may be called the **egocentric viewing arrangement**. It is characterized by an expansion of the objective scene beyond the region of perceptual optimality to include the observer and his immediate surroundings. This is the arrangement presupposed by deictic expressions that designate either a ground element or a relation in which a ground element functions as a major participant. The pronoun *I*, for example, designates the speaker, who thus puts himself on stage as the focal point within the objective scene. Barring special mechanisms like those discussed below, this represents the highest degree of objectivity that the speaker can achieve in a linguistic predication: in addition to being the conceptualizer, he is also the primary object of conceptualization. The speaker is objectified to a lesser degree in sentences like (10)(c) and (d), and serves only in the capacity of an implicit point of reference; though the speaker is necessarily internal to the scope of predication, he remains offstage.

A high degree of speaker objectification can be achieved through the mechanism of mental **transfer** (cf. Vandeloise 1984), which is diagrammed in Fig. 3.6(a) and exemplified in (11).

(11)(a) *The person uttering this sentence is quite intelligent.*
   (b) *Don't lie to your mother!* [said by mother to child]

The speaker mentally transports himself from his actual position, indicated by *G* (ground element) in Fig. 3.6(a), to another position, *G'*, that he assumes

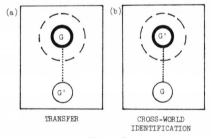

TRANSFER   CROSS-WORLD
                  IDENTIFICATION

Fig. 3.6

for expressive purposes. From the perspective of *G'*, the speaker views himself just as he would observe another individual; hence he employs a third-person form for *self*-description. In (11)(a), it is only by attending to the contents of the description that one can determine that the subject nominal actually refers to the speaker. The sentence in (11)(b) is perhaps more realistic. Here the speaker presumably employs a descriptive phrase rather than a deictic pronoun in order to underscore the gravity of the offense (a mother in particular should not be lied to).[15]

The mechanism depicted in Fig. 3.6(b), **cross-world identification**, is quite different despite its superficial diagrammatic resemblance to transfer.

---

[15] Observe that this transfer, even though it results in the selection of a third-person form, does not affect the person of the possessor pronoun: the nominal is *your mother* rather than *his/her mother*. As a general matter, a single vantage point is not necessarily adopted for all aspects of a clause or even a phrase: cf. *I'll come there tomorrow.*

As exemplified in (12), it involves a correspondence established between a ground element G and some entity G' in a distinct "world," such as the world of a picture, movie, or novel (cf. Fauconnier 1985).

(12)(a)   *That's me in the top row.* [said when examining a photograph]
   (b)   *In my next movie I play a double agent, and the CIA is trying to kill me.*

The designated entity G' is in fact fully objective in this situation, but its correspondence to G can be regarded as a kind of subjectification. The use of a first-person form to describe the objective entity marks this shift.

3.3.3. *Abstraction*

Abstraction is the final type of focal adjustment to be considered. The term abstract and its derivatives can mean a multiplicity of different things. In one usage, abstraction is equivalent to what we have called selection and involves nothing more than the omission from consideration of certain domains or properties (e.g. we can abstract away from the size, color, material, function, etc. of physical objects and concentrate solely on their shapes). In another usage, we can speak of something being abstract to the extent that it departs from immediate physical reality. Something can be abstract because it is imaginary (*unicorn*), inhabits a nonphysical domain (*seven*), or is not directly revealed by immediate sensory experience (*atom*).

Our main interest here is the abstractness of a schema relative to its instantiations, which is distinct from the other types just mentioned (a schema may cover all the domains and properties of its instantiations, and schematicity is possible in any kind of domain). The notion of schematicity pertains to level of specificity, i.e. the fineness of detail with which something is characterized; the notion always pertains, primarily if not solely, to precision of specification along one or more parameters, hence to the degree of restriction imposed on possible values along these parameters. A schema is thus abstract relative to its nonzero elaborations in the sense of providing less information and being compatible with a broader range of options, even should it cover the same domains and basic properties as its elaborations. If I say that a person is *tall*, this characterization is schematic—abstract—relative to the more precise specification that he is *over six feet tall*, for the latter restricts the permissible values to a narrower range along the height parameter. The latter expression is in turn schematic for *about six feet five inches tall*, and so on, as illustrated in Fig. 3.7, where the permissible range of values for each expression is indicated with heavy lines.

A number of linguistically significant observations follow fairly directly from this characterization of schematicity. First, linguistic expressions are seldom fully precise. Even an elaboration of a schema typically allows a range of variation rather than pinning things down to an exact value. Without this in-

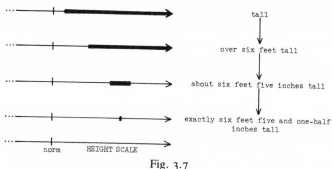

Fig. 3.7

herent imprecision and the flexibility it affords, language could hardly have become a viable instrument of thought and communication. Second, schematicity is a relative matter, as shown by the examples in Fig. 3.7; this necessitates the postulation of hierarchies of schematicity. Third, the range of values permitted by a particular schema can be restricted in numerous mutually inconsistent ways. At a given level of schematicity in a hierarchy, then, it is typical for the various instantiations to contrast in specifications with one another, each nevertheless being fully compatible with the superordinate schema.

Although schematicity is not the same as selection, the distinction is not absolute, for often an instantiation is specified for domains or properties to which the schema makes no essential reference. This comes about as a consequence of the very nature of schematicity: elaborating a schema in a particular way commonly introduces a domain (or realm of potential value) that would not be expected without the elaboration and is essentially irrelevant at the more schematic level. In phonology, for example, an obstruent has a range of possible values pertaining to release of the obstruction (unreleased, delayed release, etc.), but the question of value along this dimension does not even arise until the notion of obstruction is introduced. Hence no direct reference to release is plausibly attributed to the abstract schema [SEGMENT] or even [CONSONANT]; only when the schema [CONSONANT] is elaborated to [OBSTRUENT] is the potentiality for a specification of release created. Similarly, the concept [POLYGON] introduces the notion of sides and creates the potential for a specification of their number, but the more schematic concepts [THING] and [GEOMETRICAL FIGURE] are too abstract for this parameter to be highly salient within them.[16]

By the same token, a focal adjustment from a lower to a higher level of schematicity often entails the disappearance of minor features. The difference

[16] Given the encyclopedic view of meaning, knowledge of the typical members of the class can be regarded as one facet of a concept like [GEOMETRICAL FIGURE]. Number of sides is then included at least peripherally in this notion, but not centrally and directly as for [POLYGON].

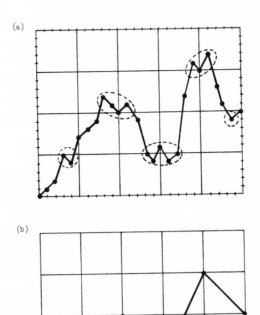

Fig. 3.8

is akin to that between representing a structure by plotting it on a fine grid (where even minor features show up) and on a coarse grid (where only gross features are preserved). In Fig. 3.8, compare the fine-grid representation of (a) to the coarse-grid representation of (b) (think of them as graphs of stock market values, partial shape specifications, or whatever). They are the same, except that five intervals along either axis in (a) count for one in (b), with specifications rounded off to the nearest integral value in either case. Not only is (b) less precise than (a), but certain features of (a) are too fine to be captured by the coarse-grid representation of (b) at all. There is no indication in the more schematic diagram of the local peaks, valleys, upturns, and downturns circled in (a).

Our cognitive ability to conceptualize situations at varying levels of schematicity is undeniable. It is manifested, for instance, in our ability to interpret schematic diagrams like those in Fig. 3.3, and linguistically in the existence of terms for superordinate as well as subordinate terms in schematic hierarchies (*tool, hammer, claw hammer; thing, animal, mammal, rodent, squir-*

rel, ground squirrel; move, locomote, run, sprint). The linguistic significance of this ability is hard to overstate, and will be dealt with constantly in the pages that follow. At this point I offer only two additional remarks.

First, a subtle but important distinction must be made between a structure being specified only schematically for a certain domain and a structure failing to occupy or interact with that domain at all; i.e. a schematic specification (a nonspecific value) along a parameter is different from the absence of a value. Thus, though [CLAW HAMMER] has a fairly precise shape specification, and [HAMMER] a somewhat less precise one, [TOOL] is quite nonspecific in regard to shape; supposing the notion of shape to be irrelevant would nevertheless be erroneous: [TOOL] is maximally nonrestrictive (schematic) in its shape specification, but it does imply that there is a shape, introducing this parameter for more restrictive specifications by its instantiations. In similar fashion, [POLYGON] is nonspecific about number of sides (except that the number must be greater than two), but this is quite different from saying that a polygon has no sides. The schema neutralizing [RED], [BLUE], [YELLOW], [GREEN], etc. is [COLORED] rather than [COLORLESS].

The second remark pertains to the viability of the conceptual theory of meaning and the role within it of visual images. Numerous writers have correctly pointed out that many concepts pertain to domains with no direct ties to sensory experience, and that others, which do occupy sensory domains, are too abstract (schematic) to correspond to any single sensory image (consider the shape specifications of [TOOL] and [POLYGON]). This is sometimes taken as invalidating the conceptual theory, but of course it does not: a conceptual theory of meaning need not rely crucially or exclusively on the postulation of either visual images in particular or sensory images more generally.

Although sensory images do not provide a full account of conceptualization and meaning, it would be wrong to conclude their irrelevance to linguistic semantics. I would argue that they constitute a substantial part of human conceptual activity and are important to the meaning of many linguistic expressions. More to the point here, the recognition of schematicity as a fundamental cognitive phenomenon vitiates the standard argument against an imagistic view of meaning. Kempson (1977, p. 15) conveniently summarizes this argument: "The problem here is to know what form the images take. The most obvious point is that these images cannot be visual. For suppose my image of a triangle is an equilateral. If this is said to constitute for me the meaning of the word *triangle*, then either *triangle* has to mean equilateral triangles only, or *triangle* has to be said to be ambiguous according as the image is equilateral, isosceles, or scalene. . . . In a similar vein, an owner of an Alsatian may have a radically different image of dogs from an owner of a miniature poodle, but it is not obvious that they thereby speak a different language.

There is no image corresponding to what is shared between dogs, and none either which has just those features shared by all triangles."

Quite a number of responses can be made to this passage from the standpoint of the present framework. The passage is meant to discredit imagery altogether in linguistic semantics, but as already noted, imagery can be an essential aspect of meaning even if it is insufficient by itself. The comment about owners of different kinds of dogs speaking different languages is particularly misleading. No two people speak the same language if "a different language" is established by a single point of variation, irrespective of one's view of meaning. Given an encyclopedic account of meaning,[17] two speakers seldom if ever have precisely identical conceptions of any notion, particularly one like [DOG]; their conceptions vary with experience, but nevertheless often have enough in common to permit successful communication. If Alsatians are prototypical for one owner, and poodles for another, the two owners may nevertheless have basically the same range of conventional knowledge about dogs, so that for most linguistic purposes their conceptions are functionally equivalent.

But let us focus on the heart of the matter, the claim that a visual image for [DOG] or for [TRIANGLE] (each as a general category) is impossible. This claim is simplistic, and hinges on the implicit and erroneous assumption that a visual image is a "mental picture" exactly analogous to a photograph, necessarily precise and fully specific in all details (of course, this is not even true of photographs, which are often blurry and imprecise about particular features). A perfectly straightforward conception of visual imagery is available, however, which does not embrace this assumption (cf. 3.2.1; also ch. 2 of Kosslyn 1980). A visual image, on this account, is an autonomous cognitive event that is equivalent in certain respects to a peripherally connected event but is not evoked by actual visual stimulation. Even peripherally connected visual experience varies in its level of specificity; our view of an object is less precisely specified (i.e. more schematic) when it lies outside the focal area of the visual field, when lighting conditions are poor, when it is seen at a distance, when there are tears in one's eyes, etc. With autonomous processing the potential is even greater for focal adjustments in the level of schematicity. We have already observed (Fig. 3.8) that shifting to a higher level of schematicity (a coarser grid) results in the disappearance of fine details, without a visual image ceasing thereby to be visual in character. Hence it is possible in principle to conceive of a shape specification schematic enough to neutralize the difference between an Alsatian and a poodle, while still being recognizable as that of a

---

[17] Presumably Kempson would rule out this alternative, since it precludes the possibility of an autonomous formal account of semantic structure. However, the assumption of such autonomy for natural language is gratuitous (cf. Ch. 1).

dog. In the same way we can recognize the schematic diagrams in Fig. 3.3 as a face, a snake, and so on.[18]

What about triangles? Is it possible to have a visual image of a triangle that is unspecified in regard to the relative length of its sides? Though nothing crucial hinges on the answer to this question (cf. fn. 18), a realistic assessment of the nature of sensory images makes this possibility less implausible than one might suppose. A visual image is not a photograph or a photographic analog, but rather a series of mental events. We saw in 3.1.4 that the perception of a straight line against a contrastive background can be treated as the occurrence of a scanning chain of the form $(A > B > C > D \ldots)$. Minimally, the perception of a triangle requires three such chains, integrated in a specific fashion. If we abbreviate these scanning chains as (X), (Y), and (Z), then $((X)\text{-}(Y)\text{-}(Z))$ represents the minimal set of cognitive events involved in perceiving a triangle. This event complex may be peripherally connected (i.e. it may be induced by sensory input and constitute an actual perceptual experience), but it can also occur autonomously, in which case it constitutes a visual image.

We have yet to accommodate the relative length of the sides. Observing the relative length of two sides clearly requires a cognitive event above and beyond those considered so far. It can be analyzed as a higher-order act of comparison (cf. 3.1) with respect to the complex scanning events involved in the perception of individual sides; specifically, it compares the magnitude (length) of these event chains. For example, perceiving that two sides are the same length consists in the comparison event $X > Y$, with no discrepancy registered for the parameter in question. Three events of this kind are implied by the perception of a triangle as being equilateral: $X > Y = 0$, $Y > Z = 0$, and $Z > X = 0$. Nonzero discrepancies are registered when a triangle is perceived as isosceles or scalene, but whatever the precise judgment, any assessment of the relative length of sides presupposes some set of cognitive events in addition to $((X)\text{-}(Y)\text{-}(Z))$. This basic core of events, required for the perception of any triangle, can be taken as schematic for the more elaborate set of events involved in the perception of a triangle with a specific shape. Observe, now, that it is at least coherent to suppose that $((X)\text{-}(Y)\text{-}(Z))$ might occur without the additional events corresponding to length comparison, especially in cases of autonomous processing. To the extent that this is possible, $((X)\text{-}(Y)\text{-}(Z))$ constitutes the visual image of a schematic triangle unspecified as to the relative lengths of its sides.

[18] There are other options for an advocate of visual imagery as one aspect of linguistic semantics: a person may rely on the more precise shape specification of a prototypical dog, recognizing other shapes as extensions from the prototype; or he may have a series of alternative shape specifications as part of his encyclopedic knowledge of the category. I think all of these figure in our understanding of such a concept; to insist on only one option would be to embrace the exclusionary fallacy.

3.4. Transformation

Mind is mental activity, and a conceptualization is the occurrence of a cognitive event. In this sense the conception of even a simple, static situation must be considered dynamic and consists in the execution of a complex pattern of neurological processes. Now, though, we turn to conceptualizations that are inherently complex and dynamic in a different sense pertaining to a higher level of cognitive organization, namely those which do not reduce to a single, consistent configuration, but rather involve a number of such configurations integrated in a specific manner. To put it in process terms (since the conceptions are seldom if ever coequal and simultaneous), they involve the **transformation** of one conceptualization to another, possibly a series of such transformations. The capacity to carry out such operations is the last of the basic cognitive abilities to be examined as background for our discussion of linguistic semantics. First we consider transformations pertaining to how a scene is construed, particularly with respect to focal settings. Then we turn to cases where the conceived situation itself is intrinsically complex.

3.4.1. *Alternate Construals*

Grammatical structure is based on conventional imagery, which reflects our ability to construe a conceived situation in alternate ways. The full conceptual or semantic value of a conceived situation is a function of not only its content (to the extent that one can speak of content apart from construal), but also how we structure this content with respect to such matters as attention, selection, figure/ground organization, viewpoint, and level of schematicity. In regard to all of these we are capable of making adjustments, thereby transforming one conceptualization into another that is roughly equivalent in terms of content but differs in how this content is construed. This is particularly evident in the case of autonomous processing, but is true for peripherally connected experience as well.

Let us consider a very simple case, namely a shift in visual attention, as sketched in Fig. 3.9. The box represents a person's visual field, and the circle within it is the focal area. In the initial state, at the left, two dark spots are

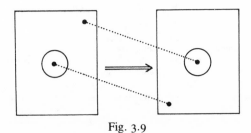

Fig. 3.9

perceived against an otherwise uniformly white background; one happens to fall within the focal area, while the other is in the upper right-hand corner at the periphery of the field. The perception of each spot (individually) consists in the occurrence of a complex scanning event of the sort discussed in 3.1.4; it involves the comparison of contiguous points and the registration of contrast with respect to brightness. As we have seen, this type of scanning is ubiquitous and has nothing directly to do with attention or with the shift of attention through a domain; it is this latter, higher-order phenomenon that is our present concern. Fig. 3.9 diagrams a shift in visual attention from one dot to the other: an eye movement causes an adjustment in the scope of the visual field and its focal area. As a result the originally peripheral dot is brought into the focal area, and the other dot is shifted from the focal area to the lower left-hand corner of the periphery.

Disregarding the slight adjustment in the scope of the visual field, we can say that the two diagrams in Fig. 3.9 represent alternate construals of the same conceived (in this case perceived) situation. What concerns us about this shift in construal is the fact that we are capable of experiencing it as an integrated event. In directing our attention from one dot to the other, we are aware of the continuous transition and recognize its initial and final states as two views of the same scene rather than totally separate and unrelated visual experiences. We keep track of the two dots and recognize that the one within the focal area at the initial stage is the same as the peripheral one at the final stage, and conversely. This is the import of the lines of correspondence in Fig. 3.9. These correspondences derive from the very act of transformation and constitute in effect a record of the distortions it engenders. Our ability to establish such correspondences enables the separate stages to be integrated into a coherent higher-order perceptual experience.

Parallel observations hold for viewpoint. Most physical objects in our experience can be seen from different directions, at different distances, and with different orientations. As viewpoint varies along these parameters, the visual impression we receive of an object also varies in absolute terms (Fig. 3.3). We are nevertheless able to identify the different impressions as alternate views of the same object rather than unrelated visual experiences. Given a particular view of an object, we are capable of transforming this viewpoint either physically (and hence perceptually) or mentally and interpreting the transformation as a coherent, integrated experience. Keeping an object in sight while moving closer to it, for example, we interpret the varying series of visual impressions as a continuous change in vantage point, not as a set of unconnected sensations. Or given the canonical front view of an object we can easily transform it mentally (through visual imagery), imagining what it would look like were it turned upside down or seen from the side. These abilities involve correspondences established between particular substructures in the contrasting visual impressions, just as in our preceding discussion of attention. The mental rotation of a triangle, for example, establishes correspondences between individual sides and angles, as illustrated in Fig. 3.10.[19]

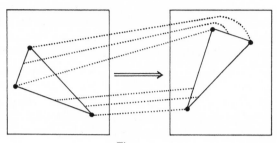

Fig. 3.10

These phenomena have direct implications for semantic structure. The semantic characterization of a term that designates a physical object must include some specification of its conceived shape. One aspect of this shape specification is most probably a cognitive routine whose autonomous activation constitutes a visual image. But typically there is no single visual image that is invariably associated with a particular object: our conception of the appearance of an object involves a family of different visual impressions together with a grasp of the transformations relating one impression to another. These images differ not only with respect to the various parameters of viewpoint, but also in their level of schematicity; highly schematic images like the ones in Fig. 3.3 coexist with those of greater specificity (and may even be the most salient for a category). An encyclopedic account of linguistic semantics must accommodate this range of images and transformations to whatever extent they have unit status and represent shared knowledge. Though certain images are far more important than others (in the sense of being prototypical, entrenched, or conventional), it cannot be supposed that a single image adequately or accurately reflects our grasp of shape specifications.

Our ability to effect mental transformations of viewpoint has important ramifications in another area of semantic structure. In construing a situation for linguistic purposes, the speaker is able to conceptualize how it would appear from different vantage points and to portray it accordingly, irrespective of his actual vantage point. This capacity for mental transfer (studied extensively in Vandeloise 1984) has numerous linguistic manifestations, the most obvious involving the use of deictic forms like *I/you*, *come/go*, and *left/right*. The ability to mentally adopt (or at least perceive and accommodate) the vantage point of my interlocutor is one factor in allowing me to avoid

---

[19] Intuitively, I judge two triangles to be congruent by mentally rotating one of them and then superimposing the resulting visual image on my direct impression of the other. The judgment is one of congruence if the two merge into a single, consistent image.

confusion when the two of us use the terms *I* and *you* in referentially contradictory ways. The sentences in (13) can both be employed in the same situation, e.g. the speaker might be in San Diego talking on the phone to somebody in Chicago; in (a) the speaker's actual location then serves as point of reference for *go*, whereas in (b) he must in some sense adopt the location of the listener to motivate the use of *come*.

(13)(a) *I will go to Chicago tomorrow.*
   (b) *I will come to Chicago tomorrow.*

(14) *Ed Klima is sitting to the left of Sandy Chung.*

Sentence (14) is ambiguous depending on whether the left/right alignment is calculated with respect to an external vantage point (most likely the actual vantage point of the speaker) or that of Sandy Chung.[20] Transfer also figured significantly in our discussion of subjectivity/objectivity (3.3.2.4).

Our ability to make other types of focal adjustments is also linguistically important. I will argue, for example, that figure/ground alignment constitutes the major point of difference between the sentences in (15), and that the semantic effect of passive participial inflection on a verb stem amounts to a kind of figure/ground reversal (cf. Langacker 1982a).

(15)(a) *The cat is under the blanket.*
   (b) *The blanket is over the cat.*

Shifts in level of schematicity are especially significant. A language provides alternate expressions suitable for coding conceived situations at varying levels of specificity; this enables a speaker to abstract away from details considered irrelevant on a particular occasion (cf. Fig. 3.7). Obviously the existence of schematic expressions greatly enhances the flexibility of a linguistic system. Furthermore, transformations pertaining to level of schematicity are implicated in the process of capturing generalizations, which is analyzed as the extraction of schemas. Extracting a schema to represent the commonality of two structures A and B requires finding a structure A' that is minimally schematic for A, and B' minimally schematic for B, such that A' and B' are identical $(A' > B' = 0)$.

3.4.2. *Complex Scenes*

We turn now to instances where two conceptualizations are inconsistent by virtue of their inherent content (not simply the construal of this content). It is important to realize that the inconsistency of two conceptualizations does not

---

[20] In figuring out who is to Sandy Chung's left or right from her viewpoint, what I do is (1) mentally transpose myself to her position and orientation; (2) imagine what the scene would look like viewed from there; and (3) compute left/right relations in the usual egocentric way with respect to my imagined perspective on the scene.

prevent their integration: we are perfectly capable of conceiving situations that are complex in the sense of not reducing to a single, consistent configuration, and many linguistic expressions have such a conception as their semantic value. For a conceptual theory of linguistic semantics, an inconsistent conceptualization is nevertheless a conceptualization and hence a meaning.

Illustrating this point are cases of semantic anomaly of the sort produced by the violation of "selectional restrictions." The expression *happy child* is unproblematic, for example, whereas **happy molecule* and **happy brick* are anomalous (assuming that the component words are interpreted with their normal value). We must assume that the latter two expressions, despite their inconsistency, are both meaningful and semantically distinct, if only on intuitive grounds. This assumption is also necessary to accommodate the fact that the sentences in (16) are neither anomalous nor paraphrases; similarly for those in (17).

(16)(a)   *There is no such thing as a happy molecule.*
   (b)   *There is no such thing as a happy brick.*
(17)(a)   *It is meaningless to speak of a happy molecule.*
   (b)   *It is meaningless to speak of a happy brick.*

The cognitive-grammar analysis of anomalous expressions is straightforward. All grammatical valence relations depend on correspondences established between substructures of the elements combined, at both the semantic and the phonological poles (cf. Fig. 2.11). The semantic pole of *happy* makes internal reference to a schematically characterized entity that is presupposed capable of emotions; when *happy* combines with a noun in a grammatical valence relation, this entity is put in correspondence with the generally more precisely specified entity designated by the noun. In the case of *happy child*, the corresponding entities are fully compatible, and the two semantic structures merge into a single, consistent conceptualization in accordance with the schematic-transparency principle (cf. 2.3.2.2). With **happy molecule* and **happy brick*, on the other hand, certain specifications of the noun's designatum contravene those of its schematic correspondent internal to *happy*. This results in a conflict when the specifications of corresponding entities are superimposed, and renders impossible a fully consistent composite conceptualization. But though their component conceptualizations remain disjoint to some degree, anomalous expressions nevertheless have semantic value, given by their components together with the correspondences indicating which substructures they supposedly share. Further, because **happy molecule* and **happy brick* have a different nominal concept as one of their component semantic structures, they are conceptually and semantically distinct.

Similar remarks were offered previously (2.3.2.2) concerning figurative language, which also involves a relationship between two semantic structures (but one of sanction rather than syntagmatic combination). Recall that semantic incompatibility between corresponding entities is precisely what distinguishes an instance of semantic extension or figurative language from normal cases of unproblematic categorization and full sanction (cf. Fig. 2.10). Only by attributing to speakers the ability to form complex conceptualizations incorporating mutually inconsistent scenes can we account for the interplay between literal and figurative semantic values that constitutes the very essence of metaphor and extension.

Since phonological space is treated as a subregion of semantic space (cf. 2.2.1, and Fig. 2.6), we expect these notions to have phonological analogs. Parallel to semantic extension is **phonological extension**, i.e. instances where a phonological target conflicts with certain specifications of the sanctioning structure instead of merely elaborating it. Just as the relation between two incompatible semantic structures often achieves unit status (e.g. in a standard idiom), so it is possible for two incompatible phonological structures to become associated in a conventional unit. This unit may constitute a general pattern of the language (a phonological "rule"), or else it may be of restricted scope. In a "process morpheme," the association of incompatible phonological structures takes on symbolic import. Let us briefly consider such morphemes (see Ch. 9 for more precise characterization).

A form like *sat* poses well-known problems of segmentation if one's conception of phonological structure is limited to physically manifested sounds: segmenting [æ] as the past-tense morpheme leaves the discontinuous residue [s...t] for the stem, and also suggests that the vowel [æ] per se marks the past tense (the way [d] does in a form like *feared*). Most analysts would say, instead, that the past tense is marked by the change of [ɪ] to [æ] in *sat*, or, to state it in nonprocess terms, by the discrepancy between the vowel of *sat* and the vowel [ɪ] that normally appears in the stem for this verb. I attribute to this past-tense allomorph a two-level phonological structure quite analogous to the two-level semantic structure in a standard idiom. One level, corresponding to the literal sense (or sanctioning structure) of an idiom, contains the vowel [ɪ]; the other, corresponding to the figurative sense (target structure) of an idiom, contains the vowel [æ]. It is the latter (as the target) that is actually implemented phonetically, but the full phonological value of the morpheme consists of the one in relation to the other and therefore constitutes an internally inconsistent phonological conceptualization: $[[\mathrm{ɪ}]--\!\!\rightarrow[\mathrm{æ}]]$.

Our capacity to deal with mutually inconsistent conceptual scenes is further reflected in our ability to conceive of changes. To qualify as a change at all, a conceptualization must involve at least two nonidentical configurations that nevertheless have certain features in common and are integrated to form a coherent mental experience. Any verb, I will claim, designates a **process**, defined as a sequence of configurations (or **states**) conceived as being distributed over a continuous series of points in time. Usually the separate configurations are distinct, i.e. a verb typically designates a change through time; a normal verbal predication is therefore highly complex, for it incorporates as many separate conceptual situations as there are recognizably different states in the designated process. That we do not consider a process predication to be intrinsically anomalous is due to the conflicting states being conceived as distributed through time (which represents a further increment of conceptual complexity).

It is useful to distinguish two modes of cognitive processing that may be invoked for the conceptualization of a complex scene, such as the one in Fig. 3.11. Part (a) diagrams five representative states (abbreviating a continuous series of such states) in a conceived process, namely the schematic conception of an object falling onto a flat surface. Consider first just the initial state in (a). Conceptualizing even this single, relatively simple configuration (whether as a perceptual experience, a visual image, or something more abstract) requires a complex array of cognitive events. These include at least the following: (1) a set of scanning events (acts of comparison) constituting recognition of the top-most structure as a separate entity (with a particular shape) distinct from its background; (2) a similar set of scanning events constituting recognition of the lower structure as a distinct entity; and (3) a comparison of the two entities so recognized with respect to their relative position in the field of representation. Each of these sets of scanning events pertains to a different aspect of the configuration; moreover, they are crucially simultaneous: they proceed roughly in parallel, and only through their coactivation (and reactivation as necessary) does one experience them as a coherent gestalt. Let us refer to this mode of

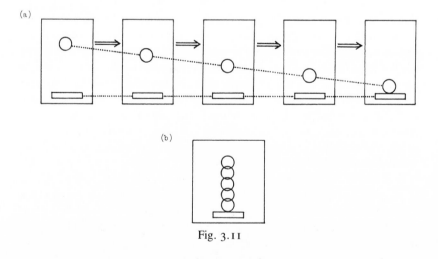

Fig. 3.11

cognitive processing as **summary scanning**. It is basically additive, each set of events contributing something to a single configuration all facets of which are conceived as coexistent and simultaneously available.[21]

The alternative mode of cognitive processing can be called **sequential scanning**. As the term implies, sequential scanning involves the transformation of one configuration into another, or a continuous series of such transformations, as in Fig. 3.11(a). For a series of distinct configurations to be perceived as a coherent evolving scene, correspondences must be established among them, and each configuration serves as standard for an act of comparison (possibly quite complex) that constitutes a recognition of disparity between it and the next. Because the scenes are viewed successively rather than simultaneously, recognition of disparity amounts to recognition of change. In contradistinction to summary scanning, the separate components (states) are conceived as neither coexistent nor simultaneously available; hence there is no judgment of inconsistency. It is not at all farfetched to compare the difference between summary and sequential scanning to that between examining a photograph and watching a motion picture (though I have taken pains to characterize the notions independently of this analogy); indeed, our ability to view both photos and motion pictures nicely exemplifies these respective modes of processing and argues strongly for their validity.

A brief note about time is necessary in conclusion. The difference between summary and sequential scanning pertains to the relative timing of **processing events**—whether the scanning events corresponding to different facets of a complex scene are activated simultaneously or successively—not to the conceived location of a scene or its components in the flow of objective time.[22] Given an ordered sequence of states like those in Fig. 3.11(a), it is natural for them to be conceived as situated successively in a continuous series of points in time, and this is indeed the case in a typical process predication. We nevertheless have the mental flexibility to dissociate processing time from our conception of objective time, a fact of considerable import for the analysis of linguistic structure, particularly in regard to aspect. Thus we are perfectly capable of carrying out sequential scanning with respect to a situation conceived as being stable through time; sentences like (18) can be explicated in these terms (cf. Ch. 7):

[21] In a very complex static configuration—for example, a complicated chess position or an intricate diagram—simultaneous activation of all the requisite cognitive events may surpass the limits of our processing capacity or what is accessible to conscious attention. We nevertheless accomplish summary scanning in cases like this by "fading in" and "fading out" various facets of the scene, or by directing our attention from one facet to another, keeping as many component events activated simultaneously as possible.

[22] Conceiving the location of a configuration in objective time requires a set of cognitive events above and beyond those implied by the conception of the configuration itself. Conceptualization takes place *in* and *through* time, but this is quite distinct from our conceptualization *of* time.

(18)   *This road winds through the mountains.*

By the same token, a situation that changes through time can be construed by means of summary scanning; i.e. its separate phases can be mentally superimposed and viewed as a single complex configuration all of whose facets are coactivated and simultaneously available. This is an important factor in nominalization, as illustrated by the contrast between the sentences in (19) or in (20).

(19)(a)   *The ball curved.*
   (b)   *He threw a curve.*
(20)(a)   *He fell.*
   (b)   *He took a fall.*

If Fig. 3.11(a) is taken as a first approximation to the conceptual value of (20)(a), involving sequential scanning of the process of falling, Fig. 3.11(b) suggests the semantic import of the noun *fall* in (20)(b), where the same event is construed with summary scanning.

CHAPTER 4

Domains

EVERY PREDICATE is characterized relative to one or more cognitive **domains**, collectively called its **matrix**. This chapter explores the nature of domains and how they combine to form multidomain matrices. It is argued that the linguistically relevant portion of our knowledge of familiar entities is open ended and essentially encyclopedic; the distinction between semantics and pragmatics is basically a matter of degree and descriptive convenience. Also discussed are notions related to the conceptualization of movement. Physical motion in the spatial domain is regarded as a special (though prototypical) manifestation of more abstract conceptions with great linguistic significance.

4.1. Types of Domains

All linguistic units are context-dependent to some degree. A context for the characterization of a semantic unit is referred to as a domain. Domains are necessarily cognitive entities: mental experiences, representational spaces, concepts, or conceptual complexes. They are conveniently discussed with respect to three properties. The first is whether a domain can be reduced to more fundamental conceptual structures. The second pertains to **dimensionality**. The third involves a distinction between **locational** and **configurational** domains.

4.1.1. Basic vs. Abstract Domains

Most concepts presuppose other concepts and cannot be adequately defined except by reference to them, be it implicit or explicit. The concept [KNUCKLE], for example, presupposes the conception of a finger. It would be virtually impossible to explain what a knuckle is without somehow invoking the conception of a finger as a holistic entity; it would also be misguided, for the position of a knuckle in relation to the finger as a whole is surely a central and crucial feature of our understanding of the notion. Given the concept [FINGER], however, [KNUCKLE] is easily and straightforwardly characterized. [FINGER] provides the necessary context—or domain—for the characterization of [KNUCKLE] and hence constitutes one of its primary conceptual components.[1]

Of course [FINGER] is itself far from being a primitive notion. One of the defining features of a finger is its position within the overall configuration of a hand, so [FINGER] has for one of its domains our knowledge of this configuration. [HAND] is similarly characterized in part by its position relative to an arm, and [ARM] in relation to the body as a whole. To some substantial (though undetermined) extent, therefore, concepts form hierarchies of complexity, such that concepts at one level are presupposed by those at the next higher level. To properly characterize a particular notion, one must invoke appropriate levels in relevant hierarchies, i.e. whichever levels make available those concepts by means of which a characterization is easily and naturally achieved. [KNUCKLE] is much more cogently defined in relation to a finger than directly (without specific reference to arm, hand, or finger) in terms of the human body as a whole.

Although it is typical for one concept (or conceptual complex) to serve as domain for the characterization of another, there must be a point beyond which no further reduction is possible. If [FINGER] is the domain for [KNUCKLE], [HAND] for [FINGER], [ARM] for [HAND], and [BODY] for [ARM], what is the domain for [BODY]? The notion [BODY] (so far as shape is concerned) is a configuration in three-dimensional space, but it hardly seems appropriate or feasible to consider three-dimensional space as a concept definable relative to some other, more fundamental conception. It would appear more promising to regard the conception of space (either two- or three-dimensional) as a basic field of representation grounded in genetically determined physical properties of the human organism and constituting an intrinsic part of our inborn cognitive apparatus. That is, our ability to conceive of spatial relationships presupposes some kind of representational space creating the potential for such relationships, but it is doubtful that conceptual analysis can go beyond positing this representational space and elucidating its properties.

I will refer to a primitive representational field of this sort as a **basic domain**. A fair number of basic domains must be posited on the grounds that one cannot be fully reduced to another, but they are certainly not all unrelated, and we are hardly able now to present a definitive list or a description of their interconnections. The experience of time certainly suggests itself as a primitive dimension of cognitive representation. The fact that we often conceive and speak of time in spatial terms only shows the utility of such metaphor for higher-level conceptualization. It does not imply that the experience of time is reducible to a purely spatial one; if anything, the opposite would seem more

---

[1] Other components include the conception of a part/whole relation as well as the notion of bending.

plausible. I incline to agree with Givón (1979, ch. 8) that time is in some sense more fundamental than space: the conception of spatial relationships involves scanning, which requires processing time, and our notions of spatial extension are intimately bound up with time-extended physical actions (e.g. movement and the manipulation of objects). Be that as it may, we must certainly posit some kind of inborn field of spatial representation.

Our sensory capacities provide a variety of basic domains. The visual system defines the potential for two- and three-dimensional visual sensations, coordinated with a multidimensional color domain. Observe that the visual and spatial domains cannot be fully assimilated (even ignoring color), despite their close association, since even a blind person is perfectly capable of grasping spatial relations. At the very least we must posit a scale of pitch as a basic domain for hearing. Taste and smell are closely related; it is largely a matter of definition whether we assign them to one domain or consider them separate. For touch we may consider the scales of temperature, pressure, and pain as basic domains. Beyond this we must postulate one or more emotive domains, one or more domains to accommodate kinesthetic sensations, and perhaps others. At this point the precise inventory is not so important as the matter of irreducibility: despite various interrelationships, we cannot reasonably hope, for example, to explicate a taste sensation in terms of space, time in terms of color, smell in terms of pitch, kinesthetic sensations in terms of temperature, or pressure in terms of emotion.[2]

By definition, basic domains occupy the lowest level in hierarchies of conceptual complexity: they furnish the primitive representational space necessary for the emergence of any specific conception. Basic domains constitute a range of conceptual potential, and particular concepts can be taken as exploiting that potential in various ways. More precisely, a concept can be characterized as a location or a configuration in a domain (or in each of a set of domains). Color space defines a range of color sensations, for example, and a particular color concept like [YELLOW] or [BLACK] can be identified as a restricted region within this domain. Similarly, the domain of two-dimensional space creates the potential for an endless variety of shape conceptions, and a specific conception such as [LINE] or [CIRCLE] is definable as a configuration (set of points) in this domain.[3]

All human conceptualization is presumably grounded in basic domains, but for the most part this grounding is indirect, being mediated by chains of inter-

[2] We can indeed perceive similarities across basic domains (note *sharp* in relation to touch, taste, visual resolution, as well as the musical scale and other abstract domains), but admitting this is quite different from claiming that one such domain is fully reducible to another.

[3] Cognitive grammar is not necessarily committed to the existence of any finite set of conceptual primitives; it is only committed to the existence of a number of basic domains and cognitive abilities. A single basic domain (e.g. pitch or color) may create the potential for an essentially unlimited number of distinct first-order concepts.

mediate concepts derived through cognitive abilities of the sort considered in
Ch. 3. Once characterized relative to a basic domain, a concept creates the
potential for an array of higher-order concepts and thus functions as their domain; these latter concepts in turn provide the domain for the emergence of
still further concepts, and so on indefinitely. In this manner—as well as
through the coordination of conceptions to form conceptual complexes that
may also serve as domains—vast and intricate hierarchies of conceptual complexity evolve over the long course of our mental experience. Any nonbasic
domain, i.e. any concept or conceptual complex that functions as a domain
for the definition of a higher-order concept, will be called an **abstract domain**.[4] For instance, the basic domain of three-dimensional space gives rise to
the shape specification of [BODY], which then constitutes an abstract domain
for the characterization of [ARM] (and [ARM] for [HAND], [HAND] for
[FINGER], and so forth). Most concepts are defined at least partially in reference to abstract domains. The distinction between basic and abstract domains
may not always be clear, but nothing hinges on it being absolute rather than a
matter of degree. The essential claim is simply that not all concepts are op-
timally characterized directly in terms of primitive notions.

4.1.2. *Dimensionality*

Postulating an inventory of basic domains is only one step in elucidating the
architecture of human conceptualization. Another step is to describe the array
of cognitive processes and abilities that give rise first to concepts in these domains and then to concepts of progressively higher order, which thus form
hierarchies of complexity. Yet another step is to characterize the intrinsic organization of each basic domain. Though a basic domain cannot be described in
terms of more fundamental concepts, the field of conceptual potential it defines may nevertheless be structured: the concepts it permits can be ordered
and grouped in various ways and be determined to lie at different "distances"
from one another.

To the extent that ordering and distance can be specified in a coherent, systematic way for certain concepts in a domain, we can reasonably describe this
domain in terms of one or more **dimensions**. Time, pitch, and temperature
exemplify one-dimensional basic domains, since a single, consistent ordering
can be determined for the entities that occupy them. We are capable of dealing
with space in either two- or three-dimensional terms. Psychophysical research
has shown that the color domain is resolvable into the three dimensions of

---

[4] An abstract domain is essentially equivalent to what Lakoff (1982, 1987) terms an **ICM** (for
idealized cognitive model) and what others have variously called a **frame, scene, schema**, or
even **script** (at least in some uses). I have referred to it as a **functional assembly** in previous
works, but being both opaque and dispensable, that term should be allowed to die.

brightness, hue, and saturation. Dimensionality is equally important for abstract domains. Knowledge of the counting numbers (1, 2, 3, ...) constitutes a one-dimensional abstract domain; the same is true for a scale of similarity (even though the similarity of two entities can be assessed for numerous parameters, for any given parameter the similarity scale itself is unidimensional). Several dimensions figure in the conception of a network of kinship relations: one is the "vertical" dimension of ascending/descending generations; another is the "horizontal" dimension of collateral relationships; in addition, each node in a kinship network is potentially specified for gender and other properties.

Not every domain organizes notions with sufficient coherence and consistency to lend itself, in any obvious way, to characterization in terms of a small number of essentially linear dimensions. Consider, for example, the emotive domain(s). We can hardly expect emotional states and experiences to be adequately described by their position along a handful of strictly ordered parameters analogous to the pitch scale. At the opposite extreme it might be claimed that every emotion is a separate experience bearing no special relation to any other, but this too is simplistic. Though the domain appears to be only loosely coherent, a number of dimensions suggest themselves as being of fairly general utility: one parameter is reflected in the intuitive classification of some emotions as positive (happiness, joy, enthusiasm, excitement, love) and others as negative (sadness, fear, anger, anxiety, depression, hate); crosscutting this is a distinction between "active" emotions (joy, excitement, anxiety, enthusiasm, fury) and those of a more "quiescent" nature (sadness, depression, calm, happiness, resentment). Taste (including the contribution of smell) further illustrates a loosely coherent domain within which a number of pertinent dimensions can nonetheless be discerned. Because of its chemically complex nature, a typical taste sensation is sui generis and cannot be reduced to a small number of nonarbitrary feature specifications. Still, such parameters as sweetness, spiciness, acidity, etc. are likely candidates for partially structuring the domain.

Domains are either **bounded** or **unbounded** with respect to a given dimension. We are capable of perceiving only a specific range of pitches, hues, and temperatures, for instance, whereas time and space are essentially unbounded. In the case of abstract domains, bounding is possible at both extremes of a dimension, at one extreme only, or at neither. Our ability to recite the alphabet is an abstract domain bounded at both extremes (there is no letter before A or after Z). A scale of similarity, by contrast, is saliently bounded at only one extreme (that of identity, i.e. full coincidence with the standard of comparison), whereas the "vertical" dimension in a kinship network is potentially unbounded. The values permitted along a given dimension can be either **con-**

tinuous or **discrete**. The dimensions of basic domains are generally continuous,[5] but discreteness is often a crucial property of abstract domains. Within a kinship network, for example, an individual can be conceived as occupying any node, but not as falling between two adjacent nodes; there is nothing intermediate between, say, parent and child in a parent/child relationship. Nor is there anything intermediate between two adjacent letters in the alphabet, which is consequently a one-dimensional, discrete, abstract, fully bounded domain.

The coordination of dimensions to form domains (or at a higher level of organization, of domains to form a complex matrix) depends on the capacity of entities to simultaneously occupy two or more dimensions (domains) and thus establish a link between them. With basic domains this coordination is largely intrinsic and easily taken for granted: a point is located simultaneously with respect to each of the two or three spatial dimensions; a color sensation has simultaneous values for brightness, hue, and saturation; and a taste sensation involves, say, the simultaneous components of sweetness and acidity. With abstract domains the associations are often more contingent. The position of a letter in the alphabet is quite unrelated to its shape, for instance, and we find it easier to dissociate the two properties. Moreover, the distinction between dimensions and domains is to some degree arbitrary and a matter of convenience. Consider taste once more. A typical taste sensation is highly complex, involving both temperature and texture in addition to chemically-based specifications. It makes little difference whether we add temperature and texture dimensions to the chemically based ones and analyze them all as forming a single multidimensional domain, or regard them instead as constituting a complex matrix with three distinct domains as components. Similarly, the olfactory components of taste can be treated either as dimensions of a single complex taste domain, or else as a separate but coordinated domain within a complex matrix.

4.1.3. Locational vs. Configurational Domains

A predicate specifies a location or a configuration in some domain (or in each domain of a complex matrix). Accordingly we can speak of a domain as being either **locational** or **configurational**. The spatial domain supports the conception of both two- and three-dimensional configurations and can be taken as prototypical for configurational domains. Locational domains are exemplified by temperature and color. A temperature sensation is not defined by a configuration, but rather by a location on a one-dimensional scale. A simple

---

[5] To say that a dimension is continuous is not to imply that all points along it are of equal status. The hue dimension of color space is continuous in the sense that every wavelength within the limits of perception gives rise to a color sensation, but it has nevertheless been established that certain focal areas have special cognitive and developmental salience.

color sensation is similarly given by a value with respect to each of the three parameters of color space.

The distinction between locational and configurational domains is elusive; let me briefly note a few of the subtleties involved. It seems natural to regard a location as a single "point" (cf. fn. 6 of Ch. 3) and a configuration as a set of points. A location can then be seen as a degenerate configuration, and the difference between the two kinds of domains viewed as a matter of the complexity of the configurations they permit. If this is correct, it is nevertheless only part of the story. A location presupposes some frame of reference making it possible to distinguish one location from another, whereas a configuration may be independent of any specific position within a coordinate system. Thus a triangle is recognized as such regardless of its position and orientation within the visual field or two-dimensional space, but changing the specifications of a color sensation with respect to the dimensions of color space results in a different color sensation (not simply the same color sensation in a different location).

This suggests that the distinction between a locational and a configurational domain hinges on whether or not its dimensions are intrinsically calibrated in some way, so that different locations correspond to different sensations instead of being functionally equivalent and interchangeable. This correlation works out fairly well, since the major configurational domains (time and space) are calibrated only to the extent that we impose on them some extrinsic set of coordinates. The pitch domain provides a counterexample, however: it is certainly inherently calibrated (one pitch is qualitatively different from another), and to that extent it is a locational domain, but we are nonetheless capable of perceiving chords, which seem best analyzable as configurations of distinct tones. Moreover, it is well known that people are more adept at perceiving the contrast between two sensations in calibrated domains than at ascertaining their absolute value in isolation (cf. 3.1.2). This would further appear to blur the distinction between the two kinds of domains.

What makes a domain configurational, in the last analysis, is our capacity to accommodate a number of distinct values as part of a single gestalt. This presupposes some means of keeping the values separate and preventing them from merging to give a single value representing their average or their vector sum. We might speculate that pitch is a configurational domain because our auditory apparatus, both physical and neurological, is geared to the analysis of complex sounds into their components at different frequencies. Space and time are configurational domains because they are inherently extensional, in the sense that they provide an indefinite number of separate points at any (or all) of which essentially the same range of experiences can occur. Similarly, any point within the two-dimensional visual field can be the locus for any of the sensations defining color space.

Locational domains become configurational when coordinated with others that lend them the necessary extensionality. For instance, color is a locational domain in the sense of it being impossible to experience more than a single color sensation at a given instant in one particular point within the visual field (or its counterpart in autonomous processing). However, by coordinating color space with the two dimensions of this field, we obtain a five-dimensional domain (or complex matrix) within which color configurations are possible; terms like *plaid, striped,* and *speckled* designate complex configurations in this domain. A color configuration is similarly possible when color space is coordinated with time, for example in the conception of a point that changes back and forth from one color to another. The earlier characterization of domains like temperature, pressure, and pain as one-dimensional and locational can now be seen as incomplete. The sensations in each of these domains are localized to particular regions of the body, so we can distinguish, for instance, between a pain in the elbow and a comparable pain in the knee. Coordination with the cognitive representation of bodily locations gives these domains the extensionality to make them configurational to a certain degree. Pains, for example, can be perceived as either sharply delineated (e.g. a pinprick) or diffuse.

4.2. Dictionaries and Encyclopedias

Most concepts require specifications in more than one domain for their characterization. The concept [BANANA], for example, includes in its matrix a specification for shape in the spatial (and/or visual) domain; a color configuration involving the coordination of color space with this domain; a location in the domain of taste/smell sensations; as well as numerous specifications pertaining to abstract domains, e.g. the knowledge that bananas are eaten, that they grow in bunches on trees, that they come from tropical areas, and so on. The following question then arises as a particular instance of a pivotal problem of linguistic semantics: Which of these specifications belong to the meaning of the lexical item *banana* and are therefore included in the grammar of English? Otherwise phrased, which of these specifications are linguistic (or semantic) in nature, and which are extralinguistic (pragmatic)? Which ones constitute the **predicate** [BANANA], i.e. the semantic pole of the morpheme *banana*?

My answer should hold no great suspense for the reader: All of these specifications are part of the meaning of *banana*. The distinction between semantics and pragmatics (or between linguistic and extralinguistic knowledge) is largely artifactual, and the only viable conception of linguistic semantics is one that avoids such false dichotomies and is consequently **encyclopedic** in nature. The present section attempts to justify this position, render it more precise, and explore some of its implications.

4.2.1. *Why an Encyclopedia?*

The rationale for choosing an encyclopedic conception of linguistic semantics has been laid out both elegantly and forcefully by other scholars. Haiman (1980), for example, has examined with care the various distinctions that might be employed for purposes of isolating a restricted range of specifications as constituting the linguistic characterization of an entity (thus permitting one to posit a dictionary entry of limited scope for the grammar of a language instead of an open-ended, essentially encyclopedic description). He argues quite persuasively that all of these grounds for delimiting the scope of linguistic knowledge are inadequate, and concludes that "the distinction between dictionaries and encyclopedias is not only one that is practically impossible to make, but one that is fundamentally misconceived" (p. 331). In a similar vein, Moore and Carling (1982) argue that linguistic expressions are not meaningful in and of themselves, but only through the access they afford to different stores of knowledge that allow us to make sense of them (see also Rumelhart 1979). I will try to articulate this conception with reasonable precision, and show how it provides the foundation for a workable account of semantic and grammatical structure.

Language is learned and used in context. We can talk about any facet of our conceptual universe, and a given expression permits indefinitely many specific interpretations depending on the conceived situation to which it is applied. Consider *The cat is on the mat.* Prototypically it describes a situation where a mat is spread out on the ground and a cat is sitting or lying on it. Already there is indefinite variability, since the cat can be of any size, coloring, or subspecies; the mat is similarly variable; the cat can assume many different postures; and so on. But this is only the beginning. Possibly the mat is rolled up in a bundle and the cat is sitting or lying (etc.) on top of it. Maybe the operator of a slide show has just managed to project the image of a cat onto a mat being used for a makeshift screen. The sentence is appropriate in a mat factory where a worker has just finished decorating a mat with the outline of a feline. Conceivably a wrestler is holding an exhibition match with a tiger and has just succeeded in pinning its shoulders to the floor of the ring. The possibilities are obviously endless.

In view of these considerations, the burden of proof would appear to lie with anyone who would claim that linguistic semantics is autonomous, either in the sense that a brief dictionary entry is sufficient to characterize the "linguistic meaning" of a lexical item (distinguishable in a principled manner from our overall body of knowledge about the designated entity), or in the sense that the meaning of a complex expression can be determined out of context as a regular compositional function of the meanings of its component lexical items. Certainly an autonomous semantics of this kind can be formulated, but the account it offers of the meanings of linguistic expressions is apt to be so restricted and impoverished relative to the full richness of how we actually understand them that one can only question its utility and cognitive reality. Only limited interest attaches to a linguistic semantics that avoids most of the relevant phenomena and leaves recalcitrant data for an ill-defined "pragmatic component."

Why would one opt for an autonomous, dictionary-type conception of linguistic semantics? Certainly not because models of this sort have proved themselves fully adequate and deeply revelatory for all aspects of meaning and usage. Instead, I suggest, the reasons have been methodological and aprioristic. For one thing, only by assuming the privileged status of a restricted class of semantic properties can one hope to describe language as an autonomous formal system; otherwise the task of semantic description is essentially open-ended, and linguistic analysis is inextricably bound up with the characterization of knowledge and cognition in general. However, the assumption that language (and in particular semantics) constitutes an autonomous formal system is simply gratuitous. The fact that the autonomy of language would be highly convenient for linguists does not amount to valid evidence for its reality. A second reason for embracing autonomous semantics is the view that human conceptualization is not amenable to empirical inquiry and precise description. This is a view I do not share. Moreover, since meaning is, in the last analysis, a matter of conceptualization (what else could it possibly be?), it strikes me as pointless to avoid the challenge of describing it in these terms, whatever the limitations on our present ability to do so. A third reason is the availability of systems of formal logic, which appear to offer a rigorous account of semantic structure based on truth conditions. Here I will say only that the availability of this formal machinery does not establish its correctness or appropriateness. Even advocates of formal semantics admit that there are aspects of meaning and language use it is simply not designed to accommodate.

To put the case in positive terms, I suggest that an encyclopedic conception of linguistic semantics permits a natural and unified account of language structure that accommodates, in a coherent and integral way, such essential matters as grammatical valence relations, semantic extension, and usage. Let us briefly consider these matters in turn.

Valence relations involve the integration of two or more component structures to form a composite structure. They depend on correspondences established between substructures within the component elements, at both the semantic and the phonological poles (cf. Ch. 8 and Langacker 1981b). Typically these corresponding substructures are quite prominent within the components, but this is not invariably the case. Often valence relations depend crucially on properties that are too marginal or too context-dependent to figure in any plausible dictionary-type characterization of a component; a restrictive view of meaning thus precludes the parallel treatment of these and more prototypical instances. Noun compounds furnish many striking examples, e.g. *buggy whip*. Only a fairly inclusive characterization of *buggy* (one incorporating the notion of a driver and the means he uses to encourage the horse pulling the buggy) brings into the picture an entity that can be placed in correspondence with the referent of *whip* (or conversely), thereby permitting the integration of the two component structures to form a coherent composite scene.[6]

Semantic extension is invariably based on some perception of similarity or association between the original (sanctioning) sense of an expression and its extended sense. Observe that the basis for extension is not limited to core specifications that would be appropriate in a dictionary entry, but may lie at any distance from this core within our encyclopedic knowledge of the designated entity. For example, it is not unusual for expressions meaning 'in' and 'out' to be extended to mean, respectively, 'invisible' and 'visible' (or more generally, 'inaccessible' and 'accessible').[7] The basis for this extension is obviously the fact that an object is commonly hidden from view when contained in another, and visible otherwise. But this fact, though quite apparent from our experience with objects participating in locative relationships and thus part of our overall knowledge of such relationships, is hardly intrinsic to the original 'in' and 'out' meanings and would have to be excluded from a dictionary-type characterization of them. Naturally one could attribute this semantic extension (and countless others) to pragmatics or extralinguistic factors; I will argue only that the implied distinction is arbitrary and gratuitous. Semantic extension is such a pervasive and central linguistic phenomenon that one can legitimately question the wisdom of an approach to semantics that fails to account for it in a unified way.

The problem of usage centers on the coding relation between conventional units in the grammar and the specific usage events they sanction (cf. Ch. 2, especially Fig. 2.5). The semantic pole of a usage event is the *contextual meaning* of an expression, i.e. the richly detailed conceptualization that constitutes our full understanding of the expression in context and includes all relevant aspects of the conceived situation. Contextual meaning is clearly encyclopedic in scope and cannot be determined algorithmically as a compositional function of component lexical items. For one thing, it includes particulars of the speech situation that are not linguistically coded. More importantly, the contextual meaning of an expression is often an *emergent* property: though perfectly evident in context and *consistent* with the meanings of the lexical

---

[6] Downing (1977) insightfully addresses the problems posed by compounds, particularly novel ones whose interpretation is apparent only from context. Their treatment in the present framework is straightforward.

[7] This extension is documented for Cora (a Uto-Aztecan language of Mexico) in Casad and Langacker (1985). Lindner (1981) discusses it for English as part of her analysis of verb-particle combinations (note *The stars came out*).

items employed, it goes beyond anything computable or predictable from their individual conventional values. Consider once more *The cat is on the mat*. For someone watching a wrestler triumph over a tiger in an exhibition match, it is straightforward to interpret this sentence as meaning that the wrestler is pinning his adversary; however, this interpretation is far more specific than anything suggested by the established meanings of the lexical items, singly or in combination. Thus, it is not that the expression intrinsically *holds* or *conveys* the contextual meaning, but rather, that conventional units *sanction* this meaning as falling within the open-ended class of conceptualizations they *motivate* through judgments of full or partial schematicity. These conceptualizations may draw on any facet of a speaker's conceptual universe.[8]

From the encyclopedic nature of contextual meaning, that of conventional meaning follows fairly directly. The latter is simply contextual meaning that is schematized to some degree and established as conventional through repeated occurrence. Whatever systems of knowledge are invoked for the contextual understanding of an expression must be imputed as well to its conventionalized meaning, provided that they are constant in the series of usage events leading to its conventionalization. In our previous example, the contextual meaning of *The cat is on the mat* presupposes an elaborate knowledge structure pertaining to wrestling; it involves the conception of a wrestler pinning his adversary, the climactic role this plays in a match, and so on. Suppose now that tiger-wrestling becomes a fad, and that sports commentators hit upon *The cat is on the mat* as a cliché to describe the moment of defeat for the tiger. In this case *The cat is on the mat* quickly becomes a conventional unit of English whose semantic pole refers specifically to an act of tiger-pinning in the overall context of a tiger-wrestling event. To be sure, this conventionalized notion of tiger-pinning is somewhat schematic: in forming it speakers abstract away from many specifics that differ from one usage event to another (age of the tiger, time and place of the match, and so forth). But even the schematic conception representing the commonality of typical tiger-pinning events presupposes an elaborate knowledge structure that approaches encyclopedic proportions.

4.2.2. *Centrality*

One objection certain to be raised against encyclopedic semantics runs something like this: "Surely you can't be claiming that everything I know about bananas is part of the meaning of *banana*, or that everything I know

---

[8] To the extent that semantic composition is regular, cognitive grammar accommodates it by means of the schemas describing grammatical constructions: at the semantic pole, these schemas specify conventional patterns for integrating component semantic structures to form composite structures. However, the model neither claims nor requires that composite structures be exhaustively definable or algorithmically computable from their components (cf. Ch. 12).

about cats is part of the meaning of *cat*. That would be absurd! For example, I know that my sister put sliced bananas on her cereal for breakfast this morning, but obviously this fact cannot be listed in the lexicon of English. The cultural association of cats with witchcraft and Halloween cannot be put on a par with a specification of their size and shape: the former is purely contingent, whereas the latter are essential properties that have to be adduced in any serious attempt to explain to someone what a cat is." These points are well taken, but they constitute a valid objection to the encyclopedic view only in its most naive and simplistic form. They are fully accommodated in the more elaborate formulation I propose.

I do not specifically claim that all facets of our knowledge of an entity have equal status, linguistically or otherwise—quite the contrary. The multitude of specifications that figure in our encyclopedic conception of an entity clearly form a gradation in terms of their **centrality**. Some are so central that they can hardly be omitted from even the sketchiest characterization, whereas others are so peripheral that they hold little significance even for the most exhaustive description. Distinctions of this kind can perfectly well be made within the encyclopedic approach. The thrust of this view is simply that no specific point along the gradation of centrality can be chosen nonarbitrarily to serve as a demarcation, such that all specifications on one side can uniformly be attributed linguistic significance and all those on the other side are linguistically irrelevant. From the practical standpoint, of course, sensible investigators focus their attention primarily on the more central specifications. The encyclopedic view does not entail that *all* aspects of our knowledge of an entity must be described before *any* sort of linguistic analysis can begin; how many aspects must be considered, and which ones, depends on what is required for specific analytical objectives. It is important, however, that practical limitations of this kind not be objectified into a sharp dichotomy granted unwarranted credence by virtue of its enshrinement in linguistic theory.

The notion of centrality requires elucidation. The centrality of a particular specification within the encyclopedic characterization of an expression is a matter of its relative entrenchment and likelihood of activation in the context of that expression. The inherent nature of a specification does not fully determine its degree of centrality (cf. 4.2.3), but several contributing factors can be discerned: centrality tends to correlate with the extent to which a specification is **conventional, generic, intrinsic**, and **characteristic**.

In 2.1 I defined the grammar of a language as an inventory of conventional linguistic units and noted that conventionality is a matter of degree. A specification achieves linguistic significance, and can be regarded as part of the meaning of a lexical item, only to the extent that it is shared by a community of speakers. I know, for example, that two of my linguistic colleagues are allergic to cats, but I would hardly be justified in viewing this knowledge as part of the conventional meaning of *cat*, even though it enriches my understanding of the notion. This is nevertheless a matter of degree, and the knowledge is more accurately seen as extremely peripheral to the meaning of *cat* than absolutely irrelevant. For one thing, there are other English-speakers who also know that these linguists are allergic to cats, so the knowledge has some small measure of conventionality. Suppose, moreover, that the fame of my two colleagues continues to grow, and that one day they become such prominent figures on the American scene—and their health an item of such general concern—that now the very mention of cats immediately calls their allergy to the mind of virtually any speaker; among the most salient properties of cats for such speakers is the threat thus posed to the well-being of our nation. It would be odd in this circumstance to deny that the specification is part of the conventional meaning of *cat* within the speech community. The example is not so farfetched as one might think (consider the transient impact that Jimmy Carter had on the semantic value of *peanut*). It shows that conventionality is partially independent of the other parameters contributing to centrality, and is not fully predictable from a specification's intrinsic nature. Further, there is a nontrivial theoretical sense in which every experience that somehow involves an entity has an impact on our understanding of it (and consequently on the meaning of an expression that designates it), be the effect minor or even infinitessimal. Though these impacts seldom have direct practical consequences, collectively and cumulatively they are the determinants of semantic structure.

The second factor contributing to centrality is the degree to which a specification is generic rather than specific. The information that two of my colleagues are allergic to my cat Metathesis is quite specific, whereas the fact that they are allergic to cats in general is partially generic, and the knowledge that many people are allergic to cats is highly generic. Generic specifications are clearly more likely than specific ones to achieve centrality in the meaning of a form. This factor too is an independent parameter, though it naturally tends to correlate with both conventionality and intrinsicness. The more generic a specification is, the greater is its chance of being known throughout a speech community, since individual experience varies greatly at the level of particulars. Large communities nevertheless share a great deal of specific information, and occasionally an individual is privileged with unshared generic knowledge. More-intrinsic properties are obviously more likely to be common to all members of a class, but here too the independence of the parameters is easily demonstrated. The allergic reaction of many people to cats is not an intrinsic property of cats, yet it is a generic property of cats for those who react in this way.

A property is intrinsic to the extent that its characterization makes no essential reference to external entities. Shape, for example, is a highly intrinsic property of physical objects, as it reduces to relations between the parts of an object and does not require interaction or comparison with other entities. Size, on the other hand, implies comparison either with other objects or with some scale of measurement; hence it is not quite so intrinsic as shape. Behavioral properties tend to be less intrinsic, for most behaviors involve interaction with other entities. Some behaviors are fairly intrinsic, e.g. the sounds that cats emit, and their techniques for washing themselves. The postures they assume are extrinsic to the extent that their characterization makes reference to vertical/horizontal orientation or to external surfaces (e.g. the ground). Such activities as chasing mice and scratching furniture bring external entities into the picture more saliently and are consequently more extrinsic. The cultural role of cats, for instance their association with witchcraft and Halloween, is highly extrinsic; it has little to do with cats themselves, but is rather a matter of how others regard them.[9]

The final factor contributing to centrality is the extent to which a specification is characteristic, in the sense of being unique to the class of entities designated by an expression and consequently sufficient to identify a class member. Shape is generally more characteristic than color: a cat can be recognized as such by its shape alone, but the observation that something is black would not suffice to identify it as a (black) cat since many noncats are also black. Shape is not always fully characteristic, of course (the shape of Colorado is less characteristic than that of California). Moreover, a moment's reflection reveals that this parameter is independent of the other three.

4.2.3. *Access*

One final objection that might be raised against the encyclopedic view is the following: "This view lacks cognitive plausibility. When someone uses a term like *cat* or *banana*, I grasp its meaning, yet it is certainly not the case that everything I know about cats or bananas flashes through my mind, not even everything that might be considered central. I can understand the term *cat* without thinking about how cats wash themselves, and *banana* without thinking about their tropical origin." This is true, but in no way does it conflict with the encyclopedic conception as I intend it. Let me therefore attempt to sharpen this conception in relevant respects.

The crux of the misunderstanding is the **conduit metaphor**, which pervades our thinking about language and often leads to conceptual difficulties that disappear once we recognize its inappropriateness.[10] The conduit meta-

---

[9] Degree of intrinsicness sometimes has direct grammatical consequences; e.g. it is one factor in determining the order of noun modifiers relative to their head (note *big round table*, where the more intrinsic shape specification is closer to the head than the size specification).

[10] Reddy (1979) examines the conduit metaphor in great detail. It is also considered in Lakoff and Johnson (1980), which pursues the linguistic ramifications of metaphor more generally, and in Moore and Carling (1982), which introduces the alternative conception of a lexical item providing access to a store of knowledge.

phor views lexical items as *containers* for meaning: meaning is stored in these containers, and it is *carried along* with the lexical items as a linguistic expression is *conveyed* from the speaker to the hearer. This metaphor leads to the natural conclusion that all facets of the linguistic meaning of a lexical item are carried along together, and thus to the hypothetical objection raised in the preceding paragraph. In actuality, of course, nothing travels from the speaker to the hearer except sound waves. To the extent that the two speech-act participants employ the same symbolic system and command comparable knowledge structures, the listener is able to reconstruct from the acoustic signal a reasonable hypothesis about the nature of the conceptualization that prompted the speaker's utterance. Instead of regarding expressions as containers for meaning, we must focus on the symbolic **correspondence** between a phonological and a semantic structure (cf. 2.2, and specifically Fig. 2.6). Our immediate task is to clarify this notion.

Mind is neurological activity, and established concepts are simply entrenched cognitive routines (cf. 3.1.1). Thus far I have spoken of a predicate like [CAT] or [BANANA] as if it were a unitary concept, i.e. a single complex routine that is activated as a whole and executed in toto if at all. Despite its expository convenience, this conception must be recognized as an oversimplification not to be taken seriously as a claim about the cognitive representation of predicates. A complex predicate like [CAT] or [BANANA] is more accurately viewed as a *set* of routines, which are interrelated in various ways facilitating their coactivation (e.g. by inclusion or by the sharing of subroutines) but nevertheless retain enough autonomy that the execution of one does not necessarily entail the activation of all the rest. The encyclopedic characterization of a typical predicate involves many such routines (possibly quite complex), each representing a separate specification.

To further articulate this conception, we must reconcile the process view of cognitive structure with a network model of knowledge systems. The standard mathematical definition of a network specifies a finite number of vertices (or "nodes") linked pairwise by a number of arcs. As a first approximation, then, we can describe a knowledge system as a network where nodes correspond to conceived entities, and arcs to the conceived relationships in which they participate. However, cognitive and linguistic considerations suggest the need for a model that is more elaborate in certain respects than a simple, well-behaved network. For one thing, some relationships involve more than just two direct participants.[11] A more significant factor is that any relationship in the network can itself be construed as a higher-order entity, and thus adopted as one of the nodes participating in a higher-order relation, and so on recursively. Because an entity can participate simultaneously in any number of relations, possibly

---

[11] We will not concern ourselves with the extent to which such relationships might be decomposable into binary relations.

at different hierarchical levels, knowledge structures grow to be extraordinarily intricate and convoluted. The total body of our knowledge (i.e. the conceptual universe we construct, maintain, and modify throughout our lives) can be thought of as an interlocking set of networks of this sort, or alternatively, as a single vast network of almost unimaginable proportions.

We can now identify every entity or relation in a knowledge system with a cognitive routine, typically decomposable into subroutines or even hierarchies of subroutines. Consider a simple relation involving two entities. Each entity corresponds to a cognitive routine, and the relation in which they participate corresponds to a higher-order routine that includes these individual routines as components (together with the mental operations serving to connect them). Activation of the higher-order relational routine thus presupposes—and is facilitated by—the activation of the two components. However, the activation of a component routine does not entail that of the relational routine as a whole.

Sketchy though it is, this scheme provides a sufficient frame of reference for exploring the notion of correspondence as it pertains to symbolic units. The matrix for most predicates is complex, requiring specifications in numerous domains, both basic and abstract. What ties these specifications together is the fact that all of them make reference to a common entity that has special status as the one **designated** by the predicate (its **profile**). In terms of the network model, each of the specifications in a complex matrix is a relation, and the entity designated by the predicate is a node shared by all of these relations. Each of the nodes and relations, moreover, can be equated with a cognitive routine.

The entity designated by a symbolic unit can therefore be thought of as a **point of access** to a network. The semantic value of a symbolic unit is given by the open-ended set of relations—simple and complex, direct and indirect—in which this **access node** participates. Each of these relations is a cognitive routine, and because they share at least one component the activation of one routine facilitates (but does not always necessitate) the activation of another. The correspondence between the phonological pole and the semantic pole of a symbolic unit implies the ability of the phonological routine to activate the subroutine constituting the access node together with an indefinite number of relational routines that incorporate this subroutine. It cannot be expected that precisely the same group of relational routines will be activated on every occasion, or that all of them will ever be activated on the same occasion. We can suppose, however, that some relational routines have sufficient centrality (4.2.2) that they are activated virtually every time the symbolic unit is invoked. In fact, some relational routines (representing more intrinsic properties) are plausibly analyzed as components of others, making their activation essentially obligatory. A likely candidate for this status is a characteristic shape specification in a predicate designating a physical object; it is difficult, for example, to conceptualize a cat chasing a mouse without in some measure evoking a conception of their shapes.[12]

The network model avoids a problem of infinite regress that arises when the encyclopedic view of linguistic semantics is interpreted on the basis of the conduit metaphor. It is part of our popular conception of cats that they chase mice, so the encyclopedic view requires this relational specification to be included in the meaning of *cat*. By the same token, one thing we "know" about mice is that they are chased by cats, so the same relational specification figures in the meaning of *mouse*. If lexical items are construed as containers for their meanings, in accordance with the conduit metaphor, a problem then obviously arises: the concept [CAT] incorporates [MOUSE] as a component in one of its specifications; at the same time, however, [MOUSE] includes [CAT] as a component in one of its own specifications; thus [CAT] contains [MOUSE] contains [CAT] contains [MOUSE], etc. No doubt things can somehow be patched up, but the problem never even arises in the network conception, where a lexical unit provides a conventionally determined point of access to knowledge systems. The concept of a cat chasing a mouse is a relation represented in the network model as a connection between two nodes, one constituting the point of access to the network for *cat*, and the other the point of access for *mouse*. A single specification functions simultaneously in the encyclopedic characterization of both lexical units, each providing access through the entity it designates.

Further refinement of the network model permits the resolution of an additional problem, illustrated by the contrast between *roe* and *caviar*. Each term designates a mass of fish eggs, and the same mass of eggs can qualify as either roe or caviar (at least at a certain stage of preparation). For sake of argument, we can thus assume that the two expressions are not distinguished with respect to their designata. Moreover, if we take seriously the encyclopedic view of linguistic semantics, neither are they distinguished by the array of domains in their complex matrices, nor by the specifications in these domains: it is part of our encyclopedic knowledge of roe that it is sometimes made into caviar, and part of our knowledge of caviar that it consists of roe prepared in a certain way. What, then, is responsible for the semantic contrast between *roe* and *caviar*, which are definitely nonsynonymous?

The difference, I suggest, lies in the relative prominence of certain domains in the matrices of these lexical items. In the case of *roe*, the role of the designated mass with respect to the reproductive cycle of fish is central and obliga-

---

[12] All of this apparatus is necessary to accommodate a single predicate representing one consistent (though multifaceted) sense of a lexical item. It should not be confused with the schematic network uniting the alternative senses of a lexical item (cf. Ch. 10).

torily accessed, whereas its role in abstract domains pertaining to the preparation and (conspicuous) consumption of foods is peripheral and activated only on a contingent basis. This ranking is reversed in the case of *caviar*: the domains that construe the designated mass as an item of consumption are salient and obligatorily activated, but the relation of this mass to fish reproduction is secondary (and often suppressed).

The semantic value of an expression is consequently not exhausted by specifying its designatum and listing the inventory of domains in its matrix. A predicate is further characterized by its ranking of domains in terms of their prominence and likelihood of activation. Contrastive pairs like *roe* vs. *caviar* demonstrate that the ranking of constituent domains is not fully predictable from the centrality factors discussed in 4.2.2, but is to some degree subject to conventional determination. A domain that is highly ranked will be referred to as a **primary domain**. The choice of primary domain is therefore responsible for the semantic contrast between *roe* and *caviar*.[13]

Finally, a word is necessary about the complexity of possible relations in the network model and the effect of unit status in this regard. Suppose a network includes the four nodes $[A]$, $[B]$, $[C]$, and $[D]$, each an entity with unit status (i.e. an established routine). Suppose further that relations $[[A]-[B]]$, $[[B]-[C]]$, and $[[C]-[D]]$ also have unit status, but that higher-order relations such as $([[A]-[B]]-[[B]-[C]])$ and $([[A]-[B]]-[[B]-[C]]-[[C]-[D]])$ do not. The question to be addressed is this: Given a predicate designating entity $[A]$, relation $[[A]-[B]]$ naturally figures in its encyclopedic characterization, but can the same be said for entities $[C]$ and $[D]$, or for relations $[[B]-[C]]$ and $[[C]-[D]]$? These entities and relations are accessible from $[A]$ by following arcs from node to node through the network. But taking things to the extreme, the same can be said for every node in a network, no matter how distant and indirectly connected. The mere fact that a chain of relations can be observed leading from $[A]$ to $[D]$ therefore does not imply that $[D]$ is part of a predicate designating $[A]$—not unless one is willing to say that every entity and relation in a network is part of a predicate designating any of them, and ultimately that all facets of one's knowledge figure at least peripherally in the meaning of every symbolic unit. Although this is not inherently unreasonable, neither is it terribly useful. Let us therefore delimit the semantic pole of a symbolic unit in the following way: a structure $[X]$ figures **directly** in the encyclopedic charac-

---

[13] Classic examples illustrating the Fregean sense/reference distinction are treated similarly: *the morning star* designates an entity construed in relation to the stellar configuration of the morning sky, and *the evening star*, to that of the evening sky. For a person who knows that the morning and evening stars are the same, both expressions include these abstract domains in their encyclopedic characterizations; they differ in their choice of primary domain, through which access to the overall knowledge system is achieved. *Venus* is yet another expression with the same designatum but a different primary domain (knowledge of the planetary system).

terization of a symbolic unit with access node [A] only if there is a structure of the form [A . . . X . . .] that has unit status; otherwise it figures only indirectly and is not an established part of the unit's meaning.

It must be remembered, though, that unit status is a matter of degree and subject to change. Because [[A]-[B]] and [[B]-[C]] share a subroutine, activation of the former facilitates the latter, which in turn facilitates the activation of [[C]-[D]]. If anything encourages the repeated coactivation of these relations, the complex structure [[[A]-[B]]-[[B]-[C]]-[[C]-[D]]] quickly achieves the status of a unit, and all of its substructures then figure directly in the meaning of an expression with access node [A].

Let us take a concrete example. The notions *cat* and *cheese* are linked in our culture through a chain of associations: we conventionally attribute to cats the property of chasing mice, and to mice that of eating cheese. We would nevertheless not say that the concept [CHEESE] figures directly in the meaning of *cat* (or [CAT] in that of *cheese*); neither has any particular tendency to elicit the other, since the associative chain lacks the status of a unit and hinges on noncentral specifications activated only on a contingent basis. Consider now a community of cheesemakers that is suddenly overrun by hordes of mice. To protect their livelihood, the cheesemakers sensibly decide to import a felony of cats, which chase away the mice and then remain to ward off any further threats. It is reasonably maintained that [CHEESE] now figures directly in the meaning of *cat* for members of this community. Their sole purpose in tolerating the continued presence of cats is to protect their cheese from mice; this conceived relationship linking cats, mice, and cheese is a well-entrenched unit that is central to the expression's semantic value.

4.3. Motion, Ordering, and Distance

The motion of physical objects through space is fundamental to our experience, so an explicit analysis of its conceptualization is important for linguistic semantics. The analysis offered in this section sheds some light on related problems, e.g. the frequent extension of expressions describing spatial motion to "motion" in abstract domains, and even to very general concepts of change and directionality. It is suggested that abstract notions of ordering, directionality, and distance are essential to linguistic structure, and that their conception necessarily involves the sequencing of cognitive events.

4.3.1. *Spatial Motion*

Even in its simplest form, the conception of spatial motion implies a complex train of cognitive events. Let us begin the analysis by making explicit the construal relationship (3.3.2.4), i.e. the relation between a conceptualizer, C, and his conceptualization. The formula in (1)(a) indicates that C conceptualizes situation S_i at moment T_i of **processing time**. We may assume for now that neither C nor the construal relation itself figures in the conceived situation S_i. Consequently the role of C in this relationship is maximally subjective, and S_i is purely objective.

$$(1)(a)\quad \begin{bmatrix} S_i \\ C \end{bmatrix}_{T_i} \qquad (b)\quad \begin{bmatrix} S_0 \\ C \end{bmatrix}_{T_0} > \begin{bmatrix} S_1 \\ C \end{bmatrix}_{T_1} > \begin{bmatrix} S_2 \\ C \end{bmatrix}_{T_2} > \cdots$$

Formula (1)(a) corresponds to the momentary conception of a single, possibly static configuration. The conceptualization of movement is necessarily more elaborate, for it involves the transformation of one configuration into another, in fact a continuous series of such transformations. A first approximation to this complex occurrence is offered in (1)(b), where $>$ indicates the sequenced occurrence of cognitive events. Through span $[T_0 > T_1 > T_2 \cdots]$ of processing time, the conceptualizer carries out a sequence of cognitive events $[S_0 > S_1 > S_2 > \cdots]$, such that each event S_i represents the specific configuration conceived at moment T_i. The discreteness of this informal notation should not be allowed to obscure the essential continuity of these events and the mental experience they constitute.

Spatial motion is change through time in the location of some entity. Notions of time and location therefore figure somehow in each component state S_i, as do specifications pertaining to the entity construed as moving. Let m represent those cognitive events required for the conception of the mover. A locative relationship involving m implies a more elaborate set of cognitive events of the abstract form $[m/l_i]$, where l_i is a conceived location and / specifies the coincidence of m and l_i. The formula $[[m/l_i]/t_i]$ then corresponds to the still more elaborate conception of m coinciding with l_i at moment t_i; observe that t_i does not refer to processing time, but rather what we may call **conceived time**. How l_i and t_i are characterized is unimportant for present purposes, but the suggested bracketing is nonarbitrary. Intuitively it is natural to think of a locative relationship being situated in time (and easy to conceptualize it atemporally). It is much more difficult to think of motion as an evolving temporal relationship distributed through space.

To simplify formulaic representations, let us adopt $[m/l_i]t_i$ as a notational variant of $[[m/l_i]/t_i]$. Formula (2) then characterizes the minimal set of cognitive events required for the conceptualization of spatial motion.

$$(2)\quad \begin{bmatrix} [m/l_0]t_0 \\ C \end{bmatrix}_{T_0} > \begin{bmatrix} [m/l_1]t_1 \\ C \end{bmatrix}_{T_1} > \begin{bmatrix} [m/l_2]t_2 \\ C \end{bmatrix}_{T_2} > \cdots$$

It indicates that C requires the span of processing time $[T_0 > T_1 > T_2 > \cdots]$ to conceptualize the movement of m along path $[l_0 > l_1 > l_2 > \cdots]$ during the span $[t_0 > t_1 > t_2 > \cdots]$ of conceived time. For the motion to be coherent, m must be basically the same from one state to the next; l_i and l_{i+1} must always be contiguous in some appropriate sense; and t_i and t_{i+1} must be successive points in time.[14] Moreover, higher-order events assessing the disparity between successive configurations can also be assumed, though the formula does not specifically represent them.

The distinction between conceived time and processing time—i.e. between time as an *object* and as a *medium* of conceptualization—is crucial to linguistic analysis. The occurrence of any complex conceptualization occupies an interval of processing time, irrespective of whether time is included as a conceived entity or a relevant domain. Moreover, the co-occurrence in (2) of $[t_0 > t_1 > t_2 > \cdots]$ and $[T_0 > T_1 > T_2 > \cdots]$ does not imply their equivalence, despite the identical subscripts. The passage of conceived time requires a span of processing time for its conception, but whereas processing time defines the "present," a segment of conceived time is free to vary in both length and temporal location. For conceived and processing time to be specifically equated, the latter must be incorporated in the scope of predication, and point-by-point correspondences established between the two.

4.3.2. *Abstract Motion*

Terms for motion and other spatial relationships are commonly extended to nonspatial domains. For example, the basic sense of *go* pertains to the movement of a physical object through space, as in (3)(a), but this verb has many other conventional uses, exemplified in (b)–(e).

(3)(a) *A train went through the tunnel.*
   (b) *It takes only five seconds to go through the alphabet.*
   (c) *I went through the book in just three hours.*
   (d) *He can go quickly from one mood to another.*
   (e) *This milk is about to go sour.*

In analyzing such data, one's first inclination is to appeal to spatial metaphor, making the intuitively natural claim that (b)–(e) involve the spatial construal of basically nonspatial domains. However, recognizing that metaphor is a factor marks only the beginning of the descriptive task. Explicit analysis is required for both the nature of the metaphorical extension and the structures it relates.

If $A \dashrightarrow B$ represents the extension, and something like the set of events in

[14] Recall that "point" refers to a quantum of cognitive processing (it is not interpreted in a strict mathematical sense). What constitutes a point for conceptual purposes—in time, space, or other domains—is quite variable.

(2) is assumed as a characterization of *A*, what is then the nature of *B*? The answer depends on the extent to which the domains and relationships of (3)(b)–(e) are susceptible to independent (i.e. nonspatial) conception. At one extreme, it could be maintained that spatial metaphor is "constitutive" of these domains in the strongest possible sense: no independent conception is possible, and *B* is in fact a conception of physical motion through space, albeit one that is at odds with physical reality. This analysis would claim, for example, that *alphabet* in (3)(b) is necessarily construed as a hypothetical physical object (something like a road with letters painted on it), and that the implicit subject of *go* moves from point to point along its length. In (3)(e), the analysis conceives the milk as transporting itself across a boundary into a spatially interpreted region of sourness, somewhat like a ball rolling out of bounds. If this hypothesis is correct, then (2) applies without modification to all the expressions cited in (3). Cases like (3)(b)–(e) are special primarily because they presuppose for their domain a fanciful version of physical space.

We frequently do entertain such conceptions, but I find it rather doubtful that this type of analysis can be maintained for all instances of extension from space to other domains. Alternatives hinge on the possibility of an independent, nonspatial construal of the target domains and relationships. I do believe we can conceptualize a person reciting the alphabet without reifying the alphabet into a roadlike object, and that we can conceive of milk changing in quality without construing it as moving from one spacelike region to another. The possibility of independent conception is strongly suggested by the existence of alternate expressions that do not rely in any obvious way on spatial metaphor. Compare (3)(b)–(e) to (4)(a)–(d), respectively:

(4)(a) *It only takes five seconds to recite the alphabet.*
  (b) *I read the book in just three hours.*
  (c) *He can quickly change moods.*
  (d) *This milk is about to become sour.*

Let us assume, then, that some instances of spatial metaphor pivot on a perceived similarity between the standard *A* (a spatial notion) and the target *B*, where *B* is an independent conception that is not spatial in the narrowest sense of the term. The coactivation of *A* and *B* as the literal and figurative senses of the expression constitutes the recognition of its metaphorical nature.[15] However, once *B* is established as a conventional value of the expression, it may sometimes be activated in this role without the coactivation of *A*: metaphors gradually fade and eventually lose their metaphorical character.

This type of analysis presupposes a generalized notion of extensionality

[15] We can further speculate that in some instances, to some degree, *A* and *B* are capable of merging into a single, internally coherent conceptualization. The "hybrid" notion that results amounts to a "spatialized" construal of *B* along the lines described above.

(4.1.3) that is not specifically tied to our conception of physical space. It is a property of many domains, both basic and abstract, though the spatial domain stands out among them for its prototypicality and cognitive salience. By making this distinction between extensionality in general and physical space in particular, we can characterize "motion" in abstract terms applicable to any extensional domain, without prejudging the extent to which spatial metaphor is constitutive of these domains.

If the elements of relationship $[m/l_i]$ are properly interpreted, formula (2) will be appropriate for this more abstract conception of motion. Thus l_i need not be a point in space, but can be an entity of any sort, so long as multiple entities of the same basic type figure in the domain (thereby providing the requisite extensionality). Similarly, the mover m is not restricted to physical objects, but need only be capable of selectively "interacting" with entities of the type represented by l_i; the symbol / specifies this interaction.[16] By this definition, reciting the alphabet is an instance of abstract motion: m is the person reciting it, l_i is the process of articulating a particular letter, and $[m/l_i]$ is the execution of this process. In the case of milk going sour, $[m/l_i]$ represents the conception of the milk (m) having one particular degree of freshness (l_i) along a graded scale. The abstract motion characterized in this fashion presumably constitutes per se the primary semantic value of expressions like *recite the alphabet* and *milk . . . become sour.* For the corresponding expressions based on spatial metaphor (*go through the alphabet, milk . . . go sour*), it functions as the target of the extension $A - - \rightarrow B$.

Occurrence in a nonspatial domain is only one of the ways in which motion can be abstract. Others are illustrated in (5):

(5)(a) *A black dog walked across the field, through the woods, and over the hill.*
   (b) *The Linguistics Hall of Fame is across the plaza, through the alley, and over the bridge.*
   (c) *There was a fire last night across the river, through the canyon, and over the mountain.*

Sentence (a) is a straightforward example of physical motion, in which the subject nominal designates the mover, and the path of movement is specified by the prepositional phrases. Spatial motion would not appear to figure in the other two sentences: certainly neither the subject nor any other explicit nominal is construed as moving along an extended spatial path. Yet both (b) and (c) are parallel to (a) in containing prepositional phrases that describe such a path, and one can argue on intuitive grounds that some kind of motion is indeed involved.

[16] If we are permissive enough in spelling out what qualifies as a mover, as a location, or as interaction, any type of change whatever can be regarded as an instance of abstract motion. We will not pursue the interesting question of whether change and motion are in fact ultimately distinguishable, but focus instead on examples with some appreciable similarity to physical motion.

An obvious suggestion is that (5)(b) is the type of sentence that would be used in giving directions to a disoriented tourist who has never before been privileged to visit the Hall of Fame. Under this analysis, the meaning of the sentence does incorporate reference to physical movement along the path in question, but it is potential rather than actual movement, and the projected mover is specifically the addressee rather than anyone designated by an overt nominal. However, (5)(b) does not have to occur in such a context; it might well be employed simply for purposes of geographical orientation, when neither the speaker, nor the addressee, nor anybody else is known to be interested in spending a boring afternoon at the shrine. Similarly, a forest ranger might produce (5)(c) in reference to a fire that broke out in utterly inaccessible terrain, with no thought of anybody traveling to the spot. As an alternative analysis, one might suggest that in sentences (b) and (c) the speaker is merely specifying the position (relative to his own) of the entity designated by the subject nominal, and does so by describing the path that one would have to follow in order to reach it (should anybody wish to do so); motion along this path is therefore purely hypothetical, with no specific mover or movement event implied. Yet another possibility is that the speaker somehow moves subjectively along the path in question; i.e. he mentally traces along this path for purposes of computing the location of the subject.

I believe that all of the above are possible ways of construing a sentence like (5)(b) or (5)(c). Sometimes context dictates a particular construal (e.g. when (5)(b) occurs in response to a request for directions), but often it does not, nor are the various alternatives sharply distinct. The difference between strictly hypothetical movement along the indicated path (where both the mover and the time of the event remain unspecified) and the projected movement of the addressee upon receipt of directions is essentially a matter of specificity: the former notion is a schema instantiated by the latter. Moreover, we will see that the contrast between hypothetical motion and subjective motion is very subtle, reducing to a maximally schematic specification on the one hand vs. the absence of a specification on the other (cf. 3.3.3).

The analysis of (5) can be summarized as follows. Sentence (5)(a) is canonical for sentences referring to physical motion: an overt subject nominal designates the mover, and the movement per se is what the clause as a whole designates. The most prominent aspect of its semantic value is therefore a sequence of cognitive events of the sort described in formula (2). The meaning of a sentence like (5)(b) or (5)(c) incorporates a comparable sequence of events, but the conceived motion is not selected as the designated entity at the clausal level (it is simply used to identify a location), and the mover is not equated with the clausal subject nor even overtly specified. Several conventionally sanctioned construals appear possible. In two of them the motion is construed objectively (at least from the speaker's standpoint), so that (2) is applicable as it stands: the movement may be purely hypothetical, in which case both m and the time span $[t_0 > t_1 > t_2 > \cdots]$ are maximally schematic; or it may be interpreted as projected movement on the part of the addressee, in which case m is so identified and the time sequence is specified as subsequent to the time of speaking. A third possible construal involves subjective motion by the speaker. How is subjective motion to be characterized?

The idea is not at all mysterious; in fact, the characterization of subjective motion is straightforward, granted certain constructs already introduced (notably abstract motion and the construal relation). Let us begin again with formula (2), representing physical motion objectively conceived. Recall that (2) comprises an ordered series of states, each conforming to the pattern of (6)(a).

$$(6)(a) \quad \begin{bmatrix} [m/l_i]t_i \\ C \end{bmatrix}_{T_i} \qquad (b) \quad \begin{bmatrix} [\ldots/l_i]\ldots \\ C \end{bmatrix}_{T_i} \qquad (c) \quad \begin{bmatrix} l_i \\ C \end{bmatrix}_{T_i}$$

Formula (6)(a) indicates that the speaker/conceptualizer C, at moment T_i of processing time, conceptualizes the spatio-temporal configuration $[m/l_i]t_i$. For a sentence like (5)(a), this configuration is largely objective and non-schematic: C is not a central participant (in particular, $C \neq m$),[17] and both m and t_i are specified to some degree. What about the motion implied by sentences like (5)(b) and (c)? For the projected motion involved in giving directions, m is equated with the listener and t_i is specified as subsequent to the moment of speaking. For hypothetical motion, (6)(a) is still valid, but m and t_i are maximally schematic (and hence nonsalient). The limiting case for (6)(a) is represented in (6)(b), where ellipses (...) indicate the minimal salience and specificity of a participating element.

The final step in diminishing the salience of m and t_i is to eliminate any reference to them at all, schematic or otherwise. The resulting structure is (6)(c); it indicates that C conceptualizes location l_i at moment T_i of processing time. Letting l_i vary continuously through a span of processing time, we obtain a complex conceptualization that amounts to the ordered conception of a linear path:

$$(7) \quad \begin{bmatrix} l_0 \\ C \end{bmatrix}_{T_0} > \begin{bmatrix} l_1 \\ C \end{bmatrix}_{T_1} > \begin{bmatrix} l_2 \\ C \end{bmatrix}_{T_2} > \cdots$$

The experiential import of (7) is that C mentally traces along path $[l_0 > l_1 > l_2 > \cdots]$; i.e. he activates in sequence those cognitive events that constitute the conception of particular points on the path, thus scanning along it

[17] The conception in (5)(a) is not fully objective—e.g. the position of the speaker serves as point of reference for the path of motion, and the time of speaking is the reference point for the past-tense specification. The ground is therefore included in the scope of predication, but remains "offstage" (cf. Langacker 1985).

from one end to the other. Observe that C does this in (2) as well. The difference is that in (2) this mental path is embedded in a more elaborate conceptualization (l_i is only one facet of $[m/l_i]t_i$ at each stage), whereas in (7) it stands alone.

Why do I refer to (7) as "subjective motion" on the part of the speaker? Because it meets the definition of abstract motion offered earlier in this section, but is not objectively construed. To see this, observe that conceptualizing a particular location can be regarded as an abstract sort of "interaction" with that location, so the successive conceptualization by C of the points along path $[l_0 > l_1 > l_2 > \cdots]$ amounts to an abstract movement of the speaker along this path (in his role as conceptualizer, not as a physical object). Note further that $[C/l_i]T_i$ can be adopted as an alternate notation for (6)(c), without distorting the import of either representation; (8) then constitutes an alternate notation for (7).

(8) $[C/l_0]T_0 > [C/l_1]T_1 > [C/l_2]T_2 > \cdots$

We can now describe the difference between (2) and (8) as residing in whether the conceived motion is viewed objectively or subjectively. It is viewed objectively in (2), provided that m is distinct from C and t_i is not equated with T_i. These distinctions are lost in (8), which can be seen as the degenerate case of (2) obtained by collapsing m with C and conceived time with processing time. Since objectivity requires a sharp distinction between the observer and the observed (or between the conceptualizer and the object of conceptualization), the basis for an objective construal of the motion is lacking in (8). In fact, if C's conceptualization at each stage is limited to l_i (as per assumption), his conception is, strictly speaking, not one of motion at all (since there is no conceived mover), but simply a sequential scanning of a linear path. Formula (8) constitutes a conception of abstract motion only to an external observer, for whom $[C/l_i]T_i$ in its entirety represents the object of conceptualization.[18]

4.3.3. *Ordering and Directionality*

By distinguishing between conceived time and processing time, we can account explicitly for the ordering, directionality, and subjective "motion" we find intuitively in conceptions pertaining to static situations. We can reasonably conjecture that an ordered conception always involves the sequenced occurrence through processing time of cognitive events corresponding to the entities that participate in the ordering, as illustrated in (7). The passage of conceived time is itself an ordered conception, and it is natural for an ordered set of entities $[e_0 > e_1 > e_2 > \cdots]$ to correlate, in the fashion of (2), with the "points" of a conceived time span $[t_0 > t_1 > t_2 > \cdots]$. However, there are many

---

[18] C himself qualifies as such an observer to the extent that he is aware of his role as conceptualizer, so that the object of conceptualization at any instant is not just l_i, but rather C *conceptualizing l_i (at T_i)*.

ordered conceptions in which the passage of conceived time is not a factor, and many others in which $[e_0 > e_1 > e_2 > \cdots]$ and $[t_0 > t_1 > t_2 > \cdots]$ fail to correlate.

Let us briefly explore some descriptive applications of these notions. Consider first the expressions in (9):

(9)(a)   *Jan walked from Reno to Las Vegas.*
   (b)   *the road from Reno to Las Vegas*
   (c)   *the road from Las Vegas to Reno*
   (d)   *the line from A to B*
   (e)   *the line from B to A*

Sentence (9)(a) is once again a canonical motion sentence. It designates a process conforming to the specifications of (2), and the mover is equated with the person designated by the subject nominal. In conceptualizing Jan's progress along the path specified by the prepositional phrases, C is claimed to activate sequentially the cognitive events $[l_0 > l_1 > l_2 > \cdots]$ corresponding to points along this path, and to coordinate these events with $[t_0 > t_1 > t_2 > \cdots]$, corresponding to the passage of conceived time. The sequential nature of that activation implies that both $[l_0 > l_1 > l_2 > \cdots]$ and $[t_0 > t_1 > t_2 > \cdots]$ are further coordinated with the passage of processing time: $[T_0 > T_1 > T_2 > \cdots]$.

The expressions in (9)(b)–(e) are not clauses but rather nominals, so the designated entity is a thing instead of a process. While sequential scanning through conceived time is critical for any processual notion (cf. Ch. 7), time is hardly a primary domain for these nominal predications. Of course, fairly central to the encyclopedic characterization of *road* is our knowledge that people use roads for travel; in schematic form this process therefore functions as one domain in the complex matrix of this morpheme, though it is not in profile (i.e. not designated) as it is in (9)(a). This unprofiled process is one possible source of the directionality responsible for the semantic contrast between (9)(b) and (c). I suggest, however, that we perceive this contrast and impose a directional construal on these expressions even when we simply conceive of the road as a spatially extended entity (the notion of travel along it remaining latent). Conceived time is not a major factor under this construal; the conception of a physical object as such is essentially atemporal. The directionality must be attributed, then, to subjective motion on the part of the conceptualizer along the specified path, as formulated in (7). Path $[l_0 > l_1 > l_2 > \cdots]$ can be identified with the ordered set of "points" constituting the road (or their spatial location), and the semantic contrast hinges on whether the "origin" l_0 is equated with Reno or with Las Vegas. The importance of subjective motion to such expressions is underscored by (9)(d) and (e), in which objective physical motion is not a salient specification.

From directional expressions that make no essential reference to conceived time, we turn now to cases where the passage of conceived time is indeed significant but fails to correlate with the ordering that provides the directionality. Consider the sentences in (10):

(10)(a) *This artery branches just below the elbow.*
   (b) *The mountain rises sharply out of the plain.*
   (c) *Near the ceiling the crack widens.*

Their directionality is quite apparent intuitively. In (10)(a), for instance, one mentally traces downward along the artery and notes the "changes" in its configuration that are encountered along the way. I analyze this motion as subjective motion by the conceptualizer: the artery defines the path of movement, but does not itself move. The applicable formula is (1)(b), the general scheme for ordered conceptualizations, which is restated here as (11):

(11) $[C/S_0]T_0 > [C/S_1]T_1 > [C/S_2]T_2 > \cdots$

At each instant T_i, the situation S_i conceptualized by C involves not only a particular location along the path of the artery, but also its configuration at that spot and how this diverges from its configuration at the preceding location. By proceeding along the course of the artery in this fashion, C cumulatively builds up a global conception of its shape.[19]

The ordering involved in building up to this global conception has nothing to do with conceived time—in fact the full configuration is construed as simultaneously valid and stable through conceived time. An analysis that properly accommodates this mixture of subjective motion and temporal stability requires two levels of organization. At the first level of organization, represented in (11), the ordered sequence of cognitive events $[S_0 > S_1 > S_2 > \cdots]$ constitutes a global shape conception that makes no internal reference to conceived time; its directionality reflects the course of its progressive assembly through processing time. At the second level of organization, the full shape configuration so obtained is followed through conceived time and construed as being stable along this axis. This second organizational level establishes the processual character of the predications in (10) (cf. Ch. 7): these sentences designate the perpetuation through conceived time of a spatial configuration. Belonging to different hierarchical levels, the directionality of the configuration and the passage of conceived time are uncoordinated.

Finally, let us apply these notions to an insightful analysis of French *avant* 'before' and *après* 'after' due to Claude Vandeloise (1984). A sentence of the form *A est avant B* '*A* is before *B*' can be used for many kinds of situations, in both spatial and nonspatial domains. Vandeloise adopts a construct that he

---

[19] Summary scanning is involved (cf. 3.4.2). Observe that the notational alternates (7) and (8) represent a special case of (1)(b) and (11), where each S_i is limited to the conception of a location.

calls the "pole" (*P*) to achieve a unified account of these variegated conventional usages. If *P* is moving physically along a spatial path, *A est avant B* indicates that *P* must traverse the location of *A* along this path in order to arrive at that of *B*. When *P* is stationary with no thought of moving, the same expression can be employed with reference to perception, in particular to indicate that *A* is closer to *P* than *B* is along *P*'s line of sight. It can also be employed for abstract domains, e.g. the alphabet or the set of counting numbers; *P* proceeds through this domain by counting or reciting the letters in their proper sequence, and *A est avant B* if *A* is encountered first. It is also possible for *A* and *B* to be the movers, for example in a race. In this event *P* is equated with the goal or finish line, and *A est avant B* if *A* is projected to reach *P* before *B* does. Vandeloise thus arrives at the following generalization, based on relative "motion" in any domain where an ordering is established: *A est avant (après) B* if, in terms of relative motion, "contact" occurs between *P* and *A* prior (subsequent) to contact between *P* and *B*.

This analysis brings out several points of general significance. First, it shows the effective equivalence, for purposes of linguistic expression, of physical motion, perceptual motion, and the abstract motion of processes like counting or reciting the alphabet. An appropriately abstract characterization of motion along the lines suggested in 4.3.2 is required to capture the proper generalization and explicate the perceived similarity motivating the common symbolization of these very different situations. A second point is the validity of a notion "origin" sufficiently abstract to include as special cases such diverse entities as the first letter in the alphabet, the point of departure for physical motion, and the vantage point for perception. Similarly, there is need for a notion of "interaction" or "contact" that is abstract enough to embrace spatial coincidence, the recitation of a particular letter of the alphabet, or contact in the perceptual sense. Third, it illustrates once more the parallelism between objective motion on the part of a conceived entity (for instance, *P* moving along a spatial path), and subjective motion on the part of the conceptualizer (e.g. in traversing the alphabet to determine which letter is encountered first).

Lastly, it demonstrates the semantic significance of ordering and abstract motion even for expressions that designate a static situation. *A est avant B* profiles a relationship between *A* and *B* that is portrayed as stable throughout the temporal scope of predication; yet crucial to computing this relationship is unprofiled motion on the part of a mover who remains implicit. When *A* and *B* are themselves in motion (the race scenario), the expression still designates this one, stable aspect of their spatial relationship, and not their movement per se. Moreover, for purposes of computing this relationship it is only *relative* motion with respect to the goal that counts, i.e. whether the initial "contact" is between the goal and *A* or between the goal and *B*. For this critical but unprofiled relationship, the goal might perfectly well be considered the mover.

This would make the race scenario precisely parallel to the other cases cited, in that *P* (which remains implicit) is always the mover in ascertaining the designated relationship between *A* and *B* (respectively the subject and object of *avant/après*).

4.3.4. *Distance*

Given the linguistic importance of suitably abstract definitions of motion, directionality, origin, and location, the need for a comparably abstract notion of "distance" is readily apparent. Let me offer some programmatic suggestions concerning a possible characterization of distance applicable to any cognitive domain.

The requisite notion makes reference to cognitive events. I will say that two events are **coordinated** when they are incorporated as facets of a more inclusive, higher-order event. No particular constraints are imposed on the nature of their relationship: it is only specified that some relationship must exist, i.e. that the component events in question not constitute totally unconnected occurrences. The simplest type of coordination—where the component events are essentially exhaustive of the higher-order event—is perhaps the association in classical conditioning between a conditioned stimulus and a conditioned response. Event coordination is more elaborate when the component events are related through various mental operations. In an act of comparison, for example, a scanning operation coordinates the standard and target to form the higher-level event $S > T$. Any of the focal adjustments discussed in 3.3 (e.g. figure/ground reversal, or a shift in vantage point) can be regarded as an operation effecting the coordination of two conceptions that differ precisely by virtue of the operation. A further possibility is for two events, each responsible for the conception of a simple entity or relationship, to be coordinated through the conception of a more complex entity or relationship having them as substructures.

I will speak of a **transition** between two cognitive events, and symbolize this $A > B$, when temporal sequencing figures in their coordination. As suggested by the common notation, an act of comparison $S > T$ qualifies as a transition; though temporal overlap between *S* and *T* may well be required for the scanning operation, we can nevertheless assume that the role of *S* as standard for the assessment of *T* (rather than the converse) is determined by its prior onset. As defined, however, the class of transitions is considerably more inclusive than the class of comparison events. If ordering and directionality reduce to the sequencing of cognitive events, as suggested, motion and other ordered conceptions can be interpreted as **transition chains**. These are illustrated in (1)(b), (2), and (7).

These notions must eventually be spelled out in far more explicit detail, but at present I can only hope to clarify a few points. Any assembly of cognitive structures and abilities defines a class of potential transitions and transition chains. Only a small proportion of these are likely to occur, and of those that do, only a certain number become entrenched as units. For example, we are all exposed to a huge number of tunes during our lifetime, and manage to learn only a small proportion of these, yet even the former quantity is vanishingly small compared to the number of potential tunes that are conceivable given the array of relevant structures and domains (the basic domains of time and pitch, the musical scale, and so on). Once a potential transition chain actually occurs, it constitutes an abstract domain and thereby creates the potential for additional transitions and chains of transitions. Out of individual transitions such as $[1>2]$, $[2>3]$, $[5>6]$, $[11>12]$, etc. we eventually master a chain consisting of those counting numbers we can run off in sequence by rote: $[1>2>3>4> \cdots]$. The ordering established by this knowledge structure renders likely the emergence of other, derivative transition chains that might otherwise never arise: by suppressing every other number, for instance, we have learned the derivative sequence $[2>4>6>8> \cdots]$. This in turn makes it a simple matter to actualize the potential chain $(\cdots >8>6>4>2)$, which can easily achieve unit status and function as another abstract domain.

Transition chains are directional by definition, but they differ in the extent to which a particular directionality is inherent, and chains with opposite alignment often co-occur. The alphabet is directional to such a degree that we cannot recite it backwards without laboriously computing each successive letter in the reversed sequence (we compute the predecessor to a given letter by first running *forward* through a substring containing it to determine which letter is adjacent). By contrast, the following sentences describe situations in which directionality is imposed rather than intrinsic, hence freely reversible:

(12)(a)   *The road narrows just outside Escondido.*
(b)   *Pacific Beach is adjacent to La Jolla.*
(c)   *Wilson sold a condominium to Rafferty.*

(13)(a)   *The road widens just outside Escondido.*
(b)   *La Jolla is adjacent to Pacific Beach.*
(c)   *Rafferty bought a condominium from Wilson.*

Given one of the sentences in (12), a speaker finds it easy to effect a shift in image and recognize its basic equivalence to the corresponding expression in (13).

Despite their essentially linear character, the notion of hierarchy is important for the understanding of transition chains. In fact, a transition is intrinsically hierarchical: $A>B$ involves the coordination of components A and B to produce a sequenced, higher-order structure. Transitions can be established and activated simultaneously at multiple hierarchical levels. Consider our ability to recite the first few letters of the alphabet. The individual transitions

[A > B], [B > C], [C > D], [D > E], etc. are well entrenched, and we can carry out the task by simply chaining these together. However, we have also learned various longer sequences as units, e.g. [A > B > C > D] and [E > F > G], and have established transitions between them at a higher level of organization: [[A > B > C > D] > [E > F > G]]. D and E are therefore directly related by transition [D > E] at the first level, but at the second their relationship is only indirect, being mediated by the unit subchains [A > B > C > D] and [E > F > G]. When we recite the alphabet and manage to come up with E as the successor to D, both paths of association may be active.

It is significant that transitions can hold between different levels in a hierarchy (thus establishing a new hierarchy whose "horizontal" axis runs along the "vertical" axis of the original). Suppose you attempt to recite the alphabet backwards for the very first time, so that finding the new "successor" for each letter demands a constructive effort. Having arrived at G, you might well determine the next letter by activating the familiar structure [E > F > G], from which you observe that F is adjacent to G and thus the next to be produced. The sequence (G > F) is what you recite, but the underlying mental events take the approximate form (G > [E > F > G] > F). The transition between G and [E > F > G] is a matter of a higher-order structure being elicited by the activation of one of its components. A computational operation then effects the transition between [E > F > G] and F, which proceeds from a higher- to a lower-level structure.

The cognitive distance between two events can be measured by the number of intervening transitions in a transition chain that connects them (at least in principle—an operational transition-counter is beyond the capabilities of current technology). Thus E is closer to F than to G with respect to the transition chain [E > F > G], and the distance between G and K in the alphabet as a whole is the same as that between S and W (when reckoned on the basis of individual, letter-to-letter transitions). Why the definition makes reference to a particular transition chain is readily apparent: the same two elements lie at different distances from one another depending on which chain is employed. The numbers 4 and 8, for example, are closer in the series [2 > 4 > 6 > 8 > 10] than they are in the regular counting sequence. Moreover, in the absence of a connecting chain there is no meaningful measure of distance between two events. Barring very special circumstances, there is no way to assess the cognitive distance between my conception of the number 12 and the itch I feel on the sole of my left foot, nor to compare this distance to that between the letter Q and the taste of a pear.

Of course, comparing distances across transition chains is hazardous at best in any case. Many chains are essentially continuous (e.g. the conception of an object falling to the ground), so there is no meaningful way to count the transitions and compare the number to that of any other chain. Even for discrete chains, comparability is a serious problem. Does it make any sense to say that the cognitive distance between A and D in the alphabet (three transitions) is the same as that between the concepts [ARM] and [KNUCKLE]? It too requires three transitions, each of which involves an established whole/part relation (cf. 3.3.1): [ARM] > [HAND] > [FINGER] > [KNUCKLE]. Yet we have no basis for asserting that this identity in number of transitions implies an equal amount of mental effort in executing the two chains or has any psychological significance.

Though less severe, there are also problems of comparability with two chains of the same basic type, or even two portions of a single chain. It seems reasonable that the distance between 1 and 3 in the regular counting sequence is identical to that between 3 and 9 in the series $[3 > 6 > 9 > 12 > \cdots]$. However, there may be a difference of cognitive significance that attaches to the substantially greater entrenchment of the former chain and its component transitions. Restricting our attention to the counting numbers, it is not unlikely that early transitions like $[2 > 3]$ are more deeply entrenched and easily effected than later ones like $[18 > 19]$, though both have unit status. There is one case in which these problems do not arise at all: when one transition chain includes another, as shown in (14).

(14) $[\cdots > E_i > \cdots > E_p > \cdots > E_q > \cdots > E_j > \cdots]$

Since $[E_p > \cdots > E_q]$ is a subpart of $[E_i > \cdots > E_j]$, the execution of the former is inherent in that of the latter; I will say that $[E_p > \cdots > E_q]$ is **immanent** to $[E_i > \cdots > E_j]$ (this notion will prove useful later on). If A is immanent to B (but not the converse), the cognitive distance between the endpoints of A is necessarily smaller than that between the endpoints of B.

There is a fundamental respect in which entrenchment and unit status are pivotal to a workable notion of cognitive distance: by redefining what effectively counts as a single mental operation, they determine the character and the length of the transition chain that links two entities. Compare the following two ways of conceiving and expressing the same relationship:

(15)(a)   *Jan is Harvey's parent's sibling's child.*
    (b)   *Jan is Harvey's cousin.*

Sentence (a) essentially takes us on a tour through the family tree, from Harvey to the child, who is equated with Jan. Each possessive expression in the series (e.g. *Harvey's parent*) involves a conceptual transition between two adjacent individuals along the path; the full transition chain has three links: [HARVEY] > [PARENT] > [SIBLING] > [CHILD]. However, we also have available to us the concept [COUSIN], which evokes the transition chain [PARENT] > [SIBLING] > [CHILD] as a unitary gestalt. The unit [COUSIN] incorporates all the elements of this chain, but its status as a unit implies their manipulability as a single element. Sentence (b) therefore takes us through the family tree in one giant bound: [HARVEY] > [COUSIN]. A conceived relationship defines a transition between its participants, and an internally complex relationship is effectively equivalent to a simple one in this regard provided that the conceptualizer deploys it holistically as a preassembled package.

Despite the obvious problems in arriving at a rigorous characterization of cognitive distance, I believe this construct has far-reaching implications for linguistic analysis. Let me conclude by hinting at just a few. I need not belabor the point that distance expressions are commonly extended from spatial to more abstract domains; an abstract notion of distance is required to explicate the basis for such extension.[20] Besides their pervasiveness in the content of linguistic expressions, distance relations are significant in linguistic form, and also in the organization of knowledge systems (which underlie both form and content). The case of linguistic form is self-evident: a speaker produces the sounds of an utterance in an ordered sequence through time, so some sounds and groups of sounds are closer together than others. In regard to knowledge systems, the network model adopted earlier is readily interpreted in terms of transitions. The relation associating two nodes represents an established transition between them, and a network defines a set of actual and potential transition chains. Distances can thus be computed for various paths through the network.

These seemingly very different kinds of distance relations interact in linguistically significant ways. Most obvious is the oft-noted iconicity between form and content, which is very common for the linear ordering of constituents (cf. (5)(a)) but also extends to distance. For example, Lakoff and Johnson (1980, ch. 20) posit for English the conventional metaphor "closeness is strength of effect," citing examples like (16):

(16)(a)　*Sam killed Harry.*
　　(b)　*Sam made Harry die.*
　　(c)　*Sam caused Harry to die.*
　　(d)　*Sam brought it about that Harry died.*

Such paradigms indicate that greater phonological distance between a predication of cause and one of effect correlates with greater conceptual distance in the domains of time and cause-effect linkages (cf. Fodor 1970; Wierzbicka 1975; Langacker 1976; Haiman 1983).

The organization of knowledge systems is not really distinct from either the form or the content of linguistic expressions, since both receive their value

---

[20] Here are a few examples chosen at random: *distant relative, distant possibility, distant past, close friend, close resemblance, close succession, near panic, near impossibility, near miss, near beer.*

from such systems and constitute knowledge structures in their own right. Beyond this, we can observe that the distance between nodes in a network has an impact on the likelihood of particular entities being exploited in a grammatical valence relation. The entity designated by a symbolic unit (its profile) can be regarded as a point of access to one or more networks. Moreover, a grammatical valence relation always depends on correspondences established between substructures of the symbolic units being combined; in the network model these substructures are identified as nodes. Generally, the pivotal correspondence in a valence relation is established between the access nodes of the component predications (i.e. between the profiled entities or subparts of the profile); the distance between an access node and the node which participates in this correspondence is therefore zero. It appears that the possibility of a valence relation becomes more and more tenuous (though never really nonexistent) as the distance of the corresponding node from the access node increases. With reference to the body, for example, we can posit direct transitions between [FINGER] and [NAIL], between [TOE] and [NAIL], and also between [EYE] and [LID]; in each case the former defines the immediate scope of predication for the latter (3.3.1).[21] Noun compounds like *fingernail*, *toenail*, and *eyelid* are therefore straightforward instances of valence relations, since the access nodes and correspondence nodes are adjacent. Less expected are nonexistent compounds like *handnail*, *legnail*, or *headlid*, where the comparable nodes are connected by a longer path.

---

[21] [EYE] is here construed inclusively (as the eye region, not just the eyeball). The claims advanced in Brown (1979) might profitably be examined in connection with the notion of cognitive distance.

CHAPTER 5

Things

COGNITIVE GRAMMAR makes specific claims about semantic structure and the notional basis of fundamental grammatical categories. A pivotal construct is **designation**, characterized by the elevation of some entity to a special level of prominence within a predication. Two fundamental classes of predicates are definable in terms of the nature of the designated entity: a **nominal predication** designates a **thing**, while a **relational predication** designates either an **atemporal relation** or a **process**. The definition of a thing is abstract: it makes reference not to physical objects but rather to cognitive events. A symbolic structure whose semantic pole designates a thing is categorized as a **noun**.

5.1. Profile and Base

A predication always has a certain scope (3.3.1), and within that scope it selects a particular substructure for designation. To suggest the special prominence of the designated element, I refer to the scope of a predication and its designatum as **base** and **profile**, respectively. Perceived intuitively, the profile (in the words of Susan Lindner) "stands out in bas-relief" against the base. The semantic value of an expression resides in neither the base nor the profile alone, but only in their combination; it derives from the designation of a specific entity identified and characterized by its position within a larger configuration.

A few brief examples should make these notions clear. Consider first the predicates [CIRCLE] and [ARC], i.e. the respective semantic poles of *circle* and *arc*. The base for [CIRCLE] is the basic domain of two-dimensional space. Its profile is a configuration (set of points) in this domain; for now we can simply observe that the points in the profile are crucially situated relative to one another rather than to any external landmark. An informal, essentially pictorial representation for this predicate is offered in Fig. 5.1(a). The box enclosing this diagram delimits the base, and the domain is labeled in the

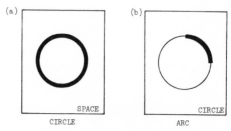

Fig. 5.1

lower right-hand corner. Heavy lines will be used throughout to identify the profile.[1]

There is a sense in which an arc is a two-dimensional figure, but it cannot be simply and directly described as a configuration in two-dimensional space. This is because [ARC] presupposes the conception of a circle: only when a set of points is identified with a portion of a circle is it recognized as constituting an arc (and not just a curved line segment). [CIRCLE] is consequently an abstract domain that serves as the scope of predication for the higher-order concept [ARC], as shown in Fig. 5.1(b); whereas undifferentiated space functions as the base for [CIRCLE], [ARC] has for its base the two-dimensional configuration that [CIRCLE] profiles. [ARC] designates only a segment of this configuration (continuous but unspecified for size and position), so only a representative portion of it is shown with a heavy line. This example nicely illustrates the interdependence of base and profile in the characterization of a predicate. Without the profiling in Fig. 5.1(b), the structure is simply that of a circle (not an arc). Without the base, the profiled configuration can only be identified as a curved line segment. The conception of an arc emerges only when the two are properly construed in relation to one another.

[UNCLE] provides a more complex example.[2] An uncle is a physical object in three-dimensional space, but it should be obvious that a direct characterization relative to this basic domain is out of the question. A straightforward description of [UNCLE] presupposes more fundamental notions that can themselves be regarded as knowledge systems situated rather far up in hierarchies

---

[1] A diagram like this makes no commitment to visual imagery. It is analogous to the drawing a biologist might make of a cell to show the relative positions of the cell wall, the nucleus, the mitochondria, etc.; it is not a formal representation, but a sketch (or crude graph) of the relations among entities in a domain. Although such diagrams have considerable heuristic value, the structures they represent should ultimately be characterized in terms of their constituent cognitive events (just as cell bodies are analyzed for their molecular composition).

[2] We will confine our attention to the prototypical sense of *uncle*, leaving aside its conventional application to such individuals as the husband of an aunt. Moreover, the genetic relationship sketched in Fig. 5.2 is only a single (though primary) domain in the complex matrix defining this predicate (omitted, for instance, is a characterization of social attitudes and expected behaviors involving uncles). Restrictions of this sort on the scope of discussion must be assumed for virtually every example treated in this monograph.

of conceptual complexity. Among these notions are the following: the conception of a person; the differentiation of people by gender, and the associated notion of sexual intercourse; the concepts of birth and the life cycle; the parent/child relationship resulting from mating and birth; and the sibling relationship based on the sharing of parents. By coordinating these notions in the appropriate manner, a speaker forms the conception of a network of persons linked together through spousal and parent/child relationships. This conceived network is the primary domain for [UNCLE], and it is only when a conceptualization of this order of complexity has been assembled that a plausible and straightforward characterization becomes possible.

The specifics are less important at present than the following points, illustrated in Fig. 5.2. A conceived network of kinship relationships is an abstract

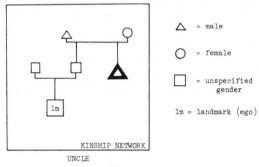

Fig. 5.2

domain. The network can clearly be extended indefinitely far from the landmark (ego), but only a fairly restricted region within this expanse is actually required for the characterization of [UNCLE] and hence necessarily included in its scope of predication. A configurational relationship vis-à-vis the landmark constitutes the crucial characterization of the profiled substructure, so it is essential to *uncle*'s meaning, but this relationship is not per se in profile. *Uncle* is a noun precisely because it designates a thing rather than a relation.

Profiling is an important component of imagery (in the sense of 3.2.1). By imposing alternate profiles on a given base, we obtain distinct but related predications. For example, the concept [CIRCLE] is the base not only for [ARC], but also for such predicates as [DIAMETER], [RADIUS], and [CHORD]. The base of [UNCLE] yields [NEPHEW] and [NIECE] when its profile and landmark assignations are reversed (and appropriate gender adjustments are made). The verb *paint* is semantically complex and designates a process; this process itself functions as the base for the semantic pole of derivative expressions such as *painter* (which designates a participant in the process), the adjectival *painted* (which designates only the final state), and *painting* (which designates an indefinite sequence of internal states, construed atemporally). By treating two predications as alternate profilings on the same base, we account automatically for their semantic relationship; the account is explicit to the extent that the underlying conceptualization (the domain or base) is explicitly characterized. Meaning postulates or comparable devices invoked to capture the relation, say, between *uncle/aunt* on the one hand and *nephew/niece* on the other are seen to be superfluous in this kind of framework. This approach also avoids a problem of circularity that arises when one attempts to describe the semantic value of an expression through some sort of linguistic paraphrase. For instance, defining *parent* as 'one who has a child' runs into difficulty because *child* (in the 'offspring' sense) would have to be defined as 'one who has a parent'. We can say instead that the base for both notions is the conception of two persons mating and one of them consequently giving birth. [PARENT] and [CHILD] profile different substructures within this conceptualization.

As I define the term, **designation** is distinct from both **symbolization** and **coding** (cf. Fig. 2.5). The differing functions of the three kinds of relationships should be apparent from Fig. 5.3. Coding (*cod*) is the relation between a linguistic unit and a usage event, at either the phonological or the semantic pole. Symbolization (*sym*) is the relation between a phonological structure and a semantic structure, regardless of whether the correspondence between

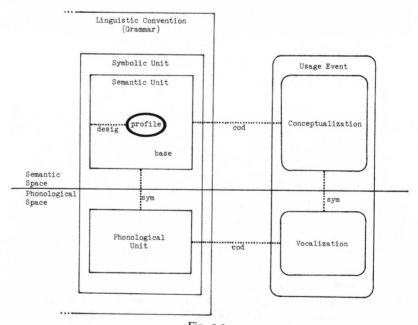

Fig. 5.3

them has unit status. Observe that symbolization relates the phonological and semantic structures as wholes; it does not associate the phonological structure solely or specifically with the profile, since the semantic value of a symbolic expression is given only by the base and profile together. Designation (*desig*) is an internal relation within a semantic structure, holding between the full base and some substructure selected as the profile. In the strictest sense, therefore, it is a predicate (rather than a phonological structure) that designates an entity. Derivatively, we can say that a phonological structure designates the entity profiled by the predication it symbolizes. With respect to Fig. 5.2, then, both the predicate [UNCLE] and (secondarily) the phonological unit [uncle] can be said to designate the profiled person in the conceived kinship network. By further extension we can say that the symbolic structure as a whole—e.g. [[UNCLE]/[uncle]]—designates the profiled entity.[3]

What is the nature of the special prominence that distinguishes the profile of a predication from the remainder of its base? Since the profile/base distinction is fundamental to the present view of semantic and grammatical structure, if necessary it can be adopted as a primitive of the theory. One would certainly prefer to explicate the notion and relate it to general cognitive phenomena. I must leave the matter open at this point, however, because none of the obvious suggestions seems fully satisfactory.

One proposal is that profile/base organization should be related to figure/ground alignment. The proposal is correct so far as it goes, if only because the heightened prominence of the profile is itself sufficient to make it stand out as a figure. However, the notion of figure is far more broadly applicable than that of designation, and there are situations in which the designated entity does not coincide with what would normally be considered the figure. In *the plane's descent*, for instance, the plane is the mover and thus (in standard terms) the figure, yet the expression designates the path of motion or the movement itself (*descent*). Moreover, I will argue (6.3.1) that the subject of a relational predication is the figure with respect to that predication (e.g. *the plane* is the figure in *The plane is above the clouds*), but the profiled entity in such predications is the relationship rather than the subject. Level of organization must be taken into account, so different entities can serve as figure (each at its own level). Still, it is not sufficient to characterize the profile as figure and let it go at that.

Another proposal is that the profile is the focus of attention within a predication. Intuitively, this strikes me as quite reasonable: I do indeed feel that I focus my attention on the plane in *the plane above the clouds*, and on the clouds in *the clouds below the plane*. The apparent difficulty is that profiling

[3] Designation is not equivalent to standard notions of **reference**. It pertains to any kind of conceptualization and has nothing to do specifically with our conception of external "reality." Not only things can be designated, but also relations and processes, and even for things the specification is typically general and does not identify a particular class member.

occurs simultaneously at multiple hierarchical levels, whereas we generally think of attention as being restricted to the highest level of organization. In *the plane above the clouds*, for instance, each component expression has its own profile: *plane, cloud, above, the, -s, the plane, clouds, the clouds, above the clouds*. That of *plane* prevails at the composite-structure level for the expression as a whole, but other profiles at lower levels contribute (I maintain) to the overall semantic value of the expression. Profiling can therefore be assimilated to attention only if one is willing to say that attention is hierarchically organized, and posit numerous "local" foci of attention in addition to the "global" one.

The hierarchical aspect of profile/base organization seems less problematic when profiling is related to intensity or level of activation relative to the other cognitive events comprised by the base. For example, we can plausibly claim that *The plane descended* and *the plane that descended* involve approximately the same complex of cognitive events for the conceptualization of their meanings, but that those events constituting the conception of the plane are activated at a substantially higher level of intensity in the latter, and those pertaining to the plane's changing position through time in the former. Of course, an account along these lines might well prove compatible with one based on an appropriately generalized notion of attention.

The prominence of profiled entities in linguistic predications can also be approached from a functional perspective. By definition, the designatum serves as focal point within the objective scene (cf. 3.3.2.4); hence it is always "on stage" and to some degree objectively construed. It is also the entity that is common to the many domains in a complex matrix and functions to tie them together in a coherent assembly, as illustrated in Fig. 5.4. The notations of diagrams 4(a) and (b) are equivalent. Diagram (a) is an exploded representation; it depicts each domain separately, the identity of the profiled structure in the various specifications being indicated by correspondence lines. Diagram (b) is a compacted representation reflecting more directly the network

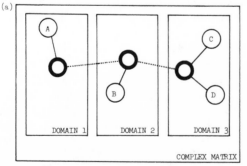
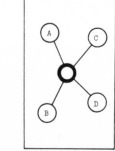

Fig. 5.4

model of knowledge systems: the profiled entity is a node participating simultaneously in several relationships (pertaining to different domains).

The domains in a complex matrix differ in their degree of centrality, which translates into the relative likelihood of their activation on any particular occasion when the symbolic unit is employed. Certain specifications of a symbolic unit are obligatorily activated on every occasion of its use, and this is true a fortiori for the subroutine constituting the profiled entity, which plays a role in all of the specifications. The profile thus functions as access node with respect to a predicate's participation in a symbolic relationship. It is also pivotal for grammatical valence relations at the semantic pole (Ch. 8). The correspondences effecting the integration of two semantic structures almost invariably involve the profile of one or both. A predication's profile thus serves as prototypical point of interaction for purposes of syntagmatic combination.

5.2. Bounded Regions

Counter to received wisdom, I claim that basic grammatical categories such as **noun**, **verb**, **adjective**, and **adverb** are semantically definable. The entities referred to as nouns, verbs, etc. are symbolic units, each with a semantic and a phonological pole, but it is the former that determines the categorization. All members of a given class share fundamental semantic properties, and their semantic poles thus instantiate a single abstract schema subject to reasonably explicit characterization. A noun, for example, is a symbolic structure whose semantic pole instantiates the schema [THING]; or to phrase it more simply, a noun designates a **thing**.[4] In similar fashion, a verb is said to designate a **process**, whereas adjectives and adverbs designate different kinds of **atemporal relations**. Our immediate task is to arrive at a motivated description of the [THING] category. I propose that a thing is properly characterized as a **region in some domain**, i.e. every nominal predication designates a region. Count nouns represent a special but prototypical case, in which the designated region is specifically construed as being **bounded** in a primary domain.

5.2.1. *Domains of Bounding*

Discussions of nouns as a possible semantic class generally focus on physical objects: witness the traditional definition of a noun as the name of a person, place, or "thing" (i.e. discrete, nonhuman object). This is understandable in view of the prototypicality of physical objects, but it dooms a notional

---

[4] Possibly the schema [THING] can be equated with the semantic pole of the morpheme *thing* in its most general sense, as represented in *something*. The apparent problems with this equation may be resolvable; for instance, the existence of more specialized pro forms like *someone* and *someplace* explains why *something* is not easily used for people or locations.

definition to failure from the very outset. Most nouns do *not* designate physical objects, and by concentrating on those that do, the best one can offer for the remainder is the assertion that they constitute extensions from the prototype, often at such a distance that the basis for extension is not apparent (how does one get from *cup* to *exacerbation*?).[5] Categorization by prototype is essential to linguistic structure (Ch. 10), and it is perfectly valid for the class of nouns (cf. Hopper and Thompson 1984). In this instance, however, I believe a schematic characterization (reflecting the commonality of all class members) to be both feasible and revealing.

The requisite schema is necessarily quite abstract. Note that the proffered definition of a thing (a region in some domain) does not refer specifically to either physical objects or three-dimensional space. Despite its cognitive salience, three-dimensional space is only one of the countless domains—basic and abstract—relative to which linguistic predications are made and regions delimited. As bounded regions in three-dimensional space, physical objects clearly satisfy the description, but many other kinds of entities also qualify as things. In fact, not even all bounded regions in three-dimensional space are physical objects: consider *sphere* (interpreted geometrically rather than concretely), or terms like *area*, *region*, and *location* (when construed in three dimensions rather than one or two). Strictly speaking, of course, a physical object *occupies* a bounded region in space but cannot be equated with that region per se.

Let us then consider some bounded regions in domains other than three-dimensional space. The objective is both to furnish enough examples of diverse character to establish the initial plausibility of this definition of count nouns, and also to note certain subtleties that arise in regard to bounding. Ultimately, the notions region and bounding require explicit description; the phrase **bounded region** must be interpreted abstractly enough to overcome the limitations of its spatial origin. For the moment, though, I will take this phrase to be self-explanatory and its import to be intuitively obvious, since our initial concern is with the domain in which bounding occurs.

To start with basic domains, nouns like *circle*, *point*, *line*, and *triangle* designate bounded regions in two-dimensional space. *Spot*, *dot*, *stripe*, and *streak* are not unreasonably analyzed as designating circumscribed impressions in the visual field, whereas *moment*, *instant*, and *period* are bounded regions in time. Color terms (when used as nouns) designate particular regions in color space; most are defined relative to the hue dimension primarily (*red*, *yellow*, *blue*, etc.), but a few are confined largely or solely to the bright-

---

[5] Thus Lyons (1968, p. 318) concludes that a notional definition is possible only for a subclass of nouns; the class as a whole must be identified by formal criteria. He suggests that a formally defined class may be identified as the noun class if all or the vast majority of lexical items referring to persons, places, and "things" fall within it.

ness dimension (*black*, *white*, *gray*). The matrix for other nominal concepts is formed by coordinating basic domains. A *beep*, for instance, is bounded in both pitch and time: it must to some degree approximate a pure tone (white noise does not qualify) and be quite short in duration as well. Duration is also limited for a *blip* and a *flash*, which display an instructive contrast. A flash must be almost instantaneous, whereas a blip can persevere (though only for a short time). Moreover, a blip (like a dot) must constitute a highly restricted region in the visual field; a flash, though it occupies the visual field, need not be bounded in this domain (it can totally suffuse the field of vision). We see from this example that the profile of a count noun is not necessarily bounded in every domain with which it interacts, a point of some significance.

Abstract domains presuppose (and thus incorporate) more-basic domains. Bounding in an abstract domain is therefore compatible with bounding in an incorporated basic domain, though the former may be primary and the latter derivative. An *arc*, for example, is a bounded region within a circle, and a *hypotenuse*, one within a right triangle. Because a circle or triangle is a two-dimensional figure, a subpart of either one also occupies two-dimensional space and even constitutes a restricted region in this basic domain. Undifferentiated two-dimensional space is not, however, the place to begin for an optimal definition of terms like *arc* and *hypotenuse*. They are best characterized with respect to abstract domains at the appropriate level in hierarchies of conceptual complexity, and it is in these domains that their primary bounding occurs. Similar remarks are valid for a host of other relational nouns pertaining to two- and three-dimensional spatial entities. Terms for body parts were considered previously: a *knuckle* is a bounded region within a finger, a *finger* within a hand, a *hand* within an arm, etc. All these entities are also restricted regions within the body as a whole and in three-dimensional space, but these latter relations are derivative rather than fundamental. A *tip* is defined more schematically, being a bounded region within an elongated object (generally a thin one); the schematic conception of such an object constitutes the base for the predicate [TIP], which designates its extremity and a vaguely delimited surrounding area. More schematic still in regard to the specification of their abstract domains are generalized relational expressions like *top*, *center*, *edge*, *surface*, and *end*.

Parallel observations can be made for examples farther up in hierarchies of conceptual complexity. A kinship network plots relations among people, so every node is equated with a person; a term like *uncle* therefore designates a person, hence a three-dimensional object, but I have suggested that this is derivative of the fact that it profiles a particular node (bounded region) in a kinship configuration. The relation of terms for musical notes (e.g. *C-sharp*, *B-flat*, *F*) to the basic domain of pitch is similarly indirect, for they designate positions on a musical scale, an abstract structure erected for the analysis and description of pitch. Expressions like *January*, *Tuesday*, *century*, *year*, *month*, *week*, and *hour* designate bounded regions within abstract constructs devised to track and calibrate the passage of time; their relation to time is consequently indirect, and they are classed linguistically as atemporal expressions (nouns rather than verbs). The terms *word*, *sentence*, *paragraph*, *section*, and *chapter* can all be used to designate bounded portions of a written work (regardless of whether it has physical instantiation). *Prolog*, *act*, *scene*, and *line* (not to mention *intermission*) indicate segments of a stage performance, and for portions of an athletic event we have words like *inning*, *period*, *quarter*, *half*, and *round*.

These examples afford some initial idea of the diversity of those entities reasonably construed as bounded regions in a domain. The viability of this characterization depends on the proper recognition of certain points, however. Typically a thing occupies or interacts with a variety of different domains, all of which are potentially included in the complex matrix of a predicate. These domains are not all on a par: they are ranked in terms of prominence and centrality, some presuppose (hence incorporate) more basic ones, and so on. There are some predicates that specifically require bounding in more than one domain (e.g. *beep* and *blip*). Others are bounded in only some of the domains central to their characterization (*flash*). Bounding in an abstract domain often implies bounding in a more basic domain that it incorporates (*arc*, *knuckle*, *tip*); but it can also happen that bounding inherited from an incorporated domain is crucial (rather than derivative) in establishing an entity as a thing. Consider deverbal agentive nouns like *painter*, *skier*, *complainer*, and so on. The base and primary domain for such nouns is the process designated by the verb stem: a *painter*, for instance, is someone who plays a specific role in the process of painting. Yet it seems implausible to say that a painter qualifies as a thing by virtue of being a bounded region within the process designated by *paint*. Indeed, the process itself presupposes the conception of a thing (prototypically a person) capable of acting in the appropriate fashion: suffixing -*er* to *paint* shifts the profile from the process as a whole to the actor specifically, but the process per se is not the domain in which the designated entity receives its primary bounding. In contrast, *arc*, *knuckle*, or *tip* itself establishes a bounded region (within a circle, finger, or elongated object) through the profile it imposes.[6]

A crucial point concerns the interaction between bounding and the scope of predication. The scope of a predication (its base) is the extension of its coverage within relevant domains. Though the limits of this extension are

---

[6] *Uncle* can be analyzed either way, and the two alternatives are not mutually exclusive (profiling in the primary domain may simply add a dimension of bounding to that inherited from more basic domains). The inheritance of bounding is not limited to derived nouns like *painter*—note *friend*, *enemy*, *chief*, *king*, *bachelor*, etc.

often rather flexible and vaguely defined, evidence has already been adduced (3.3.1) for the validity of the construct (see also Casad and Langacker 1985). When a conceived entity "overflows" the scope of a predication, only restricted portions of the entity fall within its explicit coverage, but this implicit limitation due to scope must be distinguished from bounding. We can properly speak of bounding only when an entity is fully included in the scope of predication (with respect to a particular domain), so that its outer limits are a specific matter of predication.

For example, the verb *see* establishes the visual field as a pertinent scope of predication for the characterization of its direct object, e.g. *spot* in the sentence *I see a dark spot*. A speaker could utter this sentence felicitously in the situation depicted in Fig. 5.5(a): the entire spot is included in his visual field

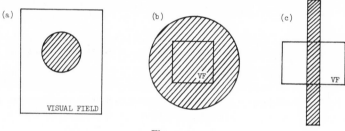

Fig. 5.5

(scope of predication), together with enough nondark background for the spot to stand out as the figure within the scene. The sentence would not be so felicitous in the situation of Fig. 5.5(b), where the speaker sees nothing but black. Because *spot* designates a bounded region contrasting visually with its surroundings, the outer perimeter—the line of visual contrast—is essential to its characterization and necessarily included in the scope of predication.[7] We can conclude that the limitation of coverage attributable to scope does not per se qualify as bounding.

Spot can instructively be compared to *stripe*. Since a spot is crucially bounded in two dimensions, but a stripe in only one, a speaker can properly say *I see a dark stripe* in the context of Fig. 5.5(c): the dark region is fully bounded with respect to the horizontal dimension of his visual field, though it overflows the scope boundaries along the vertical dimension. The speaker may know that the stripe extends vertically only a certain distance, but even so this bounding is not explicitly predicated in the sentence. We see, then, that a bounded region is not necessarily bounded in all dimensions of the primary

---

[7] *I see a dark spot* is felicitous in the context of diagram (b) if the speaker knows from other experience that what he is seeing is part of a larger bounded region and implicitly expands the scope of predication (beyond the limits implied by *see*) to include this region as a whole.

domain. *Horizon* is similar to *stripe*, but more specific. Its base consists of whatever a person can see (or potentially see) in an outdoor setting, and its profile is the line between earth and sky at the limits of vision. This line is bounded along the axis of vision, but perpendicular to this axis (i.e. to either side) it is considered to extend indefinitely, overflowing the restricted visual field. The spatially nonbounded character of *flash* can perhaps now be better appreciated. A flash may be confined to a small region of an observer's visual field, as in Fig. 5.5(a), or it may overflow it, as in (b). In either case a person can say *I saw a flash* without strain or qualification, since a flash (a brief episode of light intensity) is crucially bounded in time rather than space.

5.2.2. *Structuring*

Meaning is not objectively given, but constructed, even for expressions pertaining to objective reality. We therefore cannot account for meaning by describing objective reality, but only by describing the cognitive routines that constitute a person's understanding of it. The subject matter of semantic analysis is human conceptualization, and the structures of concern are those that a person imposes on his mental experience through active cognitive processing.

Coherent mental experience is structured with reference to previous experience (3.1). The activation of a previously established cognitive routine serves as standard (S) for an act of comparison in which some facet of current experience functions as target (T); to the extent that $S > T$ approximates zero, the overall event is one of recognition, and T is thereby interpreted as an instance of S. A great deal of variability is inherent in the process, however. For example, more than one established routine may be available to interpret T (or selected aspects of T), and there is no way to predict in absolute terms which one might be invoked on a given occasion. Recognition can operate at different levels of tolerance (i.e. the vector V_{ST} need not be precisely zero) and can be made sensitive to different parameters. Moreover, S is commonly schematic relative to T, with scanning made to assess only their compatibility (thus all of the specifications of S are recognized in T, even though T is more detailed); in this case recognition amounts to categorization.

As noted in 3.1.3, this model accounts straightforwardly for the closure phenomenon, in which recognition is achieved despite the incomplete or degraded nature of the target structure. Consider the three diagrams in Fig. 5.6, any one of which is readily recognized as a circle. Objectively, diagrams (b) and (c) consist of separate line segments or points, yet it is very hard to perceive the separate elements independent of their organization. The concept of a circle is deeply entrenched and easily elicited. Through the activation of this concept as a standard of comparison, any of the configurations in Fig. 5.6 is categorized as a circle with a minimal amount of strain. The full, autonomous conceptualization of a circle therefore occurs and functions as standard within the recognition event, and it is through their correspondence to facets of this

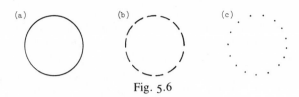

Fig. 5.6

integrated autonomous conception that the line segments and points in diagrams (b) and (c) are united in a coherent perceptual experience. Their continuity is imposed rather than being objectively given.

Taken to its extreme, this process results in the imputation of boundaries where they have no objective existence at all, even in nondegraded instances. In such cases I will speak of a **virtual** boundary. Virtual boundaries are nicely illustrated by nouns like *bump* and *dent*, sketched in Fig. 5.7; they are represented diagrammatically by broken lines, but it must be understood that no

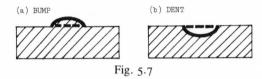

Fig. 5.7

boundary feature at all is objectively present (in contrast to Fig. 5.6(b)).[8] The domains for *bump* and *dent* are abstract, involving the conception of a three-dimensional object at least one surface of which has a canonical (typically smooth) shape. A bump or dent resides in the departure of the actual shape of the object from its expected shape; the latter therefore figures in the base of the predicates [BUMP] and [DENT] and contributes the virtual boundary to the designated entities. To see the importance of expectations, observe that the nose is not considered a bump in the middle of the face, nor is the depression in the head of a screw considered a dent. The role of expectations underscores the nonobjective nature of semantic structure.

Virtual bounding is far more prevalent than might be anticipated. Terms similar to *bump* and *dent* are not uncommon (*bulge, ridge, protrusion, hole, depression, cavity, cave*). The names of open containers (*jar, pot, box, tub, vat*) are often construed as designating the entire enclosed area, and not simply the physical object per se.[9] Nouns commonly designate parts of a

[8] Fig. 5.7 construes *bump* or *dent* as designating an entire enclosed area; an alternate construal profiles only the adjacent physical surface (indicated by the heavy solid line), relegating the virtual boundary and virtually enclosed area to the base. Comparable remarks hold for other examples, e.g. *circle*, which can be construed as designating either the curved line alone (a very thin bounded region) or else the entire area it encloses.

[9] This is so when we speak of the volume of a container; compare what is meant by the volume of a block of ice. The virtual boundary across the opening of a container also comes into play in determining whether something can be considered *in* it (see Herskovits 1982 and Vandeloise 1984 for sophisticated analysis).

larger whole that are not necessarily separated from the rest by any distinct objective boundary. Often, for example, there is no discontinuity of any kind between the *handle* of a baseball bat and its *barrel*. The body parts designated by *elbow*, *waist*, *shoulder*, and *side* are neither saliently nor sharply delimited. A boundary can be virtual in its entirety: the *middle* of a floor is typically not set off from the rest in any way, but though its extension is subject to highly variable interpretation, certainly it constitutes a bounded region. In the last analysis, then, something is a bounded region because a conceptualizer imposes a boundary in structuring a conceived situation, irrespective of how the requisite cognitive events are prompted. The perception of an objective line of demarcation greatly facilitates these events, but it is neither necessary nor sufficient for their occurrence.

By recognizing the importance of closure and virtual bounding, we can account for nouns designating collections of separate entities, for instance *swarm*, *archipelago*, and *forest*. The individual entities in the collection (bees, islands, or trees) are more or less contiguous, but nonetheless they are separated by appreciable gaps. Closure is responsible both for the association of peripheral members to form a largely virtual boundary delimiting the populated region from its surroundings, and also for the connection of internal members to provide a conception of continuity (even homogeneity) within the bounded area. Observe that the farther apart the bees, islands, or trees are (on a given scale, and in relation to other entities in the scope of predication), the more difficult it is to impose a virtual boundary and use the nouns in question to describe them. Space is therefore a primary domain for these nouns, and it is in this domain that their most salient bounding occurs. *Group*, *assembly*, and *collection* also incline towards a spatial construal, but they are more flexible in this regard, and specify their component members far more schematically, than *swarm*, *archipelago*, and *forest*.

Up to this point, the import of the term bounded region has been clear enough. Many illustrations have been spatial, and even for more-abstract examples it has been easy to conceive of the designated entity as a continuous region separated by a boundary from other portions of the domain. Matters become more difficult when we turn to nouns like *team*, or to more-abstract notions like *set* and *class*. At first they appear comparable to *archipelago*, *forest*, *group*, and *assembly* in that they designate an entity comprising an indeterminate number of component members that are not themselves separately profiled: the profiling is collective rather than individual. There is an important difference, however. The bounding in *archipelago* and the others pertains to space, where the nature of a boundary is fairly evident, even a virtual boundary imposed by closure. An *archipelago* or a spatially defined *group* also has some kind of shape determined by its peripheral members (though these predicates specify the shape of their designatum only in the most schematic terms). A *team*, *set*, or *class*, on the other hand, is apparently nonspatial in its bounding. We recognize a set of individuals as a *team* even if they are scattered all over a playing field and intermingled with members of the opposition; if relevant at all, spatial relations are less important than cooperative activity towards a common objective. Similarly, a *set* or *class* is defined by some kind of commonality regardless of where (and whether) its members are located in space. It is not obviously reasonable to speak of a boundary, and the concept of shape seems altogether inappropriate.

One might try to bridge the differences in profiling between *archipelago* and *team* by claiming that nouns like *team*, *set*, and *class* do indeed involve spatial (or quasi-spatial) bounding. In conceptualizing a team, for example, I tend to visualize them huddled together plotting strategy or posing for a team picture. Even for a class defined by an abstract property, e.g. the set of odd numbers, I can hardly avoid the image of the entities in question being extracted from a larger population of diverse objects and assembled into a compact spatial group whose peripheral members are linked by closure to form a virtual boundary (in the fashion of *archipelago*). Spatial metaphors and mental transformations of this kind are undeniably important to the semantics of the collective-noun class.

I doubt that spatial bounding tells the whole story, however. I have already suggested (4.3) that abstract conceptions of motion, directionality, and distance are linguistically important, and are in fact presupposed by an explicit account of spatial metaphor. A semantic characterization of the collective-noun class requires comparably abstract definitions of bounding, and more fundamentally, of what constitutes a region. These definitions should accommodate regions in space and spatial bounding as prototypical instantiations, and yet be applicable to the full spectrum of abstract domains. We should not expect any direct analog of shape at this highly schematic level, inasmuch as shape is tied more closely to spatial domains.

5.3. An Abstract Characterization

Our abstract characterizations of motion, directionality, and distance prove applicable to an extremely broad array of linguistic phenomena. They derive their flexibility from the fact that they refer directly to cognitive events (e.g. transition chains). This is also the level at which it is possible to achieve workable notional definitions of basic grammatical categories: we must focus our attention not on conceived entities per se, but rather on the cognitive events whose occurrence constitutes their conception. Couched in these terms, an appropriate schematic characterization of the [THING] category is capable of accommodating both count and mass nouns, as well as nouns whose content is highly abstract (e.g. deverbal nominalizations).

5.3.1. *Interconnectedness*

The defining property of a nominal predication is that it designates a **region** in some domain. Presumably this exhausts the content of the [THING] schema: no restrictions are placed on the domain (i.e. the domain specification is itself fully schematic), bounding is neither specified nor precluded, and nothing specific is attributed to the profiled region other than the very fact that it qualifies as a region. But what is a region? We can no longer rely on an intuitive, spatially grounded understanding of the notion. We require instead an explicit characterization compatible with the full class of nominal predications. To be viable, this characterization must refer to cognitive events.

A region will be defined as a **set of interconnected entities**. The requisite notion of interconnection is explicated with reference to event coordination (4.3.4): conceived entities are **interconnected** when the cognitive events constituting their conception are coordinated as components of a higher-level event. Recall that events are coordinated in a variety of ways: by simple association, through various operations (e.g. scanning, focal adjustment), or by incorporation as constituents of a more elaborate conception (e.g. a conceived relationship). It is important to observe that these interconnections (i.e. the coordinating operations or relationships) are not themselves profiled by a nominal predication; they serve to establish a set of entities as a region, but are not per se constitutive of the region. Note further that the profiling of the interconnected entities is collective: the region as a whole (the full *set* of entities) functions as the designatum and constitutes one instance of the [THING] category.

Certain matters require clarification before the intended import of this characterization can be assessed. First, the term **entity** must be understood in a maximally general sense. I use it as a convenient cover term for anything we might conceive of or refer to for analytical purposes: things, relations, locations, points on a scale, sensations, interconnections, values, etc. It is especially important to note that an entity is not necessarily discrete, separately recognized, or cognitively salient. With respect to Fig. 5.5(a), for example, the entities that constitute a dark spot can be identified as color sensations associated with various locations in the visual field. This does not imply, however, that the viewer perceives the spot as a constellation of individuated dots at any stage or level of processing; it is only claimed that input from different locations is coordinated to produce the spatially extended sensation.

Next, I assume that any concept involving continuous extension along some parameter necessarily incorporates a transition chain whose occurrence constitutes the conception of this extensionality. The conception of a line, for instance, is assumed to include at some level of processing an event sequence representing its continuous one-dimensional extensionality. Similarly, the perception of a dark spot involves scanning chains establishing the omnidirectional continuity of the dark sensation throughout a certain portion of the visual field. Transition chains representing the spatial extension of material substance are posited for the conception of physical objects, and more abstractly, the absence of a specified activity is scanned through conceived time for nouns like *intermission, pause,* and *halftime*.

Once these points are understood, it is apparent that the definition of a region as a set of interconnected entities is potentially applicable to the diverse nominal predications considered in 5.2. The definition accommodates continuous extensionality, and in fact the transition chains presumed responsible for the conception of this extensionality are themselves sufficient to establish the interconnectedness of the entities concerned, irrespective of their character and degree of individuation (possibly zero). Also accommodated, however, are cases that are problematic so long as our conception of a region retains the limitations suggested by its spatial origin.

Consider some examples. It is not obvious that an *alphabet* constitutes a region in anything approaching the spatial sense of the term, but it certainly qualifies under our abstract definition: the individual letters are interconnected by virtue of the transition chain representing the knowledge of their proper sequencing. Although the noun *constellation* is in some respects parallel to *forest* and *archipelago*, it differs in that the component stars need not form a spatially contiguous cluster; they can be distributed over a large area of the nighttime sky, and even lie interspersed with stars that are "external" to the constellation. The component stars cohere as an abstract region because a cognitive routine effects their interconnection as points in a schematic image. The members of a *team* are interconnected through their role as participants in a conceived relationship, namely a cooperative effort towards the attainment of a common goal.

Many nouns resemble *team* in emphasizing functional interrelations, where each member of a collective entity is conceived as having a specific role within an integrated whole: some examples are *orchestra, ensemble, quartet, crew, cast, staff, jigsaw puzzle, deck of cards, league, place setting, army,* and *family. Set* has comparable import in one of its senses (*set of golf clubs, set of china, set of false teeth*). What about *set* in its categorical sense, and similar terms, such as *class*? To the extent that spatial metaphor is not constitutive of their conception, the attribution of a common property or schematic characterization establishes the requisite interconnections among the members. When an arbitrary class is specified by stipulation, the very act of enumerating its members serves to interconnect them.

If entities are interconnected merely by their co-conception, it would seem that virtually any combination of entities has the potential to be construed as a region and designated by a noun. That this is not beyond reason is suggested by the ability of some people (including philosophers, mathematicians, and the authors of textbooks on set theory) to devise and label heterogeneous classes whose members have nothing significant in common. However, the absence of absolute restrictions does not imply that every theoretically possible region is equally natural. The likelihood of interconnection for a particular array of entities is doubtless determined by a variety of cognitive factors, an obvious one being proximity within a domain. Moreover, out of the countless regions that emerge in the course of cognitive processing, only a tiny proportion ever achieve sufficient entrenchment, cognitive salience, and communicative utility to be established as the profile of a nominal predication. Hence the generality of the definition is not intrinsically at variance with differences in the relative prototypicality of nominal expressions or with the strong tendency for certain types of phenomena to be construed as regions and designated by nouns.

A set of entities approaches optimality as a region as the **density** of their interconnections increases, and as their **cognitive distance** decreases.[10] In domains with continuous extensionality, these factors favor the emergence of regions whose component entities show a compact, preferably continuous distribution. It is not entirely accidental, then, that we have a monomorphemic nominal expression (*spot*) for the configuration in Fig. 5.5(a), which is optimal in this regard, but none for an otherwise comparable configuration involving separate discolored areas scattered about the visual field. Similarly, we have the term *intermission* for a single hiatus between segments of a performance, but we must resort to a composite expression (e.g. the plural *intermissions*) to designate the full amount of unoccupied time during a performance with multiple pauses. Whereas nouns like *archipelago* show that a discontinuous region certainly can be designated by a noun, *island* is closer to the category prototype, and a set of islands is most easily construed as an archipelago when their distribution is compact. And we hardly expect to find in any language a noun that designates a fancied region consisting of the hump of a camel in the morning, the letter R in the afternoon, and a color television set at night.

[10] On the basis of psychological research, Gentner (1981, 1982) has speculated that perceptual elements packaged into "noun referents" (physical objects in particular) are very cohesive in the sense of having many internal relations to one another, whereas those packaged into "verb referents" are more sparsely distributed through the perceptual field and have fewer internal relations. She explains a number of behavioral, acquisitional, and linguistic differences between nouns and verbs in terms of the claim that object concepts have a greater density of internal "links" or relationships than do similarly basic relational concepts, and that the ratio of internal links to external links is higher for object concepts.

The same factors, taken conversely, are relevant to bounding. A region is **bounded** when there is some limit to the set of interconnected entities it comprises, i.e. it does not extend indefinitely. Bounding is optimal to the extent that the interconnections among "internal" entities are of maximal density and minimal distance, while those between internal and "external" entities are of minimal density and maximal distance (at least in aggregate terms). Let us see how this works in a few specific instances.

A *constellation* is bounded because only a small, fixed set of stars participate in defining the schematic image that interconnects them. The scanning operations responsible for this shape conception associate particular stars to the exclusion of others in the same region of the sky (despite their possible intermingling). With reference to these operations, then, the component stars all connect with one another (at least in pairwise fashion), but not with any neighboring, nonconstellation stars. The stars of the constellation thus constitute a bounded region, with interconnections of variable distance among its members, but no interconnections at all between members and nonmembers. To be sure, various sorts of interconnections can be established between members and nonmembers: we can assess their spatial proximity, note that they instantiate the same category (*star*), and so forth. However, the predication in question structures the scene by seizing upon a specific type of interconnection for the characterization of its profile.

Team is fairly similar to *constellation*. Its domain is a population of individuals capable of pursuing objectives and interacting in various ways. The relevant interconnections are established through co-participation of members in the conceived relationship of cooperative interaction towards a common objective. There is no absolute requirement that every team member interact with every other in this fashion, or that there be no such interaction between members and nonmembers (a player on one team can help a member of the opposition to his feet). Still, a set of individuals approaches optimality as a team as their interconnections approach maximal density (every member cooperating with every other), and as comparable interconnections with nonmembers are minimized. A team is not generally recognized as such unless their efforts towards a common goal set them apart from other people in this regard.

It is not specifically required, for a region to be bounded, that it stand in contrast with its surroundings (i.e. that the scope of predication include both members and nonmembers among its salient entities). It is only required that the component entities be limited in some fashion; the limit may be imposed by either internal or external factors. A *constellation*, for example, is often recognizable on the basis of its internal configuration alone—the presence of nonmember stars merely complicates the task of construing the component stars with reference to the proper schematic image. Similarly, the bounding of an *alphabet* is effected solely on the basis of internal relationships among its component letters: the existence of a specified initial letter (which is not the target of any letter-to-letter transition), and also of a final letter (which is not the origin of any transition). It is not by virtue of any salient contrast with its "surroundings" that an alphabet constitutes a bounded region.

Spot lies at the opposite pole of the spectrum: a spot can be internally homogeneous, and its bounding is effected solely through contrast with its background. The component entities are color sensations associated with various points in the visual field. With respect to distribution in the visual field, the region defined by these entities must display connectivity, i.e. uninterrupted scanning chains must lead through the field from any one entity to any other (at least potentially). Moreover, the optimality of a discolored region as a category exemplar correlates with its compactness—a roughly circular discoloration is far more prototypical as a spot than a long thin one resembling a line (assuming both have equal areas). When a spot of given area is circular, the average distance through the visual field between its component entities is minimized, whereas the average distance between an internal point and the closest external point is maximized.

We must also consider cognitive distance with respect to color space. If a spot is uniform in color throughout, scanning chains through the discolored region register a value of zero for color parameters. When a component sensation is compared to one outside the region, on the other hand, a positive value is registered (i.e. a disparity is noted). It is natural to suggest that cognitive distance correlates with the magnitude of the disparity. Thus the distance between any two component sensations is zero for a spot of uniform color, whereas the distance between internal and external entities is nonzero and increases with the magnitude of their color contrast. The boundary of a spot is then determined by the distance of interconnections in color space: the boundary is so placed that internal distances are minimized, though distances between the "inside" and the "outside" are maximized. It follows that the optimality of a discolored region as a spot correlates positively with both the degree of its internal homogeneity and the magnitude of its divergence from the background color.

To obtain this result, we must refine our notion of a comparison event. As things presently stand, there is no correlation between cognitive distance and the magnitude of a perceived discrepancy: a single act of comparison $S > T$ has been posited (a transition chain with a length of one) regardless of how radically T might diverge from S. Instead, we want greater disparity between S and T to require a longer transition chain, hence greater distance. We can achieve this by resolving a single event $S > T$ into the sequence $[s_0 > s_1 >$

$s_2 > \cdots > s_i > \cdots > s_n]$, where $s_0 = S$, $s_n = T$, and each transition $s_i > s_{i+1}$ represents a quantum value for the scanning operation, i.e. a minimally detectable discrepancy along the parameter of comparison. When $s_n = s_0$ (that is, when no discrepancy at all is registered between standard and target), the distance value of transition $S > T$ is effectively zero.

5.3.2. Mass Nouns

A number of grammatical properties support the traditional distinction between count nouns and mass nouns. For example, only count nouns pluralize (*knobs*; **golds*); only count nouns take the indefinite article (*a knob*; **a gold*); only mass nouns occur with certain quantifiers (*a lot of gold*; **a lot of knob*); and only mass nouns occur as full noun phrases without any sort of determiner (*He found gold*; **He found knob*).[11] It is my contention that the count/mass distinction has a notional basis. A count noun designates a region that is specifically construed as being bounded within the scope of predication in a primary domain. By contrast, a mass noun designates a region that is not so construed.

Suggesting the plausibility of this characterization is the existence of many nouns for physical substances that can function in either category: *rock/a rock*; *brick/a brick*; *stone/a stone*; *fur/a fur*; *hide/a hide*; *glass/a glass*; *tile/a tile*; *cloth/a cloth*; *rope/a rope*; *diamond/a diamond*; *beer/a beer*; *ice cream/an ice cream*; etc. The relevant domain, in the case of physical substances, is space. When they function as mass nouns, these expressions simply name the substance without imposing any inherent limitation on its spatial extension. The corresponding count nouns do indeed imply a boundary; in each instance they designate a discrete object, bounded in space, that is composed of the substance in question. The specification of a boundary falls within the scope of predication, for it is essential to the identification of these objects.

Let us return to Fig. 5.5 for another sort of example. It was noted earlier that the sentence *I see a dark spot* is appropriate for the situation in diagram (a), but not the one in diagram (b). The interaction between bounding and scope of predication is responsible for this difference. *See* suggests the visual field as the scope of predication for its direct object, *spot*, which is a count noun and necessarily bounded. Diagram (a) accommodates this specification, but (b) does not, because only in the former are the boundaries delimiting the spot included within the scope of predication. Observe, however, that a sen-

---

[11] Proper names have special properties and are omitted from consideration. Observe that plurals behave like mass nouns: **a knobs*; *a lot of knobs*; *He found knobs in the drawer*. While pluralizability is a hallmark of count nouns, the plural forms that result constitute a special subclass within the mass-noun category.

tence like *I see (nothing but) black* is perfectly natural in the context of diagram (b), where a single color sensation totally suffuses the visual field. *Black*
functions as a mass noun in this sentence, designating a color sensation of
indefinite spatial extension. Hence there is nothing problematic about the absence of bounding in the scope of predication.[12]

The proposed characterization of mass nouns does not preclude the possibility of bounding for the designated region; bounding is just not specifically
imposed by the nominal predication itself. A mass noun is therefore compatible with the situation in Fig. 5.5(a) as well as 5.5(b): *I see (some) black*;
There's a lot of black in this picture. Often bounding is imposed by other
predications that occur in syntagmatic combination with a mass noun. Quantifiers commonly serve this function (*a little wine, some gravel, a cup of
flour*), but so can many other elements. For instance, in the sentence *Joyce ate
ice cream yesterday* the mass designated by the object nominal is bounded
through the interaction of all the other constituents: it is limited to ice cream
that was in existence yesterday, and of that to quantities a single person can
consume in one day. The complete absence of bounding is found only in expressions that are fully generic with respect to the designated mass (e.g. *Ice
cream is a dairy product*; *I'm doing a research paper on ice cream*).

The proposed characterization of the count/mass distinction accounts for
the fact that only count nouns pluralize. The region profiled by a count noun is
specifically bounded, i.e. there is some limit to the set of entities the region
comprises. Whether this limit is given by internal configuration (*alphabet*),
contrast with surroundings (*spot*), or a combination of the two, its existence
implies that at some point one instance of the category is exhausted, so that
further incrementation is possible only by initiating another instance. This
replicability—the possibility of multiple instances of the same category—is
precisely what pluralization demands. On the other hand, the region designated by a mass noun lacks this property of replicability because there is no
specification of bounding. In surveying such a region, one never reaches the
point where a single instance of the category is definitely exhausted. The profiled mass extends without inherent limit, and consequently grows by expansion rather than replication.

I will say that the designatum of a mass noun displays indefinite **expansibility** and **contractibility**. Given a volume of *water*, for instance, we can
add more and more water to it, and the resulting mass is still properly identified by that term. In similar fashion, we can remove as much water as we like
from the initial volume, but we still have *water* if any at all remains. Consequently, any subpart of the designated mass—however large or small—counts

---

[12] Sentences like these are similar: *I see nothing but water*; *I hear only silence*; *There is sand
all around*; *There is rubble everywhere you look.* In each case a mass fully occupies the relevant
scope of predication and remains unbounded within it.

as a valid instance of the category (cf. Carlson 1981).[13] This is not in general the case with the entities designated by count nouns. Arbitrary fragments of a pencil or a cat certainly do not qualify as unproblematic, nondegraded instances of the *pencil* or *cat* categories.

The source of indefinite expansibility and contractibility, I suggest, is the effective **homogeneity** of a mass. It cannot be maintained that a mass is always homogeneous in any strict literal sense—only that it is *construed* as homogeneous for expressive purposes, i.e. its internal variability is not in focus as a salient or explicit matter of predication. Instead, the focus is on properties that (within limits) can be recognized in portions of arbitrary size and that distinguish the designated mass from other substances. This construal of effective homogeneity in fact establishes the mass as a region.

There are two respects in which a mass is not homogeneous in any strict sense: (1) it may be individuated to some degree; and (2) its various subportions (regardless of individuation) may not be precisely identical. Progressively greater individuation is illustrated within the sequence *water* > *dust* > *sand* > *grass* > *tile* > *cattle* > *timber*. My suggestion here is that the categorization of these expressions as mass nouns reflects a canonical construal in which the scope of predication is quite large relative to the size of individual members. The mass is then effectively homogeneous in the sense that any subregion (of a certain minimal size) is equivalent to any other in containing multiple representatives. *Grass*, for instance, calls to mind a lawnlike expanse, where more blades than one would care to count are observed regardless of what portion is examined.[14] Individual blades are readily apparent, but the predication highlights those respects in which the mass displays internal uniformity.

The same is true in regard to different subportions not being precisely identical. Speakers realize that water is variable in certain specific properties, that no two blades of grass are alike in all respects, and that cattle have individual personalities (for those who concern themselves with such matters); the important thing, though, is that an expression such as *water*, *grass*, or *cattle* ignores these points of variation, and construes the component entities at a level of schematicity that ensures their uniformity. The requisite abstraction is more extreme in cases like *equipment* and *furniture*, where the component entities may be highly diverse, but its fundamental character is the same. The heterogeneous objects that count as pieces of equipment or furniture are

---

[13] A fully generic construal of a mass-noun category can be taken as maximally expansive. At the opposite extreme, contractibility is limited by the requirement that enough of the substance remain to preserve its identifying properties. In the case of water, for instance, a single H_2O molecule is the absolute minimum for a valid instantiation.

[14] Nothing prevents this canonical construal from being modified or even overridden by other predications in a complex expression; the image embodied by this initial lexicalization represents only the first step in a longer compositional path (cf. Ch. 8).

equivalent given an appropriately schematic representation,[15] so the designated mass is effectively homogeneous when construed in this fashion.

We have concentrated on mass nouns designating physical substances, for which space appears to be the primary domain, at least in the sense that the absence of inherent spatial bounding determines their mass-noun status. Note that the bounding imposed by a quantifier generally restricts the designation of these nouns to a spatially limited portion (i.e. a limited volume) of the potentially available mass (*a little water, some gravel, a dab of glue*). In the case of count nouns, we observed (5.2.1) that the bounding responsible for their categorization often occurs in just one of the occupied domains (e.g. *flash* is bounded in time but not in the visual field). It should therefore come as no surprise that a mass noun can perfectly well be bounded in a secondary domain.

The specific domain I have in mind is quite abstract, and might be called **quality space**. It is defined by ranges of alternative properties that an entity or substance might possess, with respect to which comparisons can be made. At least for the sake of discussion, we can think of quality space as a multidimensional domain organized in terms of specific qualitative parameters (solidity, color, taste, discreteness/continuity, texture, and so on). A substance can then be characterized as having a restricted range of possible values along each applicable parameter, and a predication designating a substance does so by profiling a region that is bounded to one degree or another (depending on its level of schematicity) along a certain number of dimensions in this abstract domain.

This notion allows us to characterize a behavior of certain mass nouns, among them *wine*, *glue*, and *beer*. Specifically, they are employed as count nouns (N) with the approximate semantic value 'brand or type of N': *They have several dry wines in stock; We need a strong glue to fix the cabinet; Most beers have too much malt.* Bounding is implied, but it can hardly be the spatial bounding of examples like *I'll have a beer.* My proposal is that these extended senses of *wine*, *glue*, etc. reflect a reranking of domains, where quality space supplants physical space as the primary domain determining basic categorization.

Consider the predications constituting the semantic pole of *wine* as a mass noun and a count noun, respectively, i.e. the relation between [WINE] and [WINE']. [WINE] designates a substance whose physical extension is primary, but which also occupies a circumscribed region of quality space; let us call this region W. Since the count-noun sense [WINE'] indicates a 'type' or 'brand' of wine, quality space is primary, and W defines its scope of predication. [WINE'] does not profile W as a whole, but rather some bounded region

---

[15] In the case of *furniture*, for instance, the component elements are specified as falling within a particular size range; as being permanent artifacts in a dwelling; as being potentially movable (not built-in); and as having certain general types of functions.

within it, W', that is obtained by narrowing certain specifications of W to encompass a more restricted range of possible values. Because it profiles a bounded region within the scope of predication in its primary domain, [[WINE']/[wine]] is a count noun and behaves accordingly. However, no particular restriction of values is specified (it is specified only that they are restricted in some fashion, i.e. that W' is a proper subpart of W), so a given construal of W' is nonunique. Pluralization is therefore possible: I can speak of many different *wines*, each with special (but contrastive) properties relative to the generic, mass-noun term.

5.3.3. *Abstract Nouns*

A comprehensive analysis of the many sorts of abstract nouns lies outside the scope of this work. Only limited discussion is offered, focusing on the relevance to abstract nouns of the count/mass distinction. It is intended only to establish the plausibility of accommodating abstract count and mass nouns under the schematic definitions advanced earlier.

It is well known that the count/mass distinction applies to abstract nouns, but the significance of this fact is perhaps not sufficiently appreciated. By way of illustration, the following deverbal nominalizations are all count nouns that designate a single episode of the process indicated by the verb stem: *jump, walk, drink, dance, complaint, fight, argument, throw, turn, yell,* and *descent*. Many nominalizations, on the other hand, behave as mass nouns: *jumping, despair, destruction, love, hope, concern, sleep, help, procrastination, envy*, etc. (Some nominalizations can of course function in either class.) If the count/mass distinction is an arbitrary grammatical classification, then its applicability to abstract nouns holds little interest. However, if the distinction has a conceptual basis, then its applicability is of considerable interest, for it strongly suggests that abstract nouns—like their more concrete counterparts—designate regions that can be either bounded or unbounded.

Given how abstractly the relevant notions have been defined, their potential applicability to nominalizations is not really surprising. Consider the episodic interpretation of deverbal count nouns: *His first jump was impressive*; *She gave out a yell*; *He made a good throw*. Each of these nominal concepts is defined in terms of a process that functions as its base. A process predication describes the evolution of a configuration through conceived time; it is resolvable into an ordered sequence of component states whose temporal distribution is continuous (cf. 4.3 and Ch. 7). By definition, an episodic nominalization refers to just a single instance of the process, i.e. a single pass through the component states. I suggest, in fact, that the bounded region it designates has these component states as its constitutive entities. These entities are interconnected because they are scanned continuously and sequentially through processing time, with each employed as a standard of comparison for evaluating its successor. This interconnection establishes them as a region, which is bounded because the processes in question have both an initial and a final state.

Episodic count nouns like *jump* are instructively compared to mass nouns derived from the same stem. A noun like *jumping* does not describe a single episode of the process, but instead refers to it in a generalized, even generic fashion: *Jumping is good for the leg muscles but very hard on the knees.* Jumping is therefore neither continuous nor bounded in time, being instantiated whenever some instance of the base process occurs. It is analogous in this respect to a physical substance: the maximal reference of *water*, for instance, is neither continuous nor bounded in space, but lies scattered about in lakes, rivers, puddles, drops, and oceans; the category is instantiated wherever there is some quantity of a substance with certain properties (as characterized in quality space). Moreover, because it represents a single type of process, jumping is readily construed as being effectively homogeneous. Recognition of this common processual source provides a qualitative unity to instantiations of jumping and establishes them as a region, just as a physical substance like water qualifies as a region by virtue of qualitative homogeneity rather than spatial distribution.

These limited remarks on abstract mass nouns are at best programmatic. They do however suggest that it may not be vacuous to regard *jumping*, *destruction*, *love*, *hope*, *concern*, *envy*, etc. as abstract "substances" analogous in many ways to physical substances. It is worth observing, in this connection, that many dimensions of quality space posited for physical substances pertain to interactive experience with these substances and most likely derive from processual concepts. Rigidity, for example, is a parameter that characterizes and differentiates such substances as rock, wood, plastic, cloth, and so on. When we explore the conceptual basis for the concept of rigidity, it is hard to avoid referring to what happens when we try to bend an object or otherwise deform it.

5.4. Spatial Bounding and Shape

I have adopted an abstract notion of bounding that neither implies nor requires an external perimeter of the sort that defines shape in spatial domains. For instance, the cooperative interaction that unites the members of a *team* also sets them apart from other persons with whom they do not so interact, but a team has no specific shape (in the usual sense of the term); neither is it divided into interior and peripheral members, with only the latter coming into contact with external entities.

The related notions of spatial boundaries and shape are nevertheless of prime importance for the semantic value of prototypical nouns. Shape is a highly intrinsic property of physical objects, and is salient and characteristic for many spatial entities. It is therefore appropriate that shape specifications receive at least preliminary explication in terms of the kinds of cognitive processes considered earlier. To keep things simple, we will confine our attention at first to a single example of minimal complexity. Let us thus return to our stock illustration: the perception of a dark spot in an otherwise uniformly white visual field.

What kinds of cognitive events are required? Acts of comparison are crucial, since the registration of contrast is obviously fundamental to this example. Consider the comparison of two cognitive events A and B, where A is a brightness sensation associated with one point in the visual field, and B is that associated with an adjacent point. If the comparison $A > B$ is carried out for both location and brightness, then V_{AB} (the vector value of the scanning operation) has two components: the registration of positional disparity (which can be further resolved into the subcomponents of direction and distance); and the registration of any brightness contrast (possibly zero). I will represent the components of location and brightness in the formula $V_{AB} = (P, Q)$, where P is mnemonic for "position" in a configurational domain, and Q is mnemonic for "quality," i.e. location in a nonconfigurational domain. The value P is therefore not the position of A or B in the visual field, but rather the value of their positional discrepancy, as embodied in the scanning operation connecting them; similarly, Q is the value of the contrast in brightness between A and B rather than the absolute value of either one along this parameter.

The essential elements in our example are depicted in Fig. 5.8, where the box delimits the visual field and arrows represent different kinds of complex scanning operations. All of them are chains of scanning events of the form

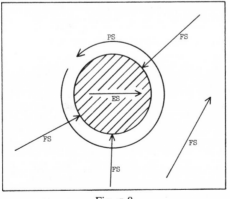

Fig. 5.8

$(A > B > C > D > \cdots)$, where the target for one component event is the standard for the next. Let us begin with **field scanning** (*FS*), and in particular with the isolated arrow at the right. Starting from an arbitrary point A in the visual field, comparison with an adjacent point B yields some nonzero value (i.e. registers a discrepancy) for the locational parameter, but a zero value (judgment of identity) for the brightness parameter. Letting x and y stand for nonzero values of P and Q respectively, we can represent this as follows: $V_{AB} = (xP, oQ)$. The occurrence of a cognitive event facilitates its recurrence, and since the scanning operation connecting A and B is a cognitive event, its occurrence in the comparison $A > B$ facilitates its recurrence in the comparison $B > C$, where C has the same positional displacement from B that B has from A, i.e. $V_{AB} = V_{BC} = (xP, oQ)$. In this way a scanning operation with the vector value (xP, oQ) can be perpetuated in a straight line through the visual field, and the chain $(A > B > C > D > \cdots)$ amounts to the perception of uniform brightness along the path. By hypothesis, most of the randomly occurring scanning chains through the field are of this type, since the field is for the most part uniformly white.

Let us now shift our attention to **expanse scanning** (ES), which is analogous to field scanning, except that it occurs within the dark region instead of the surrounding background area. The absolute value for the brightness parameter is different, but once again a scanning chain—so long as it is confined to the dark area—has a constant vector value of the form (xP, oQ). The occurrence of such chains constitutes the perception that the dark region has some extension in the visual field rather than being limited to a single point. Moreover, these chains establish the qualitative uniformity of the dark area as well as its spatial connectivity, thereby accounting for its recognition as a region.

The scanning chains encountered thus far establish the existence of a bright region and a dark region in the visual field, but nothing has yet been said about the relation between them. Obviously some of the randomly occurring scanning chains register a contrast in brightness; when continuation along a path results in the comparison of a white point with an adjacent dark point, a positive value is registered for both the locational and the brightness parameters: $V = (xP, yQ)$. If the dark region is sufficiently small, most of the scanning chains of this sort originate in the white region, and the dark point responsible for the contrast is consequently the target in the comparison event that registers the contrast; several field-scanning chains of this nature are indicated in Fig. 5.8. Because it is the target in the preponderance of scanning events registering a contrast, the dark region stands out as figure against the white background rather than the converse (cf. 3.3.2). It is thus the dark area that is recognized as a bounded region.

The final type of scanning indicated in Fig. 5.8 is **periphery scanning** (PS). This is a higher-order comparison chain that constitutes the perception of a boundary, i.e. an interface between two regions. It presupposes the registration of contrast between adjacent points by field scanning, and amounts to recognition of the boundary as a continuous and unified entity. Note that the boundary line between a bright region and a dark region consists of neither bright points nor dark points alone, but is formed by the contrast between contiguous points. I will say that the boundary consists of a continuous series of **boundary points**, each defined by two adjacent points in the domain, between which a contrast is registered. Because the boundary points it associates are higher-order entities (established by first-order comparison), periphery scanning amounts to higher-order comparison.

To see how this might work, let us assume momentarily that the boundary between the bright and dark regions is a straight line. The component points along the border in the bright region can be given as $(A_1, A_2, A_3, ...)$, and their contiguous counterparts along the border in the dark region, as $(B_1, B_2, B_3, ...)$. Then $(A_1 > B_1)$, $(A_2 > B_2)$, $(A_3 > B_3)$, and so on are the boundary points that constitute the interface. Each boundary point $(A_i > B_i)$ on the line terminates a first-order field-scanning chain and has the vector value (xP, yQ), i.e. a contrast in brightness is registered between the adjacent points A_i and B_i. In the simplest kind of situation, this vector value is identical for every boundary point $(A_i > B_i)$ along the interface. The brightness disparity (yQ) is constant throughout under the assumption that the brightness within each region is uniform. Since adjacent points are compared in each instance, the distance component of the locational discrepancy (xP) is consistently positive but minimal, and its directional component is invariant provided that the boundary line is straight.

Inasmuch as periphery scanning—the perception of the total boundary as a continuous, linelike entity extending through the visual field—is a higher-order comparison chain that operates on the first-order comparison events $(A_i > B_i)$ defining the points of the boundary, the form of the chain is thus $((A_1 > B_1) > (A_2 > B_2) > (A_3 > B_3) > \cdots)$. For each link $((A_i > B_i) > (A_{i+1} > B_{i+1}))$ in the chain, a comparison is made with respect to two parameters, which we can label P' and Q', since they are analogous to P and Q in the first-order comparison chains but pertain to higher-order relationships. The parameter P' is simply the positional discrepancy between the boundary points $(A_i > B_i)$ and $(A_{i+1} > B_{i+1})$ in the visual field; this has some nonzero value, and insofar as the boundary is a straight line the value remains constant for each higher-order comparison. The parameter Q' is the discrepancy in quality between the boundary points, where "quality" is to be interpreted as (yQ), i.e. as the contrast in brightness registered in the first-order comparisons $(A_i > B_i)$ and $(A_{i+1} > B_{i+1})$. By assumption, Q' has a zero value throughout, for all the boundary points along the interface have the same (internal) brightness contrast. We can let z stand for a nonzero higher-order comparison value; each higher-order act of comparison in the periphery-scanning chain therefore has the form $((A_i > B_i) > (A_{i+1} > B_{i+1})) = (zP', oQ')$.

Under our simplifying assumption that the boundary is a straight line, periphery scanning is essentially a higher-order equivalent of the basic examples of field and expanse scanning that we began our discussion with. But now it is time to discard the simplifying assumption and return to Fig. 5.8, where the boundary is curved rather than straight. The effect of this curvature is that the value of P' is still identical at each step in the comparison chain with respect to distance (adjacent boundary points are still being compared), but not with respect to direction. The directional discrepancy of P' may well be negligible from one pair of boundary points to the next, but the cumulative effect is substantial, for it permits the boundary line between the two regions to close on itself, making the dark area a bounded region in the fullest sense. This occurs when the first-order comparison event $(A_1 > B_1)$ initiates the higher-order periphery-scanning chain by serving as standard at its first stage and yet also serves as target in a later (possibly final) stage.

It is readily apparent that periphery scanning bears a close relation to shape. The strongest claim, in fact, would simply equate periphery scanning and shape perception, attributing differences in perceived shape to differences in the responsible scanning chains.[16] Matters are not this simple, however. Even if something akin to periphery scanning is a fundamental aspect of shape conceptualization, considerably more is required than a single scanning operation around the periphery of a bounded region. Let us conclude our discussion by glancing at a few of the complicating factors.

One class of problems arises as soon as we go beyond maximally simple examples like Fig. 5.8 to consider more prototypical instances of shape conceptions. For one thing, nothing has been said about three-dimensional shapes. A three-dimensional analog of periphery scanning can be envisaged, but that alone would tell only part of the story. Also to be accounted for is our capacity to recognize a familiar shape despite variations in vantage point, orientation, and distance, and further, to accommodate shape transformations in the perceived object itself (e.g. when an animal changes posture). Additionally it is worth noting that physical objects—despite their concreteness and prototypicality—are rather abstract in certain fundamental respects. Internal heterogeneity often precludes there being any single perceptual property (comparable to degree of brightness in Fig. 5.8) that sets an object off from its surroundings at every point around its periphery. The fact that all parts of a physical object typically move in tandem relative to its environment, maintaining their internal relationships in the process, is sometimes quite important to its recognition, yet this property is both complex and abstract. A physical object normally possesses the property of blocking visual access to

---

[16] The path of periphery scanning is determined by the directional component of P' for transitions in the scanning chain. Changes in shape are therefore generated by altering the value of this component for various links.

anything lying behind it; it also perseveres through time, resists physical penetration and separation, and so on. All these properties are basic to human interaction, but none is simply or directly definable with reference to a basic domain.

Even restricting our attention to two-dimensional shapes we find added complexities. It is unrealistic to think that our conception of a complex shape resides solely in the execution of a single periphery-scanning operation around its perimeter. More likely the processing of complex shapes involves operations at different levels of schematicity. In mastering a complex figure, e.g. the outline of a state such as California or Tennessee, we might first observe only that it is relatively long and narrow—a highly schematic shape specification that is quite vague about the nature of the perimeter. Further examination might reveal that certain segments are straight lines while others are curved and irregular. Only later (if at all) might it become apparent that two straight sides form a right angle, that there is a slight jog in one of the otherwise straight sides, that the irregular portions of the boundary form a particular configuration, and so on. We can plausibly suppose that all of these specifications, at different levels of schematicity, remain part of our knowledge of a complex shape even after it has been mastered in detail.

CHAPTER 6

Atemporal Relations

LINGUISTIC PREDICATIONS are either nominal or relational. A nominal predication designates a thing, and functions as the semantic pole of a noun. Relational predications divide into two basic groups, depending on whether they designate a **process** or an **atemporal relation**. Processual predications correspond to the class of verbs, and are analyzed in Ch. 7. The present chapter focuses on atemporal relations, corresponding to adjectives, adverbs, prepositions, and similar classes. We first consider how an atemporal relation differs from a thing (which is also atemporal). We then discuss the internal structure of a relational predication, with special reference to a small class of **basic conceptual relations**. Finally we explore some of the subtleties of the **trajector/landmark** asymmetry, which is fundamental to relational predications and underlies the distinction between subjects and objects.

6.1. Relational Profiles

What is an atemporal relation? Three aspects of this notion require explication: (1) the nature of a relational profile; (2) the asymmetry responsible for the subject/object distinction; and (3) what it means for a relation to be atemporal. We will consider them in that order.

6.1.1. *Things vs. Relations*

A nominal predication profiles a thing, i.e. a region in some domain, where a region is characterized abstractly as a set of interconnected entities. Fig. 6.1(a) diagrams such a predication. The component entities are shown as boxes, and the requisite interconnections as lines between them. Observe that these interconnections are not in profile, despite their importance in establishing the region; it is to the region per se that the special prominence of profiling attaches. The component entities partake of this prominence, but not individually, since their profiling is collective; to indicate this, I have enclosed the

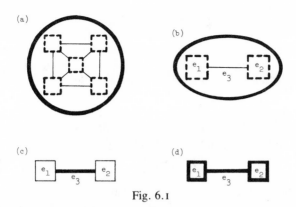

Fig. 6.1

region as a whole in a solid, heavy-line circle, using broken lines for the entities it comprises. A region approaches optimality as the density of its interconnections increases, and as the cognitive distances separating entities approximate zero. To the extent that it is optimal, the distinctness of component entities is subordinated to their place in what amounts to a continuous region of high activation.

In Fig. 6.1(b), I have reduced the configuration of diagram (a) to its simplest terms, namely the case of a region with only two component entities. I have also included labels for cognitive events: e_1 and e_2 stand for those events whose occurrence constitutes the conception of the component entities; e_3 represents the additional cognitive operations (e.g. scanning) responsible for the coordination of e_1 and e_2. By hypothesis, e_3 is activated at a lower level of intensity than e_1 and e_2, even if the component entities fail to be separately recognized.

If nominal predications crucially involve interconnections, what distinguishes them from relational predications? The essential difference, I maintain, is that a relational predication puts interconnections in profile (rather than simply presupposing them as part of the base). The distinction between a nominal and a relational predication does not necessarily imply any difference in the inventory or the organization of constituent events, but only in their relative prominence. In contrast to diagram (b), then, a relational predication has the minimal form of Fig. 6.1(c), where the coordinating operations e_3 are highly activated. Let me suggest one slight adjustment, however. Relations are **conceptually dependent**, i.e. one cannot conceptualize interconnections without also conceptualizing the entities that they interconnect (cf. 8.3). With respect to diagram (c), the interconnecting operations e_3 cannot occur without the supporting occurrence of e_1 and e_2. By the same token, e_3 presumably cannot achieve a high level of activation unless e_1 and e_2 are activated at a comparably high level. Fig. 6.1(d) is thus proposed for relational predications: the interconnected entities are treated as elements of the relational profile.

In summary, an optimal nominal predication profiles a unitary entity that is so construed because the cognitive operations providing interconnections among its constituents are minimal both in magnitude (i.e. their distance approximates zero) and in prominence (the interconnections are not themselves in profile). By contrast, a relational predication focuses on interconnections and profiles the cognitive events in which the conceptualization of these interconnections resides. A nominal and a relational predicate are therefore distinguished by the nature of their profiles even should they have the same entities and interconnections for their base. Suppose, for example, that e_3 represents an assessment of spatial proximity. The relational predicate [NEAR] is then obtained by imposing the profile of Fig. 6.1(d), whereas the profiling of Fig. 6.1(b) yields a special case of the nominal predicate [GROUP] (it designates a spatial group with just two members).

In subsequent diagrams, consequently, a nominal predication can be identified by its profiling of a single, continuous region of some kind, often simply represented as a circle (especially when its characterization is schematic). In the diagram for a relational predication, on the other hand, two or more distinct entities are commonly shown as profiled, together with their interconnections. In schematic representations like Fig. 6.1(d), these interconnections are shown with heavy lines. In more-elaborate diagrams, however, the relationships among participating entities are projected onto the two dimensions of the page (in accordance with transparent notational conventions); the nature of these relationships is thus conveyed by the relative position of participants within the diagram, and need not be separately indicated.

Let us consider some specific examples. Fig. 6.2(a) shows the semantic value of [RED] in one of its nominal uses (e.g. *Red is a warm color*), where it

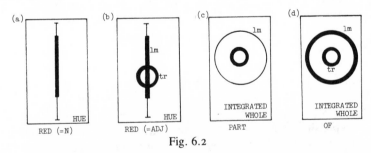

Fig. 6.2

designates a region in color space (the hue dimension being primary). Contrasting with this nominal predication is [RED] in its adjectival use, diagrammed in Fig. 6.2(b). The region profiled in (a) is also profiled in (b), but

(b) is relational and locates a second profiled entity (represented by a circle) within this region. Since the relative position of the two profiled entities is given directly in the diagram, there is no need to show it separately (e.g. by a line connecting them), even though this relationship is itself an essential aspect of the profile.[1] Diagrams (c) and (d) of Fig. 6.2 depict the contrast between [PART] as a noun and one sense of the preposition [OF] (as in *part of the wall*—cf. Langacker 1982a). Each of these predicates has for its base the conception of an integrated whole, which is represented by the outer circle in (c) and (d). *Part* designates a restricted portion of this integrated whole, but aside from this specification it is fully schematic; its profile is identified only as a bounded region contained within the larger configuration at an arbitrary location. *Of* imposes a relational profile on the same base. Both entities shown in (c) are profiled in (d), as is their interconnecting relationship, which is indicated diagrammatically by the inclusion of one entity inside the other.

6.1.2. *Trajector vs. Landmark*

In virtually every relational predication,[2] an asymmetry can be observed between the profiled participants. One of them, called the **trajector** (*tr*), has special status and is characterized as the **figure within a relational profile** (see 6.3.1 for discussion). The term trajector suggests motion, and in processual predications describing physical activity (presumably the prototype for relations) the trajector generally does move through a spatial trajectory. Note, however, that the definition makes no reference at all to motion, either physical or abstract, so this schematic description is applicable to both static and dynamic relations. Other salient entities in a relational predication are referred to as **landmarks** (*lm*), so called because they are naturally viewed (in prototypical instances) as providing points of reference for locating the trajector. The notions subject and object prove to be special cases of trajector and landmark respectively, but separate terms are needed for the general case if confusion is to be avoided.

It is common for there to be multiple landmarks in a relational predication. Two examples are sketched in Fig. 6.3, [WITH] and the variant of [ACROSS] found in sentences like *There's a mailbox across the street*. *With* situates its trajector in the **neighborhood** of its landmark; this neighborhood can itself be regarded as a kind of landmark.[3] *Across* locates its trajector on the opposite

---

[1] The location of an entity in color space is unproblematic when this entity is a color sensation (as in *red flash* or *red light*), since the domain of color space is defined by such sensations. For the treatment of other cases (e.g. *red table*), see 7.3.4 and Langacker 1984.

[2] Certain conjunctions are possible exceptions.

[3] Note the composite expressions *within* and *without* (e.g. *Please wait within/without*), where *-in* and *-out* imply a bounding enclosure. The broken arrow in Fig. 6.3(b) indicates potential or hypothetical movement, possibly subjective movement by the speaker (cf. 4.3.2).

side of one landmark relative to a point of reference (a second landmark) normally equated with the position of the speaker unless otherwise specified. The multiple landmarks of a complex relational predicate generally differ in their salience; I have noted this diagrammatically in Fig. 6.3 by leaving the neighborhood in (a) and the reference point in (b) unprofiled. I should emphasize,

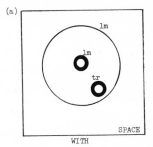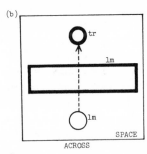

Fig. 6.3

though, that no strict dichotomy is contemplated: as a type of prominence, profiling is reasonably considered a matter of degree. For diagrammatic convenience it is necessary to depict an entity of only secondary salience either as profiled (in heavy lines) or unprofiled, but no particular significance should be attached to where the cutoff is chosen in these informal diagrams.

It is important, however, to distinguish between a relational predicate whose profile details the interconnections between two distinct entities, and a nominal predicate in which an unprofiled entity figures prominently in the base. We have already seen this in the contrast between *of* and *part* (Fig. 6.2), the former a relational predicate and the latter a **relational noun**. *Part* profiles only a schematically characterized internal region of a larger entity (also schematic); this larger entity is not in profile, but it is obviously a salient facet of the base and is reasonably regarded as a landmark. Another example is *uncle* (Fig. 5.2), which designates one participant in a kinship network but relies crucially on another (ego) for its landmark. Although English *uncle* is a noun, its counterpart in another language could perfectly well be relational: by additionally profiling ego as well as the interconnections between the two nodes (and making the "uncle" node the trajector), one obtains a relational predicate with the approximate value '(be) an uncle to'. One virtue of this framework is how straightforwardly it captures both the similarities and the differences between variants of a morpheme that represent different parts of speech (note also the nominal and adjectival *red* in Fig. 6.2).

Two relational predicates may be essentially identical apart from their trajector/landmark assignation. An example is [ABOVE] vs. [BELOW], sketched in Fig. 6.4. Their domain is abstract, for it involves the organization

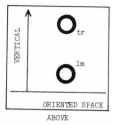 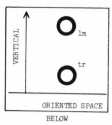

Fig. 6.4

of space into horizontal and vertical dimensions. The only substantial differ-ence between the two predicates is that an expression of the form *X is above Y* takes *Y* as a point of reference (landmark) for locating *X*, while *Y is below X* takes *X* as a point of reference for locating *Y*. This is analyzed as a figure/ground contrast (since the trajector is the figure in a relational profile), and amounts to the imposition of slightly different images on the same scene. It is important to observe that trajectors and landmarks are internal structures within a relational predication, and bear no necessary relation to other expres-sions that it combines with syntagmatically. *Below*, for instance, designates an atemporal relation with a profiled trajector and landmark regardless of whether the latter is spelled out by an explicit nominal (*Those clouds are be-low the airplane; There are clouds below*). Similarly, both *with* and *red* are relational predications each profiling at least two entities, but *with* requires explication of its landmark by a nominal object whereas *red* does not tolerate an explicit landmark. As an aspect of its internal structure, the profile of a predicate must be distinguished from its valence properties, though the two are naturally connected.

A relational predication profiles the interconnections among conceived en-tities. Since the term entity is understood in a maximally general way (5.3.1), this definition places no inherent restrictions on the nature of trajectors and landmarks. In particular, they need not be things, as they have been in all the examples considered so far, but can themselves consist of component rela-tions. There are four possible combinations given a relation of a trajector and a single landmark, and all four are readily found. The adjectival *red* has a thing for both its trajector and its landmark (the latter is the region in color space designated by the nominal *red*). *Fast* is considered adverbial rather than adjectival in its basic use (e.g. *She works fast*) because its trajector is a pro-cess (hence a relation) rather than a thing; its landmark is a region along a comparison scale for rate, and is thus construable as a thing, though it hap-pens not to be singled out as the profile of a nominal predicate (i.e. there is no noun *fast* parallel to the noun *red*). *Before* predicates a temporal relationship between two events (*She left before I arrived*), so both its trajector and its landmark are processual relations. The other possibility, where the trajector is a thing and the landmark a relation, is illustrated by certain uses of *want* and *appear* (*He wants to experiment further*; *Your sister appears intelligent*).

As notational devices, I will commonly use a circle to indicate a thing, a box for an entity, a line connecting two entities for a relation between them, and an arrow for conceived time. The notations in Fig. 6.5 therefore serve as

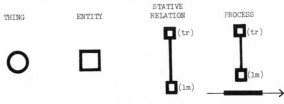

Fig. 6.5

simple abbreviations for basic types of predications when it is unnecessary or inconvenient to go into further detail about their internal structures. In abbreviatory diagrams of this sort I will understand the upper profiled entity in a relation to be its trajector, and the lower one its landmark. Observe that a relation obtains between the trajector and landmark of a process at every point during its evolution through time; each such point defines a separate **state** within the process. Only a single (arbitrary) state is explicitly shown in the schematic diagram.[4]

6.1.3. *Stativity*

An atemporal relation is **simple** or **complex** depending on whether or not it reduces to a single consistent configuration. A simple atemporal relation defines a **state** and can also be termed a **stative relation**. Complex atemporal relations do not reduce to a single consistent configuration, hence they define complex scenes in the sense of 3.4.2. Our concern in this chapter is largely confined to stative relations, though many remarks hold for atemporal relations of both sorts. Complex atemporal relations are considered in Ch. 7 in connection with processual predications.

The sense in which simple atemporal relations are stative needs to be clarified. For one thing, time can perfectly well be an important parameter in a stative predication, i.e. a predicate does not constitute a process simply because the temporal domain figures prominently in its matrix. This is most easily observed in cases where a process functions as the base for a higher-order predication that is nonprocessual in character. For instance, the nomi-

---

[4] The heavy-line portion of the time arrow in the notation for a process represents its **temporal profile**, i.e. the stretch of conceived time through which it is profiled and scanned sequentially (see Ch. 7).

nalizing suffix -*er* (and also any noun it derives, e.g. *runner*, *winner*, *mixer*)
designates a thing identified by virtue of its role in a process (normally the
trajector role). This is diagrammed in Fig. 6.6(a): a process, which inherently

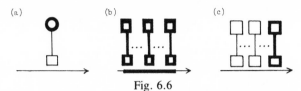

Fig. 6.6

involves the passage of time, figures centrally in this nominal predication, but
it is not in profile, and the predication as a whole is categorized as a thing.
Much the same is true for the adjectival sense of the past-participial morpheme as well as the participles it derives, for example *broken* (*a broken cup*;
This cup is already broken). The base for these stative construals is a processual predication such as *break*, which designates a continuous series of
states distributed through time, as seen in Fig. 6.6(b). The stative participle,
however, designates only the final state in the overall process, as indicated
in diagram (c). The evolution of a situation through time is thus a prominent facet of the participle's meaning, but it is confined to the base and left
unprofiled.

A second point is that the stative character of a relation says nothing at all
about how long the situation it describes may endure. The fact that *red*,
broken, and *ill* are stative does not entail that an object or person with such a
property has it only instantaneously. Stativity implies only that the specifications of the profiled situation can all be satisfied in an atemporal construal of
that situation. All the specifications of *red*, for example, can be satisfied simultaneously in a static conceptualization that is not construed as unfolding
through conceived time. The conception of a process evolving through time
provides the necessary context for *broken* (i.e. something cannot be broken
unless it has gone through the process of breaking), but the specifics of the
profiled state itself (e.g. the parts of a cup lying scattered about rather than
forming a continuous whole) can be conceptualized atemporally. *Ill* locates a
person on a conceived scale of systemic well-being, and an abstract locative
relationship of this sort lends itself naturally to an atemporal construal. It is
part of our encyclopedic knowledge of illness that it generally involves a de-
cline from good health, that it can be of variable duration (but hardly just
instantaneous), and so on, but these processual notions can be put in profile
only by integrating *ill* with other expressions (e.g. *fall ill*, *be ill*, *remain ill*).[5]

---

[5] Parallel comments can be made about things. Object permanence (i.e. persistence through
time) is an important specification of many nominal predications, but this does not make them
processual in the sense of Ch. 7.

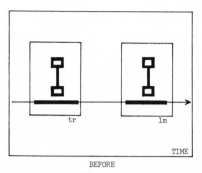

BEFORE

Fig. 6.7

Finally, a predicate need not be processual even when time is its primary domain. We can illustrate this with [BEFORE], diagrammed in Fig. 6.7. *Before* specifies the relative position of two events (processes) in time, but it nevertheless profiles a stative relation and is consequently an adverb (rather than a verb). We must consider both **level of organization** and the specific **role of time** within the predication. The trajector and landmark of *before* are both processes internally, but that is irrelevant to its basic categorization, which pertains to higher-level relationships: the profiled interconnections are those that hold *between* these two processes and treat them as unitary entities for this purpose. Moreover, the interconnections at this higher level of organization qualify as a stative relation (a single consistent configuration) in the domain of conceived time. Time functions here as the **primary** domain of predication, quite analogous to space in the locative sense of *before* (e.g. *He stood before the throne*). All facets of the scene are coactivated and simultaneously available, i.e. its conception involves summary rather than sequential scanning (3.4.2). In a process, by contrast, time is a **subsidiary** domain of predication, the locus for relationships defined with respect to some other domain (recall the formula $[m/l_i]t_i$ from 4.3.1). A process also represents a complex scene rather than a single configuration, and by definition is scanned sequentially (Ch. 7).

6.2. Basic Conceptual Relations

A relational predicate profiles interconnections among participating entities. The nature of these interconnections is to some degree apparent from informal diagrams in the genre of Figs. 6.2–4 and 6.7, but these are at best approximate and rely on the reader's knowledge of implicit conventions for interpreting graphic representations. It is therefore important to examine more explicitly the internal structure of relations, and to elucidate the constructs required in more precise formulations.

6.2.1. *Relational Decomposition*

Relational interconnections involve the coordination of cognitive events. Let us consider in this fashion the interconnections profiled by [ABOVE] and [BELOW] (sketched previously in Fig. 6.4). The domain for these predicates is oriented space: the trajector and landmark are differentially located with respect to a dimension of verticality whose origin (in canonical instances) can be equated with either the center of the earth or the horizontal plane of the earth's surface. Fig. 6.8 depicts the various constructs needed for the characterization of *X above Y* and *Y below X*. Let us assume that the interconnections between *X* and *Y* reside in a complex act of comparison that assesses the

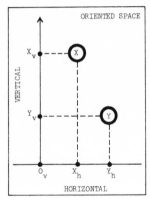

Fig. 6.8

disparity of their location in oriented space. Under the further assumption that a figure constitutes a target of scanning (3.3.2), we can say that the spatial comparison $Y > X$ is fundamental to the predicate [ABOVE] (where X is the figure or trajector), whereas $X > Y$ is central to [BELOW].[6]

The spatial discrepancy between X and Y has both horizontal and vertical components, with very different specifications. Consider first the horizontal plane. Under normal circumstances, the use of *above* or *below* is most felicitous when one participant is precisely underneath the other; this construal can be made explicit by such qualifiers as *right, precisely, directly,* and *exactly* (e.g. *The picture is directly above the plaque on the dining room wall*). As is often the case, however, conventional usage permits a certain amount of

---

[6] The internal structure of relational predications can be extraordinarily complex, and it cannot be maintained that the trajector is the target of every scanning operation that figures in such a structure. As a fully general matter, it can only be claimed that the trajector stands out against its background (i.e. is assessed as the target in relation to a standard) at some cognitively salient level and domain of organization.

leeway. *Above* and *below* are readily tolerated for the configuration of Fig. 6.8 provided that the horizontal divergence of X and Y is not too great. When their horizontal divergence becomes substantial, however, categorizing their relationship as an instance of [ABOVE] or [BELOW] is problematic: ?*The picture is above the plaque on the dining room wall and twelve feet off to the side of it.* Thus, in an optimal instantiation of [ABOVE] (or [BELOW]) the horizontal projections of X and Y coincide, i.e. $Y_h > X_h = 0$ (or $X_h > Y_h = 0$). Conventional usage also sanctions these predicates in situations where X_h and Y_h fail to coincide, provided that one is plausibly construed as located in the neighborhood of the other.

The vertical relationships are very different. For one thing, the vertical projections of X and Y must not coincide: $Y_v > X_v$ (or $X_v > Y_v$) must register some nonzero value. Secondly, the concept of a neighborhood is not applicable: X_v and Y_v can lie at any distance in the scope of predication without prejudice to the appropriateness of [ABOVE] or [BELOW]. Finally, though it is sufficient in the horizontal plane to consider the relation of X_h and Y_h to one another, in the vertical dimension it is necessary to accommodate as well the relation of X_v and Y_v to the origin O_v. Basically, we want to say that the distance between O_v and X_v is greater than that between O_v and Y_v. This relationship is readily described with reference to acts of comparison. The comparison event $O_v > X_v$ registers the displacement of X from the vertical origin, and $O_v > Y_v$ the displacement of Y. The pivotal relationship then resides in a higher-order act of comparison assessing the relative magnitude of the scanning operations in these lower-order events. Specifically, [ABOVE] involves the higher-order comparison $(O_v > Y_v) > (O_v > X_v)$, and [BELOW] the inverse comparison $(O_v > X_v) > (O_v > Y_v)$.

Let us consider these comparisons more carefully. Recall (from 5.3.1) that an event $S > T$ is decomposable into the sequence $[s_0 > s_1 > s_2 > \cdots > s_n]$, where $s_0 = S$, $s_n = T$, and each transition $s_i > s_{i+1}$ represents a minimally detectable discrepancy along the parameter of comparison. The two comparison events $O_v > X_v$ and $O_v > Y_v$ can each be decomposed in this manner; we can represent the transition chain for $O_v > X_v$ as $[x_0 > x_1 > x_2 > \cdots > x_n]$, and that for $O_v > Y_v$ as $[y_0 > y_1 > y_2 > \cdots > y_m]$. Comparison requires correspondences, so the higher-order comparison of $O_v > X_v$ and $O_v > Y_v$ implies the correspondences indicated in 1(a). Moreover, only the magnitude of the scanning chains is at issue in the higher-order event, and not, for example, their location with respect to time or the horizontal plane. Once we abstract away from irrelevant factors, the corresponding elements in the two transition chains become effectively equivalent. The two transition chains of 1(a) can therefore be conflated in the manner of (b) for purposes of the higher-order comparison in question.

(1)(a) $\quad x_0 > x_1 > x_2 > \cdots > x_m > x_{m+1} > \cdots > x_n$

$$y_0 > y_1 > y_2 > \cdots > y_m$$

(b) $\quad z_0 > z_1 > z_2 > \cdots > z_m > z_{m+1} > \cdots > z_n$

In terms of formula (b), the first-order comparison event $O_v > X_v$ consists of the transition chain $[z_0 > z_1 > z_2 > \cdots > z_n]$, whereas $O_v > Y_v$ involves only a subpart of that chain, namely $[z_0 > z_1 > z_2 > \cdots > z_m]$. The comparison $O_v > Y_v$ is therefore **immanent** to that of $O_v > X_v$, and by the definition formulated in 4.3.4, the **distance** between X_v and O_v is consequently greater than that between Y_v and O_v with respect to the vertical axis in the domain of oriented space. Although this relationship based on distance holds for both [ABOVE] and [BELOW], it is determined by distinct higher-order comparisons whose difference may well also be cognitively significant. In the case of [ABOVE], where the standard $[z_0 > \cdots > z_m]$ is immanent to the target $[z_0 > \cdots > z_n]$, the scanning operation is **expansive**: execution of the standard leaves a residue $[z_{m+1} > \cdots > z_n]$ for the target to supply. The scanning operation is **contractive** in the case of [BELOW], where the target is immanent to the standard. The contrast in directionality between [ABOVE] and [BELOW] thus entails a qualitative difference in assessing the common distance relationship.

The examination of [ABOVE] and [BELOW] has revealed the necessity of referring to a number of more fundamental relational notions. I will call these **basic conceptual relations**, for they can be characterized in terms of rudimentary cognitive operations and prove useful if not essential to the description of all relational predications. The notions in question are identity (or coincidence); separation (or noncoincidence); association (i.e. location within a neighborhood); and inclusion. The last of these appears to be primary, in the sense that it permits a natural characterization of the others. Let us then begin with inclusion.

6.2.2. *Inclusion*

When characterized at the level of cognitive events, inclusion reduces to immanence. The basic conceptual relation [A IN B] holds (as does its inverse [B INCLUDE A]) whenever A and B are transition chains and A is immanent to B. In view of the generality of this notion, such relationships are of course ubiquitous, inclusion holding implicitly between every cognitive routine and its substructures. For example, the well-entrenched transition chain [A > B > C > \cdots > Z] constituting our ability to recite the alphabet incorporates subroutines corresponding to the individual letters, each of which is immanent to it; there is consequently a latent [IN]-relation between each of the subroutines and the chain as a whole. Our interest, however, lies in those instances where an implicit [IN]-relation is raised to the level of explicit concern and made a specific matter of predication. In constructing or interpreting the expression *C is in the alphabet*, for instance, a speaker must direct his attention specifically to the relation between the transition chains [A > B > C > ⋯ > Z] and [C] (rather than merely activating the former, or activating the two as independent entities). This implies some type of higher-order event of the form [A > B > C > ⋯ > Z] > [C], where the two components are coordinated by an operation that specifically registers the immanence of one to the other.[7]

A few examples will teach us a number of things about [IN] that are applicable as well to other basic conceptual relations. It is possible for such a relation to constitute the primary or even the sole semantic content of a predicate (apart from its domain specification); I assume, for example, that the basic [IN]-relation accounts more or less fully for the relational interconnection implied by the predicate [IN] (i.e. the semantic pole of *in*). When this is so the content it contributes is highly salient, for it stands in profile and directly relates the prominent trajector and landmark. Certain factors nevertheless reduce the cognitive salience of a basic conceptual relation even when its contribution is critical to a predicate. First, it may be only one of many specifications, which renders it **sublexical** and therefore less salient. Second, salience is reduced when a relationship holds not between the profiled trajector and landmark, but rather between less prominent (possibly unprofiled) entities, especially derivative ones that are intrinsically abstract. Both of these factors are illustrated in [ABOVE] and [BELOW] by the inclusion relation between the magnitude of $(O_v > X_v)$ and that of $(O_v > Y_v)$. This relationship coexists with other specifications (nonidentity of X_v and Y_v; identity or association of X_h and Y_h). Moreover, it does not pertain directly to the trajector and landmark per se—instead, it assesses the relative magnitude of their displacement from the vertical origin (as revealed by first-order acts of comparison). The abstractness of the entities compared renders the inclusion relation fairly nonsalient despite its centrality to the value of the predicates.

It can also happen that different predicates invoke the same basic conceptual relation as their primary semantic content and yet contrast semantically owing to their domain specifications. For example, the [IN]-relation would appear to exhaust the relational content of both [IN] and [OF], but the latter predicate (diagrammed in Fig. 6.2(d)) is more specific in that its domain (equivalent in this case to its landmark) is specified to be an integrated whole; the [IN]-relation defining its landmark-trajector interconnection must be con-

---

[7] Basic conceptual relations are fully schematic in their domain specifications. The generality of [IN] makes it possible to describe sentences like *C is in the alphabet* without appealing to spatial metaphor (though it is not unlikely that such metaphor contributes to their value).

strued with reference to this domain in particular. Consider first the similarities of the two predicates. For both [IN] and [OF], the conception of extensionality for the trajector (in the relevant domain) implies a transition chain that is immanent to the chain responsible for the conception of the landmark's extensionality. Naturally this expanse scanning (cf. Fig. 5.8) sometimes pertains only to selected facets or dimensions of the entities concerned. Terry Kennedy is a three-dimensional object, but when I say *Kennedy is in the batter's box* my use of *in* concerns only his horizontal projection, for this alone is included in the two-dimensional expanse of the batter's box. Moreover, closure is often invoked in assessing the landmark's expanse, particularly when the trajector is a foreign entity. *A fish is frozen in that block of ice* describes a situation where the expanse of the fish interrupts that of the ice in a physical sense, but this is ignored linguistically. The spatial extension of the ice is construed as stretching from each outer surface of the block to the opposite one, and the spatial extension of the fish is thus included within it.

To the extent that the trajector is viewed as an inherent facet of the landmark rather than something foreign, conditions arise for the use of *of*, where inclusion relates to the interconnected entities that as such constitute the landmark, rather than to the region in space they happen to occupy. Hence the contrast between *the tip of my finger* and *the splinter in my finger*: the former describes the inclusion of the tip as part of the very substance of the finger, whereas the latter only situates the splinter within its spatial confines.[8] *In* and *of* are not mutually exclusive, however, especially since *in* can be applied to almost any domain, even the conception of an integrated whole. When convention permits the use of both predicates, the choice between them amounts to a matter of contrasting images. Both *in* and *of* can be applied to the relation between a specific letter and the alphabet as a whole (*C is in the alphabet*; *C is part of the alphabet*; *C is a letter in/of the alphabet*), but *of* highlights more strongly the role of the trajector as an integral facet of the landmark.

The case of [RED] (Fig. 6.2(b)) displays further subtleties. I have already observed that a physical object per se cannot occupy color space. In an expression like *red table*, consequently, the putative [IN]-relation between the trajector and landmark of [RED] involves only selected facets of the former, typically the color sensation associated with its outside surface. Beyond this, it must be noted that color space is a nonconfigurational domain, and we are not accustomed to scanning through this domain in the way that we scan through physical space, the visual field, or even our conception of the alphabet. Nevertheless, the landmark of [RED] is a continuous region along the hue

---

[8] What is "foreign" to an entity and what is "inherent" are obviously subject to interpretation. Observe that a gap present in an object by design may count as an integral facet of it (*the hole of the doughnut*). *That brown spot in the lawn* suggests that the spot is considered extrinsic, even though it is composed of grass.

dimension (designated by the noun *red*), and the very notion of continuity implies a set of transitions relating contiguous points in the domain; each transition corresponds in this instance to a minimally observable contrast between two shades of red. Thus it is possible to speak of a chain of transitions (or a set of such chains) leading from one extreme of the landmark region to the other. To posit an [IN]-relation between the trajector and landmark of [RED] we need not suppose that a speaker activates this entire transition chain (and successively imagines every possible shade of red) each time he employs the predicate. It is sufficient to establish that full activation of such a chain, were it to occur, would include among its components the color sensation attributed to the trajector.[9]

6.2.3. *Other Relations*

It remains to consider briefly the other basic conceptual relations posited for the internal structure of predicates. The relation [A IN B], based on immanence, specifies that the cognitive events constituting the conception of A (in a given domain) are included among those comprised by B. The relation of separation, which I will give as [A OUT B], is based on the absence of such inclusion. One way to formulate it is by specifying that the transition chain required for the interconnection of A and B is not immanent to the chain defining the extensionality of B. We saw that $[X_v$ OUT $Y_v]$ is one specification of [ABOVE] (and its inverse $[Y_v$ OUT $X_v]$ a specification of [BELOW]). The trajector and landmark of [BEFORE] (Fig. 6.7) also bear an [OUT]-relation to each other, as do those of *with* and *across* as diagrammed in Fig. 6.3.

Identity (or coincidence) is essentially the opposite of separation. It can be defined as mutual inclusion: [A ID B] holds (equivalently, [B ID A]) when [A IN B] and [B IN A] both obtain. When A and B are extensional (in a particular domain or dimension), the transition chain defining the extensionality of A is immanent to the one for B, and conversely. We can also say that the distance between every point of A and the corresponding point of B is zero; there is only one such point in degenerate instances. As an example, we saw that the use of *above* (or *below*) is optimal when the horizontal projections of the trajector and landmark are identical, i.e. $[X_h$ ID $Y_h]$ (or $[Y_h$ ID $X_h]$).

Finally we come to the relation of association, where one entity is situated in the neighborhood of the other. As a first approximation, we can decompose [A ASSOC B] into the component relations [A OUT B], [A IN C], and [B IN C], where C is a third entity, the neighborhood. These three specifications can

---

[9] This analysis predicts that some languages might express a similar concept by means of an oblique phrase (literally, *in red*) rather than an adjective (Jim Fife informs me that such a construction is found in Welsh). As an alternative, we might posit a relation of identity between the sensation attributed to the trajector and a particular *exemplar* of the red region (treating this region as a complex category—cf. Ch. 10).

all be observed for the sense of *with* depicted in Fig. 6.3(a); we have also noted that *above* and *below* tolerate nonidentity (an [OUT]-relation) between the horizontal projections of their trajector and landmark provided that the two can be construed as occupying the same neighborhood. The problem resides in determining what constitutes a neighborhood. The notion of proximity is obviously relevant, but what is proximity?

Clearly scale (3.3.1) is important. What counts as proximity in regard to the objects inside a room is quite different from proximity with respect to the clustering of galaxies. Scope is also relevant, since associative relationships on a given scale are computed only for those entities a speaker chooses to include within the scope of predication. Once scale and scope are established, proximity is a matter of relative distance with respect to actual or potential alternatives, and assessments of relative distance imply comparisons.

All the elements depicted in Fig. 6.9 therefore function either implicitly or explicitly in the relation [*A* ASSOC *B*], which requires the following cognitive events: (1) $B>D$, the transition chain connecting *B* and *D*; (2) $B>A$,

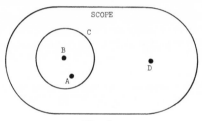

Fig. 6.9

the chain connecting *B* and *A*; (3) the higher-order comparison $(B>D)>(B>A)$ assessing the relative magnitude of these chains—*A* is judged proximal to *B* (with reference to *D*) when the scanning operation is contractive; and (4) the conception of a neighborhood, *C*, consisting of points judged proximal to *B* in this fashion.

The status of *D* and of *C* is quite variable in associative relations. Entity *D* may be specific and contextually salient (*Helen is standing with Jason, not with her mother*), but it may also be left unspecified and be construed, in effect, as an average or representative entity (actual or potential) within the scope of predication. Similarly, the neighborhood *C* can either be specified and contextually prominent (*Helen is with Jason in the Jacuzzi*) or else left vague and unspecified. There is some reason to believe that *with* reifies the neighborhood as a fairly salient entity and then situates the trajector *A* inside it, whereas *near* computes the proximity of *A* and *B* directly in terms of elements (1)–(3) above (the neighborhood notion remaining latent). Consider the contrast between *Helen is with Jason in the Jacuzzi* and *Helen is near*

Jason in the Jacuzzi (focusing solely on the primary interpretation of each). In the former I understand the locative phrase *in the Jacuzzi* as elaborating on the character of the neighborhood implied by *with*. This is not at all the case in the latter, where *near Jason* and *in the Jacuzzi* are more like separate specifications. To put it otherwise, in the first expression Helen is construed as being *with Jason* precisely because both are *in the Jacuzzi*, whereas in the second she is *near Jason* in addition to being *in the Jacuzzi* with him. This evidence is admittedly tenuous, but it does suggest that the neighborhood region is more salient in the case of *with* than for *near* (also see fn. 3).

Fig. 6.10 summarizes the basic conceptual relations introduced to characterize the internal structure of relational predications, and the notations com-

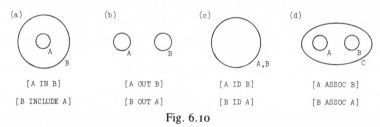

Fig. 6.10

monly employed for them. Observe that the [IN]-relation is asymmetrical, since [*A* IN *B*] is incompatible with [*B* IN *A*] except in the limiting case of identity; it contrasts with [OUT] and [ID] in this regard. Though only one circle is explicitly shown in the notation for the identity relation, it should be emphasized that this is nevertheless a relational notion: it involves two conceived entities plus the additional specification that they coincide with respect to the parameters of comparison. This additional specification may be profiled as the primary content of a predication (e.g. *same, identical*), which is thereby categorized as a relation rather than a thing. One must be more careful in speaking of the symmetry of the associative relation. Perhaps it is always true that [*A* ASSOC *B*] implies [*B* ASSOC *A*], but to the extent that the neighborhood *C* achieves cognitive salience there is a difference between the two with potential linguistic consequences. In [*A* ASSOC *B*] the neighborhood *C* is defined as the set of points in proximity to *B*, whereas in [*B* ASSOC *A*] it is the set of points in proximity to *A*. These two construals of the neighborhood *C* need not coincide fully, even if *A* and *B* are each consistently included in the neighborhood of the other.

Systematic exploitation of these basic conceptual relations carries us surprisingly far towards an explicit description of the internal structure of relational predicates. I do not wish to understate the inevitable problems in moving beyond this programmatic characterization towards something approximating a formal account, but the preceding discussion is at least suggestive of how an explicit descriptive framework might work in principle. There is nothing particularly surprising about the relations proposed; analogs are readily found in other approaches (e.g. set theory and formal logic). More novel, and far more problematic from a rigid empiricist standpoint, is the characterization of these relations in terms of cognitive events rather than objective entities or purely mathematical constructs. The speculative aspects of this move hardly need emphasis, yet I see no suitable alternative if one takes seriously the idea of cognitive semantics.

6.3. Trajector and Landmark

The trajector/landmark asymmetry is fundamental to relational predications and underlies the universal subject/object distinction. I have defined a trajector as the figure in a relational profile; other salient entities are identified as landmarks. Though grammatical relations are not a major focus of the present volume, these notions nevertheless require a certain amount of initial elaboration and clarification. First to be discussed are grounds for treating the trajector/landmark asymmetry as a special case of figure/ground alignment. We will then examine various types of landmarks and how they are related to trajectors. Offered in conclusion are some comments on the characterization of traditional grammatical classes.

6.3.1. *The Trajector as Figure*

With few if any exceptions, relational predications display an inherent asymmetry in the presentation of their participants. This asymmetry is not reducible to semantic roles, i.e. the nature of participant involvement in the profiled relationship. For one thing, it is observable even for predications that designate symmetrical relationships: *X equals Y* is not precisely equivalent semantically to *Y equals X*, nor is *X resembles Y* equivalent to *Y resembles X*. Moreover, otherwise identical relationships can be presented with opposite alignment. From the standpoint of semantic content, the roles of *X* and *Y* are the same in *X above Y* as they are in *Y below X*, yet a subtle difference in meaning remains to be accounted for.

In the expression *X equals Y*, *X resembles Y*, or *X above Y*, *X* is referred to as a trajector, and *Y* as a landmark. This terminology reflects the intuitive judgment that *Y* provides a reference point with respect to which *X* is evaluated or situated: *X* stands out as the entity being assessed, and this assessment takes the form of its relationship to *Y*. As a working hypothesis, I maintain that the trajector/landmark asymmetry is one linguistic instantiation of figure/ground alignment. From among the entities participating in the profiled interconnections, a relational predication selects one to be construed as figure and "tracked" against the background provided by other elements. The selection is not predictable in absolute terms and constitutes a dimension of conventional imagery.

The trajector/landmark distinction is far more general and broadly applicable than the subject/object distinction as this is traditionally understood. The terms subject and object are normally reserved for overt nominals (i.e. noun phrases) with specifiable roles in clause-level syntax. By contrast, trajector/landmark alignment pertains to the internal structure of relational predications, at any level of organization. Trajectors and landmarks need not be spelled out overtly, and are often relational (rather than nominal) in character.

The internal structure of a predicate must be distinguished from its combinatorial properties (despite their mutual influence). The verb *read*, for example, has both transitive and intransitive uses (*David read his new book*; *David reads quickly*), but a schematically characterized landmark is included in its relational profile irrespective of the presence or absence of a direct-object nominal. The adjective *red* has both a trajector and a landmark (Fig. 6.2(b)) regardless of whether the former is specified by a nominal expression, and despite the fact that the latter never can be. Strictly speaking, then, a trajector or landmark belongs to the internal structure of a relational predication. It does, however, provide the fulcrum for syntagmatic combination. In the phrase *red vase*, for instance, the integration of the component expressions is effected by a correspondence established between the schematic trajector of *red* and the profile of *vase*. *Vase* thus **corresponds to** the trajector of *red*, and **elaborates** its schematic characterization, but only in a derivative sense will I say that it *is* the trajector. Similarly, the integration of *read* with *his new book* in *David read his new book* reflects a correspondence between the landmark of *read* and the profile of the nominal expression, whereas that of *David* and *read* hinges on a correspondence between the former's profile and the latter's trajector. Though I will refer to *David* and *his new book*, in shorthand fashion, as the trajector and landmark of *read*, they are more accurately described as **correspondents** of these elements.

It is customary to speak of subjects and direct objects only for nominals at the clausal level. For instance, in the sentence *Helen left quickly before Jason entered the tiny Jacuzzi*, there are only two subjects (one in each clause) and a single object. The population of trajectors and landmarks is considerably larger. *Left* can be attributed an internal landmark despite the absence of an elaborating nominal (cf. *Helen left the room*). *Quickly* has neither a subject nor an object in the usual sense, but it does have a trajector and landmark: its trajector is a process, elaborated by *left*; the predication situates this process within a certain region along a scale of rate, which functions as an unelaborated landmark. In similar fashion, *tiny* has both a trajector that corresponds to the profile of *Jacuzzi*, and a landmark (pertaining to a scale of size) that is not separately expressed. Finally, the initial clause elaborates the trajector of *before* (cf. Fig. 6.7), and the second clause its landmark, but neither is generally considered a subject or object.

Because subjects and objects elaborate the trajectors and landmarks of relational predications, the subject/object distinction reflects the trajector/landmark asymmetry. The issue we now address is the nature of this asymmetry. If a schematic characterization is sought, it must not be tied to the special properties that distinguish subjects and objects from trajectors and landmarks in general. My specific proposal is to identify a trajector with the figure in a relational profile. I cannot offer an incontrovertible proof that this is the proper definition, but it does have the advantage (over obvious alternatives) of being applicable to the full range of instances.

Attempts to define the subject role in notional terms generally focus on verbs and bring forth notions like "agent," "topic," "energy source," and "controller" (or some combination thereof). A characterization based on these concepts is problematic even for the class of verbs, since many verbs designate processes that involve no action, energy, or control at all (e.g. *resemble, cost, seem, inhere*).[10] If notions like "agent," "topic," "controller," etc. cannot provide a workable schematic characterization for the full class of verbal subjects, certainly they cannot do so for the far broader class of relational trajectors. None of these terms, interpreted in any standard way, is reasonably applied to the trajectors of *red, of, with, above, before, quickly*, etc. at all levels of clausal organization. If a schematic description of the trajector construct is possible, it must approximate the proposed definition in its abstractness and generality.

What are some positive reasons for believing that a trajector is definable as the figure in a relational profile? For one thing, the analysis has a certain fundamental plausibility. Figure/ground organization is pervasive in human cognition, so we expect it to be operative in language; the trajector/landmark asymmetry—virtually universal for relational predications—seems a natural place to look. Moreover, our capacity for dealing with hierarchies of figure/ground organization can be related to the simultaneous trajector/landmark alignment found at different hierarchical levels within a clause. I would also suggest, on intuitive grounds, that the contrast between *X above Y* and *Y below X* (Fig. 6.4) is plausibly regarded as an instance of figure/ground reversal.

More persuasive, no doubt, is a cross-linguistic tendency for the unmarked choice of trajector to correspond to the entity that would normally be construed as the figure on general perceptual grounds. This is perhaps most evi-

---

[10] A characterization along these lines is appropriate, however, for the subjects of prototypical verbs (those describing overt physical activities), and extensions from this prototype can account for the subject role in a great many others.

dent in cases of physical motion. An object moving in relation to a fixed setting is almost invariably perceived as the figure in the scene, though the
opposite alignment can be imposed with some effort. Linguistically this is reflected in the overwhelming tendency with motion verbs for the mover to be
selected as the subject.[11] Sporadic lexical exceptions to this tendency (e.g.
receive), as well as the existence of grammatical constructions like the passive that reverse the expected alignment, only serve to underscore the basic
pattern, for their marked character is quite evident. If the subject/object distinction instantiates figure/ground asymmetry, we should anticipate the possibility of figure/ground reversal occasionally overriding the unmarked choice
of subject.

That verbs of physical motion and activity are commonly recognized as
prototypical may be due in part to the clear basis they provide for determining
figure/ground alignment. The analysis predicts, I think quite correctly, that
the choice of subject (trajector) among the participants in a relationship
should become more variable as the natural grounds for picking out any one in
particular to be the figure become more tenuous. For physical motion/action
verbs like *run, kick, move, approach, slap,* etc. we therefore expect relatively few lexical exceptions to the selection of the mover/actor as subject. In
contrast, verbs of perception and mental or emotional attitude provide less
basis for an intrinsic figure/ground asymmetry (for example, does a viewer's
gaze move towards a perceived object, or does a visual signal travel from the
object to the viewer?); the choice of subject is consequently more flexible and
depends on the image selected to structure the scene. Opposing pairs such as
like vs. *please, think about* vs. *preoccupy, see* vs. *be visible to,* etc. are quite
common in these domains, but comparable lexical oppositions for verbs of
asymmetrical physical activity are unusual. Moreover, since a primary function of the passive construction is to permit a marked choice of subject (for
discourse purposes), we can expect this construction to be most deeply entrenched with prototypical action verbs where natural figure/ground alignment has the strongest effect in dictating a particular selection. This certainly
appears to be the case (cf. Ch. 1).

The natural basis for a figure/ground distinction is weakest for stative relations between participants of equal status, by which I mean, for instance, that
both are processes or both are physical objects.[12] The frequent occurrence of

[11] I refer in particular to simple situations involving only one mover; with multiple movers
other considerations enter the picture. (Relevant here is my discussion of *hit* (Langacker 1979,
p. 102). I should also note, in relation to causatives and similar expressions, that the transfer of
energy can be regarded as an abstract type of motion attributable to the energy source.)

[12] A physical object is intrinsically more salient than, say, a region on a scale. When a physical
object interacts with a region on a scale to define a stative relation, the former is consequently the
natural choice for figure and trajector. It is hardly surprising, then, that we seldom (if ever) find
inverses of predicates like [RED] and [CLEVER] such that the scalar region functions as trajector
and the physical object as landmark.

contrasting pairs like *above* vs. *below*, *in front of* vs. *in back of*, *over* vs. *under*, *before* vs. *after*, and so on is therefore in accordance with our predictions. It is also significant that the first member of each pair (*above*, *in front of*, *over*, *before*) is judged intuitively to be "positive" or unmarked, and will generally be used in preference to the second member (*below*, *in back of*, *under*, *after*) unless the speaker has some reason for making the opposite selection. Observe, now, that *above*, *in front of*, and *over* all have for their trajectors the entity that is most readily perceived in canonical viewing situations. In the normal course of our experience, an object that is *above*, *in front of*, or *over* another is typically more likely to be visually accessible and salient, and hence to stand out as figure in perceptual terms. As a temporal predication, *before* does not yield an exact parallel, but there is nevertheless a suggestive similarity: as one progresses through its domain (conceived time), its trajector is the first of the participating processes to be encountered.

The proposed characterization is at least compatible with the well-known tendency across languages for clausal subjects to display certain syntactic properties (Keenan 1976). A subject is more likely than other nominals to be the controller for verb agreement, the antecedent for reflexivization and pronominalization, the pivot for relativization, the controller for complement-subject deletion, the source of floated quantifiers, the understood subject of adverbs and subjectless adverbial clauses, and so on. There are obvious problems with trying to *define* the notion subject by means of such properties (cf. Foley and Van Valin 1977), but from my standpoint this effort misses the point in any event. The trajector/subject notion is not at root syntactic, but rather semantic, and its attendant grammatical correlates are not *criterial*, but rather *symptomatic* of the special salience that trajectors (and in particular, clausal subjects) have by virtue of their role as relational figure. The intrinsic salience of a clausal subject (as opposed to a direct object or an oblique) naturally makes it the most readily accessible nominal for purposes of integration with other elements in grammatical constructions of these sorts. Because salience is a matter of degree, and since factors other than figure/ground alignment enter into it, a certain amount of language-specific variation is to be expected; the grammatical properties in question should be associated with subjects only *preferentially* instead of *exclusively*.

A further consideration depends on an analysis of head/modifier constructions, presented in Ch. 8. It is claimed that a head is a type of figure (specifically, a **profile determinant**—the entity designated by the head is also profiled by the construction as a composite whole), whereas the relation designated by the modifier constitutes the ground. If this analysis is correct, it is significant that the head is almost invariably placed in correspondence with the trajector of a nonfinite relational modifier (and thus *is* its trajector in the derivative sense described earlier). In *clever girls*, for example, the head *girls* elaborates the trajector of *clever*. *Magazine* similarly elaborates the trajector of *on the floor* in *the magazine on the floor*, and *run* the trajector of *fast* in *run fast*.[13] This tendency is weaker with modifiers of a more sentential character (and is essentially absent with finite-clause modifiers, where other factors come into play). Still, even nonfinite clauses typically modify through their subjects. We find many more constructions like *the person fixing my car*, where the head corresponds to the trajector of the participle, than cases like *the person to see about that*, where it corresponds to the infinitival landmark.

It has often been argued (e.g. Givón 1979) that clausal subjects manifest greater "topicality" than other nominal complements. Indefinite or nonspecific subjects are sometimes tolerated reluctantly or not at all; singular, animate, and count nouns are favored in subject position over plural, inanimate, and mass nouns; new information is more likely to be introduced through an object than a subject; and so on. At the risk of oversimplifying a subtle and difficult area of investigation, let me summarize these tendencies by saying that subject position favors reference to elements that have been clearly identified to the speaker and hearer and sharply delimited as discrete and well-articulated entities set off from the largely undifferentiated mass of entities constituting the potential universe of discourse. Phrased in this manner the similarity of the subject/nonsubject distinction to the figure/ground asymmetry is perhaps apparent. A figure is defined by contrast with its surroundings, and the likelihood of an entity being construed as figure is enhanced to the degree that the contrast is sharp and the entity discrete.

Though I do not regard these arguments as conclusive, they add up to a reasonably strong circumstantial case. I am aware of nothing that argues against the workability of characterizing a trajector as the figure in a relational profile, and quite a number of phenomena begin to fall into place once this is done. The special status of the subject as a relational figure may help explain its relative autonomy vis-à-vis the verb, as compared to the direct object in particular. In English, for example, it is difficult to insert anything (e.g. an adverb) between the verb and its object, but many things commonly separate the verb from its subject. It is often observed that verb-object idioms are more frequent than subject-verb idioms, that object incorporation in the verb predominates over subject incorporation, and so on. To the extent that differences like these are found even in "nonconfigurational" languages, where conventional word order does not permit the analysis of verb and direct object as a constituent in the usual sense, an explanation based on the more abstract figure/ground distinction seems more promising.

[13] As evidence for these trajector/landmark assignations, note that *girls* and *magazine* function as clausal subject when the equivalent predication is made at the clause level: *Girls are clever*; *The magazine is on the floor*. For the claim that *run* is the trajector of *fast* (rather than its landmark) in *run fast*, see fn. 12.

6.3.2. *Trajector/Landmark Coincidence*

Every relational predication is attributed a landmark of some kind as part of its profile, regardless of whether this landmark receives overt expression through syntagmatic combination with other symbolic elements. There are various reasons why linguistic convention might permit a relational landmark to remain unelaborated (see Tuggy 1981 for incisive discussion). For one thing, the landmark may be unique, so that no information is required to identify it beyond that conveyed by the relational predicate itself. Though any number of different entities can function as the landmark in an [OF]-relation— so that an additional predication is needed to identify it with any specificity— the landmark of [RED] is unique, a specific region in color space fully identified by this predicate standing alone (cf. Fig. 6.2). When the landmark is not unique, it may nevertheless be sufficiently elucidated by context or by the content of the predicate that explicit elaboration can be dispensed with. Consider *Is your brother around?*, which lacks a prepositional object. *Around* situates its trajector in the vicinity of a landmark specified only in the vaguest terms (essentially any point in space), but in context this landmark is equated with the location of the speech event (or identified in some other manner). Given the meaning of *smoke*, the range of inherently plausible landmarks is limited enough that a sentence like *My father smokes* is quite informative even without a direct object.

A landmark may also be left unelaborated because identity with the trajector makes its separate specification redundant. There are several ways in which this can come about. If the trajector and landmark of a predication are normally distinct, they may nevertheless happen to be identical on a particular occasion. We will concern ourselves no further with this possibility, and concentrate instead on cases where reflexivity is inherent rather than contingent. In certain expressions, e.g. *X is identical to Y*, the identity of trajector with landmark is specifically predicated; the basic conceptual relation [ID] furnishes the primary relational content. This relationship is symmetrical, but not reflexive in the usual sense, since *X* and *Y* are in fact represented by distinct nominals (i.e. identity is asserted rather than presupposed). However, consider the alternative expression *X and Y are identical*. Here it is neither *X* nor *Y* individually that is singled out as the relational figure to serve as trajector—this honor is accorded instead to the collective entity *X and Y*. The contrasting expressions imply that *identical* has two semantic variants, which profile the same interconnections but differ in their "packaging" of participants. In *X is identical to Y*, these interconnections equate two separate entities, and the possibility of construing them as a higher-order entity remains latent. This possibility is exploited in *X and Y are identical*, with the result that the interconnections hold not between separate entities, but rather between subparts of the global trajector *X and Y*.

The expression *X and Y are identical* is inherently reflexive, since—by virtue of how the relational predication structures the scene—the coincidence of trajector and landmark is necessary rather than contingent. The same entity (*X and Y*) is both the relational figure and the point of reference for evaluating the figure. That the interconnections associate differentiable *subparts* of this global entity, instead of relating it to itself as an undifferentiated whole, is unproblematic in this framework; it turns out to be the rule and not the exception for trajector-landmark interconnections even in the case of nonreflexive predications (cf. 7.3.4). This simply reflects the ability of speakers to deal simultaneously with structures and relationships at different levels of organization: even though speakers recognize low-level structures for purposes of establishing crucial interconnections, they are nonetheless able to construe these structures as constituting a higher-level entity of special salience. There is considerable flexibility in choosing the relational figure (and also in the relative prominence accorded various landmarks) even when relational interconnections are held constant.

Inherent reflexivity of this sort is not restricted to expressions like *identical*, which are actually atypical of reflexive predications. Many relational predicates have reflexive components (i.e. certain interconnections hold between subparts of the trajector), and often these components furnish their primary content. In the realm of atemporal relations, predicates describing shape (e.g. *round, straight, square*) should probably be regarded as prototypical for this class. We are now in a position, in fact, to characterize explicitly the semantic contrast between a form like *square* when used as a noun and as an adjective.

To clarify what is involved, let us first consider nonreflexive stative relations in which the trajector and the landmark are fully distinct. An example is the spatial *with* of Fig. 6.3(a) (e.g. *Helen is with Jason*). The primary content of [WITH] is given by the basic conceptual relation [*TR* ASSOC *LM*], where *TR* and *LM* stand for the trajector and the landmark as integrated wholes. What is true for *TR* and *LM* as unitary entities is true as well for their subparts in this instance. Suppose we resolve *TR* into the component entities [tr_1, tr_2, tr_3, ...], and *LM* into the component entities [lm_1, lm_2, lm_3, ...]. For any pair of components *tr* and *lm*—for example tr_i and lm_j—it is evident that the proximity relationship [tr_i ASSOC lm_j] holds between them, just as for *TR* and *LM* overall; *TR* and *LM* are both **coherent** with respect to the associative relation, to the point that analyzing it into component relationships seems a rather pointless exercise.

Such coherence is not always observed, however, and typically the relationship between *TR* and *LM* must be resolved into component subrelations if a revealing analysis is to be achieved. A case in point is the variant of [THROUGH] illustrated in Fig. 6.11 and exemplified by the sentence *A nail is sticking through that board*. Here it is obvious that the relation between tr_i

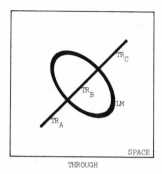

THROUGH

Fig. 6.11

and lm_j is not uniform for every such pair, and that this variation is important to the semantic value of the preposition. In particular, *TR* can be segmented along one axis into three continuous subparts TR_A, TR_B, and TR_C such that every point within TR_A and TR_C bears an [OUT]-relation to *LM*, whereas every point within TR_B bears an [IN]-relation. Crucially, though, the set of entities $[tr_1, tr_2, tr_3, ...]$ are collectively construed as a thing identified on a global level as the predicate's trajector (*TR*), despite the recognition that the component entities, as well as the intermediate-level substructures TR_A, TR_B, and TR_C, are differentially located with respect to the global landmark (*LM*).

Let us now apply these constructs to instances where *TR* and *LM* coincide. Consider the notion of parallelism. The minimal base for a predication of parallelism is sketched in Fig. 6.12(a), which has two lines labeled *A* and *B*.[14] Each line is resolvable into indefinitely many points, of which just three are singled out diagrammatically for illustrative purposes. For each point b_i on line *B*, an assessment of its distance from the point a_i directly opposite on line *A* implies an act of comparison $b_i > a_i$. A judgment of parallelism then resides in a series of higher-order comparisons, which determine this distance to be the same for every first-order comparison that happens to be carried out: $(b_1 > a_1) > (b_2 > a_2) = 0$; $(b_2 > a_2) > (b_3 > a_3) = 0$; and so on.

This characterization of the requisite cognitive events makes no inherent reference to their relative prominence, hence it is independent of profiling.

[14] To keep things simple I examine only the case of two straight lines; an elaboration of the analysis accommodates situations where there are more than two lines, where the lines are not straight, where the parallel entities are facets of more complex objects, and so on. A mathematical definition of parallelism simply specifies that parallel lines never intersect however far they are extended. While nonintersection is certainly part of the encyclopedic characterization of *parallel* for anyone schooled in geometry (and possibly also for the mathematically naive), what we will focus on here is an aspect of parallelism that I suspect to be cognitively more fundamental.

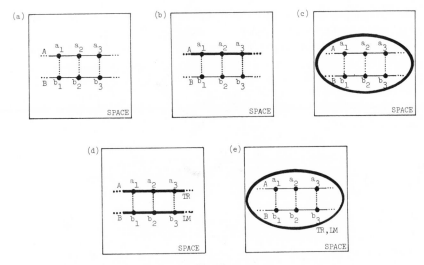

Fig. 6.12

Quite a number of predications are found in English that reduce in essence to
alternate profiles on this base. By profiling a single line (i.e. by according this
special prominence exclusively to those cognitive events constituting the conception of *A* or *B*) we obtain a nominal predication designating this line; Fig.
6.12(b) so construes line *A*, which can then be referred to as *a parallel*. We
can invoke the parallelism of *A* and *B* as the interconnection needed to establish them as a region—let us call this higher-order entity [*A-B*]—and thus
refer to this region with the plural noun *parallels*, diagrammed in Fig. 6.12(c).
The other two senses of *parallel* in Fig. 6.12 are relational: they profile the
interconnections between *A* and *B* (i.e. the first- and second-order comparison
events described above) rather than these lines per se (singly or collectively).
The difference between diagrams (d) and (e) resides in the choice of relational
figure from among those entities that we have already seen to be construable
as things. In (d), line *A* is selected as figure and hence trajector, leaving *B* as a
salient landmark. This is the variant of *parallel* occurring in sentences like *A
is parallel to B* (by extending it through conceived time, we obtain the associated verb: *A parallels B*). When *A* and *B* are construed collectively as a thing
and elevated as such to the level of relational figure, what results is the plural-
trajector variant found in expressions like *parallel lines* or *A and B are parallel*. This variant is diagrammed in (e). It is very similar notationally to the
plural noun *parallels* of (c), but the two are quite different in their profiling.
The structure in (c) profiles the region [*A-B*], whereas (e) profiles instead the
interconnections that establish it as a region.
    Consider now the status of [*A-B*] as both the trajector and the landmark in

Fig. 6.12(e). An overall relational predication R can be decomposed into an indefinite number of component subrelations $[r_1, r_2, r_3, \ldots]$, each of which represents the interconnections between two entities; in the present example, these entities are individual points of A and B (for first-order comparisons). Each subrelation therefore has the form $[a_i \, r_i \, b_i]$, in which a_i can be thought of as subtrajector at this "micro" level, and b_i as sublandmark. Consider now the sets of entities $[a_1, a_2, a_3, \ldots]$ and $[b_1, b_2, b_3, \ldots]$, consisting respectively of those that serve as a_i and b_i (i.e. subtrajector and sublandmark) in one of these subrelations. It often happens that these two sets correlate with facets of distinct higher-order entities recognized within the scene. If so, and if one of these higher-order entities is singled out as figure, we obtain a canonical relational predicate with separate overall trajector and landmark; an example is Fig. 6.12(d), in which $[a_1, a_2, a_3, \ldots]$ and $[b_1, b_2, b_3, \ldots]$ are recognized as constituting the separate lines A and B, with A selected as figure. But it can also happen that the higher-order entity selected as the relational figure subsumes both sets. This is so in diagram (e), where the figure $[A\text{-}B]$ includes within it not only all the subtrajectors $[a_1, a_2, a_3, \ldots]$ but also all the sublandmarks $[b_1, b_2, b_3, \ldots]$; thus $[A\text{-}B]$ functions simultaneously as the overall trajector TR and the overall landmark LM. The profiled interconnections hold between different substructures within $[A\text{-}B]$ construed as a unitary entity.

Within the class of inherently reflexive relations, characterized by the coincidence of TR and LM, the plural-subject variant of *parallel* is perhaps atypical. It is by no means always true that the overall TR/LM has salient substructures lending themselves equally well to construal as separate TR and LM (in the fashion of Fig. 6.12(d)). Consider adjectives like *compact* and *dense*, which specify the various component entities of TR/LM as lying in exceptionally close proximity to one another. Every such entity functions simultaneously as subtrajector and sublandmark for numerous subrelations of proximity with its neighbors, and there are no salient substructures within TR/LM that can naturally be construed as differentially assuming the trajector and landmark roles. The same is generally true of shape predications, which specify relations between subparts of a unitary object: no differentiation of TR/LM into salient substructures is implied by predicates like *round* and *straight*.

The difference between contrasting expressions like the nominal vs. the adjectival *square* should now be evident. The same complex of component entities and interconnecting operations function in both the nominal and the relational predications. In the case of *square*, these include the conception of four line segments whose endpoints coincide in pairwise fashion; comparison events specifying opposite sides as being parallel (as in Fig. 6.12); additional comparisons specifying the identity of length for any pair of sides; and also, cognitive events representing the perpendicularity of intersecting sides. The difference resides in the profile imposed on this common base. The nominal predication designates the bounded region comprising the four line segments; the interconnections establish these segments as a region and specify its configuration, but they are not themselves in profile. The adjectival predication does profile these interconnections. The bounded region comprising the line segments is selected as the figure within the relational profile, and since it includes both participants (subtrajector and sublandmark) of the pivotal subrelations, it functions as both the global trajector (TR) and the global landmark (LM).

6.3.3. *Classes of Atemporal Relations*

I have claimed that major grammatical classes are notionally definable, and have attempted a rudimentary characterization of the requisite constructs. The semantic pole of a noun designates a thing, defined as a region in some domain, whereas adjectives, adverbs, prepositions, and certain other classes profile atemporal relations. In seeking to explicate traditional categories, however, I do not mean to imply that these categories, as normally interpreted, are necessarily optimal in all respects. From the perspective of cognitive grammar, the implicit criteria for these categories are occasionally seen to be mixed or confused, and certain limits on category membership are rather arbitrary. But by and large the traditional categories are quite useful, so it is worth pointing out how they differ from the fundamental notional classes posited in this model.

If a noun is a symbolic expression that designates a thing, it would seem most rational to employ the term for all such expressions, and I will do so in the context of my own framework. Traditionally, though, the term is limited to expressions of a certain size, typically words and compounds. I thus depart from traditional practice and categorize phrases and even longer expressions as nouns (e.g. *lazy cat, people with cats, that man out walking his cat*), including full nominals (noun phrases). Pronouns are also sometimes excluded from the traditional noun category, apparently because they have special properties (and another name happens to be available for them). Pronouns do satisfy the cognitive-grammar definition for the noun class, however, and will be considered a special case within the category.

Traditional grammatical categories are especially problematic in regard to atemporal relations. Among the basic distinctions traditionally drawn, the only one that I interpret as resting solely on semantic grounds is the broad contrast between **adjectival** expressions, which have a thing for their trajector, and **adverbial** expressions, which have a relation.[15] There are difficulties, however, as soon as we turn to prepositions, postpositions, and the second

---

[15] Thus I agree in essence with the definition of an adjective as something that modifies a noun, and an adverb as something that modifies a verb, an adjective, or another adverb (cf. Ch. 8).

member of "verb-particle" constructions, whatever it is called. The very terms preposition and postposition reveal the core of the problem: they pertain to syntagmatic relations between the relational element and a nominal expression serving to elaborate its landmark; by their very nature, then, they go beyond the internal properties of the relational predication and include information about the larger grammatical context in which it functions. Something is not called a preposition, for example, unless it precedes (or typically precedes) an overt nominal; bipolar syntagmatic considerations are therefore combined with internal semantic factors.

It may be useful (and is certainly possible in cognitive grammar) to posit such classes, so long as we are clear about what is at issue and do not let erroneous suppositions lead us astray. Suppose we define a preposition as a symbolic expression categorized semantically as an atemporal relation, whose landmark is commonly elaborated by an overt nominal that directly follows it: the definition thus involves both semantic and formal factors. Observe now that all these factors are consistent with the previous characterizations of both adjectival and adverbial expressions, which mention only the trajector of an atemporal relation. It follows that prepositions should not be considered mutually exclusive with adjectives or adverbs—instead they constitute a class defined along different lines that can overlap with either one. An atemporal relation is prepositional when its landmark is commonly elaborated as specified; a preposition is also an adjective when its trajector is a thing (*a girl like Sally*), and an adverb when its trajector is a relation (*walk with a limp*), but there are both adjectives and adverbs that are nonprepositional because their landmarks cannot be elaborated (*red, fast*). It is misguided on this view to treat adjectives, adverbs, and prepositions as separate classes all on a par with one another.

The "particle" in "verb-particle" constructions has long been considered taxonomically problematic (see Lindner 1981 for a survey). Though most particles are identical in form and related in meaning to prepositions, they are generally either treated as adverbs or else assigned to a special class because of their distinct behavior, in particular their variable position with respect to a direct object and the lack of an object of their own (e.g. *She turned the lights on/She turned on the lights*). There is again no harm in recognizing particles as a separate class by virtue of their grammatical behavior, but we should avoid the spurious conceptual difficulties entailed by regarding this class as comparable to but disjoint from the others. Considered as predicates, these particles are not distinct from the class of prepositions: they are simply prepositions employed in grammatical constructions where the landmark happens not to be elaborated, as it otherwise normally is.

CHAPTER 7

Processes

A VERB IS a symbolic expression whose semantic pole designates a **process**. A processual predication has a **positive temporal profile**; i.e. its evolution through conceived time is scanned in sequential fashion. Our first objective in this chapter is to explicate this characterization and render it more precise. A second is to introduce the aspectual distinction between **perfective** and **imperfective** processes, which is based on whether the conceived situation is construed as changing during the course of its temporal profile. We will also examine certain complexities pertaining to the internal structure of processual predicates.

7.1. The Temporal Profile

As a first approximation, we can say that the conceptualization of a process follows the temporal evolution of a situation. It involves a continuous series of states representing different phases of the process and construed as occupying a continuous series of points in conceived time. The span of time during which its evolution is tracked is referred to as the **temporal profile** of the process. Because evolution *through* time is criterial, the temporal profile of a process is necessarily **positive**, i.e. nonzero. However, any of its component states occupies just a single point within its temporal profile and can be thought of as having a temporal profile of zero.[1]

7.1.1. Notation

Fig. 7.1 diagrams the purely spatial construal of the processual predicate [ENTER]. The essential import of this predicate is that a trajector, through time, progresses from an [OUT]-relation to an [IN]-relation with respect to some landmark. An indefinite number of component states are involved, but

---

[1] A time interval counts as a "point" because it is construed as minimal (effectively zero) at a certain level of cognitive processing, not necessarily because it has no actual temporal extension whatever.

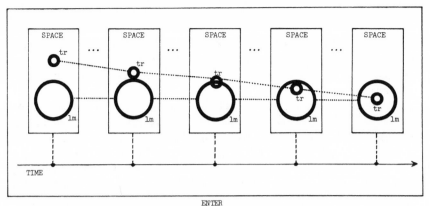

ENTER
Fig. 7.1

in practical terms it is possible to show only a few of them explicitly. Each of these states consists of a relation between the landmark and trajector in the spatial domain; dotted correspondence lines indicate that the landmark is the same from one state to the next, as is the trajector. Moreover, the trajector is shown as changing position vis-à-vis the landmark, which is portrayed as constant in location. It is not precluded that the landmark might be in motion, but no motion is attributed to it by the predicate [ENTER] itself. A broken line connects each component state to its projection in the temporal domain. The full set of projections (including those of states left undepicted) constitutes the temporal profile of the process.

Fig. 7.2 diagrams the same predicate in a simplified format that I will generally use for processes. Only a few states are shown explicitly, normally including both the initial and the final state. The labels for the trajector and

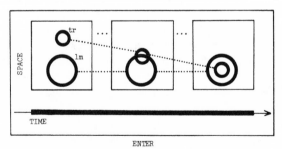

ENTER
Fig. 7.2

landmark (*tr* and *lm*) are given only once, wherever it is convenient to do so. The domain specification for the component states is similarly given only once, at the left. Finally, the temporal profile is indicated simply by representing the proper portion of the time arrow with a heavy line.

7.1.2. *Profiling*

A predicate is not processual simply because the temporal dimension figures saliently in its characterization (6.1.3). To see what else is necessary, let us begin with the notion of a complex scene in the sense of 3.4.2, namely one that does not reduce to a single, consistent configuration. If time is left aside, the component states of [ENTER] clearly amount to a complex scene—the initial state [*tr* OUT *lm*] is grossly inconsistent with the final configuration [*tr* IN *lm*], and some kind of discrepancy can be found between any two states. It is the distribution of these component states through conceived time that avoids the potential contradiction and renders the overall conceptualization coherent rather than semantically anomalous.

Consider, then, a complex scene made coherent by the component configurations being fully ordered and conceived as occupying a continuous series of points through time. Such a conceptualization has all the ingredients for a process, but to actually constitute a processual predication it must satisfy a number of additional requirements. The first of these, and the easiest to grasp, is that a *series* of component states (not just a single state) must be profiled. We saw this previously in regard to stative participles like *broken* (e.g. *a broken cup*), diagrammed schematically in Fig. 6.6. The evolution of a configuration through time furnishes the necessary context for such a participle, but within this base the participial predication designates only the final state; hence it is stative (adjectival) rather than processual. Categorization as a process thus requires that the profile not be restricted to a single state. However, it does not require that every state be put in profile. [ARRIVE], for example, presupposes an extended path of motion on the part of its trajector, but only the final portions of this trajectory—those where the trajector enters the vicinity of its destination and then reaches it—are specifically designated by this verb. The remainder of this trajectory nevertheless functions as part of the base, as shown in Fig. 7.3.[2]

For a predicate to be processual, however, it is not sufficient that a series of component states be included within the profile. To see this, consider episodic nominalizations derived from verbs (5.3.3), e.g. *entrance* (*His entrance was greeted with general gaiety*). Clearly these are nouns rather than verbs, hence they designate abstract things rather than processes. Yet it is equally clear that they refer in some fashion to all the component states profiled by the corresponding verbs (not, say, just the final state), and that these states are recognized as being distributed through time (*His entrance through the grand foyer*

---

[2] There is not necessarily any specific point where the profile abruptly terminates. Profiling is a matter of degree, and it is often helpful to think of it in terms of a focal area (in this instance the final state, where the trajector makes contact with the goal) and a surrounding region that gradually decreases in prominence with increasing distance from the focus.

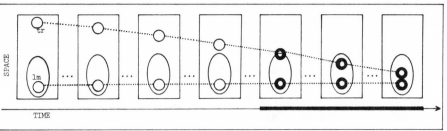

ARRIVE

Fig. 7.3

took a full minute). What, then, is the difference between a verb like *enter* and a noun like *entrance*? I suggest the following: the component states within a process are all profiled individually as relations, but in the corresponding noun they are instead profiled collectively as a thing. In other words, a nominalization like *entrance* construes the component states of the corresponding process as a set of interconnected entities and imposes on them the collective profile of a thing (in the fashion of Fig. 6.1), thus overriding—at this higher level of organization—the relational character that each of these component entities has internally. For the same sequence of states to constitute a process, the possibility of their higher-order construal as a thing must remain latent, and each must retain its relational profile. In short, a process must have the profile of a relation throughout its temporal extension.

We can summarize matters as they stand so far by observing the contrast between (a) and (c) in Fig. 7.4, which employs notational conventions introduced earlier (cf. Figs. 6.5 and 6.6). A process is relational (i.e. it profiles

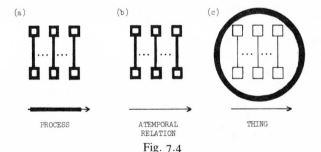

Fig. 7.4

interconnections) at every point throughout its temporal profile, which must be positive (i.e. nonzero). A process can then function as the base for defining an episodic noun, which collectively profiles as a thing the set of component states comprised by the base process. The resulting noun is nonrelational by virtue of its profiling, and is claimed to be atemporal despite the fact that its component entities are conceived as being distributed through time. Observe that the contrast between (a) and (c) in Fig. 7.4 involves two separate distinctions: (1) the difference between a relational and a nonrelational profile; and (2) the difference between a positive temporal profile (where the evolution of a relation is followed through time) and an atemporal construal of the scene. The first should by now be fairly clear, but the second may still be problematic. What does it mean for an event to be construed atemporally? In what sense is an event not "followed through time" even though its occurrence requires the passage of time?

7.1.3. *Summary vs. Sequential Scanning*

The key to the matter is the distinction made in 3.4.2 between summary and sequential scanning. These are contrasting modes of cognitive processing that serve to structure a complex scene in ways that are experientially quite different. Summary scanning is basically additive, and the processing of conceptual components proceeds roughly in parallel. All facets of the complex scene are simultaneously available, and through their coactivation (with reactivation as needed) they constitute a coherent gestalt. This is the mode of processing characteristic of things and atemporal relations, even those for which conceived time is a central domain. Sequential scanning, on the other hand, involves the successive transformations of one configuration into another. The component states are processed in series rather than in parallel, and though a coherent experience requires a certain amount of continuity from one state to the next, they are construed as neither coexistent nor simultaneously available. This is the mode of processing that characterizes processual predications and defines what it means to follow the evolution of a situation through time. In short, summary scanning is the ability we display when examining a still photograph, and sequential scanning is what we do in watching a motion picture.

Crucially, we have the conceptual flexibility to process a complex scene in either mode. Given a complex scene whose component states are conceived as being distributed through time, it is natural to structure them as a process by activating them sequentially and thus experience them successively with the passage of processing time. We are nevertheless capable of activating the component states simultaneously by means of summary scanning, with the experiential effect that they are superimposed to form a single gestalt (this composite gestalt is roughly analogous to a photograph made from multiple exposures—cf. Fig. 3.11). The simultaneous availability of all the component states makes it possible to profile them collectively as a thing.

The twofold difference between a complex scene construed as a process (e.g. *enter*) and the same scene construed as an episodic noun (*entrance*) can thus be restated as follows: (1) the component states are profiled individually as relations in the former, and collectively as a thing in the latter; and (2) sequential scanning is employed for the process, and summary scanning for the noun. If this analysis is correct, we might predict the possibility of an intermediate type of predication that is like a process with respect to one of these properties and like a thing with respect to the other. Though full discussion cannot be offered at this juncture, I will claim the existence of a substantial class of **complex atemporal relations** that have precisely this character. These have a relational profile, as shown in Fig. 7.4(b), but they are scanned in summary rather than sequential fashion. An example is the infinitival *to* in certain of its uses, including its role in forming noun modifiers (e.g. *She was the first person to enter the cave*). *To* derives from the processual *enter* a predication that, like nonfinite noun modifiers in general, is both relational and atemporal; *to enter* is thus adjectival rather than verbal, though it clearly profiles all the component states of its base process.[3]

The partial schematic hierarchy in Fig. 7.5 summarizes the basic classes of predications introduced so far. The highly schematic notions [THING] and [RELATION] are immediate instantiations of the all-embracing category

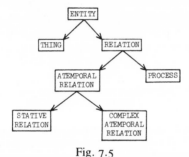

Fig. 7.5

[ENTITY], which neutralizes the difference between a nominal and a relational profile. Within the broad class of relations, a fundamental distinction is made between those that involve sequential scanning and therefore have a positive temporal profile (i.e. processes), and those that do not and are thus construed as atemporal relations even when time is a salient dimension. Atemporal relations are of two sorts. Complex atemporal relations (e.g. infinitivals used as noun modifiers) resemble processes in profiling a series of relational configurations. A simple atemporal relation—one that profiles only a single relational configuration—is the same as a stative relation (6.1.3); examples include *red*, *above*, and the stative participle *broken*.

---

[3] See Langacker (1982a) for arguments characterizing English passive participles as complex atemporal relations. Active participles derived by *-ing* are also atemporal relations; they differ from infinitivals by construing the component states of the base process as effectively homogeneous and profiling only a representative series of these states. Both *to* and *-ing* have nominal variants as well. The rather subtle difference between a complex atemporal relation and an abstract nominalization is well within the range of what we can expect from semantic extension and normal polysemy.

7.1.4. *Formulation*

We can clarify these notions further by employing the formulaic notations devised in 4.3 to characterize motion and other ordered conceptions. The most general form of an ordered conceptualization is given in (1), where C is the conceptualizer, $[T_0 > T_1 > T_2 > \cdots > T_n]$ represents the passage of processing time, and any S_i within the range $[S_0 > S_1 > S_2 > \cdots > S_n]$ is the situation as momentarily conceived, i.e. the set of cognitive events activated by C at T_i.

$$(1) \quad \begin{bmatrix} S_0 \\ C \end{bmatrix}_{T_0} > \begin{bmatrix} S_1 \\ C \end{bmatrix}_{T_1} > \begin{bmatrix} S_2 \\ C \end{bmatrix}_{T_2} > \cdots > \begin{bmatrix} S_n \\ C \end{bmatrix}_{T_n}$$

In the case of spatial motion, S_i has the special form $[[m/l_i]/t_i]$, where m is the mover, and l_i is the location of the mover at moment t_i of conceived time.

Spatial motion is a particular kind of process. To accommodate processes in general, we can replace the locative relationship $[m/l_i]$ with a less specific construct; let R_i then stand for any structure profiled as a relation. My hypothesis concerning the nature of processual predications can now be represented as follows:

$$(2) \quad \begin{bmatrix} R_0/t_0 \\ C \end{bmatrix}_{T_0} > \begin{bmatrix} R_1/t_1 \\ C \end{bmatrix}_{T_1} > \begin{bmatrix} R_2/t_2 \\ C \end{bmatrix}_{T_2} > \cdots > \begin{bmatrix} R_n/t_n \\ C \end{bmatrix}_{T_n}$$

In (2), $[R_0 > R_1 > R_2 > \cdots > R_n]$ are the component states of the process, each with a relational profile. These states are construed as being distributed through the span $[t_0 > t_1 > t_2 > \cdots > t_n]$ of conceived time. Sequential scanning—viewing the stages of a process successively rather than simultaneously—amounts to a correspondence between conceived time and processing time; more specifically, each moment T_i of processing time witnesses the activation of $[R_i/t_i]$ alone, and its activation is limited to T_i. When all these conditions are met, the conceptualization constitutes a process with $[t_0 > t_1 > t_2 > \cdots > t_n]$ as its temporal profile.

Using (2) as our point of departure, we can now characterize various sorts of nonprocessual conceptions by modifying it in different ways. Complex atemporal relations (e.g. *to enter*), schematized in Fig. 7.4(b), have the structure given abstractly in (3).

$$(3) \quad \begin{bmatrix} R_0/t_0 \\ C \end{bmatrix}_{T_0} > \begin{bmatrix} R_0/t_0 \\ R_1/t_1 \\ C \end{bmatrix}_{T_1} > \begin{bmatrix} R_0/t_0 \\ R_1/t_1 \\ R_2/t_2 \\ C \end{bmatrix}_{T_2} > \cdots > \begin{bmatrix} R_0/t_0 \\ R_1/t_1 \\ R_2/t_2 \\ \vdots \\ R_n/t_n \\ C \end{bmatrix}_{T_n}$$

All the component states that figure in the process also figure in the corresponding atemporal relation, and these states are still conceived as being distributed through time. The contrast between (3) and (2) comes down to the difference between summary and sequential scanning. In scanning sequentially through the complex scene $[R_0/t_0 > R_1/t_1 > R_2/t_2 > \cdots > R_n/t_n]$, the conceptualizer C activates only a single component $[R_i/t_i]$ at a particular moment T_i of processing time. Summary scanning relaxes this restriction, and with the passage of processing time the components are accessed cumulatively and simultaneously. In saying that the relation is atemporal, therefore, I certainly do not imply that time is not an important factor—just the opposite is true. Instead, the relation is atemporal in the sense that the strict correspondence between conceived time and processing time is suspended; C activates the successive phases of the process as a simultaneously available whole rather than simply following its evolution through time state by state. By definition, a complex relation is said to have a (positive) temporal profile only in those instances where the correspondence between conceived time and processing time is maintained.

It is actually only the final stage in (3) that is crucial, namely T_n, where all the component states are simultaneously activated. This is the stage represented directly in Fig. 7.4(b), which shows the overall relational profile as incorporating that of each component state. The preliminary stages in (3) are included to indicate that the activation of a complex conceptualization is most likely not an instantaneous affair. It is plausible to suppose that the conceptualizer builds up a complex structure of this sort by first activating certain substructures, then maintaining their activation as further substructures are activated, and so on until all component substructures are active simultaneously. When the component substructures are inherently ordered—which is certainly the case in an atemporal relation derived from a process—it is reasonably conjectured that this ordering is reflected in the sequence of their initial activation during the summary scanning that eventuates in their coactivation at T_n. None of this implies that the buildup from T_0 to T_n necessarily has any great cognitive salience, or that any substantial amount of processing time is required. The span $[T_0 > \cdots > T_n]$ may well be instantaneous for most practical purposes, and it may be construed as a single point in processing time with respect to higher levels of organization (cf. fn. 1).

Consider now the contrast between a complex atemporal relation and the corresponding episodic noun, e.g. between *to jump* as a noun modifier (*The last one to jump is a coward*) and *jump* as a noun (*That was a good jump*). This contrast, diagrammed in Fig. 7.4(b)–(c), amounts to the imposition of different profiles on the same atemporally construed base process. Profiling is not specifically indicated in formulaic representations couched in the format of (1)–(3), so (3) is actually appropriate for both concepts, provided that the proper profile is attributed to it. If the relational profile of each component state R_i is retained in the aggregate structure, the result is a complex atemporal relation as depicted in diagram (b). On the other hand, an event noun is obtained by construing $[R_0 > \cdots > R_n]$ as a set of interconnected entities (a region) collectively profiled as a thing. But in either case the atemporal predication observed in T_n is based on an ordered series of states distributed through conceived time and presumably activated successively but cumulatively through processing time during the buildup phase.

To make the episodic-noun construal of (3) more perspicuous, we can replace $[R_0 > \cdots > R_n]$ with the symbols $[e_0 > \cdots > e_n]$, to emphasize that the component relations lose their individual relational profiles and are taken instead as entities collectively profiled as a thing:

$$(4) \quad \begin{bmatrix} e_0/t_0 \\ C \end{bmatrix}_{T_0} > \begin{bmatrix} e_0/t_0 \\ e_1/t_1 \\ C \end{bmatrix}_{T_1} > \begin{bmatrix} e_0/t_0 \\ e_1/t_1 \\ e_2/t_2 \\ C \end{bmatrix}_{T_2} > \cdots > \begin{bmatrix} e_0/t_0 \\ e_1/t_1 \\ e_2/t_2 \\ \vdots \\ e_n/t_n \\ C \end{bmatrix}_{T_n}$$

This formula is appropriate for a thing whose component entities are ordered by virtue of being distributed through conceived time, but clearly there are many nominal concepts that lack this property. Some involve ordering that is independent of conceived time; simple examples include the concept of a line segment or any sort of scale, either of which is resolvable into a fully ordered set of points. To the extent that a single ordering predominates, the formula in (5)(a) is applicable; it accommodates a broader class of ordered conceptions than (4), whose temporal ordering makes it a special case.

$$(5)(a) \quad \begin{bmatrix} e_0 \\ C \end{bmatrix}_{T_0} > \begin{bmatrix} e_0 \\ e_1 \\ C \end{bmatrix}_{T_1} > \begin{bmatrix} e_0 \\ e_1 \\ e_2 \\ C \end{bmatrix}_{T_2} > \cdots > \begin{bmatrix} e_0 \\ e_1 \\ e_2 \\ \vdots \\ e_n \\ C \end{bmatrix}_{T_n} \quad (b) \begin{bmatrix} r_0 \\ r_1 \\ r_2 \\ \vdots \\ r_n \\ C \end{bmatrix}_{T_n}$$

Of course the component entities of many things cannot be fully or uniquely ordered. The scheme in (5)(a) is in that case oversimplified with respect to the buildup phase, if not altogether inappropriate. But it is the final stage T_n that is crucial and taken to be characteristic of things as a class.

For sake of completeness, the representation of a stative relation is given in (5)(b). We saw in 6.2 that a stative relation (e.g. *above*—cf. Fig. 6.8) is decomposable into component subrelations that are not necessarily ordered with respect to one another. These subrelations, indicated by $[r_0, \ldots, r_n]$ in (5)(b), are coactivated by summary scanning and may be completely independent of conceived time. All of them taken together constitute a single higher-order relation, which is then capable of being situated in conceived time as one state R_i in a series of such states defining a process or a complex atemporal relation, as sketched earlier in (2) and (3). When this occurs, however, location in conceived time (i.e. $[R_i/t_i]$) involves a relationship above and beyond those (namely $[r_0, ..., r_n]$) that figure in R_i internally.

With all this in mind, let us return to *before* (as in *It began to rain before we finished painting*), which was diagrammed in Fig. 6.7 and claimed to be a stative relation, despite its manifest connection with conceived time. The basis for this claim should now be evident. For *before*, conceived time is the basic domain of predication; its function is quite analogous to that of space with *above*. That is, the component subrelations $[r_0, ..., r_n]$ defining the stative relation R_i are computed from the relative positions of its trajector and landmark in conceived time, but these are coactivated through summary scanning in the manner of (5)(b) and pertain to its internal structure alone. A processual predication based on R_i would require the further steps of (1) placing R_i within a series of distinct relations of this sort; (2) locating these relations successively in conceived time (this step might be automatic since time is the primary domain); and (3) scanning through them sequentially. These happen not to be part of the conventional content of *before*.

7.1.5. *Motivation*

A hard-nosed linguist will doubtless ask for evidence to support these claims. How can one prove that the conception of a process (hence the meaning of every verb) requires sequential scanning and has the schematic form indicated in (2)? The request for justification is certainly legitimate, but we must take some care that the form of the request does not embody methodologically unreasonable expectations. In particular, one cannot necessarily expect or demand the existence of direct empirical evidence that bears on this question alone considered in isolation from the overall descriptive context in which the analysis of processes is embedded: I can no more substantiate the claim that verbs imply sequential scanning—directly, and without regard to how the total descriptive system meshes together—than the proponent of a more fashionable model can prove that movement rules leave traces without explicating the function of these constructs as part of a much larger theoretical and descriptive framework. The absence of direct and conclusive empirical support is unfortunate, but no linguistic theory can provide such motivation for all its constructs taken individually.

The motivation I can offer has two aspects. The first, by far the weaker, is simply an assertion of plausibility. Verbs are a universal and fundamental grammatical category, so it should not be surprising to find that they have an equally fundamental cognitive basis. The intimate association between verbs and temporal notions makes the time-based characterization I offer a natural one in a priori terms, and it relies only on constructs that I consider to be of undeniable cognitive validity (sequential vs. summary scanning, conceived vs. processing time). I further believe that the characterization is revelatory and intuitively satisfying, for it explicates the oft-noted "dynamic" quality that sets verbs apart from nouns and other categories.

The second, more substantial aspect is an assertion of descriptive adequacy. The battery of constructs and descriptive devices I have introduced and employed in the characterization of processes (profiling, ordering, things vs. relations, the construal relationship, modes of scanning, conceived time, processing time) all have independent justification and constitute the minimal apparatus needed to characterize nonarbitrarily the varied types of predications summarized in Fig. 7.5, their subtypes and interrelations, and how they interact in larger grammatical constructions. The full import and descriptive utility of this apparatus may not yet be apparent, but it has all been evolved to permit the explicit description—and to some degree the explanation—of a considerable body of previously intractable or mysterious linguistic data. This can only be judged by assessing the coherence, naturalness, breadth, and insightfulness of the overall descriptive system as it emerges in later chapters and subsequent works.

7.2. Perfective vs. Imperfective Processes

A process is a relationship scanned sequentially during its evolution through conceived time. This type of predication is ideally suited to the description of change. Most verbs do in fact predicate a change of some kind, but we must nevertheless recognize a substantial class that do not. Processes that involve a change through time will be called **perfective**, for reasons to become apparent; other processes will be called **imperfective**.[4] The contrast between these basic classes is of prime importance for understanding the English aspectual system, particularly as it pertains to the auxiliary.

7.2.1. The Nature of the Contrast

The existence of imperfective processes and their nonprototypical character are both predicted from the definition of processes summarized in formula

---

[4] A similar distinction is made by Smith (1983), whose results are quite compatible with my own. **Active** and **stative** are common terms for the classes I am calling perfective and imperfective, but active suggests **action** (and agent), which is not always appropriate for a perfective predicate, and stative is most felicitous for a simple atemporal relation (i.e. a state). The problem of linguistic terminology is notorious, and not just in the domain of aspect. Though I do not claim to have a fully optimal terminological system, I have felt it necessary to devise many terms of my own (sometimes by redefining standard ones), since established terms are either unavailable or carry too much "excess baggage."

(2). This definition requires a series of states $[R_0 > R_1 > R_2 > \cdots > R_n]$ distributed along the temporal dimension, but nowhere is it specified that these states are necessarily distinct. One should therefore anticipate—as the limiting case of variability from one state to the next—the possibility of a process in which all component states happen to be identical and the degree of variability falls to zero. Because they represent the perception of constancy through time instead of change, imperfective processes are qualitatively different from perfectives, and have special grammatical properties that are in some measure explained by this qualitative difference. But the endpoint of a scale is nevertheless still a part of it. Despite their extreme character, imperfective processes group with perfectives to jointly define the class of verbs, which function alike in many ways.

Let me offer a prefatory comment about the grammatical properties distinguishing perfectives and imperfectives. Although the behaviors in question permit one to determine the classification of verbs and may in fact be the only overt indication of their aspectual character, I emphasize that they are *symptomatic* of perfectivity/imperfectivity rather than *definitional*—the definition of perfective and imperfective processes is semantic, consisting of the specifications in (2) together with an indication of whether or not the component states are construed to be effectively identical. There is no circularity here, for our enterprise is not one of constructing operational definitions or discovery procedures. It is rather to construct a coherent and revelatory descriptive system that accommodates a broad array of facts with economy and insight. I cannot prove in absolute or autonomous terms that *resemble* has all the properties I attribute to imperfective processes (e.g. a positive temporal profile, in contrast to the stative *like*); nor can I specify a simple empirical check, independent of the analysis, which might falsify the claim. What I can do, however, is show that this claim is part and parcel of a comprehensive analysis of the English aspectual system in which everything falls neatly into place and many apparent peculiarities are explained.

The verbs in (6) exemplify imperfective processes:

(6)(a) *J.P. resembles his father.*
  (b) *The Smiths have a lovely home in the country.*
  (c) *Your sister believes that the earth is flat.*
  (d) *An empty moat surrounds the dilapidated castle.*
  (e) *This road winds through the mountains.*

Just two distinguishing properties of English imperfectives will be mentioned at this point. First, as (6) shows, they can be used in the simple present tense without a "special" interpretation; the present-tense perfectives in (7), by contrast, must be construed as habitual, as instances of the "historical present," as part of a play-by-play account, or in some comparable fashion.

(7)(a)   *The middle linebacker kicks his dog.*
  (b)   *This guy comes up to me and tries to sell me some Charger tickets.*
  (c)   *Payton fights his way into the end zone!*

Second, perfectives occur in the progressive construction marked by *be . . . -ing*, while imperfectives do not:

(8)(a)   *The middle linebacker is kicking his dog.*
  (b)   *Payton is fighting his way into the end zone!*
  (c)   **J.P. is resembling his father.*
  (d)   ** The Smiths are having a lovely home in the country.*
  (e)   ** Your sister is believing that the earth is being flat.*
  (f)   **An empty moat is surrounding the dilapidated castle.*

This second difference has a ready functional explanation. *Be* is itself an imperfective verb,[5] and the progressive construction overall has the effect of imperfectivizing what would otherwise be a perfective expression. Adding *be . . . -ing* to imperfectives would therefore be superfluous, and it is understandable that the evolving conventions of English have not pursued this redundant path.

That imperfective processes profile a relation construed as constant through time is perhaps apparent from the examples cited. All of the situations described in (6) would be presumed stable under normal circumstances, and the sentences themselves do not impute to them any change through time.[6] Suppose, however, that we employ the same verbs in a context most plausibly interpreted as involving a change; in this case they receive a perfective construal and consequently occur felicitously in the progressive, as seen in (9):

(9)(a)   *J.P. is resembling his father more and more every day.*
  (b)   *The Smiths are having a lovely argument.*
  (c)   *That guy is spinning your sister a line, and she's believing every word of it.*
  (d)   *The SWAT team is surrounding the dilapidated castle.*
  (e)   *This road is winding through the mountains.*

Most of these examples are straightforward. *Resemble* in (9)(a) is inchoative and describes an increase in the degree of similarity, in contrast to the constant degree of similarity imputed by (6)(a). As for the (b) sentences in (6) and (9),

---

[5] In most of its common uses, *be* designates a maximally schematic imperfective process, i.e. it has no content other than that serving to characterize imperfective processes as a category. The auxiliary *do* (also the passive *be*) is schematic for the class of processes as a whole, both perfective and imperfective. (Cf. Langacker 1981c, 1982a.)

[6] Imperfectivity does not imply that the designated situation is immutable and will necessarily endure forever: observe that (6)(c) is felicitous even if the speaker thinks that the sister might change her opinion any moment. It only specifies that the situation is construed as being effectively constant for the duration of its temporal profile, which is limited by the scope of predication and in the simple present is restricted to the time of speaking.

having a home in the country is a matter of ownership that endures until something occurs to change it, but to have an argument is to carry out a certain type of activity. In (6)(c) the sister's belief is part of her already existing theory about the nature of reality, but in (9)(c) *believe* describes a change in her belief system (such as it is) and means, roughly, 'accept a claim'. The locative configuration in (6)(d) is obviously stable, whereas (9)(d) pertains instead to activities having a comparable configuration for the resultant state.

The contrast between (6)(e) and (9)(e) merits closer examination. Both can be used without strain to describe the same objective situation, i.e. the same road whose winding course through the mountains is not at all affected by the passage of time. They are nonetheless quite distinct in meaning, in a way that accords perfectly with the hypothesized difference between perfective and imperfective processes. *Wind* in (6)(e) is imperfective. Its scope of predication is sufficiently broad to encompass the entire road (or a substantial portion of it) as a simultaneously accessible whole. The stative relation predicated as being constant through time incorporates the entire complex locative configuration involving the road and the mountains, including the curved shape of the road as a complete unit as well as the intermingling of mountain slopes with the loops of the road's curves. Sentence (6)(e) is therefore most aptly used in circumstances affording an overview of the entire scene, for example in consulting a road map or discussing the desirability of choosing one route over another. By contrast, (9)(e) would more likely be spoken by someone actually travelling along the road as a description of his current experience. For each component state in the process, its scope of predication is highly restricted, essentially confined to what the speaker can actually see at the moment. What constitutes the *road* in this situation is limited to whatever segment of it falls within the current scope of predication, and this segment changes from one instant to the next. Consequently the position vis-à-vis the mountains of the "road" (i.e. that segment of the road to which the speaker has immediate perceptual access) also changes from one instant to the next, making *wind* a perfective process. Sentences (6)(e) and (9)(e) therefore structure the same objective scene by means of alternative images, particularly in regard to scale and scope of predication. The perfectivity of the verb is determined by whether the scope of predication encompasses the entire scene simultaneously or only successively through time.

These examples show that the perfective/imperfective contrast is not appropriately viewed as a rigid dichotomy partitioning the class of verbs into disjoint subsets. For many verbs, both perfective and imperfective variants are firmly established in linguistic convention. Though some processual notions lend themselves far more readily to one particular construal, others are ambivalent, their categorization easily influenced by seemingly minor matters, like the choice of subject or object. *See*, for example, is imperfective in (10)(a), but perfective in (10)(b); only the former is well formed in the simple present without a special interpretation.

(10)(a)   *I see the mountains.*
    (b) **I see a flash.*

Mountains endure through time and are capable of supporting a perceptual relationship that is essentially stable throughout a positive temporal profile, but the instantaneous character of a flash renders an imperfective construal most unlikely. Flexibility of categorization is further enhanced by conventional patterns allowing a verb to be extended from one category to the other, often with no morphological consequences. The element of inchoation making *resemble* perfective in (9)(a) can be added to other imperfectives as well (e.g. *I'm liking my teacher better and better*). Almost any perfective can be construed as habitual with no special marking, as in (7)(a), and habituals are classed as imperfectives.

Predicting whether a given verb will behave as a perfective or an imperfective is therefore not always possible given its basic semantic value alone. Absolute predictability may not even be feasible when the verb, the other major lexical items, and the objective situation to be described are all specified beforehand (consider *wind* in (6)(e) and (9)(e)). If absolute prediction remains beyond our grasp, there is nevertheless much that we can properly and usefully attempt to do: define the relevant categories; list conventionally established usages and patterns of extension; and explore the factors that might influence a speaker to structure a scene in one way rather than another.

7.2.2. *Temporal Bounding*

Many aspectual subclasses can be recognized for verbs (cf. Vendler 1967; Dowty 1972; Talmy 1977), and crosscutting schemes of classification may be equally valid both cognitively and linguistically. I am focusing on the perfective/imperfective contrast, which is fundamental for English in terms of the number of its grammatical ramifications; in view of its primal character (simply the presence vs. absence of change) it can be expected to have substantial significance for other languages as well. Reinforcing this expectation is the close parallel that exists between the perfective/imperfective distinction for verbs and the elemental count/mass distinction for nouns (cf. Mourelatos 1981).

I suggested in 5.3.2 that the hallmark of a mass noun is effective homogeneity. It is not required that the mass be continuous in any strict sense, or that every portion be fully identical to every other—we know, for instance, that *corn* consists of individual kernels that vary somewhat in size and other properties—but construal as a mass does require that internal variability be subordinated to an overriding conception of continuity and uniformity. For physical substances, effective homogeneity is attributed to a mass throughout its spatial expanse. In imperfective processes, time is the relevant domain: the component states in such a process are construed as being identical throughout its temporal profile. Once again, however, it is *effective* homogeneity rather than actual identity in any strict sense that is pivotal. For example, in using (8)(b), *Payton is fighting his way into the end zone!*, one is certainly aware that Payton is carrying out an activity and that his situation is changing through time. This inherently perfective activity is central to the meaning of the sentence, but it functions as a base and is not profiled per se by the overall expression. The imperfectivizing progressive construction superimposes its own profile on this base and structures it in a manner that highlights those respects in which the profiled states of the process are constant; the component states are viewed at a level of abstraction sufficient to neutralize their differences and are thus construed as a kind of mass. The individual elements of this mass (analogous to the kernels with *corn*) lose their separate identity and are considered effectively equivalent owing to their shared participants and their common status as facets of the same base process.[7]

In the case of mass nouns, effective homogeneity is the source of indefinite expansibility and contractibility. Any portion of a mass entity, however large or small, constitutes a valid instance of the category. Imperfective processes also manifest indefinite expansibility and contractibility in their temporal profiling, which—as before—is the analog of spatial expanse for a physical substance. This flexibility in the temporal profile proves crucial for understanding how imperfectives function grammatically and interact with other predications. For one thing, it explains why imperfectives can be used in the simple present. In brief, their expansibility/contractibility ensures that the temporal profile can always be made to coincide precisely with the time of speaking. This is not so with perfectives, and the only perfectives that occur in the simple present are performatives, where this coincidence holds as a matter of definition. (See Langacker 1982b for extended discussion.)

Also explained is a difference between perfectives and imperfectives that emerges when they are put into the past tense:

(11)(a)　*The Smiths had an understanding about that, and in fact they still do.*
(b)　**The Smiths had an argument about that, and in fact they still do.*

Have an understanding describes a stable arrangement and is thus imperfective, whereas *have an argument* is perfective because it describes an event. Let us assume that the past-tense form of a verb implies full instantiation of the process it designates prior to the time of speaking. Because an imperfective process is indefinitely expansible/contractible along the temporal dimen-

---

[7] The requisite degree of abstraction might appear extreme, and the similarities tenuous, but they are within the range of what is attested for mass nouns (note *furniture* and *equipment*).

sion, so that any subpart is representative of the category, existence of the Smiths' arrangement through any positive span of time should constitute a valid instance of the processual category *have an understanding*, regardless of whether it exhausts the full duration of the arrangement. With this in mind the felicity of (11)(a) is easily explained. The Smiths' understanding is specified as enduring from the past right through the present (i.e. the time of the speech event). Any subpart of its duration prior to the moment of speaking is sufficient to instantiate the category, so the requirements imposed by the past-tense predication of the first clause are satisfied; this is fully consistent with continuation of the Smiths' arrangement through the present, so the specifications of the second clause are also met and the sentence is consequently well formed. An inconsistency arises in (11)(b), however. A perfective category lacks the property that any subpart of an instance is also a valid instance: its members qualify as such only holistically. Putting *have an argument* into the past tense therefore implies that this perfective event has been carried out in its entirety prior to the time of speaking. The result is a conflict with the second clause, which specifies the continuance of the event through the present.

Count nouns further contrast with mass nouns in being bounded within the scope of predication. Bounding implies the possibility of exhausting one instance of a category and initiating another, with the result that count nouns are replicable (i.e. they pluralize); masses are expanded rather than replicated. Translating this into the temporal domain, we find as expected that a perfective process is bounded and replicable, while an imperfective process is unbounded and nonreplicable. This contrast in bounding is in fact what motivates the terms perfective and imperfective. We have already observed it in relation to (11): full instantiation of the perfective process prior to the speech event implied its completion, but full instantiation of the imperfective process was consistent with its continuation beyond the profiled time span up to and even through the present. The associated contrast in replicability is illustrated in (12).

(12)(a)   *The linebacker kicked his dog again and again.*
     (b) ?*The linebacker liked his dog again and again.*

The adverb *again and again* induces a repetitive construal of the verb, and though this replication is felicitous with the perfective *kick* of (12)(a), it is incompatible with the imperfective *like* of (12)(b). It is of course possible to give (12)(b) a consistent (though unlikely) interpretation, one requiring a perfective variant of *like* that is not currently established in conventional usage. In this perfective variant *like* would designate the full cycle of starting to like some entity, holding this attitude for an indeterminate period, and then ceasing to hold it; bounding is thus brought within the scope of predication. Once made perfective in this fashion, the process designated by *like* can be replicated, yielding the repetitive interpretation of (12)(b).

The schematic diagrams in Fig. 7.6 provide a summary of our central observations. A perfective process profiles a change through time, which I have

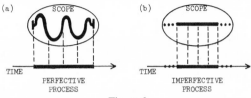

Fig. 7.6

indicated by a wavy line, whereas an imperfective process profiles a relationship construed as holding constant through time, represented by a straight line. Moreover, a perfective process is specifically bounded within the scope of predication, whereas an imperfective process is not; the relation profiled by the latter may completely occupy the scope of predication and even overflow its boundaries. Below, along the time arrow, I have marked the temporal projections of the relational profiles. Being bounded, the temporal profile of the perfective process is represented as a discrete line segment; to indicate the expansibility/contractibility of an imperfective process (where no specific endpoint is specified), its temporal profile is shown with a series of dots at each end. These contrasting notations for the temporal profiles will be employed in certain diagrams in the format of Figs. 7.2 and 7.3, to mark the difference between the two aspectual classes. With regard to formulaic representations, that given in (2) above is now seen to be appropriate only for perfective processes, since it includes specific initial and final states. More accurate for imperfective processes is the formula in (13), which is open ended and employs the symbol R in unsubscripted form throughout to indicate that all the component states are construed as identical.

$$(13) \quad \ldots > \left[\begin{array}{c} R/t_i \\ C \end{array} \right]_{T_i} > \left[\begin{array}{c} R/t_{i+1} \\ C \end{array} \right]_{T_{i+1}} > \left[\begin{array}{c} R/t_{i+2} \\ C \end{array} \right]_{T_{i+2}} > \ldots$$

For the most part, the covariant properties of change and bounding can be regarded as two sides of the same coin (as can their opposites, namely constancy and open-endedness). However, bounding requires only that there be some limit to the participating entities, and change is not absolutely indispensable for limiting the sequence of component states. Some processes are internally homogeneous but construed as occurring in limited episodes (e.g. *sleep, wear a sweater, walk*); the bounding implied by this episodic construal results in their categorization as perfectives (e.g. they take the progressive). Observe that this internal homogeneity makes them analogous to count nouns like *spot*. Of course the onset and termination of an otherwise homogeneous process can be interpreted as representing a type of change (a limiting case). A processual predication that specifically includes them in the scope of predication may be perfective for that very reason.

7.2.3. *Directional Imperfective Processes*

One problem that remains is to account for the semantic contrast between pairs of sentences like the following:

(14)(a)   *That road leads from Reno to Las Vegas.*
   (b)   *That road leads from Las Vegas to Reno.*

(15)(a)   *This nerve branches just below the elbow.*
   (b)   *These nerves merge just below the elbow.*

(16)(a)   *The hill gently rises from the bank of the river.*
   (b)   *The hill gently falls to the bank of the river.*

Since both members of each pair can be used to describe exactly the same objective scene, the difference in their meanings must reside in alternate images being employed to structure the scene. There seems little doubt that directionality figures crucially in this imagery. For example, (15)(a) is appropriate in the context of tracing the path of certain nerves outward from the central nervous system, and (15)(b) in tracing their path inward from the periphery. But how, specifically, are these sentences to be described with reference to the constructs now at our disposal?

One's first thought might be to analyze them in the manner of (9)(e), *This road is winding through the mountains*: the speaker scans mentally along the path of the road, nerve, or hill in one direction or the other; only a limited part of the path falls within the scope of predication at any one moment, and with the passage of processing time the accessible part is perceived as "moving" in the direction of scanning. This cannot be correct, however. The verb *wind* in (9)(e) is perfective, but the verbs in (14)–(16) are imperfective (note their occurrence in the simple present), implying constancy rather than change through time. Moreover, we saw that (9)(e) would be appropriate for someone actually driving along the road and having immediate perceptual access only to a small segment of it at any one time, but analogous remarks do not hold for (14)–(16); these sentences are compatible with the holistic view afforded by a road map, a comprehensive diagram in a medical handbook, or a ride in a helicopter. Hence they are parallel not to (9)(e), but rather to (6)(e), *This road winds through the mountains*, where the entire configuration of the road and mountains is claimed to fall within the scope of predication for every component state of the imperfective process. But if all these component states are identical and the situation is portrayed as constant through conceived time, how is directionality to be accommodated?

The answer, in brief, is that different levels of organization must be taken into account. We have already seen how ordering is possible in an atemporal conception involving summary scanning (cf. formulas (4) and (5)). The directionality observed in (14)–(16) has this basic character; it holds for a single component state and derives from the manner in which the specifications of the complex stative configuration are progressively activated during the buildup phase. The summary scanning that eventuates in this complex stative conception constitutes the first level of organization. At the second level, the directional conception derived in this manner is followed as a unit through conceived time, giving the predication the temporal profile of an imperfective process.

To see this in concrete detail, let us focus on the imperfective *rise* of (16)(a); the verb is crucial, for it lends its profile to the sentence as a whole at higher levels of grammatical organization. We had best begin, however, with the perfective *rise* of sentences like *The balloon rose slowly*. The perfective variant is diagrammed in Fig. 7.7.

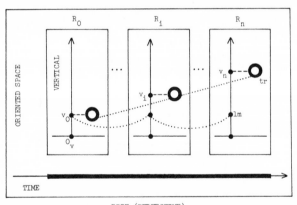

RISE (PERFECTIVE)

Fig. 7.7

The domains are time and oriented space. Three component states are explicitly shown, labeled R_0, R_i, and R_n. Crucial to this predicate are the projections of the trajector along the vertical axis at successive points in time; for any moment t_i within the temporal profile, this vertical projection is designated v_i. The trajector's initial position along the vertical axis, v_0, is especially significant and has been marked in Fig. 7.7 as the landmark.[8] The dis-

---

[8] Identification as a landmark is not the exclusive property of any one entity. In some expressions, the entire vertical path $[v_0 > \cdots > v_n]$ achieves special salience and can be so identified (e.g. *The balloon quickly rose 200 feet*).

placement of v_i from O_v, the origin of the vertical axis, increases from one component state to the next. As for *above/below* (analyzed in 6.2.1), detection of such change is presumed to involve higher-order acts of comparison. Thus, if $O_v > v_0$ is the cognitive event that registers the displacement of v_0 from the vertical origin, and $O_v > v_1$ is the corresponding event for the immediately following state, an increase in the trajector's vertical displacement between t_0 and t_1 is given by the comparison $(O_v > v_0) > (O_v > v_1)$ with respect to the magnitude of the first-order scanning events. For *rise* (as opposed to *sink* or *fall*) the transition from standard to target in the higher-order comparison is expansive (rather than contractive), i.e. $O_v > v_0$ bears an [IN]-relation to $O_v > v_1$. In a prototypical instance, the same is true for each pair of adjacent states R_i and R_{i+1}. The relationship is uniformly expansive throughout the temporal profile: $[(O_v > v_i) \text{ IN } (O_v > v_{i+1})]$.

Fig. 7.8 diagrams the imperfective variant of *rise* employed in (16)(a). In effect, all the component states of the perfective variant are telescoped into a single state in its imperfective counterpart, reflecting the fact that the trajector

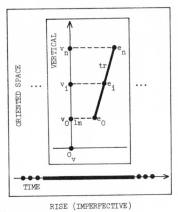

RISE (IMPERFECTIVE)

Fig. 7.8

occupies all the positions in its vertical trajectory simultaneously rather than successively, in a configuration that is conceived as stable through time. Only a single state is shown explicitly; this is sufficient, for all of the indefinitely many states in the expansible/contractible temporal profile are construed to be identical. It is important here to resolve the trajector (or at least the relevant facet of it) into an ordered sequence of entities $[e_0 > \ldots > e_n]$ profiled collectively as a thing; the vertical projection of any entity e_i is given as v_i. As before, we can consider either v_0 or the entire set of projections $[v_0 > \ldots > v_n]$ to be a landmark.

To explicate the directionality of the imperfective *rise*, it is helpful to consider the formulaic representation of its perfective and imperfective variants. For both the perfective predicate and its imperfective counterpart, the set of first-order comparisons of the form $O_v > v_i$ are pivotal, as well as the second-order comparisons assessing their relative magnitude for each v_i and v_{i+1}. The difference between the two variants resides in how these specifications are distributed with respect to conceived and processing time. The perfective *rise* presents the situation formulated in (17); for sake of convenience, the first- and second-order comparison events are given separately, in (17)(a) and (b) respectively.

$$(17)(a) \quad \begin{bmatrix} (O_v > v_0)/t_0 \\ C \end{bmatrix}_{T_0} > \begin{bmatrix} (O_v > v_1)/t_1 \\ C \end{bmatrix}_{T_1} > \begin{bmatrix} (O_v > v_2)/t_2 \\ C \end{bmatrix}_{T_2} >$$

$$\cdots > \begin{bmatrix} (O_v > v_n)/t_n \\ C \end{bmatrix}_{T_n}$$

$$(b) \quad \begin{bmatrix} (O_v > v_0) > (O_v > v_1) \\ C \end{bmatrix}_{T_1} > \begin{bmatrix} (O_v > v_1) > (O_v > v_2) \\ C \end{bmatrix}_{T_2} >$$

$$\cdots > \begin{bmatrix} (O_v > v_{n-1}) > (O_v > v_n) \\ C \end{bmatrix}_{T_n}$$

The formula in (17)(a) simply states that the trajector, at each point in conceived time t_i, has the displacement $O_v > v_i$ from the vertical origin, and that this relationship is scanned sequentially through the span $[T_0 > \cdots > T_n]$ of processing time. The formula in (17)(b) pertains to the sequential scanning of second-order comparisons. Part of the structure activated at T_1, for example, is the second-order comparison representing the assessment by the conceptualizer C of the relative magnitude of the trajector's displacement from the vertical origin at t_0 and t_1. The transition from standard to target for these higher-order comparisons is in each case expansive (though this is not shown explicitly in the formula as written). The directionality of the perfective *rise* stems from the distribution of these first- and second-order locative specifications through both conceived time and processing time.

In the case of the imperfective *rise*, all of the same specifications are present and simultaneously available internally to a single component state, as seen in Fig. 7.8. The directionality observed in this predicate must also be attributed to the internal structure of a single state, at the first of the two levels of organization referred to at the outset. More precisely, this directionality reflects the order in which the various specifications are activated (through summary scanning) in the buildup phase for the conceptualization of a single representative state. This is formulated in (18).

(18)(a) $\begin{bmatrix} O_v > v_0 \\ C \end{bmatrix}_{T_0} > \begin{bmatrix} O_v > v_0 \\ O_v > v_1 \\ C \end{bmatrix}_{T_1} > \begin{bmatrix} O_v > v_0 \\ O_v > v_1 \\ O_v > v_2 \\ C \end{bmatrix}_{T_2} > \cdots > \begin{bmatrix} O_v > v_0 \\ O_v > v_1 \\ O_v > v_2 \\ \vdots \\ O_v > v_n \\ C \end{bmatrix}_{T_n}$

(b) $\begin{bmatrix} (O_v > v_0) > (O_v > v_1) \\ C \end{bmatrix}_{T_1} > \begin{bmatrix} (O_v > v_0) > (O_v > v_1) \\ (O_v > v_1) > (O_v > v_2) \\ C \end{bmatrix}_{T_2} >$

$\cdots > \begin{bmatrix} (O_v > v_0) > (O_v > v_1) \\ (O_v > v_1) > (O_v > v_2) \\ \vdots \\ (O_v > v_{n-1}) > (O_v > v_n) \\ C \end{bmatrix}_{T_n}$

Here $[T_0 > \cdots > T_n]$ represents the processing time required for building up a single, complex stative relation; conceived time is not yet a factor, since all of the specifications are construed as holding simultaneously at any moment of conceived time. The import of (18) is that the conceptualizer, C, initiates his buildup of the stative scene with e_0 and its vertical projection v_0 (see Fig. 7.8). By scanning along the path $[e_0 > \cdots > e_n]$, and assessing its vertical projection at every stage, he progressively and cumulatively activates the full set of locative specifications indicated for T_n. It will be noted that these are precisely the same specifications found in (17).

Collectively, the locative specifications in (18) constitute a single stative configuration that we can label R. The ordered buildup leading to the full activation of R is the first of the two levels of organization involved in the imperfective *rise*. At the second level of organization, R—as a structured whole with built-in directionality—is situated with respect to conceived and processing time in accordance with formula (13). That is, R is conceived as holding constant through an indefinite span of conceived time, and the sequence $[\cdots > R/t_i > R/t_{i+1} > R/t_{i+2} > \cdots]$ is scanned sequentially. Observe that processing time figures at both levels of organization. In (18), at the first level, $[T_0 > \cdots > T_n]$ is the time required for the buildup phase in activating the conceptualization of a single state. In (13), at the second level, $[\cdots > T_i > T_{i+1} > T_{i+2} > \cdots]$ is the time involved in the sequential scanning (where the state is followed through conceived time) that makes the structure processual. The sequentiality of $[T_0 > \cdots > T_n]$ is quite important at the first level of organization (it is the basis for the directionality of the predication); however, this entire span counts as a single point of processing time at the higher organizational level.

The perfective and imperfective *rise* therefore differ not in their locative specifications, but rather in the distribution of these specifications with respect to conceived and processing time. The contrast between them also correlates with the difference between physical and abstract motion (4.3). With the perfective *rise* of (17) and Fig. 7.7, the trajector is a mover progressing through physical space. With the imperfective *rise* of (18) and Fig. 7.8, on the other hand, there is no physical motion. It is possible, however, to consider the speaker/conceptualizer as the mover in an abstract sense, since he activates successively the various locative specifications pertaining to the trajector's vertical projection; these correspond to the points in the physical trajectory followed by the trajector in the perfective predication.

7.3. Dimensions of Complexity

The internal structure of processual predications is complex in various ways that merit brief consideration. These include the relation between trajector and landmark; the resolution of a process into component subprocesses; verbs with multiple semantic variants; and the differential participation of various facets of the trajector and landmark in processual relationships.

7.3.1. *Trajector/Landmark Differentiation*

The first matter is the degree to which the landmark and trajector of a process are distinct and salient entities differentiated from their surroundings and from one another. We can regard as prototypical a process involving separate and well-defined physical objects as participants, but obviously there are many process predicates that deviate from this prototype in various respects. The landmark of *rise*, for example, is simply the trajector's location along the vertical axis at the initial stage of the process (Fig. 7.7); this point is not otherwise identified and has no independent salience or special status.

Many processual predications are inherently reflexive (6.3.2) in the sense that they specify coincidence of their trajector and landmark as an intrinsic part of their internal structure. Processes of this kind typically give rise to intransitive verbs describing the relationship that different facets of the trajector bear to one another (*break, stretch, bend, curve, blink*, and so on). One such example is *disperse* (e.g. *The crowd dispersed*), diagrammed in Fig. 7.9. The same complex entity functions as both the overall trajector (*TR*) and the overall landmark (*LM*). It is a higher-order construct (e.g. a crowd) consisting of a substantial though indeterminate number of component entities that, at

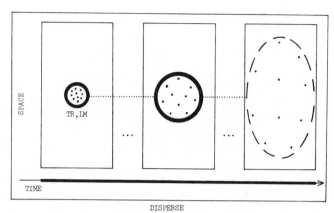

DISPERSE

Fig. 7.9

the initial stage, are in close proximity to one another. The import of *disperse* is that the distance among these component entities increases through time (at least in aggregate terms), to the point where the higher-order construct functioning as *TR/LM* ceases to be recognizable as such at the final stages. Just as *TR/LM* decomposes into component entities, so the overall process can be decomposed into subrelations. For a given pair of component entities, we can speak of a subrelation [*tr_i r_i lm_i*] representing the distance between them, which is specified as increasing through conceived time. Since every component entity participates in a subrelation of this sort with every other, it is evident that the set of subtrajectors [*tr_1, tr_2, ..., tr_n*] and the set of sublandmarks [*lm_1, lm_2, ..., lm_n*] are extensionally identical. The former is construed collectively as a higher-order thing that functions as overall trajector for the process, and the latter as a higher-order thing that functions as overall landmark, but since the two sets are identical, the trajector and landmark coincide.

7.3.2. *Subtrajectories*

For *disperse*, no particular subtrajector, sublandmark, or subrelation has any special status relative to any other; all the relationships are essentially symmetrical, and only collectively do the component entities or subrelations achieve any substantial salience. Often, though, prominent substructures can be discerned that are intermediate between the predicate as a whole and what can be recognized for all practical purposes as its smallest components. Consider the verb *walk*, for instance. If we refer to the actions carried out by its trajector as a **trajectory**, it is readily seen that this trajectory is complex and resolvable into two component subtrajectories. One subtrajectory is reflexive: the trajector's legs move relative to one another in a characteristic, cyclically repetitive manner. The other subtrajectory, nonreflexive, consists of the trajector's motion through space relative to his surroundings. Obviously, the two are coordinated and closely interrelated.[9] At present, though, we need only observe that these subtrajectories occupy neither the highest nor the lowest level in the hierarchy of descriptively significant constructs.

Another type of example is the predicate [THROW]. Like [WALK], it comprises two salient subtrajectories (call them R_1 and R_2), but it differs from [WALK] in that these subtrajectories have different subtrajectors. An expression of the form X *throw* Y can thus be resolved into the components $[X R_1 Y]$ and $[Y R_2 Z]$. The first component involves an action by subtrajector X that transfers energy to Y; this could be broken down further into subcomponents (including a reflexive subcomponent pertaining to how portions of X's body move in relation to others), but we will not pursue the matter here. The second component, $[Y R_2 Z]$, consists of subtrajector Y moving in relation to its surroundings (Z) as a result of the energy transferred from X by $[X R_1 Y]$. Though both subtrajectories are central to the meaning of *throw*, they are not of equal status. Note, for example, that the progressive construction can be used to describe $[X R_1 Y]$ as an ongoing event, but not $[Y R_2 Z]$: I can say X *is throwing* Y quite felicitously if X's arm is in motion and Y has not yet initiated its subtrajectory, but the sentence is inappropriate if X's activity is already completed and Y is in midflight. We see, then, that the components of a complex trajectory can differ in their relative prominence. Naturally this correlates with the relative prominence of their participants.[10] In the case at hand, the subtrajector (X) of the more prominent subtrajectory functions as the overall trajector for the predicate. Though Y is the most salient and highly differentiated entity in the less prominent subtrajectory $[Y R_2 Z]$, this subtrajector is only the landmark of $[X R_1 Y]$ and has the same secondary role at the predicate level.

7.3.3. *Multiple Variants*

A further dimension of complexity is the existence of verbs having an array of interrelated senses. Some of these senses differ primarily in the relative prominence of substructures within a common base. *Throw*, for instance, has (at least marginally) a variant in which Y rather than X is selected as figure and overall trajector (cf. van Oosten 1977):

(19)(a) *This new Frisbee throws easily.*

    (b) *This knife throws well.*

A more elaborate example of this sort is provided in (20).

(20)(a) *Sally teaches handicapped children.*

    (b) *Sally teaches mathematics.*

[9] Equally important for some purposes is a third subtrajectory, reflexive in character, pertaining to the volitional control exerted by the trajector over his motor activity.

[10] Recall the suggestion (6.1.1) that a high level of activation for a relational conception implies a correspondingly high level of activation for its participants.

(c)   *Sally teaches third grade.*
(d)   *Sally teaches Sunday school.*

Besides an agent, the concept of teaching makes intrinsic reference to the learner, to the subject matter, and—on a more contingent basis—to the level of instruction and its institutional setting. All of these elements are present in the base of *teach* and consequently figure to one degree or another in the semantic structure of all the sentences in (20). The verb *teach* itself introduces these various entities schematically; it is only through syntagmatic combination with other expressions that they are specified in any detail. The conventions of English permit various options for the elaboration of these entities by a nonoblique nominal. These options are accommodated in the present framework by different variants of *teach*, which share a common base but vary in the relative prominence of components. All the variants in (20) select the agent as the figure and overall trajector, and the nominal that elaborates it syntagmatically is what we recognize as the subject. They differ in their choice of **primary landmark**, i.e. the most salient profiled participant apart from the trajector; when this substructure is a thing, a nominal elaborating it syntagmatically is recognized as the direct object. These different variants of *teach* (and the constructions in which they function) impose contrasting images on essentially the same conceived situation.[11]

We can briefly note certain other ways in which the senses of a verb commonly differ in semantic value. Most familiar is the presence in one variant of a subtrajectory that is lacking in another. For example, the transitive *roll* of (21)(a) is parallel to *throw* in having two components that we can represent as $[X R_1 Y]$ and $[Y R_2 Z]$; the intransitive *roll* in (21)(b) contains only the latter, so Y is left as the relational figure.

(21)(a)   *The elephant rolled the log down the hill.*
    (b)   *The log rolled down the hill.*

Often two senses of a verb involve the same (sub)trajectory but contrast in regard to whether the (sub)trajector instantiates this trajectory successively through time or simultaneously for any given moment. Previous examples include the difference between the perfective and imperfective variants of *rise* (Figs. 7.7 and 7.8) and also of *wind*: recall the comparison of (6)(e), *This road winds through the mountains*, with (9)(e), *This road is winding through the mountains*.[12] Yet another source of variation concerns how much of a tra-

---

[11] None of these variants of *teach* is derived from any other in the sense of generative grammar (though one may provide the source for another through semantic extension). In the usage-based model I propose, the variants in (20) are all listed in the grammar, together with a schema representing their commonality (this schema specifies trajector status for the agent but is neutral in regard to the choice of primary landmark).

[12] A similar contrast is observed with atemporal expressions, e.g. *around*. In *The scout hiked all around the lake*, the scout occupies the points of the indicated path only successively with the

jectory is included within a relational profile. Profiling is a matter of degree, and even when a particular portion of a trajectory can be identified as a kind of "focal area," there is often considerable flexibility as to how far the profiled region extends outward from this focus. In the case of *jump*, for instance, the focal area is the moment when the trajector leaves the ground; possibly the profile incorporates nothing other than this transition, as in (22)(a). The remaining examples show that other facets of the overall event (e.g. the activity leading up to departure from the ground, the subsequent spatial path, and even the planning/scheduling phase) can nevertheless be rendered more prominent and brought within the profile.

(22)(a) *Without even bending his knees, Superman jumped (and remained suspended in the air).*
  (b) *Myricks is jumping now, gathering speed as he sprints down the runway.*
  (c) *His horse jumped all the way over the moat.*
  (d) *Dwight Stones is jumping at noon.*

·The difference between the imperfective *believe* of (23)(a) and the perfective *believe* of (23)(b) hinges on whether the profile is restricted to the constant situation of holding a belief, or is expanded to include the initial judgment through which this situation comes about:

(23)(a) *My wife believes that I was working at the office last night.*
  (b) *My wife believed what I told her.*

Here it is not obvious that either the initial judgment or the resulting belief stage should be considered primary.

7.3.4. *Active Zones*

The final dimension of complexity to be considered is illustrated by the sentences in (24).

(24)(a) *We all heard the trumpet.*
  (b) *Don't ever believe Gerald.*
  (c) *I finally blinked.*
  (d) *Bring me a red pencil.*

What these expressions have in common is a relational predication in which a highly prominent substructure within the profile (i.e. the trajector or primary landmark) does not precisely coincide with the entity that participates most directly and crucially in the designated relation. *Trumpet* profiles a physical object, but a physical object per se does not impinge on our auditory apparatus; rather it is the sound emitted by the trumpet that does so. Similarly, the

---

passage of time. In *the fence around your garden*, on the other hand, the fence occupies all of these points at once. *Around* is thus a complex atemporal relation in the first example, but a stative relation in the second.

process of believing pertains to propositions (as in (23)), not to people as such, yet the conventions of English include a variant of *believe* whose primary landmark corresponds to the person who is the source of a proposition rather than to the proposition itself. Blinking directly involves only the eyelid and associated portions of the body (muscles, nerves, the surface of the eyeball), but *blink* selects for its trajector the body as a whole; other options are generally not even permitted in the trajector role, though they may be accommodated as an explicit landmark:

(25)(a)   *My eyelid blinked.*
   (b)   ?*His left eye blinked.*
   (c)   *He kept blinking his eyes.*
   (d) ??*He kept blinking his eyelids.*

Finally, a *pencil* cannot per se occupy color space; only the light sensations associated with it can interact with this domain. In expressions like *red pencil*, English usage sanctions in this role the sensations associated with either the outer surface of the pencil or the marks it creates when used for writing.

This type of phenomenon is far more pervasive and important than is generally realized, and its treatment in the present framework is relatively unproblematic (cf. Langacker 1984). All semantic structure is claimed to derive from the profiling of substructures within a base, an inclusive conceptualization that may approach encyclopedic proportions. Since the base is inherent in the meaning of an expression, alternate expressions formed on the same base may have largely the same conceptual import despite minor differences in their profiles. *Teach*, for example, means largely (but not precisely) the same thing in (20)(a)–(d), even though its four variants select different substructures within the common base for the special prominence accorded the primary landmark. In similar fashion, the verbs in (26)(a) and (b) are almost equivalent to those in (24)(a) and (b) respectively, and the meaning of *blink* is not drastically different in (24)(c) and (25)(c).

(26)(a)   *We all heard the sound of the trumpet.*
   (b)   *Don't ever believe what Gerald says.*

Within limits, then, the choice of trajector and primary landmark is free to vary within a scene with only minor effect on the semantic value of an expression. Languages commonly exploit this flexibility to accommodate the greater cognitive salience of concrete objects over abstract entities, wholes over parts, and so on.

Entities are often multifaceted, only certain facets being able to interact with a particular domain or play a direct role in a particular relationship. Those facets of an entity capable of interacting directly with a given domain or relation are referred to as the **active zone** of the entity with respect to the domain or relation in question. Thus the sound emitted by a trumpet when played (or perhaps when dropped) is the active zone of *trumpet* with respect to the process of hearing, whereas the entity it designates is the physical object rather than the sound. What the examples in (24) demonstrate is that active zones and profiles do not always coincide. What Gerald says is the active zone with respect to *believe* in (24)(b), but it is not what the noun *Gerald* designates. The active zone of *I* with regard to blinking is the eye or eyelid, and that of *pencil* with regard to *red* is the color sensation associated with the outer surface or with the marks it makes, but these nouns profile the speaker and pencil as holistic entities.

We see from (24) that the substructure profiled by a relational predicate as its trajector or primary landmark cannot necessarily be equated with the active zone of the participating entity. Sometimes two variants of a verb differ on precisely this point: in (26)(a) the primary landmark of *hear* is specified to be a sound (hence it is felicitously elaborated by the nominal expression *the sound of the trumpet*), so profile and active zone coincide; in (24)(a), on the other hand, its primary landmark is specified as an object capable of emitting a sound (not the sound itself), implying a discrepancy between active zone and profile. The two variants of *believe* illustrated in (26)(b) and (24)(b) are exactly parallel in this respect. *Blink* has two variants both of which manifest a discrepancy between active zone and profile in regard to its trajector. The trajector in (24)(c) is identified as an entire person (or animal), though only the eye region is directly involved in the designated activity. The variant in (25)(c) also identifies the trajector with the entire person, but the discrepancy between profile and active zone is to some degree made explicit by elevating the eye region to the status of primary landmark. The contrast between these two variants of *blink* is schematized in Fig. 7.10, where *AZ* indicates the active zone.

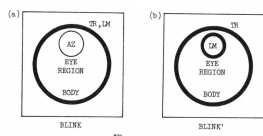

Fig. 7.10

Note, in conclusion, that both interpretations of the stative *red* in *red pencil* involve a discrepancy between active zone and profile with respect to the trajector, but not the same discrepancy. The trajector is in both cases the writing implement overall, and the active zone is a color sensation, associated with either its outer surface or the marks it leaves on paper. Two points worthy of mention emerge from this observation. First, this analysis explains the possibility of sentences like (27) being noncontradictory:

(27)   *This red pencil isn't red.*

The interpretation of (27) is unproblematic if the first instance of *red* has for its active zone the color of marks left on paper, and the second instance that of the pencil's outer surface. Second, the importance of an encyclopedic view of linguistic semantics comes to the fore. The color of marks left on paper would figure marginally at best in a restricted, dictionary-type characterization of *pencil*, and the notion of a writing implement would not figure at all in that of *red*. Yet these are crucial in (27) to explicating the pertinent sense of *red*, the grammatical valence relation permitting the composite expression *red pencil*, and even the sentence's logical properties.

□ Part III □
GRAMMATICAL
ORGANIZATION

PART I OF THIS MONOGRAPH laid out the fundamental assumptions of cognitive grammar, and Part II provided a programmatic account of semantic structure. We can now begin to examine how the framework accounts for grammatical structure. Part III is devoted to general principles of grammatical organization. Subsequently (in Volume II), Parts IV and V will apply these principles to restricted but significant domains of English grammar: nominal structure in Part IV, and the verbal structure of finite clauses in Part V.

The objective in Part III is to show in general terms how grammar works, and to indicate how a model of the sort proposed can say the kinds of things a grammar has to say. Ch. 8 deals with valence relations, i.e. the integration of symbolic structures to form composite symbolic expressions. In Ch. 9 we probe further into the nature of symbolic units; a particular concern is the asymmetry between autonomous and dependent elements. Ch. 10 presents a unified discussion of categorization, schematic networks, and the relation between structure and context. A variety of interrelated problems are treated in Ch. 11: distribution, grammatical classes, structural descriptions, well-formedness, and the computation of novel expressions. Finally, Ch. 12 examines the compositional relationship between component and composite structures in a grammatical construction, with special reference to the notions of analyzability and partial compositionality.

CHAPTER 8

Valence Relations

WHEN TWO OR MORE symbolic structures combine to form a more elaborate expression, I speak of there being a **grammatical valence relation** between them. The structures that combine are referred to as **component structures**, and the integrated entity that results as the **composite structure**. The term **grammatical construction** is applied to this entire ensemble: the component structures, their mode of integration, and the resulting composite structure.

Valence theorists have often recognized the relevance of meaning to their enterprise, but owing to the absence of an appropriate or sufficiently articulated account of semantic structure—or to their belief in the autonomy of grammar—they have generally concentrated on working out taxonomies based on formal criteria (Allerton 1982 is an example). The present approach is quite different. Though distribution is explicitly accommodated (cf. Ch. 11), taxonomy is not regarded as an end in itself: the ultimate objective is to understand grammatical behavior on the basis of a deeper analysis that explicitly describes the internal structure of the participating elements and details the nature of their integration.

Valence relations are not a simple matter, but the major factors are reasonably well understood. There are four primary valence factors: (1) correspondence; (2) profile determinacy; (3) conceptual (as well as phonological) autonomy and dependence; and (4) constituency. We will consider these in the order stated.

8.1. Correspondence

In chemistry it has long been recognized that the valence properties of atoms—their combinatory potential—can only be understood and explained with reference to their internal structure. The matter is not quite so clear-cut in linguistics owing to the prime importance of conventionality. How a symbolic unit interacts with others cannot be predicted in any absolute way from its internal structure alone, because at any one time the established conventions of a language strongly sanction only a relatively small proportion of the potentially available combinations. Nevertheless, it is the internal structure of component expressions that determines the vast range of potential combinations from which the selection is made, as well as the likelihood that particular sorts of combinations will actually be conventionally exploited.

Valence relations between atoms are based on the sharing of electrons. The valence relations uniting linguistic expressions depend in similar fashion on the sharing of elements. It is only by virtue of having certain substructures in common that two component expressions can be integrated to form a coherent composite expression. To the extent that we regard the component structures as distinct and separable entities, we can speak of **correspondences** between their shared substructures, i.e. between certain substructures within one and those substructures within the other to which these are construed as being identical. Such correspondences are found at both the semantic and the phonological poles, and they constitute the one invariant feature of valence relations. We will concentrate for now on integration at the semantic pole.

8.1.1. *Its Significance*

It is worth pausing to consider why composite predications are necessary in the first place. The reason, quite obviously, is that linguistic convention cannot provide a fixed, unitary expression for every conceivable situation that a speaker might wish to describe. Instead it furnishes a limited inventory of fixed expressions, which are generally appropriate for coding only certain aspects of complex conceptualizations, together with a set of conventional patterns for combining these as needed. More often than not the speaker wishes to symbolize a coherent conceived situation that is relatively complex and for which no fixed expression is available. For purposes of linguistic coding, then, he is forced to dissociate his integrated conception into separate but overlapping "chunks" for which conventional symbols are provided, and to invoke a number of compositional patterns sufficient to specify at least approximately the nature of their intended integration.[1]

One way to think of correspondences, then, is to view them as a record of the distortions engendered by dissociating an integrated scene into separately symbolized chunks of conceptual content, and more specifically, by the occurrence in separate components of what is really understood to be the same entity. It is equally valid to regard correspondences as indications of the overlap between two conceptions that permits their integration to form a coherent scene. Still another approach is to treat correspondences as instructions for assembling a composite structure from its components, i.e. as instructions

---

[1] At best the combinatory principles of a language provide an incomplete account of how a composite expression is actually understood in context. This notion of **partial compositionality** will be developed in later chapters.

for superimposing the specifications of corresponding substructures. These alternate descriptions represent mutually compatible perspectives on the phenomenon.[2]

Let us take a simple illustration. Suppose I wish to tell someone where he can locate his football. Finding no single morpheme or other fixed expression to convey the desired notion, I construct the novel sentence *Your football is under the table*. I can achieve appropriate linguistic symbolization only by isolating and separately symbolizing various facets of my unified conception, such as the objects most saliently involved (*football, table*), their relative position in space (*under*), their relation to me and my interlocutor (*your, the*), and the status of the conceived situation in time and reality (*is*). Established combinatory principles of English (in the form of schematic symbolic units) give me guidelines for assembling the complex expression out of these components, and sanction the result. Also, it is not implausible to suppose that some of the higher-order structures, e.g. *the table* and *under the table*, have the status of units and thus require little constructive effort for their activation. In short, my knowledge of the conventions of English makes this particular task relatively straightforward (though by no means trivial from the analytical standpoint), and if I utter the sentence properly my interlocutor will have little difficulty using these same conventions to reconstruct my intent.

Consider just one small part of this task, the integration of *under* and *the table* to form the prepositional phrase *under the table*. I have already suggested that this phrase most likely has unit status for a typical speaker and need only be activated, but we can nevertheless examine its internal composition. The two semantic components are [UNDER] (a predicate) and [THE-TABLE] (a more elaborate predication that can itself be analyzed into component predicates). [UNDER] profiles a stative relation in the domain of oriented space. [THE-TABLE] has a complex matrix that includes such domains as three-dimensional space (for a shape specification), oriented space (for canonical orientation), and the abstract domain supporting the predication of contextual uniqueness (identification by both speaker and hearer). For diagrammatic ease, I have omitted from Fig. 8.1(a) any indication of contextual uniqueness and have given explicitly only a schematic shape specification and an indication of canonical alignment in oriented space.

As diagram (a) indicates, the integration of the two predications depends on a correspondence between the landmark of [UNDER] and the profile of [THE-TABLE].[3] These are the substructures within the component predica-

---

[2] Yet another description, based on categorizing relationships between the component and composite structures, is presented in Ch. 12.

[3] My choice of correspondences depends on what I want to say and how I want to say it. With other communicative objectives, I might establish instead a correspondence between, say, the trajector of [UNDER] and the profile of [TABLE], or between the landmark of [UNDER] and the profile of some other nominal predication.

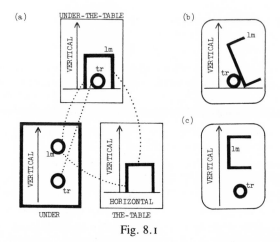

Fig. 8.1

tions that I construe as identical with reference to the unified conceptualization for which I am seeking linguistic symbolization. Observe, however, that
the two predications differ markedly in regard to how they characterize the
corresponding substructures. The landmark of [UNDER] is specified only
schematically—basically only as a thing capable of being located in oriented
space. The profile of [THE-TABLE], by contrast, is embedded in an essentially open-ended complex matrix, some of whose specifications are quite
detailed.

A composite structure is formed by superimposing corresponding entities
and merging their specifications. The component predications are thereby integrated by virtue of their overlapping substructures, and the matrix of the
composite structure consists of the union of the matrices of its components. In
the case at hand, the matrix of [UNDER-THE-TABLE] is equivalent to that of
[THE-TABLE], since the latter includes the domain of [UNDER] (oriented
space). The composite structure [UNDER-THE-TABLE] is an integrated
conception equivalent to [UNDER] in that it profiles a stative relation in oriented space. In contrast to the schematic landmark of [UNDER], however, that
of [UNDER-THE-TABLE] is fairly specific, for it inherits all the specifications of [THE-TABLE]. It is pertinent at this juncture to recall the schematic-
transparency principle (Ch. 2), which states that the result of merging a
schema with an instantiation of that schema is a unified conception equivalent
to the instantiation. Consequently, when the corresponding entities are superimposed, the schematic landmark of [UNDER] is "swallowed up" by the more
elaborate specifications of [THE-TABLE] in forming the composite structure.

A number of general points concerning correspondences and the formation
of composite structures can be made with reference to this basic example. For
one thing, we must also recognize correspondences between the composite

structure and its components. The composite structure represents an integrated conception that must be specifically accommodated as such: it is experientially distinct from the recognition of individual components plus instructions for their integration, and it may involve entities and specifications beyond those provided by the components. Normally it inherits most of its features from the component structures, simply effecting their union through the merger of shared entities; establishing the "vertical" correspondences is therefore largely automatic. Identifying these correspondences is nevertheless prerequisite to the full description of a construction, since they make explicit the nature and degree of its compositionality. The vertical correspondences required for [UNDER-THE-TABLE] are shown in Fig. 8.1(a), but in most diagrams I will simply indicate the overall compositional relationship by means of single lines between the composite structure and each component structure.

Observe, next, that the composite structure in Fig. 8.1(a), as depicted, is rather more specific than anything necessarily implied by its components. For example, it shows the table resting in its canonical orientation on a horizontal surface (though this is certainly not the only position that tables can assume), and it further represents the trajector as a relatively compact object resting on the same horizontal surface between the table's legs. Though this is naturally how I would most likely construe the scene in the context described earlier, numerous other configurations, equally compatible with the components and with the basic correspondence between the landmark of [UNDER] and the profile of [THE-TABLE], can be evoked in other circumstances. The scene in Fig. 8.1(b) is quite plausible in the context of describing the wreckage left by a tornado, and that of diagram (c), in describing the results of temporarily suspending the law of gravity. The question that arises, then, is to what extent one is justified in attributing to the composite structure any of the properties that distinguish these various possibilities from one another. To what extent are these matters of linguistic convention rather than our pragmatic understanding of the world and the context of the speech event?

That question loses much of its force in a usage-based model that eschews full compositionality and embraces an encyclopedic conception of linguistic semantics. It is probably not at all uncommon for most speakers to use the expression *under the table* to describe a relationship with the specific properties of the composite structure in diagram (a); this construal is reasonably taken as prototypical for the location of objects under tables, and is likely to be invoked in lieu of special circumstances that lead the speaker to structure things differently. If so, this particular construal of *under the table* can be regarded as an established unit representing the most frequent conventional usage of the expression, and as such it is included in the grammar of English (as defined in Ch. 2). Other construals of *under the table* may have the status of conventional units as well, for example its idiomatic interpretation with the implication of drunkenness (e.g. *She drank me under the table*). A structure schematic enough in relevant respects to neutralize the substantial differences among the diagrams in Fig. 8.1 may or may not constitute a conventionalized unit, but in any case its cognitive salience would seem to be less than that of diagram (a). In short, it is claimed that the meaning of an established composite expression—like the meaning of an individual morpheme—is best conceived as a network of interrelated senses, which differ in such properties as prototypicality, schematicity, domain, entrenchment, and so on.

Finally, I return to the topic of selectional restrictions and the anomaly that results from their violation (cf. 3.4.2). A violation of selectional restrictions is nothing more than a conflict in specifications between two entities placed in correspondence. No special apparatus is needed in this model to deal with selectional violations, since all valence relations depend on correspondences, and since the detection of conceptual inconsistency is a problem of cognition in general. Automatically accommodated as well is our intuition that anomalous expressions have semantic import (even if they have no truth value), and that sentences like those in (1) are semantically well formed.

(1)(a)   *There is no such thing as a charismatic neutrino.*
   (b)   *It is meaningless to speak of a charismatic neutrino.*

As defined in cognitive grammar, the meaning of an expression is given not by its composite structure alone, but rather by its composite structure in relation to its components (cf. 8.2). When integrating two component structures, a speaker can perfectly well establish correspondences between substructures with conflicting specifications. When he does establish such correspondences—as in (1), where the trajector of *charismatic* corresponds anomalously to the profile of *neutrino*—the resulting clash in specifications precludes the formation of a coherent composite structure. The expression is nevertheless meaningful, even though no composite structure emerges as a unified entity, because the component structures together with their putative mode of integration are an inherent part of its semantic value. The semantic pole may be defective, but it is not contentless. Two different anomalous expressions are thus nonsynonymous, and sentences like those in (1) are semantically well formed precisely because they comment on the defectiveness of the anomalous constituent.

8.1.2. *Properties*

Correspondences between substructures of the components are claimed to be an invariant feature of valence relations. As one might expect, the relative prominence of substructures correlates with the likelihood of their participation in such correspondences. There is a notable tendency for the profile or one of its salient subparts to correspond in a valence relation, and it is in fact difficult to find instances in which this is not true of at least one component predication.[4] The valence relation in Fig. 8.1(a) is a typical example in this respect: the major correspondence holds between the profile of one predication ([THE-TABLE]) and a subpart of the profile, namely the primary landmark, in the other ([UNDER]).

It is nevertheless quite common for an unprofiled substructure to participate in a correspondence, even the pivotal correspondence in a valence relation. Consider the word *gone*, in particular the version of *gone* that appears in sentences like *He is gone*, where it designates the locative relation resulting from the process *go*. The valence relation combining [GO] and [PRTC] (the past-participial predicate) is diagrammed in Fig. 8.2. [GO] is a process predication, in which the trajector moves from a position inside the neighborhood of

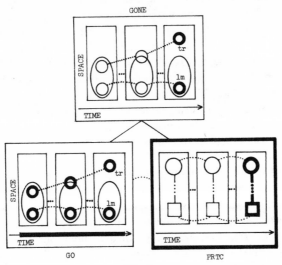

Fig. 8.2

some landmark (often equated with the location of the speaker) to a position outside this neighborhood. The past participle has a number of semantic variants (cf. Langacker 1982a); the one relevant here profiles a stative relation that constitutes the final state of a schematically characterized process functioning as its base.[5] The valence relation hinges on a correspondence established be-

---

[4] What would an example look like? Suppose a zoo manager gives presents to his keepers, and uses a different kind of ribbon to wrap the present depending on what type of animal each keeper cares for. He might then say: *Let's see, where did I put the elephant ribbon?*, meaning the ribbon with which he intends to wrap the package he is giving to the elephant keeper. The correspondence linking [ELEPHANT] and [RIBBON] holds between two unprofiled entities, namely the keeper and the recipient; the former functions in the encyclopedic base of [ELEPHANT], and the latter in that of [RIBBON] (via the specification that ribbon is used for the wrapping of gift packages).

[5] For each component state of [PRTC], three dots appear in the vertical line representing the relational interconnection. They indicate that the base process is characterized only schematically.

tween the process profiled by [GO] and the schematic process serving as the base of [PRTC]. By superimposing the specifications of these corresponding entities (and adopting the profile of [PRTC]) we obtain the composite structure: it designates the stative relation constituting the resultant state of the process [GO].[6]

A number of significant points concerning correspondences can be illustrated by this example. First, as noted, an unprofiled element—in this case the base of [PRTC]—can be a correspondent. Second, the substructures participating in a correspondence need not be things (as in Fig. 8.1); they can also be relations, as in the present example, or indeed any kind of entity. Third, the substructure of a predication that participates in a correspondence does not have to be a proper substructure. The corresponding substructure of [PRTC] in Fig. 8.2 is the schematic process that constitutes its base, and since the profile is included in the base, the correspondent is in fact exhaustive of the content of the predicate. Finally, when a substructure of any complexity functions as correspondent, it is often useful to resolve the global correspondence into a number of more basic ones. Only one correspondence line is shown between [GO] and [PRTC] in Fig. 8.2, but this overall correspondence between the two processes must be understood as subsuming a series of more restricted correspondences: between their trajectors; between their sequences of component states; between the projections of these sequences in conceived time; and so on.

Valence theorists have focused most of their attention on verbs and their nominal complements, where verbs are taken as describing an action or relationship and their complements as designating its participants. There has consequently been a tendency to assume that only relational elements are capable of bearing valence relations: something akin to a "predicate"/"argument" distinction is often taken for granted. Predicates (i.e. verblike elements) are divided according to their valence potential into one-place predicates, two-place predicates, and so on, depending on the number of their participants. Nominal elements function as arguments or elaborators of these relational predicates but are presumed incapable of bearing valence relations of their own. This type of arrangement is not without insight, but it proves too limited to accommodate the full range of combinatory relationships to be found in the varied domains of grammatical structure. A relational predication bearing a valence relation to a nominal participant is no doubt prototypical, but it is nonetheless only a special case in the full spectrum of possibilities (cf. Langacker 1981b).

The relation between [UNDER] and [THE-TABLE] in Fig. 8.1 conforms to this prototype, but the relation in Fig. 8.2 does not: [GO] and [PRTC] are both relational, and neither is reasonably considered a participant of the other. The

---

[6] *Away* and *gone* profile similar relations but differ in their bases. *Away* directly describes a relation of nonproximity in the spatial domain. The domain for *gone*, by contrast, is the process designated by *go*: something can be gone only by virtue of having executed the process of going.

cognitive-grammar account of valence relations has the flexibility to deal with this and many other deviations from the prototype, since it requires only correspondences between substructures; nothing is specified concerning the nature of the predications overall or the role of the corresponding substructures within them. Thus it is possible even for two nominal predications to participate in a valence relation, and such cases are straightforwardly accommodated. One type of instance is provided by noun compounds on the model of *puppy dog*, *killer bee*, and *sailor boy*, where each member of the compound profiles a thing and the two profiles correspond. Very similar, but at a higher level of organization (involving full nominals—i.e. noun phrases), are appositional expressions such as *Jack the Ripper* and *my good friend Henry Kissinger*.[7]

Since valence relations provide for the linguistic coding of a unified conceptualization, it is not surprising that many such relations involve multiple correspondences. One simple example of multiple correspondences is brought out by the well-known ambiguity of expressions like *big elephant*, which can be interpreted to mean either that the elephant is large relative to the norm for elephants (cf. *As elephants go, that one is pretty big*), or else that it is big in terms of the typical human scale (a parent might point out a normal-sized elephant to a young child and say *Look at that big elephant!*). *Big* designates a stative relation in which the dimensions of a trajector are matched against a scale and predicated to fall substantially beyond the norm; the existence of an implied norm is the only important point for present purposes. In forming the valence relation, the profile of *elephant* is placed in correspondence with the trajector of *big*, under either interpretation of *big elephant*. The difference between the two interpretations reduces to whether or not there is a second correspondence, namely between the scalar norm implied by *big* and the category norm that functions as one specification in the encyclopedic conception that constitutes the meaning of *elephant*. The possibility and the optionality of this second correspondence give rise to the alternate construals of the phrase.

As the example shows, correspondences can hold between abstract or nonsalient entities. The same point is illustrated by expressions like those in (2), which exhibit what might be called a "nested locative" construction.

(2)(a) *The heating pad is upstairs in the bedroom in the closet on the top shelf.*
   (b) *The axe is outside in the back yard near the picnic table.*

The order of locative phrases is clearly relevant in this construction, with each locative serving to confine the location of the trajector to a smaller region than

---

[7] In such languages as Luiseño (Uto-Aztecan, southern California) where adjectives are morphologically parallel to nouns, one might analyze expressions like *yot hunwut* '(the) big bear' as appositional constructions (roughly, 'the big one, the bear'). Section 8.3 offers a definition of the head/modifier relation that makes no reference to the distinction between relational and nominal predications.

the preceding. In (2)(b), for example, *outside* specifies the location of the trajector only as being exterior to some unspecified landmark. The second locative, *in the back yard*, narrows down the position of the trajector to a subportion of this broad domain, and the third, *near the picnic table*, narrows it down still further. There is no intrinsic limit to the number of locatives that may be nested in this fashion.

Fig. 8.3 outlines schematically the essential relationships between any two successive locatives in the nested-locative construction. One requirement of this construction is that the trajectors correspond. The second correspondence

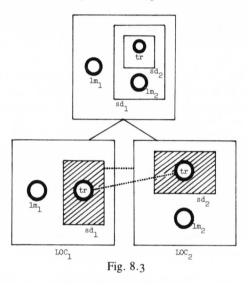

Fig. 8.3

relates two constructs considerably more abstract than those previously considered in this regard. One of the constructs involved is the **search domain**, which was introduced by Bruce Hawkins (1981). The search domain (sd) of a locative predication (LOC) is defined as the region to which it confines the trajector, i.e. the set of points such that the location of the trajector at that point is compatible with its specifications. By definition the trajector is located within the search domain for each component predication; I have crosshatched these regions in Fig. 8.3. The nesting effect of this construction is achieved by a correspondence that equates the search domain of one locative with the scope of predication of the second: the first locative confines the trajector to a particular region, and the specifications of the second all pertain to relationships within this region. The result, as indicated in the composite structure, is that the trajector is simultaneously confined to both search domains, one of which is included in the other.

I conclude this section by noting that the presence vs. the absence of a particular correspondence—seemingly a minor factor in the characterization of a construction—often has striking consequences for the construction's semantic value and grammatical behavior.[8] Consider, for instance, the following well-known sentence type of French:

(3)(a) *Il ouvre la bouche.* 'He opens his mouth.'
  (b) *Il lève la main.* 'He raises his hand.'
  (c) *Il ferme les yeux.* 'He closes his eyes.'

Although the object nominal appears with a definite article and no possessive, the primary interpretation of such sentences construes this nominal as designating an inherent part of the body of the person referred to by the subject. In a transformational analysis of this construction, one might account for the understood possessive relationship by means of a deletion rule erasing the possessor of the object by virtue of coreference to the subject.[9] The cognitive-grammar analysis achieves a comparable result with far less formal machinery. The requisite grammatical construction, depicted in Fig. 8.4, is

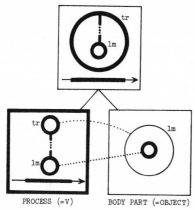

PROCESS (=V)   BODY PART (=OBJECT)

Fig. 8.4

simply a special case (subschema) of the general schema for the integration of verbs with direct-object nominals.

In the general schema for the verb-object construction, the landmark of the process designated by the verb is placed in correspondence with the thing pro-

---

[8] See Casad (1981) and Langacker (1981c) for an example of another sort, concerning the particle *núʔu* in Cora (Uto-Aztecan, western Mexico). Briefly, the different apparent grammatical functions of this morpheme (quotative particle, complementizer, and main-clause verb of saying) stem from how *núʔu* is integrated through correspondences with other predications, not from any variation in its own semantic content.

[9] See, for instance, Langacker (1968), where it is also pointed out that the construction requires the action to be *carried out by* (rather than *applied to*) the body part in question. In the present framework such factors can easily be built into a fuller analysis of the construction.

filed by the object nominal; this is true for the subschema as well. Two additional factors distinguish the subschema from the general construction: (1) the object nominal designates a body part, which necessarily includes within its base, as a salient landmark, the conception of the overall body that it is a part of; and (2) a second correspondence is established, namely between the trajector of the process and the unprofiled landmark of the object nominal. This second correspondence is crucial. It is the functional equivalent of the deletion rule of transformational grammar, since it equates the trajector of the process with the person whose body part is affected, as seen in the composite structure. When the trajector is elaborated by the subject nominal at a higher level of constituency, therefore, the identity of the possessor is specified as well, since this special construction equates the two; there is no need for a separate nominal or possessor element to accomplish this. The occurrence of the definite article is then seen as a natural consequence of the fact that the construction identifies the possessor with the subject: given their equation, the body part designated by the object nominal is contextually unique.

8.2. Profiling Within Constructions

In this section we consider two related topics: **analyzability** and **profile determinacy**. Both pertain to the profiles of component structures and their contribution to the overall meaning of an expression. We may speak of profile determinacy to the extent that the profile of a component structure is adopted as the profile of the composite structure. Analyzability, on the other hand, involves the augmented salience of the substructure designated by a component regardless of how it relates to the composite-structure profile.

8.2.1. *Profile Determinacy*

The issue of profile determinacy, the second valence factor to be considered, can be posed as follows: given the profiles of the component structures in a valence relation, what will be the profile of the composite structure? In Fig. 8.1, for example, [UNDER] designates a stative relation, whereas [THE-TABLE] profiles a thing that corresponds to the landmark of this relation. What then will be the profile of the composite structure [UNDER-THE-TABLE]?

There is no absolute predictability in this matter, i.e. no simple rule that works in all instances. Thus, from constructions like those in Figs. 8.1 and 8.4, one might formulate the natural hypothesis that the profile of a relational predication always prevails over that of a nominal predication when the two are integrated in a valence relation. But this hypothesis (like other obvious candidates) turns out to be false, since the nominal profile can also prevail; at best the hypothesis can be said to hold for prototypical instances. Consider the expressions in (4).

(4)(a) *that football under the table*
   (b) *That football is under the table.*

In both expressions, *football* elaborates the schematic trajector of the relational predication (*is*) *under the table*. Yet (4)(a) designates the football (hence it is nominal in character) whereas (4)(b) profiles the relation. The characterization of a grammatical construction must specifically indicate the profiling of its composite structure, since this is basically an independent feature (despite certain tendencies and limited regularities).

For the most part, a composite structure simply inherits the profile of one of its components. The component structure whose profile is inherited will be termed the **profile determinant** of the construction. I will identify this component notationally by using heavy lines for the box (or closed curve) surrounding it, as I have already done in Figs. 8.1–2 and 8.4. In Fig. 8.1, for example, [UNDER] is the profile determinant in its construction with [THE-TABLE], since the overall predication designates the stative relation profiled by [UNDER]. Similarly, [PRTC] is the profile determinant in Fig. 8.2, since the composite structure [GONE] accords with [PRTC] in profiling only the final state of the process designated by [GO].

Fig. 8.1 can be profitably compared to Fig. 8.5, which diagrams the integration of its composite structure [UNDER-THE-TABLE] with [FOOTBALL] as one step in the formation of (4)(a). This integration implies a correspondence between the profile of [FOOTBALL], a thing, and the schematic trajector of the relational [UNDER-THE-TABLE]. [FOOTBALL] is clearly the profile

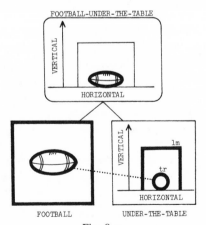

Fig. 8.5

determinant, since (4)(a) is a nominal expression that designates the football
rather than the locative relationship in which it participates. The composite
structure in Fig. 8.5 shows that this locative relationship is part of the semantic characterization of (4)(a), but constitutes an unprofiled facet of the base.[10]

Despite the nonavailability of a fully predictive universal principle (i.e. one
valid for all valence relations in all languages), significant regularities can be
discovered and described. Thus Fig. 8.1 instantiates a general pattern of English for the combination of prepositions with their objects. This pattern is
represented in the grammar as a schema equivalent to its instantiations except
that both the preposition and the nominal are schematic rather than specific: it
specifies that the landmark of the relation corresponds to the profile of the
nominal, and further, that the relational predication is the profile determinant.
Similarly, the schema describing the basic pattern for English compounds
identifies the second member of the compound as the profile determinant:
football thus designates a ball rather than a body part, *carrot juice* names a
liquid rather than a vegetable, *blackbird* is a noun rather than an adjective,
and so on. Such schemas embody the generalizations observable in specific
combinations, but of course the specifications assigned to the schema do not
cease thereby to be specifications of its instantiations as well (indeed, just the
opposite is true). Note, however, that in a usage-based model these schemas
are not invalidated by individual expressions having conflicting properties,
nor do they preclude the possibility of alternate constructions with opposite
specifications, in the same language or another.

Although the canon in valence relations is clearly for one component to
predominate over the others by imposing its profile on the composite structure, this arrangement is far from universal. Several kinds of exception can be
noted. One kind, already illustrated in Fig. 8.3 and by the examples in (2),
involves complex relational predications that inherit as equally salient facets
of their profile the relational profiles of all their component structures. For
example, in (2)(b) there is no reason to think that the composite locative structure profiles any of the component relations (*outside, in the back yard*, or
near the picnic table) at the expense of the others; instead it seems that the axe
is being located simultaneously with respect to multiple landmarks (cf. Fig.
8.3). Another, somewhat clearer example of this kind is a paradigm of locative particles in Cora that situate a trajector (generally the process designated by a clause) with respect to its topographical setting (see Casad 1982;
Casad and Langacker 1985). A typical exponent is *mah* 'away up there to the
side in the face of the slope'. The initial morpheme, *m*, indicates medial
distance from the speaker; the second, *a*, situates the trajector outside the

---

[10] Note that the composite structure is surrounded by a closed curve rather than a box on the
assumption that *football under the table* is probably not an established conventional unit. I assume
that this entire structure combines with *that* at a higher level of constituency to derive (4)(a).

speaker's line of sight up the face of the slope; and the third, *h*, specifies that the trajector is nevertheless in the face (as opposed to the foot or the top) of the slope. The composite conceptualization symbolized by *mah* does not profile any one of these relationships in particular, but rather adopts them as simultaneously valid and coequal specifications.

In cases where the component structures contribute equally to the profile of the composite structure, it makes no real difference whether we say that all of the component structures are profile determinants or that none of them are. To keep things simple, though, I will adopt the latter alternative, and speak of a profile determinant only when there is an asymmetry among component structures in this regard.[11] There is also no intrinsic basis for identifying a profile determinant in constructions for which the profiles of the component structures correspond. We have already noted noun compounds like *puppy dog*, *killer bee*, etc.: each stem designates a thing and a correspondence links their profiles. Superimposing the specifications of corresponding entities yields the same composite structure in such examples regardless of which component is identified as the profile determinant.[12] The same is true in expressions like (5), from Cahuilla (Uto-Aztecan, southern California) (cf. Seiler 1977 and Langacker 1981b):

(5)(a)   *ne-ʔaš kiyul*   'my fish'
  (b)   *ne-ʔaš tamawet*   'my mockingbird'

The stem *ʔaš* 'possessed animal' (with *ʔ* designating a glottal stop) is a kind of classifier that obligatorily carries the possessor prefix when possession of an animal is expressed. Each word in the composite expression (such as *ne-ʔaš* 'my possessed animal' and *kiyul* 'fish') designates a thing, and the two profiled entities correspond in the valence relation forming the nominal constituent. Since each profile corresponds to that of the composite structure, neither component can be singled out as the profile determinant.

Finally, the profile of the composite structure may diverge from those of all the component structures, so that no component qualifies as a profile determinant. This is illustrated by compounds like *yellowjacket*, *pickpocket*, and *redhead*. *Pick*, for instance, designates a process, and *pocket* a thing corresponding to the landmark of that process; the composite structure of *pickpocket* profiles neither, however; it designates the entity corresponding to the trajector of *pick*. A rather different sort of case is given by verbs in Eastern Mono (Uto-Aztecan, central California) formed by adding an instrumental prefix to a stem (cf. Norris 1980). Many of these prefixes designate body parts, and

---

[11] Hence neither component structure in Fig. 8.3 is enclosed in heavy lines.

[12] We can reasonably assume nevertheless that the second member of the compound is a profile determinant, since that is the pattern observed for English compounds in general. We have no guarantee, however, that independent evidence of this sort will always be available.

they appear from examples like (6)(a) to be nominal in character (' is a morphological feature that makes the following consonant fortis):

   (6)(a)   *ma'-tua-'ci?* 'little finger'
          hand-child-DIMINUTIVE

      (b)   *ma-ma'-k^waca?i-'ti* 'He dropped it.'
          it-hand-descend-TENSE

When they combine with an intransitive stem, however, such as $k^w aca?i$ 'de-
scend' in (6)(b) (the superscript *w* indicating labialization of the preceding
sound), the resulting verb is often transitive and causative. The processual
profile of the composite structure clearly centers on the causative activity, yet
this activity is not the designatum of either component.[13]

Such examples are in no way problematic for the cognitive-grammar theory
of valence relations, since there is no claim to the effect that the composite
structure is fully compositional or derives in any mechanical way from the
semantic specifications of its components. The composite structure is recognized as a distinct facet of a grammatical construction even in cases of regularity and full compositionality, and since the description is nonreductive,
there is no inherent difficulty when full reduction cannot be achieved. As a
general matter, it is somewhat inaccurate to regard the composite structure as
being constructed out of its components (though it is convenient to speak in
these terms, as I commonly do). It is more appropriate to say that the component structures *motivate* aspects of the composite structure, and that the degree of motivation is variable (though typically quite substantial). We will explore this approach in Ch. 12.

8.2.2. Analyzability

The semantic pole of a grammatical construction is multifaceted. The
meaning of a complex expression is not its composite semantic structure
alone, but includes as well the separately symbolized semantic structures of
its components and the relation that each of these bears to the composite
whole. These three facets of linguistic meaning are functionally and experientially distinguishable. The composite structure is a unified, "seamless" conceptualization that includes the full content of the expression. The component
structures represent limited "chunks" of this content dissociated from the
whole for coding purposes. The third facet is **analyzability**: recognition of the
contribution that each component makes to the composite conceptualization.

I have already advanced two considerations that motivate the adoption of

---

[13] A third kind of example is found in American Sign Language: a list of terms designating
prototypical instances of a category serves to name the category as a whole ('tool', for instance,
is given literally as 'hammer-saw-screwdriver').

this rather elaborate view of meaning. One is its ability to accommodate the semantic value of anomalous expressions, where a coherent composite structure fails to emerge from the specified mode of integrating the component structures. A second consideration is that the meaning of a composite expression is often not a regular function of the meanings of its parts; composite structures are therefore not in general eliminable in favor of component structures plus a set of compositional rules. The semantic import of analyzability reinforces the need for a view of meaning that takes both component and composite structures into account.

The effect of analyzability can be illustrated by the semantic contrast between pairs of expressions such as these: *father* vs. *male parent*; *triangle* vs. *three-sided polygon*; *acorn* vs. *fruit* (or *nut*) *of an oak tree*; *puppy* vs. *puppy dog*; and so on. Even ignoring the "connotational" aspects of certain terms (like *father*) and concentrating on their central denotational properties, it can reasonably be maintained that the members of each pair are nonequivalent. It can be argued, for example, that *male parent* renders the notions [MALE] and [PARENT] more salient than does *father*, even though both concepts are conveyed by the latter expression. In similar fashion, the notions [POLYGON] and [OAK] are considerably less prominent in *triangle* and *acorn* respectively than in their periphrastic counterparts, which mention these concepts explicitly. The differences are often subtle, and naturally it would be possible to devise a semantic theory that ignored them altogether; to do so, however, would not only be gratuitous, but also misguided given the many indications that relative prominence is an important (if not preeminent) dimension of semantic and grammatical organization.

To state it directly, I claim that the explicit symbolization of a notion augments its prominence and renders it more salient than it would otherwise be (cf. Langacker 1985). Even though *father* fully conveys the concepts [MALE] and [PARENT], it does not specifically designate either of them individually, hence it fails to highlight them to the same degree as *male parent*. The contrast is accounted for automatically in a framework that recognizes both component and composite structures as aspects of the meaning of linguistic expressions. There are two levels of organization in the symbolic and semantic structures of *male parent*. At the first level, the components *male* and *parent* specifically symbolize [MALE] and [PARENT], according them a certain individual prominence that remains despite their subordination, at the second organizational level, to the unified conception functioning as the composite structure. *Father*, by contrast, is basically unanalyzable (any morphemic segmentation is tenuous), so its semantic value involves only a single, unified conception; there is nothing to make [MALE] and [PARENT] stand out individually as specially highlighted facets of it. Even if we assume that the composite structure of *male parent* is identical to the single conceptualization conveyed by *father*, the former expression is nevertheless distinct and more complex semantically.[14]

Father and *male parent* arrive at their common composite structure by way of alternate **compositional paths**—by direct symbolization in one, and by the integration of component symbolic structures in the other. The semantic contrast is a matter of imagery, for it involves the relative salience of various facets of the conceived situation. The contrast is present to some degree even in expressions like *puppy dog* and *oak tree*, where the second element is fully schematic for the first and therefore neither imparts additional information nor imposes added truth conditions: the inclusion of the second element highlights the status of the designated entities as members of the broader *dog* and *tree* categories. The semantic distinctiveness of *triangle* and *three-sided polygon* is even clearer. Explicit mention of *polygon* in the latter calls attention, in a way that *triangle* simply does not, to the status of the designated figure as one member of a class that also includes rectangles, pentagons, etc. Moreover, if *triangle* and *three-sided polygon* were semantically equivalent, the same claim would have to be made for *triangle* and *three-angled polygon*; this would imply the semantic equivalence of *three-sided polygon* and *three-angled polygon*, which hardly seems plausible, intuitively or otherwise. Observe that a person could understand both expressions and yet not realize—before thinking the matter through—that each was applicable only to triangles.

The grammatical significance of these claims and observations is not easily overstated. They imply that a grammatical construction not only provides for the symbolization of a complex notion, but also inherently serves to structure this conceptualization in a particular manner. At the very least, the use of a compositional expression to convey the notion results in greater salience for the explicitly mentioned substructures than with a noncompositional equivalent. Often there are alternate grammatical constructions allowing the speaker to arrive at identical or comparable composite structures via different compositional paths, resulting in contrasting images and nuances of meaning. Since other phenomena may be sensitive to these meaning contrasts, even when seemingly minor, the constructions are capable of exhibiting differential grammatical behavior and combinatory potential at higher levels of organization.

Elsewhere (Langacker 1982a), for example, I have argued that the grammatical differences between plurals and underived mass nouns reflect the greater individuation of plurals wrought by their compositionality (hence

---

[14] It is important to distinguish between unipolar and bipolar componentiality (2.3.1.2). We are concerned here with the latter, i.e. the hierarchical organization of symbolic structures. By definition a predicate is minimal from a symbolic standpoint, but in unipolar terms it may nonetheless have many semantic components and be defined at any level with respect to hierarchies of conceptual complexity.

many boards vs. *much lumber, four boards* vs. **four lumber*).[15] Consider
also the following (no special context is to be assumed for (9)):

(7)(a)   *Oak trees are the best kind for your yard.*
   (b)   *Deer meat is the only kind I eat.*
(8)(a)   *Oaks are the best kind of trees for your yard.*
   (b)   *Venison is the only kind of meat I eat.*
(9)(a)   **Oaks are the best kind for your yard.*
   (b)   **Venison is the only kind I eat.*

Kind refers to some general class, but is too schematic to be felicitously used
unless this class is identified in some way. Explicit mention of the superordinate category (*trees, meat*) is accomplished via the subject nominal in (7),
and through an *of*-phrase in (8). However, the infelicity of the expressions in
(9) shows that implicit reference does not suffice, even when there is little
doubt about what class is involved. Explicit symbolization affords the superordinate category sufficient prominence for its construal as the category implied by *kind* to be unproblematic.[16]

For an illustration of two polymorphemic expressions that arrive at the
same composite structure via distinct compositional paths, consider the subtle
contrast between the compound *corn kernel* and the phrase *kernel of corn*.
Transformational accounts (from Lees 1960 onward) generally derive the former from the latter, but the present framework necessarily treats them as separate constructions and imputes to them slightly different meanings. The valence relation for *corn kernel* is sketched in Fig. 8.6(a). *Corn* designates a
mass consisting of indefinitely many individual objects. *Kernel*, in the sense
relevant here, designates a single grain representative of a larger set of such
objects generally constituting a mass. The valence relation involves a correspondence between the schematically characterized mass in the base of
[KERNEL] and the specific mass profiled by [CORN]. Since [KERNEL] is
the profile determinant, the composite structure designates a single grain from
a mass with the specific properties of [CORN].

---

[15] The issue of whether expressions like *many* and *four* specifically require composition with
the plural morpheme, or whether they demand only a certain level of prominence for individual
members of the mass, is not of great significance in the present framework, which can accommodate either type of analysis. A stipulation of compositionality for the noun in these constructions
would not establish the existence of purely "grammatical" structures and restrictions, since only
symbolic elements figure in the composition of plural nouns.

[16] It will not really do to argue that the requirement is purely formal, with *kind of N* reducing to
kind only when N is named elsewhere in the sentence or discourse. Consider the following
(uttered in a butcher shop, where *meat* has not previously been mentioned): *We have venison,
pork, and beef; what kind do you want?* If not ideal, this sentence is at least much better than
those in (9), and in fact it would be a bit odd to use the fuller expression *what kind of meat* in the
interrogative clause. (See Postal 1969 and Gensler 1977 for pertinent discussion of kindred
phenomena.)

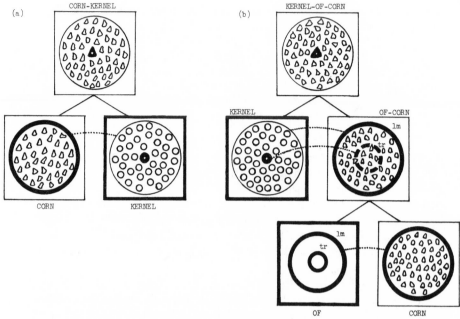

Fig. 8.6

We see from Fig. 8.6(b) that *kernel of corn* has the same composite structure, but a more elaborate array of component structures at two levels of constituency. At the lower level, *of* and *corn* combine to form a prepositional phrase. Recall that [OF] profiles a stative relation, whose landmark (and domain) is specified simply as an integrated whole of some sort, and whose trajector is some subpart of this whole. [OF] is the profile determinant, and its landmark is put in correspondence with the mass profiled by [CORN]; the intermediate-level composite structure [OF-CORN] therefore designates a stative relation between the specific mass profiled by [CORN] and some schematically characterized subpart of this mass (the trajector). At the second level of constituency, the valence relation between [KERNEL] and [OF-CORN] is accomplished through two correspondences: the profile of [KERNEL] corresponds to the trajector of the prepositional phrase, and the schematic mass in the base of [KERNEL] corresponds to its landmark. [KERNEL] is the profile determinant, so once again the overall composite structure designates a single grain within a larger, specified mass.

Corn kernel and *kernel of corn* differ semantically because the presence of *of* in the latter renders more salient the notion of a relation between an integrated whole and a restricted subpart. The difference is subtle, since the import of the preposition is fairly abstract, and also since a comparable part/whole relation is implicit in both *kernel* and *corn*. There is consequently a sense in which *of* does not add anything to the meaning of the other morphemes, but it would be wrong to conclude from this that it is meaningless or that *corn kernel* and *kernel of corn* are fully synonymous. I cannot emphasize too strongly that *meaningfulness is not the same as nonoverlapping meaning*. All valence relations depend on some kind of overlap in meaning, so it is to be expected that in some instances the meaning of one component would be wholly included in that of another. This makes it harder to detect the semantic contribution of the included element, but it is nonetheless present, having an impact on the relative salience of substructures if not on their informational or truth-value content.[17]

I should note in conclusion that analyzability is a matter of degree. It seems intuitively obvious that speakers are far more aware of the contributions of individual morphemes in forms like *swimmer*, *mixer*, and *complainer* than they are in *professor*, *propeller*, or *screwdriver*. We can reasonably posit a scale of analyzability, which finds at one extreme expressions that are novel and fully analyzable (e.g. *regurgitator*), and at the other extreme, etymologically composite expressions such as *drawer* (e.g. *It's in the bottom drawer*) that for all synchronic purposes are monomorphemic and fully unanalyzable. A novel expression is necessarily fully analyzable, because the speaker, in putting it together, must attend specifically to each component and its contribution to the desired composite sense. Once a complex expression achieves unit status, however, there is at least the potential that its composite structure—itself now a unit—may be activated autonomously (i.e. without the supporting activation of the component structures). Certainly this does not happen immediately; the component and composite structures may continue to be coactivated indefinitely. It is nevertheless the composite structure that furnishes the primary content of an expression, the role of component structures being subsidiary and dispensable. With continued use, then, a fixed expression will tend to gravitate toward the negative pole of the analyzability scale (though local reversals are possible), until its compositionality fades away entirely.

We can therefore equate position on the analyzability scale with the likelihood that the use of an expression will involve the activation of component structures, as well as the cognitive salience of their contribution if activated. When employing the word *swimmer* I am very much aware of the semantic import of *swim*, but often I say *computer* without thinking of it specifically as 'something that computes', and in expressions like *propeller* and *ruler* (the

---

[17] Recall examples like *oak tree* and *puppy dog*, where the second element of the compound is implied by the first. Despite the full inclusion, one cannot plausibly maintain that *tree* and *dog* are meaningless in these expressions.

latter an 'instrument for drawing straight lines and measuring') it is quite un-usual for me to perceive the presence of *propel* or *rule*. If one accepts the reality of such differences, they further support the contention that the seman-tic value of an expression is complex, involving the composite structure, the component structures, and the relations between the two.

Observe that this view resolves in a plausible way the apparent dilemma posed by fixed expressions like *computer*, *blackbird*, and countless others, which do appear to be compositional and yet mean something more than (or different from) their expected compositional value. Treating them as simply compositional cannot account for their full or precise semantic value, but list-ing them as unanalyzable forms in the lexicon with their composite structure alone seems grossly counterintuitive. (Clearly *black* and *bird* contribute to the meaning of *blackbird*!) In the present theory, both composite structures and component structures function as aspects of the meaning of such forms, and there is no expectation of full compositionality.

8.3. Autonomy and Dependence

A third valence factor involves the distinction between **autonomous** and **dependent** elements. Though subtle and often a matter of degree, this distinc-tion is crucial for the explication of grammatical structure. The notions of autonomy and dependence are applicable to both phonological and semantic structures, and to elements defined in either unipolar or bipolar terms. We can most easily begin with unipolar elements.

8.3.1. Unipolar Dependence

Unipolar elements are those defined independently of symbolic considera-tions. In phonology, unipolar elements include such entities as segments, syl-lables, words, phonological phrases, and intonation groups. Morphemes, by contrast, are bipolar in nature, since a phonological sequence is accorded morphemic status only by virtue of its participation in a symbolic relation-ship. Observe that the segmentation of a phonological sequence into bipolar elements is often at variance with its inherent (unipolar) phonological organi-zation. For example, a unipolar analysis decomposes *picnics* into the syllables *pic* and *nics* (each of which is further decomposable into segments); bipolar analysis divides the word quite differently, into the minimal symbolic units *picnic* and *-s*, with the division falling in the middle of a syllable.

Within the class of phonological segments, vowels are clearly autonomous, and consonants dependent. For one thing, a vowel can stand alone as a syl-lable, a word, or an entire utterance, but (with only marginal exceptions) a consonant cannot.[18] However, it is not this fact of distribution per se that moti-

[18] Syllabic resonants are categorized as vowels.

vates my use of the terms autonomous and dependent, but rather a deeper factor, pertaining to the very nature of vowels and consonants, that is ultimately responsible for it: consonants presuppose vowels, and require vowels for their full phonetic implementation, but the converse is not true. The most fundamental property of a vowel, I suggest, is a period (however brief) of essentially stable sonority. The hallmark of consonants, by contrast, is change: consonants can be seen as operations on the sonority provided by vowels. The relation between the two is asymmetrical, in that the stable sonority of a vowel in no way requires consonantal modification for its manifestation, though a consonant does require a vowel to provide the sonority it modifies.[19] It is this asymmetry that I wish to single out as the basis for the distinction between autonomous and dependent segments. Consonants are dependent because their characterization makes crucial reference to their effect on the sonority provided by vowels. This is equivalent, in the present framework, to saying that a schematically specified vowel is included as part of the internal structure of a consonant (i.e. modification presupposes some reference to the entity modified). Vowels are autonomous because they do not similarly (in any salient or crucial fashion) make internal reference to a schematically characterized consonant.[20]

For meaning too it is important to distinguish between unipolar and bipolar elements. The distinction is equivalent to that between conceptual and semantic structure: unipolar elements are natural conceptual units (irrespective of linguistic considerations), whereas bipolar elements are predications, i.e. the semantic poles of linguistic expressions. It is essential to realize that there can be a certain amount of divergence between unipolar and bipolar elements, just as we saw in regard to phonological structure. Conceptually, for example, it might be argued that a single corn kernel represents a simpler notion than that of a mass of such kernels—the former concept is a component of the latter in unipolar terms. Linguistically, however, the simple expression *corn* lexicalizes these entities at the level of the mass, whereas a composite expression like *kernel of corn* is required to designate a single member. The bipolar compositionality is therefore at odds with the nonlinguistic conceptual organization.

It is not at all difficult to find an analog in conceptual structure for the distinction just made between phonological autonomy and dependence. A conceptually dependent structure would be one that presupposes another and requires it for its full implementation. In this sense any relational notion can be

[19] It is not denied that consonants can be articulated in isolation, but a vocalic element is needed to support their optimal implementation. Note, for instance, that the perception of stops is heavily dependent on their formant transitions with adjacent vowels, but vowels are easily perceived and distinguished by themselves.

[20] Recall that sounds are treated as cognitive entities for many linguistic purposes. Physical implementation is not required for their cognitive activation and manipulation, and is not possible in the case of phonological schemas.

regarded as conceptually dependent, since it requires for its conceptualization some intrinsic reference—however schematic—to the entities that participate in the relation. One cannot, for example, conceptualize the process of chasing without conceiving to some extent of the thing doing the chasing and the thing being chased, even if the idea formed of them is maximally vague. We can say that the chase concept makes essential internal reference to these schematically characterized things. The conception of a physical object like a tree or a cat, by contrast, is more autonomous. We can conceptualize a cat without activating to any significant degree the notion of its participation in a relationship with other objects (e.g. we can simply visualize a cat). It is part of what we know about cats that they participate in external relations, but no such relation is obligatorily accessed.

I therefore draw a parallel between vowels and things as autonomous entities, and also between consonants and relations as dependent entities. I must caution that the distinction is a matter of degree, especially at the semantic pole, and that sometimes there is no observable asymmetry. This will become more evident when we apply these notions to bipolar elements.

8.3.2. Bipolar Dependence

A dependent structure is one that is characterized to a significant degree in relation to another and consequently makes salient internal reference (at least in schematic terms) to a structure of the requisite type. This description is valid for both semantic and phonological elements. It derives from our examination of unipolar elements, but carries over to bipolar elements without essential change. The bipolar elements of relevance are those that integrate with one another in a valence relation.

Whenever two structures combine in a valence relation, one can ask whether either structure qualifies as dependent with respect to the other, in accordance with the following definition: **One structure, D, is dependent on the other, A, to the extent that A constitutes an elaboration of a salient substructure within D.** This definition is equally applicable to the semantic and the phonological poles, and in fact the two poles show a notable tendency to correlate in this regard. The definition is inherently a matter of degree, since it rests squarely on two scalar notions (elaboration and salience). Canonically the structures in a valence relation manifest substantial asymmetry, with one of them (on balance) clearly dependent, and the other autonomous. As always, though, recognition of the prototype must not be allowed to obscure the existence of other possibilities. Nothing in the definition precludes a relation of mutual dependence between the two structures, or guarantees that there will always be a significant relation of dependence in one direction or the other.

Let us be more precise about the central notions. Suppose two predications, X and Y, are integrated at the semantic pole of a valence relation. How do we determine whether X is conceptually dependent on Y? We do so by considering the substructure of X that corresponds to the profile of Y—call this substructure x_e. The degree to which X is dependent on Y ($D_{X \to Y}$) correlates positively with the following two factors: (1) the salience of x_e within X; and (2) the extent to which Y constitutes an elaboration of x_e.[21] One can similarly evaluate the degree to which Y is conceptually dependent on X ($D_{Y \to X}$). This involves identifying the substructure y_e within Y that corresponds to the profile of X; determining the salience of y_e; and assessing the extent to which X elaborates it. Comparison of the two values $D_{X \to Y}$ and $D_{Y \to X}$ is then the pivotal factor. If, for example, $D_{X \to Y}$ is substantially greater than $D_{Y \to X}$, then X can be identified (in relative terms) as the conceptually dependent member of the valence relation, and Y as the conceptually autonomous member. It should be clear, though, that designating Y as conceptually autonomous does not preclude its being to some degree dependent on X.

Some examples will clarify these notions. Fig. 8.1(a) diagrams the valence relation between [UNDER] and [THE-TABLE]; which of these predications is conceptually dependent on the other? We must first consider the substructure of [UNDER] that corresponds to the profile of [THE-TABLE]. This substructure is the primary landmark of [UNDER], and is quite salient by virtue of being included in its relational profile. Moreover, this landmark is highly schematic, and is elaborated to a substantial degree by the far more precise specifications of [THE-TABLE]. With respect to both factors, then, [UNDER] is notably dependent on [THE-TABLE]. We must next evaluate the possible dependence of [THE-TABLE] on [UNDER]. Does [THE-TABLE] contain a substructure that corresponds to the profile of [UNDER]? Certainly it does given our encyclopedic account of semantic structure. It is part of what we know about tables that they participate in locative relationships with other objects, so the conception of the table in a schematically characterized locative relationship can be identified as the relevant substructure. However, this schematic locative relationship is not profiled, nor is it obligatorily accessed when a table is conceptualized. Because of this low degree of salience, [THE-TABLE] is less dependent on [UNDER] than conversely. On balance, then, we can identify [THE-TABLE] as the conceptually autonomous component, with [UNDER] conceptually dependent. By exactly parallel considerations, [UNDER-THE-TABLE] is seen to be conceptually dependent in the valence relation of Fig. 8.5, and [FOOTBALL] (which elaborates its trajector) is conceptually autonomous. We can see from these two examples that the direction of dependence and the choice of profile determinant are independent parameters: in both Figs. 8.1(a) and 8.5 the relational predication is conceptually de-

---

[21] The salience of x_e is based on its degree of centrality (cf. 4.2.2), on whether or not it is profiled, and so on. In regard to the second factor, full schematicity counts for more than partial schematicity; dependence also increases with the **elaborative distance** between x_e and Y (i.e. how much precision and detail Y adds to the schematic characterization furnished by x_e).

pendent relative to the nominal predication, but only in the former is it the profile determinant.

Finally, let us examine the relation between *go* and the past-participial morpheme as diagrammed in Fig. 8.2. I will argue that [PRTC] should be regarded as the dependent predicate, but the issue is fairly subtle. What is the substructure of [GO] that corresponds to the profile of [PRTC]? It is the final state of [GO], which is reasonably prominent by virtue of inclusion in [GO]'s relational profile. However, it is in no way elaborated by [PRTC], since [GO] is more specific than [PRTC]. [GO] is thus dependent on [PRTC] with respect to only one of the two relevant factors. What, now, is the substructure of [PRTC] that corresponds to the profile of [GO]? It is the schematic process that constitutes the base of the participial predication. Though not in profile, this base is clearly highly salient within [PRTC], since it contributes the *only* semantic content of this predicate. Moreover, it is obligatorily accessed, since the whole raison d'être of this morpheme is to define an atemporal relation in terms of a process. It is also apparent that [GO] substantially elaborates the schematic base process of [PRTC], so the latter is dependent on both counts. In relative terms, then, [GO] should be recognized as the autonomous predication, and [PRTC] as dependent.

Let us turn now to phonological elements, confining our attention to single morphemes. An element is dependent to the extent that it makes salient and schematic reference to a second element as part of its own internal characterization. I suggest that this description is perfectly applicable to the class of affixes (as opposed to roots). A suffix, for instance, is characterized partially as an element that follows a stem; since no particular stem is specified, reference to it is schematic within the suffix. A root, by contrast, is autonomous and makes no essential internal reference to a schematically characterized affix.

We can illustrate this with the English plural morpheme, as in *tables*. The semantic pole of this complex form is given in Fig. 8.7(a). *Table* is a count noun, but *tables*—like all plurals—is a type of mass noun. The plural predicate, which functions as profile determinant, designates a **replicate mass**, i.e. one that consists of indefinitely many instances (or replications in type) of a particular nominal category. These discrete entities are identified only schematically within [PL] itself, and taken individually they can be considered unprofiled (their profiling is only collective, and no single instance has any particular salience vis-à-vis the others). The valence relation is effected by means of a correspondence between the discrete object profiled by [TABLE] and an arbitrarily selected member of the replicate mass profiled by [PL].[22] The com-

---

[22] Since all the members are by definition instances of the same nominal category, attributing the properties of [TABLE] to any arbitrarily chosen member has the effect of attributing them to all members. I am glossing over some important questions here (pertaining to "referentiality" and the type/token distinction) because they are irrelevant to present concerns (cf. Part IV, Volume II).

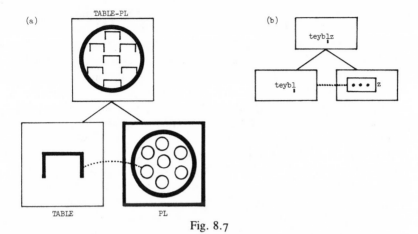

Fig. 8.7

posite structure therefore profiles a replicate mass consisting of indefinitely many instances of the [TABLE] category.

The phonological pole of *tables* is sketched in Fig. 8.7(b). Symbolizing [TABLE] is the phonological sequence [teybl], which should be regarded as an integrated structure organized into syllables, etc., even though I have simplified things in the standard way by showing only a string of segments. Symbolizing [PL] is a phonological structure considerably more complex than just the segment [z]. The box preceding [z] stands for a schematically characterized phonological structure; it can be specified that the final segment of this structure is voiced, and that there is at least one syllabic element, but there is little if any additional specific content. Once again the diagram oversimplifies matters, for [z] is not simply juxtaposed to this schematic phonological structure, but instead is specified as having a particular role in its syllabic organization: it functions as the outermost consonant in the coda of its final syllable. Naturally a speaker cannot actually pronounce a schematic phonological structure, or pronounce [z] as part of the syllabic organization of one; for actual implementation, this schematic structure must be replaced by specific phonological content. This is accomplished by a correspondence linking the schematic stem of the plural morpheme with [teybl] (or more generally, linking this schema with whatever happens to be the phonological pole of the noun stem). The resulting composite structure, [teyblz], is specific and fully integrated in terms of syllabic structure and other unipolar considerations. It is this composite structure that receives physical manifestation.

This initial description of phonological valence relations requires elucidation and refinement, but already one can note a number of similarities to semantic valence relations. Integration at either pole depends on correspondences between substructures of the components, with the composite structure derived by superimposing the specifications of corresponding entities.

More often than not a schematically characterized substructure within one component functions as a correspondent, being elaborated by the other component. This makes it possible to distinguish between autonomous and dependent structures at either pole. [PL] is semantically dependent in Fig. 8.7(a): [TABLE] elaborates a salient but schematic substructure within [PL], but not the converse. Relations at the phonological pole are parallel, with the autonomous [teybl] elaborating a schema internal to the plural suffix. There is a notable cross-linguistic tendency for the alignment of autonomous and dependent structures in a valence relation to "harmonize" in this way at the two poles, a fact of substantial grammatical significance (cf. Langacker 1981b).

8.3.3. *Elaboration Sites*

In a typical valence relation with components X and Y, there is some substructure of X—referred to earlier as x_e—that corresponds to the profile of Y, such that x_e bears a relation of schematicity to Y as a whole. Since x_e is elaborated by Y, we can call it an **elaboration site** (or more briefly, **e-site**). In Fig. 8.1(a), for example, the e-site is the landmark of [UNDER]; it corresponds to the profile of [THE-TABLE], and this autonomous predication spells out its properties in finer detail. Similarly, the e-site in Fig. 8.5 is the trajector of [UNDER-THE-TABLE], which is elaborated by the autonomous predication [FOOTBALL]. The landmark of [OF] functions as e-site at the first level of constituency depicted in Fig. 8.6(b), and its trajector at the second level. These are elaborated by [CORN] and [KERNEL] respectively.

The examples so far cited have a number of common properties. In each the dependent predication is relational, and the autonomous structure designates a thing. Moreover, the e-site is in each case a thing saliently included (as trajector or landmark) within the relational profile. It is not unreasonable to regard this configuration of properties as prototypical for valence relations. Relations of this type are the ones most commonly dealt with in classic valence theory, and also the ones most straightforwardly represented in standard predicate/argument accounts of semantic or grammatical structure. Importantly, however, there are no inherent restrictions along these lines in the present framework. The e-site can be any sort of entity whatever. It is not necessarily included in the profile of the dependent predication, and this latter need not be relational. In Fig. 8.6(a), for instance, the dependent [KERNEL] is nominal instead of relational, and its e-site (elaborated by [CORN]) is an unprofiled mass in its base.[23] In Fig. 8.2, [GO] elaborates a schematic and unprofiled process that constitutes the base of the participial predication; since [PRTC] has no other content (apart from the profiling of its final state), we may conclude that the substructure functioning as e-site is not always a proper substructure, i.e. it may be exhaustive of the dependent predication.

[23] [KERNEL] is dependent because the unprofiled mass it introduces is characterized only schematically, whereas the individual objects implied by [CORN] are quite specific.

A point of some significance is that the e-site implied by a valence relation is not always directly discernible within the dependent predication given the way it structures the scene. Each of the component predications organizes the scene in its own fashion with respect to the parameters of selection, perspective, and abstraction (cf. Ch. 3), and there may in this regard be some divergence in how they portray the pivotal shared substructure. To find within the dependent predication a substructure that is fully schematic for the autonomous component, it may therefore be necessary to carry out a focal adjustment of some kind, such as reversing figure/ground alignment or abstracting away from certain domains or dimensions. For example, the passive version of the English past-participial predication chooses for its figure (trajector) a different nominal entity than the one selected by the stem it combines with. One must consequently look past the figure/ground alignment imposed by the profile of the passive participle to find a base process that can be judged fully schematic for the process designated by the stem (cf. Langacker 1982a).

Another kind of example is found in the valence relation between the verb and prepositional-phrase complement in sentences like (10).

(10)   *The little girl crawled through a tunnel.*

Crawl implies that its trajector follows a spatial path but specifies nothing very precise about its nature. This path functions as e-site in the valence relation, being elaborated by the more detailed path-specification *through a tunnel*. Observe, however, that the e-site within *crawl* is not easily isolated or represented diagrammatically as a discrete entity, for it involves only selected aspects of the process. *Crawl* combines two kinds of relational specifications: (1) the schematic path followed by its trajector with respect to external surroundings; and (2) the activity the trajector carries out to propel itself through this spatial trajectory. The two are intimately related, and for every component state of the process the trajector is specified as being both located in space and engaged in some phase of its locomotive activity. Nevertheless, it is only the locative specifications that correspond to the profile of the prepositional phrase, and only by abstracting these specifications from the larger matrix of relationships constituting each component state does one obtain the schematic entity that constitutes the e-site. Nor do matters stop there. Since *crawl* is processual, its component states are scanned sequentially, but *through a tunnel* is a complex atemporal relation; it designates an ordered series of distinct locative relationships between the trajector and landmark, which avoid inconsistency by being distributed through conceived time, but these relationships are accessed cumulatively by means of summary scanning. Only by suspending the mode of scanning implied by the process *crawl* do we arrive at a conception internal to it that is schematic in all respects to the elaborating predication.

The description of valence relations in terms of conceptual autonomy and dependence therefore involves a number of subtleties. An asymmetry along these lines is not always observed, and when it is the distinction is often a matter of degree. Even when one predication clearly serves to elaborate some facet of another, discerning a schematic e-site within the dependent component may require a focal adjustment of selection, perspective, mode of scanning, etc., since the shared entity may be structured very differently by the overlapping predications. Fuller illustration and more precise analysis of these phenomena will come in later chapters.

8.3.4. *Grammatical Import*

Terms like **dependency** are commonly used in linguistics in a manner that not only diverges from my notion of dependence but even runs counter to it for the most part. Thus, in the various sorts of "dependency grammar" (cf. Robinson 1970; Anderson 1971; Hudson 1976; Matthews 1981), nominal arguments are said to be dependent on a relational element such as a verb or adjective, which is said to have a particular valence potential and consequently determines how many nominals are allowed in the clause (I would say instead that the relational predication is conceptually dependent on the nominals). Distribution is considered a major factor; often one element is said to be dependent on another because it only occurs when the second element also does. My own contention is that distribution is sometimes a treacherous guide to linguistic structure, being influenced by a variety of factors that may not be apparent prior to analysis.[24]

Though my choice of terminology is unorthodox and a possible source of confusion, it is nonetheless deliberate and strongly motivated: **autonomy** vs. **dependence** is the most natural way to describe an opposition that is fundamental to all facets of linguistic structure and has important consequences for the elucidation of grammar. To emphasize that I have something nonstandard in mind, I employ the term **dependence** instead of the usual **dependency**, and often include it in larger expressions like **conceptual dependence** or **phonological dependence**. As defined, these notions pertain to the intrinsic character of the elements involved, and represent an attempt to articulate the underlying conceptual or phonological factors that are largely responsible, in the final analysis, for their combinatory behavior. For example, the fact that consonants seldom appear except in combination with a vowel is a natural expectation given their characterization as operations on vocalic sonority.

Our concern in this section is with the bipolar elements participating in valence relations and with the grammatical implications of the asymmetry they frequently exhibit in regard to autonomy/dependence. At the phonological pole, this *A/D* **asymmetry** can be used to explicate the distinction between

---

[24] See Langacker (1982b) for a striking example of how reliance on distribution can lead one astray.

roots and nonroot morphemes, including both affixes and more abstract symbolizations such as process morphemes. Roots are autonomous, providing an initial array of phonological content; nonroot morphemes are dependent and can be viewed as operations on the initial content provided by the root in much the same sense that consonants modify the sonority furnished by a vowel.[25] Observe that this characterization of nonroot morphemes gracefully accommodates such phenomena as ablaut, reduplication, and truncation, and that affixes fall into place as a special (albeit prototypical) kind of modification, namely that consisting primarily in the appendage of segmental material.

I believe this proposal reconstructs quite well the usual, rather impressionistic description of a root as the "core" morpheme within a word. It also generalizes straightforwardly to provide an account of the "layering" characteristic of word structure at all levels of organization. Consider a complex word like *unlawfully*, which most analysts would bracket as follows: [[un[[law]ful]]ly]. *Law*, as a root, is defined phonologically without salient reference to other elements. By contrast, each of the other three morphemes is defined as an operation on a more autonomous structure. To specify this operation, which is simply one of appendage (to a following structure for *un-*, and a preceding structure for *-ful* and *-ly*), each nonroot morpheme must refer internally to the element it modifies. This reference is highly schematic, essentially requiring only that the modified structure have segmental content consisting of at least one syllable; in particular there is no restriction concerning its possible morphemic complexity, so it need not be a root. A multilayered word can therefore be constructed out of these morphemes by means of valence relations at several levels of constituency. First, the dependent *-ful* combines with the autonomous root *law* to yield the composite structure *lawful*. This stem is itself autonomous, for it contains no unelaborated schematic substructure and is not defined as an operation on such a substructure. *Lawful* is perfectly compatible with the specifications of the schematic stem referred to by *un-*, permitting a valence relation that derives *unlawful* as the autonomous composite structure. This in turn combines felicitously with *-ly* at the highest level of constituency. Note that *law*, *lawful*, *unlawful*, and *unlawfully*—i.e. the root, the stems at different levels, and the word as a whole—are all autonomous structures in this account, and that only the three affixes are dependent.

For expressions larger than words, we can similarly speak of the dependence of (bipolar) phonological structures whenever there is some indication that one of the participants in a valence relation, asymmetrically, must be defined in relation to the other. A clitic, for example, resembles an affix in that its position with respect to a more autonomous element (and also its rhythmic

---

[25] To say that a root is autonomous does not, as I have defined the term, imply that it can always stand alone as a word, though this is frequently the case. The issues raised in this passage are treated more fully in Ch. 9.

association with this element) is an inherent aspect of its phonological value. Elements restricted to clausal second position provide further illustration (e.g. the Cora quotative particle *nú?u* of fn. 8). The phonological pole of such an element specifies its segmental content as being situated in post-initial position within a schematically characterized clause. Matters are perhaps more obvious in valence relations where one component is manifested solely by an intonation pattern, which requires the segmental content of the other component as a "carrier" for its full implementation. Similarly, if one component is analogous to a process morpheme in comprising a modification of the other (e.g. duplication or a change in order), its characterization necessarily makes inherent reference in schematic terms to the structure it modifies.

The distinction between conceptually autonomous and dependent predications is crucial for characterizing a number of important grammatical notions. One of these is the contrast, noted often by valence theorists and others, between what are variously called "central" vs. "peripheral" elements in a clause, "complements" vs. "modifiers" of a verb, or "actants/participants" vs. "circumstantials." [26] Subjects and direct objects are always considered central elements (participants). The status of other elements, e.g. prepositional phrases or adverbs, is not always so evident or immune to controversy; nevertheless, there would be general agreement about many cases, including those in (11) and (12).

(11)(a)   *The verdict rendered him speechless.*
    (b)   *I put the sweater in a box.*
(12)(a)   *Before she left the phone rang.*
    (b)   *We chased squirrels in the park.*

Speechless in (11)(a) would be considered a central element or complement of the verb, as would the prepositional phrase of (11)(b). In (12), on the other hand, the adverbials *before she left* and *in the park* are treated as peripheral elements of the clause, and more specifically as modifiers.

The distinction between (11) and (12) in the present framework revolves on the direction of conceptual dependence between the verb and the other relational constituent. In (11) the verb is straightforwardly regarded as the dependent member of the relationship. *Render* describes a process inducing a change of state, so the notion of a resultant state is inherent in this verb and salient within it; this state functions as an e-site in the valence relation with *speechless*. Similarly, *put* implies a final destination for its primary landmark, so *in a box* elaborates a substructure already prominently introduced by *put*.

---

[26] Cf. Tesnière (1959); Matthews (1981); Allerton (1982). In generative grammar this type of distinction goes back to Chomsky (1965), which distinguishes between adverbials internal to the verb phrase vs. those external to it, or more generally, between constituents that subcategorize verbs and those that do not.

In (12), however, it is the adverbial that is conceptually dependent in its relation to the verb. The constituent formed by the verb together with its subject and object nominals designates a process that in each instance corresponds to the trajector of the adverbial and substantially elaborates it: *the phone rang* elaborates the trajector of *before she left*, and *we chased squirrels* elaborates the trajector of *in the park*. The constituent formed by the verb and its nominals is by contrast not dependent on the adverbial predication to any significant degree. It is known that events like the phone ringing bear temporal relations to other events, and that acts like squirrel-chasing take place in some spatial setting, but these are basically extrinsic specifications and are neither prominent nor central to the designated processes.

The constructs now available to us also permit the resolution of another classic problem, namely the character of the head/modifier relation. Both complement relations (like those in (11)) and head/modifier relations (as in (12)) are defined for situations where two predications in a grammatical construction show a notable A/D asymmetry. Let us call these component predications A and D respectively. When D is the profile determinant in this situation, as in (11), we speak of **complements** (rather than heads and modifiers): A is recognized as a complement of D. Complements can be of various sorts. For the time being it is sufficient to note that complements can have either a nominal or a relational profile. Subjects and objects qualify as **nominal complements** (or **arguments**), whereas *speechless* and *in a box* are **relational complements**.[27]

We therefore speak of complements when the dependent predication is the profile determinant in valence relations with notable A/D asymmetry. When, instead, the autonomous predication functions as the profile determinant in such valence relations, we speak of a head/modifier relation: structure A is the **head**, and structure D a **modifier** of this head. This is the situation in (12), where the adverbials were seen to be dependent on the constituent formed by the verb and its nominal arguments. Since this latter constituent contributes the processual profile to the clause as a whole, it is the profile determinant as well as the autonomous component in the valence relation. The definition properly characterizes the verbal constituent as the head, and the adverbials as modifiers of this head.

Because the definition makes no reference to the type of predication (it mentions only autonomy, dependence, and profile determinacy), its characterization of the head/modifier relation is fully general. The head can be a constituent of any size, and it can profile a process (as in (12)), an atemporal relation, or a thing. Here I will simply observe that the definition correctly

---

[27] Some other kinds of relational complements are illustrated in sentences like these: *They elected me chairman*; *I ran three miles*; *Farnsworth expects to prevail*.

identifies the two instances of noun modifiers from the array of examples diagrammed previously. In Fig. 8.5, corresponding to (4)(a), *that football under the table*, [FOOTBALL] is autonomous, elaborating the trajector of [UNDER-THE-TABLE]. Since [FOOTBALL] is also the profile determinant, the prepositional phrase *under the table* is correctly described as a modifier of the head noun *football*. The other example is exactly parallel: *of corn* functions as a prepositional-phrase modifier of the head noun *kernel* in *kernel of corn* (Fig. 8.6(b)).

The importance of the constructs head, modifier, and complement has been widely recognized, but the present account goes beyond merely acknowledging them, or seeking to define them in distributional terms, by proposing a reasonably explicit characterization of their conceptual basis. Moreover, since the definition of conceptual dependence makes it inherently a matter of degree, the difficulty scholars have encountered in finding any clear line of demarcation between complementation and modification is both expected in this analysis and unproblematic from the descriptive standpoint. Note, in conclusion, that the analysis is grounded in more general considerations. Conceptual dependence for predications is seen as but one manifestation of a far broader distinction between autonomous and dependent structures that is described in unified fashion for the many facets of linguistic organization where it is relevant. Further, the notions invoked by its definition (salience, correspondence, profile) are part and parcel of an overall account of semantic structure and valence relations and were adopted for independent reasons.

8.4. Constituency

Three of the four valence factors have now been considered: correspondence, profile determinacy, and the distinction between autonomous and dependent components. The final valence factor is **constituency**, which pertains to the order in which component structures are successively combined to form progressively more elaborate composite structures. The choice of a particular constituency arrangement is often not critical in this framework, and constituency appears in fact to be quite variable. Moreover, the present theory of valence relations allows one to establish a closer relationship between constituency at the semantic and the phonological poles than is generally thought possible.

8.4.1. Constituents

Hierarchy is fundamental to human cognition. Cognitive processing involves multiple levels of organization, such that elements at one level combine to form a complex structure that functions as a unitary entity at the next higher level, and so on. Prominent among the linguistically relevant hierarchies are those defined by the successive integration of symbolic structures in valence relations. The same hierarchical organization can be observed whether we consider semantic, phonological, or symbolic structures.

Multiple levels of constituency have already been exemplified. Fig. 8.6(b) shows the semantic integration of *of* and *corn* to form the composite structure *of corn*, which then combines with *kernel* at the next higher level of organization to yield *kernel of corn*. Similarly, Fig. 8.1(a) depicts the semantic pole of *under the table*, whose composite structure functions as one component of the higher-level valence relation deriving *(that) football under the table* in Fig. 8.5. It is precisely by virtue of their integration to yield a composite structure that two or more components are recognized as forming a constituent.

A different kind of example is provided in Fig. 8.8, which represents the semantic pole of the compound *pole climber*. At the first or lower level of constituency, the processual predicate [CLIMB] is integrated with [ER] to form the nominal predication [CLIMB-ER], which is certainly an established unit of English. [CLIMB-ER] then combines with [POLE] at the second or

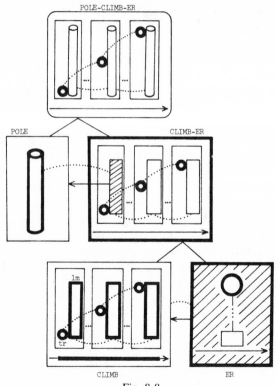

Fig. 8.8

higher level of constituency, deriving the composite structure of the overall expression. A closed curve surrounds this composite structure on the presumption that it is novel; all the other structures are surrounded by rectangles to indicate their unit status.

Consider first the lower level of constituency. [CLIMB] designates a process in which a trajector, through time, assumes a succession of positions on the surface of a landmark, thereby defining an upward path along the vertical axis. [ER] is a nominalizing predicate, profiling a thing identifiable solely by its role as trajector in a schematically characterized process; the process constitutes the base of the predicate. This schematic base process functions as the e-site in the valence relation: it corresponds to the profile of [CLIMB], and is elaborated by that predicate. [ER] is the profile determinant, so the composite structure [CLIMB-ER] designates a thing characterized solely as the trajector of the process [CLIMB]. Because [ER] is both conceptually dependent and the profile determinant, [CLIMB] is a complement of [ER].[28]

I have introduced in Fig. 8.8 an additional notational device to clarify the nature of valence relations: cross-hatching is used to identify the e-site, and an arrow indicating a relation of schematicity leads from the e-site to the elaborating predication. At the lower level of constituency, the schematic process constituting the base of [ER] is marked by cross-hatching as the e-site, and an arrow indicates the elaborative relationship between this process and [CLIMB]. The process profiled by [CLIMB] functions as the base for [CLIMB-ER] at the second level of constituency, and the landmark of this base process is selected as the e-site: a correspondence line equates this landmark with the profile of [POLE], and an arrow shows the relation of schematicity that the landmark bears to this predicate. [CLIMB-ER] is specified as the profile determinant in this construction (in accordance with the general pattern for compounds), so the composite structure (POLE-CLIMB-ER) designates the trajector of the base process instead of its landmark (the pole). Once more the dependent predication (the one containing the e-site) is the profile determinant as well, so [POLE] is a complement of [CLIMB-ER].

Quasi-pictorial diagrams like Fig. 8.8 are very helpful in coming to grips with the many structures and relationships that are crucial in valence relations, since they force one to make these factors explicit (even if only informally, and to a limited depth of analysis). Obviously, though, they are very awkward, and often it is useful or necessary to talk about valence relations without going into a great deal of detail about the internal structure of predications. As a less explicit alternative, then, I will often employ constituency-tree

---

[28] [ER] is conceptually dependent because [CLIMB] substantially elaborates its base process, whereas [ER] fails to elaborate the trajector of [CLIMB]. I have shown the trajector as a heavy circle for all three of the component states depicted in the base of [CLIMB-ER]. Since the trajector corresponds from one state to the next, the profile consists of just one thing, not several; its multiple representation is an artifact of the type of diagram employed.

diagrams in the format of Fig. 8.9, which convey only selected aspects of the valence relations represented.[29]

Fig. 8.9(a) sketches the semantic pole of the plural noun *undressers* (i.e. 'those who undress'), and (b) its phonological pole. Square brackets and parentheses enclose structures that have unit status and structures that lack it,

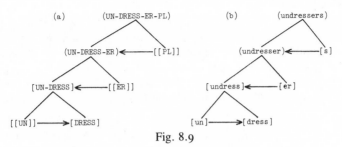

Fig. 8.9

respectively; Fig. 8.9 therefore indicates that *undress* is a unit, whereas *undresser* and *undressers* are novel. At the semantic pole, the profile determinant is marked by doubling the brackets or parentheses surrounding it. [[UN]] is thus the profile determinant at the first level of constituency, [[ER]] at the second, and [[PL]] at the third. Finally, arrows (for schematicity) indicate *A/D* alignment; each arrow leads from the dependent component to the autonomous component that elaborates one of its substructures. We see that at the semantic pole the dependent structure and the profile determinant always coincide, so at each level we have a complement relation. At the phonological pole, the direction of the arrows marks [un], [er], and [s] as dependent (i.e. affixal). As the autonomous component at the lowest level of morphological constituency, [dress] is identified as the root. Observe that at each constituency level the direction of dependence is the same at the semantic and the phonological poles, as is generally (but not always) the case.

There are some subtle matters that merit discussion concerning the relation between **units** and **constituents**. It must first be noted that the concepts are quite distinct and defined in ways that imply no special connection between them: a unit is a thoroughly mastered routine, a structure that can be activated and manipulated more or less automatically, without attending to the details of its internal composition; constituency, however, is determined by the order in which component structures are integrated in the assembly of progressively more elaborate composite structures. Either a novel structure or a unit can function as a constituent (e.g. *undressers* vs. *undress*). Moreover, it would appear that a unit can be either a constituent or a nonconstituent. Examples of nonconstituent units would include such entities as discontinuous expressions (*either . . . or*, *if . . . then*, etc.), idioms with open slots for variables (such

---

[29] Constituency, profile determinacy, and *A/D* asymmetry are indicated, but not correspondences, since these presuppose the resolution of components into substructures.

as a nominal in *lose . . .'s cool*), and even recurring affix sequences (*-er-s*, *-ist-ic*, *-ful-ly*).

In fact, though, the constructs unit and constituent interact. It is natural for a speaker, in putting together a complex structure, to employ established units as a first resort, expending the constructive effort of assembling a novel constituent only when no constituent with unit status is available. It is also apparent, as a matter of definition, that when a constituent has unit status all its subconstituents are units as well. Constituency trees therefore consistently show something akin to the pattern of brackets and parentheses illustrated in Fig. 8.9. The smallest (i.e. noncomposite) structures are nearly always units, and units predominate at lower levels of constituency; nonunit structures are virtually always composite and predominate at higher levels of constituency. Moreover, a composite structure with unit status has only units for components, but a nonunit composite structure may have for components a mixture of units and nonunits. It follows that a so-called novel structure may in actuality be largely preassembled, its novelty confined to a limited zone at the higher reaches of the constituency tree.

A certain amount of importance attaches to the issue of whether nonconstituents can achieve the status of units. No one could seriously question the unit status of many apparent examples (e.g. *either . . . or, lose . . .'s cool*, and *-ful-ly*), but the analysis of these examples as nonconstituents is another matter. I suggest, in fact, that the structures to which unit status can be attributed involve more than just the elements with explicit segmental manifestation. The instances just cited are more adequately given as [either CONJUNCT or CONJUNCT], [lose PRONOUN's cool], and [STEM-ful-ly], where the entities represented by capital letters are substructures characterized only schematically (at both poles). Because these substructures have only schematic phonological content, they cannot be overtly manifested per se, and so the specific segmental content of these units appears to be discontinuous or to represent a nonconstituent. I would argue, however, that the overtly manifested portions of these units achieve structural coherence only by virtue of being embedded as parts of a more inclusive, fully integrated structure certain facets of which are schematic rather than specific. The structures that have unit status therefore belong to the schematic and not the syntagmatic plane (cf. 2.1.5), i.e. they represent the generalizations extracted from specific instances, but do not themselves appear overtly in linguistic expressions.

Let me therefore advance the working hypothesis that all units are constituents. The suffix combination *-er-s* provides a convenient illustration of the type of analysis proposed. It is perfectly reasonable to suppose that speakers of English, familiar with large numbers of nouns ending in this combination (e.g. *divers, workers, marchers, computers, sprinklers*), have learned it as a unit and are consequently quite prepared to deal with it in novel forms like *undressers*. This does not, however, imply that *-er-s* is a unit lacking constituency, since what actually achieves unit status is the partially schematic structure [STEM-er-s], which is in fact a constituent. The situation is depicted in Fig. 8.10.[30] This diagram represents the categorizing judgment (cf. 2.1.4) by

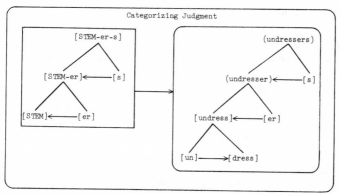

Fig. 8.10

which the schema [STEM-er-s], shown at the left, sanctions the novel form *undressers*. The sanctioning schema has unit status and embodies the morphological generalization speakers have abstracted from numerous specific instances (many of which are also listed in the grammar as established units). The schema fully sanctions the novel expression, which is compatible with its specifications and elaborates its schematically characterized stem. Observe that all units in this diagram are also constituents. The portions of the sanctioning schema that are fully specified and require no significant elaboration for their overt manifestation, namely *-er-s*, do not form a constituent, but neither is there any necessary reason to suppose that they constitute a unit to the exclusion of the schematic stem. A region of maximal specificity within a partially schematic structure does not necessarily qualify as either a constituent within this structure or as a unit on the basis of its level of specificity alone.

These points are directly applicable to expressions like *talk to, look at, quarrel over, marvel at, deal with*, etc., where the verb governs a particular preposition, yet does not necessarily form a constituent with it: to some degree at least, the preposition and its object nominal behave as a syntactic constituent to the exclusion of the governing verb.[31] The apparatus at hand allows

---

[30] I simplify by showing only the phonological pole, but the analysis is bipolar.

[31] For present purposes, we may factor out the problem posed by competing synchronic analyses: certain grammatical properties argue for the preposition forming a prepositional-phrase constituent with the following nominal, and others for its combination with the preceding verb to form a complex verb taking the nominal as direct object. Only the former analysis is considered at this juncture. (Competing analyses—unproblematic in this framework—are dealt with in Ch. 11.)

us to reconcile the apparently conflicting demands of government and constituency. The actual units include not only the verb and preposition, but also a schematic nominal, e.g. [talk [to NOMINAL]]. *To* and the following nominal form a schematic prepositional-phrase constituent within the larger unit, and this prepositional phrase functions as a complement of *talk*. The fixed unit is generally taken to be *talk to* rather than [talk [to NOMINAL]] simply because *talk* and *to* are the only facets of the structure susceptible to overt phonological manifestation.

One last point to be considered is how the present notion of constituent structure relates to the one assumed in generative grammar. They are not equivalent.[32] Generative grammar's tree structures are conceived as syntactic entities. A node like VP (verb phrase) or NP (noun phrase) is neither a semantic nor a phonological structure: it may be associated with semantic and phonological representations by interpretive rules, but this happens in separate components of the grammar. By contrast, every constituent and every structure (node) in a cognitive-grammar constituency tree is bipolar, with both semantic and phonological content, and has no existence apart from this content. Moreover, though the nodes in a generative phrase tree function as labels of syntactic categories, the cognitive-grammar conception makes a clear distinction between constituency and categorization. The nodes in a constituency tree are symbolic entities (component or composite structures), not category labels. Categorization is effected by relationships in the schematic rather than the syntagmatic plane (cf. Fig. 8.10), and the categorizing elements are themselves symbolic structures. Though schematic, they manifest internally the same sorts of relationships (including constituency) that are found in the content structures they sanction. Finally, sister nodes in a generative phrase-structure diagram are associated only through the higher node that immediately dominates them, but in cognitive grammar the components that participate in a construction are directly integrated via correspondences and elaborative relationships.

8.4.2. *Variability of Constituency*

The four valence factors are not of equal significance. Correspondence is fundamental in the sense that it is the only factor that figures in every valence relation. Correspondence and profile determinacy are together sufficient to specify the composite structure in constructions exhibiting full compositionality, but we have seen that some valence relations provide no basis for identifying a profile determinant. The distinction between autonomous and dependent structures is similarly appropriate only for a subset of valence relations.

---

[32] The conception I have outlined shows certain affinities to dependency-tree diagrams, but here too there are substantial differences (see Langacker 1981b).

There is also a clear sense in which constituency is a secondary factor. It tends to be binary, so in constructions of any complexity constituency groupings can almost invariably be observed. These groupings are not themselves essential to the derivation of a composite structure, however, and the same composite structure can generally be derived from its components through alternate compositional paths. The same correspondences can be established between the component and composite structures regardless of the order in which the component structures are combined.

Consider a simple transitive clause like *The arrow hit the target*. There are three main elements: *hit* is processual, whereas *the arrow* and *the target* are nominal. *Hit* is the profile determinant in the valence relations deriving the composite structure, for the clause as a whole inherits its processual profile. The process [HIT] is sketched in diagram (a) of Fig. 8.11, and the composite structure for the clause (omitting tense and articles) in diagram (b). [HIT] designates a process in which a trajector moves through space until it makes forceful contact with a landmark. In the valence relations leading to the composite structure, the schematic landmark of [HIT] is an e-site that corresponds to the profile of [TARGET], and its schematic trajector an e-site that corresponds to the profile of [ARROW]. The composite structure [ARROW-HIT-TARGET] is therefore exactly parallel to [HIT] except that its trajector and landmark are nonschematic, having inherited the specifications of these nominal predications.

No mention of constituency was made in this characterization, and it is readily seen that the same composite structure results irrespective of the order

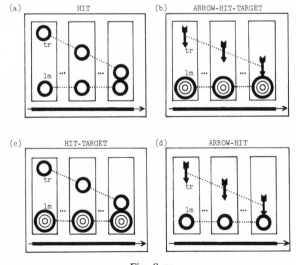

Fig. 8.11

of combination. Suppose that [TARGET] elaborates the landmark of [HIT] at the lowest level of constituency. This produces the intermediate-level composite structure depicted in diagram (c), where the landmark has the specifications of [TARGET] but the trajector remains schematic. We then derive structure (b) by selecting as e-site the schematic trajector of [HIT-TARGET]; [ARROW] elaborates it at the second level of constituency. Suppose, on the other hand, that the trajector of [HIT] functions as e-site at the first constituency level, being elaborated by [ARROW] to yield the intermediate-level structure in diagram (d), with specified trajector and schematic landmark. Elaborating this landmark with [TARGET] at the higher level of constituency once again results in structure (b). Nor is any constituency grouping necessary at all. Perfectly conceivable is a tripartite valence relation in which [HIT], the profile determinant, is simultaneously elaborated by two nominal predications, [ARROW] corresponding to its trajector and [TARGET] to its landmark.

The notion that constituency might be fluid, variable, and relatively inessential to grammatical relationships is quite at odds with generative theory, which treats it as a basically fixed and constant aspect of grammatical organization that serves as foundation for the definition of grammatical relations. However, the reasons for this position are largely internal to generative theory, and its empirical liabilities are many. With the exception of a handful of categories whose status as constituents is fairly obvious (e.g. noun phrase, prepositional phrase), there has always been a notable lack of consensus among generative linguists concerning virtually every aspect of phrase structure at the level of specific detail, even for English, despite over a quarter century of intensive investigation. Moreover, to maintain the position it has been necessary to invoke a suspiciously broad array of theoretical devices (some of them notably ad hoc), including "readjustment rules" to mediate between the output of the syntax and the input required for the phonological component (cf. Chomsky and Halle 1968), rules of "restructuring" to change the constituency grouping of elements in the course of a syntactic derivation (cf. Akmajian, Steele, and Wasow 1979), and various kinds of transformations.

To question the primacy and the fixed character of constituent structure is not, however, to claim that chaos reigns supreme. Like any other aspect of linguistic activity, compositional paths specifying the organization of components into constituents are subject to conventionalization and entrenchment. Patterns of constituency invariably emerge to be incorporated in the complex schematic units that constitute a speaker's knowledge of grammatical constructions (cf. Fig. 8.10). The expressions of a language therefore show a considerable measure of regularity in their constituency groupings, certain patterns becoming so deeply entrenched that variability is essentially precluded. Usually, though, a significant amount of flexibility remains. Often there is a dominant, default-case pattern that can nevertheless be overridden when special circumstances motivate another option. Sometimes alternate constituency groupings are conventionally established to a comparable degree, the choice being either free or conditioned by other factors. The constituent structure of a particular expression is thus determined through the interaction of conventional patterns, the broader grammatical context, and considerations of a functional, communicative, or stylistic nature.

Consider the constituency of English transitive clauses consisting of nothing more than a subject, verb, and direct object. The dominant pattern for such clauses groups the verb and direct object as a constituent—this is the pattern that prevails in the absence of special, overriding circumstances. We can see this in (13), where the slash indicates a slight pause or the demarcation of rhythmic groups within a sequence.

(13)(a) *The arrow/hit the target.*
(b) ?*The arrow hit/the target.*

It is far more natural to put this intonational break after the subject, suggesting that the verb and object form a constituent, than between the verb and object. The standard NP + VP analysis of English clause structure therefore has a certain amount of validity.

There are numerous instances, however, where special circumstances dictate some other constituency, and there is no reason whatever in this framework to discount the surface evidence by positing a "deeper" level of NP + VP organization distorted by the application of transformations or comparable rules. In the topic construction of (14)(a), for example, intonation and word order indicate rather unequivocally that the subject and verb form a constituent:

(14)(a) *This target/the arrow hit/(but not that one).*
(b) *The arrow hit/but the bullets missed/the target.*

Here I offer no analysis of topic constructions, except to note that the canonical NP + VP organization is readily suspended when communicative factors favor isolating the direct object as a separate major constituent. The landmark of the designated process thus remains unelaborated until a higher level of constituency, where the object nominal is integrated with a composite structure incorporating all the other clausal elements. Something similar is observed in (14)(b). Transformational analysts consider such sentences to involve the conjoining of nonconstituents, and generally posit a rule of Right Node-Raising to derive it from an underlying structure displaying the orthodox NP + VP constituency. The cognitive-grammar account is much less contrived. The desire to express a parallel relation between two processual notions that share a landmark but otherwise diverge is sufficient motivation for overriding the canonical constituency in favor of one that permits this parallelism to be structurally expressed. The conventions of English sanction an alternate constituent grouping for such instances: the subject and verb are first integrated to form a composite structure with unelaborated landmark (cf. Fig. 8.11(d)); two composite structures of this sort are then joined as conjuncts at a higher level of organization; and finally, at the highest level of constituency, the complex structure so derived is integrated with a nominal that simultaneously elaborates the landmark of both conjuncts. The hypothesized constituency is perfectly consistent with the surface evidence and requires no apparatus not independently justified. The analysis claims that (14)(b) does in fact involve the conjoining of constituents, even though the constituency grouping is noncanonical.

The examples in (15) illustrate how constituency interacts with stylistic factors pertaining to "balance" and the relative "weight" of constituents.

(15)(a)   *I sent the artifacts to an anthropologist.*

(b)   ??*I sent to an anthropologist the artifacts.*

(c)   ?*I sent the artifacts that had been sitting in the attic for seventeen years collecting dust to an anthropologist.*

(d)   *I sent to an anthropologist the artifacts that had been sitting in the attic for seventeen years collecting dust.*

The basic facts are well known: in normal circumstances (i.e. when the direct and indirect objects are approximately equal in length), the direct object precedes—this is the dominant pattern; when, however, the direct object is extremely long and cumbersome relative to the indirect object, the order is reversed. Though one pattern is predominant in neutral situations, there is no theory-independent reason to suppose that either is derived from the other or that (15)(d) really involves two levels of grammatical organization, one with the canonical order of constituents and the other with the order actually observed. Instead, I posit two alternate constituency groupings. In (15)(a), the direct object first elaborates the primary landmark of the verb; then, at a higher level of constituency, the indirect object elaborates a substructure within the composite structure so derived. The order of integration is reversed in (15)(d). The indirect object first elaborates the schematic path-specification of the verb, forming a processual constituent with an unelaborated primary landmark; this landmark functions as the e-site for the direct-object nominal at the higher level of constituency. Whereas the alternate compositional paths are reflected in contrasting word order at the phonological pole, the composite semantic structure is the same.

We can carry this example even further. There is no necessary reason to believe that (15)(a) and (d) preserve the canonical clausal organization of NP + VP—the major intonation break comes after the first postverbal complement:

(16)(a) *I sent the artifacts/to an anthropologist.*
   (b) *I sent to an anthropologist/the artifacts that had been sitting in the attic for seventeen years collecting dust.*

Nothing in the framework posited here precludes a conventional constituency pattern that accords with the intonational evidence in (16), where the subject, the verb, and one postverbal complement form a constituent that combines at a higher level with the second postverbal complement. Adhering to the ortho- dox NP + VP pattern in sentences like these would produce a massive dis- crepancy in the weight of the two major constituents. It is hardly astonishing that the dynamics of language use might result in the emergence and conven- tionalization of secondary constituency patterns permitting the construction of expressions with greater intonational balance.

There are open questions concerning how the constituent grouping of expressions is to be determined (for example, intonational factors cannot always be accepted at face value). Nevertheless, the overt evidence, examined without theoretical prejudgment, suggests rather strongly that this aspect of grammatical organization is subject to considerable variation. The proposed framework tolerates the observed fluidity because it does not rely on phrase- structure configurations for the definition of crucial grammatical relation- ships. Instead, such relationships reflect correspondences established between the substructures of components, and the same correspondences can be estab- lished (directly or indirectly) through alternate orders of integration and composition.

8.4.3. *Semantic and Phonological Constituents*

A consequence of the model presented here, as opposed to certain others, is that a very close relationship can be established between the constituency attributable to expressions on phonological grounds (e.g. linear contiguity, intonational considerations) and that necessary for the characterization of se- mantic relationships. Exactly how close this relationship is remains to be de- termined; certainly a mechanical segmentation procedure applied to a mor- phemically analyzed string and relying only on observable phonological cues would not unerringly yield constituency groupings reasonable from the stand- point of semantic and grammatical analysis.[33] It is nonetheless possible to conjecture that the relationship is very close indeed, and that by and large— with allowances for certain phenomena of identifiable kinds—constituency groupings suggested by phonological considerations can be reconciled with the structures necessary for grammatical and semantic purposes.

Preliminary illustration was provided by our discussion of (14)–(16). We

[33] Consider examples (analyzed in 9.3.2) like *hand-held cameraman* (which is someone who operates a hand-held camera, not a cameraman of small stature) or *the queen of England's con- sort* (where the monarch, not the nation, is understood as the possessor).

saw in each instance that the proposed scheme of valence relations makes it both possible and unproblematic to group together as (bipolar) semantic constituents those elements that correspond to major intonational groups, even when the groupings in question conflict with the canonical NP + VP organization generally assumed to be the only one permitted in English.

A different class of examples is represented by the compound *pole climber*, diagrammed earlier in Fig. 8.8. On first examination this expression appears to show a discrepancy between semantic and phonological constituency: (1) phonologically (since a compound involves the juxtaposition of two stems) the constituents are clearly *pole* and *climber*; (2) semantically, however, *pole* is the object of *climb*, and *climber*—as a noun rather than a verb—cannot be said to have an object; (3) consequently, *pole* and *climb* must be grouped as a semantic constituent in opposition to *-er*, which conflicts with the grouping established on phonological grounds.

The fallacy in this argument is the assumption in (2) that a noun like *climber* cannot support an object. The contrary position has already been spelled out in Fig. 8.8, showing the semantic pole of *pole climber* under the assumption that its semantic and phonological constituency are parallel. In particular, the noun stem *climber* has for its base the processual notion *climb*, with schematic landmark and trajector. *Climber* profiles the trajector of this base process, but nonetheless it contains a salient landmark, equated (through a vertical correspondence) with the landmark of the verb root, capable of serving as the e-site in the valence relation with *pole* at the second level of constituency. The assumption that *climber* cannot take an object is seen as erroneous in the context of the present account of semantic structure and valence relations.

We find a more dramatic example in English sentences where an auxiliary verb agrees with the subject, e.g. *Your football is under the table*. Here many linguists (e.g. Keyser and Postal 1976) have posited a transformation that raises the subject nominal out of a lower clause and inserts it as the subject of a higher clause (the auxiliary is treated as the higher verb). The rationale, based once more on a putative discrepancy between surface and semantic constituency, is roughly as follows: (1) a verb in English agrees with its surface subject; (2) in sentences like these, it is the auxiliary verb that shows agreement, so the nominal must be the surface subject of the auxiliary; (3) semantically, however, this nominal is the subject only of the content predicate (e.g. *under*), not of the auxiliary; (4) therefore a raising rule must extract the nominal from its subject relationship with the content predicate in underlying structure and reattach it as the derived subject of the auxiliary.

The problem lies in point (3), and specifically in the assumption that the nominal bears a semantic subject relation only to the content predicate. Observe that this assumption is made in the absence of any explicit account of the meaning of *be* or the nature of valence relations, but surely these are relevant to the problem. Only minimal discussion is appropriate here (fuller treatment is given in Part V), but I suggest the assumption is groundless. In the present framework it is reasonable to claim that *your football* is the semantic subject of *is* in the sentence *Your football is under the table*.

Be is analyzed as a maximally schematic imperfective-process predication. That is, it profiles an imperfective process (cf. Ch. 7), but is schematic for the class of such predications and has no content apart from that expressing their commonality. Finite verb-inflection (for tense and "agreement") is itself treated as a predication, with actual (though limited) semantic content. It is sufficient here to note that one such predication combines with [BE] to yield the composite semantic structure [IS], sketched in Fig. 8.12. [IS] also designates a schematic imperfective process: it follows through conceived time a

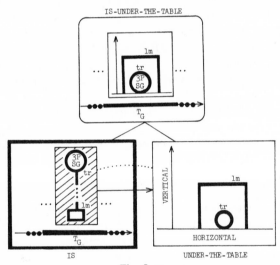

Fig. 8.12

schematic stative relation construed as being constant throughout its temporal profile. The contribution of the finite verb-inflection to this structure is twofold. First, the trajector is identified as being third person (3P), i.e. other than speaker and hearer, as well as singular (SG). Second, the temporal profile of the process is equated with the time of speaking, labeled T_G (for "ground time") in Fig. 8.12.

The pivotal claim is that the auxiliary verb has semantic content, and specifically that it profiles a process, albeit one characterized only in schematic terms. Consequently it makes inherent reference, as part of its own internal structure, to a trajector and a landmark, though they too are only schematic. A further point of significance is that the relational predication [UNDER-

THE-TABLE] does *not* correspond to the trajector of [IS]: in this analysis it is neither a subject nor a nominal, but a relational complement: it elaborates the stative relation followed by [IS] through conceived time. Since [IS] functions as the profile determinant, the composite predication (IS-UNDER-THE-TABLE) profiles an imperfective process; predicated as holding constant during the time of speaking is the state in which a thing (identified only as third person and singular) bears an [UNDER]-relation to a particular table.

At the highest level of constituency, [YOUR-FOOTBALL] elaborates the schematic trajector of the composite structure (IS-UNDER-THE-TABLE); the latter is the profile determinant, so the overall expression is clausal rather than nominal. What do we then say about the subject nominal *your football*? In particular, what is it the subject of? In terms of the present analysis, it is simply false to claim that it bears a semantic subject-relation only to *under*. Because of the correspondences established by valence relations—both horizontal and vertical correspondences—the profile of *your football* is equated with the trajector of *all* the pertinent relational predications. It corresponds to the trajector of [BE], [IS], [UNDER], [UNDER-THE-TABLE], and (IS-UNDER-THE-TABLE), since all these trajectors are themselves linked by correspondences. In effect it elaborates all the trajectors simultaneously, even though the valence relation that effects the elaboration refers specifically to the trajector of (IS-UNDER-THE-TABLE). No raising rule whatever is needed to achieve the desired result, and the semantic constituency is perfectly compatible with the one suggested by phonological considerations.

8.5. Canonical Valence Relations

Each of the valence factors has been seen to exhibit a significant range of possibilities. These possibilities are not all equal in status, however: in each instance one particular configuration appears to be canonical or prototypical, so far as one can judge (at least impressionistically) on the basis of frequency and the unmarked character of the constructions.

The single constant factor in valence relations is the existence of correspondences linking substructures of the component predications. In the canonical configuration, at least one correspondence associates highly salient entities—in particular, the profile of one predication and the trajector or primary landmark of the other. We have seen a number of cases, though, where the correspondent of a profile is an unprofiled entity in the base, and there is probably no absolute requirement on its degree of salience.

With regard to profile determinacy, the canonical situation is for the composite structure to inherit the profile of one of its components, which is then referred to as the profile determinant. There are several kinds of circumstances, however, where the grounds for identifying a profile determinant are lacking. One such case is when the profiles of the components correspond; the same composite structure then results regardless of which component is selected. In other instances the composite structure appears to conflate the profiles of its component structures rather than choosing one at the expense of the others. There are also valence relations in which the composite-structure profile is distinct from that of all its components.

Typically the components in a valence relation show a notable asymmetry permitting one of them to be identified as conceptually autonomous and the other conceptually dependent. A predication is conceptually dependent when it contains a salient but schematic substructure (e-site) corresponding to the profile of another predication that substantially elaborates it. In canonical instances the dependent predication is relational, and the autonomous predication profiles a thing that corresponds to its trajector or primary landmark. All of these matters are variable, however. A dependent predication may be nominal, and an elaborating predication may be relational. Structures other than trajectors and primary landmarks can function as e-sites; an e-site need not be in profile, nor does it require any specific level of prominence. The distinction between autonomous and dependent predications is further a matter of degree: there may be a certain amount of dependence in both directions (or very little in either direction), and often the asymmetry required for a meaningful distinction is lacking.

Finally, the integration of components into progressively more elaborate predications tends to proceed in binary fashion. In a structure of any complexity, then, we typically find a number of hierarchical levels, where at each level a constituent is defined by the integration of precisely two components to form a composite structure. Constructions involving three or more components at a single level can nevertheless be found, and it appears that some constructions (e.g. certain types of coordination) permit an indefinite number of component structures with no hierarchical grouping among them.

Pulling together the canonical situations for each valence factor, we arrive at the configuration in Fig. 8.13 as the apparent prototype for grammatical constructions. There are two component structures, one relational and the other nominal. The relational predication is conceptually dependent, containing a salient substructure—part of its profile—that corresponds to the profile of the autonomous nominal predication and bears to it a relation of schematicity. Moreover, the dependent predication functions as profile-determinant, making the nominal predication a complement (in particular, an argument). A number of previous examples meet all these specifications, including the prepositional-object relation between *under* and *the table* (Fig. 8.1) and the subject-verb and verb-object relations of *The arrow hit the target* (Fig. 8.11).

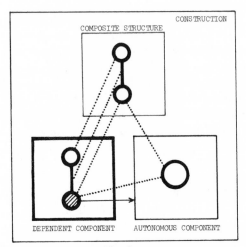

Fig. 8.13

These are the kinds of constructions that valence theorists normally take as their point of departure, but a valence theory must be flexible enough to accommodate the full range of relationships actually encountered.

If such a prototype proves empirically motivated, it can be included among the substantive specifications constituting a linguistic theory. Presumably speakers employ this structure to the maximal extent feasible in organizing their linguistic experience, structuring their knowledge of linguistic convention along these lines so long as this is compatible with the data. Nevertheless, they must be prepared to depart from the canon in regard to any or all of the valence factors, as needed. Indeed, certain noncanonical configurations no doubt themselves have special linguistic status, for instance the head/modifier relation (obtained from Fig. 8.13 by making the autonomous component the profile determinant). These can be accommodated in linguistic theory as secondary prototypes, and attributed to speakers as part of the cognitive apparatus they bring to the task of mastering linguistic convention.

Fig. 8.13 incorporates certain notational features that have been omitted from various diagrams for one reason or another but call attention to points of some significance. First, I have used cross-hatching to identify the e-site within the dependent predication, as well as the arrow of schematicity between this substructure and the autonomous predication that elaborates it. Second, since Fig. 8.13 is abstract and nonpictorial, the nature of the profiled interconnections defining the relational predications is not apparent from the configuration of the diagrams themselves; heavy lines have thus been included specifically to represent these relational interconnections. Third, both horizontal and vertical correspondences have been indicated. For the profile determinant, there are vertical correspondences involving both participants in the profiled relation and also the relational interconnections themselves.

Finally, I call attention to the outer box in Fig. 8.13. This box represents the grammatical construction as a whole, i.e. the composite structure, the component structures, and the relations these bear to one another. This is a distinct higher-order construct, and if the construction as a whole has unit status it is included in the grammar of the language as a conventional unit: it represents the cognitive routine having all the other structures as subroutines. For purposes of diagrammatic simplicity, I generally omit the box or closed curve enclosing the overall construction. It is nevertheless important that the construction be recognized as a distinct and significant structural element. One reason is that the construction as a whole is what represents a constituent at a given level of hierarchical organization. This should be apparent from Fig. 8.14, showing the phonological pole of *undressers*; it is equivalent to

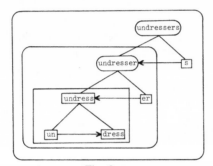

Fig. 8.14

Fig. 8.9(b), except that constructions are explicitly indicated. Note further that the construction as a whole may have a status different from that of its subparts; in particular, the overall construction may in some instances be novel even if its component and composite structures are deeply entrenched units. Suppose, for example, that a speaker realizes for the very first time that *propeller* (previously seen as opaque) is analyzable into *propel* and *-er*: though all three (taken individually) have been established units, their association to form a construction constitutes a novel configuration.

CHAPTER 9

Symbolic Units

THE ELEMENTS that participate in valence relations are symbolic structures, each associating a predication with its phonological realization. The definition of predications and their realizations is bipolar: they are delimited by the very fact that they stand in a symbolic relationship, and do not always coincide with the entities that are recognized as natural building blocks of conceptual or phonological structure when these are considered individually. Our examination of symbolic units begins with the phonological pole of morphemes; fairly abstract constructs prove necessary to their description. Some of the requisite notions are then applied to the semantic pole, where they clarify the nature of dependent predications. We then explore the implications of these findings for the determination of constituency.

9.1. The Phonological Pole

Semantic structure and phonological structure are parallel in many significant respects. I have argued, for example, that the notions of autonomy and dependence are applicable in both domains (for elements defined in both unipolar and bipolar terms). I have further suggested that valence relations at the two poles require essentially the same apparatus for their description. Though our discussion will focus on bipolar units, a brief examination of unipolar phonological structure will serve as a useful preface.

9.1.1. *Phonological Structure*

Phonological hierarchies have long been recognized: segments are grouped into syllables, syllables into words, words into phonological phrases, and so on. Let us concentrate on the lower levels of this hierarchy, namely the organization of segments into syllables and of syllables into words. At each level the component elements manifest important asymmetries and even intralevel constituency groupings—a word is not simply an unstructured sequence of syllables, nor is a syllable just a linear sequence of segments. This has prompted generative phonologists, in recent years, to analyze words as hierarchies of syllables, where at each level of constituency a distinction is made between strong vs. weak components; they have similarly begun to posit significant constituent structure for the grouping of segments within a syllable.[1]

The asymmetries and relationships that require such analyses can be explicated using notions that are broadly grounded in the present framework. The relevance of constituency is self-evident, and also its generality. Somewhat less obvious, perhaps, is the role of A/D alignment, particularly at the word level. I suggest that the concepts of autonomy and dependence, properly interpreted for the domains in question, are applicable to both the vowel/consonant distinction and the contrast between strong and weak syllables.

At the segmental level, I have already characterized vowels as phonologically autonomous and consonants as dependent. A vowel provides a period of essentially stable sonority and can be fully implemented without the support of a consonant. A consonant, on the other hand, is reasonably described as a modification of the sonority furnished by a vowel and is therefore asymmetrically dependent on a vowel for its full manifestation. There are of course degrees, even though a categorical C/V (consonant/vowel) distinction can be made and is appropriate for many purposes. Syllabic resonants instantiate the vowel schema because they involve a period of stable sonority, but the presence of a significant obstruction in the oral tract renders them nonprototypical for the vowel class. Voiceless vowels depart from the prototype because of their greatly attenuated level of sonority, even if they are briefly stable and produced without oral obstruction. Voiceless stops are maximally opposed to vowels in their properties and would generally be considered "optimal" or prototypical consonants. Other types of consonants deviate from this prototype in different ways and degrees that lessen their distinctness from vowels (by virtue of voicing, the continuous and possibly nonturbulent flow of air through the oral or nasal tract, and so on). A partial gradation can therefore be observed between the two prototypes despite the categorical C/V distinction and the susceptibility of the two classes to schematic characterization (cf. Jaeger and Ohala 1984).

Let us now consider these factors in relation to the internal constituency of a syllable. In one form or another, the analysis of a syllable into structural "layers"—at least to the extent of recognizing the vowel as the "core" or "nucleus"—is universally accepted. What does it mean, precisely, to say that the vowel is the "core" or "nucleus" of a syllable? What is the nature of the functional asymmetry between the vowel and the consonants of a syllable that is responsible for our applying such terms to the former rather than the latter? The answer, I submit, lies in the notions of phonological autonomy and de-

---

[1] See, for instance, Liberman and Prince (1977); Prince (1980); Selkirk (1980); Cairns and Feinstein (1982).

pendence. A vowel is essentially prerequisite to the implementation of a consonant, but the converse is not true. A vowel is therefore the "starting point" for the construction of a syllable in the sense that it can be implemented autonomously and creates the conditions necessary for the occurrence of an associated consonant.

It has frequently been observed that the consonants within a syllable are not arranged in random fashion. Despite some exceptions, there is a strong tendency for the members of a consonant cluster to align themselves so that their distance from the syllabic nucleus correlates with their prototypicality. Moving from the nucleus outward, in either the onset of a complex syllable or the coda, one first encounters the most vowel-like of the consonants (glides in particular, which are often analyzed as part of the nucleus), then others of intermediate status (e.g. liquids), then finally the most prototypical consonants (obstruents). A natural way of accounting for this is to posit multiple layers of *A/D* organization. In the word *child*, for example, the nucleus and coda would be organized hierarchically as shown in Fig. 9.1(a). Three levels of

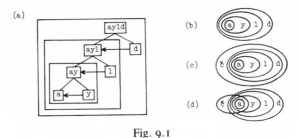

Fig. 9.1

constituency are involved; at each a phonologically dependent segment (i.e. consonant) is appended to a more autonomous structure. The autonomous structure is a vowel at the first level (or inner layer), but at higher levels it consists of the vocalic nucleus together with previously appended consonantal increments.

I will assume that something along these lines correctly represents one important aspect of syllabic organization.[2] It will be convenient, though, to have a somewhat simpler form of diagrammatic representation. A full constituency tree like Fig. 9.1(a) is needed to depict all the structures and relationships that must actually be recognized in a complex syllabic structure, but for many purposes compacted representations in the format of Fig. 9.1(b) are adequate ab-

---

[2] Incrementation at a given level need not be restricted to a single consonant. Conceivably, for instance, [s] and [p] form a constituent in words like *spin*, being integrated as a composite unit with the vocalic nucleus. (This would correlate with the exceptionality of the consonantal layering, where [p] is directly adjacent to the nucleus despite being less vowel-like than [s]. In purely local terms, [s] is autonomous relative to [p], and this may be sufficient to permit their forming a constituent.)

breviations. Each circle (or ellipse) in such a diagram stands for an autonomous structure at a particular level of organization, and the element just outside this circle indicates a dependent structure that combines with it to form a higher-order autonomous structure. (Circles are employed purely for diagrammatic ease in these representations of canonical A/D layering—they say nothing about degree of entrenchment.)

Yet to be considered is the relation between the consonant or consonant cluster in the onset of a syllable and the one that functions as its coda. Under one common analysis, the nucleus and coda form a constituent that combines as a unit with the onset at a higher level of organization. *Child* would then have the structure shown in Fig. 9.1(c). A plausible alternative is given in Fig. 9.1(d): it assumes that the nucleus is capable of anchoring chains of successive consonantal increments extending from it in either direction, simultaneously and more or less independently of one another. I have no real basis at this point for choosing one option over the other, nor would I be surprised to learn that constituency is variable even at this level. I will arbitrarily choose the analysis of diagram (d) for expository purposes.

A/D asymmetry is plausibly invoked as well for the organization of syllables into words. To see the parallelism, note that constituency at this level and the distinction between strong and weak syllables were first proposed (and are most convincingly motivated) for the analysis of rhythmic and accentual phenomena. To the extent that a strong syllable is identified on the basis of relative accentual prominence, its function is analogous to that of a syllabic nucleus: each is a sonority peak at its own level of organization. I suggest further that the grouping of strong and weak syllables to form "feet" or comparable constituents within a word resembles the rhythmic association of consonants as "satellites" of a preceding or following vocalic nucleus.

More specifically, let us suppose that the phonological autonomy of a syllable (or higher-order constituent) is manifested by its occurrence in full, unreduced form—approximately as if it were pronounced in isolation. The effect of phonological dependence, by contrast, is reduction and compression: as rhythmic "satellite" to an autonomous structure, a dependent syllable is compressed along such phonetic parameters as time, amplitude, and pitch range. The rhythmic subordination of a dependent structure thus confines it to a narrower region of phonological space, resulting in an overall decrease in its sonority and prominence (and often in the maintenance of fewer phonological distinctions). Though it is generally possible to pronounce a dependent syllable by itself, in doing so a speaker is almost certain to render it with the phonological range and sonority of an autonomous, unreduced syllable. To be implemented with the actual phonetic properties characteristic of its subordinate status, a dependent syllable must be pronounced in combination with an autonomous one. This is equivalent to saying that a dependent syllable makes schematic reference to an autonomous structure as part of its own internal characterization.

Consider, then, a word like *macaroni*, whose phonological structure (at the level of syllables and above) is sketched in Fig. 9.2. At the first level of constituency, the dependent status of [kə] and [ni] is shown in two ways: (1) each

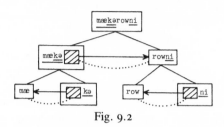

Fig. 9.2

is underscored, to represent the phonological compression entrained by rhythmic subordination; and (2) each follows a schema (crosshatched) standing for the autonomous structure it presupposes. These schematic substructures of [kə] and [ni] are elaborated by [mæ] and [row] respectively to yield the composite structures [mækə] and [rowni], where the second syllable is in each case reduced and compressed relative to the first. The dependence of [mækə] on [rowni] at the second level of constituency is shown in parallel fashion: the former makes schematic reference to an autonomous structure, and an additional underscore indicates its role as rhythmic satellite to this structure. The overall composite structure is therefore [mækərowni], where only [row] appears in unreduced form. Both [ni] and [mækə] are compressed in relation to [row], and within the narrowed phonetic range of the latter the second syllable is compressed relative to the first. This reduction and compression is intrinsic to the composite structure (not something requiring separate specification), for it constitutes per se the phonetic value of phonological dependence at these higher levels (cf. Prince 1983).

We must therefore posit schematic structures even for unipolar phonological organization. While articulation and audition determine the parameters of phonological space, they are nevertheless cognitively grounded phenomena. They are subject to abstraction and other mental operations, resulting in the emergence of cognitive structures that can be activated even in the absence of peripheral implementation, or which are too abstract—in whole or in part— for such implementation. There is nothing inherently implausible, then, in positing a schematic vowel for the internal structure of a consonant, or an autonomous syllable for a dependent syllable, even though these schematic substructures cannot be directly manifested per se. More broadly, phonological rules and categories take the form of schematic structures in phonological space whose connection with peripheral activities may be quite distant.

I assume, for example, that speakers extract and manipulate the schemas [VOWEL] and [CONSONANT], together with various subschemas (e.g. [HIGH VOWEL], [OBSTRUENT]); these may function as substructures of other elements. Generalizations about conventionally permitted syllable structures are similarly represented in the form of schematic syllables equivalent to the traditional syllable canons (e.g. CV, CVC, CCVC). These notions will be developed more fully as we proceed.

9.1.2. *Phrase Trees*

With this background, we turn now to morphological structure and the phonological pole of morphemes. Our attention thus shifts to units determined by symbolic relationships, which often crosscut natural (unipolar) phonological constituents. I have already invoked the *A/D* asymmetry of such units to explicate the root/affix distinction. This conception can now be made more precise.

Ch. 8 outlined a nonstandard view of constituency, applicable—at each pole—to both morphological and syntactic structure. The phonological pole of morphological structure provides additional motivation for this rather elaborate conception, which posits a considerable array of distinct entities for every hierarchical level: component structures, the composite structure, the correspondences among these (both horizontal and vertical), as well as the overall constituent that embodies all of these elements. A brief critique of the standard phrase-tree model of morphological structure will serve as a basis for comparison.

Fig. 9.3 exemplifies the tree structures typically employed in generative grammar to represent the morphological layering of complex words. Every

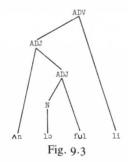

Fig. 9.3

node corresponds to a constituent, and node labels represent their grammatical class. The root is identified as the smallest constituent with a node label; in the labeled-bracketing format, the innermost set of brackets enclose it. Observe that affixes do not themselves have node labels, since they do not represent "lexical" categories. Fig. 9.3 correctly depicts many important aspects of the structure of *unlawfully*. Trees of this type work well for many examples, and are highly perspicuous for various purposes.

A number of points nevertheless suggest that the optimality of phrase trees as normally conceived cannot be granted by default. It might first be questioned whether affixes are properly said to have no category status, as implied by the absence of node labels. Previous examples should make my own position clear: affixes have semantic content (if only highly schematic) and they are subject to categorization on the basis of this content in exactly the same way as roots and stems. Thus *-ful* is analyzed as a schematic adjective, *-er* as a schematic noun, the plural morpheme as a noun designating a schematic replicate mass, and so forth. These morphemes function as profile determinants in their valence relations with a stem, and consequently they impose their categorization on the stem's generally more elaborate semantic content. Some linguists may doubt the appropriateness of such analyses for the cases cited, but there are other instances where the meaningfulness of an affix is beyond dispute, and the failure to imbue it with category status can only be considered arbitrary. One example will suffice:

(1)(a) *ni-k-neki ni-k-iʔta-s*   'I want to see it.'
         I-it-want I-it-see-FUT

   (b) *ni-k-iʔta-s-neki*   'I want to see it.'
         I-it-see-FUT-want

These sentences illustrate the dual function of the verb *neki* 'want' in Classical Nahuatl. It can occur as the content verb of the main clause, as in (1)(a), in which case it constitutes the verb root; but as (1)(b) shows, it can also function as a derivational suffix, where it designates the process profiled by the clause as a whole. To claim that the suffixal manifestation of *neki* obviates its categorization as a verb would be gratuitous at best. Many more examples of this kind can be adduced.

I assume, then, that at least some affixes have category status. However, it will not do simply to add the requisite node labels to phrase trees like Fig. 9.3: this would obliterate the root/affix distinction, which is marked only by the presence vs. the absence of such labels. I would argue in any case that the deployment of labels for basic grammatical categories (N, V, ADJ, etc.) is an inappropriate way of identifying roots and affixes, for it has no intrinsic connection with the notion of "layering" or the "core"/"satellite" asymmetry that is fundamental to morphological structure. Categorization defines a plane of relationships (the schematic plane) that is essentially orthogonal to the one given by relationships of layering and constituency (the syntagmatic plane).[3] I suggest that morphological layering and the root/affix asymmetry must be de-

---

[3] This statement is qualified in Ch. 12, but not in any way that affects the present discussion.

scribed in their own terms, and that crucial reliance on class labels for their characterization serves only to confuse the issues.

Yet another difficulty with phrase trees is their inadequacy for representing nonroot morphemes other than affixes, including such entities as discontinuous morphemes, zero morphemes, suprasegmental morphemes, and process morphemes of all kinds (e.g. truncation, ablaut). Phrase-tree representations presuppose linear sequences of discrete morphemes, each consisting of a linear sequence of segments. How is one then to draw the tree diagram for the nonagglutinative morphological structure of, say, the plural noun *sheep*, the past-tense form *sat*, or a perfective verb in Papago derived by truncating the final CV of the stem? Certainly some kind of notation can be devised that will allow at least the appearance of a canonical tree structure to be maintained. One such notation is illustrated in Fig. 9.4; *sat* is diagrammed in (a), and *fearful*—on the assumption that the noun *fear* derives from the verb— in (b).

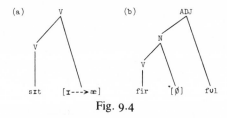

Fig. 9.4

In this notation, brackets are used to enclose morphemes that in one way or another are more abstract than simple segment sequences. Some version of the notation is occasionally found in the generative literature, and it is not intrinsically objectionable; it recognizes both the existence of these abstract morphemes and the layered character of morphological structure, attempting to reconcile the two within the confines of the phrase-tree model. The notation is nevertheless both arbitrary and inexplicit in certain respects. It is arbitrary, for example, in that it reflects no comprehensive view of the nature of morphemes as phonological entities and does not automatically accommodate nonsegmental morphemes as expected, easily described phenomena rather than entities that are essentially unanticipated and problematic for standard formal devices. More concretely, it is arbitrary to show a process or zero morpheme as occupying any particular position in the linear sequence (e.g. why should [ɪ—→æ] or [Ø] in Fig. 9.4 be represented as "suffixes" rather than "prefixes"?), but the standard tree notation forces one to make such a choice. The notation is inexplicit because it does not inherently indicate how the component morphemes are to be integrated. The problem may seem trivial when only segmental morphemes are involved: the adjacency of elements in the terminal string specifies their phonological concatenation. This is hardly adequate for nonsegmental morphemes, however. The adjacency of [Ø] and [fʊl] in diagram (b) cannot be taken to mean that the latter combines with zero, and concatenation is hardly the way to speak of the relation between [sɪt] and [ɪ--→æ] in diagram (a). What is needed is a more sophisticated notion of phonological integration, and an explicit account of composite phonological structures at different levels of organization. In the case of *fearful*, for instance, we want to be able to say that [fʊl] combines with the composite structure obtained by previously integrating the component morphemes [fɪr] and [Ø] (the result of which is of course identical to [fɪr]).

The more elaborate conception of constituency I have proposed, together with other concepts already introduced on independent grounds, provide the descriptive machinery necessary to resolve these problems in a reasonable way. In fact, they overcome certain conceptual and terminological difficulties encountered in traditional views of morphology. One is the inability to explain with any precision what a "root" is.[4] Normally we provide linguistics students with impressionistic statements to the effect that the root is the "core" of the word, to which other morphemes are "appended," but such comments are barely adequate even from a pedagogical standpoint, let alone a theoretical one. A second problem, already alluded to, is the lack of a general perspective allowing nonsegmental morphemes to be accommodated as natural, fully unproblematic phenomena. In particular, let me call attention to a significant lexical gap in the traditional vocabulary for dealing with morphological structure: I am aware of no standard term that excludes root morphemes but includes both affixes and nonsegmental morphemes of the kinds mentioned above. We can call them both "nonroot morphemes," but this negative characterization hardly does justice to their functional equivalence (indeed, there is no clear dividing line between them). Since both affixes and nonsegmental morphemes require the support of a stem, I will refer to them as **dependent** morphemes.

9.1.3. *Dependent Morphemes*

A phonologically dependent morpheme (at the level of word structure) is one that makes salient internal reference to a schematically characterized stem. Because its own value is defined at least partially in reference to this schematic substructure, such a morpheme requires the support of an actual stem for its full manifestation. To use one metaphor, we can say that a dependent morpheme "modifies" or "operates on" the stem in much the same way that a consonant modifies the sonority provided by a vowel. Using an alternative metaphor, we can regard a dependent morpheme as a "function" that maps one stem onto another.

---

[4] Simple distributional definitions are inadequate, since many roots are bound morphemes and certain affixes (e.g. the Nahuatl suffix *neki* cited above) can also occur as independent words.

However we choose to talk about dependent morphemes, the characterization offered above provides a unified account of the many different morpheme
types that must be included in the class. Some dependent morphemes modify
a stem by supplying it with additional segmental content, appended at a specified location.[5] A suprasegmental morpheme (e.g. a particular tone pattern)
modifies a stem by giving it values along certain phonological parameters for
which it would otherwise be differently valued or unspecified. Process morphemes are those for which the modification is not simply one of addition or
elaboration: with reference to a stem, a process morpheme defines a higher-
order stem whose phonological properties conflict in certain respects with
those of the original. A zero morpheme represents the limiting case of modification, the case of no change at all. It is reasonably viewed as an analog of
the identity function.

Let us begin with affixes. Fig. 9.5 conveys the difference between the verb
stem *neki* 'want' of Classical Nahuatl and its suffixal counterpart. The stem,

Fig. 9.5

in diagram (a), is simply a bisyllabic sequence all portions of which are fully
specified (i.e. nonschematic).[6] The suffix -*neki* has the same overtly manifested segmental content, but its phonological pole also contains schematic
elements, as seen in diagram (b). In particular, [neki] follows (as part of the
same word) a segment string specified only as a nonzero sequence consisting of at least one syllable (*S*). The schematic substructure is enclosed in a
box simply for purposes of diagrammatic clarity (it need not be a unipolar
constituent); it functions as the e-site in a valence relation joining -*neki* to a
verb stem.

In stating earlier that the phonological boundaries of bipolar units often
conflict with those of unipolar constituents, I was referring in particular to the
fully specified, overtly manifested portions of bipolar elements. The plural
suffix -*s* of *tables*, for instance, is neither an autonomous segment nor a syllable, and when the plural noun is segmented into morphemes the boundary
falls in the middle of a syllable: *table-s*. I am arguing, however, that this segmentation oversimplifies matters by ignoring the schematic content of the plural morpheme, as well as the overlap between constituents characteristic of
valence relations. The actual phonological structure of this morpheme includes more than just [z]: it consists of [z] embedded as an integral part of the

---

[5] Reduplication can be treated as a special case of affixation, where the specific segmental
content to be appended is determined by that of the stem itself.

[6] The organization of syllables into larger units is ignored except when directly relevant.

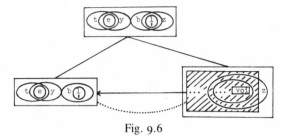

Fig. 9.6

syllabic organization of a schematic stem, as seen in Fig. 9.6. This morpheme is a natural phonological constituent when both overt and schematic content are taken into account, and this may be true in general (cf. 8.4.1). The actual discrepancy is between unipolar constituency and those portions of the morpheme susceptible to direct physical implementation.

Fig. 9.6 is more explicit about the phonological pole of *tables* than a previous diagram (Fig. 8.7). The overtly manifested segment [z] is shown as the outermost consonantal increment in the coda of a schematically characterized syllable; the autonomous structure it attaches to has little specific content apart from the specification that its final segment is voiced.[7] It is unspecified whether the syllable has an onset, and also whether there are preceding syllables in the stem (note the three dots outside the larger ellipse). The schematic portions of the dependent morpheme are once again crosshatched to indicate that they serve as the e-site in the valence relation with *table*. A correspondence line equates the stem with the e-site, and their relationship of schematicity is shown by the arrow. Superimposing the specifications of corresponding entities derives the composite structure: a bisyllabic sequence having [z] as the sole consonantal increment in the coda of its second syllable.

Other morpheme types involving only the addition of phonological content to the stem are similarly accommodated. Prefixes are equivalent to suffixes except for temporal sequencing. Infixes are allowed by the already-attested possibility (8.4.1) of intermingling between schematic and specific substructures. Thus, if [ta...] is a prefix, and [...ta] a suffix—the dots representing schematic content—an infix with the same segmental shape can be given as [...ta...], where the overtly manifested segments constitute an island of specificity within an otherwise schematic structure.[8] A suprasegmental morpheme takes the form of a generally schematic segmental or syllabic sequence that is nevertheless specific in regard to certain prosodic properties. Fig. 9.7(a), for instance, represents a morpheme manifested as high tone on the

---

[7] This autonomous structure contains a syllabic nucleus, incremented by an unspecified number of consonants. (The voiced segment must not have a sibilant release, or [əz] is used instead.)

[8] The discontinuity of a schematic region does not preclude its functioning as an e-site (cf. 8.3.3).

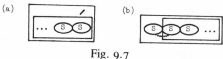

Fig. 9.7

final syllable of the stem; one variant of the plural morpheme in Cora has this shape (e.g. *ša?irú* 'flies').[9]

Reduplication is also nonproblematic, but it forces us to distinguish two constructs that have coincided in the examples considered so far. In Figs. 9.5(b), 9.6, and 9.7(a), the inner box within the dependent morpheme demarcates a region that can be described in either of two ways: (1) it is the region characterized only schematically; and (2) it is the phonological pole of a schematic stem and consequently functions as the e-site in a valence relation (where it corresponds to a specific stem). These are not equivalent descriptions, and the regions they delineate sometimes diverge. On the one hand, a dependent morpheme may occur only with stems that have a particular segment in a certain position; this segment then has to be included in the otherwise schematic e-site despite its specificity. On the other hand, the schematically characterized region may extend beyond the boundaries of the e-site corresponding to the stem. This happens in reduplication, where the segmental content of the dependent morpheme is variable and therefore schematic. Fig. 9.7(b) sketches a simple reduplicative morpheme that copies the initial stem syllable. The inner box stands for the schematic stem, characterized only as a sequence of syllables. The reduplicated element is also given schematically, but an internal correspondence line specifies its identity with the initial stem syllable. Its value is determined simultaneously with that of the stem syllable when the e-site is elaborated by a specific stem in a valence combination.

Already our discussion of dependent morphemes has led to the postulation of highly abstract phonological structures. Neither of the morphemes depicted in Fig. 9.7 has specific segmental content; hence they cannot per se receive peripheral implementation, requiring the support of a specified stem for their physical manifestation. Since I have taken the position that phonological structures are conceptual in nature (albeit peripherally grounded), the existence of abstract morphemes having only schematic segmental content is in no way surprising and poses no descriptive problems. Nor is there anything problematic about the existence of process morphemes, which are abstract in a somewhat different way. The basic analysis has already been introduced (cf. 3.4.2). Like other dependent morphemes, a process morpheme is defined in reference to a largely schematic stem that is consequently part of its own in-

---

[9] There are some affinities here to certain ideas of autosegmental phonology (cf. Goldsmith 1976; McCarthy 1981; Marantz 1982), but I will not pursue them.

ternal structure. It differs from other dependent morphemes in that some aspect of its overtly manifested content corresponds to some portion of the schematic stem but stands in conflict with its specifications. A process morpheme therefore embodies a **complex scene** in the phonological domain. It requires for its description two separate structures, linked by correspondences, that nevertheless cannot be reduced to a single, internally consistent configuration. In this way it resembles metaphor and semantic extension (in the schematic plane) as well as semantic anomaly (in the syntagmatic plane).

The internal structure of a process morpheme thus involves two separate phonological configurations; correspondences are established between them, but to some degree they are mutually inconsistent. One of these structures is the stem in reference to which this dependent morpheme derives its phonological value. The stem often contains specified segments, but it is basically schematic, and functions as the e-site in morphological valence relations. The second structure is the one destined for physical implementation; let us call it the **target structure**, for reasons that may be evident. The target may itself contain schematic elements, but once these are elaborated in a valence relation, the resulting structure is fully specific and susceptible to peripheral connection. As the "output" of the function constituting the process morpheme, the target—in accordance with the specifications supplied by the stem—determines the composite structure in the construction.

All this is illustrated in Fig. 9.8, depicting the phonological pole of *sat*. As with certain other verbs (e.g. *ring*, *begin*), the past tense of *sit* is marked by

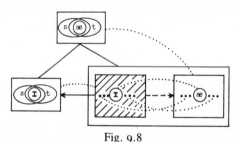

Fig. 9.8

ablauting the stem vowel from [ɪ] to [æ]. The component structure on the right is the process morpheme responsible for this ablaut. It is abstract and internally complex, as just explained, involving two phonological configurations as subcomponents together with certain relationships between them. The subcomponent on the left is the schematic stem; it must contain [ɪ] as a vocalic nucleus, but the material flanking it on either side is variable and therefore schematic within this morpheme itself. The subcomponent on the right is the target structure. It contains the vowel [æ], shown by a dotted line to be a correspondent of the stem vowel [ɪ]; the schematically specified contexts on both sides of [æ] are similarly put in correspondence with the respective left-side and right-side contexts of the stem vowel. The broken arrow connecting the stem and the target structure indicates a relation of partial schematicity: taking the stem as standard in an act of comparison, we perceive the target as conflicting with certain of its specifications, making the relation between them one of extension rather than simple elaboration.[10]

Within the process morpheme, then, the direction of the arrow indicates that [...ɪ...] is the stem, and [...æ...] the target structure intended for physical implementation. The former serves as the e-site in the valence relation, being elaborated in this instance by [sɪt]. The resulting composite structure is the same as the target structure, except that the schematic content on either side of the vocalic nucleus is replaced by the specific context inherited from [sɪt] (as determined by vertical and horizontal correspondences, including those between subcomponents). It is claimed that the phonological value of *sat* is not exhausted by its overt segmental content: analyzability is as much a factor at the phonological pole as it is at the semantic pole. Consequently the phonological value of this expression consists of *sat*, overtly manifested, construed in relation to the component structure *sit*; the discrepancy between *sat* and the otherwise-expected *sit* is recognized as the symbolization of past tense. Observe that only constructs introduced and justified for other purposes have been employed in this account.[11] The possibility of process morphemes is therefore inherent in the overall descriptive apparatus we have slowly been developing.

No a priori restrictions are imposed on the distribution of schematic and specified substructures within either subcomponent of a process morpheme, nor on the degree to which these subcomponents can be allowed to diverge. It is readily seen as a consequence that this framework accommodates the full range of process morphemes. In lieu of additional examples, then, I will comment on the distinction between process morphemes on the one hand, and "additive" morphemes (notably affixation) on the other. My basic point is that the distinction is not at all sharp, and that the two types can be treated in parallel fashion—in regard to both notation and functional description—without obscuring the special character of process morphemes. Obviously, many morphemes represent a mixture of the two ideal types (e.g. *brought*,

---

[10] This is directly analogous to the situation found at the semantic pole of metaphorically extended expressions (cf. Fig. 2.10), where the literal sense bears a relation of partial schematicity to the figurative sense. Just as the phonological target structure is the one physically implemented, so the figurative sense of a metaphorical expression is the one the speaker matches directly (in the coding process) to the conceptualization for which he seeks linguistic symbolization.

[11] These constructs include: valence and constituency; schematic structures; partial schematicity; internal correspondences; the distinction between the e-site (or internal reference to a stem) and the region characterized schematically; the conceptual nature of phonological structure, not all of which is physically implemented; and the notion of complex scenes.

kept, swollen). A deeper connection can be discerned, however, and an adequate description even of simple affixes ultimately requires the descriptive apparatus invoked for process morphemes.

Observe, first, that affixes are easily represented in the format used for process morphemes. The structure of Nahuatl *-neki* 'want' is reformulated in Fig. 9.9(a) (cf. Fig. 9.5(b)). The subcomponent on the left in Fig. 9.9(a) is the

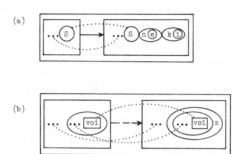

Fig. 9.9

stem and e-site, characterized only as a phonological structure containing at least one syllable. The target structure, on the right, is partially schematic and partially specific; the bisyllabic sequence [neki] follows a schematic substructure equated with the stem by correspondence lines. Figs. 9.5(b) and 9.9(a) are notational variants (compacted and exploded representations of the same structure); some analog of the exploded representation (treating dependent morphemes as functions mapping stems onto stems) will be required in a formal treatment. This format revision is not a notational trick, but rather an attempt to highlight the special property that characterizes dependent morphemes as a unified class. The special status of process morphemes within this class is preserved, though its description must be slightly rephrased. In Fig. 9.9(a), exemplifying an affix, the standard (i.e. schematic stem) and target are fully compatible; in particular, corresponding entities are identical, so the superposition of correspondents yields a coherent phonological conceptualization equivalent to the target (as in Fig. 9.5(b)). This is not the case in process morphemes (Fig. 9.8), where certain correspondents in the standard and target have conflicting properties. Full merger being precluded, the standard and target retain the character of a complex scene.

But even redefined in this manner, the distinction between affixes and process morphemes cannot be maintained as any kind of sharp dichotomy. The addition of an affix always has some impact on the phonological properties of a stem (however minor), and to this extent a discrepancy is implied between the standard and target. Certain affixes appear to have no stem-modifying effect—if we ignore such matters as allophonic variation, prosody, and syllabic organization—but this is an idealization valid only for limited purposes.

The appropriateness of the solid arrow in Fig. 9.9(a), indicating full rather than just partial schematicity, therefore depends on our objectives and the delicacy of our analysis.

Fig. 9.9(b) reformulates the description of the plural morpheme [z] (cf. Fig. 9.6). If we seek in the target of diagram (b) an exact duplicate of the standard, we will not find it. The reason is that the voiced segment is syllable-final in the standard, but not in the target, where [z] is appended as a consonantal increment; correspondences thus equate a full syllable in one structure with only part of a syllable in the other, and this difference has necessary (though perhaps negligible) consequences for other phonetic properties. The analogous contrast is sometimes quite substantial. An affix containing a vowel may trigger a notable syllabic or prosodic reorganization of the stem, as well as segmental modifications that even a syntactician might notice (e.g. *átom/ atómic*). The boundary between process morphemes and affixes is therefore rather tenuous, coming down to the nature and degree of discrepancy between standard and target. It may be useful for practical and descriptive purposes to maintain the distinction (which is clear enough for simple, prototypical instances), but it should not be adopted as a rigid dichotomy accorded theoretical significance as such.

Two objections are bound to be raised against this conception of dependent morphemes. First, it will certainly be argued that this approach does not properly separate what is intrinsic to the morpheme itself from those properties that are a function of general phonological rules and consequently omissible from the morpheme's characterization. For instance, when the final consonant of a stem is resyllabified as the syllabic onset to a vowel-initial suffix (as in *musical*), this can be attributed to general rules of syllabification; syllabic organization of the target structure need not be specified as a property of the suffix. Comparable remarks can be made for the effects of a dependent morpheme on prosodic features and segmental quality.

Quite tentatively (lacking a well-articulated phonological theory), I am inclined to respond along the following lines. The criticism regards a rule system as a **constructive device**, and it embodies the **exclusionary fallacy** (cf. Ch. 1). It assumes, for instance, that syllabification rules impose syllabic organization on input forms that have no syllabic specifications (or at least not those of the final output). By contrast, the present model accommodates general patterns through sanctioning schemas rather than constructive rules. Crucially, the relation between a schema and its instantiations is elaborative and not exclusionary: the specifications of a schema are also intrinsic to its instantiations, which are however characterized in finer detail. Whereas a schema reflects the commonality observed in specific forms, and may in fact be employed in the assembly of novel exemplars, none of this implies the existence or the coherence of specific forms from which the sanctioned properties have been factored out. When the syllabification specified by a dependent morpheme accords with a schema, this facet of its phonological organization is thereby motivated and not idiosyncratic, i.e. it conforms to a broader pattern established in linguistic convention. This syllabification is nonetheless characteristic of the morpheme itself as well as the complex expression it derives.

The second objection concerns the proliferation of units that results if these notions are taken seriously. Obviously, the specific phonetic effect of integrating a dependent morpheme with a stem depends on the stem's own properties; for example, a suffix might induce a realignment of the accentual pattern on some stems, but not on others with different syllabic organization. Are we not then forced (superfluously) to posit two allomorphs of the suffix, one inducing an accent shift and the other not? [12]

Brief comment can hardly do justice to the issues (see Ch. 10). I would argue, however, that such proliferation is justified in a usage-based model describing fully a speaker's grasp of linguistic convention, and that it is objectionable only under spurious assumptions about the proper role of simplicity in linguistic analysis (cf. Ch. 1). In all facets of linguistic structure, specific units coexist in the cognitive representation of language with the generalizations (at varying levels of schematicity) that speakers have succeeded in abstracting from them. A lexical item is typically not a single structure, but rather a multitude of closely related structures constituting a schematic network. The more highly specified structures in this network reflect specific facts of conventional usage, and at the phonological pole they incorporate phonetic properties localized to particular environments. The postulation of multiple low-level variants of a morpheme, each with very specific phonological properties, accommodates a real and significant aspect of linguistic knowledge; it does not preclude the postulation of more-schematic variants neutralizing low-level differences and capturing essential generalizations. The relative cognitive salience of structures at different levels of schematicity is an open question (and possibly variable), but a full account of linguistic ability cannot focus exclusively on the highest levels.

One last point of business concerns the treatment of zero morphemes, e.g. the past tense of *cut* or the plural of *sheep*. Their analysis is quite straightforward. At the level of word structure, a dependent morpheme defines one stem (the target) as a function of another (the standard). In general, of course, there must be some discrepancy between the standard and target, for otherwise the dependent morpheme is not overtly signaled. Languages nevertheless tolerate,

---

[12] Consider Hopi, where accent generally falls on the initial syllable (in trisyllabic and longer words) when this syllable is "heavy," but on the second syllable otherwise. Adding the future -*ni* to *náani* 'laugh' therefore yields *náanini* 'will laugh', without a stress shift, but the stress shifts in *maqáni* 'will give', from *máqa* 'give'. Do we then posit two allomorphs of the future morpheme, roughly $[[\acute{S}S]-->[\acute{S}S\text{ni}]]$ and $[[S\acute{S}]-->[S\acute{S}\text{ni}]]$ (where $\acute{S}$ and S denote stressed and unstressed syllables)?

on a limited basis, dependent morphemes where the standard and target happen to be identical. The present framework allows this situation as a limiting case and requires no special provisions; in this sense it actually predicts the existence of zero morphemes, which have the following form: $[[...] \leftrightarrow [...]]$. The double-headed arrow (for mutual full schematicity) signals identity of the standard and target. These structures correspond, and are characterized at an appropriate level of schematicity.[13] In a valence relation, the composite structure inherits the phonological shape of the stem—it reflects the target structure, which is identical to the standard that the stem elaborates. The equivalence of the stem and composite structure leads us to speak of a zero morpheme, but it is a feature of this framework that the so-called zero morpheme does indeed have a phonological pole with actual content, schematic though this content may be.

9.1.4. *Morphological Constituency*

The proposed account of morphological structure has a number of advantages. For one thing, it permits a precise characterization of central notions with reference to broadly grounded concepts: (1) morphemes are minimal symbolic units; (2) within this class, the defining property of roots is their phonological autonomy—affixes and other nonroot morphemes are phonologically dependent; (3) a stem is an autonomous phonological structure at any level within a word: a root is a stem, and so is each successive composite structure obtained by combining a stem with a dependent morpheme. A further advantage of this scheme is the unified description it affords of the many different types of dependent morphemes: affixes, reduplication, ablaut, truncation, suprasegmental phenomena, and even zero morphemes. Common to them all is their status as functions mapping stems onto stems. The gradations among these types (including their frequent conflation in a single morpheme) is unproblematic.

An additional advantage is the handling of morphological layering by the same devices employed for valence and constituency in general. These devices overcome the various problems associated with the phrase-tree model (see 9.1.2). (1) The root/affix distinction is treated as a matter of autonomy vs. dependence, which is properly distinct from the question of grammatical category; by contrast, the phrase-tree model distinguishes roots from affixes through node-labeling conventions that we have seen to be unmotivated at best. (2) Nonsegmental morphemes are accommodated in natural fashion, and their functional equivalence to affixes is captured on a principled basis. (3) Un-

---

[13] If the morpheme occurs with any type of stem whatever, the standard and target are maximally schematic. If it occurs only with stems having certain phonological properties (e.g. only with monosyllables), these properties are included in the specification of standard and target. (Comparable remarks can be made for other dependent morphemes.)

like standard phrase trees, constituency trees are not temporally ordered.[14] We therefore avoid the problem (evident in Fig. 9.4) of having to choose an arbitrary position for a nonsegmental morpheme in a linear sequence. (4) Finally, the descriptive devices render explicit the nature of the integration between stems and dependent morphemes, as well as its result. Phrase trees per se specify no details of this integration (particularly for nonsegmental morphemes), nor do they include composite structures at any level.

Let me pull things together with a final example, articulated in some detail. Fig. 9.10 shows the phonological pole of the plural noun *swings* (the noun

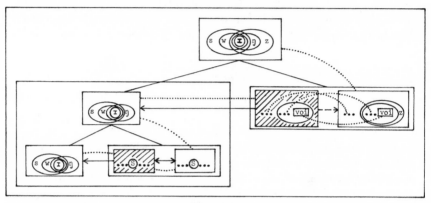

Fig. 9.10

swing is analyzed as a zero nominalization of the verb). There are two levels of constituency, each characterized by an *A/D* asymmetry. At the lower level, *swing* (autonomous) combines with a zero morpheme (dependent). *Swing* is the root, i.e. the autonomous element at the lowest constituency level (or innermost layer). Being dependent, the zero morpheme maps a schematic standard onto a target; it specifies the standard and target as being identical, and as containing at least one syllable (since all verb stems in English have this much content). The standard serves as the e-site in the valence relation, where it is elaborated by *swing*. Since the target corresponds to the standard and is identical to it, elaboration of the one entails elaboration of the other; and since the composite structure is determined by the target, it is identical to the root.

At the second level of constituency, the component structures are *swing* and the plural ending. Though identical in composition to the root, the former must be recognized as a separate construct: it is a composite stem (a zero derivative of the root), symbolizing a nominal predication. *Swing* is autono-

---

[14] Temporal ordering is a dimension of phonological structure that is referred to as part of the *internal structure* of each node in a constituency tree (cf. Figs. 9.6 and 9.8), but these nodes are not themselves temporally ordered with respect to one another.

mous, and elaborates the standard of the dependent plural morpheme, whose target diverges from this standard by the increment of [z] in the coda of the final syllable. The composite structure thus computes to *swings* when the specifications of corresponding entities are systematically superimposed. As the highest-level stem, *swings* is a word; as the highest-level composite structure, it is susceptible to peripheral implementation.

All the phonological structures in Fig. 9.10—from individual morphemes to the entire complex construction enclosed by the outermost box—bear symbolic relations to corresponding structures at the semantic pole. There is a symbolic correspondence, for example, between the composite structures at the two poles: *swings* symbolizes a nominal predication designating a particular sort of replicate mass. Similarly, the large inner box contains three phonological structures (the root, the zero morpheme, and the first-level composite structure) that symbolize three corresponding elements at the semantic pole (a process predicate, a nominalizing predicate, and the nominal predication resulting from their integration). If the noun *swings* is well entrenched, all these structures are established units.

Orthogonal to these structures and relations are categorizing relationships in the schematic plane. There are many such relationships, reflecting various aspects of linguistic organization. For instance, both *swing* and *swings* instantiate the syllable schema, as well as subschemas representing syllable canons at different levels of specificity. In symbolic space, the verb schema categorizes the root, whereas the derived stem *swing* instantiates the count-noun category, and *swings* the mass-noun category. There is also categorization involving complex schematic structures that characterize grammatical constructions. The inner layer of morphological structure in Fig. 9.10 is categorized by a schema describing the zero-morphemic derivation of nouns from verbs. The second level of organization is similarly sanctioned by a schema representing one pattern of plural formation (cf. Fig. 2.9).

To the extent that the expression has unit status, all these structures and relationships are part of a speaker's knowledge of linguistic convention. The same is true for all morphologically derived expressions with the status of units, regardless of complexity or whether they constitute stems or full words. This is partially independent of their degree of regularity or analyzability, and also of any putative distinction between "derivational" and "inflectional" morphology; such factors fail to correlate consistently with an expression's degree of entrenchment or the distinction (actually a gradation) between fixed and novel expressions. Variation along these parameters may well be significant. Behavioral consequences may attach to the degree of analyzability or regularity, for instance, or there may be a structural basis (in a particular language or in general) for according special status to stems at a certain level of organization. The present account of morphological structure can accommodate such differences, but it also explicates the common structural basis of morphological organization discernible for the full gamut of derived expressions.

A final point to consider is the relation between phonological elements defined in unipolar and in bipolar terms. Though structures delineated on the basis of symbolic relationships need not coincide with unipolar constituents (at least in their overt content), they are nonetheless phonological entities, representing a second mode of organization superimposed on the intrinsic organization of phonological content. The relationship between unipolar and bipolar constituents is unlikely to be fully arbitrary. We can reasonably anticipate a rough parallelism between the two modes of organization.

They do indeed correlate with respect to A/D alignment. Roots and stems (autonomous in bipolar terms) almost invariably have sufficient phonological content to stand alone as independent words (though this potential is not always exploited[15]): a root or stem without a syllabic nucleus is at best a rarity. Often roots and stems are bi- or polysyllabic, but seldom if ever do we encounter one consisting of nothing more than a consonant or a prosodic feature. There are no such restrictions on dependent morphemes. Affixes tend to be short, and often lack a syllabic nucleus. Many dependent morphemes (involving ablaut, truncation, reduplication, or suprasegmental phenomena) are too abstract for independent manifestation. Observe that the exclusion of such morphemes from the role of root or stem is automatic in the present framework, as they presuppose another, more autonomous structure for their implementation.

9.2. The Semantic Pole

Phonological space has many special features reflecting its peripheral connection to the auditory and vocal apparatus, but it is nevertheless a subdomain of semantic space. Parallels between semantic and phonological organization are therefore to be expected. We have already noted a variety of constructs applicable to both poles, among them autonomy/dependence, correspondence, schematicity, elaboration sites, constituency, and complex scenes. Perhaps, then, our analysis of dependent phonological structures may have some relevance for their semantic counterparts. In particular, we have determined that a uniform account of dependent morphemes—one that accommodates

---

[15] *Distribution* must be distinguished from *internal structure*. Distribution can be influenced by many extrinsic factors; e.g. grammatical conventions might require that every root take some affix, so that no root stands alone. The status of a morpheme as autonomous or dependent pertains to its internal structure, hinging on whether it makes salient internal reference to a schematic stem.

process morphemes without special provisions—requires the postulation of two internal substructures (standard and target). Might this conception be useful for dependent semantic structures as well? As a background for discussion, let us examine more carefully the nature of the standard/target asymmetry.

9.2.1. *S/T Asymmetry*

A standard (S) and target (T) are essential to any act of comparison (cf. Ch. 3). The standard/target asymmetry reflects a fundamental aspect of cognitive functioning, namely the exploitation of previous experience for the structuring and interpretation of novel experience. The activation of a standard provides a baseline for the assessment of subsequent events, which derive their value from the nature and magnitude of their departure from this baseline.

The inherent asymmetry of the standard/target relation is not confined to the evaluation of immediate experience. Like any sequence of cognitive events, an act of comparison is subject to entrenchment and routinization when it recurs with sufficient frequency. The result is a unit of the form $[S \rightarrow T]$ (or $[S \dashrightarrow T]$ for partial schematicity); it embodies a fixed categorization, which is no less asymmetrical for having achieved unit status. Large numbers of categorizing relationships in the schematic plane are included among the conventional units of a grammar. Each evaluates a target with reference to a standard and represents an established judgment of category membership.[16]

Consider the phonological pole of a dependent morpheme, e.g. the vowel ablaut marking the past tense of *sit*, *ring*, *begin*, etc. In describing such a morpheme with reference to a standard, a target, and a relation of partial schematicity between them (cf. Fig. 9.8), I have equated its internal structure with a comparison event. This is not implausible from the developmental standpoint. The past-tense morpheme is never presented to the language learner in isolation; what he hears instead is forms like *sit* and *sat*, typically as part of larger meaningful expressions. From a multitude of such expressions that share the processual notion [SIT] but contrast in tense, aspect, and so on (e.g. *sits*, *will sit*, *is sitting*, *sitter*, *to sit*), the learner extracts the basic symbolic correspondence [[SIT]/[sɪt]]. *Sat*, on the other hand, occurs only when the process designated by [SIT] is located in the past, so once he has isolated [[SIT]/[sɪt]], the learner can assign the value [PAST] to whatever it is that differentiates [sɪt] and [sæt] phonologically. An act of comparison of the form ([sɪt] $\dashrightarrow$ [sæt]) is therefore implied, representing the learner's percep-

---

[16] We cannot conclude that the standard in a categorizing relationship is always mastered before its instantiation. People obviously have the ability to notice similarities among established notions and extract a novel schema to categorize them; the schema then serves as standard in the resulting categorical judgments.

tion of how the past tense is signaled with this particular verb. Similar acts of comparison occur for pairs like *ring/rang*, *begin/began*, etc. The dependent morpheme [[...I...] --→[...æ...]] is then a schema extracted by the learner to embody the commonality of these different comparison events.[17]

It is not implied that all dependent morphemes are necessarily acquired in precisely this way; I only suggest that assimilating their internal structure to acts of comparison is neither arbitrary nor mysterious. It should also be apparent why the target (not the standard) determines the composite structure in a morphological valence relation. By definition, a composite structure derives from a stem (rather than conversely). This derivation is effected by a dependent morpheme, whose internal structure therefore mirrors the asymmetry between the two elements: it embodies a schematic characterization of how the composite structure diverges from the stem. Our analysis equates this asymmetry with that inherent in a comparison event, where the standard is the baseline relative to which the target is evaluated. It follows that the standard of a dependent morpheme corresponds to the stem, and its target to the composite structure.

We must now consider whether dependent predications are parallel to phonologically dependent morphemes. Are they profitably conceived as "functions" mapping one type of predication onto another? Is it useful or appropriate to describe them as categorizing relationships involving a standard and target? Despite certain qualifications, I will answer in the affirmative.

9.2.2. *Dependent Predications*

One predication, D, is conceptually dependent on another, A, when D contains a salient substructure D_e, such that D_e corresponds to the profile of A and is schematic for A at a substantial elaborative distance. The substructure D_e is the pivotal element in this characterization; as the e-site in the valence relation between D and A, it is the entity that is functionally equivalent to the standard within a dependent morpheme. Is it reasonable, then, to represent D in the format $[D_e --→ T]$, where D_e is a standard relative to which the target structure T derives its value?

The desirability of such a representation, at least in certain instances, is suggested by a previous observation (8.3.3), namely that a focal adjustment is often necessary to discern within a dependent predication a substructure that is fully schematic for an autonomous predication that combines with it. The A and D predications in a valence relation sometimes structure corresponding entities by means of different images, with the consequence that D_e—construed in a way that makes it fully schematic and parallel in organization to A—is observable within D only if one suspends or modifies certain aspects of

---

[17] There is no distinction in this framework between a dependent morpheme and a rule or pattern deriving one type of stem from another (cf. Anderson 1982).

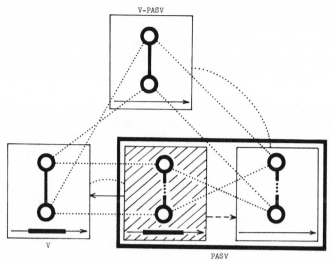

Fig. 9.11

the structure that *D* itself imposes on the entity in question. This is comparable to the situation characteristic of process morphemes, where portions of the standard and target correspond but are nevertheless attributed conflicting properties.

A striking example of this is the passive variant of the past-participial morpheme in English.[18] The function of this morpheme is twofold: (1) it suspends the sequential scanning of the verb stem, converting it into a complex atemporal relation (hence the temporalizing *be* is required in a finite clause); and (2) it imposes a figure/ground alignment distinct from that of the stem, specifically with respect to the choice of trajector. Because the passive participial predication structures the scene differently from the verb stem in regard to both figure/ground organization and mode of scanning, an e-site within this predication fully compatible with the specifications of the stem cannot be accommodated unless we resort to a bipartite representation analogous to that employed for process morphemes, where correspondences link a separately depicted standard and target each structured in its own fashion.

Fig. 9.11 sketches the valence relation between the verb stem and the passive participial predication, [PASV]. The standard and target of [PASV] have conflicting specifications, so the relation between them is one of extension rather than simple elaboration. The standard of [PASV], the subcomponent shown on the left, is a schematic process; its trajector and primary landmark are both things (by convention, the trajector is on top). The target structure

[18] Langacker (1982a) discusses the family of predicates symbolized by the participial inflections, including the one that occurs in *gone* (Fig. 8.2); DeLancey's notion of "terminal viewpoint" (1981) goes a long way towards explaining their interrelationships.

lacks sequential scanning, as indicated by the absence of a temporal profile marked with a heavy line along the time axis. Moreover, its trajector corresponds not to the trajector of the standard, but to its primary landmark (note the correspondence lines). The effect of this predicate, then, is to define a complex atemporal relation with reference to a schematic process, but one that imposes on the scene a figure/ground organization distinct from that of the process. By definition, the target structure determines the value and category membership of the predicate, which is consequently nonprocessual.

The internal structure of this predicate is indicative of its valence relation with a verb stem. The stem is a specified process predication that corresponds to the schematic standard of [PASV] and elaborates it. It is a complement of [PASV], since the latter is both dependent and the profile determinant. The composite structure (the semantic pole of the passive participle) inherits its profiling and mode of scanning from the target of [PASV], and through horizontal and vertical correspondences this structuring is imposed on the more specific content provided by the verb stem. The passive participle (e.g. *helped, bitten, examined,* etc.) is therefore nonschematic; it profiles a relation construed atemporally (despite its distribution through conceived time) and with a figure/ground alignment distinct from that of the stem.

Another example is the nominalizing suffix -*er*, whose semantic pole is diagrammed in Fig. 9.12. The standard, on the left, is a schematic process. An

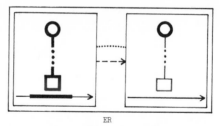

ER

Fig. 9.12

identical and corresponding process is found in the target, but there it is not in profile, and functions only to identify the profiled thing as a processual trajector. The target determines the categorization of the predicate, so [ER] is nominal—it designates a thing identified solely by its role in a process. The process serving as standard can be regarded as the baseline relative to which the target is evaluated. Alternatively, to use a more "active" metaphor, we can think of the predicate as a function that maps processes onto things.

The exploded representation of Fig. 9.12 can be compared to the compacted representation of the same predicate, given previously (Fig. 8.8). It will be noted that the compacted representation is identical in appearance to the target in Fig. 9.12. Is there any purpose, then, in resorting to the more complex notation depicting the standard and target as separate entities? This question can be posed in either practical or substantive terms. As a practical matter, the compacted format is obviously simpler, and I will employ it unless the exploded format is needed for greater clarity. The substantive issue is whether the standard and its categorizing relation with the target should be accorded explicit formal status. I believe they should be, because of the standard's clear functional significance. It constitutes the overlap between two structures in a valence relation, and the disparity between the standard and target represents the specific contribution of the dependent predication to the composite scene—what it brings to the scene above and beyond the content and organization furnished by the autonomous predication.

Described in this manner, the *S/T* format is reasonably considered appropriate for all dependent predications. Moreover, its general applicability is assured (albeit trivially), since no restrictions have been imposed on the mapping between standard and target. How far do we really want to push it, though? Dependent predications are a disparate lot. It seems quite natural to characterize the passive participial morpheme as an "operator" that derives an atemporal relation from a process, and *-er* as a "function" mapping processes onto things. But can we plausibly treat [TALL] as a function converting a thing into a relation, or [CHASE] as an operator deriving a process from two things? In part the grounds for hesitation are spurious. Terms like "function," "mapping," and "operator" are metaphorical in this context; the aptness of the metaphor does not per se reflect on the validity of the constructs. When the *S/T* relationship is described in neutral fashion (in terms of e-sites and their role in the overall predication), the problem does not arise.

At issue here is the putative distinction between "lexical" and "grammatical" morphemes. I see no reason to impose a rigid boundary, or to isolate a restricted class of dependent predications characterized as operators and accorded special status; instead I see gradations and the need for a unified description. As it turns out, the constructs adopted for dependent predications allow us to explicate the apparent contrast. Variation along two continuous parameters makes the distinction between lexical and grammatical morphemes seem plausible when intermediate cases are ignored. These parameters are (1) the level of specificity at which the dependent predication characterizes a situation; and (2) the amount of overlap between standard and target (i.e. how close the e-sites come to exhausting the content of the predication).

With respect to the first parameter, consider the contrast between the agentive nominalizer *-er* and the agentive noun *thief*. As analyzed in this framework, each predication defines a thing by virtue of its trajector role in a process. The difference between them—clearly a matter of degree—is that this process is relatively specific in the case of [THIEF], but quite schematic for [ER]. It is important that schematicity not be mistaken for the lack of semantic content. Speakers have the ability to conceptualize situations at varying levels of specificity, and predications that occupy a position towards the non-specific pole of this continuum are meaningful nonetheless.

The second parameter concerns the proportion of semantic content in a dependent predication that is subsumed by its e-site(s). Observe that the standard (e-site) of [ER] is coextensive with the schematic process that constitutes its base; beyond what is included in the standard, the semantic value of this predicate consists solely in the nominal profile it imposes on the schematic scene. Consider, then, what happens in a valence relation, where the standard is elaborated by a predication that designates a specified process. By virtue of the schematic-transparency principle, this e-site effectively merges with its instantiation (as in any valence relation) and achieves no cognitive salience as a distinct entity. With its standard thus "absorbed," only the nominal profile of [ER] stands out in contrast to the value of the stem. For this reason, [ER] is easily interpreted by analysts as an operator deriving nouns from verbs. However, I have demonstrated the coherence of a position that treats such elements as meaningful predications.

In contrast to [ER], a "lexical" predicate like [CHASE] involves many specifications beyond those that characterize its principal e-sites (its schematic trajector and landmark). These specifications are also fairly detailed. When [CHASE] participates in valence relations, then, only a relatively small proportion of its content is "swallowed up" by the overlapping nominal predications that elaborate its e-sites. [CHASE] is easily perceived as meaningful because it introduces a richly specified process not necessarily conveyed or suggested by its complements, and its characterization as a function or operator thus seems peculiar. The apparent contrast between operators (like [ER]) and other dependent predications therefore reduces to expected variation along two continuous parameters. A unified account of the full range of dependent predications is both possible and to be desired.

The proposed framework predicts the possibility of yet another type of dependent predication, one that represents the limiting case of overlap between standard and target, namely complete identity. We have seen that the standard and target of [ER] are identical in basic content, differing only in the nominal profile imposed by the target on the schematic base process. However, it is perfectly conceivable that a standard and target might agree in profile as well as basic content. The resulting predication would be the exact analog of a zero morpheme at the phonological pole (a phenomenon not generally considered controversial). Can we then find an actual example of a "zero predication"?

I have argued elsewhere that this is the proper semantic analysis for the auxiliary verb *do* in English (cf. Langacker 1981c, 1982a). Its semantic pole is sketched in Fig. 9.13. As with [ER], the standard for [DO] is a schematic process;[19] unlike [ER], however, [DO] adopts the profiling of its standard for

---

[19] In fact, [DO] is maximally schematic for process predications: it can be elaborated by any nonauxiliary verb.

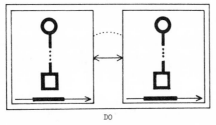

DO

Fig. 9.13

its target as well, so the standard and target are identical. When the standard is elaborated by another verb in a valence relation, therefore, the overlap between [DO] and its complement is complete: all the specifications of [DO] (both standard and target) are inherent in the less schematic complement and are "absorbed" in accordance with the schematic-transparency principle. It is easy to understand, then, why *do* is commonly considered a meaningless grammatical morpheme. Still, it is undeniably a verb, and in cognitive grammar there is no reason whatever to deny it the minimal semantic content characteristic of process predications. Neither its identifiable grammatical function nor the full inclusion of its meaning in that of its complement constitutes valid grounds for the opposite conclusion.

Despite the significant parallels between dependent structures at the two poles, certain differences can be observed that doubtless reflect the distinctive character of phonological space. A dependent phonological structure (e.g. an affix) combines with only one stem at a time. By contrast, a dependent predication may have multiple e-sites and be elaborated simultaneously (though possibly at different levels of constituency) by a number of separate complements. A second difference clearly derives from the grounding of phonological structure in our vocal and auditory apparatus. The physical implementation of sounds in either domain implies essentially full specificity: we cannot hear or articulate a schematic vowel, for instance, but only one with specific values in all relevant dimensions. It stands to reason, then, that phonological e-sites are obligatorily elaborated; i.e. dependent morphemes necessarily participate in valence relations with autonomous structures. The situation is quite different at the semantic pole, since schematic notions can be grasped and manipulated even in the absence of concrete instantiation. Dependent predications can therefore be flexible in regard to elaboration. Verb complements are sometimes optional as a result, and in certain constructions (e.g. nominalizations) direct elaboration of an e-site is precluded:

(2)(a) *She tossed the keys (into the pool).*
   (b) *Her toss (*the keys) was accurate.*

In other instances the omission of an elaborator is permitted, but produces an expression whose semantic schematicity renders it useless out of context:

(3)(a)   *They do.*
   (b)   *We found several.*

More is obviously involved than just optional participation in a valence relation, but the contrast with dependent phonological structures is nevertheless striking.

9.3. Symbolic Relationships

The distinction between autonomy and dependence hinges on whether one structure presupposes another for its full implementation. More technically, structure D is dependent on structure A if they participate in a valence relation where A elaborates a salient but schematic substructure of D. This definition is valid for both poles, but so far we have focused primarily on either the semantic pole or the phonological pole taken individually. These notions must now be examined in bipolar terms.

9.3.1. A/D Alignment

A/D alignment tends strongly to be parallel at the two poles (cf. Fig. 8.9). For example, when a stem (phonologically autonomous) combines with a phonologically dependent morpheme (e.g. an affix), the semantic pole of the stem generally elaborates a prominent e-site within the predication symbolized by the affix; hence the affix is semantically dependent as well. Typically, then, we observe a strong correlation between morphological layering and "semantic scope" (cf. Langacker 1981b): at each level of constituency, the phonologically dependent morpheme is also a semantic "operator," i.e. it takes the predication symbolized by the stem as a complement (has it "in its scope"). Starting from the root, each successive morphological increment mapping a basic stem onto a derived stem represents a dependent predication that effects a corresponding mapping at the semantic pole. From the autonomous predication symbolized by the basic stem, it derives another such predication that constitutes the composite structure of the higher-order stem.

In the standard situation, therefore, a symbolic structure is consistent with respect to A/D alignment: either it is autonomous at both poles, or else dependent. Valence relations strongly incline to configurations like Fig. 9.14, where one component structure shows bipolar autonomy, and the other bipolar dependence.[20] At each pole the component on the right is dependent because it contains a prominent e-site elaborated by the autonomous component on the left. The bipolar character of this A/D alignment allows us to speak of autonomous and dependent **symbolic** structures. Observe that a correspondence line connects the semantic and phonological e-sites, since the structures that

---

[20] Fig. 9.14 is a compacted representation (the standard is not shown separately from the target); composite structures are omitted.

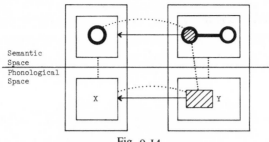

Fig. 9.14

elaborate them stand in a symbolic relationship defining the autonomous component. The dependent structure thus contains a bipolar e-site.

Parallel A/D alignment at the two poles is canonical, but it cannot be imposed as an absolute restriction. Though a definite minority, constructions with reversed alignment at the two poles are not at all difficult to find. A common type of example is the occurrence of a nominal affix on a verb stem, such as the Nahuatl *ni-nemi* 'I live' (cf. (1)). Semantically, *ni-* 'I' is autonomous relative to *nemi* 'live' and elaborates its trajector; phonologically, however, the stem *nemi* is autonomous, and *ni-* dependent. Cases from English are provided by the cliticization of certain pronouns. Consider the prepositional phrase *with her*, which has alternate pronunciations. The pronoun may be unreduced and carry the primary accent, in which case it is the autonomous element within the phrase. However, we also find the expression *wíth'ĕr*, where the pronoun appears as an unstressed clitic on the preposition and is consequently phonologically dependent. With either pronunciation the pronoun is semantically autonomous and elaborates the preposition's primary landmark. The existence of semantically equivalent but phonologically contrastive pairs of this sort suggests quite forcefully that the "harmonization" of A/D alignment at the two poles is in no way a structural necessity.

The skewing of alignment between the two poles makes things harder to conceptualize, but it does not actually pose any descriptive problems for the present framework. Correspondences can be established, profile determinacy indicated, and the relation between component and composite structures ascertained regardless of the location of e-sites and the direction or degree of A/D asymmetry at the two poles. Observe that A/D alignment is not something that is separately or formally specified in the characterization of a construction. It is inherent in the nature of the component structures (given a particular set of correspondences linking them), and is made explicit for analytical purposes only in order to explicate various grammatical phenomena (e.g. the complement/modifier distinction). Recall, moreover, that A/D alignment is a relative matter, reflecting two essentially continuous parameters (elaborative distance; e-site prominence). Some measure of semantic or phonological dependence—however tenuous it might be—can always be observed in either direction between two component structures in a valence relation. Labeling one component structure "autonomous" and the other "dependent" is therefore a quantitative judgment and does not imply that the dependence is unidirectional.

A valence relation with skewed A/D alignment is schematized in Fig. 9.15. The component structures are labeled A and B. At both the semantic and the

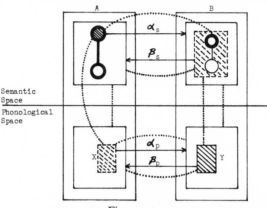

Fig. 9.15

phonological poles, each of these structures is evaluated for its degree of dependence on the other. Four evaluations are consequently represented in the diagram; each revolves on an elaborative relationship (shown by an arrow) that one structure bears to some substructure (e-site) within another. Two of these e-sites are attributed a relative lack of prominence, indicated by enclosing them in broken lines. The skewing of A/D alignment simply reflects the relative prominence of e-sites at the two poles.

Consider first the semantic pole, where α_s represents the degree to which A is dependent on B, and β_s the degree to which B is dependent on A. If elaborative distance is held constant, the former value is clearly greater (i.e. A is semantically dependent). This follows from the definition of dependence, given the relative salience of the e-sites. The e-site of A is highly prominent: as part of the relational profile (trajector or primary landmark), it is central to the value of A and obligatorily activated. By contrast, A elaborates an unprofiled substructure of B that is assumed to be peripheral and nonessential. We can think of it as an extrinsic relationship (4.2.2) that is part of the encyclopedic characterization of the designated entity but is accessed only under special circumstances. In the case of *wíth'ĕr*, for instance, the substructure of [HER] that corresponds to the profile of [WITH] is the rather banal specification that the designated person sometimes participates in stative relationships.

The phonological poles of A and B are presumed to include both specific segmental content—represented by X and Y—and more-schematic elements, notably those that function as e-sites. The relative salience of these e-sites determines that B is dependent on A—that is, β_p is greater than α_p. At the level of word structure, we can interpret this A/D asymmetry as indicating that A is a stem and B a suffix. Structure B is characterized as an operation on a stem (primarily the addition of segmental content), so its internal reference to a schematic stem (its e-site) is both intrinsic and prominent. In contrast, the autonomy of A implies that any reference it makes to other structures is both extrinsic and relatively nonsalient.

A question arises at this point: if A is a stem, why does its phonological pole make any reference at all to another structure? What does it mean for a supposedly autonomous structure to contain an e-site? The answer is suggested by the extensive parallelism attributed to semantic and phonological structures. At the semantic pole, the analogous situation was taken as indicating the graded nature of A/D alignment, and hence of the complement/modifier distinction. Its basic import at the phonological pole is that here too A/D alignment is a matter of degree, and consequently that the stem/affix distinction may not always be clear-cut.[21]

If semantic space includes phonological space as a subdomain (cf. 2.2.1), the encyclopedic approach we have adopted for the former should be applicable to the latter as well. This is not a standard view of phonological (or even semantic) structures, but the lack of precedent hardly establishes inherent implausibility. The encyclopedic view is in fact quite natural granted that phonological structures have a conceptual basis, and that only certain facets of them are susceptible to peripheral implementation.

In the encyclopedic analysis of semantic structure, a predication's profile is the access node to a network of relationships. The centrality of these specifications is highly variable: more-intrinsic properties (e.g. shape for physical objects) are incorporated in the representation of others and activated with virtually every use; extrinsic properties (e.g. locative relationships with external objects) are activated on a more contingent basis. A similar gradation can be posited for the phonological pole. Overtly manifested content (X and Y in Fig. 9.15) is maximally central to the value of a phonological structure. Since dependent elements are defined as operations on more-autonomous structures, their schematic reference to such structures is also both intrinsic and obligatorily activated. The extrinsic specifications of a phonological element derive from its participation in larger configurations. Our knowledge of words, for example, includes their linear sequencing to form phrases and more-elaborate expressions. Similarly, part of what we know about a typical stem is that it permits the appendage of additional segmental content in the

[21] The following discussion owes much to conversations with David Tuggy (cf. Tuggy 1981).

formation of a word. A specification of this sort provides the phonological e-site of *A* in Fig. 9.15.

These notions are better understood from the standpoint of language acquisition. Consider the stem/affix distinction. Seldom if ever is the learner exposed to an affix occurring alone; the sequence he learns as a suffix, for instance, consistently follows additional segmental material within the same word. The preceding sequence is variable, but some such sequence is always present, and is susceptible to uniform characterization at an appropriate level of schematicity. Schematic reference to a stem will therefore be salient at the phonological pole of the suffix granted the plausible assumption that a morpheme is extracted from the various contexts in which it appears and incorporates whatever is common to these contexts.

For a stem, the situation is typically quite different. Often a stem occurs alone, and even if additional material is required, this may be furnished by a prefix on some occasions and a suffix on others. Consequently, when the learner extracts invariant features from the contexts in which a stem appears, neither prefixal nor suffixal elements survive the cancellation process to become enshrined as obligatorily activated facets of its phonological value. Nothing precludes the incorporation of schematic reference to such elements as contingent specifications of the stem; however, circumstances dictate that such reference will be optional, nonsalient, and extrinsic (i.e. not required for the implementation of its overt content). To this extent a stem remains autonomous even though its potential for combining with other elements in a word is part of its encyclopedic characterization.[22]

On the basis of this analysis, we expect *A/D* asymmetry and the stem/affix distinction to be more tenuous in composite forms where neither morpheme can occur alone. An example is provided by the large family of forms having *re-*, *ex-*, *trans-*, *per-*, *de-*, etc. as initial elements, and *-ceive*, *-port*, *-fer*, *-duce*, *-tain*, etc. as final elements (e.g. *receive*, *pertain*, *export*, *deduce*, *transfer*). Despite their limited semantic analyzability, speakers can segment these forms into structurally significant subparts because of the many combinations observed. To claim that there is no stem/affix distinction in these forms would probably be an exaggeration, but certainly it is less clear-cut than in expressions like *houses*, *rapidly*, and *twisted*. The stem/affix contrast should also be more tenuous when both morphemes can occur alone; this is illustrated by complex prepositions like *into*, *onto*, *within*, *without*, *inside*, and *outside*, where the applicability of the distinction is less than obvious.[23]

[22] It is important not to be misled here by the container metaphor (see 4.2.3 and Reddy 1979). Despite the nested boxes in diagrams like Fig. 9.15, phonological units should not be regarded as separate containers with a clearly defined "inside" and "outside." It is better to think in terms of certain structures providing access to others, in the sense of facilitating their activation.

[23] If both component morphemes are construed as phonologically autonomous we have an instance of compounding.

It should not be concluded that distributional factors alone determine the stem/affix analysis. In prototypical instances where the distinction is clear, a number of mutually reinforcing properties contribute to the perceived asymmetry. We can reasonably assume that speakers employ the prototype to impose a stem/affix analysis on examples where certain contributing factors are inapplicable or inconclusive. At least the following properties are prototypical. (1) A stem can occur alone, but an affix requires a stem. (2) A stem has greater phonological "weight" than an affix: it is more often polysyllabic, and virtually always contains a syllabic nucleus. A morpheme that is inherently dependent phonologically (e.g. a suprasegmental or process morpheme) cannot function as a stem. (3) A stem also has greater semantic "weight." By and large, the notions symbolized by stems are more complex, specific, and concrete than those symbolized by affixes. (4) Stems are drawn from large, open-ended classes, whereas classes of dependent morphemes are restricted in membership. (5) Autonomy and dependence are in parallel alignment at the two poles.

9.3.2. *Implications for Constituency*

A maxim of grammar holds that elements that "belong together semantically" tend to "occur together syntactically" (Behagel's law). Vague though this principle is, both its significance and its essential correctness are beyond dispute. The iconicity it implies between semantic and formal relationships is naturally expressed in the present framework, where the bipolar character of grammatical structure is fundamental.

The principle pertains to combinatorial relationships, and hence to grammatical constructions. The tendency for semantic proximity to be matched by "syntactic" proximity is thus to be sought, in cognitive grammar, at the semantic and phonological poles of valence relations, which characterize these constructions. In a valence relation, the integration of two predications at the semantic pole is symbolized by the parallel integration of their phonological correspondents. It is to this symbolic relationship that the principle attributes iconicity: at each pole the associated structures are said to display a certain "togetherness."

Obviously, this notion of togetherness must be spelled out more precisely if the principle is to be regarded as substantive. We must therefore consider the sense in which the predications integrated by a valence relation "belong together semantically," and also what it means to say that their phonological correspondents "occur together." This notion of semantic togetherness can be explicated by a general property of valence relations: correspondences virtually always equate highly prominent substructures in the component predications. In particular, the profile of one component typically corresponds either to some portion of the other's profile or else to an unprofiled substructure that

is nevertheless quite salient (cf. Ch. 8). One of the predications thus elaborates an element that is central to the value of the other.

The requisite notion of phonological togetherness has more subtleties than
one might suppose. The most straightforward kind of togetherness is perhaps
to be identified as simple juxtaposition: one structure, A, is placed immediately adjacent to the other, B: [A B]. Linear adjacency of this sort is employed in English to symbolize the head-modifier relation (e.g. *black cat*), the
verb-object relation (*eat snails*), the preposition-object relation (*under the
table*), and so on; the juxtaposition of two stems to form a compound is also
of this type. Several factors contribute to the optimality of linear adjacency as
a symbolic device. For one thing, the component structures A and B are fully
manifested and can be directly observed within the composite structure.
Moreover, a relationship of adjacency (as opposed, say, to inclusion) pre-
serves the integrity of both components, requiring neither the interruption of
their internal structure nor any other substantial modification. Finally, a specification of simple adjacency has minimal complexity, for it makes no essential
reference to any elements other than A and B themselves.

If we assume that simple adjacency is an unmarked and fairly ubiquitous
type of phonological integration, tentative conclusions can often be drawn
about grammatical constituency on the basis of linear ordering. In the absence
of evidence to the contrary, for instance, we would assume that *send* and *the
peaches* form a constituent in (4)(a) (with *send the peaches* and *to Harry*
being integrated by adjacency at a higher organizational level), whereas *send*
and *Harry* form a constituent in (4)(b).

   (4)(a)   *Send the peaches / to Harry.*
     (b)   *Send Harry / the peaches.*

Nothing, in absolute terms, rules out the more complex alternative positing
the opposite constituency. A conceivable analysis of (4)(a) would integrate
send and *to Harry* at the first level of constituency, yielding the composite
sequence *send to Harry*; integration at the second level then requires the insertion of *the peaches* in the middle of this sequence. We will see that the
insertion of one component at a specified location inside the other is indeed a
possible mode of phonological integration, but invoking this less obvious
analysis would be gratuitous in the absence of semantic motivation. Presumably speakers adopt the more straightforward account of phonological constituency whenever this is consistent with semantic relationships (as it is in (4)).

"Simple adjacency" is not all simple, however. For one thing, phonological
constituency is intimately associated with intonational phenomena. In (4), the
evidence derived from linear order for the postulated constituency groupings
is corroborated by the evidence from rhythmic cohesiveness and the location
of intonational boundaries. Rhythmic cohesiveness is to some substantial de-

gree a matter of timing. If *A* and *B* form a rhythmic group within the sequence [*A B C*], suggesting the constituency [[*A B*] *C*], we recognize this in part by the greater temporal proximity between *A* and *B* than between *B* and *C*. There are doubtless other factors besides constituency that are capable of influencing rhythm and timing, but the tendency for rhythmic groups to coincide with constituents is plausibly attributed to the intrinsic character of hierarchical organization.

Hierarchy implies the incorporation of component elements as facets of a composite structure that is manipulated as a whole for purposes of higher-order combination. The natural consequence of incorporation is compression: as manifested within the unitary composite structure, the component elements are generally more restricted than they would be in isolation, i.e. they show more-limited variation and occupy narrower ranges of values along relevant parameters. Compression is cumulative in multilevel hierarchies, with the result that greater variation and fuller ranges of values are most always observed at the upper levels of constituency.[24] In phonological hierarchies, the temporal axis is one dimension where compression can be expected. In general, a phonological sequence incorporated as a constituent in a larger expression should occupy a somewhat shorter time interval than when it occurs alone; we further expect tighter temporal proximity between adjacent components at lower levels in a constituency hierarchy. Other things being equal, then, an expression with the constituency [[*A B*] *C*] should manifest a greater degree of rhythmic cohesiveness between *A* and *B* than between *B* and *C* (or between [*A B*] and *C*).

"Simple adjacency" is further complicated by *A/D* relationships, which I have also described in terms of compression. It is possible, particularly at higher levels of organization, for each of the phonological components in a valence relation to resist the compression that generally accompanies composition, and for both components to be manifested essentially as they would be in isolation. For example, one natural pronunciation of *Sally succeeded* puts unreduced stress on both words; in this event pitch does not fall so sharply on the second syllable of *Sally* as it does in utterance-final position, but otherwise the phonetic concomitants of composition are negligible. More commonly, though, one of the two components in a valence relation is more successful than the other in resisting the tendency towards compression, and the result is some degree of *A/D* asymmetry. One of the component structures retains its basic autonomy, remaining essentially unreduced. The second structure suffers compression along certain phonetic parameters, and to the extent that its properties thus diverge from those of an independent expression, it becomes a satellite to its autonomous companion, requiring the support of the latter for its undistorted implementation. A gradation of *A/D*

[24] Ross (1973) discusses the grammatical repercussions of this differential.

asymmetry can be observed, and the further one progresses along the scale, the less appropriate it becomes to speak of juxtaposition or even adjacency. Cases of minimal asymmetry are illustrated by phrases where one component shows reduced stress but is otherwise unmodified; the choice may be variable, depending on discourse factors (e.g. *nèar Tóm* vs. *néar Tòm*). Cliticized pronouns display a higher degree of compression and dependence, being fully unstressed and even reduced in segmental content (*néar'ĭm, wíth'ĕr*). Clitics or affixes without a syllabic nucleus are more dependent still, as they inherently require the support of a syllabic element for their implementation. At the extremity of the scale are dependent morphemes (e.g. suprasegmentals, process morphemes) that coincide with their supporting structure along the temporal axis.

We see, then, that the "togetherness" established by phonological integration ranges from simple juxtaposition—actually quite atypical—through a spectrum of more-intimate relationships that extends to the full commingling of component structures. I have already argued (9.1.3) that affixation involves more than simple adjacency, even for prefixes and suffixes. The occasional occurrence of infixes demonstrates in more dramatic fashion that phonological integration does not invariably respect the integrity of component structures. More specifically, it shows that the inclusion of one component inside another is among the types of proximity effected by valence relations at the phonological pole.

At higher levels of organization such inclusion is neither uncommon nor unfamiliar. The following example (Casad 1981) involves the quotative particle *nú?u* of Cora (cf. Ch. 8, fn. 8) (DISTR and REFL indicate morphemes whose basic values are distributive and reflexive, respectively):

(5)   *t^yám^wa?a nú?u   citá   t^yú?-uh-m^wa?ati*
      lots   QUOT cucuixtle DISTR-REFL-pure
      'The area, they say, was completely covered by a stand of cucuixtle.'

The particle *nú?u* is adjacent to both *t^yám^wa?a* 'lots' and *citá* 'cucuixtle', but obviously it forms a grammatical constituent with neither the quantifier nor the noun per se. Semantically, *nú?u* specifies the location of a proposition (its trajector) in an abstract domain; it indicates that the validity of this proposition is beyond the firsthand knowledge of the speaker. The expected valence relation thus hinges on a correspondence between the trajector of *nú?u* and the overall finite clause *t^yám^wa?a citá t^yú?uhm^wa?ati* 'The area was completely covered by a stand of cucuixtle'. Under this analysis, *nú?u* does not form a grammatical constituent with either of the words adjacent to it, but rather with the clause as a whole. This is corroborated by distributional evidence: *nú?u* does not regularly occur next to any particular clausal element, but is found instead in a certain clausal position, namely (to simplify) after the first word, whatever this word might be.

Fig. 9.16 sketches the integration of *nú ʔu* with the clause in (5) (spaces delimit words and *W* stands for the word-schema). The component on the

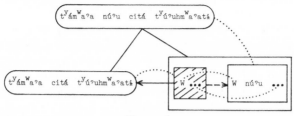

Fig. 9.16

right is the phonological pole of *nú ʔu*, which is dependent. Its standard is characterized schematically as a phonological sequence consisting of at least one word (in a bipolar diagram it would be shown as the correspondent of a schematic finite clause). What identifies *nú ʔu* as a second-position element is the placement of this specified segmental sequence in the otherwise schematic target, namely after the initial occurrence of *W*. As always, the standard functions as e-site in the valence relation, and the composite structure accords with the specifications of the target.

The possibility of one component structure being included in another has important implications for the determination of grammatical constituency. It demonstrates that constituency cannot be ascertained on the basis of phonological cues alone. Given a sequence like (5), for example, together with the information that *nú ʔu* participates in a valence relation, we cannot determine conclusively—in the absence of semantic considerations—whether this word forms a grammatical constituent with the preceding word, the following word, or some larger structure such as the clause as a whole.[25] We can ascertain the most likely analysis only by weighing the superficial phonological evidence with other factors, most notably the plausibility of the valence relationships implied for the semantic pole.

The primary source of indeterminacy appears to be disparity in the relative size of component structures, in particular their location in the unipolar phonological hierarchy. When both structures occupy the same hierarchical level (e.g. when both are syllables, or both are words), their phonological integration can perhaps be accomplished by simple juxtaposition. However, since notions like "juxtaposition" and "simple adjacency" suggest the continued au-

---

[25] This is so even when rhythmic and intonational factors appear to indicate co-constituency with an adjacent element. A case in point is the Luiseño second-position "auxiliary" (cf. Steele et al. 1981), which cliticizes to the preceding word despite its status as co-constituent with the clause containing it.

tonomy and coequal status of the associated elements, their applicability is problematic to the extent that these elements manifest a substantial disparity in size and organizational complexity. We can observe this in (5), where one component (*nú ʔu*) is a single word and the other a multiword clause (which could be of indefinite length).

Disparity in size between the phonological components in a valence relation is commonplace, and by recognizing its consequences we can explicate some initially very puzzling examples of constituency, showing them to be nothing more than extreme cases of rather ordinary phenomena. Consider the phrase *England's throne*. Semantic and phonological considerations both suggest that *England* and -*'s* form a grammatical constituent, with *England's* and *throne* then combining at a higher level of organization. At this second level, the phonological components (*England's* and *throne*) are of comparable complexity (single words); their integration can be effected by simple juxtaposition. But what about *England* and -*'s* at the lower level?

To say that *England* and -*'s* are simply juxtaposed would be a substantial oversimplification. They are not phonetic coequals, and occupy nonadjacent levels in the hierarchy of phonological complexity: -*'s* is a single segment, and *England* a polysyllabic stem capable of standing alone as a word. In purely phonetic terms, it is somewhat misleading to say that -*'s* combines with the stem as a whole. It bears a direct relationship only to the final syllable of the stem, and still more narrowly, to that portion of the final syllable consisting of the nucleus and coda, where it functions as the outermost consonantal increment: $(((\eta)d)z)$.[26] In terms of unipolar organization, $(...z)$ forms a constituent with $((\eta)d)$, not with the full polysyllabic stem.

The point of this example is twofold. First, it shows that symbolic considerations are critical to the determination of grammatical constituency, being necessary for the proper interpretation even of seemingly clear-cut phonological evidence. There is no real doubt that *England* and -*'s* form a constituent, but strictly speaking the phonetic evidence would indicate that -*'s* forms a constituent with -*and*, not with *England* as a whole; the linguist (and the speaker too, presumably) overrides this evidence, and specifies the full stem to be the component integrated with -*'s* in the valence relation, because he knows that the -*and* of *England* has no symbolic import of its own. Parallel remarks apply to almost any composite expression.

Second, the example shows that certain facets of a phonological component participate far more directly and crucially in a valence relation than others.[27] In the case of *England's*, the directly relevant portions of the stem include the nucleus and coda of its final syllable: -*'s* refers to these explicitly as part of its

[26] We can ignore the coalescence of [dz] to an affricate.
[27] This is directly analogous to the phenomenon of **active zones** at the semantic pole (cf. 7.3.4).

internal structure and specifies their properties in some detail; other aspects of the schematic stem constituting the standard of -'s are optional and character-ized with maximal schematicity. This was illustrated for -s, the plural analog of -'s, in Fig. 9.9(b).

These two factors—level disparity, and the direct involvement of only cer-tain facets of phonological structures—are therefore typical even in run-of-the-mill valence relations. Once this is realized, we can deal with a variety of examples that appear at first blush to be exotic and problematic. Consider the nominal expression *the queen of England's consort*: it is the queen (not En-gland) who has a consort, yet the possessive ending occurs on the word *En-gland*. The apparent anomaly is easily accounted for. Both *queen* and *the queen of England* designate the possessor (their profiles are linked by a ver-tical correspondence), so either one could reasonably be integrated with the possessive predication from the semantic standpoint. The actual valence com-ponents appear to be *the queen of England* and -'s, despite their substantial level disparity. As in our previous example (*England's*), -'s is attached as the outermost consonantal increment in the coda of the final syllable of the autono-mous structure. The only difference is that here the autonomous component is more complex, and its active substructure—the part of it that interacts di-rectly with the dependent structure—constitutes a smaller proportion of the whole. We need only specify that the possessive -'s can attach to a multiword autonomous structure; within this sequence the active zone for the valence re-lation is the final syllable of the last word.[28]

Parallel examples are easy to find. *The*, for instance, often cliticizes to the following word, whatever it might be. Typically it is the head noun (e.g. *th'dog*), but it can just as well be a modifier. On semantic grounds we would not want to posit a valence relation between *the* and *big* in *th'big dog*, despite their rhythmic grouping. Instead we must say that the article integrates with the remainder of the nominal (*dog* and *big dog* have the same designatum, so this poses no problems for the semantic integration); the phonological pole of the autonomous structure can therefore be a multiword sequence, and its ac-tive zone is the initial word in this sequence. Another type of example is pro-vided by compounds functioning as constituents of larger expressions derived by inflection or further compounding. Often the added phonological con-tent—though integrated with the compound as a whole—combines with a single member of the compound in just the way that it does when that element occurs alone as an uncompounded stem. An instance attested in English is *hand-held cameraman*, designating a person who operates a *hand-held cam-*

---

[28] The plural -s, by contrast, limits the autonomous structure to a single word or compound. Apart from this difference in scope, the possessive -'s is equivalent to the plural -s diagrammed in Fig. 9.9(b).

era; *man* combines phonologically with *camera* just as it does when *camera* stands alone. *Hand-held cameramen* (the plural of *hand-held cameraman*) is a similar, inflectional example. This model requires no devices for their description that cannot be motivated for completely straightforward cases of phonological integration.

CHAPTER 10

Categorization and Context

MOST SYMBOLIC UNITS are variable in both form and meaning. How to account for this variation is a pivotal issue for our understanding of grammatical organization, despite its general neglect in contemporary theory. The present chapter argues that the semantic and phonological poles of a symbolic unit are analyzable as complex categories, and that these are best conceived and described as schematic networks. The connection between rules and schematic networks is explored, as well as the nature of symbolic relationships as they pertain to complex categories. Finally, we examine the essential relation between linguistic structures and their contexts.

10.1. Complex Categories

Linguists are gradually coming to appreciate the critical significance of categorization to linguistic structure. The role of categorization is especially prominent in cognitive grammar, which invokes it for several basic functions not generally associated with it. These include judgments of well-formedness (conventionality); certain types of rules; the assignment of structural descriptions; A/D alignment in syntagmatic relationships; and even composition (cf. Ch. 12). It is therefore essential that we develop a coherent view of the process of categorization and the structures it produces.

10.1.1. *Categorization: A Synthesis*

Linguistic categories are typically complex: they group together, and treat as equivalent for certain purposes, a variety of distinct and sometimes quite disparate elements. Though similar to varying extents, these elements are not always susceptible to a uniform characterization affording absolute predictability of class membership; i.e. it is not always possible to find a description valid without qualification for all class members and inapplicable to all nonmembers. Hence it cannot in general be presumed that membership in a linguistic category is a predictable, all-or-nothing affair. Membership is commonly a matter of degree, resistant to strict delimitation, and subject to the vicissitudes of linguistic convention.

The facts of language thus dictate a nonreductive approach to categorization. Important though it is to capture generalizations by describing any commonality among the members of a category, the analyst who seeks a comprehensive description will not invariably escape the task of enumerating established class membership. Nor should he desire to do so, since established categorization is part of a speaker's knowledge of linguistic convention. To the extent that specific categorizing judgments have the status of conventional units, they are properly included in the grammar of a language even when they follow as special cases of a general characterization.

Any serious examination of lexical items, the initial focus of our discussion, reveals the necessity for a nonreductive, usage-based model of this sort. A lexical item of frequent occurrence displays a substantial, often impressive variety of interrelated senses and conventionally sanctioned usages; its set of established values can be regarded as a complex category, the members of which are treated as equivalent for symbolic (and possibly other) purposes. A speaker's conventional knowledge of such a category cannot be reduced to a single characterization. Even when all its attested values are plausibly analyzed as instantiations of a single abstract schema, or as extensions from a single prototype, there is no way to predict from the schema or prototype alone precisely which array of instantiations or extensions—out of all the conceivable ones—happen to be conventionally exploited within the speech community. This knowledge is separated only arbitrarily and infelicitously from other aspects of the speaker's grasp of linguistic structure: the facts of conventional usage lie at the very foundation of linguistic structure and are properly included in the grammar of a language.

In eschewing a reductionist approach to lexical categories, we are by no means committing ourselves to an atomistic approach that treats every attested value as a separate lexical item (resulting in a claim of massive homonymy). There is a far more viable middle alternative, namely to attempt what Lindner (1981) calls a **unified** account of lexical (and other) categories. This usage-based conception requires the listing of all conventionally established values of a lexical item, as a minimal description of the empirical data. It further demands an analysis of how the category is structured, i.e. how the different senses are related to one another. The principal types of relationship to be accommodated are elaboration (the relation between a schema and its instantiations) and extension (the relation between prototypical and peripheral values). Multiple instances of such relationships unite the various senses of a lexical item in a network that incorporates (as schemas) whatever generalizations can be extracted from specific instances and reflects the many categorizing judgments through which the complex category has evolved.

Alternate models of categorization were first discussed in 1.1.4.2. There it was argued that the strict criterial-attribute model, despite its dominance in the Western intellectual tradition, cannot be accepted unquestioningly as the basis for language structure and behavior.[1] Two other models, more directly grounded in cognitive concerns, appear to offer more revelatory and empirically adequate accounts of linguistic categorization: the prototype model, and a model based on schematicity (cf. 3.3.3). They are not fundamentally incompatible, and both prove essential for a reasonable description of natural language. What I therefore propose is a synthesis that treats them as special cases of a unified phenomenon and relates them in integral fashion to the network conception of complex categories.

Categorization by prototypes at first appears quite different from categorization by schemas. A prototype is a typical instance of a category, and other elements are assimilated to the category on the basis of their perceived resemblance to the prototype; there are degrees of membership based on degrees of similarity. A schema, by contrast, is an abstract characterization that is fully compatible with all the members of the category it defines (so membership is not a matter of degree); it is an integrated structure that embodies the commonality of its members, which are conceptions of greater specificity and detail that elaborate the schema in contrasting ways.[2] The two modes of categorization are nonetheless inherently related and describable as aspects of a unified phenomenon.

Whether by schema or by prototype, categorization resides in a comparison event of the form $S > T = V$. It is achieved when the conceptualizer succeeds in observing within the target (T) a configuration that satisfies some or all of the specifications of the standard (S). More precisely, V—the magnitude of discrepancy between the standard and target—is required to fall below a certain threshold of tolerance. When all the specifications of S are satisfied by T, so that $V = 0$, S is referred to as a **schema**, and the categorizing relationship $S \rightarrow T$ is one of elaboration or specialization; there is full compatibility between S and T, even though the latter is specified in finer detail. When there is some inconsistency between S and T, so that V has a nonzero value, S can be referred to as a **prototype**, in a generalized sense of the term; the categorizing relationship $S \dashrightarrow T$ then involves extension rather than simple elaboration, as some of the specifications of S must be modified or suspended if this configuration is to be observed in T.

The two modes of categorization are reconcilable because a gradation of

---

[1] See Lakoff (1982, 1987) for extensive treatments of categorization that deal with this issue in some detail.

[2] By virtue of being an integrated structure, i.e. an abstract concept in its own right, a schema differs from a list of criterial attributes. The two are similar to the extent that each is taken as being compatible with all category members.

values is possible for V: schematicity occupies the endpoint of the scale, where $V = 0$ by virtue of the full compatibility of S and T. From this perspective it is neither surprising nor a matter of concern that the two modes are sometimes difficult to distinguish in practice. There is nevertheless a qualitative difference to be accounted for. Categorization based on schematicity provides **full sanction**, which corresponds to the linguistic notion of well-formedness. By contrast, categorization based on extension provides only **partial sanction** and figures in assessments of deviance (nonconventionality). This distinction may have substantial cognitive salience.

Schematic relationships have special status precisely because they represent the limiting case (zero) of S/T discrepancy. Qualitative distinctness and special cognitive salience often attach to an element that occupies the extremity of a continuous scale. For instance, there is a mathematical sense in which a point is the limiting case of a circle (it is a circle with a radius of zero), but cognitively the two are treated quite differently even when the relationship is recognized. The contrast between perfective and imperfective processes is a convenient linguistic example. A perfective process profiles a change through time; an imperfective process represents the limiting case of change, namely no change at all. The seemingly minor quantitative difference between imperfectives and many perfectives is sufficient to endow the former with special properties according them unique status in the English aspectual system (cf. 7.2). The apparent significance of discrete well-formedness judgments can therefore be accommodated even in a model describing sanction and conventionality in continuous terms.

The two modes are even more intimately associated, in that categorization by extension typically presupposes and incorporates schematic relationships. Consider the assimilation of a concept X to the category defined by a prototype PT. There are two basic possibilities, corresponding to the difference between central and peripheral members of the category. If X accords fully with the specifications of PT, it is recognized as a central or prototypical instance of the category. There being no conflict in specifications, PT is judged schematic for X in the categorizing relationship: $PT \rightarrow X$. Suppose, on the other hand, that X is inconsistent with certain specifications of PT. Concept X can nevertheless be assimilated to the category provided that the conceptualizer observes a measure of similarity between PT and X and is willing, for the purposes at hand, to overlook their discrepancies. This perception of similarity is pivotal to the categorization and consequently merits explicit treatment. Three cognitive entities thus figure in the judgment, not just two: PT, X, and some representation of their perceived similarity.

As a representation of the commonality perceived in PT and X, this third element amounts to a schema (SCH) that PT and X elaborate in alternate ways. Categorization by extension from a prototype therefore has the form

Fig. 10.1

depicted in Fig. 10.1. It is certainly not claimed that the schematic notion always attracts the conceptualizer's attention as an object of explicit awareness. Nor is it claimed that entrenchment of the relationship $PT--\rightarrow X$ necessarily entails either unit status or cognitive salience for the schema. An extension by similarity does however imply at least the transitory occurrence of those cognitive events which constitute the perception of commonality.

Grasping the commonality of two structures requires abstraction. By suspending certain specifications of PT, and relaxing certain others to allow a wider range of variation, the conceptualizer arrives at a schematic construal of PT that is compatible with both PT and X.[3] If we think of extension as a "horizontal" relationship, and schematicity as a "vertical" one, we can say that the "outward" growth of a lexical network by extension from prototypes is inherently associated with its "upward" growth by extraction of schemas. One is not impossible without the other, but they tend to co-occur as interrelated facets of the same expansive mechanism.

10.1.2. *A Lexical Category*

For illustrative purposes, let us sketch a plausible (though simplistic) scenario for the evolution of a complex category. Consider a child in the process of learning the various senses (conventional usages) of the word *tree*, and suppose the term is first applied, in his early experience, to such ordinary specimens as oaks, maples, and elms. Their perceptual prominence and obvious gross similarities enable the child to extract a conception that embodies their commonality, while excluding the many properties that vary from one instance to the next. Presumably this conception emphasizes intrinsic, characteristic, and cognitively salient properties (e.g. shape, size, color, brachiation, leaves); subtler and more contingent properties are either ignored or factored out. Hence the notion is fairly concrete and specific compared to many the child deals with, but as an abstraction from varied experience, it nevertheless constitutes a low-level schema. With continued usage, this initial conception becomes more deeply entrenched, and comes to be invoked for the categorization of more divergent experience. As the starting point for the gradual evolution of a complex category, it can be recognized as the category prototype.

---

[3] In the limiting case, namely categorization by schema, PT and SCH coincide (i.e. the requisite abstraction is zero).

Suppose, then, that our child has mastered the concept [TREE] (the eventual category prototype), as well as the symbolic relationship [[TREE]/[tree]]. When he encounters a tall plant with branches, leaves, and bark he readily sees it as conforming to the specifications of [TREE] and takes it as a straightforward instance of the *tree* category. What happens, now, when he first encounters a pine, which is [TREE]-like in most respects but has needles instead of leaves? He will quickly learn to call it a *tree*, either from hearing someone refer to it in this way or because this is the most nearly applicable term at his disposal.[4] This usage implies the symbolic unit [[PINE]/[tree]], derived by extension from the original [[TREE]/[tree]]. The two symbolic units are identical at the phonological pole, but at the semantic pole [TREE] is only partially schematic for [PINE], since they conflict in one of their specifications (leaves vs. needles).

The extension is based on the categorizing judgment [[TREE]--→[PINE]]. The observation of similarity permitting this judgment takes the form of a conception (TREE') that embodies the commonality of [TREE] and [PINE] but is sufficiently schematic in relevant respects to eliminate their conflicting specifications (in particular, it must neutralize the difference between leaves and needles). Possibly this similarity-perception endures for only a fleeting moment. It is not unlikely, though, that it eventually achieves the status of a unit with a certain amount of cognitive autonomy, i.e. the child develops a schema for the *tree* category that abstracts away from specific properties of the foliage. The result is then the schematic network depicted in Fig. 10.2(a),

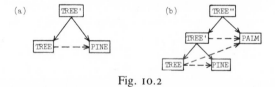

Fig. 10.2

representing the different concepts that function as the semantic pole of *tree* together with their interrelationships. Through extension to a broader, more variegated class of objects (including pines), the term *tree* acquires an abstract sense that it would not otherwise have. The meaning of *tree* for the child at this point is not just the schematic [TREE'], nor is it just the prototype [TREE]; rather its meaning is given by the entire schematic network, any node of which can be accessed by the phonological unit [tree].

This process can be repeated. Suppose the child next acquires the unit [[PALM]/[tree]]; i.e. he learns that a palm can be called a *tree* in conventional English usage. Either [TREE] or [TREE'] is plausibly invoked as a basis for

---

[4] I simplify by assuming that more specialized terms (*pine*, *oak*, *maple*, etc.) are not presented to the child until a later stage.

extension, the former because of its entrenchment as the category prototype, and the latter because its specifications, being more abstract, conflict less sharply with those of [PALM]. Fig. 10.2(b) depicts the schematic network that results if comparisons are made with both [TREE] and [TREE'], and if the requisite similarity-perception [TREE''] is incorporated as a higher-order schema with unit status. Whatever its details, the extension is somewhat more radical than the preceding one: since a palm lacks branches and leaves, instead having fronds concentrated at the very top of the trunk, additional specifications of the standard must be suspended or relaxed to achieve compatibility with the target. [TREE''] is therefore quite abstract, being neutral as to degree of brachiation, the size and nature of the foliage, and the distribution of branches and foliage along the length of the trunk.

Our child will learn much more about the conventional usage of *tree*, but let us pause at this juncture for some general discussion. A point of overriding significance is the extreme complexity of many linguistic categories.[5] Only a fragment of the complex category defining the semantic pole of *tree* is depicted in Fig. 10.2(b); *tree* is by no means atypical in this regard, but already the description is more complicated than many analysts would contemplate. Can it really be maintained that a linguistic description, ideally, should accommodate the full schematic network, in all its elaborate detail?

If our goal is a characterization of cognitive reality, the exclusion of such complexity from the domain of linguistic inquiry and description is both arbitrary and self-defeating. All of the nodes and relationships in a network like Fig. 10.2(b) stand for distinct facets of a speaker's linguistic knowledge. The inclusion of [PALM], for instance, specifies the conventionality of referring to a palm as a *tree* (the facts could well be otherwise); the categorizing relationship [[TREE]--→[PALM]] indicates that [PALM] is a peripheral member of the class. Moreover, a reductive characterization of schematic networks is not in general feasible, since no single node affords absolute predictability for the remainder. Giving only the prototype [TREE] as the meaning of *tree* would fail to indicate that a palm is conventionally labeled by this term, and giving only the higher-order schema [TREE''] would fail to indicate that a palm is more peripheral to the category than an oak or even a pine.[6] A viable linguistic description must therefore embrace the entire network (in principle if not in practice). The methodological objections to this position are fallacious (cf. 1.2).

---

[5] See Lindner (1981) and Brugman (1981) for extended lexical examples, insightfully analyzed. In the syntactic domain, Lakoff (1984a) analyzes the large family of *there*-constructions as a complex category.

[6] Expressions pointing out the prototypicality of class members provide direct linguistic evidence that speakers are sensitive to the structure of a complex lexical category, not just to individual nodes (cf. Lakoff 1982). Observe that an oak (but not a palm) is *your common*, or *run-of-the-mill*, or *garden-variety tree*.

Equally significant is the dynamic, continually evolving nature of a complex category, whose structure reflects the previous experience and linguistic activity of the language user and is subject to continued expansion and modification by these factors. Every usage event has some impact (even if very minor) on the structure of the categories it invokes. We have already seen how usage—in particular the need to find linguistic expression for novel conceptions—drives the initial acquisition of a lexical network, starting from the category prototype. Any facet of a schematic network, once established, is maintained or further entrenched by its continued activation in subsequent usage events. For this reason, changes in patterns of experience and communicative needs can alter the specific configuration of a network even for a mature speaker. Elms and maples may not survive as prototypical trees for a speaker who has lived for forty years in the desert.[7]

It is conceivable, then, that speakers vary considerably in the specifics of the schematic network they construct to represent a particular class, depending on the range of their experience, the order of their exposure to relevant data, the similarities they happen to perceive, the generalizations they manage to extract, and so on. Variation does not preclude effective communication, for this requires little more than substantial overlap from one speaker to the next in the range of senses that are somehow incorporated in the network. The consequence that no two speakers share precisely the same linguistic system may be considered unfortunate by some, but it is realistic nonetheless (if not self-evident).

How is it possible to discover and verify the precise structure of a complex category? How can we tell, for example, if there should be an arrow from [TREE'] to [PALM] in Fig. 10.2(b)? Does the node [TREE''] exist, and if so, should it be accorded unit status? At a minimum, we can affirm the accessibility to empirical investigation of at least certain facets of these networks. Speakers do have relevant intuitions: they judge the 'celebrity' sense of *star* to be extended from its astronomical sense (rather than conversely); that an apple is more central than a tomato to the *fruit* category; and that certain senses of a word are more closely related than others.[8] Moreover, prototypicality can be established through a variety of experimental techniques, shown capable of yielding consistent rankings for centrality or degree of category membership. One can also adduce a substantial range of purely linguistic evidence, both lexical and grammatical. As for the former, we have already noted (fn. 6) the existence of qualifiers that specify status within a complex category. Composite lexical items can tell us something about the structure

---

[7] Conceivably there are speakers for whom the term *apple* now designates a fruit only by virtue of semantic extension, based on its similarity (when a byte is removed) to a computer logo.

[8] Intuitions cannot be taken at face value, but there is no a priori reason to regard such judgments as any less reliable and informative than, say, the grammaticality judgments that guide research in generative syntax.

and membership of a category; the existence of *palm tree*, for instance, corroborates the inclusion of palms in the *tree* category (cf. *beanbag chair, mechanical pencil*). Differences in the natural and cultural salience of category members have been related by Witkowski and Brown (1983) to certain types of lexical change. Grammatical behavior sometimes reflects the distance between nodes in a lexical network. It is intuitively obvious, for example, that the extension of *star* from 'celestial body' to 'celebrity' is much greater in magnitude than that of *tree* from the category prototype to 'pine' or 'palm'. This is witnessed grammatically by the infelicity of a sentence like (1)(a) or (1)(b) when one of the two stars is taken to be an astronomical object and the other a famous person:

(1)(a) *Tony saw a star, and Georgia saw one too.*
   (b) *Tony saw two stars.*

However, if *star* is replaced by *tree* in these sentences, they are perfectly acceptable even when one of the trees referred to is taken to be a maple and the other a palm.

We are therefore not without potential resources for elucidating the structure of a complex category. Seldom, though, can we expect a clear-cut basis for determining all the specific features of a schematic network; in practice many points of detail are bound to remain uncertain if not indeterminate. However, the importance of this limitation should not be overstated. The specifics of particular networks are less important than having a realistic conception of their general character. Our inability to demonstrate directly and conclusively that a particular schema has been extracted, or that a particular categorizing judgment has been made, does not invalidate the claim that speakers do extract schemas and make categorizing judgments, and that these are crucial aspects of linguistic organization. In the present framework, moreover, much less hinges on the specific details of a network than one might think. With respect to Fig. 10.2(b), for instance, a speaker has learned the conventionality of referring to a palm as a *tree* regardless of whether [TREE″] (the similarity-perception motivating its extension to this notion) is incorporated in the network. The entrenchment and cognitive salience of such structures is in any case a matter of degree.

10.2. Schematic Networks

A complex category is reasonably described as a schematic network. Though we have focused on the interrelated senses of a lexical item, the network model is applicable to any category of linguistic relevance. The structure attributed to schematic networks must now be examined in more systematic detail. We will first consider the constructs required for their characterization, turning subsequently to their growth and modification.

10.2.1. A Static View

A network is defined by a set of nodes (or vertices) and a set of arcs that connect these nodes in pairwise fashion. Any kind of linguistic structure—semantic, phonological, or symbolic—can function as a node in the schematic networks that concern us. The arcs connecting these structures are categorizing relationships, based primarily on full and partial schematicity. Since a categorizing relationship (e.g. $[[A] --\rightarrow [B]]$) is itself a linguistic structure in semantic, phonological, or symbolic space, it can also function as a node in some schematic network; however we will ignore this possibility at present.

A node can be a structure with any degree of internal complexity. In a lexical category like *tree*, for instance, a single node (e.g. [PINE]) consists of a complex matrix that incorporates numerous domains, some of them representing substantial knowledge systems. It is inappropriate to conceive of the nodes in a network as discrete containers, each holding a separate body of "content." Certain knowledge systems serving as domains for one sense of a lexical item must be included in the matrix for other senses as well; no reasonable view of cognitive organization could maintain that duplicates of these knowledge systems are stored as distinct modules "inside" each of the nodes for which they are relevant. To take just one example, the knowledge that trees are the source of wood could be accessed through any of the senses of *tree* depicted in Fig. 10.2.

We can realistically assume that certain nodes in a lexical network share a substantial knowledge base. Each of them structures and organizes this content in its own way, combining it with additional specifications not appropriate for all the others. [PINE], for example, augments the common knowledge base for *tree* by specifying the traditional role of pines as Christmas trees, whereas [PALM] evokes the conception of a tropical setting. Schemas and their instantiations represent shared content at different levels of specificity; in contrast to [TREE] and [PINE], for instance, the schema [TREE'] abstracts away from the difference between leaves and needles. Selection is another factor: [TREE'] makes reference to branches, but the higher-order schema [TREE''] does not, as it accommodates palms as well as less peripheral members of the category. The nodes in a lexical network can also structure a knowledge base contrastively by their choice of profile or primary domain. A typical example is Luiseño *kulaawut* 'tree', whose conventional usages also include 'stick' and 'wood'. Of the entity profiled by 'tree', 'stick' profiles only a small (and detached) subpart. Moreover, domains pertaining to substance and function are primary for 'wood', but only secondary for 'tree'.

Thus, rather than being separate, self-contained entities, the nodes in a lexical network provide alternate "windows" on a common knowledge base; each affords a different view by structuring this base in its own fashion, and by introducing supplementary specifications. Although we are concentrating on the alternate senses of a single lexical item, comparable remarks can be made for distinct lexical items that refer to overlapping systems. The semantic relations among *pine*, *oak*, *palm*, etc. are basically parallel to those linking the individual senses of *tree*. In fact, their central values might be identified with nodes in the latter's schematic network.

The structure of a lexical network is given by a set of categorizing relationships between nodes. Each such relationship is a cognitive routine, more specifically an established comparison event assessing one node in relation to another. Two basic types have been recognized: specialization ($A \rightarrow B$) and extension ($A \dashrightarrow B$), the former analyzed as a limiting case of the latter (note the terms **full** vs. **partial schematicity**). Starting from these basic notions a broader variety of categorizing relationships can be defined. For one thing, both specialization and extension are matters of degree. The **elaborative distance** between [TREE] and its immediate subordinate [OAK] is considerably less, for example, than that between the higher-order schema [TREE″] and the subtype [BLACK OAK] (assuming a direct assessment of their relationship). Degree of extension (S/T discrepancy) is obviously variable as well, as we saw for [[TREE]$\dashrightarrow$[PINE]] vs. [[TREE]$\dashrightarrow$[PALM]]. More-extreme instances are considered metaphorical, especially when domain shifts restrict the similarity between standard and target to abstract configurational properties, as they do for *tree* in *phrase tree*, *decision tree*, etc.

If A categorizes B, nothing rules out a simultaneous relationship wherein B categorizes A. The simple, unidirectional relations of full and partial schematicity can therefore be compounded to form various kinds of bidirectional relations. With full schematicity, there is an inherent asymmetry: if B is characterized in finer detail than A (i.e. $A \rightarrow B$), A cannot simultaneously be characterized in finer detail than B ($B \rightarrow A$). The inverse of an elaborative relationship is consequently not itself elaborative, but rather extensional. The inverse of [[TREE]$\rightarrow$[OAK]], for instance, is [[OAK]$\dashrightarrow$[TREE]], as the target [TREE] does not satisfy the detailed specifications of the standard [OAK]. The single case where full schematicity can be bidirectional is when the elaborative distance is zero in both directions. This amounts to identity, which is therefore conveniently symbolized by a two-headed, solid-line arrow (for mutual full schematicity): $A \leftrightarrow B$.

With partial schematicity, nothing precludes a bidirectional relationship $A \dashleftrightarrow B$. If a perceived similarity motivates the extension of A to B, the same similarity can motivate the extension of B to A. Often there are grounds for positing a particular direction of extension: speaker intuition, the obvious prototypicality of A or B, or general principles of semantic extension (e.g. it typically proceeds from concrete to more abstract domains). However, nothing guarantees that a nonarbitrary choice can always be made. The relationship

$A \leftarrow - \rightarrow B$ then indicates that the speaker perceives the similarity of each element to the other without attributing primacy to either one. By my own intuitions, various specific senses of *drive* are related to one another in this way (*drive a car*, *drive a ball*, *drive a nail*).

A further dimension must be recognized for the structure of a schematic network, namely the cognitive salience of its individual nodes and categorizing relationships. Their prominence varies over a wide range. Some are readily accessible to intuition and crucial to a linguistic description, whereas others are so marginal that we can ignore them for all but theoretical purposes. Several partially independent factors apparently contribute to the status of a particular element. One factor is the prominence of its domain. Some domains are intrinsically salient and pervasive in cognitive processing (e.g. those pertaining to space and vision). Moreover, structures in highly abstract domains are generally less salient than those related more directly to sensory experience. Also significant is level of schematicity, i.e. position in a taxonomic (schematic) hierarchy. It has been found that **basic-level categories** (e.g. *apple*, *hammer*, *table*) manifest psychological primacy in various respects relative to either superordinate notions (*fruit*, *tool*, *furniture*) or subordinate ones (*McIntosh*, *claw hammer*, *coffee table*) (cf. Rosch 1975, 1977, 1978; Lakoff 1982). An additional factor is degree of entrenchment, which presumably correlates with frequency of activation. It is by virtue of this correlation that a complex category is shaped in accordance with a speaker's previous experience and is continually adapted to accommodate changing experiential patterns. A high degree of entrenchment is a major determinant of prototypicality.

To summarize, a schematic network includes a finite set of nodes, which can be linguistic structures of any sort. Every node is linked to at least one other through a categorizing relationship, of which there are several types: full schematicity (at varying elaborative distances); partial schematicity (with varying degrees of S/T discrepancy); or a bidirectional relationship decomposable into component relations of the aforementioned kinds. Each of the nodes and categorizing relationships in the network has a certain degree of cognitive salience, as determined by entrenchment and other factors.

Within a schematic network, therefore, certain nodes and relationships are far more prominent and important than others, both cognitively and linguistically. In particular, special significance attaches to the nodes that function as the category prototype and as the highest-level schema. The prototype is significant because of its developmental priority and notable cognitive salience. As the primary basis for extension, it defines the center of gravity for the category. The highest-order schema is significant because it embodies the maximal generalization that can be extracted as a characterization of the category membership. With respect to Fig. 10.2(b), then, both [TREE] (the prototype) and [TREE″] (the topmost schema) have a privileged standing.

Matters are not really this simple, however. For one thing, neither schematicity nor prototypicality is absolute. A "local" schema and prototype can be identified for every instance of extension, as shown in Fig. 10.1, and any number of such entities can be observed in a network. In Fig. 10.2(b), for example, [TREE] is the local prototype, and [TREE′] the local schema, in the extension [[TREE]--→[PINE]]; for the extension [[TREE′]--→[PALM]], on the other hand, [TREE′] is the local prototype and [TREE″] the local schema. The status of a node is thus relative to a particular subconfiguration. [TREE′] instantiates the schema [TREE″], but it itself is a schema relative to [TREE]. By the same token, the instantiations of [TREE′] (both pines and "run-of-the-mill" trees) are prototypical and central to the category in relation to palms, but within this subclass [TREE] defines the prototype and pines are more peripheral.

Furthermore, not every complex category offers viable or unique candidates for the roles of prototype and schema at the "global" level. A particular node can be recognized as the global prototype if it is substantially more salient than any other and functions as the apparent basis of more extensions. Nothing intrinsic to the structure or the dynamics of complex categories guarantees that a single node will always distinguish itself in this way, however, or that multiple prototypes of considerable local prominence will not arise in different portions of an extensive network. There is similarly no assurance that a schematic network will always be graced with a single "superschema" fully compatible with all other members of the category; extensions can occur without the motivating schemas (similarity-perceptions) achieving the status of conventional units. Thus a network need not incorporate a well-behaved schematic or taxonomic hierarchy, with a single topmost node that dominates all the others.[9] Moreover, even if an all-subsuming superschema can plausibly be posited for a category, it may well be only minimally entrenched and have very little cognitive salience. Although such a schema would define the commonality of the entire category, its cognitive and linguistic significance might be negligible.

10.2.2. *A Dynamic View*

Our characterization of schematic networks has emphasized their "static" properties, but it is important to regard them as dynamic, continually evolving structures. A schematic network is shaped, maintained, and modified by the

[9] In her examination of English verb-particle combinations, Lindner (1981) uncovered three basic values for *out*, and noted the plausibility of a superschema representing their commonality. The senses of *up*, on the other hand, cluster under two schemas for which no obvious superschema can be proposed.

pressures of language use. The locus of these pressures is coding, i.e. the interactive relationship—in the form of categorizing activity—between established conventional units and the specific usage events they are invoked to sanction. In the final analysis, a schematic network is a set of cognitive routines, entrenched to varying degrees: despite our inevitable reifications, it is not something a speaker *has*, but rather what he *does*.

We must attribute to the language user various capacities that effect the evolution of a network. Most fundamental, perhaps, is the ability to extract schemas that embody the commonality of more specific structures. Without this ability every experience would remain sui generis; it enables the speaker to unite certain experiences as tokens of the same general type, through cancellations of idiosyncratic detail and adjustments in level of specificity. The emergence of an initial category prototype has been characterized as the extraction of a low-level schema. I have also claimed that schematization figures in the second basic capacity, namely that of perceiving the similarities that motivate extension. The outward growth of a category from its prototype thus tends to be accompanied by upward growth in the form of higher-order schemas.

This canonical growth pattern is not the only possible one, however, nor is the original category prototype always found among the lowest-order generalizations represented in a schematic hierarchy. We must also credit the language user with the ability to make progressively finer distinctions, i.e. to effect the continued elaboration and differentiation of a category after an initial generalization has been achieved. Let us return, for illustration, to the child abandoned earlier in the process of learning the conventional senses of *tree*. We assumed that he extracts the prototype [TREE] from exposure to typical instances (oaks, maples, elms, etc.) prior to the realization that these various exemplars can further be grouped into subtypes with distinctive properties. That is quite plausible, but cognitive development will not be frozen at this stage. Having succeeded in analyzing his experience coherently at a certain level of specificity, the child is now prepared to refine his categorization, making finer discriminations among the entities previously considered equivalent and noting the common properties of various subgroups.

As the child becomes aware that "just plain trees" are a heterogeneous lot, his conception of the *tree* category might evolve from the network of Fig. 10.2(b) to that of Fig. 10.3(a). [TREE] remains salient and deeply entrenched, tending to be activated in preference to its instantiations, so it can still be regarded as the prototype for the overall category. It is nonetheless schematic relative to notions like [OAK], [ELM], [APPLE TREE], etc., which are themselves low-level schemas extracted from the conception of specific instances. We see again the relativity of the distinction between schemas and prototypes. At a certain level of specificity, where only gross features are

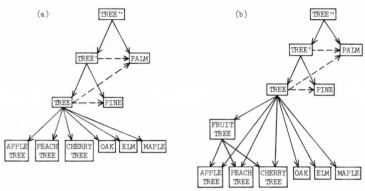

Fig. 10.3

taken into account, [TREE] and [PINE] count as instances of the schema [TREE'], [TREE] being prototypical. At a finer level of specificity, [OAK], [ELM], [APPLE TREE], etc. count as instantiations of the schema [TREE]; if one of them is cognitively salient relative to the others, it constitutes a local prototype.

I assume that speakers continually engage in structuring activity, perceiving and establishing additional relationships whenever existing structures happen to be construed together. Given the instantiations of [TREE] in Fig. 10.3(a), for example, the child will not long fail to notice the special similarity that sets apple, peach, and cherry trees apart from other kinds. This perception involves the extraction of a subschema, [FRUIT TREE], which takes its place in the network as an elaboration of [TREE], as shown in Fig. 10.3(b).[10] Any number of further developments are possible, starting from network (b). When he learns that dates come from palm trees, the child may establish the extensional relationship [[FRUIT TREE]--→[PALM]]. He may differentiate and elaborate the [PINE] and [PALM] categories, just as he did for [TREE]. He may arrive at bidirectional relationships such as [[OAK]←-→[MAPLE]] or [[APPLE TREE]←-→[PEACH TREE]] by observing the similarity between sister nodes. The eventual network is bound to be highly intricate and subject to individual variation.

Yet to be considered are semantic extensions that appear not to be based on any judgment of similarity. A classic example, cited by Stern (1931) and many others, is the extension of Middle English *bedes* from 'prayers' to 'beads'; clearly this shift reflects the cultural association of prayers and beads

---

[10] Direct classificatory relationships such as [[TREE]→[APPLE TREE]] are not necessarily lost when an intermediate structure like [FRUIT TREE] is incorporated in the network. Thus a rectangle may be directly categorized as a polygon despite the intervening subschema [QUADRANGLE], and [i] as a vowel despite the subschemas [HIGH VOWEL] and [FRONT VOWEL]. Each categorizing relationship is a cognitive routine capable of coexisting with many others.

in the practice of using rosaries. Despite their qualitative distinctness, extensions of this sort are readily accommodated in the present model. They are analyzable as a special case of extensions motivated by perceived resemblance. Several factors account for the special character of extension based on association. First, the connection between the original and extended values is limited to a single domain—most of the domains in their complex matrices are irrelevant in this regard.[11] Second, and quite crucially, the operative domain is shared by the two meanings. In the case of *bedes*, the notion of a person keeping track of a cycle of prayers by counting the balls on a rosary figured prominently in the encyclopedic description of both [PRAYERS] and [BEADS] during Middle English times. This common domain is what provided the association that motivated the extension.

A third factor emerges when the extension is examined more closely with reference to the pivotal domain. The global categorization (([[PRAYERS]/[bedes]]--→([BEADS]/[bedes])) resolves itself into an identity relation at the phonological pole, and a relationship of partial schematicity, namely ([PRAYERS]--→[BEADS]), at the semantic pole. In the operative domain, both [PRAYERS] and [BEADS] evoke the conception of a one-to-one correspondence between prayers in a cycle and balls on a rosary; they contrast only by their choice of profile. If we abstract away from this point of difference, and consider the one-to-one correspondence without imposing a profile, the resulting conception is schematic for both [PRAYERS] and [BEADS]: it is compatible with their specifications and reflects their extensive commonality. Since it is mediated by a schema, the extension is quite comparable to those based on similarity; the qualitative difference that leads us to speak of association rather than resemblance derives from the fundamental contribution of profiling to the semantic value of an expression. Association is therefore analyzable as the attenuated similarity that remains when this critical specification is suspended.

A final point to consider is how a network, once established, is invoked in actual language use. We have already noted that each node in a lexical network represents a different established usage; in combination with the phonological pole, it defines a distinct **semantic variant** of the lexical item. In a specific usage event, a speaker presumably activates a particular node that approximates the notion he wishes to convey; we can refer to this as the **active node** of the network with respect to the event (by analogy to **active zone**—cf. 7.3.4). For a speaker who utters (2)(a), the active node could be any of the lower-level structures in Fig. 10.3(b) (e.g. [OAK], [ELM], [APPLE TREE],

[11] Extension by similarity may also pivot on single domains within the complex matrices. Consider *star*, where the 'celestial body' and 'celebrity' senses are similar only if most of their respective specifications are ignored.

[PINE], [PALM]); regardless of the choice, he knows that established convention sanctions the label *tree*.

(2)(a) *Look at that tree!*
  (b) *There are trees along the river.*
  (c) *How many trees are there in this orchard?*
  (d) *The trees in this forest are mostly oaks and pines.*
  (e) *A palm is a tree.*

The other sentences in (2) most likely invoke a more schematic variant of *tree*. If (2)(b) is uttered with reference to elms, maples, and peach trees, the speaker must construe the individual objects at a level of abstraction sufficient to render them equivalent, presumably by means of the prototype [TREE]; at this level of schematicity they constitute a replicate mass, as required by the plural morpheme. In similar fashion, (2)(c)–(e) suggest the respective schemas [FRUIT TREE], [TREE'], and [TREE"].

It is unlikely, however, that all nodes other than the active node remain dormant in a usage event. The categorizing relationships in a schematic network are cognitive routines that incorporate as subroutines the cognitive events corresponding to individual nodes. Each routine thus provides an ingrained transition between the component subroutines, so that activation of one tends to facilitate activation of the other. By virtue of the entrenched relationship [[TREE]→[OAK]], for example, the activation of [OAK] tends to elicit the activation of the overall structure [[TREE]→[OAK]] and ipso facto that of its substructure [TREE]. The primary activation of one node in a usage event can thus induce the secondary activation of an indefinite and variable array of other nodes connected to it through categorizing relationships, either directly or indirectly.[12] Even if activated with lesser intensity, these additional nodes and relationships enrich the semantic value of the expression, and contribute a portion of the meaning it assumes on a particular occasion of its use.

Consider, for example, the different nuances conveyed by referring to a tiger with the alternative expressions *tiger* and *cat*. Both are conventionally applied to large, wild, striped felines. In the case of *tiger*, this conception defines the category prototype: [[TIGER]/[tiger]]. The prototype for *cat*, by contrast, is the conception of a small domestic feline (not necessarily striped): [[CAT]/[cat]]. *Cat* applies to tigers by virtue of its generalization to designate any type of feline, regardless of size, domesticity, etc. The schematic [[FELINE]/[cat]] is therefore a unit in the network for *cat*, as are various instantiations, including [[TIGER]/[cat]]. This latter is linked to the prototype by a chain of categorizing relationships; let us assume, for sake of discussion,

---

[12] I assume the validity of a **spreading-activation** model, as proposed by cognitive psychologists (e.g. Collins and Loftus 1975).

the direct relationship [[[CAT]/[cat]]--→[[TIGER]/[cat]]].[13] This relationship is the source of the special nuances that accompany the use of *cat* to designate a tiger. In such a usage the active node is [[TIGER]/[cat]], which has the same semantic pole as [[TIGER]/[tiger]]. By virtue of the categorizing relationship, however, the primary activation of [[TIGER]/[cat]] elicits the secondary activation of the prototype [[CAT]/[cat]], whose properties (including such notions as domesticity and gentleness) thereby color the expression's semantic value.

Precisely the same mechanism is responsible for the more obvious semantic complexity of metaphorical expressions. For instance, the extension of *star* to designate a celebrity implies the categorizing relationship [[[STAR]/[star]]--→ [[CELEBRITY]/[star]]]. When *star* is used in this metaphorical sense, the primary activation of [[CELEBRITY]/[star]] may elicit the secondary activation of [[STAR]/[star]]. This coactivation of [STAR] and [CELEBRITY] at the semantic pole characterizes a metaphorical understanding of the expression. However, the existence of the categorizing relationship between [[CELEBRITY]/[star]] and [[STAR]/[star]] does not guarantee that the former will activate the latter on every occasion of its use: it is possible for [[CELEBRITY]/[star]] to be activated without inducing the coactivation of [[STAR]/[star]], in which case *star* is understood to mean 'celebrity' without any awareness of the metaphorical origin of the usage. The variable "transparency" of conventional metaphors can therefore be accommodated by positing different degrees of cognitive salience for the categorizing relationships that originally motivated them. Lessening salience (i.e. the "fading" of a metaphor) translates into a reduction in the likelihood that the literal sense will be activated when the term is applied with its extended value.

10.3. Bipolar Networks

The schematic-network model is not domain-specific. It proves applicable to the complex categories observable in all areas of linguistic structure, and reveals their common organizational principles. In this section we examine the emergence, coherence, and interaction of such categories, with special reference to phonological structures and symbolic (bipolar) relationships.

10.3.1. *The Emergence of Categories*

The emergence of coherent categories is guided by both intrinsic and extrinsic factors. We have emphasized the former, notably the perceived resemblances that motivate extension and schematization. Extrinsic factors

---

[13] Equivalently for present purposes, we could assume an indirect relationship mediated by the schema [[FELINE]/[cat]], which is elaborated by both [[CAT]/[cat]] and [[TIGER]/[cat]]. (There are other possibilities as well.)

are equally significant, and influence categorization in either of two ways. On the one hand, commonality of behavior can itself be taken as an abstract type of similarity and exploited as a basis for categorization (cf. 11.1.3). More obviously, parallel interaction with other elements induces a speaker to make particular comparisons in preference to many others that are perfectly conceivable.

A shared behavior that strongly encourages the emergence of a semantic network is common symbolization. The symbolic units [[*A*]/[*X*]] and [[*B*]/ [*X*]] establish a transition chain leading from [*A*] to [*B*]: the activation of [*A*] tends to elicit that of [*X*], which in turn facilitates the activation of [*B*]. The resulting coactivation of [*A*] and [*B*] induces their comparison, wherein any observable similarity may be seized upon as the basis for a categorizing relationship [[*A*]--→[*B*]]. Sometimes, as with the central senses of *tree*, the similarities are cognitively salient and would likely be noticed even in the absence of common symbolization. In other instances the resemblance is quite tenuous. Many speakers treat the meaning of *ear* implied by *ear of corn* as an extension from the prototypical value of *ear* as a body-part term; it is doubtful that the concepts would ever be compared were it not for their identical symbolization. The cognitive distance and entrenchment of such categorizing relationships are obviously variable. Homonymy represents a limiting case, where the comparison of two identically symbolized concepts reveals no similarity that is salient or plausible enough to establish a categorization achieving unit status. For a speaker who fails to notice any special resemblance among the meanings of *bill* (proper name; request for payment; protrusion on a bird, cap, or platypus), the semantic units do not unite to form a network and are connected only via their common symbolic correspondent.

The inverse of homonymy is **homosemy**, defined as different phonological structures related only by virtue of their symbolic correspondence to the same semantic unit. It is commonly argued that there are no true synonyms, that some semantic difference, however slight, can always be found to distinguish apparent homosemes.[14] Though this may well be true, a possible example is afforded by phonologically dissimilar allomorphs of grammatical morphemes, e.g. the plural morpheme of English. Some, notably [z], [s], and [əz], are obviously linked in a network of categorizing relationships, but there is no inherent phonological basis for relating these to the zero allomorph or to the various ablaut patterns. If the plural allomorphs are all united in a single phonological network, it is doubtless because their parallel grammatical behavior

[14] The absence of exact synonyms follows, in a rather trivial sense, from the encyclopedic view of lexical semantics, together with the fact that linguistic structure can itself be referred to as a domain of predication. Thus, pushing things to the extreme, the phonological shape of a lexical item constitutes one of its semantic specifications (albeit a maximally extrinsic one); one thing we know about dogs, for instance, is that they are designated by the morpheme *dog* in English. *Homoseme* and *synonym* are therefore nonsynonymous by virtue of their nonhomonymy alone.

prompts the extraction of a schema allowing them to be referred to collectively. At the phonological pole this schema is almost vacuous, essentially specified only as "some dependent structure."

A category is **coherent** to the extent that its members are densely linked by well-entrenched categorizing relationships of minimal distance. An example is the network for *tree* depicted in Fig. 10.3(b). In a strongly coherent category, the activation of a particular node facilitates the secondary activation of its neighbors, especially any prototype or salient schema that categorizes it. It is therefore activated as a *representative* of the category, not as an isolated or autonomous cognitive event. If I observe a palm and refer to it as a *tree*, the symbolic unit [[PALM]/[tree]] functions as the active node of the *tree* category for coding purposes. Normally this elicits the coactivation of the categorizing unit [[[TREE]/[tree]]--→[[PALM]/[tree]]], i.e. I construe the conceived entity with reference to the category prototype.

The coherence of a category is naturally a matter of degree, and within a broad, loosely integrated category there may be subcategories of greater internal cohesion. *Tree* is quite cohesive when limited to the network of Fig. 10.3(b), but it is considerably less so when this network is expanded to include metaphorical extensions (e.g. *tree* for 'phrase marker'), if only because of their cognitive distance. As the coherence of a category decreases, the possibility of autonomous activation becomes more realistic. Thus it is possible for a speaker of English to mention *ear of corn* without invoking its vague functional resemblance to the body part, to call a celebrity a *star* without activating the notion of an astral body, and (perhaps) to use *tree* in the sense of 'phrase marker' without reference to its botanical motivation. To the extent that a semantic network with common symbolization approximates a coherent category, we can reasonably speak of a **lexical item**. Despite its convenience, however, this construct is more a descriptive fiction than a natural unit of linguistic organization. Not only is coherence inherently a matter of degree, but also the definition allows a single network to be divided into lexical items in multiple and mutually inconsistent ways. I regard this as a realistic characterization of the phenomena in question.

10.3.2. *Phonemes as Complex Categories*

There is precedent in traditional phonology for a usage-based approach to linguistic description. Theoreticians might balk at accepting a full schematic network as the meaning of *tree* (Fig. 10.3(b) is only a fragment), but it has long been accepted that a complete account of the sounds of a language cannot be limited to a list of phonemes: a phonological description must also cover allophonic variation and the factors that condition it, whether specified by lists or by rules of some generality. Linguists' dedication to the elucidation of allophonic detail has been diminished, in recent years, by the call of higher glories. Still, it is realized that a speaker's command of phonetic detail is part of his competence in a language and is properly included in a comprehensive description of its structure.

Phonemes and allophones are abstract entities. One cannot articulate a phoneme or allophone per se, but only a specific sound that has precise values for pertinent phonetic parameters. Even a low-level (i.e. maximally specific) allophone represents an abstraction from actual articulatory (and auditory) events, each of which is phonetically unique in absolute terms. An allophone is characterized at a level of schematicity that makes it compatible with any number of such events: variation along relevant parameters is confined to a particular range (possibly quite narrow), but is not pinned down exactly. Allophonic variation is largely induced by the surrounding phonological environment. At the extreme, it can be recognized that every environment determines a separate and unique allophone (though an analysis to this degree of delicacy has more theoretical than practical import). The emergence of a phoneme as a unified category is therefore a process of decontextualization. It involves the extraction of schemas (at different hierarchical levels) to represent the commonality of the sounds that occur in coherent classes of environments.[15]

Consider a restricted example: the acquisition of [pa], [ta], [ka], and [a]. The child does not first learn the individual segments [p], [t], [k], and [a] in isolation, proceeding only subsequently to effect their combination. He is exposed primarily to full syllables from the very beginning, and the separate occurrence of a nonsyllabic segment is at best atypical. We may thus hypothesize an initial set of phonological routines—articulatory and/or auditory— that are syllabic in scope and constitute the cognitive representation of [pa], [ta], [ka], and [a]. Each of these units is abstracted from a series of unique and specific phonetic events and is consequently schematic to a certain degree.

The mastery of these syllabic routines does not per se establish any connection among the vocalic nuclei of the four syllables. We may suppose, however, that individual segments are recognized at some level of cognitive organization, and that phonemes are coherent categories for the mature speaker. With reference to our limited example, how might a phoneme like /a/ be acquired? Observe that the four vocalic nuclei are distinct in their phonetic properties. Acoustically, the formant structure of [a] is more or less stable throughout its duration, but the nuclei of [pa], [ta], and [ka] arrive at this stable configuration through initial transitions that differ from one to the next. The articulatory and auditory correlates of these contrasts are incorporated in the child's cog-

[15] The reader will note a resemblance to Twaddell's (1935) distinction between "microphonemes," defined in reference to specific environments, and his more abstract "macrophonemes."

nitive representation of the syllabic nuclei, which thus involve four separate segment types: [a], [ᵖa], [ᵗa], and [ᵏa] (where superscripts indicate the transitions induced by preceding consonants).

Their relationship as allophones of a single phoneme consists in the emergence of a schematic network uniting them through schemas and categorizing judgments. One possible structure for such a network is sketched in Fig. 10.4.

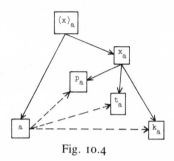

Fig. 10.4

Among the lowest-level structures, we might assume that [a] has special cognitive salience by virtue of its simplicity and frequency of occurrence, making it the category prototype. The allophones [ᵖa], [ᵗa], and [ᵏa] then constitute extensions (in more traditional terms, [a] is the "basic allophone" or "unmarked" form). The unit [ˣa] is schematic for these extensions and defines the class of postconsonantal allophones; it specifies the occurrence of an initial transition but leaves its precise character unspecified. The unit [⁽ˣ⁾a] is still more schematic, for it abstracts away from the difference between the presence and the absence of a transition. The phoneme /a/ is not identified in this model with either this topmost schema or the prototype [a]; it is equated with the entire schematic network.

Given a substantial array of low-level allophones, each localized to a particular environment, there are numerous alternative ways of grouping them into phonetically natural subclasses. A particular grouping is effected by the extraction of a schema at the appropriate level of specificity; for realistic cases we can envisage the emergence of intricate schematic networks, where hierarchies of schemas classify the allophonic variants into overlapping and crosscutting subgroups. Consider a language where /k/ occurs with each of the vowels /i e a o u/ in both pre- and postvocalic position within a syllable. This alone gives us ten low-level allophones of /k/ that we can represent as [kⁱ], [ⁱk], [kᵉ], [ᵉk], etc. For the prevocalic allophones, a subschema grouping [kⁱ] and [kᵉ] is not unreasonable, nor is one grouping [kᵃ], [kᵒ], and [kᵘ]. A crosscutting classification based on rounding instead of the front/back dimension would class together [kⁱ], [kᵉ], and [kᵃ] on the one hand, [kᵒ] and [kᵘ] on the other. A parallel array of schemas and subgroups can be posited for the postvocalic allophones. A further range of categorizations abstracts away from the difference between the pre- and postvocalic variants that occur with a given vowel or class of vowels. We can posit a schema that neutralizes the difference between [kⁱ] and [ⁱk], for example, or one that characterizes the allophones that occur adjacent to a rounded vowel.

It is not at all implausible that a speaker's cognitive representation of a phonemic category might incorporate a substantial number of schemas and intersecting subclasses of this sort. Of course a schema need not be extracted for every subgroup with potential phonetic motivation, and those that are extracted vary in entrenchment and cognitive salience. The emergence of a particular subclass is no doubt facilitated by the parallel behavior of its member allophones, which encourages the speaker to assess them in relation to one another and to extract a schema for their collective reference in characterizing the behavior.[16] It cannot be assumed that every phonemic network is dominated by a single "superschema" that is straightforwardly elaborated by all the member allophones. A superschema is easily contemplated for our simplified examples of /a/ and /k/, but consider a case like English /t/, one of whose allophones is a glottal stop (e.g. in *sentence, kitten,* or even *glottal* and *bottle* in some dialects). The schema subsuming glottal stops as well as the other allophones cannot impose any restrictions on the point of articulation. This schema thus characterizes the superordinate category of voiceless stops, not the phoneme /t/ in particular.

Let us turn now to syntagmatic relationships. The simplest example is a bisegmental sequence, e.g. the morpheme *pa.* How do we describe its phonological composition? The normal approach is to specify the phoneme sequence /p/-/a/ in the lexicon, as all that the grammar has to say about the phonological shape of this morpheme per se; the specification of its phonetic detail is left to the operation of general phonological rules. In our usage-based model, however, the motivation of phonetic detail by schemas describing regular phonological patterns does not entail its removal from the characterization of individual instantiations. Moreover, it is not immediately clear what constitutes a phoneme sequence when a phoneme is analyzed as a complex category and represented in the form of a schematic network.

The traditional approach separates distinctive, unpredictable, and idiosyncratic phonological properties of a lexical item from those that follow from more general statements, and describes these sets of properties in different components of the grammar (lexicon vs. phonology). I argue against this compartmentalization on several grounds. There is first the problem of forms

---

[16] For example, a schema grouping [tⁱ] and [ⁱt] could be extracted on the basis of their common palatalization to [č] under certain conditions. A schema for the category permits a unified characterization of the two extensions.

that violate the predictions of general rules. Special devices (e.g. exception features) can always be invented to handle such discrepancies, but the problem does not arise at all in a nonconstructive, usage-based account, where specific forms with unit status are listed in addition to sanctioning schemas. Moreover, the rationale for separating general from idiosyncratic properties rests ultimately on the exclusionary fallacy, the rule/list fallacy in particular (see Ch. 1). Phonetic details are no less properties of an individual morpheme by virtue of conforming to general patterns: such features are simply motivated within the system, being supported by corresponding features of other expressions and by the schema that unites them. Finally, the program of separating regularity from idiosyncrasy leads to incoherence when pushed to its logical conclusion. A linguistic structure is an integrated system, not a set of atomistic elements sortable into arbitrary packages. If all the regularity is factored out of a linguistic structure, the residue is seldom if ever recognizable as a coherent entity plausibly attributed cognitive autonomy. The phoneme sequence /pa/, for example, is not confined to wholly idiosyncratic specifications, for it is a regular instantiation of the CV (consonant-vowel) pattern of syllabic organization. If we factor out this regularity by abstracting away from the consonantal character of /p/ and the vocalic character of /a/, we are left with isolated features (e.g. [LABIAL] and [BACK]) that have no import except as facets of integrated consonantal or vocalic segments (cf. 1.1.4.4).

To the extent that a speaker has mastered the pronunciation (or audition) of *pa* as an established unit, we must posit as part of his linguistic competence the precise articulatory (auditory) routine that defines its detailed phonetic properties. Thus, if [p^a] is the specific, low-level allophone of /p/ that occurs before /a/, and [^{p}a] the low-level allophone of /a/ that occurs after /p/, the composite structure [[p^a]-[^{p}a]] represents the speaker's knowledge of the actual phonetic shape of the morpheme. Each of the segments, [p^a] and [^{p}a], is an extension and/or specialization with respect to other elements in the complex category that constitutes its respective phoneme. The phonetic properties that set them apart from other allophones are induced by the very fact of their integration, and reflect the mutual **accommodation** that permits their coordination as a smooth, well-entrenched routine. In short, [[p^a]-[^{p}a]] is an integrated system, and—if our analysis is sufficiently delicate—the components [p^a] and [^{p}a] occur as such only within the confines of this system.

The situation is depicted in Fig. 10.5. Each of the component structures, [p^a] and [^{p}a], is a context-induced allophone representing an elaborate schematic network that defines its respective phoneme. These networks are indicated by circles; only a few of the associated nodes and categorizing relationships are shown explicitly. As the category representatives that participate directly in the syntagmatic relationship, [p^a] and [^{p}a] are the active nodes of

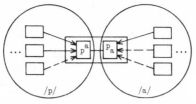

Fig. 10.5

the networks with respect to the relationship. Since phonemes are highly coherent categories, the activation of $[[p^a]-[^pa]]$ has extensive ramifications in both phonemic networks. The activation of $[^pa]$, for example, elicits that of categorizing relationships such as $[[a]-->[^pa]]$ and $[[^xa]\rightarrow[^pa]]$, possibly even chains of relationships like $[[^{(x)}a]\rightarrow[^xa]\rightarrow[^pa]]$ (cf. Fig. 10.4). The secondarily activated nodes and relationships contribute to the phonological value of the expression. They constitute its **structural description**, i.e. they specify the nature of its **systemic motivation**.

The articulation (also the audition) of *pa* is a well-rehearsed routine for any fluent speaker of English; $[[p^a]-[^pa]]$ is therefore a conventional unit, i.e. one of the cognitive entities to be accommodated in a comprehensive linguistic description. In a sufficiently delicate analysis, we can interpret this unit as a low-level structure capable of actual peripheral implementation: it represents the speaker's ability to direct the motor (or sensory) activities that constitute a successful articulation (audition) of the form. However, the inclusion of $[[p^a]-[^pa]]$ in the grammar does not rule out the possibility that more abstract characterizations of *pa* might also be included: the cognitive representation of a phonological sequence need not be unique. The existence of multiple characterizations is in fact quite plausible. When $[p^a]$ and $[^pa]$ occur, they do so as representatives of complex categories, and elicit the secondary activation of other, more salient structures within these categories. It is quite conceivable, then, that the coordination of $[p^a]$ and $[^pa]$ to form a low-level representation of *pa* is accompanied by the emergence of additional representations based on schemas and prototypes from their respective categories, e.g. $[[p^{(x)}]-[^{(x)}a]]$. Such a structure would not itself be subject to peripheral implementation, but for certain purposes it might have greater cognitive salience than $[[p^a]-[^pa]]$.

The type of analysis proposed is quite foreign to contemporary linguistic thought: a phoneme is not regarded as a unitary entity, but rather as a complex category; instead of rules and representations, one speaks of schematic networks and categorizing relationships. This model does not, however, deny the valid insights of more traditional approaches. In particular, it readily accommodates the generalizations expressed in such approaches by phonological rules. How does it accomplish this in the specific case of allophonic variation?

Where are the "detail rules" that capture regularities in the phonetic manifestation of phonemes?

Rules of this sort are inherent to schematic networks. In a nonconstructive model that avoids the insidious process metaphor, the categorizing relationships that organize schematic networks reveal themselves as statements of the very patterns and regularities that phonological rules are devised to accommodate. With reference to Figs. 10.4 and 10.5, the context-induced extension [[a]-->[ᴾa]] is equivalent to a rule that takes the basic allophone [a] as input and applies (in the appropriate environment) to give [ᴾa] as its output. More dramatically, the glottal stop occurring before [n̩] in *kitten, sentence, button,* etc. is categorized as an extension from more central nodes in the network for /t/; the categorizing relationship is equivalent to a rule reducing /t/ to a glottal stop in this context. Rules affecting natural classes of phonemes are simply schemas extracted from the categorizing relationships in the networks of individual phonemes. Suppose, for instance, that /p/, /t/, and /k/ all merge to a glottal stop in a certain environment; [ʔ] is thus an allophone of each of these phonemes. A speaker who grasps the commonality of the individual categorizing relationships [[p]-->[ʔ]], [[t]-->[ʔ]], and [[k]-->[ʔ]] does so by extracting the schema [[T]-->[ʔ]] (where [T] is the schema for voiceless stops). We observe in this example a natural but essential feature of the framework: categorizing relationships can themselves function as standard and target in higher-order categorizations, e.g. [[[T]-->[ʔ]]→[[p]-->[ʔ]]].

10.3.3. *Morpheme Variants*

Like its semantic counterpart, the phonological pole of a lexical item is analyzed as a complex category. A typical expression has numerous **phonological variants**, linked by categorizing relationships to form a schematic network. Although the existence of allomorphic variants is hardly revealed here for the first time, it is natural in the present framework to construe the notion quite broadly. Allomorphic variation is both extensive and ubiquitous when conceived in this fashion.

We can reasonably posit a network even for seemingly invariant morphemes like *tree* and *pa.* For one thing, a single pronunciation may have multiple cognitive representations, at different levels of abstraction. It was suggested above that a familiar form like *pa* is represented not only as a fully specific, low-level structure capable of peripheral implementation (i.e. an auditory/ articulatory routine), but also more schematically in structures that may well have greater cognitive salience despite their confinement to autonomous processing.[17] We can further assume that the phonetic variants associated with

---

[17] We might speculate that the linguist's description of *pa* as a simple phoneme sequence (/pa/) has a cognitive analog, most likely a representation involving the basic-level category prototypes for /p/ and /a/.

different tempos and registers are commonly mastered by speakers as well-entrenched routines, bringing them within the purview of a grammar. The fast-speech rendition of *tree*, for instance, constitutes an extension vis-à-vis its careful pronunciation. The partially conflicting properties of these variants reflect the temporal compression of the fast-speech form, as well as the phonetic adjustments that ensue (e.g. the affrication of *tr*).

More obvious are variants involving different phonemic compositions, as exemplified by the alternate pronunciations of words like *economics*, *route*, *tomato*, *either*, *aunt*, and *pa*. Most of these are lectal variants, but it is not uncommon for a single speaker to employ alternate forms more or less interchangeably (as I do for *route* when used as a noun); in any case a speaker's familiarity with different lects is a significant aspect of his linguistic ability (cf. Bailey 1973). The close resemblance of the variants makes their comparison inevitable. The result is a minimal phonological network, where they are linked by a categorizing relationship (e.g. [[rawt] ←–→ [rut]] for *route*).

The more traditional conception of allomorphy is restricted to variation conditioned by syntagmatic relationships. A convenient example is *leaves*, whose composition is sketched in Fig. 10.6. Even ignoring subphonemic variation, the phonological pole of each component morpheme must be given as a

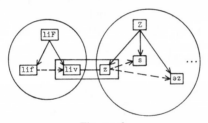

Fig. 10.6

network. The major allomorphs of *leaf* are [lif] and [liv]. The former is analyzed as the basic allomorph (since it occurs in uninflected forms), and the latter as an extension. Presumably they instantiate the schema [liF], where [F] neutralizes the voicing distinction between [f] and [v].[18] For the plural morpheme, [s] and [əz] are depicted as extensions from [z]; [Z] is a schema that subsumes these three variants—it specifies an alveolar fricative, but is neutral with respect to voicing and the option of a preceding schwa. (The remaining allomorphs are omitted.) Note the similarity to Fig. 10.5. Though we are dealing here with morphemes rather than phonemes, the integration of two complex categories is once again effected through specific, mutually compatible representatives: [liv] and [z] constitute the active nodes of their respec-

---

[18] [F] is thus equivalent to an "archiphoneme" or "morphophoneme," which are simply schemas in the present framework.

tive networks with respect to this particular construction. The primary activation of these nodes elicits the secondary activation of others. Thus, when [liv] occurs in [[liv]-[z]], it is analyzed as an extension from [lif] and an elaboration of [liF]; the categorizing relationships [[lif]--→[liv]] and [[liF]→[liv]] constitute its structural description. Also, at the segmental level, [v] elaborates [F] and is extended from [f]—hence its phonemic and morphophonemic status is different from that of other occurrences of the sound. It must be borne in mind that Fig. 10.6 shows only the phonological pole of what is really a bipolar construction; the full construction further identifies [liv] as the symbolic correspondent of [LEAF], and [z] as the correspondent of [PL]. In the possessive construction, different active nodes are specified at the phonological pole: [[lif]-[s]].

With respect to the schematic networks of individual phonemes, it was observed that categorizing relationships are equivalent to phonological rules specifying phonetic detail in particular environments, and that schemas express the regularities in such relationships across natural classes of phonemes. The same is true at the morphemic level, except that the rules are "morphophonemic" rather than phonetic. In Fig. 10.6, for example, the categorizing relationship [[lif]--→[liv]] can be interpreted (in process terminology) as a statement to the effect that [lif] "changes" to [liv] when it combines with the plural [z]. A number of other nouns behave in parallel fashion (*elf, scarf, knife, hoof, wife, sheaf, life,* etc.), and for each of them the grammar of English contains a bipolar construction directly analogous to the one posited for *leaf*. From these a speaker presumably extracts a schematic construction that differs from the individual constructions only in that the stem is schematic rather than specific: its semantic pole designates a bounded region (not further identified), and its phonological pole specifies [...v], further identified as an extension from [...f]. This schematic categorizing relationship [[...f]--→[...v]] is equivalent to a morphological rule deriving the combining allomorphs from their basic forms in the appropriate morphological environment.

10.3.4. *Coherence and Differentiation*

Each pole of a lexical item has been characterized as a coherent complex category. A category achieves coherence to the extent that its defining nodes are densely associated through categorizing relationships of minimal cognitive distance. At the center of such a network, and contributing greatly to its coherence, we commonly find a node of special prominence and cognitive significance: the overall category prototype (e.g. [TREE] in Fig. 10.3(b)). This node functions as the starting point for the category's acquisition, as its default-case representative, and as the standard for a large number of categorizing relationships.

At its simplest, the symbolic relationship between the networks at the two poles is effectively global: any node of one can be coactivated with any node of the other to produce a conventionally sanctioned variant of the lexical item. (We do not, for example, find that the fast-speech rendition of *tree* indicates a pine in particular, or that more-schematic representations of its phonological shape correspond to more-schematic construals of its meaning.) However, we cannot assume that every individual symbolic pairing between a semantic and a phonological node has the status of a unit in its own right—there are too many combinations, and in any event a speaker can immediately apply any phonological variant to a novel semantic construal (e.g. an innovative metaphorical extension). I suggest, instead, that the global symbolic relationship between two complex categories resides in an indeterminate number of local relationships, primarily involving highly salient nodes at one pole or the other. These local symbolic associations, together with the associations established through categorizing relationships at either pole, assure the ready availability of a derivative symbolic relationship between any pair of nodes (cf. Ch. 11).

This notion is quite plausible developmentally. When a term undergoes semantic extension, there is no reason for the learner to compute the symbolic relationship between the new sense of the lexical item and every phonological variant he presently controls. The only symbolic pairings he invokes are those that associate the new semantic variant with phonological structures implicated in the requisite usage event: the active node of the phonological network with respect to the usage event, and other nodes activated secondarily. Salient nodes are the most susceptible to secondary activation, and over a number of usage events the category prototype may be the only structure to participate consistently in the symbolic pairing. In the resulting network, consequently, the most deeply entrenched of the newly established symbolic relationships may well be the one that associates the new sense with the phonological category prototype.

Similarly, in the acquisition of a new phonological variant, the learner has no reason to compute its symbolic relationship with every previously mastered sense of the lexical item. The variant will tend instead to form local symbolic pairings with highly salient nodes in the semantic network, and with the active nodes in the relevant usage events.

Matters are more complicated when the categories are less coherent. Often a network divides naturally into subregions, each centered on a node of considerable local prominence, between which there are comparatively few (and more-distant) categorizing relationships. To the extent that a network is thus differentiated, it can be expected to participate less globally in external relations (both symbolic and syntagmatic): such relations are first established with respect to individual nodes, and extend to closely associated nodes in largely automatic fashion, but the lesser density and greater distance of associations between subregions tend to inhibit their spread from one subregion to another. A subregion is therefore capable of behavioral autonomy, which is one of the factors that leads us to posit separate lexical items.

As an example of behavioral autonomy, consider the verb *fly*. In most of its uses, the past-tense form is *flew*, as illustrated in (3)(a)–(c).

(3)(a) *A bird just flew in the window.*
   (b) *Our plane flew high above the clouds.*
   (c) *My neighbor flew to Norway last Sunday.*
   (d) *McReynolds flied to right field in the second inning.*

The senses implied by the conventional usages of (a)–(c) are quite similar (in each instance the trajector moves swiftly through the air) and thus constitute a reasonably coherent category. The usage of (3)(d) is no less conventional in the context of baseball, but here there is a notable meaning shift: it is not the trajector (i.e. subject) that moves through the air, but rather a baseball that the trajector propels by hitting it with a bat.[19] The distance and special domain of this extended semantic value set it apart as a distinguishable subregion in the network of *fly*. Because of its peripheral status, the resulting lexical variant has substantial potential for distinct behavior. This potential is realized (for most speakers) in its selection of the regular pattern of past-tense formation, as opposed to the ablaut pattern associated with the central variants.

Since well-delineated subregions within a network are capable of divergent behavior, separate specifications are implied when they do in fact behave alike. A convenient illustration is *route*, which displays a differentiated network at both poles. At the semantic pole, its nominal and verbal senses constitute subregions that are clearly distinct in view of their contrasting profiles.[20] At the phonological pole, major subregions are established by the alternate pronunciations [rawt] and [rut], representing different phoneme sequences. In my own speech, either pronunciation can be used with the nominal senses, as in (4)(a), but only [rawt] is possible when *route* is employed as a verb; [rut] is thus precluded in (4)(b):

(4)(a) *Which route did he take?*
   (b) *Where did they route it?*

Symbolic correspondences have therefore been established between the phonological subregion for [rawt] and each of the two semantic subregions, but

---

[19] There are further specifications, e.g. that the ball is caught (or catchable) for an out. Despite the distance of the extension and the special behavior of the lexical variant it defines, one cannot plausibly maintain that speakers establish no association between this sense of *fly* and the others.

[20] For many scholars, the noun/verb distinction is sufficient to establish two separate lexical items. Though this criterion is not unreasonable, I have suggested that category coherence is a matter of degree, so that the segmentation of networks into discrete lexical items is bound to involve a measure of arbitrariness.

[rut] is associated symbolically only with the subregion defined by the nominal senses. For a speaker who allows either pronunciation regardless of semantic value, we must posit four symbolic relationships, to accommodate all four combinations of subregions at the two poles. The acceptability of all possible symbolic pairings between subregions is not automatically given, but requires specific acquisitional developments each resulting in a distinct symbolic association.[21]

Lexical differentiation is sometimes systematic, and a matter of considerable structural significance. A case in point is a widespread pattern of sound-symbolic consonantal alternations found in the Yuman languages, and reconstructed by Langdon (1971) for Proto Yuman. The following examples from Ipai (Northern Diegueño) are typical:

(5)(a) *čəkuLk* '(large) hole through something'
   (b) *čəkulk* 'small hole through something'

(6)(a) *LapəLap* 'to be (large and) flat'
   (b) *lapəlap* 'to be small and flat'

(7)(a) *xəkaL* 'to have a gap in a row' [e.g. missing tooth]
   (b) *xəkal* 'to have a small gap in a row'

Whether we analyze the members of each pair as related lexical items or as variants of the same lexical item, it is obvious that speakers must at some level (perhaps even conscious awareness) perceive their strong resemblance at both poles. Taking (5) as our example, we can therefore posit the semantic and phonological networks shown in Fig. 10.7(a).[22]

The phonemic contrast between [čəkuLk] and [čəkulk] divides the phonological network naturally into two subregions, indicated by ellipses. There is parallel differentiation at the semantic pole, with [SMALL HOLE] in particular set off as a subregion demanding special symbolization (i.e. [[SMALL HOLE]/[čəkulk]] is the marked form). While the distance between [SMALL HOLE] and the other semantic nodes is not very great, the pervasiveness in Ipai of sound-symbolic alternations based on size ensures the cognitive salience of the 'small/not small' contrast. The resulting prominence enables a node like [SMALL HOLE] to function as the locus of a coherent subregion.

The examples in (5)–(7) represent a semiproductive pattern that is manifested in many other contrasting expressions. The speaker of Ipai captures this regularity by extracting the schema depicted in Fig. 10.7(b). Instantiating this schema is the structure in diagram (a), as well as many other contrasting pairs with unit status. The schema is further available to sanction innovative pairs

---

[21] There are certain similarities here to stratificational grammar, which has long been concerned with the complexities of symbolic relationships (cf. Makkai 1969).

[22] The actual networks are presumed to be vastly more complex (e.g. at the phonological pole they include contextual variants and representations at different levels of schematicity). The diagram abstracts away from all but a minimal number of prominent nodes.

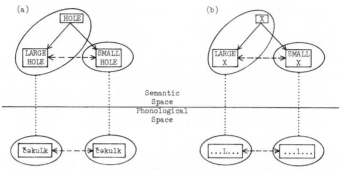

Fig. 10.7

of expressions that display the same opposition. It is functionally equivalent to a "lexical redundancy rule" (cf. Jackendoff 1975), though in our non-constructive model it differs from other sorts of rules only in the type of structure it schematizes. To the extent that parallel schemas emerge for other sound-symbolic phoneme pairs, they are subsumed under a higher-order schema that expresses the broader generalization. In fact, an elaborate schematic network may develop to accommodate the many patterns and subpatterns and their interrelationships.

Let us conclude by considering briefly the morphemic analysis of sound-symbolic forms. It seems apparent that the [l] of [čəkulk] symbolizes in some fashion the small size of the designated hole. I will assume as well that English [ɪ] has diminutive force in words like *flit*, despite the absence of opposing forms with another vowel (cf. Langacker 1973a, p. 26). How are these symbolic relationships to be expressed in a linguistic description? Observe that the answer is not at all obvious in terms of classic morphemic analysis. If the [l] of [čəkulk] or the [ɪ] of [flɪt] is segmented as a morpheme, the result is in each case a discontinuous residue that does not itself have morphemic status: [čəku...k], [fl...t].[23]

The present framework allows us to capture sound-symbolic relationships without resorting to such dubious constructs. In particular, they can be accommodated by categorizing relationships in the schematic plane, as opposed to composition in the syntagmatic plane (though these are not fully distinct—cf. Ch. 12). Note that Fig. 10.7(b) contains a symbolic unit, [[SMALL X]/ [...l...]], that expresses precisely the symbolic correspondence in question. This is not a morpheme in the standard sense, but rather a schema extracted to represent the commonality of examples like (b) in (5)–(7). To the extent that speakers of English associate the sound [ɪ] with diminutive force in certain forms, we can posit a similar schema [[...DIM...]/[...ɪ...]], which cate-

[23] A process morpheme changing [L] to [l] might be posited for the Ipai examples, but this will not work for *flit*, which has no nondiminutive counterpart.

gorizes just these forms (not every form with [ɪ]). Given the categorizing relationships [[[SMALL X]/[...l...]]→[[SMALL HOLE]/[čəkulk]]] and [[[...DIM...]/[...ɪ...]]→[[FLIT]/[flɪt]]], the sound-symbolic value of [l] and [ɪ] is specified without imposing an unworkable morphemic segmentation on [čəkulk] or [flɪt]: whenever the expressions are used, they are capable of eliciting the secondary activation of the schemas as part of their structural description. The diminutive value of [l] and [ɪ] is thus attributed to systemic motivation rather than morphemic composition.

10.4. Context

All linguistic units are context-dependent. They occur in particular settings, from which they derive much of their import, and are recognized by speakers as distinct entities only through a process of abstraction. How far this abstraction proceeds for a given unit depends on (1) the variety of its settings, which determines the level of specificity at which its context is characterized; and (2) how consistently it appears in these settings, which determines their centrality to its value. Rather than context-dependency, it is this process of partial **decontextualization** that requires explication.

Several different types of context must be recognized. One is the **systemic context**, i.e. the position of a linguistic unit within the schematic networks that collectively constitute the grammar of a language. Another is the **situational context**: the pragmatic circumstances (centered on the speech-act participants) that give rise to a particular usage event. Yet a third is the **syntagmatic context**, pertaining to the combination of units in the formation of complex expressions. All of these are crucial to a viable conception of linguistic structure.

10.4.1. *Systemic and Situational Context*

Systemic and situational context are most profitably discussed with reference to coding: the relation between conventional units and an actual usage event. Coding reduces to a set of categorizing judgments, each with a conventional unit as its standard and some facet of the usage event as its target (cf. Figs. 2.1, 2.2, and 2.5). A usage event derives much of its value from the systemic context, i.e. its categorization by conventional units. Conversely, these units are acquired, maintained, and modified through usage, and aspects of the situational context are reflected in their internal structure.

Systemic context requires only brief summary at this juncture (cf. Ch. 11). The interpretation and conventionality of a usage event depend on the particular array of conventional units relative to which it is assessed. The units selected for the primary categorization of a usage event are referred to as the active nodes of the linguistic system with respect to this event; each effects the categorization of a different facet of its structure, which is recognized as conventional (i.e. well formed) provided that the categorizing relationship is one of full (as opposed to partial) schematicity. Since the active nodes are embedded in various schematic networks, their activation has broader systemic ramifications, eliciting the secondary activation of categorizing units linking them to other nodes. The full set of nodes and relationships activated in this manner constitute the structural description attributed to the usage event, and collectively represent an assessment of its status vis-à-vis established convention.

Consider the audition of *pa*, and specifically the recognition of its vowel, assuming the partial schematic network of Fig. 10.4. The actual auditory input corresponding to the vocalic nucleus is a unique event, more specific in its phonetic properties than any conventional unit. Assuming a reasonably accurate pronunciation, however, it closely resembles the conventional post-/p/ allophone [ᴾa], so we can symbolize it as (ᴾa'). Barring special circumstances—for instance a strong expectation by the hearer that some other syllable is going to be uttered instead—[ᴾa] is most likely selected as the active node in the coding process; (ᴾa') is thus sanctioned either as a well-formed instance of the linguistic category [ᴾa] through the elaborative judgment ([ᴾa]→(ᴾa')), or else as a "deviant" (nonconventional) instance through the extension ([ᴾa]--→(ᴾa')). When [ᴾa] is activated in this sanctioning role, it facilitates the coactivation of such categorizing relationships as [[a]--→[ᴾa]], [[ˣa]→[ᴾa]], and [[⁽ˣ⁾a]→[ˣa]→[ᴾa]]; [ᴾa] thus occurs as the representative of a complex category (the phoneme /a/), and the full set of activated nodes and relationships constitute its structural description.

Every coding decision has an impact on the linguistic system that is important in a theoretical sense, even if particular instances are negligible in practical terms. Let $[A]$ be an active node, (e_1) some facet of a usage event, and $([A]--→(e_1))$ a sanctioning relationship of either full or partial schematicity. The occurrence of $([A]--→(e_1))$ has a number of consequences. For one thing, it reinforces the unit status of $[A]$, and of all the additional conventional units that are activated secondarily. Moreover, its occurrence represents the initial step in the possible conventionalization of $([A]--→(e_1))$ itself. How far this process proceeds depends on whether $([A]--→(e_1))$ recurs sufficiently often to acquire the status of a unit for a given speaker, and whether such entrenchment takes place for a substantial proportion of the speech community. To the extent that these conditions are met, the categorization is incorporated in the linguistic system and characterizes one small aspect of established convention.

Actually, $([A]--→(e_1))$ cannot per se become a conventional unit if (e_1) is understood to be some facet of a usage event, in all its specificity and idiosyncratic detail: both (e_1) and $([A]--→(e_1))$ are unique occurrences. Conventionalization is however possible given a number of usage events that are similar in many respects. From a sequence of parallel structures [(e_1), (e_2), (e_3), ..., (e_n)], each participating in a categorizing relationship of the form $([A]--\rightarrow(e_i))$, a speaker is capable of extracting the low-level schema [E] to represent their commonality. It is then the categorizing structure $[[A]--\rightarrow[E]]$ that is incorporated in the grammar as a conventional unit.

Each structure (e_i) occurs in a specific and highly elaborate situational context that includes the circumstances of the speech event itself. As a schematic representation, [E] abstracts away from much of this detail and specificity, but the extent of this abstraction depends on the diversity of its instantiations. Presumably a speaker extracts the lowest-level schema compatible with all of the structures (e_i) on which it is based. That is, he most easily arrives at a characterization describing the instantiations with maximal specificity and contextual inclusiveness. It is only by a process of **cancellation**—due to the absence of a specification in certain instantiations, or the presence of conflicting specifications—that the speaker excludes a property from his schematic representation.[24]

By and large, the more intrinsic a property is the more likely it is to survive the cancellation process. If [E] is a variant pronunciation, e.g. [ant] (rather than [ænt]) for *aunt*, the quality of the vowel is a maximally intrinsic property, and its [a]-like character is apparent in every event (e_i) supporting the extraction of this schema. Other, more extrinsic facets of the situational context vary from one usage event to the next and are therefore subject to cancellation: the words contained in the previous sentence, the age of the aunt referred to, the specific identity of the speaker, how far the speaker is standing from the hearer, the time of day, etc. Similarly, the extended value of *fly* pertaining to baseball (roughly, 'hit a catchable ball in the air') is given by a schema that abstracts away from extrinsic and variable factors such as the inning in which the event occurs, who the batter is, how heavy a bat he is using, where the game is being played, the city in which the speech event takes place, and so on indefinitely.

Nevertheless, detailed aspects of the situational context are often constant across the relevant set of usage events, and even highly extrinsic properties are capable of surviving the abstraction process to be incorporated in a conventional unit. The term *steed* designates a horse, for instance, but makes obligatory reference to its role in an extrinsic relationship, namely that of bearing a rider. The contrast between *murder* and *assassinate* does not pertain to the intrinsic characteristics of the designated process, but rather to highly extrinsic factors: the motives of the agent, and the social or political status of the

---

[24] Obviously this oversimplifies matters. For one thing, speakers may be predisposed to focus on certain traits at the expense of others. They can also "learn how to learn." Having previously acquired numerous linguistic categories, a speaker may estimate the nature and degree of abstraction most likely required for a new one.

patient. Moreover, despite the cancellations noted above, the verb *fly* as applied to baseball inherits a substantial, and in certain respects quite specific, representation of its supporting situational contexts. Included in this representation is the notion of a batter swinging with a bat at the ball hurled by a pitcher; the notion of a playing field with fielders capable of catching a ball hit in the air; the notion of an out (presupposing some knowledge of the rules and objectives of baseball); and so forth. In short, they constitute the domain required to characterize the profiled process.

Most linguistic units do not pertain directly to the speech event or its participants, and their relationship to **ground** elements (in the sense of 3.3.2.3) is consequently both extrinsic and noncentral to their value. There is nothing, for example, in the meaning of *tree* that saliently evokes the speech-act participants or attributes to them any specific properties; there is no constancy to this facet of its situational context that would lead the language learner to accord it any prominence in the value of *tree*, which represents the ground—if it does at all—only in the most schematic terms.[25] Some units do however make salient reference to ground elements, including many whose content would appear to have no inherent connection to the speech event. In cases such as these, reference to the ground is central to some degree despite its extrinsic nature (cf. 4.2.2). Moreover, certain properties of ground elements are more or less constant across usage events and thus escape the process of abstraction and cancellation that produces the units in question.

Suppose, for instance, that a phonological variant is observed only in the speech of one person; since its association with this speaker is constant over usage events, it can be incorporated as a prominent (though nonintrinsic) specification of the lexical unit.[26] More commonly, speakers attribute a variant pronunciation (e.g. [ant] for *aunt*) to a particular social or dialectal group; whether their attribution is accurate in this regard has no direct bearing on its inclusion in the cognitive representation of the form. In many languages, the social status of speech-act participants (or their relation to one another) has widespread structural significance, functioning as a central specification of numerous units that designate other entities. This is exemplified by a language like Tamil, where (to take just one example) the form *tuungu* not only means 'sleep' but also indicates that the speaker belongs to the Brahmin caste; *orangu* is used by non-Brahmins (Bright and Ramanujan 1964). Cases like these are unproblematic in the present framework because it adopts an en-

---

[25] I believe it is reasonable, for theoretical purposes, to analyze every linguistic unit as making some kind of reference to ground elements as part of its encyclopedic characterization, even if such reference is maximally peripheral and schematic. The very fact that a unit functions in a linguistic system and participates in the construal relationship (cf. 3.3.2.4) constitutes an aspect of its value (though admittedly a very minor one).

[26] The specification can even be conventional for a large speech community if the speaker with the variant pronunciation is well known. Consider *puddy tat* (a variant of *pussy cat*), associated primarily with a cartoon character.

cyclopedic account of meaning and further assumes that the schematization required in the formation of conventional units is characterized by the maximal retention of the shared situational context. Even a wholly extrinsic property like the relative social status of the speaker and hearer can be learned as part of the meaning of an expression provided that it is consistently present in the situational context for this expression across usage events.

10.4.2. *Syntagmatic Context*

In regard to syntagmatic context, a primary concern is the mutual **accommodation** that often characterizes the integration of two semantic or phonological structures. Questions of distribution must be considered, since a variant induced by a particular environment is sometimes confined to this context. A further problem that arises is the scope of a context-restricted variant: to what extent can such a variant be distinguished from the context that induces it?

Semantic accommodation occurs whenever an expression that originally violates a selectional restriction comes to be used conventionally with no sense of semantic anomaly and is thus interpreted as being compositional. Consider, once again, two conventional uses of the verb *fly*:

(8)(a) *A raven flew over my house.*
   (b) *Jets fly above the clouds.*

Developmentally (also historically), we can assume that *fly* is originally predicated of birds. This original process predication, [FLY], thus characterizes its trajector schematically as a bird or birdlike creature, and specifies that this trajector propels itself through the air by flapping its wings. What happens when *fly* is now used to describe the motion of inanimate objects like airplanes? If the verb is used without modification in its original sense, the result is a violation of selectional restrictions: the trajector of [FLY] is placed in correspondence with the profile of a subject nominal having conflicting specifications. Rather than dwell on this anomaly, however, the language user tends to interpret the component structures in such a way that the overall expression is compositional and semantically well formed. In the present example, *fly* accommodates to the new type of subject nominal via the semantic extension ([FLY]$--\rightarrow$(FLY$'$)), where (FLY$'$) designates the flight of a self-propelled machine by means other than wing-flapping. The categorizing relationship [[FLY]$--\rightarrow$[FLY$'$]] is therefore part of the semantic network of *fly* in the linguistic system of a mature speaker.

Phonological accommodation is exemplified by any type of assimilation, for instance the palatalization of [n] to [ñ] before [i], or the low-level phonetic adjustments considered earlier. The superscripts in formulas like [[p^a]-[^{p}a]] indicate those respects (perhaps quite minor) in which each segment accommodates to its neighbor in the formation of a smoothly coordinated articula-

tory (and auditory) routine. Whether an assimilated variant can occur outside
the environment that induces it depends on the delicacy of our analysis. If we
simply state that [[n]—→[ñ]] before [i], identifying the segments in fairly
schematic terms, we can say that the variant is capable of occurring outside
the specified environment; [ñ] is often a separate phoneme that can occur with
any type of vowel. If the segments are characterized in very precise detail,
however, the assimilated variants are most likely confined to the specific syntagmatic combination that induces them. Asked to pronounce the vowel of *pa*
in isolation, a speaker of English will almost certainly produce [a] instead of
[ᴾa]: the formant structure will be steady throughout, and will not display the
particular formant transition brought about by the tautosyllabic stop. We are
dealing with a level of phonetic detail too fine to be readily noticed by speakers or independently controlled.

The status of [ᴾa] as a separate segment therefore represents a kind of abstraction. Unlike [a], which stands alone as a full syllable, [ᴾa] only occurs as
such in combination with [pᵃ] (and conversely). Fig. 10.4 is consequently
misleading if the boxes around [ᴾa], [ᵗa], and [ᵏa] are interpreted as indicating
that these are self-contained cognitive routines that can be implemented by
themselves in the fashion of [a]. The legitimacy of this segmentation for analytical purposes is not in question, and speakers no doubt arrive at schematic
characterizations of these sounds (e.g. [⁽ˣ⁾a] in Fig. 10.4) that can be activated independently at autonomous levels of processing. However, if [ᴾa] etc.
are regarded as low-level structures capable of peripheral implementation, it
must be recognized that they do not themselves constitute separate routines
easily activated in isolation.

It is important, then, that we recognize the oversimplifications inherent in
diagrams like Fig. 10.4. A more elaborate representation of the same schematic network is offered in Fig. 10.8. Here the solid-line boxes are used for
self-contained cognitive routines that can be activated independently without
any difficulty. The low-level structures therefore correspond to the syllables *a*,
pa, *ta*, and *ka*; the component sounds of the latter three display mutual ac-

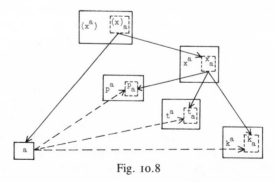

Fig. 10.8

commodation. Thus $[x^{a \ x}a]$ is schematic for *pa*, *ta*, and *ka*, and in turn is one instantiation (along with [a]) of the higher-level schema $[(x^a)^{(x)}a]$.

The arrows in Fig. 10.8 do not however represent the categorizing relationships that associate these complex units as integral wholes. Instead they show the more specific categorizations that hold between particular facets of these complex structures, those facets enclosed by the broken-line boxes. For example, it is not $[p^{a \ p}a]$ in its entirety that is depicted as an extension from [a], but rather the substructure $[^p a]$. The categorizing relationship holds between [a] and that portion of the larger structure that is deemed the **correspondent** of [a]. It is not required that this portion of $[p^{a \ p}a]$ be discrete or delineated with any great precision, nor that it be separable from the remainder; it is only necessary that speakers construe certain aspects of the complex structure as corresponding to the independently occurring [a] and constituting its context-induced variant.

Although structures like $[^p a]$, $[^\prime a]$, etc. can be counted as conventional units, and participate as such in categorizing relationships (e.g. $[[a]--\rightarrow[^p a]]$), an accurate description of linguistic organization will show them as integral facets of the more inclusive structures in which they invariably occur.[27] The schematic network given originally in Fig. 10.4 is therefore intact in Fig. 10.8, but the latter depicts its nodes as subsystems of the more elaborate, independently occurring units that provide their necessary context. These larger units represent syllables of a certain type and are themselves united in a schematic network (though the arrows have been suppressed). One such network thus occurs (node by node) within the scope of another.

This usage-based approach resolves certain problems without any special apparatus. For one thing, the restricted distribution of these allophones is automatically specified: to say that $[^p a]$ occurs after /p/ is just to say that $[p^{a \ p}a]$ is a conventional unit; to say that it occurs only after /p/ requires merely that one not posit—gratuitously and erroneously—a conventional unit where $[^p a]$ appears in some other environment. An accurate inventory of the conventional linguistic units of the language properly specifies the limited distribution without additional statements, or indeed, without any statements at all that refer to distribution per se.

A second problem pertains to phonological rules. It was noted in 10.3.2 that the categorizing relationships between nodes in the schematic network defining a phoneme are the functional equivalent of rules that specify its allophonic detail. For example, the relationship $[[a]--\rightarrow[^p a]]$ is effectively a rule that takes [a] as "input" and gives $[^p a]$ as "output" in the appropriate environment. How is this environment to be specified? The answer is immediately apparent from Fig. 10.8: $[^p a]$ is represented as a subsystem of $[p^{a \ p}a]$,

---

[27] Recall that a grammar is characterized as a **structured** inventory of conventional linguistic units: some units function as components (or subsystems) of others.

and is only activated as an integral facet of the activation of this larger structure. The "output" of the rule, [ᵖa], is defined as those facets of the complex structure that are construed as corresponding to the "input" [a]. The context for the rule can be identified as the remainder of the complex structure, i.e. as the complement of this correspondent. There is no need to assume that either the correspondent or its complement is amenable to independent activation, or that its delineation within the complex structure is discrete or precise.

What are the implications of these notions for the fundamental distinction between autonomous and dependent structures (cf. 8.3)? If [ᵖa] only occurs with [pᵃ], and conversely, to what extent can we speak of the former as being autonomous and the latter dependent? Are they not mutually dependent? And if so, how can we identify one as a vowel and the other as a consonant, since autonomy/dependence was taken as the basis for this distinction? Recall, however, that autonomy is not defined here in terms of independent occurrence. Thus a vowel is considered autonomous even in a language requiring CV as the minimal syllable, and a root or stem is autonomous even if it always takes an affix. Though it may, in the final analysis, be a matter of degree, a distinction is made between (1) one structure obligatorily *co-occurring* with another as an integral facet of a higher-order system; and (2) one structure *presupposing* another in the sense of being defined as an operation or function that maps it onto a target structure. The mutual dependence of [pᵃ] and [ᵖa] in the first sense is not inconsistent with the claim that [pᵃ] is asymmetrically dependent on [ᵖa] in the second sense. The two kinds of dependence thus pertain to different levels of organization: in sense 2 we are dealing with a consonant's intrinsic reference to a schematic vowel as the carrier of its phonetic value, whereas sense 1 relates to the phonetic fine-tuning superimposed on this basic value as a matter of mutual accommodation with a specific vowel.[28]

The need to distinguish these notions can be further illustrated in regard to morphological layering. Consider the plural noun *leaves*, whose analysis into the stem *leave-* and the suffix *-s* is uncontroversial. The stem/affix distinction pertains to dependence in sense 2: whereas a stem is autonomous, an affix is dependent, being characterized as a function that maps a basic stem onto a derived stem through the addition of segmental content. Observe, however, that *leave-* (when used as a noun) occurs only in combination with the plural ending, whereas the plural *-s* occurs with many different nouns. Both are bound allomorphs, but *-s* appears in a far broader class of environments than does *leave-*. *Leave-* is therefore more dependent than *-s* in sense 1, though it is autonomous in sense 2. Since the same element can be autonomous in one sense and dependent in the other, these notions must be distinguished. I will use the terms **autonomy** and **dependence** in sense 2 exclusively; hence they do not refer in any direct way to distribution.

---

[28] Sense 1 approximates the definition of **dependency** often assumed in dependency grammar. As a technical term of cognitive grammar, **dependence** is always to be understood in sense 2.

CHAPTER II

Sanction and Distribution

THE CENTRAL PROBLEM we address in this chapter can be stated as follows in the contemporary linguistic idiom: How do we ensure that a grammar gives the right output? In the context of cognitive grammar, of course, the question is improperly phrased; a grammar is viewed as nongenerative and nonconstructive, so it gives no output at all. We must ask instead how such a grammar makes available to speakers an open-ended range of symbolic expressions, and further, how it specifies the degree and the nature of their conventionality. We begin our examination of this problem by discussing grammatical patterns, distribution, and distributional classes. Then we turn to the question of systemic motivation, i.e. how an expression is assigned a structural description, and the sanction it thereby receives. The final section deals with the computation of novel expressions, feeding relationships, and the rule vs. analogy controversy.

11.1. Constructions and Distribution

A grammatical construction consists in the bipolar integration of two or more component structures to form a composite expression. All of the major elements of a construction are symbolic in nature: its component structures, their integration at the two poles,[1] and the composite structure that results from this integration. This characterization covers both morphological and syntactic composition, and is applicable to both fixed and novel expressions, regardless of the regularity and generality of their compositional relationships.

11.1.1. Constructions as Complex Categories

As a limiting case, a specific composite expression qualifies as a grammatical construction. Such expressions are included in the grammar of a language to the extent that they achieve the status of conventional units. Regularities in the formation of composite expressions are represented in the gram-

[1] Recall that the integration of component structures at the phonological pole symbolizes their integration at the semantic pole (cf. 2.2.2, especially Fig. 2.8).

mar by hierarchies of schematic constructions, characterized at appropriate
levels of abstraction; both subschemas and specific expressions may instantiate a particular schema (cf. Fig. 2.9). For example, the most schematic characterization of the English prepositional-phrase construction simply specifies
the sequence [P + NML] (i.e. a preposition followed by a nominal). Any
number of subschemas might be recognized, such as [P + PRON] (a preposition taking a pronominal object), [beside + NML], or even [beside + PRON]
(which instantiates the previous two). The specific expressions *beside me, beside her*, etc. instantiate all of the (sub)schemas mentioned, either directly or
through a series of elaborative relationships.

It is apparent even from this brief example that grammatical constructions
are reasonably viewed as complex categories and represented in the form of
schematic networks. A speaker's knowledge of the prepositional-phrase construction includes not only a high-level schema, but also subschemas, specific
expressions, and categorizing relationships that associate these various structures.[2] The basic difference between a network of this sort and the ones considered previously lies in the complexity of the individual nodes. Informal notations like [beside + NML] and [P + PRON] abbreviate the elaborate contingent of structures (semantic, phonological, symbolic) and relationships
(symbolization, integration, composition) that characterize any construction
(see Fig. 2.8). Practical considerations dictate the frequent use of such notations, but we should not lose sight of the structural complexity they conceal.

The complexity of the individual nodes in the network representing a grammatical construction creates a multitude of possibilities for subcategorization.
A subschema can be extracted to define a subclass on the basis of either component structure: within the class of prepositional phrases, we have considered the subclass having *beside* as the preposition, as well as the subclass
with pronominal objects. Moreover, either the semantic or the phonological
pole may be pivotal; thus we may speak of the subclass of prepositional
phrases with indefinite objects, or the subclass with only monosyllabic prepositions. Subcategorization may depend on the characteristics of the composite
structure, distinguishing, for example, between single-word expressions and
phrases. Subschemas that simultaneously specify different types of properties
are not at all improbable—the set of prepositional phrases with polysyllabic
prepositions and pronominal objects might well have structural significance in
a particular language, or even the set of such expressions whose objects have
low tone.

Any coherently describable subcategory can be represented by a subschema with the proper specifications. Out of all the cognitively plausible
subclasses, only a small proportion are likely to be established as linguis-

---

[2] The term **construction** will be used either for individual nodes (i.e. schemas and specific
expressions) or the entire schematic network.

tically significant by the speakers of a particular language. The specific inventory doubtless varies, depending on such factors as the utility of subschemas in the description of other structures. Once again, the precise geometry of the schematic network is less important than having some idea of its general nature. Every node represents either a specific fixed expression or a pattern discernible in the composition of multiple expressions. Categorizing relationships identify certain patterns as extensions from others or as special cases. In a complex construction there are numerous crosscutting subcategories, based on different types of properties and characterized by subschemas at various levels of specificity.

11.1.2. *Distribution*

Language is a mixture of regularity and idiosyncrasy. By training and inclination, linguists are better equipped to deal with the former than the latter, with the consequence that far more effort goes into the formulation of general rules than into the patient elucidation of their limitations (cf. Gross 1979). The notion of a usage-based model represents an attempt to redress this imbalance, and to overcome the problems it engenders. The central claim is that a reductive account of grammatical constructions is unworkable: a speaker's conventional knowledge of a construction is not given by any single structure (such as a prototype or high-level schema). Its cognitive representation is more adequately treated as a full schematic network, where specific structures co-occur with categorizing schemas extracted to describe their commonality at various levels of abstraction.

11.1.2.1. *Implications of a Network Model.* In the case of the English prepositional-phrase construction, the need for an elaborate schematic network may not be readily apparent. With only minor qualifications, the construction is fully productive: any preposition is allowed to combine with any nominal. A single statement to this effect, equivalent to the topmost schema in the network (i.e. [P + NML]), might therefore seem sufficient. What cognitive grammar seeks to provide, however, is not a maximally parsimonious list of statements enumerating the proper set of strings, but rather an accurate account of a speaker's mental representation of linguistic organization. When a speaker masters specific expressions that accord with a general pattern, or extracts a limited generalization valid only for certain instances, he acquires cognitive routines that structure and elaborate his knowledge of the construction. They are an integral part of his grasp of linguistic convention and thereby fall within the legitimate purview of grammatical description.

The utility of a usage-based model is more apparent in cases of defective distribution or limited productivity, where expressions that conform to a general pattern are not conventionally permitted, despite their semantic and phonological viability. Situations like this are common, and obviously their full description requires more than an unrestricted rule or high-level schema. Exceptionality is problematic when general rules are taken as paradigmatic for linguistic organization—at the very least it requires special apparatus.[3] The network conception allows a more straightforward treatment, and is broadly motivated within the cognitive-grammar framework.

Consider the following simple example from Luiseño. The language has a series of postpositional suffixes, two of which are illustrated below:

(1)(a) *ki-yk*   (b) *palvun-ŋay*
        house-to   valley-from
        'to (the) house'   'from (the) valley'

(2)(a) *ʔo-yk*   (b) *čaamo-ŋay*
        you-to   us-from
        'to you'   'from us'

As these examples show, the postpositions combine with either inanimate nouns or personal pronouns. They cannot be attached to animate nouns, however; instead they suffix to a pronoun that follows the noun as a separate word:

(3)(a) *yaʔaš po-yk*   (b) *hunwutum poomo-ŋay*
        man   him-to   bears   them-from
        'to (the) man'   'from (the) bears'

How are these data to be described? In particular, how do we account for the absence of expressions with a postpositional ending on an animate noun?

From expressions like (1)(a)–(b), the learner of Luiseño extracts the low-level schema $[N_{inan}$-P]; the inanimacy of the noun survives the cancellation process, for it is common to all the examples on which the schema is based. From expressions like those in (2), the learner extracts the low-level schema [PRON-P], which is subsequently incorporated in the higher-order structure $[N_{an}$ [PRON-P]] representing the construction illustrated in (3). All these schemas are then available to sanction novel expressions formed on the same patterns. However, nothing motivates the learner to extract the schema $[N_{an}$-P], for he is simply not exposed to expressions of this type. His grasp of established convention provides no basis for attaching a postpositional affix directly to an animate noun.

This solution is straightforward and commonsensical. It merely claims that a speaker learns the patterns he is exposed to and uses them in preference to unfamiliar ones. This approach is instructively compared to one that emphasizes global generalizations rather than local patterns. For instance, how

---

[3] An example from the generative tradition is the device of rule features (Lakoff 1970). More commonly, a vacuous appeal is made to a mysterious entity called "the lexicon," supposedly the repository of all idiosyncrasy.

would the data be treated in a classic transformational analysis? Most likely one would posit a uniform representation of postpositional expressions at the deep-structure level, both to capture a syntactic generalization and to simplify the rules of semantic interpretation. The deep-structure sequence N + P would thus be generated without regard to the character of N (animate or inanimate, noun or pronoun). A transformation would then copy an animate noun in pronominal form, followed by the attachment of P to the noun or pronoun that immediately precedes it. The desire for an all-encompassing generalization thus leads the analyst to postulate a nonoccurring sequence that is prevented from surfacing only by the intervention of an obligatory copying rule. Moreover, the patterns that actually occur (e.g. $[N_{inan}\text{-}P]$) are not specifically listed as such anywhere in the grammar.[4]

In cognitive grammar, by contrast, primacy is accorded to structures that are directly attested. In fact, the model is maximally restrictive in this regard by virtue of the content requirement (1.2.6.2): apart from categorizing relationships, the only units permitted in the grammar are structures that actually occur, or that are schematic for such structures. Hence the patterns $[N_{inan}\text{-}P]$, $[PRON\text{-}P]$, and $[N_{an} [PRON\text{-}P]]$ are represented in the grammar as schemas, but there is no such schema corresponding to nonexistent sequences. Does this account fail to capture any valid generalization? It might be argued that the transformational analysis, by positing the deep-structure sequence N + P, captures the generalization that there is *some* means of associating a postpositional ending with any sort of noun, including one that is animate. This is not so much a structural description, however, as it is a statement of **functional efficiency**. Though functional considerations are undeniably critical in the shaping of linguistic structure, it does not follow that they should be incorporated directly in the grammar as descriptive statements.

Let us consider another angle. Given our overall assumptions, we might expect the speaker of Luiseño to extract a higher-order schema representing the obvious parallelism of $[N_{inan}\text{-}P]$ and $[PRON\text{-}P]$. If so, what is its character? By virtue of the cancellation process, this higher-order schema must be neutral with respect to animacy (since the pronouns are typically animate) as well as the noun/pronoun distinction. It is therefore comparable to the structure N + P of the transformational analysis, which was just criticized for generating (at the deep-structure level) a sequence that does not occur. How does the present analysis escape this criticism? Why does the higher-order schema not sanction impermissible sequences of the form $[N_{an}\text{-}P]$?

The difference is that the higher-order schema (if it exists at all) is only a subsidiary aspect of the overall analysis. Even if a speaker observes the simi-

---

[4] This is not a straw-man analysis: I proposed it myself (Langacker 1972) for the parallel constructions in Classical Nahuatl. A cognitive-grammar analysis of the construction in (3) is presented in Langacker (1981c); the composite semantic structure is easily derived.

larity between [N$_{inan}$-P] and [PRON-P] at some level of cognitive processing, the abstractness of the resulting schema assures it of neither salience nor entrenchment. More crucially, the existence of a schema does not imply that every potential instantiation has equal standing in relation to established convention; it only represents the judgment that its actual instantiations are parallel in certain respects. Hence the existence of [N-P] does not entail that any postposition can occur on any type of noun: the conventional status of postpositional expressions in the language is specified by the entire schematic network, in all its complexity and detail.

A crucial aspect of the usage-based approach is the notion that low-level structures are often more significant than high-level schemas, notably in the selection of an active node for categorizing a usage event or computing a novel expression. The likelihood of a particular unit being selected is claimed to correlate positively with its salience, and negatively with its elaborative distance vis-à-vis the sanctioned structure. We therefore predict that units at lower hierarchical levels will generally prevail: they are preferentially selected when salience is held constant, and there is no apparent tendency for the highest-level structures to be most salient. Thus, even though high-level generalizations contribute to the unity of a category, they are not omnipotent; they may in fact be rather inconsequential in the computation of novel expressions, leaving this task to their less schematic underlings. The distribution of Luiseño postpositions is consequently unaffected by the possible extraction of the higher-order schema [N-P]. Their conventional distribution is specified instead by the presence in the grammar of the salient subschemas [N$_{inan}$-P], [PRON-P], and [N$_{an}$ [PRON-P]], and by the absence of [N$_{an}$-P].

11.1.2.2. *Further Exemplification.* We consider now a different type of distributional phenomenon, this one concerning postpositional expressions in Classical Nahuatl.[5] The problem here is that not every postposition occurs freely with both nouns and pronouns. Three basic classes can be recognized. Some, including -*k(o)* 'in/on' and -*tew* 'like', occur only on nouns:

(4)(a) *aateen-ko*   (b) *oostoo-k*
        shore-on   cave-in
        'on (the) shore'   'in (the) cave'

(5)(a) *siwaa-tew*   (b) *čaalčiw-tew*
        woman-like   emerald-like
        'like (a) woman'   'like (an) emerald'

Others, such as -*waan* '(together) with' and -*pampa* 'because of/on behalf of', attach only to pronouns:

---

[5] I simplify in unimportant respects. Whether the endings are postpositions or "relational nouns" (cf. Andrews 1975, p. 304) is of no consequence to the distributional question.

(6)(a) *no-waan*   (b) *ii-waan*
      me-with   him-with
      'with me'   'with him'

(7)(a) *mo-pampa*   (b) *tee-pampa*
      you-because:of   someone-because:of
      'for you'   'on someone's behalf'

A third class can occur with both nouns and pronouns; *-pan* 'in/on/at' and *-caalan* 'among' are examples:

(8)(a) *ii-pan*   (b) *aa-pan*
      him-on   water-in
      'on him'   'in (the) water'

(9)(a) *to-caalan*   (b) *kʷaw-caalan*
      us-among   tree-among
      'among us'   'among (the) trees'

How are these restrictions to be imposed?

To say that a particular postposition, $-P_1$, occurs on pronouns is equivalent in this framework to positing the schema [PRON-P_1] as a unit in the grammar, together with some array of instantiations having unit status. The nonoccurrence of a postposition $-P_1$ on pronouns is reflected in the grammar by the absence of the schema [PRON-P_1], or of any specific expression that might instantiate it. It is not inconceivable that in cases like this a speaker learns an explicit prohibition of the pattern as a rule of grammar. On grounds of cognitive plausibility, however, I adopt the working hypothesis that a speaker learns only positive specifications of the structures and patterns of his language, and that these will account for distributional phenomena. The initial strategy is to assume that speakers avoid a nonoccurring pattern through the absence of a direct precedent and the entrenchment of a suitable alternative. (Cf. Perlmutter 1971.)

In any event, from data like (4)–(9) the learner extracts a number of low-level schemas reflecting the co-occurrence privileges of particular postpositions. For instance, expressions like those in (4) give rise to the schema [N_{lex}-ko], which specifies the attachment of *-ko* to a stem identified as a noun with "lexical content." Similarly, the data in (6) supports the schema [N_{pro}-waan], specifying the combination of *-waan* with a noun having the minimal semantic content that characterizes a pro form. Fig. 11.1(a) shows the low-level schemas that can be extracted from the range of data being considered. Observe that *-pan* and *-caalan* each occur twice (e.g. [N_{lex}-pan] and [N_{pro}-pan]), whereas other conceivable schemas are excluded (e.g. [N_{pro}-tew]) because the learner is not exposed to data that would motivate their extraction.

Also included in Fig. 11.1(a) are certain higher-order schemas: [N_{lex}-ko], [N_{lex}-tew], etc. support the extraction of [N_{lex}-P], where the postposition is

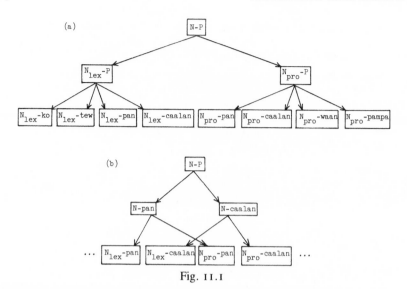

Fig. 11.1

represented schematically; $[N_{pro}$-P] similarly expresses the commonality of $[N_{pro}$-caalan], $[N_{pro}$-pampa], and so on. By further abstraction, the learner may well arrive at the topmost schema [N-P], which has all the others as either direct or indirect instantiations. In this model, however, the existence of $[N_{lex}$-P] does not imply that every postposition in the language is conventionally employed with lexical nouns, nor does the extraction of [N-P] have the consequence that any noun-postposition combination whatever is acceptable. The import of a particular schema from the standpoint of conventional distribution is spelled out by the array of lower-level units that instantiate it: the schema defines a range of potential structures, but only certain portions of that range are actually exploited in conventional usage. A schema's unit instantiations figure more directly and more significantly in the computation and sanction of novel expressions.

Recall that some of the postpositions occur on both lexical nouns and pronouns. This is reflected in Fig. 11.1(a) by their appearance in two different subschemas, e.g. $[N_{lex}$-pan] and $[N_{pro}$-pan]. We must therefore contemplate the categorizations shown in Fig. 11.1(b): [N-pan] has $[N_{lex}$-pan] and $[N_{pro}$-pan] as immediate instantiations, whereas [N-caalan] is similarly schematic for $[N_{lex}$-caalan] and $[N_{pro}$-caalan]. In turn, [N-pan] and [N-caalan] are subschemas with respect to [N-P]. Their subcategorization of postpositional expressions crosscuts the one effected by $[N_{lex}$-P] and $[N_{pro}$-P] in diagram (a). The subcategorizations are equally and simultaneously valid, and the hierarchies of diagrams (a) and (b) can be superimposed to form a single network. This is rather messy diagrammatically (at least on a two-dimensional page), but quite natural linguistically.

Despite their obvious convenience, the formulas we have been using for grammatical constructions (e.g. [N$_{\text{pro}}$-pan]) are quite ad hoc. A more principled abbreviatory notation—one that at least indicates the component and composite structures at each pole—is introduced in Fig. 11.2. The

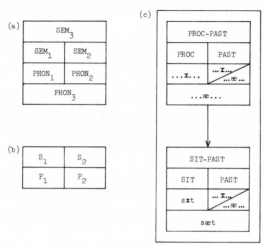

Fig. 11.2

general format is sketched in diagram (a), where [[SEM$_1$]/[PHON$_1$]] and [[SEM$_2$]/[PHON$_2$]] are component structures, and [[SEM$_3$]/[PHON$_3$]] the composite structure. I will speak of six **sectors**, and refer to them as SEM$_1$, PHON$_1$, SEM$_2$, etc. A streamlined version of this format is given in diagram (b); the composite structure is omitted, so there are only four sectors; also, the sector labels are reduced from SEM$_1$ to S$_1$, from PHON$_1$ to P$_1$, and so on. We can therefore refer quite simply to such elements as the phonological pole of the second component structure (sector P$_2$), or the semantic pole of the composite structure (S$_3$).

The six-sector format is illustrated in diagram (c). The upper structure is a schema representing a particular pattern of past-tense formation; the lower structure is *sat*, which instantiates this schema. Both *sat* and the categorizing schema contain the past-tense morpheme, so S$_2$ and P$_2$ are identical in the two structures. A special notation is used in sector P$_2$ to simplify the representation of the dependent allomorph [...ɪ...-->...æ...]: a diagonal line divides the sector into two subparts, with the upper-left portion corresponding to the "input" of the function (...ɪ...), and the lower-right portion to its "output" (...æ...). The stem, [S$_1$/P$_1$], is of course specific for *sat*, but in the schema it is identified semantically only as a process predication, and phonologically as a sequence containing [...ɪ...]; this contrast in specificity is naturally reflected in the composite structures (S$_3$ and P$_3$).

Using this style of notation, let us continue with the past-tense morpheme as a final distributional example. There are three regular allomorphs, and a number of others limited to specific, essentially closed classes of verb stems. How do we account for this distribution, and for the proper selection of allomorphs in novel expressions? We must consider the appropriate schematic network. Any facet of composite expressions provides a possible basis for subcategorization, but we are specifically concerned with sector P_2, i.e. the phonological pole of the tense morpheme. Our focus is therefore the network of constructions defined by categorizing relationships based on P_2 in particular.

We will restrict our attention to the regular forms, two ablaut patterns, and the zero allomorph. A minimal sketch of the requisite schematic network is offered in Fig. 11.3; omitted are lower-level subschemas, extensional relationships between the schemas that are included, and the elaboration of these schemas by specific expressions with unit status (as shown for *sat* in Fig. 11.2(c)). Note that all of these structures are identical and quite schematic in the semantic sectors, since there is no obvious semantic coherence to the verb stems that inflect in a particular way.

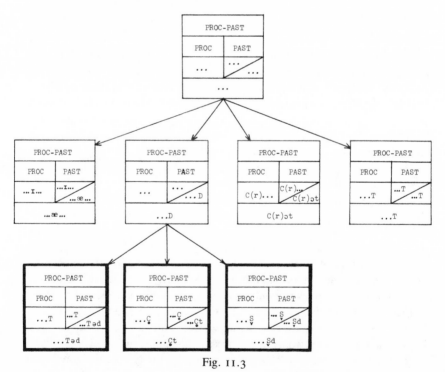

Fig. 11.3

The subschemas for the regular forms are enclosed in heavy lines, to indicate their presumed entrenchment and cognitive salience. There are three of them, each incorporating a different basic allomorph in sector P_2. The subschema on the lower left categorizes such unit expressions as *inspected*, *tasted*, *loaded*, and *waded*; it specifies the suffixation of [əd] to a stem that ends in an alveolar stop (T). Units like *kicked*, *reached*, *bounced*, and *wished* instantiate the middle subschema, which suffixes [t] to a stem ending in a voiceless consonant (Ç̥). The third subschema, describing the suffixation of [d] to stems with a final voiced segment (Ş̥), is elaborated by units like *killed*, *tied*, *prayed*, and *rubbed*. In the schema that subsumes these three patterns, D is to be interpreted as schematic for [əd], [t], and [d].[6]

The other three schemas are presumed to be less salient. The ablaut pattern [...ɪ...$--\rightarrow$...æ...] is instantiated by verbs like *sat*, *began*, *sang*, and *swam* (cf. Figs. 11.2(c) and 9.8). *Brought*, *taught*, *sought*, and *caught* are among the exponents of the [C(r)...$--\rightarrow$C(r)ɔt] pattern. The final schema represents the zero inflection, which is limited to stems with a final alveolar stop (T), e.g. *cut*, *hit*, *bid*. Since the patterns are quite diverse, the superschema that subsumes them all—if indeed there is one—is almost vacuous in its phonological specifications: P_1 and P_3 do little more than indicate the existence of segmental content, and P_2 is characterized only as a dependent morpheme of some sort.

How does this network account for distribution? Many past-tense forms are determined by being included in the grammar as conventional units. The inclusion of *brought*, for instance, automatically specifies that *bring* takes the [ɔt] allomorph, and the status of *sat* as a conventional unit specifies the proper ablaut pattern for *sit*. As entrenched units, these expressions sanction themselves at the minimal possible elaborative distance (zero), and their ready availability forestalls the search for alternatives. We can plausibly attribute unit status to all the instantiations of the minor patterns, so the schemas that categorize them are relatively nonsalient, being seldom invoked as active nodes in the coding process. The regular endings [d], [t], and [əd] occur in large classes of forms (many doubtless learned as units), and are also used for novel expressions to the virtual exclusion of other allomorphs. My working hypothesis is that the contrast between productive and nonproductive patterns reflects the greater entrenchment and cognitive salience of the former. Salient structures are easily activated, and if the disparity in prominence is sufficiently large, their ready elicitation preempts the possible selection of other sanctioning schemas.

---

[6] That is, D specifies an alveolar stop but is neutral in regard to its voicing and the possibility of a preceding schwa; it is parallel to the schema symbolized Z in our discussion of the plural (cf. Fig. 10.6). We can express the full parallelism in this framework by postulating a higher-order schematic network having as instantiations the individual networks headed by D and Z.

Suppose a speaker of English needs to express the past tense of *grit*. If he
has learned the conventional form, he can activate it as a unit without appreciable constructive effort; the appropriate schema may then be activated secondarily. Should it happen that the familiar form does not spring immediately
to mind, the speaker can employ this schema to compute it. In either case the
schema is coactivated with the actual expression and constitutes an aspect of
its structural description. The unit status of *gritted* does not remove it from
the scope of the general pattern, nor does it preclude its computation. Instead
its dual motivation—as a unit, and as a straightforward instantiation of a
salient schema—makes it accessible to the speaker by two alternate routes,
either of which may predominate on a given occasion.[7]

If the speaker happens not to be familiar with the form, he must activate a
schema to compute it. How does he determine the conventionality of *gritted*
and conclude that this (as opposed, say, to *graught*, *grat*, or *grit*) is the proper
expression? In the absence of special motivation (e.g. jocularity, or response
bias induced by a psycholinguistic experiment), his selection among the compatible schemas is a function of their prominence and elaborative distance.
The most prominent schemas available are those representing the regular patterns; of these, only two are compatible with *grit* in their characterization of
the verb stem (sector P_1): those specifying the suffixation of [əd] and of [t].
Being more specific in regard to the final stem consonant, the schema with
[əd] is selected on the basis of lesser elaborative distance. *Gritted* is therefore
judged to be the conventionally motivated form.

11.1.3. *Distributional Classes*

A major concern in Ch. 10 was the distinction between two modes of categorization: by schema, and by prototype. In this section we focus instead on
the nature of the specifications on which categorization is based (intrinsic
vs. extrinsic). To simplify matters, we will consider only categorization by
schemas.

11.1.3.1. *Natural vs. Arbitrary Classes.* Structurally significant classes
are often definable on the basis of intrinsic semantic or phonological properties. "Natural classes" in phonology are of this type: a uniform auditory/
articulatory characterization is possible for such segment classes as fricatives,
high vowels, or voiceless stops. I argued in Part II that a number of fundamental grammatical classes can be defined in semantic terms (e.g. noun, verb,
count noun, imperfective process). In cases like these, all the class members
instantiate the defining schema and are fully compatible with its specifications.

---

[7] Though I have not investigated the matter in detail, I believe this account to be compatible
with empirically observed differences (based on speech errors, etc.) in the processing of forms
instantiating productive vs. nonproductive patterns (cf. Stemberger 1981).

Obviously, though, many structurally significant classes cannot be defined in this manner. Linguists are much concerned with **distributional classes**, where the basis for categorization is participation in a certain grammatical construction. Sometimes a distributional class coincides with one determined by an intrinsic property: the set of Luiseño nouns permitting the direct suffixation of a postposition matches the set that designates inanimate entities; a specification of inanimacy is therefore included in the schema describing the construction ($[N_{inan}$-P]). Frequently, however, such coincidence is only approximate, and often there are no intrinsic grounds whatever for determining the membership of a distributional class. For all practical purposes the assignment of English verbs to the various patterns of past-tense formation is arbitrary. Given the phonological shape of the stem, there is no way to predict in absolute terms whether it is regular, or which allomorph it takes should it be irregular; nor is there any semantic predictability.[8] Even when the members of a distributional class cluster around some prototypical value, the exact inventory may be subject to conventional determination, thus requiring explicit enumeration. A case in point is the set of English verbs that participate in the passive construction (cf. Ch. 1).

It is commonly assumed that the full or partial arbitrariness of distributional classes demonstrates the autonomy of grammar (cf. Newmeyer 1983, p. 7–10). The correctness of the autonomous-syntax hypothesis, for example, is believed to follow from the impossibility of predicting in absolute terms— on the basis of intrinsic semantic properties—precisely the class of structures that participate in every syntactic construction. Apparently the reasoning goes something like this: some classes are defined on semantic grounds, others on phonological grounds; however, there are still other classes for which neither a semantic nor a phonological characterization is possible or predictive, hence there must be some other aspect of linguistic organization—distinct from both semantics and phonology—that affords the basis for such categorization; being thus distinct from both semantics and phonology, grammatical structure must reside in one or more autonomous components.

This line of argument confuses two issues that are in principle quite distinct: the **types of structures** to be found in language, and the **predictability of their behavior**. Absolute predictability cannot in general be expected for natural language, and any assumption that a certain level of predictability is criterial for a particular type of structure is essentially gratuitous. We have dealt in some detail with two instances of unpredictable distribution: the selection by verbs of past-tense allomorphs in English; and the restriction of postpositions in Classical Nahuatl to lexical nouns and/or pronouns. In both

[8] The schemas in Fig. 11.3 characterize the verb stem (sector P_1), but these specifications are descriptive rather than predictive: not every stem containing [ɪ] marks the past tense by ablauting this vowel to [æ].

instances we saw how the conventional distribution can be accounted for in a usage-based model making plausible assumptions regarding sanction and systemic motivation. Only symbolic units were posited. Many are schematic, and they are linked to one another by categorizing relationships, but all of these structures and associations inhabit symbolic space; there is no distinct "grammatical space," and no grammatical units that cannot be described in terms of semantic and phonological units together with their symbolic pairings.

Let us consider more explicitly the treatment of arbitrary distributional classes, i.e. cases where the structures that participate in a construction are not uniquely identifiable through schematic characterization. In such instances class membership must be indicated specifically for each individual participant. To identify class members, linguists often posit syntactic features or other diacritics (e.g. [+Rule 17], [Class 3A]). Since these diacritics are neither semantic nor phonological entities, does it not follow that they constitute a special group of "grammatical" properties?

A usage-based model obviates the need for such diacritics. To say that a given element unpredictably participates in a construction is equivalent to saying that the structure so defined is established as a conventional unit. For example, the fact that *bring* participates in the past-tense construction with [ɔt] is indicated in the grammar of English by the unit status of *brought*, which instantiates the schema for this construction. Similarly, the occurrence of Nahuatl *-pampa* in the [N_{pro}-P] construction is specified in the grammar of this language by the inclusion of the schematic unit [N_{pro}-pampa] (Fig. 11.1(a)), together with a series of unit instantiations. The number of units serving a "diacritic" function is finite, because a speaker can only learn the conventionality of an unpredictable form by actually observing it. The problem of specifying the membership of arbitrary distributional classes is therefore handled quite organically in the usage-based approach; in a sense the problem never arises at all.

11.1.3.2. *Reference to Arbitrary Classes.* I have suggested that a usage-based model affords a natural account of arbitrary distributional classes, and have provided an initial description of its general character. Quite a number of distributional questions merit closer investigation, but here I will focus on just one, namely whether parallel behavior might itself be seized upon as the basis for schematic characterization. Consider the parallel behavior of *bring*, *catch*, *seek*, *fight*, *think*, *buy*, *wreak*, and *teach* with respect to past-tense formation. Is it possible that speakers might construe this shared behavior as an abstract type of similarity, and establish these verbs as a distinctive class by means of a schema reflecting this common property? Could a schema be extracted to specify that certain postpositions in Nahuatl are similar by virtue of their occurrence on pronouns? By permitting collective reference to the members of a distributional class, such a schema might accord them a measure of cognitive salience and allow them to function as a group in other ways as well. A possible example involves those verbs that contain the sequence [ɪN] (i.e. [ɪ] followed by a nasal consonant) and form their past tense by ablauting the vowel to [æ]: *swim, begin, sink*, etc.[9] All these verbs behave alike as well in the formation of their past participle, ablauting the same stem vowel to [ʌ] (e.g. *swum, begun, sunk*). A schema categorizing these verbs on the basis of past-tense formation—call it *SCH_x*—therefore permits a generalization about the verbs that select a certain variant of the participial inflection. The generalization is expressed as a categorizing relationship: the participial construction schema for the ablaut of [ɪ] to [ʌ] (cf. *won, dug, spun*) has among its immediate instantiations a subschema that identifies the stem specifically as *SCH_x*. This categorizing relationship is the functional equivalent of a morphological redundancy rule.

For our purposes the central point is not the prevalence of such phenomena, or the significance of this particular example, but rather the possibility—at least in principle—of referring collectively to arbitrary distributional classes in a framework that recognizes only semantic, phonological, and symbolic structures. I will argue that this is indeed possible, and requires nothing essential beyond the constructs already introduced and motivated on other grounds. The emergence of structurally significant classes defined on the basis of their combinatory behavior is not sufficient to demonstrate the existence of a distinct syntactic or grammatical component.

Why does categorization based on distributional properties appear to be so special? Not because it refers to structures of a special character, but rather because these structures are extrinsic to the elements being categorized. Since a grammatical construction contains only semantic and phonological elements (together with their interrelationships), the property of occurring in a given construction is representable by a schema that refers only to elements of these types. Natural and distributional classes differ primarily in that the similarities defining the former pertain to intrinsic properties of the units being categorized, whereas those defining the latter pertain to their external environment. The line between internal structure and syntagmatic context is anything but sharp, however, as discrete units are recognized only through a process of decontextualization. It is reasonable, then, to seek a unified account of natural and distributional classes, where the categorizing schema specifies properties of variable intrinsicness and centrality to class members.

To arrive at a unified account, we need only distinguish two notions that have coincided in our previous discussions: the elements being categorized,

[9] This set includes most verbs that take the [...ɪ... —→ ...æ...] allomorph (*sit* is the most prominent exception).

and the **scope** of the categorizing judgments. Suppose schema $[A]$ is extracted to represent the commonality of structures $[a_1]$, $[a_2]$, $[a_3]$, etc. Up to now the similarities permitting a schema's extraction have been inherent properties of its instantiations, and we have generally employed the notation of Fig. 11.4(a)

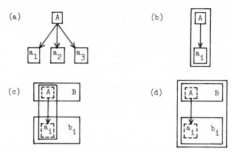

Fig. 11.4

to display these "context-free" categorizing relationships. However, each individual categorizing relationship requires a distinct comparison event and constitutes a separate unit. The network of diagram (a) is therefore more properly given as a set of structures in the format of diagram (b), all of which have $[A]$ as the standard and some unit $[a_i]$ as the target. But if the basis for categorization is limited to intrinsic specifications of the targets, $[a_i]$ still functions in each instance as both the categorized element and the scope of the requisite categorizing judgment.

We have also considered the type of situation depicted in diagram (c) (cf. Fig. 10.8). Here the categorized units are limited to appearing in a particular environment: each element $[a_i]$ occurs only in combination with another element $[b_i]$ (as a context-induced variant). However, this context-dependence is not yet quite what we are aiming at. An element $[a_i]$ may still be categorized as an instance of $[A]$ by virtue of its internal properties, despite their being influenced by the surrounding environment. Even though $[a_i]$ is confined to the higher-order structure $[[a_i]-[b_i]]$, and $[A]$ to the structure $[[A]-[B]]$ (where $[B]$ is schematic for $[b_i]$), the categorizing relationship is limited in scope to $[A]$ and $[a_i]$.

The situation that does concern us is depicted in diagram (d). Schema $[A]$ still categorizes $[a_i]$, but here the scope of the categorizing judgment is expanded to encompass its syntagmatic relationship to $[B]$. That is, only when $[A]$ occurs in combination with $[B]$ does it qualify as the standard of comparison for the categorizations in question. The instantiations of $[A]$ similarly qualify as instances of the category only by virtue of appearing in this context. Though integration with $[B]$ is not an intrinsic property of either $[A]$ or its instantiations, it is construed as one of the defining properties establishing $[a_1]$, $[a_2]$, $[a_3]$, etc. as a distinctive subgroup. Instantiations of $[A]$ that do not appear in the specified context are therefore excluded from the distributional class.

Even though these proposals for handling distributional phenomena are obviously preliminary, I believe a usage-based conception holds promise of proving both adequate and realistic. The fundamental import of these observations is that distributional considerations do not bear in any direct way on the question of what basic kinds of units are found in natural language. The arbitrariness of many distributional classes—even their possible cognitive salience and multifaceted structural significance—does not imply the existence of linguistic units that cannot be resolved into semantic, phonological, and symbolic structures, nor does it establish the organization of grammar into discrete components. Since grammar consists of interrelationships among semantic and phonological structures, and patterns of such interrelationships, grammatical description makes reference only to structures in semantic and phonological space. There is no separate domain of "grammatical content."

11.2. Systemic Motivation

Our attention now focuses on the relation between the linguistic system and individual expressions. The nature of linguistic expressions requires initial clarification. We next consider the assignment of structural descriptions and the sanction they afford. Subsequently explored are certain aspects of complexity in the systemic motivation of expressions.

11.2.1. *Expressions*

Formal studies of language generally distinguish sharply between "sentences" and "utterances." Sentences are abstract objects, defined solely by the specifications of a grammar. The grammar is conceived as an algorithmic device giving a fixed (though infinite) set of sentences as output, each with a specific and invariant structural description.[10] By contrast, utterances involve the actual use of sentences on specific occasions. Since utterances are strongly shaped by context and performance factors, they are not susceptible to algorithmic characterization.

Cognitive grammar takes a rather different view of things. It differs first in its notion of structural description: this is not (as in algorithmic models) an abstract, bipartite relationship between a grammar and a sentence, but rather a tripartite relationship centered on the speaker: it is a matter of how a speaker employs the conventional units of the grammar to structure particular usage events. Moreover, in lieu of the sentence/utterance dichotomy it posits a continuum of **linguistic expressions** that vary in their level of specificity and con-

---

[10] Ambiguity is not an issue here (cf. 11.2.3). A sentence with multiple semantic interpretations can be resolved into distinct sentences each with a single interpretation.

textual inclusiveness.[11] Utterances (usage events) represent the limiting case with respect to this parameter.

A usage event is the pairing established on a particular occasion between an actual conceptualization and an actual vocalization. An event has linguistic relevance to the extent that it is structured and evaluated with reference to the conventional units of a grammar. It thus receives a structural description, consisting of the units that are activated for its primary categorization, together with those additional units whose activation is secondarily elicited. Representations of usage events will be referred to as linguistic expressions regardless of their level of specificity. At the extreme, an expression can be a linguistically categorized usage event in all its elaborate detail; if described with sufficient delicacy, every such expression is unique. Also qualifying as linguistic expressions are more schematic representations, compatible with open-ended classes of usage events that differ in fine details and incidental contextual features. Fairly schematic expressions correspond to the entities traditionally identified as sentences.

Consider an example. While climbing out of a swimming pool, I realize that I forgot to remove my watch before entering the water. I hold the watch up to my ear, and then—with a sigh of relief—utter:

(10)   *It's running!*

Of course, I cannot literally utter this orthographic sequence. Instead I produce a specific vocalization, employing it to express a particular, context-dependent conceptualization. This utterance is a usage event, which qualifies as a linguistic expression because in large measure—down to a certain level of specificity—it is structured in accordance with certain conventional units of English.

A broad array of units contribute to the systemic motivation of this usage event. Some pertain to unipolar organization. For instance, my vocalization requires the peripheral implementation of articulatory routines corresponding to individual segments, syllables, and larger phonological structures. Others, defined in bipolar terms, include morphemes (e.g. *run*), composite lexical units (*running*), and grammatical constructions. Among the units that are activated—either primarily or secondarily—are both specific structures and schemas at different hierarchical levels. *Running*, for example, instantiates the V + -*ing* schema for present participles, which in turn instantiates the higher-order schema for the class of atemporal relations. All of these and many others are invoked for my production of the usage event. Collectively they constitute its structural description and reflect the fact that my utterance is intended as a well-formed expression of English.

[11] Hudson (1984) also argues for eliminating the traditional distinction.

Linguists generally regard *It's running* to be a single sentence, but only at the cost of considerable abstraction and oversimplification. For one thing, this position ignores a substantial amount of phonetic variation that is not only permitted by the phonological system of English but is actually characterized in fairly precise detail by low-level phonological units. One dimension of this variation, reflected to some extent in orthographic representations, pertains to register and tempo:

(11)(a)   *It is running.*
   (b)   *It's running.*
   (c)   *It's runnin'.*

A second dimension is prosodic, encompassing the possibility of alternate intonational contours and accentual patterns. My actual vocalization reflects particular choices from the conventionally provided ranges of options, but it is fully specific, more so than even the lowest-level conventional units it instantiates. However, since unit status and conventionality are matters of degree, there is no precise cutoff point for the properties attributable to the linguistic system. There is a gradation from the schematic to the maximally specific, with usage events at the endpoint of the scale.

Analogous remarks can be made with reference to the semantic pole. The conventional meaning of *run* is given by a complex network incorporating heterogeneous structures characterized at various levels of schematicity. The value it assumes in (10) depends on whether its trajector is construed as an animal, a liquid, a nose, hosiery, a computer program, a machine, or some other type of entity for which a conventional usage has been established. The conventional range of *it* must also be spelled out explicitly in a comprehensive description: it applies to animals, inanimate objects, and human infants; to bounded objects and mass substances; to both physical and abstract entities; and so on. Even the progressive construction has an array of interrelated values (e.g. ongoing vs. imminent activity). One should not underestimate the degree of specificity that such units can achieve within the legitimate confines of linguistic description. For instance, it is a conventional fact of English— not predictable in absolute terms—that *run* is predicated of watches. The semantic variant that reflects this usage is specific to the point of characterizing its trajector as a watch in particular; it elaborates a more schematic structure in which the trajector is simply characterized as a timepiece, which in turn instantiates a higher-order schema where the trajector is any sort of machine. In the actual usage event, of course, *run* is understood as being predicated of my watch in particular, but even this may have some marginal conventional standing if I and my interlocutors have frequent occasion to refer to its operation.

The point of this discussion is twofold. First, it suggests the continuity be-

tween linguistic and nonlinguistic structures, and in particular between utterances (usage events) and linguistic expressions characterized more schematically. Secondly, it indicates that *It's running*—and any other object of the
sort normally referred to as a sentence—represents not a single expression but
rather an extensive **family** of possible expressions, variable at both the semantic and the phonological poles. We can observe numerous parameters of
variation even for a simple sentence like *It's running*. Variation along just one
parameter is sufficient to define a range of alternate expressions. When every
dimension of variation is taken into account, and all compatible combinations
of values are considered, the set of alternate expressions is quite large (and
probably open ended).

Even for a single usage event, like that described above, we can recognize a
family of linguistic expressions representing its construal at different levels of
schematicity. The utterance itself is a maximally specific linguistic expression. We obtain a more schematic variant by focusing on low-level schemas.
At the phonological pole, a characterization of this sort might specify the
tempo, intonation, and accentual pattern fairly precisely, but still as types
compatible with a divergent (though circumscribed) range of tokens. Similarly, it might specify that *run* is predicated of a watch, but not of any particular watch, and that the progressive construction involves ongoing (rather than
imminent) action. Comparable representations at higher levels of schematicity
can be envisaged, each qualifying as an expression in its own right and potentially functioning as part of the structural description of the usage event. At a
sufficiently high level of abstraction, we obtain a structure resembling the type
of object normally thought of as a sentence: sounds are represented as sequences of phonemes (not by specific allophones); variations in tempo, intonation, and accentual pattern are neutralized; the semantic pole of *run* is an
all-subsuming schema for this processual category (if we assume that such a
schema exists); the progressive construction is neutral between the senses of
ongoing and imminent action; and so forth.

The potential validity of these abstract constructs is therefore not in dispute. At a certain level of schematicity, we can speak of a sentence like *It's
running* and examine those of its properties that are essentially common to all
its divergent elaborations. Possibly a representation of this kind is activated as
part of the structural description of instantiating usage events. However, it is
not the only one presumed to figure in the structural description of an utterance, nor is it necessarily the most prominent. We have assumed, in fact, that
low-level schemas are preferentially chosen as active nodes for the primary
categorization of usage events.

11.2.2. *Structural Descriptions*

How are active nodes selected? What are the factors responsible for assigning one structural description to a usage event in preference to conceivable

alternatives? This type of problem is not specifically linguistic, for it arises in all domains of cognitive processing. Consider the recognition of a familiar face. Face-recognition involves an act of comparison of the form $f > F = 0$, where f is the cognitive routine representing the perceiver's knowledge of the face, F is the immediate perceptual experience, and 0 indicates that there is no substantial discrepancy when f is used as standard for assessing the target F (cf. 3.1.3). The problem is to determine how the perceiver "finds" f: out of the countless routines at his disposal, including a large number that correspond to familiar faces, how does he manage to activate as standard in the comparison event precisely the routine (namely f) that matches the immediate percept (F)?

I will assume some kind of **interactive-activation model**, roughly along the lines proposed for speech perception by Elman and McClelland (1984). By virtue of gross similarities or shared components, any facet of the input is presumed capable of activating a variety of established routines as possible standards of comparison. The candidate routines run in parallel; their specifications are continuously matched against those of the target, and constitute "expectations" about its further, more specific properties. As the expectations of a given routine are successively satisfied, its level of activation is progressively augmented, and beyond a certain level it inhibits the other candidates. The system thus converges on a "solution," whereby the routine that most closely matches the target eclipses other alternatives and emerges as the primary categorizing structure.[12]

The analogy with perceptual recognition has its limitations, but it does suggest some further points of linguistic relevance. It is well known that a given perceptual input can often be structured in alternate ways, as in the perception of an ambiguous figure (e.g. Fig. 3.4). One structuring tends to inhibit the other, as expected in the interactive-activation model. Commonly, then, a person structures an ambiguous figure in one fashion and remains unaware of the other possibility; if he perceives the ambiguity, he does so by switching back and forth from one structure to the other—they are not just superimposed to form a single, doubly complex structure. The parallel with linguistic ambiguity is frequently noted and too obvious to require elucidation.

The biasing effects of context and previous expectations are also quite familiar. An interactive-activation model describes these factors as the pre-activation of certain potential categorizing structures. Owing to their higher initial level of activation, these structures may be selected for purposes of structural description over other candidates that match the target more closely. Suppose, for instance, that you and I are picking vegetables in my mother's

---

[12] This proposal bears a notable resemblance to Marcel's (1983) characterization of the procedure by which conscious percepts are recovered from unconscious processing. He analyzes consciousness as the imposition of **structural descriptions** (his term) on the records of such processing.

garden. Wondering what to do with the okra, you very reasonably ask me the question in (12)(a), and I respond with (12)(b) (representing my own opinion of where the okra should be sent).

(12)(a)   *Where does your mother want the okra?*
    (b)   *Alaska.*

In this context you might well construe my utterance as a mispronunciation of the sentence *I'll ask her* rather than a well-formed pronunciation of *Alaska*. This would certainly not happen if (12)(b) occurred in a list of states.

Two factors are claimed to influence the selection of a categorizing structure (active node): (1) the cognitive salience of possible candidates; and (2) their elaborative distance vis-à-vis the target. These factors are often antagonistic, and their interaction is central to questions of linguistic well-formedness. We have seen this already in our discussion of (12): when (12)(b) is construed as an ill-formed instance of *I'll ask her*, a structural description is imposed that is less than optimal with respect to factor (2); it is selected because the categorizing nodes (and the structural description as an integral whole) are temporarily rendered highly salient by the immediate context. The less transient cognitive salience associated with entrenchment and proto-typicality has comparable effects. Familiar expressions are easily recognized, and are often mistakenly recognized when something less usual was intended.

Let us explore these matters more carefully with reference to the sentences in (13):

(13)(a)   *He who laughs last laughs best.*
    (b)   *He who laughs least laughs best.*

The proverb in (13)(a) is a well-entrenched conventional unit that is readily elicited for the categorization of an appropriate usage event. In fact, a listener familiar with the expression can recognize it from the first few words alone. How might the interactive-activation model account for this phenomenon? All of the individual words are components of the complex unit, as are various word sequences (e.g. *He who*). The listener's identification of any component is capable of activating this unit (along with many others) as a candidate routine for structuring the overall usage event. As each successive word conforms to the predictions of this candidate routine, it becomes progressively more highly activated, and tends more strongly to inhibit alternatives. Convergence may be quite rapid: the sequence *He who* is already sufficient to suggest *laughs* as a likely continuation; its occurrence both confirms this expectation and disconfirms that of other candidates.

Once the expression has been provisionally identified as the well-known proverb, the remaining words are scanned for consistency with this hypothesis. Subsequent processing takes on more of a "top-to-bottom" character: insofar as possible, the usage event is interpreted according to this structural description. The closure phenomenon then comes into play (cf. 3.1.3), and discrepancies may go undetected if the remainder is not monitored closely. Thus an utterance of (13)(b) might be perceived as a well-formed rendition of (13)(a) if the listener has already, on the basis of *He who laughs*, invoked his knowledge of the proverb for primary categorization of the usage event. Suppose, however, that the listener does in fact detect the occurrence of *least* instead of the expected *last* in the utterance of (13)(b). What is then the structural description of the usage event? What is its conventional status?

The well-formedness of an expression is critically dependent on the conventional units selected for its primary categorization. Thus an impeccable utterance of *Alaska* is nevertheless ill formed when construed as an attempted pronunciation of *I'll ask her*. The status of (13)(b) is similarly determined by the structural description chosen for its evaluation. A listener who happens not to know the proverb of (13)(a) will simply judge (13)(b) to be a well-formed novel sentence, invoking for this purpose a variety of units (corresponding to words, phrases, grammatical constructions, etc.) that categorize various aspects of the usage event. For a listener who does know the proverb, these same units are invoked, but in addition the higher-order unit representing the conventional expression as a whole is almost certain to be activated. Whereas (13)(b) is then perceived as conforming in most respects to established patterns of English, it conflicts with certain specifications of the proverb, and is thus deviant (nonconventional) with respect to this particular aspect of its structural description.

The interactive-activation model is instructively compared to a conceivable and initially plausible alternative. We can call it the "minimal-deviance principle": structural descriptions are always chosen so as to maximize their compatibility with the usage event and thereby minimize any judgments of illformedness. If this were correct, primary categorization would always be effected by active nodes fully compatible with the usage event, provided that any such nodes were available; descriptions yielding judgments of well-formedness would consistently prevail if any were possible at all. Strictly applied, the principle would favor the selection of more schematic nodes (since these are less likely to conflict with the usage event), and would probably rule out any perception of linguistic deviance.[13]

The interactive-activation model is considerably more realistic, as no single factor determines the selection of categorizing nodes. The inherent and contextual salience of candidates is accommodated, as well as their compatibility

---

[13] Given the existence of high-level schemas, some categorizing structure can always be found that is fully schematic for the usage event. At the extreme, one might posit the schema [.../...], representing a speaker's knowledge of the existence of symbolic relationships. Such a superschema would be compatible with the specifications of any symbolic expression.

with the usage event. The model provides a plausible cognitive basis for the claim that low-level schemas generally predominate in the coding process: greater specificity (finer "grain") enables a routine to articulate with the target in many more points of detail, each contributing to its level of activation when the specifications match. Moreover, it permits a structural description to be imposed that nevertheless conflicts with the target in significant respects, as we saw in the discussion of (12) and (13). Judgments of ill-formedness are thus accounted for.

One additional example should bring the grammatical import of these notions into sharper focus. Suppose a child utters:

(14)   *I drinked it all!*

Though its intent is quite clear, adult speakers immediately judge this sentence ill formed from the standpoint of established convention: *drank* is the proper past-tense form of *drink*, and *drinked* is simply incorrect. What is the basis for this judgment?

The answer is less obvious than it might appear. Certainly *drank* is listed in the grammar as a conventional unit, but so is a salient schema—predicting *drinked*—that is regularly employed in the sanction of novel forms. These two units are sketched (using the sector notation) in (a) and (b) of Fig. 11.5.

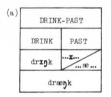 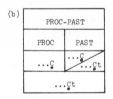 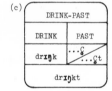

Fig. 11.5

Either might be called on to categorize the verb in (14), which is represented in diagram (c). If (b) is selected for primary categorization, the expression will be judged well formed, as (b) is fully schematic for (c). This is not, however, an option for the mature speaker under normal circumstances: *drinked* just "sounds wrong," and will not slip by unnoticed.

Consider the predictions of our two hypotheses concerning the assignment of a structural description. Our straw man—the minimal-deviance principle—wrongly predicts that *drinked* should be recognized as well formed: it is afforded full sanction by the selection of (b) as active node, and the principle maintains that a structural description providing full sanction always prevails over alternatives offering only partial sanction. By contrast, the interactive-activation model correctly predicts the judgment that *drinked* is deviant. Both (a) and (b) are well entrenched and easily elicited. However, (a) is far more specific than (b) in sectors S_1, S_3, and P_1, so given the fact that the expression is intended as the past-tense form of *drink*, (a) will be selected as the active node: it matches the target in far too many points of detail, and at a minimal elaborative distance, not to be elicited as the primary categorizing unit.[14] There is nonetheless a conflict in sector P_3: (drɪŋkt) is not an elaboration with respect to [dræŋk], but rather an extension, so it receives only partial sanction. The expression is therefore judged ill formed in regard to its phonological shape.

In contrast to *drank*, an infrequent form like *strove* does not have great cognitive salience, so it might not be invariably selected as active node when a past-tense form is needed for *strive*. Our model correctly predicts the possibility of the regular pattern being invoked: it is less specific than *strove*, but far more deeply entrenched. *Strived* might therefore slip by and be accepted as well formed.

11.2.3. *Complex Analyses*

There are several dimensions of complexity to the process of assigning structural descriptions to usage events. One is the distinction between primary and secondary categorization. Primary categorization is effected by active nodes: these are low-level structures selected from a range of candidate routines on the basis of cognitive salience and elaborative distance. The degree of compatibility between active nodes and those facets of a usage event they categorize provides an assessment of its linguistic well-formedness. Active nodes elicit secondary categorization, i.e. the activation of additional nodes and categorizing relationships, as determined by the configuration of schematic networks. A usage event is thereby characterized at multiple levels of schematicity and construed as instantiating a variety of linguistic categories. Collectively, these representations and relationships constitute its structural description.[15]

A second dimension resides in the complexity of an expression when construed at any given level of abstraction. Consider the (presumably novel) compound *arm hair* 'hair of the arm'. The expression is relatively simple, yet a substantial array of active nodes are invoked for its primary categorization, each corresponding to a particular facet of its structure. There are active nodes for the recognition of the component morphemes. Each of these is internally complex, having both a semantic and a phonological pole, which are in turn resolvable into smaller constituents (e.g. individual sound segments).

---

[14] A variety of theoretical frameworks accord precedence of application to the rule whose structural description is specified in the greatest detail. Examples include disjunctive ordering (Chomsky and Halle 1968), proper-inclusion precedence (Sanders 1974a, 1974b), and Hudson's priority-to-the-instance principle (1984).

[15] Nothing guarantees that two comparable usage events will trigger primary and secondary categorization by precisely the same array of conventional units. To some degree, then, the structural description of an expression may vary from one occasion of its use to the next.

Also required is a bipolar unit describing the grammatical construction, i.e. a low-level schema sanctioning the semantic and phonological integration of *arm* and *hair* to form a specific type of compound.[16] All the structures mentioned can be regarded as active nodes for the expression: each pertains to a particular level of organization and has its own scope of categorization. In this sense their roles are complementary (though some are components of others), and a single episode of primary categorization involves the coordinated activation of this full battery of nodes. Each active node contributes to the overall assessment of the expression's well-formedness through the full or partial sanction it affords within its scope of categorization. Moreover, it elicits the secondary activation of additional units, which are thereby also included in the expression's structural description.

The foregoing account of how structural descriptions are assigned may seem quite elaborate, but I would argue for its psychological plausibility. For one thing, it relies only on constructs that will almost certainly have analogs in any realistic model of cognitive processing. Moreover, any comprehensive analysis of linguistic expressions must accommodate their multifaceted, multilevel structure and systemic motivation. I suggest, in fact, that the account is at best a minimal one, even for a single **episode** of structural description, i.e. the imposition of one comprehensive and internally consistent analysis on a particular usage event. But we are not finished yet: it is readily apparent that many instances of language use are more complicated still, by virtue of requiring multiple episodes of this sort. Here we find a third dimension of complexity in the assignment of structural descriptions.

This can be illustrated with a previous example, namely the structural description assigned to *drinked*. It was claimed in 11.2.2 that *drank* is sufficiently well entrenched and cognitively salient, and matches the target in so many points of specific detail, that its selection as a standard (active node) is virtually inevitable for the primary categorization of an expression construed as the past-tense form of *drink* (cf. Fig. 11.5); *drinked* is therefore judged deviant because of an S/T discrepancy at the phonological pole. The single primary categorizing relationship ([dræŋk]––→(drɪŋkt)) hardly tells the whole story, however, since a speaker of English easily recognizes the nature of the error; i.e. he knows (in this case even at the conscious level) that *drinked* is perfectly reasonable given the regular patterns of past-tense formation, and would in fact be the proper form were it not for the existence of *drank*. To the extent that such a judgment is made, it presupposes a second episode of structural description: besides the construal of *drinked* with reference to *drank*, resulting in the perception of deviance, the speaker carries out

---

[16] We might identify this schema as the one having *body hair*, *head hair*, and *chest hair* as unit instantiations, i.e. a schematic compound that describes the first element as a noun designating the body or a body part, and the second element as *hair* in particular.

a subsidiary evaluation invoking as an active node the appropriate subschema that sanctions regular forms (Fig. 11.5(b)).

Our account of how structural descriptions are assigned is not intended as a comprehensive model of speech production or comprehension; it pertains only to a single instance of interpreting a usage event as the possible instantiation of a particular linguistic structure. A number of such episodes are likely to figure in the production or comprehension of an expression (even a fairly simple one), and are implied whenever the language user considers alternatives. For example, in seeking an efficient and effective way to get his idea across, the speaker often contemplates various options that structure the same basic situation through different images (e.g. *It's running* vs. *It's still ticking*). Or the hearer can be forced in mid-utterance to revise his hypothesis concerning the expression he is monitoring (led by *He who laughs* to anticipate the familiar proverb in (13)(a), the listener may change his analysis when the following word proves to be *least* instead of *last*). Each alternative considered requires the assignment of a structural description to a potential usage event.

Most obviously, multiple episodes of structural description occur in the perception of ambiguity. Here a particular phonological sequence is subject to construal as instantiating two or more alternative expressions that coincide in sector P_3 (i.e. their composite phonological structure). Of course, their phonological coincidence need only be approximate: a usage event can be structured in alternate ways even if its phonological pole is judged ill formed under one of the interpretations.[17] Observe that ambiguity is not regarded in this account as an absolute property of abstract linguistic objects (e.g. sentences), but is treated instead as a function of language use. The class of potentially ambiguous phonological sequences is not well defined, since only the tolerance level of the language user determines how divergent two expressions can be in sector P_3 and still be assignable as structural interpretations of the same vocalization.

A final matter to consider is the need for multiple analyses in the sense of Hankamer (1977). These are cases in which the grammatical behavior of a particular construction gives conflicting signals about its proper linguistic description. Either of two obvious analyses accounts for certain of its peculiarities, but neither is sufficient alone to account for all of them. Illustration is provided by an extensive set of established verb-preposition combinations in English, e.g. *talk to, quarrel over, deal with, ask for, stare at,* and so on. What is their constituency in sentences like those in (15)?

(15)(a) *The manager is talking to some reporters.*
   (b) *They always quarrel over women.*
   (c) *Martin didn't dare ask for another promotion.*

---

[17] Punsters are notorious for their tolerance in this regard.

Various considerations suggest that the verb (V) and preposition (P) form a constituent (itself a complex verb); these include the unit status and specialized meaning of the combinations, as well as the possibility of passivizing the prepositional object:

(16)(a) *He was talked to at great length.*
    (b) *She's the sort of woman who is always being quarreled over.*
    (c) *Was it specifically asked for?*

However, other phenomena suggest that the preposition forms a constituent instead with the following nominal:

(17)(a) *It was to the deputy chief executive assistant that I finally managed to talk.*
    (b) *They fight constantly about money and politics, but over women they never quarrel.*
    (c) *For what is he most likely to ask?*

Cognitive grammar straightforwardly accommodates this type of situation. We have already noted (Ch. 8) that constituency is variable, and that the same composite structure is generally derivable through alternate compositional paths. Two such paths can be noted for sentences like those in (15), and correspond to alternative structural descriptions. (1) V and P are integrated at the first level of constituency to derive a composite transitive verb, whose primary landmark corresponds to that of P; this landmark is then elaborated by a direct-object nominal (NML) at the second hierarchical level. (2) P and NML are first integrated to form a prepositional phrase; this composite expression then elaborates a relational e-site within V at the second level of constituency. Recall that in this framework both analyses are consistent with the unit status and semantic specialization of particular V + P combinations (cf. 8.4.1 and 12.2.3).

All we need say, then, is that both orders of composition have been conventionalized and are represented in the grammar by schematic units describing multilevel constructions. In certain instances, global considerations of structural consistency dictate a particular choice, as illustrated in (16) and (17). For expressions like those in (15), on the other hand, both descriptions are workable and potentially available to the language user (though (2) may be the default-case analysis). On a given occasion either type of analysis can be imposed, or even both (implying two episodes of structural description). Such expressions are therefore treated as structurally ambiguous. They differ from standard, more striking examples of ambiguity (e.g. *Visiting relatives can be a nuisance*) only because the semantic consequences of choosing one analysis as opposed to the other are relatively inconsequential—the composite semantic structure is essentially the same with either order of composition.

11.3. Actualization, Computation, and Analogy

Cognitive grammar captures generalizations by postulating schematic units. How are these schemas employed for the sanction and computation of novel expressions? The present section describes this process with reference to cognitive transitions and related constructs. "Chains" of computations are then discussed and compared to the notion of derivations in the generative tradition. Profitably examined in this context is the relationship between "rules" in the generative sense and the more traditional concept of analogy.

11.3.1. *Transitions*

Let us briefly review the notion of cognitive transitions (cf. 4.3.4). A transition between two cognitive events, A and B, consists in their sequenced occurrence as facets of a higher-order event: $A > B$. In some instances (e.g. classical conditioning) A and B are essentially exhaustive of the higher-order event. Commonly, however, their coordination as components of such an event requires some kind of mental operation. Acts of comparison imply an operation referred to previously as scanning (3.1.2). Other operations are given by the various types of focal adjustments (3.3), such as a shift in vantage point or level of abstraction.[18] A more elaborate example is the mental rotation of a figure, where A and B correspond to the conception of the figure in different orientations (cf. Fig. 3.10).

A particular array of cognitive structures and abilities defines a class of potential transitions involving the elements in this domain. A potential transition $A > B$ is **actualized** when the coordinated activation of A and B does in fact occur. With repeated actualization, a transition achieves unit status; it is then an **established** transition that can be activated like any other unit. The notions **actualization** and **activation** are thus distinguished: the former term refers to the realization of previously unexploited potential, and the latter to the execution of an established routine.

Significantly, it is possible for all the links in a chain of transitions to constitute established units without this being true for the chain as a whole. Thus, if $[A > B]$ and $[B > C]$ have unit status individually by virtue of the repeated coordination of their respective components, it may nonetheless happen that these units have never been coordinated with one another. Their chained occurrence would hardly be surprising, however, since the activation of B as part of $[A > B]$ naturally facilitates the activation of $[B > C]$. In effect, all the groundwork has been laid for the implementation of $(A > B > C)$; it simply awaits actualization, i.e. the exploitation of immediate potential.

---

[18] Suppose I see three apples on a table and observe that they form an equilateral triangle. A is then my detailed conception of the scene with the apples; B is the schematic conception of their spatial relationship; and $A > B$ incorporates the abstracting operation relating the two.

When one transition chain is included within another as a subchain, the former is said to be **immanent** to the latter; $A > B$ and $B > C > D$ are therefore immanent to $A > B > C > D > E$. This notion was previously invoked in the characterization of cognitive distance (4.3.4) and of basic conceptual relations (6.2). In a somewhat more speculative vein, I now suggest its applicability to the elaborative relationship between a schema and its instantiations.

The basic hypothesis is that greater precision of specification demands a more elaborate sequence of cognitive operations (at some level of analysis): in specifying a parameter, confining its value to a narrow range requires additional cognitive processing beyond that needed to confine its value to a broader range. Suppose that schema S is elaborated by instantiation I with respect to parameter P. For the characterization of S in regard to P, we can posit some sequence of cognitive events $[p_1 > p_2 > \cdots > p_m]$ serving to articulate this conception down to a certain level of specificity; call this sequence P_S. The finer precision of I along this parameter then implies the more inclusive sequence P_I: $[p_1 > p_2 > \cdots > p_m > p_{m+1} > \cdots > p_n]$. It is thus hypothesized that P_S is immanent to P_I, with the added subchain $[p_{m+1} > \cdots > p_n]$ corresponding to the elaborative distance between S and I along the parameter in question. If we summarize over all relevant parameters, and simplify by treating S and I as the aggregates of their many specifications, we can say by extension that S is immanent to I.

This hypothesis directly explains the schematic-transparency principle, which holds that a schema merges with its instantiation to form a composite conception equivalent to the instantiation. If S is immanent to I with respect to every parameter of specification, all the cognitive events contributed by S are also inherent in I, so their union is identical to I. It also helps explain a crucial step in the recognition process as described in the interactive-activation model, namely the presumed capacity of any facet of a target to elicit candidate routines for its potential categorization. The target is generally quite specific relative to these categorizing units, so among the cognitive events it comprises are various subsets that either constitute such units or substantially overlap them.

A subtle distinction must be drawn, however, between immanence and explicit categorization. If the hypothesis is correct, the activation of an instantiation implies the occurrence of all those cognitive events that figure in the activation of a schema. In conceptualizing a cobra, for instance, there is a sense in which we are ipso facto conceptualizing a snake. But this is quite different—experientially and analytically—from what is involved in making the specific categorizing judgment that a cobra instantiates the snake category. The latter requires a higher-order event of the form $[[\text{SNAKE}] \rightarrow [\text{COBRA}]]$, where the cognitive events constituting [SNAKE] occur as an individuated unit in addition to their occurrence as integral facets of [COBRA].

As a general matter, the occurrence of a sequence of cognitive events in the execution of a more inclusive routine does not per se establish this sequence as a unit; in reciting the alphabet, for instance, we have often uttered the letter sequence N-O-P-Q-R, but it is doubtful that many speakers have segregated this particular group and established it individually as a unit. Similarly, we cannot regard a schema as being activated simply because the event sequence it comprises occurs as part of the execution of its instantiation. Despite the immanence of [SNAKE] to [COBRA], therefore, the activation of the former is not necessitated by that of the latter. It is certainly facilitated, though, since a well-entrenched categorization like [[SNAKE]→[COBRA]] provides an easily activated transition between the component units in either direction: [COBRA] > [SNAKE] involves an operation of abstraction, and [SNAKE] > [COBRA] one of elaboration.

11.3.2. *Computation as Actualization*

The well-formedness of usage events is assessed through categorizing judgments of the general form $S--\!\!\rightarrow T$. In the simplest situation, a conventional unit functions as the standard and is directly compared to (T), some facet of the event. The categorization thus has the form $([S]--\!\!\rightarrow(T))$, and the status of (T) depends on the degree to which $[S]$ (the active node) is recognized in (T), i.e. whether $[S]$ bears to (T) a relation of full or partial schematicity. Matters are more complicated, though, whenever schemas are employed for the computation of novel expressions. When this happens, the relationship between conventional units and the usage event is mediated by additional elements of structural significance, as represented in the formula $([U]===\!=\!\!=>(S)--\!\!\rightarrow(T))$; $[U]$ is here a set of conventional units, (S) is the novel expression, and computation is indicated by the double arrow. Immediate categorization of the usage event is thus effected by a structure (S) that is not itself a unit, though it "follows" in some sense as a straightforward extrapolation from established convention.

Let us take a phonological example, namely the optional reduction of English -*ing* to [ən] or [n] (orthographic -*in'*). For many speakers, the full form is employed in careful speech, and the reduced form is a stylistically marked variant occurring in casual speech. For frequently used verbs, both variants are capable of being mastered as units; they are associated by an extensional relationship to constitute a minimal schematic network: [[work-ing]--→ [work-in']]. From an array of established units of this sort ([[talk-ing]--→ [talk-in']], [[feel-ing]--→[feel-in']], etc.), a speaker presumably extracts the schema [[V-ing]--→[V-in']]. This schema, which ˙amounts to a morphophonemic rule, describes a conventional pattern of phonological reduction affecting participial expressions.[19]

---

[19] The notation [V-ing] abbreviates a composite, bipolar structure (i.e. a construction). Note that the schema specifies the suffix -*ing* in particular: the reduction does not apply to just any occurrence of unstressed *ing* (e.g. *lemming* does not reduce to *lemmin'*).

Suppose a certain speaker possesses the units just noted, and that he witnesses an utterance of *workin'*. Categorization of this usage event is then direct, as described in the formula $([S]--\rightarrow(T))$: $[S]$ is the unit [work-in'], and (T) is the event, the utterance *workin'*. Primary categorization with [work-in'] as the active node elicits the secondary activation of [[work-ing]$--\rightarrow$[work-in']], which may in turn activate the schema [[V-ing]$--\rightarrow$[V-in']]. Though all of these nodes figure in the structural description of the utterance, the sanction it receives directly from [work-in'] determines its well-formedness.

Suppose further that the same speaker has encountered the verb *strive* on relatively few occasions, and primarily in formal contexts. It is conceivable, under these circumstances, that the unreduced participle *striving* has achieved the status of a unit (though not deeply entrenched), whereas the reduced variant *strivin'* is unfamiliar. What happens when this speaker encounters an utterance of the reduced form? If [striv-ing] is selected as the active node for categorizing the usage event, he will find *strivin'* deviant in some measure (it will "sound funny" or "feel wrong"). Nevertheless, he will likely accept it as perfectly well formed, since it follows a productive pattern. The categorizing judgment then has the shape $([U] = \doteq =>(S)--\rightarrow(T))$: conventional units $[U]$ permit the computation of a novel but "expected" intermediate structure (S), namely (striv-in'), which is fully schematic for the usage event (T). The sanction afforded by the intermediate structure is evidently responsible for the well-formedness judgment.

Our task is now to scrutinize the computational relationship $[U] = = = =>$ (S). I will speak of **computation**, and posit a sanctioning role for a computed structure (S), only in those instances in which (S) is fully prefigured by a set of established units. We can say that (S) merely awaits actualization: given set $[U]$, its implementation requires only the realization of immediate (though previously unexploited) potential.[20]

In the present example, the novel expression (S) is (striv-in'). As a conventionally determined form, it is necessarily abstract relative to the fully specific usage event, even though the phonological pattern it follows is phonetically motivated. What are the conventional units—set $[U]$—permitting the computation of (striv-in')? One of these units is obviously [[V-ing]$--\rightarrow$ [V-in']], the schema representing the general pattern of extension. Another is the unreduced form [striv-ing], constituting the "input" to the computation. We must also include the relationship [[V-ing]$\rightarrow$[striv-ing]], i.e. the categorization of [striv-ing] as a structure of the sort to which the extension is applicable.

[20] If a language were regarded as a formal system, we could say that (S) is algorithmically derivable. I am not so much opposed to this way of viewing things as I am concerned with giving it a plausible cognitive interpretation. Still, I would argue that a completely formal, algorithmic account of linguistic expressions is achievable only at the expense of imposing arbitrary boundaries.

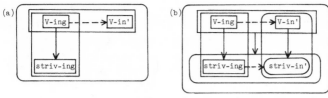

Fig. 11.6

The members of $[U]$ are depicted in Fig. 11.6(a). Observe that [V-ing] is a component of both [[V-ing]$--\rightarrow$[V-in']] and [[V-ing]$\rightarrow$[striv-ing]]; it is shown only once in this compacted diagram, despite its dual function. Because it appears in both categorizing relationships, [V-ing] provides a connection between [V-in'] and [striv-ing]. In fact, since a unit categorization establishes transitions in either direction between standard and target, the configuration in diagram (a) constitutes a bidirectional transition chain: in one direction it reads ([striv-ing]$>$[V-ing]$>$[V-in']), where the first transition is based on an operation of abstraction, and the second on extension (transformation). Note that the chain as a whole is novel, despite the unit status of the individual transitions.

Lurking within this configuration, awaiting actualization, is the novel expression (striv-in'). How does its actualization come about? Essentially, it requires only the coactivation of the two links in the transition chain, [[striv-ing]$>$[V-ing]] and [[V-ing]$>$[V-in']] (or more precisely, [[striv-ing]$\leftarrow$[V-ing]] and [[V-ing]$--\rightarrow$[V-in']]). Both transitions are units, so when [striv-ing] activates the first, its component [V-ing] is capable of eliciting the second. Recall, now, our hypothesis that a schema is immanent to its instantiations. The cognitive events constituting [V-ing] are thus embedded in the more elaborate set of events comprised by [striv-ing]. Moreover, activation of the categorizing relationship [[V-ing]$\rightarrow$[striv-ing]] implies that the former events occur as a functionally significant group in the context of the latter, i.e. [V-ing] is recognized within [striv-ing]. When [[V-ing]$--\rightarrow$[V-in']] is activated, therefore, the transforming operation it embodies does not affect [V-ing] as an isolated entity, but as an integral facet of [striv-ing]. The effect of carrying out the operation [[V-ing]$--\rightarrow$[V-in']] in this more elaborate context is the modified set of cognitive events that constitute (striv-in').

The full computation is depicted in Fig. 11.6(b). Added to the elements of 6(a) is the novel structure (striv-in'), which functions as an elaboration of [V-in'] and an extension from [striv-ing]. Further, the categorizing relationship ([striv-ing]$--\rightarrow$(striv-in')) instantiates the schema [[V-ing]$--\rightarrow$[V-in']]. All of these structures and relationships are capable of becoming units should the variant pronunciation occur with any frequency. Parallel complexes of units already exist for *workin', talkin', feelin',* etc.

In rejecting an algorithmic model, consequently, I am not denying either

computational activity or the possibility of deriving an open-ended set of
novel expressions from an array of conventional units. However, computation
is related to more broadly applicable cognitive notions and treated as a special
case of the categorizing ability employed for the structuring of usage events.
The set of structures that are fully prefigured by existing units is but a small
and otherwise nondistinctive subset of those a speaker is capable of evaluating; this larger class includes indefinitely many structures that cannot be predicted algorithmically, because they either conflict with the specifications
of conventional units or are greatly underspecified by these units. It happens
that a schematic unit sanctions the reduction of *-ing* to *-in'*, hence the form
strivin' readily computes; but even if there were no such rule, and *strivin'*
simply occurred as a slip of the tongue, a speaker would still be able to categorize it as an extension from [striv-ing], despite its unanticipated and unpredictable character.

11.3.3. *Computation Chains*

When the coding process involves the mediated relationship $([U] = = = >$
$(S) - - \rightarrow (T))$, the computed structure (S) effects the primary categorization of
(T) and determines its well-formedness. In this respect (S) is comparable to a
unit, despite its novel character. It is therefore not unanticipated that (S) can
also function like a unit in the sense of motivating further computations. That
is, (S) may combine with another set of units $[U']$ to permit the further computation of an additional element (S'): $(([U'],(S)) = = = > (S'))$. We can thus
envisage a chain of computations, where (S') in turn combines with a third set
of units $[U'']$ for the actualization of (S''), and so on, until one of the computed
structures is directly employed to categorize (T). In a chain like Fig. 11.7, the

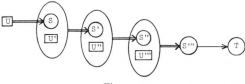

Fig. 11.7

intermediate structures correspond to sequenced stages in the coding process,
and the sequence as a whole is prefigured by conventional units.

Consider how the previous pattern of extension interacts with another,
namely the reduction of [t] to [ʔ] before [n̩]. The phonological networks of
words like *curtain, button, kitten,* etc. include categorizing relationships between the variants with [t] and those with [ʔ], e.g. [[kɪtn̩] - - →[kɪʔn̩]]. From
relationships of this sort a speaker extracts the schema [[...tn̩] - - →[...ʔn̩]].
Suppose, now, that a speaker who has mastered both patterns of extension
encounters a casual pronunciation of the progressive of *sprout*:

(18)   *They're sproutin' like crazy!*

If the reduction of *sprouting* to *sproutin'* is novel for this speaker, a computation directly parallel to Fig. 11.6 results in the actualization of the intermediate structure (sprawtn̩). The standard of [[...tn̩]--→[...ʔn̩]] is clearly immanent to (sprawtn̩), so the potential exists for a second computation. The coactivation of these structures, i.e. the transformation of [...tn̩] to [...ʔn̩] in the context of (sprawtn̩), results in the actualization of (sprawʔn̩), which is then available for categorizing the usage event.

This type of scenario is familiar to anybody who has studied linguistics. It represents the commonplace observation that certain linguistic patterns "feed" others: the applicability of one pattern presupposes a structure specified by another. In a constructive model, it is customary to employ the process metaphor and speak of the output of one rule constituting the input to the next; a sequence of rule applications effects the derivation of a surface representation from some kind of underlying structure. I have rejected most aspects of this standard view (the process metaphor, derivations, underlying structures), yet I appear to be invoking very similar notions under the guise of computation chains. Some kind of explanation is thus in order. Are the frameworks really as different as I have made them out to be?

Considering the insight often afforded by derivational analyses, it would be surprising (and disturbing) if nothing remotely comparable were found within the present framework. We may accept the existence of feeding relationships between structural patterns as a valid and important aspect of linguistic organization. Derivational models are specifically geared to accommodate such relationships; in fact, their organization is inspired by these relationships in an obvious and fundamental sense. Cognitive grammar interprets them in a very different way, however, and situates them in a broader context where they are seen as special manifestations of other phenomena. Hence they are subsidiary rather than paradigmatic, and are treated in processual terms only insofar as all linguistic structure can be said to reside in cognitive processing.

More specifically, computation is assimilated to categorization. The "derivation" of one structure from another is regarded as a manifestation of our general capacity for extension, i.e. categorization by prototype. Many such categorizations (e.g. metaphorical extensions) do not correspond to anything recognized as "rules" in derivational frameworks, and those that do are not the exclusive province of either the grammar ("competence") or its use ("performance"): for example, if *workin'* has unit status but *strivin'* does not, the categorization [[work-ing]--→[work-in']] is included in the grammar as a conventional unit, whereas ([striv-ing]--→(striv-in')) occurs by computation as part of the coding process. A schematic network often includes a series of extensions that define a node-to-node path of some length; this path then resembles the sequence of steps ("rule applications") in a complex derivation.

There are nevertheless significant differences. For one thing, the "underlying" structure in a derivation is not conceived as a prototype, nor is a rule considered to be a schema for categorizing relationships. The elements corresponding to the steps in a derivation may be split between categorizing relationships with unit status (included in the grammar) and computations actualized in the coding process; where this boundary falls can vary from one expression to another (even if they are precisely parallel), and can change fairly quickly for a particular expression. Furthermore, an established path need not be activated in its entirety on every occasion (as a unit, [work-in'] might be activated for the categorization of a usage event without eliciting the secondary activation of [work-ing]), and indeed, the network conception suggests the possibility of alternate categorizing paths leading to the same node.[21]

Patterns of phonological extension (i.e. rules like [[...tn]--→[...ʔŋ]]) are matched at the semantic pole by patterns of semantic extension. One such pattern is exemplified in (19); it permits the extension of the name of a nation's capital to designate that nation's government.

(19)(a)   *Paris refuses to consider the proposal.*
    (b)   *London, as usual, is conciliatory.*
    (c)   *Moscow rejected the treaty.*
    (d)   *Managua refuses to negotiate.*

From particular extensions of this type that constitute established units, e.g. [[PARIS/Paris]--→[GOVERNMENT-IN-PARIS/Paris]], speakers extract the schematic unit [[CITY/...]--→[GOVERNMENT-IN-CITY/...]], from which novel instances of the pattern can then be computed. By following these developments we obtain a fairly accurate picture of shifting national concerns— *Hanoi* was extended in this way about two decades ago, and *Managua* much more recently.[22]

Patterns of semantic extension can also participate in feeding relationships. A simple example involves two very general patterns that qualify as conventional units despite their being so natural and obvious from a cognitive standpoint that we normally take them for granted. One permits the term for an object to be extended to designate a replica of that object, e.g. *tiger* for a doll in the image of a tiger. The second permits a term to be extended to designate a degraded instance of the type it names. Moreover, the first pattern can feed the second; this is illustrated in (20)(a):

---

[21] Beyond this, there are many putative derivations for which analogous chains of categorization or computation are not posited. For instance, the English passive is not derived from the active (or categorized by it), but represents instead an independent construction (cf. Langacker 1982a).

[22] This and other metonymic patterns are discussed in Lakoff and Johnson (1980, ch. 8). The pattern of (19) is actually a special case of a far more general phenomenon (cf. *New York says that they can't fill our order until next month*). The schema describing it is therefore just one node in a substantial schematic network.

(20)(a) *Would you please sew the tail back on my tiger?*
(b) *Where did you put my cathedral?*

If (20)(a) is construed in the most obvious way, *tiger* refers to a degraded instance of a tiger doll. The opposite feeding relationship is also possible, though perhaps less common—an original object becoming degraded before replication, the replicate taking the name of the original; (20)(b) might be uttered by somebody searching for the model he has built of a devastated church.[23]

A final matter pertains to the growth of bipolar networks. We observed in 10.3.4 that if each pole of a lexical item consists of an elaborate schematic network, it cannot be presumed that every possible pairing of a semantic and a phonological node occurs with sufficient frequency to be established individually as a symbolic unit. In general, however, any phonetic variant is readily employed with any semantic variant (e.g. a fast-speech rendition of *tree* symbolizes any of the semantic nodes in Fig. 10.3). We can now explain the ready availability of nonunit combinations in terms of actualization. Given the unit status of particular symbolic relationships between salient nodes, established categorizations at the two poles create the immediate potential for other combinations. Suppose that $[A/a]$ constitutes the prototype for a lexical category (i.e. $[A]$ is the semantic prototype, and $[a]$ the phonological prototype). Suppose further that the extensions $[[A]--\rightarrow[A']]$ and $[[a]--\rightarrow[a']]$ have been effected (individually) at the two poles: these extensions have resulted in the symbolic units $[A'/a]$ and $[A/a']$, but the specific combination (A'/a') has never occurred. Its actualization requires only the coactivation of two units constituting a transition chain, e.g. $[A'/a]$ and $[[a]--\rightarrow[a']]$. The effect of carrying out the transformation $[[a]--\rightarrow[a']]$ in the context of the symbolic unit $[A'/a]$ is precisely the structure (A'/a').

11.3.4. *Rule vs. Analogy*

The notion of actualization is further applicable to the computation of novel expressions instantiating grammatical constructions. Let us choose for illustration the [V-er] pattern of subject nominalization, and assume that *striver* is a novel exponent of that pattern. Two different representations are offered in Fig. 11.8 for the relationship between the schema for the construction and its novel instantiation.[24] In diagram (a), the schematic unit is shown on the left.

---

[23] Just as orders of composition can be conventionalized (cf. 8.4.2), so can feeding relationships between particular patterns of extension. Higher-order schematic units are thereby incorporated in the grammar, e.g. $[[OBJECT/...]--\rightarrow[REPLICA-OF-OBJECT/...]--\rightarrow$ $[DEGRADED-REPLICA-OF-OBJECT/...]]$. Such units are the analog of rule-ordering relationships in derivational models. I will not explore the implications of the present conception for the many well-known problems and issues associated with the ordering of rules.

[24] The letter V stands for the verb schema; the lexical units *strive* and *-er* are given by their orthographic representations. Despite these abbreviations, all the structures in Fig. 11.8 are bipolar.

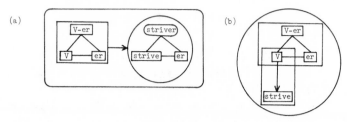

Fig. 11.8

The component structures [V] and [er] integrate to form the composite structure [V-er]. The novel expression *striver* is sketched on the right. Its composite form is assembled from the unit components [strive] and [er] in accordance with the specifications of the constructional schema. *Striver* thus bears an elaborative relationship to this schema.

Diagram (b) does not show *striver* directly; instead it depicts the transition chain that underlies its actualization (cf. Fig. 11.6). The unit status of the constructional schema (given at the top) implies established transitions between any pair of its elements ([V], [er], and [V-er]), if only because any one of these elements is capable of activating the schema as a whole. Unit [V] is the pivotal element in the transition chain, for it is also a component of the categorizing relationship [[V]→[strive]], the other link in this chain. Observe now that [V] is immanent not only to its elaboration [strive], but also to the composite structure [V-er]: since this latter structure defines a (schematic) noun with reference to a (schematic) verb, it incorporates the cognitive events comprised by the verb schema. Consequently, the actualization of *striver* is effected simply by the coactivation of the schema and the categorizing unit. *Striver* (as depicted on the right in diagram (a)) is the structure that results when the elaborative operation [[V]→[strive]] is carried out in the context of the constructional schema, wherever those cognitive events constituting [V] occur.

It is instructive to compare this rule- or schema-based account of the formation of novel expressions to an alternative that has often been proposed, namely the mechanism of analogy (cf. Bloomfield 1933, sec. 16.6; Householder 1971, ch. 5; Langacker 1973a, p. 22). Analogy is typically presented as equivalent to the mathematical task of solving a proportion, as in (21).

$$(21)\quad \frac{search}{searcher} = \frac{lecture}{lecturer} = \frac{examine}{examiner} = \frac{complain}{complainer} = \frac{strive}{?}$$

It can thus be claimed that a speaker forms the novel expression *striver* from *strive* by analogy to familiar pairs like *search/searcher*, *lecture/lecturer*, *examine/examiner*, *complain/complainer*, etc., obviating the need for an abstract nominalization rule.

From the perspective of cognitive grammar, these two approaches are effectively equivalent. If the notion of analogy is made explicit, and if rules are conceived as schemas, there is no substantial difference between analogical and rule-based descriptions. The model therefore achieves a significant conceptual unification.

What is required for an explicit account of analogical formation? For example, what is it that enables a speaker to figure out that the correct solution to the proportion in (21) is *striver* as opposed, say, to *golfer*, *shark*, or *vacillate*? The ability to make the proper analogy implies the perception of a pattern, together with some means for extending the pattern to a novel instance. What are the elements of the pattern in (21)? The established pairs *search/searcher*, *lecture/lecturer*, *examine/examiner*, etc. are parallel in numerous respects. The first member of each pair is a verb, and the second member is a noun. Moreover, there is a systematic semantic relationship between the two members: the noun denotes a person who performs a particular role in the process described by the verb (it designates the trajector of the corresponding process). There are also obvious phonological parallels. In particular, the noun is in each case identical to the verb except for the addition of the suffix *-er*.

When considered collectively, together with the symbolic relationships implicit in the above, these specifications are effectively equivalent to the schema that characterizes the nominalizing construction. The verbs in (21) correspond to the component structure labeled [V] in the constructional schema of Fig. 11.8, and the nouns correspond to the composite structure [V-er]. Once the schema is extracted to represent the parallelism of *search/searcher*, *lecture/lecturer*, etc.—i.e. once the basis for the analogy has been established—the solution to the proportion is fully prefigured. Extending the pattern to the novel exponent *striver* is only a matter of actualization.

The one remaining issue is whether or not the speaker possesses the constructional schema as a preestablished unit. If he does, *striver* can be actualized without the concomitant activation of *search/searcher*, *lecture/lecturer*, etc. (cf. Fig. 11.8(b)). If he does not, he must activate these forms and extract the requisite schema—representing a fleeting perception of structural parallelism—as immediate and essential steps in computing the novel expression. The difference is not terribly significant in the present framework, as both alternatives require the same basic operations: extracting the schema, and computing the novel form. The distinction comes down to whether the schema has previously been extracted, and whether this has occurred sufficiently often to make it a unit. One would presume so in the present instance, but we certainly have the ability to extract new schemas and analogize in unprefigured directions. The importance of this ability to language change is readily apparent (cf. Bolinger 1961).

CHAPTER 12

Composition

IN THIS FINAL CHAPTER we return to valence relations and grammatical constructions. Ch. 8 emphasized the "horizontal" relationships within a construction, namely component structures and their mode of integration. Here we probe more deeply into the "vertical" dimension, examining **composition**, i.e. the relation between component structures and the composite structure that derives from them. Our first order of business is to supplement the earlier discussion of analyzability (8.2.2). We then consider the implications of describing composition in terms of categorizing relationships. Problems concerning zero morphemes and composite lexical units are dealt with in conclusion.

12.1. Analyzability and Related Phenomena

In considering the compositional aspects of grammatical constructions, it is important that we distinguish clearly between the closely associated notions of **analyzability** and **compositionality**. Analyzability pertains to the ability of speakers to recognize the contribution that each component structure makes to the composite whole; the question of analyzability thus arises primarily at the level of individual composite expressions. Compositionality, on the other hand, pertains to the regularity of compositional relationships, i.e. the degree to which the value of the whole is predictable from the values of its parts. It therefore concerns the relationship between a constructional schema and its instantiations: Is the integration of component structures to form a composite structure sufficiently regular to be susceptible to schematic characterization? Is it possible to formulate a schema for a particular construction that will enable one to predict, for every potential choice of component structures, precisely what the composite structure will be?

12.1.1. *Compositionality*

These questions can be posed in bipolar terms, but we will concentrate on semantic compositionality. The standard view attributes full compositionality to grammatical structure: the meaning of an expression generated by grammatical rules is a regular compositional function of the meanings of its parts. For every grammatical rule effecting the combination of elements, an associated rule of semantic interpretation is normally posited that computes the semantic value of the higher-order structure through an operation on the values of its immediate constituents. The assumption of semantic compositionality is considered necessary to account for the ability of speakers to construct and understand an open-ended set of novel expressions.

The validity of this assumption is less an empirical issue than a matter of defining the scope of grammar and linguistic semantics. It is usual to exclude from the domain of grammatical description—by assigning it to the lexicon—any established expression whose semantic value diverges from the predictions of regular compositional rules. For a novel expression whose interpretation is too specific to be predicted in full detail by general rules, the analyst relies on the putative distinction between semantics and pragmatics, holding the grammar responsible only for the obviously compositional aspects of its meaning. Hence the claim of full compositionality is hardly forced upon us by the overwhelming weight of empirical observation and all-embracing descriptive triumphs: it is true instead by virtue of definitions that restrict its scope to a highly limited domain. Since many important aspects of meaning are left to be accounted for in some other manner, one can legitimately question the significance and internal coherence of what is left.

I do not believe that either the distinction between grammar and lexicon or that between semantics and pragmatics can ultimately be maintained. Nevertheless, some degree of compositionality must obviously be assumed. There is certainly a large measure of regularity in the meaning of composite expressions vis-à-vis the meanings of their components, and speakers rely on this regularity in determining the semantic value of novel expressions. Patterns of compositionality are represented in the grammar as schematic constructions that specify the integration of component structures and the relation that each of them bears to the composite structure. The existence of such patterns does not substantiate the claim that composite expressions are *fully* compositional, however, nor does it establish the nonarbitrary nature of the dichotomies required to maintain this claim. Linguistic phenomena lend themselves more easily to a claim of *partial* rather than full compositionality. Such a claim is perfectly natural in view of the fact that language is learned and used in context by speakers who bring many shared knowledge systems to the communicative endeavor.

To clarify this notion, let us consider abstractly the elements that figure in a construction. There are three primary structures, and three relationships, as sketched in Fig. 12.1: [A] and [B] stand for component structures, whereas [C] is the composite structure. These are associated pairwise by correspon-

Fig. 12.1

dences to form the relationships indicated by solid lines. Horizontal correspondences establish the relationship [A]-[B], which is one of integration.
Vertical correspondences establish the compositional relationships [A]-[C]
and [B]-[C]. A full description of the construction must specify all of these
structures and relationships.

We must also consider a fourth structure, [AB], representing the "expected" outcome of the integrative relationship [A]-[B]. Structure [AB] is defined as being computable from this relationship in the following sense:
(1) [AB] has no content that is not contributed directly by [A] and/or [B];
(2) it is a unified conceptualization that respects the correspondences constituting relationship [A]-[B] (i.e. it is the structure that results from superimposing the corresponding substructures of [A] and [B]); and (3) it inherits
its profile from one of the component structures. In fully compositional expressions, the composite structure [C] is computable in this sense, hence
[C] = [AB]. An example is the phrase *black bird*, whose composite structure
inherits the profile of *bird*, and whose content is exhausted by that of its components. However, since the composite structure has separate identity and requires separate characterization, nothing in this model prevents [C] from
having content that is contributed by neither [A] nor [B] (so that [C] = [ABX]),
or from conflicting in certain respects with the specifications of one or both
components (i.e. [C] = [A'B']). The former circumstance is illustrated by the
compound *blackbird*, which designates a specific type of black bird and is
consequently more precise in content than anything deducible from *black* and
bird alone. The latter is illustrated by *blackboard*, which is not a board in the
usual sense, and is not necessarily black.[1]

Though [C] = [AB] in fully compositional expressions, their identity is not
sufficient as a characterization of full compositionality. As generally understood, this notion additionally implies a substantial regularity across expressions with respect to how [A] and [B] combine and the relationship they bear
to the composite structure: [C] is a **regular compositional function** of [A]
and [B]. In more standard approaches, this is interpreted to mean that [A] and
[B] combine by virtue of a regular syntactic rule, with [C] algorithmically
derivable from [A] and [B] by an associated rule of semantic interpretation.

---

[1] The first of these discrepancies has been alleviated to some extent by the truncation of *blackboard* to *board* (e.g. *Go to the board, Johnny, and do the first problem*). One extended sense of
board is consequently available that matches the pertinent specifications of the composite
structure.

The cognitive-grammar translation of this requirement is that relationships [A]-[B], [A]-[C], and [B]-[C] all conform to the specifications of a salient schema.

These two aspects of full compositionality are distinct and independently variable. The identity of [C] and [AB] is possible even for an expression that is syntactically and semantically idiosyncratic. Consider a language exactly like English, except that by some accident of linguistic history the phrase *black bird* has come to designate a color, namely the shade of black characteristic of the pupil of a bird's eye. It can still be maintained that [C] = [AB] for this expression, since all the content of the composite semantic structure is inherent in either *black* or *bird*. However, the relationships among [A], [B], and [C] conflict with those of the schema defining the general construction ADJ + N. With respect to [A]-[B], the schema specifies a correspondence between the trajector of the adjective and the profile of the noun; in our fancied expression, the adjectival trajector corresponds instead to a nonsalient subpart of the nominal profile. With respect to composition, the schema specifies that [C] inherits the profile of the noun, but the composite structure of our expression inherits the profile of neither component; the entity it designates (a color) corresponds to the landmark of the adjectival predicate.

It is equally possible for an expression to be fully sanctioned by a schema even though [C] and [AB] diverge. This is shown in Fig. 12.2. Three specific

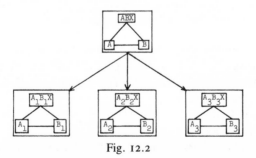

Fig. 12.2

expressions are shown, the first with components $[A_1]$ and $[B_1]$, the second with $[A_2]$ and $[B_2]$, and the third with $[A_3]$ and $[B_3]$. In each instance the composite structure has content beyond that inherited from the component structures—the composite structure for the first expression is thus $[A_1B_1X]$ (rather than just $[A_1B_1]$), and so on. The significant point is that the nature of the discrepancy is constant from one expression to the next (the same additional specifications, X, consistently appear), so a regular pattern can be discerned. The regularity is captured in the schema, which displays internally the same disparity between component and composite structures manifested by its instantiations. Given this schema and the units $[A_4]$ and $[B_4]$, a speaker is able to compute the composite value of a novel expression formed on the same pattern: (A_4B_4X).

A likely example is provided by the following data from Eastern Mono (cf. 8.2.1):

(1)(a) *ma'-kʷaca?i* 'drop'
      hand-descend

  (b) *ci'-weepuhi* 'knock over (with tip of stick)'
      tip-fall:over

  (c) *wɨɨ'-koti?i* 'break (something)'
      side-break

These composite expressions are transitive verb stems with causative force. Each is formed from an intransitive root by attaching a formative that is often referred to (not entirely felicitously) as an instrumental prefix. The causative/transitive value of the composite stem does not appear to be inherited from either component. The root is intransitive and noncausative. The precise meaning of the prefix is harder to ascertain; it would seem to designate part of the body or of an object, and refers in its base to a canonical motion of this object (e.g. grasping for *ma'-*, poking for *ci'-*). Although there are ways to analyze these expressions that would render them fully compositional (e.g. by positing a causative zero-morpheme), there is no direct support for such an analysis, and on the face of it the composite structure incorporates specifications that are not contributed by either component.[2]

12.1.2. *The Building-Block Metaphor*

Our conception of composition is greatly influenced by certain metaphors whose appropriateness for natural language cannot be accepted uncritically. They are valid and useful up to a point, but cannot pretend to universal applicability and lead to conceptual difficulty when pushed too far. One is the container metaphor—an aspect of the more inclusive conduit metaphor (Reddy 1979)—which views linguistic expressions as containers for a substance called meaning. The second is the **building-block metaphor**, which sees the meaning of a composite expression as being constructed out of the meanings of its parts simply by stacking them together in some appropriate fashion. These metaphors do not facilitate our understanding of the many instances in which a composite structure has substantial semantic content not attributable to either component. Noncompositionality is necessarily regarded as problematic, to be dealt with outside the confines of grammatically based linguistic semantics (as a matter of lexicon, pragmatics, or performance).

---

[2] See Norris (1980) for data and illuminating discussion. Conceivably the causative/transitive value can be attributed to the prefixes, but their other uses do not encourage this interpretation; they also occur with inherently causative/transitive stems, and some appear on noun stems.

We have no reason to subscribe to these metaphors beyond the limits of their usefulness, so let us consider some alternatives with broader applicability. Instead of viewing an expression as a container for meaning, we can regard it as providing access to various knowledge systems of indefinite expanse (possibly to be conceived as networks—cf. 4.2.3). And rather than seeing a composite structure as an edifice constructed out of smaller components, we can treat it as a coherent structure in its own right: component structures are not the building blocks out of which it is assembled, but function instead to *motivate* various aspects of it. From this perspective there is nothing problematic about a composite structure evoking a knowledge system (abstract domain) to which neither of its components provides direct access; nor is it surprising that in many instances the component structures motivate and highlight selected facets of the composite meaning, but nonetheless fail to exhaust its content.

In (1)(b), for example, the composite expression *ci'-weepuhi* 'knock over (with tip of stick)' evokes in integral fashion a complex conceptualization prominently incorporating the notions of causation and instrumentality. The stem *weepuhi* 'fall over' corresponds to one portion of this complex conceptualization (the resultant action), and the prefix *ci'*- to another (poking with the tip of a long, thin object), but the organizing conception of an overall causative event is not necessarily a central or prominent specification of either component. To the extent that speakers perceive the contribution of *ci'*- and *weepuhi* to the composite expression (i.e. to the extent that *ci'weepuhi* is analyzable), they render the global symbolic relationship nonarbitrary and enhance the salience of their symbolic correspondents. But saying that the component structures render the composite structure nonarbitrary is not equivalent to regarding them as the building blocks out of which it is constructed.

The effect of switching from one set of metaphors to the other is not to deny the importance of compositionality to linguistic structure, but rather to provide a more realistic assessment of its character and to place it in a more inclusive context. Within the full spectrum of possibilities for the motivation of a composite structure by its components, full compositionality represents a special case: the case where $[C] = [AB]$, and where the relationships $[A]$-$[B]$, $[A]$-$[C]$, and $[B]$-$[C]$ all conform to a sanctioning schema. These conditions enable the composite structure $[C]$ to be derived by computation (11.3), and when they obtain, the container and building-block metaphors are helpful and not altogether inappropriate.[3] But even if fully compositional expressions are accorded privileged status because of their systematic character, their segregation as a distinct and autonomous descriptive domain is artificial and unrevealing; many aspects of a unified phenomenon are simply ignored.

---

[3] I will continue to employ them when the purely compositional aspects of complex expressions are the sole concern; indeed, they are almost impossible to avoid.

We can profit by considering a specific example in some detail. Suppose the professional football-club owners decide, in their unbounded wisdom, that playing the national anthem before each game does not sufficiently express the deep love they hold for their country. The NFL commissioner therefore issues a decree, and the following Sunday, in stadiums across the land, the following scene is witnessed by expectant crowds just prior to the anthem: a beautiful woman dressed as a Dallas Cowgirl shinnies up a flagpole; when she reaches the top, she passionately kisses the American flag; then she waves while sliding down the pole to the sound of exploding fireworks and applauding fans. Through the public-address system an announcer shouts *Let's hear it for our patriotic pole-climber!*, and the fans—anxious to demonstrate their own patriotism—continue to applaud with even greater enthusiasm. This ritual is repeated every Sunday, before every NFL game, and the woman is invariably referred to as a *patriotic pole-climber*. Soon this expression gains currency as a well-entrenched conventional unit of English.

Our concern is with the compositionality of this expression. How much of its semantic value is determined by regular compositional principles from the meanings of its components? Certainly many central aspects of its meaning are computable in this manner. The structure of *pole-climber* was spelled out fairly explicitly in Fig. 8.8. *Climber*, with the somewhat schematic sense 'something that climbs', is constructed at the first level of constituency in accordance with the productive V + -er nominalizing pattern; it designates a thing identified as the trajector of the process [CLIMB], which constitutes its base. At the second level of constituency, *pole* elaborates the schematic landmark of this base process; this too exemplifies a productive pattern and is sanctioned by a schema (cf. *lawn mower, woodcutter, mountain climber, tea drinker*, and so on). General compositional principles (in the form of schematic constructions) thus permit the computation of *pole-climber* with the approximate value 'something that climbs a pole'. Finally, at the third level of constituency, the general schema ADJ + N sanctions the integration of *pole-climber* with *patriotic*. The schema specifies that the trajector of [PATRIOTIC] corresponds to the profile of the noun, which functions as profile determinant in this head-modifier construction. Moreover, since [PATRIOTIC] identifies its trajector as being human, this specification is inherited by the overall composite structure as a property of its designatum. Roughly, then, the conventionally determined meaning of *patriotic pole-climber* is 'patriotic person who climbs a pole'.

But does this compositional value adequately represent the actual meaning of the expression? I argue that it does not, if the term "meaning" is interpreted in any linguistically appropriate way: the compositional value gives an incomplete account of how a speaker understands the expression, as either a novel form or a familiar conventional unit.

When the expression first occurs, both the compositional value (*AB*) and the full contextual value (*C'*) are novel structures, which stand in an elaborative relationship: $((AB) \rightarrow (C'))$. We have no reason to doubt that a speaker computes (*AB*) as part of the coding process, but 'patriotic person who climbs a pole' grossly underspecifies the richness of the conceptualization that constitutes the semantic pole of the usage event. Nothing in the previously established conventions of English allows a speaker to deduce that *patriotic pole-climber* designates a beautiful woman dressed as a Dallas Cowgirl, that the pole in question is a flagpole, that the climber kisses the American flag before sliding down the pole to the accompaniment of fireworks, or that this is part of a ritual that precedes the opening of NFL football games. It is also not evident from conventional principles alone that the patriotism of the designated individual is manifested specifically in the climbing of the pole and the ensuing activity (i.e. *patriotic pole-climber* could simply mean 'person who climbs a pole and is also patriotic'). Yet all this is part of the contextual understanding of the expression by every fan who is initially exposed to it.

The situation does not appreciably change as the expression becomes a conventional unit designating the performer of this familiar (and increasingly tedious) pregame ritual. Speakers may or may not still compute the compositional value, but if so it has unit status and participates in an elaborative relationship with the composite structure: $[[AB] \rightarrow [C]]$. The composite structure [*C*] is schematic relative to (*C'*)—the semantic pole of the original usage event—for in mastering the expression speakers obviously abstract away from many precise details that vary from one occasion to another (the date and city, the specific identity of the pole-climber, the color of her hair, and so on). Still, all the features mentioned in the preceding paragraph are essentially constant from one occasion to the next and consequently survive the cancellation process. The script for this pregame ritual is entrenched as a knowledge system that functions as the base for the unit expression; *patriotic pole-climber* profiles a woman identified with reference to her role in this abstract domain. Once the expression is established as a lexical unit, its conventional semantic value presupposes this abstract domain in just the same fashion that *hypotenuse* presupposes the conception of a right triangle, *January* presupposes the conception of a calendrical cycle, and *onside kick* presupposes some appreciation of the rules and strategy of football.

There is nothing particularly farfetched about this example (at least from the linguistic standpoint). Virtually all linguistic expressions, when first constructed, are interpreted with reference to a richly specified situational context, and much of this context is retained as they coalesce to form established units; this is why most composite expressions have a conventionalized meaning more specific than their compositional value. As a conventional unit, *patriotic pole-climber* does not mean simply 'patriotic person who climbs a pole', just as a *computer* is not simply 'something that computes', a *propeller* 'something that propels', or a *linebacker* 'something that backs a line'. At the same time, though, one would be mistaken to swing to the opposite extreme and claim that the expression is semantically opaque, listed in the lexicon as an unanalyzable unit. It does not lose its internal grammatical structure or cease to instantiate schematic constructions simply by virtue of achieving unit status. Moreover, it is not unlikely that its compositional value remains a significant factor in its meaning, i.e. that its use induces the activation of $[[AB] \rightarrow [C]]$, either consistently or sporadically.

We can draw several useful conclusions from this extended example. First, instances of noncompositionality are not confined to the realms of morphology and compounding. *Patriotic pole-climber* involves the noun-modifier construction ADJ + N, which is syntactic by any reasonable criterion; moreover, the noncompositional aspects of its meaning include the specific way in which the notion of patriotism is integrated with the act of pole-climbing, as noted earlier. Although word structure generally displays a greater proportion of noncompositionality than higher levels of organization, it would be wrong to single out any particular structural level as a line of absolute demarcation in this respect.

Second, it would be equally misleading to claim that noncompositionality is restricted to the lexicon, or that full compositionality is criterial for syntax in particular or grammar in general. If the notion "lexicon" has any content, it refers to fixed expressions, and primarily those that are less than fully compositional. Many expressions that meet these conditions nevertheless display internal grammatical organization, even of an obviously syntactic character. By the same token, we have observed that a novel expression (e.g. *patriotic pole-climber* on the first occasion of its use) is quite likely to have a contextual interpretation that is far more specific than its compositional value. One might choose to discount these aspects of its meaning: since the expression is novel, they are not (yet) conventional. There is nevertheless a certain arbitrariness in this procedure, for nothing stands in the way of their conventionalization except a certain amount of repetition.

Finally, an essential point emerges that eliminates a potential source of conceptual confusion: the composite structure can perfectly well be characterized relative to an abstract domain distinct from any that its component structures have in isolation. The composite semantic structure of *patriotic pole-climber* incorporates the full conception of the pregame ritual of pole-climbing, flag-kissing, and fireworks-accompanied descent. This entire knowledge system constitutes its base, but neither *patriotic* nor *pole* nor *climber*, taken individually, evokes or presupposes this domain. This state of affairs reflects the genesis of the composite expression, which was coined specifically to describe the central participant in the ritual. No such reference to the ritual is evoked by *patriotic*, *pole*, or *climber* taken individually, for these were preexisting units defined with respect to other, more fundamental domains.

12.1.3. *The Nature of Analyzability*

Compositionality refers to the degree of regularity in the assembly of a composite structure out of smaller components. It is to be distinguished from analyzability, which pertains instead to the extent to which speakers are cognizant (at some level of processing) of the contribution that individual component structures make to the composite whole. While the regularity of composition obviously affects the potential for such recognition, the two notions are nevertheless distinct. Speakers can be quite aware of individual components within a structure that manifests only partial compositionality. By the same token, they may be relatively unaware of the components within a familiar expression that is fully compositional.

The notion of analyzability is subtle. It does not refer to the intrinsic complexity of a structure, but rather to a person's awareness of certain aspects of this complexity. As the term suggests, analyzability implies some kind of *analysis* of a complex structure, and thus involves cognitive events above and beyond those that constitute the structure per se; the structure retains its intrinsic complexity regardless of whether it is subjected to such analysis. We must therefore distinguish between two types of componentiality, i.e. two distinct senses in which we can say that a composite structure [*C*] has the simpler structures [*A*] and [*B*] as components. On the one hand, we can mean that the content of [*A*] and [*B*] is included in that of [*C*], perhaps as coherent substructures (subroutines). Or on the other hand, we can mean that a person specifically *ascribes* to [*C*] the contents of [*A*] and [*B*], i.e. that he analyzes [*C*] in these terms. The former type of componentiality does not entail the latter.[4]

The distinction has a ready phenomenological interpretation in nonlinguistic domains. Consider the sensory experience induced when you sample some spaghetti sauce. This sensation has numerous components, including temperature, texture, and a complex array of properties registered in the domain of taste and smell. The degree to which you consciously analyze this experience is subject to considerable variation: you may fail to take explicit note of the texture; unless the sauce is too hot or too cold, you may not notice the temperature; you may observe that the sauce is rather spicy without specifically identifying the presence of salt and oregano; and so on. Noting such factors heightens and enriches your taste experience, but there is a fundamental sense in which all of these components contribute to your experience irrespective of whether you subject it to any type of conscious analysis: you

---

[4] We might relate this distinction to the difference between conscious and unconscious processing as described in Marcel (1983) (conscious processing is claimed to involve the assignment of a structural description to the records of unconscious processing). However, I do not specifically claim that the "awareness" implied by analyzability is always at the conscious level.

simply taste the spaghetti sauce, and either like it or dislike it. Parallel remarks describe the process of listening to an orchestral performance. Your experience of the performance is greatly enriched if you manage to perceive the
sounds of the individual instruments and observe the complex interplay of
their parts. The sounds of the separate instruments contribute to your auditory
sensations, however, and are in that sense components of the overall experience, regardless of whether you carry out this type of analysis. The contrast
between unified sensation and explicit analysis is what permits us to experience a musical work differently from one performance to the next, deepen-
ing our appreciation of it as we succeed in observing additional structural
relationships.

Shifting to the level of cognitive events, we can identify the first type of
componentiality—pertaining to inherent structural properties, independent of
possible analysis—with the notion of **immanence** (cf. 11.3.1). Structure [A]
is a component of [C] in this sense if the cognitive events comprised by [A]
are included among the more extensive set of cognitive events constituting
[C]; the occurrence of the former set of events is thus intrinsic to the execution of the latter. The second type of componentiality involves a more elaborate configuration of events: beyond the immanence of [A] to [C], analysis
involves the **recognition** of [A] in this context. The overall event therefore
requires not only the occurrence of [C] (and thus of [A]), but also the separate
occurrence of [A] as the standard in an act of comparison resulting in recognition of the immanent structure.

Some diagrammatic conventions for these notions are given in Fig. 12.3.
The dashed lines in diagram (a) indicate that structures [A] and [B] are immanent to [C]; neither [A] nor [B] is necessarily recognized as such, though

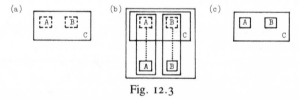

Fig. 12.3

their constituent events are all to be found within the larger structure. Diagram
(b) represents the successful analysis of [C]. Besides the execution of [C], [A]
and [B] are run separately as standards of comparison; the targets of comparison are their correspondents within [C], and each comparison event results in recognition (that is, [A] > [A] = 0; [B] > [B] = 0). Diagrams (b) and
(c) are notational alternatives: (b) (in exploded format) shows separately the
functionally distinct occurrences of [A] and [B], whereas the solid-line boxes
in (c) (a compacted representation) signal the recognition of [A] and [B]
within the composite structure. Diagrams (a) and (c) therefore contrast: the
former specifies immanence, the latter recognition.

The distinction between immanence and explicit recognition is not restricted to any particular domain or type of phenomenon. We discussed it above in regard to sensory experience, and in 11.3.1 with reference to schematicity and semantic categorization. With respect to unipolar phonological structure, we can note that speakers often produce and recognize syllables without any real appreciation of their segmental composition. Important though it is for a linguist, segmental analysis is rather marginal for the language user (at least at the level of conscious awareness).

However, our immediate concern is the analysis of bipolar expressions into their symbolic components. The pertinent situation is depicted in Fig. 12.4,

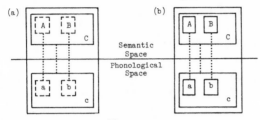

Fig. 12.4

showing the composite expression [[C]/[c]] as decomposable into the component expressions [[A]/[a]] and [[B]/[b]]. Diagram (a) indicates only that these components are immanent to [[C]/[c]]; diagram (b) goes further and specifies (in compacted format) that these components are actually recognized.[5] To the extent that a speaker is accustomed to activating the full set of cognitive events implied by diagram (b), we can say that expression [[C]/[c]] is analyzable.

If ((C)/(c)) is a novel composite expression, it is necessarily fully analyzable. The speaker can hardly fail to recognize the contribution made by [[A]/[a]] and [[B]/b]] to the composite structure on the very occasion when he assembles it out of these smaller components. Once ((C)/(c)) becomes established as the unit [[C]/[c]], however, it is at least conceivable that it might be activated independently of the more elaborate structure implied by the recognition of its components. A speaker may employ the term *computer*, for example, without any cognizance of its relation to *compute* and -*er*; the structure he activates then corresponds to diagram (a). If he happens on some occasion to be aware of the contributions made by these components, he activates instead the more complicated structure of diagram (b).

What is the import in this context of terms like "aware," "cognizant," and "recognize"? Does the claim that a speaker is "aware" or "cognizant" of the components within a composite structure imply that these components are consciously recognized and attended to? Not necessarily. There is nothing in

[5] Note that Fig. 12.4(b) is the bipolar counterpart of Fig. 12.3(c); it is not directly parallel to Fig. 12.3(b), despite their superficial diagrammatic resemblance.

the definition of analyzability (characterized at the level of cognitive events) that inherently restricts it to the domain of consciousness. Recognition is accomplished through acts of comparison, which are assumed to be ubiquitous to all domains and levels of cognitive processing (Ch. 3). Speakers do however have reasonably clear intuitions about the analyzability of symbolic expressions. They can tell you that the components of *complainer* are more salient than those of *computer*, for example, and we have all had the experience of suddenly becoming (consciously) aware of the componentiality of a previously opaque expression. I assume that these intuitions are as valid as any others that linguists rely on, and that they do reflect on the phenomenon in question. Still, I have no basis for asserting that analyzability occurs only at the conscious level, so I will leave the question open.

12.1.4. *Descriptive Significance*

When a speaker wishes to express a complex notion, (C'), the options available depend on the conventional symbolic resources of his language. If a structure approximating (C') happens to function as the semantic pole of a symbolic unit, he has only to activate this unit, $[[C]/[c]]$, in order to effect the desired symbolization. In the absence of an appropriate unit, he must resort to composition. His task (in simplified form) is to find two symbolic units, $[[A]/[a]]$ and $[[B]/[b]]$, which have the following properties: (1) both $[A]$ and $[B]$ can be recognized as prominent aspects of (C'); (2) the integration of $[A]$ and $[B]$, in accordance with the pattern of an established constructional schema, yields a composite structure (C) that approximates (C'); and (3) $[a]$ and $[b]$ are phonologically compatible, permitting their integration as specified by the phonological pole of the schema. The resulting symbolic structure, $(([A]\text{-}[B])/([a]\text{-}[b]))$, is novel but conventionally motivated.

The compacted notation of the formula must not be allowed to obscure the structure's complexity. The semantic pole $([A]\text{-}[B])$ consists of three separate elements linked by correspondences: $[A]$, $[B]$, and the composite notion (C).[6] Similarly, the phonological pole consists of $[a]$, $[b]$, and the composite phonological structure (c), also interconnected by correspondences. The speaker's original desire to find symbolic expression for conception (C') is satisfied by the relationship $((C)/(c))$ established between the composite structures at the two poles. However, arriving at this symbolic relationship requires a constructive effort in which the speaker activates units $[[A]/[a]]$ and $[[B]/[b]]$ and assesses the result of integrating them in a specific fashion. When $((C)/(c))$ is first constructed, therefore, it necessarily occurs within the context of the more elaborate configuration $(([A]\text{-}[B])/([a]\text{-}[b]))$. It is the occurrence of $((C)/(c))$ in this larger context that constitutes the analyzability of the composite expression.

[6] We can assume for now that the expression is fully compositional; hence the composite structure (C) coincides with the compositional value (AB).

Although (*C*) is thus the overall notion that the speaker expresses, and (*c*) the phonological structure destined for peripheral implementation, these are not exhaustive of the semantic or phonological value of the expression. Its full semantic value is given by (*C*) in relation to [*A*] and [*B*], and its full phonological value by (*c*) in relation to [*a*] and [*b*]. The motivating units heighten the prominence of their correspondents within the composite structures and thereby enrich the value of the expression at both poles. All of this, however, is predicated on the novelty of the expression. What happens when the expression achieves the status of a unit?

Unit status does not per se affect analyzability, so the resulting structure has the form [[[*A*]-[*B*]]/[[*a*]-[*b*]]] (cf. Fig. 12.4(b)). The potential impact of entrenchment is nevertheless substantial. For one thing, it tends to reduce the salience of individual components, because it is no longer necessary to attend to them individually in a constructive effort: coordinated by an established routine, their coactivation is essentially automatic. More significantly, the unit status of [[[*A*]-[*B*]]/[[*a*]-[*b*]]] creates the potential for the independent occurrence of the bipolar composite structure [[*C*]/[*c*]]. Like any other substructure of the complex unit [[[*A*]-[*B*]]/[[*a*]-[*b*]]], [[*C*]/[*c*]] now has unit status itself. It is a privileged unit, moreover, since an expression's composite structure is the one that participates directly in coding and higher-level composition.

The independent occurrence of [[*C*]/[*c*]] is therefore not unanticipated. An event of this sort requires only actualization, i.e. the realization of potential inherent to the existence of [[[*A*]-[*B*]]/[[*a*]-[*b*]]] as an established unit. The independent occurrence of [[*C*]/[*c*]] amounts to a kind of decontextualization: originally confined to a particular systemic context, it comes to be used outside that context. When it occurs in this fashion, [[*C*]/[*c*]] is unanalyzed, as the systemic motivation afforded by [[*A*]/[*a*]] and [[*B*]/[*b*]] fails to be recognized. In lieu of the building-block metaphor, we might adopt the **scaffolding** metaphor: component structures are seen as scaffolding erected for the construction of a complex expression; once the complex structure is in place (established as a unit), the scaffolding is no longer essential and is eventually discarded.

Clearly this decontextualization is a gradual process. The familiarity of a complex expression does not blind us to its componentiality and render us unable to perceive the contribution of individual components. If this were so, the notion of a complex lexical item would be a contradiction in terms: the unit status characteristic of lexical items would entail their immediate and automatic loss of analyzability, removing any grounds for considering them to be complex; all fixed expressions would therefore constitute single morphemes, regardless of size or any resemblance to other units. In fact, though, a fixed expression appears capable of retaining some measure of analyzability almost indefinitely. At any one time, a language has many thousands of complex symbolic units whose values are enriched by the recognition of their components. We need not assume that the component structures are accessed on every occasion when the composite structure is employed, or that when accessed they are necessarily activated at the same level of intensity as they are in a novel expression. However, only when the composite structure loses altogether its capacity to elicit the activation of its components can it be regarded as fully opaque and unanalyzable. At that point we can speak of the **reanalysis** of $[[[A]-[B]]/[[a]-[b]]]$ to constitute a monomorphemic unit $[[C]/[c]]$.

The grammatical import of this overall conception was first discussed in 8.2.2. It was noted that analyzability accounts for the semantic difference observable between two expressions with essentially the same composite structure (e.g. *father* vs. *male parent*, *triangle* vs. *three-sided polygon*, *oak* vs. *oak tree*). Because component structures contribute to meaning, the meaningfulness and nonsynonymy of anomalous expressions (in which no coherent composite structure emerges) is accounted for as well. It is further possible that certain grammatical constructions are sensitive to the added prominence of particular substructures that results from their explicit symbolization. We now consider some additional descriptive consequences of this scheme, and in particular its rejection of the building-block metaphor.

One consequence is that the analyzability of a composite expression is naturally regarded as a matter of degree. The building-block metaphor makes it hard to think in these terms—either the composite structure is built out of smaller elements or it is not—but there is no such problem when analyzability is treated as the coactivation of the composite structure and its components (as in Fig. 12.3(b)). An expression's degree of analyzability thus reflects the likelihood of the composite structure eliciting the activation of its components, as well as their prominence (level of activation) when elicited. Moreover, if analyzability is a matter of degree (which is seemingly undeniable on intuitive grounds), then we must further conclude that the question of whether a certain form is morphemically complex is not always answered adequately with a simple "yes" or "no" response. Granted, for example, that the components of *swimmer* are more frequently elicited and saliently perceived within the whole than those of *propeller*, it must also be admitted that the decomposition of *propeller* into the separate morphemes *propel* and *-er* is more tenuous than that of *swimmer* into *swim* and *-er*. The question merits an unqualified yes/no answer only when the expression is either novel or fully opaque.

A further consequence of eschewing the building-block metaphor is the unproblematic nature of complex expressions falling short of full compositionality; in these the composite structure is either a specialization or an extension vis-à-vis the expected compositional value. The building-block metaphor makes it difficult to understand how such expressions arise: if the component structures are stacked together to form the composite structure, how can the latter have content that is either absent in the former or conflicts with their specifications? The model proposed here avoids this conceptual problem, as the component and composite structures are treated as distinct facets of a grammatical construction. A composite structure derives systemic motivation from its components, but is not assembled out of them. Nothing intrinsically requires that the motivation be full rather than partial, or prevents the inclusion of unanticipated content.

The situation comes about when there is a significant discrepancy between (C'), the conceptualization that a speaker wishes to express, and (AB), representing the expected compositional result, at the semantic pole, of integrating $[[A]/[a]]$ and $[[B]/[b]]$. The speaker may nevertheless accept the adequacy of the composite expression, being either oblivious to the disparity or willing to overlook it as tolerable within the communicative context. He doubtless computes the compositional structure $((AB)/(ab))$ at some stage in the coding process, but this intermediate structure is either extended or specialized at the semantic pole to yield the symbolic relationship $((C')/(ab))$. This latter structure then gives rise (by entrenchment, conventionalization, and decontextualization) to the somewhat schematized unit $[[C]/[ab]]$; this is thereby established as a symbolic unit, even though $[ab]$ "ought to" symbolize $[AB]$ instead.

Fig. 12.5 diagrams the semantic pole of a complex symbolic unit that is analyzable but less than fully compositional. There, $[A]$ and $[B]$ are the component structures, and $[C]$ the composite structure. On the left is $[AB]$, the

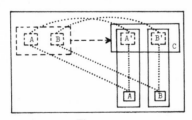

Fig. 12.5

expected compositional value of the expression; I have enclosed this structure in dashed lines, because we cannot be certain that it is always activated when the expression is employed. But when $[AB]$ is activated, it bears a relationship of either full or partial schematicity to the composite structure $[C]$, as indicated by the arrow.[7] Note that $[A']$ and $[B']$ are the substructures of $[C]$ that correspond to $[A]$ and $[B]$; $[A]$ and $[B]$ have a dual role, as component structures and as substructures of $[AB]$.

---

[7] In the case of an idiom or a metaphorical expression, $[AB]$ is the literal sense, and $[C]$ the figurative sense (cf. Fig. 2.10).

Fig. 12.5 should be compared to Fig. 12.3(b). Both represent the semantic pole of an analyzable expression; the only difference between these two exploded diagrams is the added complexity in Fig. 12.5 that is attributable to noncompositionality. A fully compositional expression can be more simply diagrammed, since in that case [C] and [AB] are identical and collapse into a single structure (also, no distinction need be made between [A] and [A'], or [B] and [B']). It is sensible in this perspective to regard the configuration of Fig. 12.3(b) as a degenerate instance of Fig. 12.5: only the latter is sufficiently articulated to accommodate the complete range of possibilities. Full compositionality is more the exception than the rule (even for novel expressions), so it is reasonable that the present model treats it as a special, limiting case.

With full compositionality, the systemic motivation of [C] is maximal, since [A] and [B] are easily recognizable within [C] and exhaust its contents. However, as [C] diverges from [AB], its systemic motivation by [A] and [B] progressively decreases. The impact is small when [C] merely elaborates [AB] (as in *blackbird*), for the substructures [A'] and [B'] are easily recognized as instances of [A] and [B] even though characterized with greater specificity (i.e. as stated earlier, [C] = [ABX]). The impact is greater when [C] diverges from [AB] by extension rather than specialization (e.g. *blackboard*). Extension implies some conflict in specifications, and to the extent that [A'] and [B'] are inconsistent with [A] and [B], the latter's recognition within [C] is rendered problematic.

The diminished systemic motivation associated with noncompositionality contributes to the gradual loss of analyzability that generally occurs with complex symbolic units, but its effect is neither automatic nor absolute. The definition of analyzability does not refer directly to either full compositionality or unproblematic recognition; it refers instead to coactivation, the likelihood that a composite structure will be construed in relation to the component structures, irrespective of their degree of compatibility. The analyzability of an expression can be maintained indefinitely despite a substantial discrepancy between [AB] and [C]; for example, the "opacity" of *yellowjacket* does not prevent the speaker from construing the composite notion in relation to the concepts [YELLOW] and [JACKET], which thereby contribute to its full semantic value.[8] Furthermore, an expression's degree of analyzability is not predictable in any consistent fashion from the character or extent of the discrepancy. A *propeller* is in fact 'something that propels', yet the term is analyzable only to a very limited degree for most speakers, if at all; *mixer* is

---

[8] That is, to some degree speakers perceive the metaphor motivating the extension: the designated insect is colored as if it were wearing a yellow jacket. The structure [AB] is [YELLOW-JACKET], the literal (compositional) sense of the expression. This is extended to designate the insect by virtue of a metaphor (the similarity of the insect's coloration to a yellow jacket) and a part/whole relationship (from the coloration of the insect to the insect as a whole).

parallel with respect to compositionality but is far more analyzable, whereas *blackboard* is reasonably analyzable even though it represents an extension rather than a specialization. Analyzability must therefore be accommodated as a basically independent parameter of variation. More specifically, it reflects the cognitive salience of [A], [B], and [AB] in the context of the expression.

A final consequence of replacing the building-block metaphor with a notion of componentiality based on systemic motivation is that component structures can sometimes be expected to differ in their salience within a construction. The building-block metaphor leads one to anticipate that a component is either present or is not, and that if one of two components is present the other must be as well. This results in certain classic problems of morphemic analysis that simply evaporate in the context of the present framework.

The framework straightforwardly allows a gradient of possibilities between the extremities of full analyzability and total opacity, represented by the respective formulas [[A]-[B]] and [AB] (or [C]). Full analyzability implies that [A] and [B] are obligatorily activated at a high level of intensity; with lesser analyzability, likelihood and intensity of activation decrease, as does the systemic motivation they afford the composite structure. Nothing dictates that [A] and [B] must always agree in this regard, and indeed there are examples where one component is intuitively much more salient than the other. My own judgment, for instance, is that *screw* is much more prominent in *screwdriver* than is the second element of the compound, *driver*. I am quite aware that the notion *screw* is essential to *screwdriver*, and figures in its meaning, but I do not think of a screwdriver as something that *drives* a screw.

The limiting case of divergence between [A] and [B] in this regard is where [A] is not recognized at all, even though [B] is salient and obligatorily accessed. I do not know whether such cases occur, but many examples approximate them sufficiently well that the notation [A[B]] is not grossly inappropriate. With regard to *inept*, for instance, speakers readily perceive the negative force of *in-* even though *ept* is not recognized.[9] Much the same is true for the *berry* of *cranberry* and *boysenberry*. It is similarly possible in this framework to recognize the presence of the common nominal suffix *-er/-or* in forms like *doctor*, *hammer*, *beaker*, and even *father*, *mother*, *brother*, *sister*, and *daughter*, even though the residue is not itself a lexical unit. These expressions have a composite structure and one component structure, the latter providing systemic motivation for only a portion of the former. Although *father* is a morpheme to the extent that we disregard the marginal morphemic status of *-er*, this ending may nevertheless be analyzed as a morpheme to a

---

[9] The recognition of *in-* and the existence of an associated derivational pattern for negative adjectives create the potential for an innovative adjectival stem *ept* 'capable'. The exploitation of this potential exemplifies the process called **back formation**: actualization that occurs in the context of a partially analyzed symbolic unit and renders it fully analyzed (i.e. [A[B]] becomes [[A-B]]).

limited degree without entailing a similar status for the residue *fath*. It is only the building-block metaphor that renders this type of analysis in any way problematic.

12.2. Composition as Categorization

In discussing analyzability, I spoke of a construction's composite structure receiving **systemic motivation** from its component structures. The same term was applied in Ch. 11 to the coding relationship between usage events and the conventional units of the grammar. This identity of terminology was obviously not fortuitous. Instead it anticipated a fundamental unification achievable in the framework as elaborated so far: the explication of composition with reference to sanction and categorization.

12.2.1. *Unification*

Let us begin by reexamining Fig. 12.5. To say that [A] and [B] are component structures with respect to [C] is equivalent, I now suggest, to saying that [A] and [B] are invoked to categorize certain facets of [C], indicated as [A'] and [B'] respectively. Construing [C] in relation to these components therefore involves the comparison events [A]>[A'] and [B]>[B'] (as well as [AB]>[C]). Recognition is optimal when [C] is fully compositional: the comparisons register no discrepancy between standard and target, even in level of specificity. Component structures [A] and [B] are also recognized in [C] (i.e. their specifications are satisfied) when [C] elaborates [AB], but standard/target disparity produces nonzero comparison values in cases of extension.

Previous discussion has largely prefigured this proposal. The integration of [A] and [B] has already been analyzed into horizontal correspondences and categorizing relationships involving either entire component structures or certain of their substructures. Moreover, the significance of vertical correspondences between elements of the component and composite structures has been acknowledged from the beginning (cf. 2.3.2.3 and Fig. 8.13). It is now proposed to complete the parallelism between the horizontal and vertical axes in a grammatical construction, by recognizing categorizing relationships along the vertical axis as well.

Concrete illustration is provided in Fig. 12.6, which diagrams the semantic pole of *above the tree*. It is assumed that the expression is novel and fully compositional. [ABOVE] is a stative relation, and imposes its relational profile on the composite structure. The broken-line boxes in these relational structures can be understood as enclosing those of their specifications that characterize the primary landmark: the characterization is schematic for [ABOVE], and more specific at the composite-structure level. The source

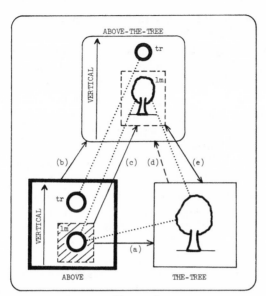

Fig. 12.6

of this greater specificity is the elaboration of [ABOVE]'s landmark by the nominal predication [THE-TREE] (abbreviated here by a mnemonic shape specification).

Among the many categorizing relationships that could be imputed to this construction, five are singled out in Fig. 12.6 for special attention. In the horizontal axis, (a) is the elaborative relationship between the landmark of [ABOVE] (its e-site) and the nominal predication. Four categorizations are depicted along the vertical axis, two involving each component structure. The one labeled (b) is the global categorization of the composite structure by its profile determinant, i.e. ([ABOVE]→(ABOVE-THE-TREE)). Observe that the profile determinant is fully schematic for the composite structure; this is consistently true with full compositionality, because the profile determinant imposes its overall organization on the composite scene. If we similarly assess the global categorization of the composite structure by the other component, it proves to be one of only partial schematicity owing to the contrasting profiles of the standard and target. This is exemplified in Fig. 12.6 by relationship (d): ([THE-TREE]--→(ABOVE-THE-TREE)).

We can also consider local categorizations between the component and composite structures. In (c), the primary landmark of the composite structure elaborates that of the profile determinant. Note that this local elaborative relationship is responsible for the global one labeled (b): the greater specificity of the composite structure relative to the profile determinant is confined to their landmarks. This obviously reflects the fact that the landmark of the profile determinant is the substructure that functions as the e-site in the valence relation: (c) is the reflection in the vertical axis of relationship (a) along the horizontal axis. Moreover, because the landmark of the composite structure receives all its detailed specifications from the nominal predication, these two entities bear to one another a relationship of identity, given as (e).

The categorizations of Fig. 12.6 typify those to be found in canonical valence relations. The two component structures categorize different facets of the composite notion: as a relational predication, the profile determinant establishes the general organization of the scene, and characterizes the participating entities in fairly schematic terms; the nominal predication corresponds to just one of these entities and describes it with greater specificity. In view of their complementarity, we can think of the components as joining in a cooperative venture to categorize the composite structure and thereby afford it systemic motivation. What makes this joint endeavor necessary is the inability of individual symbolic units to express the full conceptualization a speaker wishes to convey.

In accordance with the building-block metaphor, we have so far distinguished between two orthogonal planes of relationships—the syntagmatic and the schematic—and considered the vertical and horizontal axes of a grammatical construction to be two dimensions in the syntagmatic plane (cf. 2.1.5). We must now reassess the geometry of linguistic organization in light of our rejection of this metaphor and the decision to equate composition with categorization. The effect is to unite the two planes: the vertical axis of a construction is reinterpreted as constituting one dimension in the space (no longer just a "plane") defined by categorizing relationships. The integration of component structures along the horizontal axis can then be thought of as specifying the nature of their cooperation in jointly sanctioning the composite structure.

The naturalness of this reinterpretation is suggested by certain fundamental similarities between schematic relationships (as originally understood) and compositional relationships. Both involve a crucial standard/target asymmetry, where the target is (as it were) the "business end" of the configuration. In the case of composition, the target is the composite structure, the one that is used in the computation of higher-order compositional relationships; the topmost composite structure (i.e. the endpoint of the computation chain) corresponds most directly to the overall notion that the speaker wishes to express, and is matched against the usage event in the coding process. We can therefore refer to the topmost composite structure as the **active node** with respect to coding, thereby underscoring the parallelism with structural description and categorizing relationships in the schematic plane (Ch. 11).

In the assignment of structural descriptions, primary categorization of the usage event is effected by an active node representing the endpoint in one or more chains of categorizing relationships within a schematic network. The active node itself determines the well-formedness of the usage event; the secondary activation of additional nodes in the chains provides additional systemic motivation and is presumed to be variable in extent. The systemic motivation afforded by secondary activation is now seen as analogous to that received by the topmost composite structure from its immediate components, and in fact from the entire compositional path defining its constituency tree. For expressions with unit status, moreover, the composite structure may sometimes be activated without the support of any component structures (or of those below a certain level in the constituency hierarchy). Degrees of analyzability are therefore regarded as analogous to the variable extent of secondary activation in the assignment of structural descriptions.

Let us reexamine *above the tree* in light of these observations. The entire complex configuration in Fig. 12.6 functions as the target of categorization with respect to the schema that characterizes the prepositional-phrase construction. This schema is internally complex in the manner of Fig. 12.6, and specific subparts categorize the corresponding subparts of the instantiation. Within this instantiating configuration, the composite structure functions as the target of categorization with respect to its components, each of which also categorizes selected aspects of the target. Of all these elements, it is the composite structure of the instantiation (i.e. the target within the target) that serves as the active node. This is the entity that responds most directly to the speaker's symbolic or communicative needs; the remainder constitute the matrix of conventional structures and relationships that support its actualization.

I mention only in passing the possibility of a still broader unification. The *S/T* asymmetries just discussed, and the special status of the target as the "active" structure, are reminiscent of various other asymmetries that are fundamental to this framework: (1) the prominence of a profile relative to its base; (2) that of the trajector within a relational predication; (3) the distinction between an entity construed objectively and one construed subjectively (cf. 3.3.2.4); and (4) the internal *S/T* alignment of a dependent structure, where the target determines the character of the composite structure (Ch. 9). In each instance, there is a structure of special salience that in some sense derives its value through its departure from a standard or baseline situation; the asymmetry is that of an "event" detected against an established background. Obviously this type of asymmetry is fundamental to cognitive organization and not at all peculiar to language. It recalls not only figure/ground alignment (3.3.2.1), but also the more general point that novel experience is structured and interpreted with reference to previous experience (3.1.3). The ultimate objective of unifying these various notions—revealing them as manifestations of a single underlying asymmetry—should guide the further elaboration of this framework.

12.2.2. *Extension vs. Zero Morpheme*

Our discussion of analyzability and partial compositionality (12.1) established the wisdom of replacing the building-block metaphor with an account of composition that reduces it to categorization and systemic motivation. The rationale for this proposal was further developed in the preceding section (12.2.1), which noted significant parallels between compositional relationships and relationships defining schematic networks. We will now explore some additional considerations that support its plausibility.

In valence relations manifesting an A/D asymmetry, the dependent component contains a substructure that functions as an e-site and is elaborated by the autonomous component (cf. Fig. 12.6). Normally the e-site is a proper subpart of the dependent structure, but one does find instances of the limiting case, where the e-site is exhaustive of the whole. An example is the compound *oak tree*, whose semantic pole is sketched in Fig. 12.7(a). Because

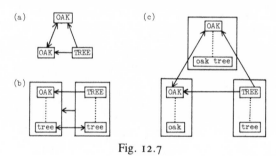

Fig. 12.7

[TREE] is fully schematic for [OAK], [TREE] as a whole can be considered an e-site elaborated by the other predicate, as indicated by the horizontal arrow.

What about relationships in the vertical axis? We obtain the composite structure from its components by superimposing the specifications of corresponding entities. Since the profiles of [TREE] and [OAK] correspond, and are characterized by these predicates at different levels of specificity, the schematic-transparency principle comes into play. Merging the specifications of a schema and its instantiation produces a coherent structure equivalent to the instantiation: in the case at hand, [TREE] and [OAK] merge to form a composite structure equivalent to the latter. As shown in diagram (a), the result is a composite structure that is identical to one of its components and elaborates the other: [[OAK] ↔ [OAK]], [[TREE] → [OAK]].

This example illustrates the interchangeability of schematic and syntagmatic relationships. Observe that [[TREE] → [OAK]], which occurs twice in diagram (a), is precisely equivalent to the categorizing relationship between

[TREE] and [OAK] found in the schematic network of *tree* (cf. Fig. 10.3). Nothing inherent in [[TREE]→[OAK]] determines whether it constitutes the vertical axis of a construction (making it an instance of composition), the horizontal axis (integration), or a categorization in the schematic plane. Its status depends solely on the use to which it is put, i.e. its role in larger, bipolar configurations.

These larger configurations are sketched in diagrams (b) and (c). [[TREE]→ [OAK]] is shown in (b) as a categorizing relationship in the schematic network of *tree*. The bipolar categorization [[TREE/tree]→[OAK/tree]] represents a fact of conventional usage, namely that *tree* is employed not only for the category prototype, but also for the special case of an oak in particular. In an actual usage event of this latter sort, [OAK/tree] functions as the network's active node, with [TREE/tree] elicited secondarily by way of systemic motivation. Diagram (c) depicts the dual role of [[TREE]→[OAK]] in the grammatical construction *oak tree*; it differs from (a) only by including symbolic correspondences with elements at the phonological pole.[10] Here the active node is the composite structure [OAK/oak tree], which induces the secondary activation of [OAK/oak] and [TREE/tree] and thereby receives their joint systemic support.

By comparing these three occurrences of [[TREE]→[OAK]], we note that [TREE] is consistently symbolized by [tree], whereas [OAK] has a different symbolic correspondent in each instance. Its correspondent is naturally [tree] in diagram (b), since this configuration represents a relationship of semantic specialization in the schematic network of the morpheme *tree*. [OAK] is symbolized by [oak tree] with respect to the vertically aligned occurrence of [[TREE]→[OAK]] in diagram (c), and by [oak] in its horizontal occurrence. Observe that [tree] categorizes the second element of [oak tree] along the vertical axis, which pertains to composition and systemic motivation. However, [tree] does not categorize [oak] in the horizontal axis; they are related instead through their joint categorization of [oak tree]. A variety of functional and symbolic relationships therefore cooperate to distinguish the uses of the semantic categorization [[TREE]→[OAK]].[11]

The interchangeability of schematic and syntagmatic relationships is further illustrated by a far more striking example, where the status of a particular

---

[10] For sake of simplicity, categorizing relationships are suppressed, apart from those at the semantic pole.

[11] The component structures are characterized by their functional roles, with respect to the composite structure and to each other: they need not be phonologically distinct. Consider the following exchange: *This chili is very hot. Do you mean spicy hot or hot hot?* Note that this construction differentiates between central and peripheral senses of the repeated lexical item, and thus indicates the direction of semantic extension. An exchange that plays on the nonprototypicality of palms within the *tree* category might go like this: *He planted a tree in back of his house. Was it a palm tree or a tree tree?*

relationship is not apparent even when both poles are taken into account. The problem concerns the derived nouns in (2):

(2)(a)   *You're a cheat!*
   (b)   *Everyone contends that Sally is a flirt.*
   (c)   *Don't be such a tease!*

There are two possible analyses, seemingly quite different. One analysis claims that the nouns are derived from the corresponding verbs by a zero derivational affix. The nouns are therefore bimorphemic, being parallel to *cheater*, *swimmer*, etc. except that the derivational morpheme has no overt phonological manifestation. The other analysis treats the nominal variants of *cheat*, *flirt*, and *tease* as semantic extensions from their processual variants. In this event the verbs are monomorphemic and the phenomenon is lexical rather than morphological.

Which is the correct analysis? I imagine most analysts would incline towards the morphological treatment, but nothing forces us to rule out the possibility of semantic extension: the choice appears to be arbitrary. I suggest that this indeterminacy is to be expected, for the analyses turn out to be equivalent under the view of composition being proposed. It is not a matter of choosing between two distinct analyses, but rather one of a single analysis that can be discussed from either of two equally valid perspectives. Pivotal to this solution is the lack of any intrinsic difference between relationships in the syntagmatic and the schematic planes. The descriptive and conceptual problem posed by the phenomenon simply disappears given a proper understanding of the character of these relationships.

Consider first the morphological analysis. The essentials of the requisite grammatical construction are sketched in Fig. 12.8, with *cheat* as the specific example. At the bottom are the two component structures: the verb stem and the nominalizing morpheme; the derived noun functions as the composite structure and is shown at the top. All three structures, abbreviated V (verb), NR (nominalizer), and N (noun), are shown explicitly as bipolar units, with the semantic pole above and the phonological pole below. Observe that no attempt is made to characterize the process [CHEAT] beyond specifying its processual nature. Also, for sake of simplicity and comparability, certain notational features have been suppressed (e.g. correspondence lines, the crosshatching of e-sites, and the heavy-lined enclosure identifying NR as the profile determinant).

The nominalizing morpheme is dependent at both the semantic and the phonological poles. It thus consists, at each pole, of a standard that functions as an e-site in its valence relation with V, and a target that corresponds to the composite structure N and determines its organization. Semantically, the

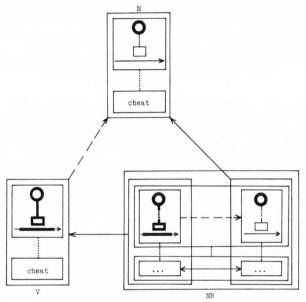

Fig. 12.8

nominalizing morpheme is equivalent to -*er* (cf. Fig. 9.12): its standard is characterized as a schematic process, and its target profiles the trajector of this process.[12] The categorizing relationship between the standard and target is one of extension (partial schematicity) because of this contrast in their profiles. Phonologically, NR is a zero morpheme. Its standard and target are therefore identical at the phonological pole, and each is highly schematic (cf. Fig. 9.10).

Once the internal structure of NR is understood, the overall construction is straightforward. The bipolar standard of NR serves as the e-site in the valence relation and is elaborated by V; the standard is fully schematic for V at both poles: [[PROC/...]→[CHEAT/cheat]]. As the profile determinant, NR imposes its organization—more specifically, that of its target—on the composite structure N.[13] Note that the target is fully schematic for N at both poles (just as the standard is for V): the target designates the trajector of a schematic process, whereas N designates the trajector of the specific process [CHEAT]; the phonological relationship [[...]→[cheat]] is similarly elaborative. Finally,

[12] The schematicity of the process is indicated diagrammatically by the dots in the vertical line connecting its trajector and landmark. Note that the process is schematic in NR, but specific in both V and N.

[13] In the terminology of Ch. 11, we can say that the bipolar transformation embodied by NR is carried out in the context of the specific structure V, resulting in the actualization of N.

the compositional relationship between V and N is one of identity at the phonological pole, but at the semantic pole (and overall, consequently) it is extensional.

Let us now consider the alternative analysis, where the noun *cheat* is treated as a semantic extension from the verb. This analysis posits for the schematic network of *cheat* the categorizing relationship [[CHEAT/ cheat]--→[CHEAT'/cheat]], where [CHEAT] is processual and [CHEAT'] designates the trajector of the same process. Parallel extensions grace the schematic networks of other lexical items with both nominal and verbal senses, e.g. [[FLIRT/flirt]--→[FLIRT'/flirt]] and [[TEASE/tease]--→[TEASE'/ tease]]. From these specific categorizing relationships, a speaker is capable of extracting a schema representing a pattern of semantic extension: [[PROC/ ...]--→[PROC'/...]] (where [PROC'] profiles the trajector of [PROC]).

Observe, now, that this analysis matches Fig. 12.8 in every particular. We need only reorient this diagram and construe NR as the schema for the pattern of extension; the relationship between V and N then constitutes an instantiation of that schema (the former elaborates its standard, the latter its target). Precisely the same configuration is involved whether we (1) interpret V and NR as components of the composite structure N, or (2) interpret the extensional relationship between V and N as instantiating the schematic pattern NR; N functions as an active structure under either analysis—as the composite structure in (1), and in (2) as the "target within a target" (i.e. the target of a categorization that is itself the target of a higher-order categorizing relationship). Observe, however, that this result is possible only if syntagmatic and schematic relationships are considered interchangeable in the manner outlined earlier. More specifically, NR participates as a component structure in a syntagmatic relationship under interpretation (1), but in (2) it is a categorizing schema.

12.2.3. *Composite Lexical Units*

In the generative tradition, movement rules have often been justified by a standard type of argument based on complex lexical units (cf. Perlmutter 1970; Soames and Perlmutter 1979). Normally the argument is made with idioms, though it is applicable with comparable force to any fixed expression involving semantic extension or specialization. The sentences in (3) provide a typical example:

(3)(a)   *His finest agents kept tabs on the smugglers.*
    (b)   *Tabs were kept on the smugglers by his finest agents.*

Keep tabs on is a fixed expression whose semantic value is less than fully compositional. Its discontinuous occurrence in (3)(b) is taken as prima facie evidence that this passive sentence derives from an underlying nonpassive structure like (3)(a), or at least from some structure where *keep tabs on* is inserted as a contiguous unit. This argument relies on certain assumptions about the nature of these lexical units. One assumption is that they are semantically unanalyzable (i.e. meaning is carried only by the sequence as a whole); *tabs*, for instance, has no semantic value in (3)(b), so an analysis treating it as an underlying subject would be semantically incoherent. Another assumption is that a lexical item consists of a single, fixed morphological sequence, so that any departure from this sequencing signals the operation of a transformational rule (or some comparable device). These assumptions are at best gratuitous from the standpoint of cognitive grammar. An expression like *keep tabs on* is partially analyzable despite its lack of full compositionality.[14] A complex expression involves an intricate array of semantic and symbolic relationships, including the recognition of the contribution made by component structures to the composite whole. Most of these relationships hold constant—enabling a speaker to identify the unit and grasp its import—even when its component words occur discontinuously to satisfy the dictates of higher-order grammatical constructions that incorporate it. The inability of transformational rules to accommodate all such variations in the manifestation of complex lexical units has been acknowledged even by generative theorists (Bresnan and Grimshaw 1978). Hence there is nothing inherently controversial about the necessity for a more abstract conception of such units like the one to be proposed, which handles their variable manifestation directly, without appeal to rules that modify a single underlying shape.

Everything of present relevance can be illustrated with a simpler example, so let us focus on the expressions in (4):

(4)(a) *Would you please turn on the radio?*
   (b) *Would you please turn the radio on?*

(5)(a) *The frost turned the leaves red and yellow.*
   (b) *The television was already on.*

The lexical unit of concern is the verb-particle combination *turn on* (cf. Fraser 1976; Lindner 1981). Like other V + P combinations, *turn on* can occur as either a continuous sequence preceding the direct-object nominal, or a discontinuous sequence with the object nominal intervening between the verb and the particle. The expression seems highly idiomatic when construed in relation to the prototypical, spatial senses of *turn* and *on*; it is somewhat less so when its components are identified with the extended senses of these morphemes exemplified in (5). Its actual value nevertheless represents a specialization vis-à-vis its compositional value, and the same specialization is wit-

[14] Only the building-block metaphor renders this position in any way problematic. As for *tabs* in particular, I personally construe it to mean something like 'surveillance' and/or 'contact'.

nessed in (4)(a) and (4)(b): there is no doubt that *turn on* and *turn . . . on* are variant manifestations of a single lexical item.

Let us begin our analysis at the level of the transitive-verb construction. The fact that a particular verb, V_i, conventionally takes a direct object is represented in the grammar by the existence of a schematic verb-plus-object construction that includes as component structures V_i and the schema for nominals (i.e. noun phrases). There are two such constructional schemas for a transitive verb-particle combination, corresponding to the alternate direct-object constructions it appears in. The constructions specifying the transitivity of *turn on* are sketched in Fig. 12.9 (only the semantic pole is shown).

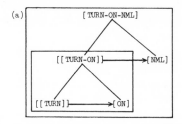 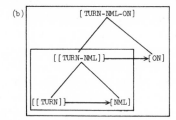

Fig. 12.9

The schemas of diagrams (a) and (b) are instantiated by the final portions of (4)(a) and (b), respectively: *turn on the radio* and *turn the radio on*.

The same components figure in the two constructions, but are assembled through alternate compositional paths, reflected at the phonological pole in contrasting word orders. [TURN] designates a process whose trajector induces a change of state in its primary landmark; this landmark serves as an e-site for the valence relation with [NML], and the resultant state for the relation with [ON]. In diagram (a), [TURN] is elaborated by [ON] at the first level of constituency, and [TURN-ON] by [NML] at the second. The dependent predication is in each case the profile determinant, so the composite structure [TURN-ON-NML] is processual. In diagram (b), [NML] elaborates the landmark of [TURN] at the first constituency level, and [ON] elaborates the resultant state at the second. The composite structure [TURN-NML-ON] is actually identical to [TURN-ON-NML]: the two are unified semantic structures, and the ordering of elements in this abbreviatory notation is simply mnemonic for the contrastive word orders at the phonological pole.

I will comment just in passing on the possibility of higher-order schemas. From some array of structures like Fig. 12.9(a) a speaker presumably extracts a schema that we can abbreviate [[V P] NML], where the verb and the particle (or the preposition) are schematic, like the nominal. From structures like Fig. 12.9(b), similarly, he extracts the higher-order schema [[V NML] P].[15] It

[15] Both are different from the schema for the construction where a verb takes a prepositional-phrase complement: [V [P NML]].

is even conceivable that a speaker perceives the resemblance between these construction types; this would imply a categorizing relationship uniting the schemas, perhaps of the form [[[V P] NML] ←–→ [[V NML] P]]. This schematic categorizing unit expresses the systematicity of the relationship between the two construction types; as such it is roughly analogous to the classic Particle Shift transformation (the putative rule deriving (4)(a) from (4)(b), or the converse). I note once again, however, that the present framework assimilates such relationships to the more inclusive notions of categorization and schematic networks. Moreover, a viable cognitive-grammar analysis does not require the extraction of any particular high-level schema or categorization (in view of its usage-based character), nor is it obligatory that the categorizing relationship between [[V P] NML] and [[V NML] P] have any particular directionality (cf. 10.2.1).

Let us return now to the level of individual lexical items. Where, in this complex of units, do we find the verb-particle combination *turn on*? We might first identify it with the bipolar unit corresponding to the inner box in Fig. 12.9(a), where component and composite structures form a constituent. However, this substructure of diagram (a) represents only the occurrence of *turn on* in sentences like (4)(a), and says nothing about cases like (4)(b). Although identifying the lexical unit with this substructure is not incorrect, doing so nonetheless tells only part of the story.

Actually, we should not expect to be able to identify it with any single unit—composite lexical items like *turn on* must be treated as complex categories and represented in the form of schematic networks (as must phonemes, individual morphemes, grammatical constructions, and so on). One possible dimension of variation distinguishing the nodes in such a network pertains to the linear ordering and contiguity of the component morphemes. *Turn on* and *turn . . . on* can therefore be regarded as variants of a single lexical item, analogous in this respect to [LEAF/lif] vs. [LEAF/liv] as phonological variants (allomorphs) of *leaf*, or [TREE/tree] vs. [OAK/tree] as semantic variants of *tree*. We should also not expect this network, or the nodes therein, to be self-contained entities observable in isolation. A grammar comprises a **structured** inventory of units: some units occur only in the context of others, and those defining a complex category may be found distributed among a set of more-inclusive units that provide the necessary environment (cf. Fig. 10.8).

At this point we can usefully recall a previous hypothesis (8.4.1), namely that units are always constituents, even when they appear not to be because certain facets of them are too schematic for overt manifestation. Hence the unit suffix-sequence *-er-s* is more accurately represented as [STEM-er-s] (cf. Fig. 8.10); the idiom instantiated by *lose my cool, lose your cool, lose his cool*, etc. can be given as [lose PRON's cool]; and the fact that *quarrel* governs *over* in a prepositional-phrase complement is expressed by the partially schematic unit [quarrel [over NML]].

Using this type of analysis, we can equate the variant *turn . . . on* with the entire schema depicted in Fig. 12.9(b). Being a constituent, the continuous variant *turn on* is in some sense self-contained, but the discontinuous variant—by definition—is only observable in the context of a larger structural configuration; in schematized form, this context therefore survives the cancellation process leading to the variant's mastery and conventionalization. It is perfectly reasonable, then, to give the major variants of *turn on* as [turn on] and [[turn NML] on], where these are identified as the bipolar units corresponding respectively to the inner box of Fig. 12.9(a) and the outer box of diagram (b). It would also be consonant with our general approach to include the direct-object construction in the representation of both variants: [[turn on] NML] and [[turn NML] on]. We have already noted the possibility of elements being categorized on the basis of their extrinsic properties, such as their occurrence in particular grammatical constructions (11.1.3.2). To the extent that transitivity is considered a property of *turn on*, the full schemas in both diagrams of Fig. 12.9 are included in the characterization of the lexical item.[16]

Still, there is probably more to a composite lexical unit than a set of context-specific structures like those in Fig. 12.9. Speakers can recognize a complex unit as being "the same" in some sense despite its highly divergent manifestations in a considerable variety of structural contexts (cf. (3), and the examples in 1.1.5). This ability suggests the extraction of a schema to represent its commonality across grammatical constructions. The approximate character of such a schema is depicted abstractly in Fig. 12.10.

Represented as component structures are the symbolic units [A/a] and [B/b]. At the semantic pole, [A] and [B] correspond to certain facets of the composite structure [C] and provide them with systemic motivation; these facets are labeled [A'] and [B'] respectively (cf. Fig. 12.5). Similarly, [a'] and [b'] are those respective facets of the composite structure [c] that correspond to components [a] and [b] at the phonological pole. The salience of these categorizing relationships between the component and composite structures determines the expression's degree of analyzability. To the extent that the expression is analyzable, the global symbolic correspondence between [C] and [c] subsumes the local symbolization of [A'] by [a'], and of [B'] by [b']; these local symbolic relationships reflect the bipolar recognition of [A/a] and [B/b] within the composite structure.

All these features are characteristic of any analyzable expression. The distinctive property of Fig. 12.10 is its schematicity, in particular its neutrality in

---

[16] Both the building-block metaphor and the container metaphor encourage us to conceive of lexical units as discrete entities with sharply defined boundaries. However, we can just as well attribute different degrees of centrality to the specifications of a lexical item, with no specific limitations on its scope. As constructions become larger and more inclusive, a lexical item's property of occurrence within the construction becomes more extrinsic and hence less central.

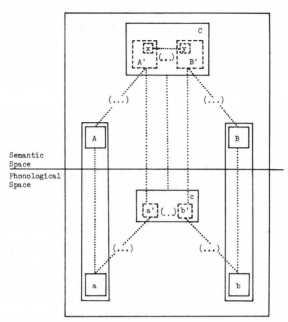

Fig. 12.10

regard to whether [A/a] and [B/b] are directly integrated to form the composite structure, or whether their relationship is mediated by other elements. The possibility of intervening elements is indicated in several places by the notation (...), which therefore marks the primary loci of schematicity in this representation. The direct combination of [A/a] and [B/b] corresponds to the special case where there are no intervening elements, i.e. (...) stands for zero; an example is the integration of [TURN/turn] and [ON/on] whose semantic pole is given in Fig. 12.9(a). Categorizing relationships are then direct (e.g. [[A]--→[A']]). Moreover, the correspondents of the component structures are essentially exhaustive of the composite structure's content (e.g. [turn] and [on] exhaust the content of [turn on]).

Suppose, however, that the content structures of the expression combine only through the mediation of other elements. Examples are *tabs . . . kep(t) on* in (3)(b), and *turn . . . on* in (4)(b); in the latter, for instance, *on* does not combine directly with *turn*, but rather with the intermediate composite structure [turn NML] (cf. Fig. 12.9(b)). In this event the scope of Fig. 12.10 is identified with a constituent that is large enough to have both [A/a] and [B/b] among its ultimate components; there is no inherent limit on its size, or on the number of elements in the path between [A/a] and [B/b] through the constituency tree. The composite structures may therefore have substantial content in addition to that comprised by the correspondents of the component structures, which may in fact furnish only a minor portion of it.

The correspondents of [A/a] and [B/b] are nevertheless present in the composite structure, and enable a speaker to recognize the lexical item, even when they have a distinctly minor role. At the phonological pole, the schema specifies the presence of [a'] and [b'], but it may be neutral about their contiguity and even their linear ordering (note *tabs . . . kep(t) on* in (3)(b)). Slightly more can be said about the semantic pole: not only are [A'] and [B'] immanent to [C], but in general there is also some point of overlap between them, as indicated in Fig. 12.10 by the correspondence line between the substructures *x* and *y*.

When [A] and [B] directly combine in a valence relation, their integration is effected by a correspondence between substructures *x* and *y*, and this overlap is of course inherited by the composite structure; in Fig. 12.9(a), the correspondence holds between the resultant state implied by [TURN] and the stative relation profiled by [ON].[17] When the combination of [A] and [B] is indirect, the same overlap is nonetheless bequeathed to the composite structure as the cumulative result of horizontal and vertical correspondences at each level of constituency. [ON] does not directly elaborate [TURN] in Fig. 12.9(b), so no single valence relation establishes a correspondence between the former's profile and the latter's resultant state. However, the resultant state of [TURN] is equated with that of [TURN-NML] through a vertical correspondence at the first level of constituency, and this correspondent within [TURN-NML] is then equated with [ON] by a horizontal correspondence specifying their integration at the second constituency level. In the overall composite structure, [ON'] (the correspondent of [ON]) is consequently identified with the resultant state of [TURN'] (the correspondent of [TURN]). The final semantic relation between *turn* and *on* is therefore the same regardless of the compositional path through which it is achieved.

---

[17] As part of this overall correspondence, the primary landmark of [TURN] corresponds to [ON]'s trajector.

Conclusion and Preview

THE CURRENT PROTOTYPE for linguistic publications is that a work should confine itself to a highly restricted topic, advance a specific claim formulated in the context of an established theory, and demonstrate the validity of this claim through rigorous argumentation. Since it fails on all these counts, the present work is at best a highly peripheral member of the category. That is by design and necessity, however. The narrowness of standard approaches could not be revealed by discussion limited to a single topic, nor could the possibility of describing the many aspects of linguistic structure in a unified manner. Moreover, definitive argumentation presupposes a well-articulated theory accepted by all concerned, and is consequently unachievable when the conceptual underpinnings of accepted theory are themselves at issue. I have therefore taken a global perspective, and attempted to sketch an overall conceptual framework rather than offer definitive proof of individual claims.

What has been accomplished? I should like to think that I have succeeded in presenting and motivating a coherent, realistic, and revelatory theoretical framework that achieves descriptive adequacy and conceptual unification— but in view of the programmatic nature of many proposals, and the lack of extensive illustration, even a sympathetic reader is well justified in withholding final judgment. I do however claim to have demonstrated the potential viability of radical alternatives to the reigning orthodoxy, and to have explored in some detail a conceivable (and not implausible) approach to characterizing language structure with reference to cognitive processing. At the very least I have shown that certain assumptions underlying current theory are less than self-evident, and that serious, open-minded examination of the conceptual foundations of linguistic thought is very much needed.

More concretely, I have in fact discussed a wide variety of linguistic problems and phenomena, some at considerable length. A number of analyses are spelled out in reasonably explicit detail (e.g. the notional definition of nouns and verbs, and the parallelism between count vs. mass nouns and perfective vs. imperfective processes), and I would argue for both their adequacy and their elegance. Moreover, time and time again we have seen that the general orientation and specific proposals of this framework permit the resolution of longstanding problems, both descriptive and conceptual, and the characterization of fundamental notions that have previously either resisted such treatment or been taken for granted. Finally, a substantial inventory of concepts, terms, notations, and descriptive constructs has been introduced. Some of these may well prove useful irrespective of one's theoretical persuasion or the ultimate validity of the model.

The basic presentation of cognitive grammar is only half-finished. The theoretical and descriptive notions advanced in Volume I must now be shown both adequate and revelatory for a representative array of grammatical problems. Volume II will consequently offer more comprehensive analyses of both nominal and verbal structure, with special (though by no means exclusive) reference to English. It will deal with phenomena that have been pivotal in the development of other frameworks (e.g. raising rules, the English auxiliary), and demonstrate that the present model accommodates them in a natural and revealing way. The conceptual unification and broad applicability of cognitive grammar are not achieved at the expense of cogent and insightful analysis.

Reference Matter

Glossary

THIS GLOSSARY was prepared by Larry Gorbet, of the University of New Mexico, whose conscientious efforts are gratefully acknowledged. The listing is selective, being restricted for the most part to recurrent terms that either are novel to cognitive grammar or assume a special value in this context; no attempt is made to list every technical term employed. (Thus, not every term in boldface type in the text is included here.) Each entry concludes by citing those sections of the text that introduce the designated notion, substantially elucidate its properties, or describe its significance within the framework. Although intended as a convenience, the glossary is not a surrogate for either the text discussion or the index.

abstract domain   Any nonbasic domain; any concept or conceptual complex that functions as a domain for the characterization of a higher-order concept. [4.1.1]

access node   The entity designated by a symbolic unit, considered as a point of access to a network. [4.2.3]

accommodation   The adjustment in details of a component required when it is integrated with another to form a composite structure. [2.1.5; 10.4.2]

activation   The execution of an established cognitive routine. (Contrasted with **actualization**.) [11.3.1]

active node   In a network, the particular node activated in a specific usage event. It approximates the notion the speaker wishes to convey. In terms of a compositional hierarchy, the active node is the topmost composite structure. [10.2.2; 11.1.2.2; 11.2; 12.2.1]

active zone   Those facets of an entity capable of interacting directly with a given domain or relation. [7.3.4]

actualization   The realization of a previously unexploited systemic potential of a cognitive system; a potential transition, $A > B$, is actualized when the coordinated activation of A and B in fact occurs. (Contrasted with **activation**.) [11.3.1]

A/D asymmetry   In a grammatical construction, the asymmetry between two component structures differing substantially in their degree of mutual dependence; on

485

balance, one of them (*A*) is **autonomous**, and the other (*D*) is **dependent**. [8.3; 9.1] (Cf. **autonomous structure**; **dependent structure**.)

adjective　An atemporal relation with a thing as trajector (this definition includes more than traditional adjectives, e.g. prepositions). [6.0; 6.1.2; 6.3.3]

adverb　An atemporal relation with a relation as trajector. [6.0; 6.1.2; 6.3.3]

analyzability　The extent to which the contribution of component structures to a composite structure is recognized (particularly the recognition of morphemes within a complex lexical item). [8.2.2; 12.1]

atemporal relation　A relation lacking a positive temporal profile; summary rather than sequential scanning characterizes the processing of the relation. [5.0; 6.0; 6.3.3] (Cf. **complex atemporal relation**; **simple atemporal relation**.)

autonomous cognitive event　Evoked in the absence of stimulation of a sense organ and not producing motor activity. (The opposite of **peripherally connected cognitive event**.) [3.2]

autonomous structure　A semantic or phonological structure that "exists on its own," not presupposing another structure for its manifestation; e.g. vowels are autonomous relative to consonants. (The opposite of **dependent structure**.) [8.3; 10.4.2]

base　The cognitive structure against which the designatum of a semantic structure is profiled; the ground with respect to which the designatum is the figure. The base includes specifications in one or more domains, which collectively are called the **matrix** of the semantic structure. [5.1] (Cf. **scope of predication**.)

basic conceptual relations　The set of relations that form the basis for more-complex relations: identity, separation, association, and inclusion. [6.0; 6.2.1]

basic domain　A domain that is primitive and not characterized in terms of more-fundamental domains. Examples are time, three-dimensional space, temperature, color space, and pitch. [4.1.1]

bipolar　Involving the relation between two poles, specifically the semantic and the phonological. [2.2.1]

bipolar componentiality　Componentiality involving structures defined on the basis of symbolic relationships rather than on the basis of semantic or phonological considerations alone. [2.3.1]

bounded　A region is bounded when there is some limit to the set of interconnected entities it comprises, determined on the basis of either internal configuration or contrast with surroundings. [4.1.2; 5.2; 5.3] (Cf. **region**.)

cancellation　The exclusion of a property from a schematic representation due to its not being specified or having conflicting specifications in certain instantiations. [10.4.1]

centrality　One of the dimensions that differentiate the elements in our (encyclopedic) knowledge of an entity: some elements are more central, and others are more peripheral, to our conception of it. Centrality, which can be equated with likelihood of activation in a neutral context, correlates with the degree to which a specification is conventional, generic, intrinsic, and characteristic. [4.2.2]

coding, and the coding problem The relation between linguistic units and usage events; the coding problem is to find an appropriate target structure that fits a sanctioning unit within some expected range of tolerance. [2.1.4; 2.2.1; 5.1] (Cf. **target structure**.)

cognitive distance A measure reflecting the number and likelihood of cognitive events needed to relate two notions, e.g. the degree to which a schema is elaborated by a particular instantiation: the distance between [THING] and [DOG] is greater than that between [THING] and [ANIMAL]. [4.3.4; 5.3.1; 11.3.1]

coherent Of a category, having its members densely linked by well-entrenched categorizing relationships of minimal cognitive distance. [10.3]

compacted Of a diagram, representing a structure holistically, not fully separated into components. (The opposite of **exploded**.) [2.1.5]

complement In a construction showing notable A/D asymmetry, and where the dependent component D is the profile determinant, the autonomous component A is the complement of D. [8.3.4]

complex atemporal relation An atemporal relation that does not reduce to a single consistent configuration. Thus it is like a process insofar as a series of states is profiled, but unlike a process insofar as the configuration is scanned in summary rather than sequential fashion. [6.1.3]

complex scene A scene that does not reduce to a single, consistent configuration. [3.4.2; 6.1.3; 7.1.2]

component structure A structure that integrates with one or more other structures in a combinatory relationship (particularly a grammatical valence relation). [8.0]

composite structure A structure that results when two or more structures in a given domain (phonological, semantic, or symbolic) combine in a valence relation. [2.1.5; 8.0]

composition The relation between component structures and the composite structure that derives from them. [12.0]

compositionality The regularity of compositional relationships; the degree to which the value of a whole is predictable from the value of its parts. A composite expression is *fully* or *partially* compositional depending on whether or not the composite structure derives from its component structures solely by virtue of regular compositional principles (as embodied in schemas). [12.1]

computation The actualization of a novel structure that is fully sanctioned by a set of conventional units. [11.3.2; 11.3.3]

conceived time Time as an object of conceptualization, as it is viewed and portrayed. (Contrasted with **processing time**.) [4.3.1]

configurational Of a domain, supporting predications specified by configuration (rather than simply location) within the domain. [4.1.3] (Cf. **locational**.)

constituency The order in which component structures are combined to yield progressively more elaborate composite structures. [8.4]

construal relationship The relationship between a speaker (or hearer) and a situation that he conceptualizes and portrays, involving focal adjustments and imagery. [3.3.2.4]

content requirement The requirement that the only structures permitted in the grammar of a language are (1) phonological, semantic, or symbolic structures that actually occur in linguistic expressions; (2) schemas for such structures; and (3) categorizing relations involving the elements in (1) and (2). Arbitrary formal devices are thus ruled out. [1.2.6.2]

contextual meaning The semantic pole of a usage event; the richly detailed conceptualization that constitutes our full understanding of an expression in context, including all relevant aspects of the conceived situation. [4.2.1; 10.4.1; 12.1.2]

conventional Widely shared (and known to be shared) by members of the relevant speech community. [2.1.3; 4.2.2]

conventional expression A multiword expression, which, though it may be largely or fully regular in its composition, is nevertheless conventionally established and learned as a unit. Examples are *good to see you, let the cat out, have great respect for, answer the phone, other things being equal*, and so forth. [1.2.2]

conventionality The degree to which an expression conforms to the linguistic conventions of a language. It is the measure of well-formedness in a cognitive grammar. [2.1.4.2]

dependence The degree to which one component presupposes another. One structure, *D*, is dependent on another, *A*, to the extent that *A* elaborates a salient substructure within *D*. In a valence relation, if this relation is asymmetrical, *D* is recognized as the dependent component, and *A* as the autonomous component. [8.3; 10.4.2]

dependent morpheme A morpheme that makes salient internal reference to a schematically characterized stem, particularly with respect to the phonological pole; a morpheme describable as a function that maps one stem onto another. [9.1.2; 9.1.3]

dependent structure A semantic or phonological structure that presupposes another for its manifestation. Phonologically, consonants are dependent on vowels. Relations are conceptually dependent, since to conceive of a relation one must conceive (at least schematically) of the related entities. (The opposite of **autonomous structure**.) [6.1.1; 8.3]

designation The relation within a semantic structure between the base as a whole and some substructure selected as the profile. [5.0; 5.1]

direct object A nominal whose profile corresponds to the primary landmark of a relation (prototypically, of a verb), generally elaborating this landmark. [7.3.3]

domain A coherent area of conceptualization relative to which semantic units may be characterized. Three-dimensional space, smell, color, touch sensation, etc. are basic domains. A concept or conceptual complex of any degree of complexity can function as an abstract domain (e.g. the human body, the rules of chess, a kinship network). [2.1.3; 3.2.2; Ch. 4]

egocentric viewing arrangement A viewing arrangement in which the objective scene is expanded beyond the region of perceptual optimality to include the observer and his immediate surroundings. [3.3.2.4] (Cf. **objective scene**.)

elaborate   To instantiate a schema (represent a special case of the structure it describes); e.g. [DOG] elaborates [ANIMAL], and [u] elaborates [VOWEL]. The elaboration of a schema is consistent with its specifications but is more fully and precisely specified. [2.1.4.3]

elaboration site   Those facets of one component structure in a valence relation that another component structure serves to elaborate. (Abbreviated as e-site.) [8.3.3]

encyclopedic   Describes the open-ended character of meanings: one cannot exhaustively characterize the meanings of linguistic expressions by short, dictionary-type definitions. [2.1.3; 4.2]

entity   Anything that may be conceived of or referred to for analytical purposes; e.g. a thing, relation, sensation, or point on a scale. An entity need not be discrete, separately recognized, or cognitively salient. [5.3.1]

epistemic grounding   An entity is epistemically grounded when its location is specified relative to the speaker and hearer and their spheres of knowledge. For verbs, tense and mood ground an entity epistemically; for nouns, definite/indefinite specifications establish epistemic grounding. Epistemic grounding distinguishes finite verbs and clauses from nonfinite ones, and nominals (noun phrases) from simple nouns. [3.3.2.3] (Cf. **nominal**.)

event   Any cognitive occurrence of whatever degree of complexity, from the firing of a single neuron to the comprehension of a complicated expression. [3.1.1]

exclusionary fallacy   The belief that one analysis, motivation, categorization, cause, function, or explanation for a linguistic phenomenon necessarily precludes another. [1.1.6]

exploded   Of a diagram, representing a structure by separately showing its various components. (The opposite of **compacted**.) [2.1.5]

expression   The pairing of a conceptualization and a vocalization, or the schematic representation of such a pairing. Linguistic expressions constitute a continuum, varying in level of specificity and contextual inclusiveness, that subsumes the traditional "sentences" and "utterances" as special cases. [1.1.1; 11.2.1]

focal adjustment   Variation in how a situation is conceived, particularly variation pertaining to selection, perspective, and abstraction. [3.3] (Cf. **imagery**.)

grammar   Those aspects of cognitive organization in which resides a speaker's grasp of established linguistic convention. The grammar of a language is a structured inventory of conventional linguistic units. [2.1]

grammatical construction   A symbolic structure involving the syntagmatic combination of morphemes and/or larger expressions. The construction consists of a set of component structures, their mode of integration, and the composite structure resulting from this integration. [2.2.2; 8.0; 11.1]

ground   The speech event, its participants, and its setting. (Distinct from the sense of ground that contrasts with figure.) [3.3.2.3] (Cf. **epistemic grounding**.)

head The profile determinant in a grammatical construction, particularly when it is the autonomous component in a construction showing notable A/D asymmetry; the autonomous profile determinant, A, is the head in such a construction, and the dependent component, D, is a **modifier**. [8.3.4]

imagery The ability to construe a situation in alternate ways for purposes of thought or expression, e.g. by effecting various types of focal adjustment. [1.2.2; 3.2.1] (Cf. **focal adjustment**.)

immanent One transition chain is immanent to another when it is included within the other as a subchain. [4.3.4; 11.3.1]

immediate scope Where the scope of predication is quantized, the innermost of its layered regions—that with the highest degree of salience and relevance—is the immediate scope; e.g. the concept [FINGER] (rather than [HAND]) is the immediate scope of predication for [KNUCKLE]. [3.3.1]

imperfective Of processes, profiling a relation as unchanging through time. (The opposite of **perfective**; *know* vs. *learn* illustrates the contrast.) [7.0; 7.2]

instantiate To elaborate; an instantiation is a subcase of a schema (consistent with its specifications, but more precise). [2.1.4.3]

integration The combination of component structures (effected by correspondences between their subparts) to form a composite structure, particularly in grammatical constructions. [2.1.5; 8.1]

interconnection Conceived entities are interconnected when the cognitive events constituting their conception are coordinated as components of a higher-order event. [5.3.1]

intrinsic property Capable of being determined without reference to external entities; e.g. shape is a more intrinsic property of physical objects, whereas size is less intrinsic, since it involves comparison with other objects or some scale. [4.2.2]

landmark A salient substructure other than the trajector of a relational predication or the profile of a nominal predication. [6.1.2]

lexical item Exists to the extent that a coherent semantic category participates in a symbolic relationship with a coherent phonological category. [10.3; 11.3.3] (Cf. **coherent**.)

linguistic creativity The creation of novel expressions, including extensions (involving figurative language, the adaptation of linguistic units to new situations, or even willful violation of convention) and also the straightforward computation of fully sanctioned expressions. [2.1.4.5]

locational Of a domain, supporting predications specified by location (rather than configuration) within the domain. Color and temperature are locational. [4.1.3] (Cf. **configurational**.)

matrix The set of domains relative to which a predication is characterized, and which constitute its base. [4.0]

modifier In a construction showing notable A/D asymmetry, and where the autonomous component, A, is the profile determinant, the dependent component, D, is a modifier of A (A is its **head**). [8.3.4]

morpheme   A symbolic structure that is not analyzable into bipolar components. The semantic pole of a morpheme is called a **predicate**. [Introduction to Part II]

nominal   An epistemically grounded expression that profiles a thing. (Roughly equivalent to "noun phrase.") [3.3.2.3]

nominal predication   A predication that designates a thing. [5.0]

noun   A symbolic structure whose semantic pole profiles a thing. (This definition subsumes more than just traditional nouns, e.g. pronouns and noun phrases.) [5.0]

objective   An entity is objective to the extent that its role as observer is minimized, and its role as object of observation is maximized. Various devices allow for the objectification of an otherwise subjective entity. [3.3.2.4]

objective scene   The general locus of viewing attention; the onstage region within the scope of predication. In the optimal viewing arrangement, it coincides with the region of maximal perceptual acuity. [3.3.2.4]

optimal viewing arrangement   A situation in which the roles of the observer and the observed are maximally distinct; the observed is sharply differentiated from its surroundings and situated in a region of maximal perceptual acuity. [3.3.2.4]

perfective   Of processes, profiling a relation as changing through time. (The opposite of **imperfective**.) [7.0; 7.2]

peripherally connected cognitive event   Evoked by stimulation of a sensory organ or producing motor activity. (The opposite of **autonomous cognitive event**.) [3.2]

perspective   The way in which a scene is viewed. Aspects of perspective include figure/ground alignment, vantage point, and subjectivity. [3.3.2]

phonological pole   A phonological structure in relation to a semantic structure that it symbolizes. [2.2.1]

predicate   The semantic pole of a morpheme. [Introduction to Part II]

predication   The semantic pole of a linguistic expression (whether a morpheme or more complex). [Introduction to Part II]

primary domain   A domain that is particularly prominent and likely to be activated in a predication. Which domains are primary may be a matter of convention (e.g. the relative prominence of certain domains in the lexical items *roe* and *caviar* is responsible for the semantic contrast between the items). [4.2.3]

primary landmark   The most salient landmark in a relational predication. When it is a thing, the nominal elaborating it is the direct object. [7.3.3]

process   A relation having a positive temporal profile: its evolution through conceived time is portrayed via sequential scanning. [5.0; 7.0; 7.1] (Cf. **imperfective**; **perfective**.)

processing time   Time as a dimension through which cognitive activity takes place. (Contrasted with **conceived time**.) [4.3.1]

profile   The entity designated by a semantic structure. It is a substructure within the base that is obligatorily accessed, functions as the focal point within the objective scene, and achieves a special degree of prominence (resulting in one level of figure/ground organization). [5.0; 5.1]

profile determinant   In a construction, a component structure whose profile is inherited by the composite structure; the profile determinant is thus schematic for the composite structure. For example, in *The man is tall*, the unit *is tall* is the profile determinant; in *tall man*, *man* is the profile determinant. [6.3.1; 8.2.1]

prototype   That unit in a schematic network which is naturally most salient, most often thought of, most likely to be chosen as representative of the category. In a generalized sense, the term is also adopted for the standard in a categorizing relationship based on extension rather than schematicity. [1.1.4.2; 10.1.1]

recognition   The limiting case of scanning, in which no discrepancy is registered between the standard and target. [3.1.3]

region   A set of mutually interconnected entities. (A noun profiles a region, which is specifically bounded in the case of count nouns.) [5.2; 5.3]

relation   Defined by interconnections among conceived entities. [6.1.1]

relational predication   A predication that profiles a relation (either an atemporal relation or a process). [5.0; 6.0; 6.1.1]

root   A phonologically autonomous morpheme. [8.3.4] (Cf. **dependent morpheme**.)

rule/list fallacy   The exclusionary fallacy holding, on grounds of simplicity, that particular statements (lists) are to be excised from the grammar of a language if general statements (rules) can be established that subsume them. [1.1.6]

sanction   The motivation afforded a novel structure by the conventional units of a grammar. **Full sanction** involves an elaborative relationship (one of full schematicity) between the sanctioning unit and target structure; **partial sanction** involves a relationship of extension (or partial schematicity, in which there is some conflict in specifications). Although partial sanction implies some degree of ill-formedness, a considerable degree of nonconventionality is tolerated and often expected in actual language use. [2.1.4., 10.1.1; 11.2.2]

scanning   The operation that relates a standard of comparison and a target, registering any discrepancy between them. [3.1.2]

schema   Structure *A* is a schema with respect to structure *B* when *A* is compatible with the specifications of *B* but characterizes corresponding entities with less precision and detail. (The relation between *A* and *B* is equivalent to that between a superordinate and subordinate node in a taxonomic hierarchy.) [2.1.4.3; 3.3.3; 10.1.1]

schematicity   Relative precision of specification along one or more parameters. Also, the relation between a schema and its instantiation; such schematicity is *full* or *partial* depending on whether or not the two are fully compatible in their specifications. [2.1.4.3; 2.1.4.4; 3.3.3]

schematic network   An assembly of overlapping categorizing units. [2.1.5; 10.1; 10.2]

schematic plane   Defined by categorizing relationships among structures organized in schematic networks (paradigmatic relationships). (The opposite of **syntagmatic plane**.) [2.1.5]

schematic-transparency principle   The tendency for the sanctioning and target structures to merge into a single, consistent conceptualization when there is full consistency between their specifications. When a schema merges with its instantiation, the resulting structure is equivalent to the instantiation. [2.3.2.2; 11.3.1]

scope of predication Base. Those aspects of a scene that are specifically included in a particular predication. The scope of a predication may sometimes constitute only a limited portion of relevant domains. [3.3]

search domain The region to which a locative predication restricts its trajector. [8.1.2]

selection Focal adjustments determining what aspects of a scene are being dealt with. Included are choices of domain, scale, and scope. [3.3.1]

semantic pole A semantic structure as it is related to a phonological structure that symbolizes it. [2.2.1]

semantic structure A conceptualization shaped in accordance with linguistic convention and functioning as the semantic pole of a linguistic expression. [Introduction to Part II]

sequential scanning The mode of cognitive processing in which a series of states are conceived through the successive transformation of one into another; noncumulative in nature. (The opposite of **summary scanning**.) [3.4.2; 7.1.3]

simple atemporal relation A relation that reduces to a single consistent configuration (or state); a stative relation. [6.1.3; 7.1.3] (Cf. **stative relation**.)

standard A baseline event, relative to which a target event is evaluated. [3.1.2]

stative relation A simple atemporal relation. Though time may be a domain, the predication profiles only a single state, not a sequence of distinct, temporally distributed configurations. [6.1.3; 7.1.3]

subject A nominal whose profile corresponds to the trajector of a relation (prototypically, of a verb), generally elaborating this trajector. [6.3.1]

subjective An entity is subjective to the extent that its role as observer is maximized, and its role as object of observation is minimized. [3.3.2.4]

summary scanning The mode of processing in which component states or specifications are activated in cumulative fashion, so that all facets of a complex structure are coexistent and simultaneously available. [3.4.2; 7.1.3]

symbolization The relation between a structure in semantic space and one in phonological space, whether this relation constitutes a unit in the grammar of a language or is created in a specific usage event. [1.1.1; 2.1.2; 2.2.1; 5.1]

syntagmatic plane Defined by combinatorial relationships, specifically the integration of component structures to form composite structures. (The opposite of **schematic plane**.) [2.1.5]

target structure The object of comparison in a scanning operation. A solution to the coding problem. In a dependent structure seen as a "function," the "output" of that function: the substructure corresponding to the composite structure and determining its organization. [2.1.4; 3.1.2; 9.1.3; 9.2; 12.2.1]

temporal profile In a process predication, the span of conceived time through which the evolving relation is profiled and scanned sequentially. [7.1]

thing   A region in some domain of conceptual space. [5.0; 5.2]

trajector   The figure within a relational profile. [6.1.2; 6.3.1]

transfer   The ability of a speaker to conceptualize a situation as it would appear from different vantage points and to portray it accordingly for linguistic purposes, irrespective of the speaker's own vantage point. [3.3.2.4; 3.4.1]

transformation   A complex conceptualization that does not reduce to a single consistent configuration, especially when the component conceptualizations are ordered. (Exemplified by the component states of a perfective process.) [3.4.1] (Cf. **complex atemporal relation; complex scene.**)

transition   There is a transition between two cognitive events when temporal sequencing figures in their coordination. [4.3.4]

unipolar componentiality   Componentiality involving structures defined on the basis of semantic or phonological considerations alone (without regard for symbolic relationships). [2.3.1]

unit   A cognitive structure mastered by a speaker to the point that it can be employed in largely automatic fashion, without requiring attention to its individual parts or their arrangement. A unit is sufficiently well entrenched to be easily evoked as an integrated whole, that is, carried out more or less automatically once initiated. (Such a structure is also said to have **unit status**.) [2.1.1; 3.1.1]

usage-based approach   Substantial importance is given to the actual use of the linguistic system and a speaker's knowledge of this use; the grammar is held responsible for a speaker's knowledge of the full range of linguistic conventions, regardless of whether these conventions can be subsumed under more general statements. A nonreductive approach to linguistic structure that employs fully articulated schematic networks and emphasizes the importance of low-level schemas. [1.2.5; 11.1.2; 11.2.2] (Cf. **rule/list fallacy**.)

usage event   · A symbolic expression assembled by a speaker in a particular circumstance for a particular purpose; the pairing of a detailed, context-dependent conceptualization and (in the case of speech) an actual vocalization. [2.1.4.2]

valence relation   The combinatory (or syntagmatic) relationship between component structures (particularly in a grammatical construction), effected by correspondences established between their subparts. [8.0] (Cf. **integration**.)

verb   A symbolic structure whose semantic pole profiles a process. (This definition subsumes more than just traditional verbs, e.g. finite clauses.) [7.0]

viewpoint   Vantage point (the position from which a scene is viewed) plus orientation of the viewer. [3.3.2.2]

References

Akmajian, Adrian, Susan M. Steele, and Thomas Wasow. 1979. "The Category AUX in Universal Grammar." *Linguistic Inquiry* 10: 1–64.

Allerton, D. J. 1982. *Valency and the English Verb*. London: Academic Press.

Anderson, John M. 1971. *The Grammar of Case*. Cambridge, Eng.: Cambridge University Press.

Anderson, Stephen R. 1982. "Where's Morphology?" *Linguistic Inquiry* 13: 571–612.

Andrews, J. Richard. 1975. *Introduction to Classical Nahuatl*. Austin: University of Texas Press.

Arnheim, Rudolf. 1969. *Visual Thinking*. Berkeley: University of California Press.

Bach, Emmon. 1967. "*Have* and *Be* in English Syntax." *Language* 43: 462–85.

———. 1977. Review of Paul M. Postal, *On Raising*. *Language* 53: 621–54.

Bailey, Charles-James N. 1973. *Variation and Linguistic Theory*. Arlington, Va.: Center for Applied Linguistics.

Barwise, Jon, and John Perry. 1983. *Situations and Attitudes*. Cambridge, Mass.: MIT Press.

Bever, Thomas G., and Peter S. Rosenbaum. 1970. "Some Lexical Structures and Their Empirical Validity." In Roderick A. Jacobs and Peter S. Rosenbaum, eds., *Readings in English Transformational Grammar*, 3–19. Waltham, Mass.: Ginn.

Block, Ned, ed. 1981. *Imagery*. Cambridge, Mass.: MIT Press.

Bloomfield, Leonard. 1933. *Language*. New York: Holt.

Bolinger, Dwight. 1961. "Syntactic Blends and Other Matters." *Language* 37: 366–81.

———. 1977. *Meaning and Form*. New York: Longman, Inc.

———. 1982a. "Intonation and Its Parts." *Language* 58: 505–33.

———. 1982b. "Nondeclaratives from an Intonational Standpoint." In Robert Chametzky, Robinson Schneider, and Kevin Tuite, eds., *Papers from the Parasession on Nondeclaratives*, 1–22. Chicago: Chicago Linguistic Society.

Bresnan, Joan. 1978. "A Realistic Transformational Grammar." In Morris Halle, Joan Bresnan, and George A. Miller, eds., *Linguistic Theory and Psychological Reality*, 1–59. Cambridge, Mass.: MIT Press.

———. 1982. "Control and Complementation." *Linguistic Inquiry* 13: 343–434.

Bresnan, Joan, and Jane Grimshaw. 1978. "The Syntax of Free Relatives in English." *Linguistic Inquiry* 9: 331–91.

Bright, William, and A. K. Ramanujan. 1964. "Sociolinguistic Variation and Language Change." In Horace Lunt, ed., *Proceedings of the Ninth International Congress of Linguists*, 1107–13. The Hague: Mouton.

Brown, Cecil H. 1979. "A Theory of Lexical Change (with Examples from Folk Biology, Human Anatomical Partonomy and Other Domains)." *Anthropological Linguistics* 21: 257–76.

Brugman, Claudia. 1981. "The Story of *Over*." M.A. Thesis. Berkeley: University of California.

Cairns, Charles E., and Mark H. Feinstein. 1982. "Markedness and the Theory of Syllable Structure." *Linguistic Inquiry* 13: 193–225.

Carlson, Lauri. 1981. "Aspect and Quantification." In Philip J. Tedeschi and Annie Zaenen, eds., *Syntax and Semantics. Volume 14: Tense and Aspect*, 31–64. New York: Academic Press.

Casad, Eugene H. 1981. "The Conversational Scheme and Cora Viewpoint Particles." *Linguistic Notes from La Jolla* 8: 41–72.

———. 1982. *Cora Locationals and Structured Imagery*. Ph.D. Dissertation. San Diego: University of California.

Casad, Eugene H., and Ronald W. Langacker. 1985. "'Inside' and 'Outside' in Cora Grammar." *International Journal of American Linguistics* 51: 247–81.

Chafe, Wallace L. 1968. "Idiomaticity as an Anomaly in the Chomskyan Paradigm." *Foundations of Language* 4: 109–27.

———. 1970. *Meaning and the Structure of Language*. Chicago: University of Chicago Press.

Chomsky, Noam. 1957. *Syntactic Structures*. The Hague: Mouton.

———. 1959. Review of B. F. Skinner, *Verbal Behavior*. *Language* 35: 26–58.

———. 1965. *Aspects of the Theory of Syntax*. Cambridge, Mass.: MIT Press.

———. 1970. "Remarks on Nominalization." In Roderick A. Jacobs and Peter S. Rosenbaum, eds., *Readings in English Transformational Grammar*, 184–221. Waltham, Mass.: Ginn.

———. 1972. "Some Empirical Issues in the Theory of Transformational Grammar." In Stanley Peters, ed., *Goals of Linguistic Theory*, 63–130. Englewood Cliffs, N.J.: Prentice-Hall.

———. 1973. "Conditions on Transformations." In Stephen R. Anderson and Paul Kiparsky, eds., *A Festschrift for Morris Halle*, 232–86. New York: Holt.

Chomsky, Noam, and Morris Halle. 1965. "Some Controversial Questions in Phonological Theory." *Journal of Linguistics* 1: 97–138.

———. 1968. *The Sound Pattern of English*. New York: Harper & Row.

Collins, Allan M., and Elizabeth F. Loftus. 1975. "A Spreading-Activation Theory of Semantic Processing." *Psychological Review* 82: 407–28.

Cooper, Robin. 1980. "Montague's Syntax." In Edith A. Moravcsik and Jessica R. Wirth, eds., *Syntax and Semantics. Volume 13: Current Approaches to Syntax*, 19–44. New York: Academic Press.

Cruse, D. A. 1979. "On the Transitivity of the Part-Whole Relation." *Journal of Linguistics* 15: 29–38.

DeLancey, Scott. 1981. "An Interpretation of Split Ergativity and Related Phenomena." *Language* 57: 626–57.

Derbyshire, Desmond C., and Geoffrey K. Pullum. 1981. "Object-Initial Languages." *International Journal of American Linguistics* 47: 192–214.

Dinsmore, John. 1979. *Pragmatics, Formal Theory, and the Analysis of Presupposition*. Ph.D. Dissertation. San Diego: University of California.

Diver, William. 1982. "The Focus-Control Interlock in Latin." *Columbia University Working Papers in Linguistics* 7: 13–31.

Dougherty, Ray C. 1973. "A Survey of Linguistic Methods and Arguments." *Foundations of Language* 10: 423–90.

Downing, Pamela. 1977. "On the Creation and Use of English Compound Nouns." *Language* 53: 810–42.

Dowty, David R. 1972. "On the Syntax and Semantics of the Atomic Predicate CAUSE." *Proceedings of the Annual Meeting of the Chicago Linguistic Society* 8: 62–74.

Elman, Jeffrey L., and James L. McClelland. 1984. "Speech Perception as a Cognitive Process: The Interactive Activation Model." In Norman Lass, ed., *Speech and Language. Volume 10*, 337–74. New York: Academic Press.

Fauconnier, Gilles. 1985. *Mental Spaces: Aspects of Meaning Construction in Natural Language*. Cambridge, Mass.: MIT Press.

Feyerabend, Paul. 1978. *Against Method*. London: Verso.

Fillmore, Charles J. 1975. *Santa Cruz Lectures on Deixis*. Bloomington: Indiana University Linguistics Club.

———. 1977. "The Case for Case Reopened." In Peter Cole and Jerrold M. Sadock, eds., *Syntax and Semantics. Volume 8: Grammatical Relations*, 59–81. New York: Academic Press.

———. 1982. "Frame Semantics." In *Linguistics in the Morning Calm* (ed. by the Linguistic Society of Korea), 111–37. Seoul: Hanshin.

Fodor, Jerry A. 1970. "Three Reasons for Not Deriving 'Kill' from 'Cause to Die'." *Linguistic Inquiry* 1: 429–38.

———. 1983. *The Modularity of Mind*. Cambridge, Mass.: MIT Press.

Foley, William A., and Robert D. Van Valin, Jr. 1977. "On the Viability of the Notion of 'Subject' in Universal Grammar." *Proceedings of the Annual Meeting of the Berkeley Linguistics Society* 3: 293–320.

Fraser, Bruce. 1970. "Idioms Within a Transformational Grammar." *Foundations of Language* 6: 22–42.

———. 1976. *The Verb-Particle Combination in English*. New York: Academic Press.

Freidin, Robert. 1975. "The Analysis of Passives." *Language* 51: 384–405.

García, Erica C. 1977. "On the Practical Consequences of Theoretical Principles." *Lingua* 43: 129–70.

García, Erica C., and Ricardo L. Otheguy. 1983. "Being Polite in Ecuador: Strategy Reversal under Language Contact." *Lingua* 61: 103–32.

Gazdar, Gerald, Geoffrey K. Pullum, and Ivan A. Sag. 1982. "Auxiliaries and Related Phenomena in a Restrictive Theory of Grammar." *Language* 58: 591–638.

Gensler, Orin D. 1977. "Non-Syntactic Antecedents and Frame Semantics." *Proceedings of the Annual Meeting of the Berkeley Linguistics Society* 3: 321–34.

Gentner, Dedre. 1981. "Some Interesting Differences Between Verbs and Nouns." *Cognition and Brain Theory* 4: 161–78.

————. 1982. "Why Nouns Are Learned Before Verbs: Linguistic Relativity Versus Natural Partitioning." In Stan Kuczaj, ed., *Language Development I: Syntax and Semantics*, 301–34. Hillsdale, N.J.: Erlbaum.

Givón, Talmy. 1979. *On Understanding Grammar.* New York: Academic Press.

————, ed. 1983. *Topic Continuity in Discourse: A Quantitative Cross-Language Study.* Amsterdam: John Benjamins.

————. 1984. *Syntax: A Functional-Typological Introduction. Volume 1.* Amsterdam: John Benjamins.

Goldsmith, John. 1976. "An Overview of Autosegmental Phonology." *Linguistic Analysis* 2: 23–68.

————. 1980. "Meaning and Mechanism in Grammar." *Harvard Studies in Syntax and Semantics* 2: 423–49.

Gorbet, Larry. 1973. "The Isthmus of Anaphor (and Idiomaticity)." *Stanford Occasional Papers in Linguistics* 3: 25–34.

Green, Georgia M. 1974. *Semantics and Syntactic Regularity.* Bloomington: Indiana University Press.

Gross, Maurice. 1979. "On the Failure of Generative Grammar." *Language* 55: 859–85.

Haiman, John. 1980. "Dictionaries and Encyclopedias." *Lingua* 50: 329–57.

————. 1983. "Iconic and Economic Motivation." *Language* 59: 781–819.

Hankamer, Jorge. 1977. "Multiple Analyses." In Charles N. Li, ed., *Mechanisms of Syntactic Change*, 583–607. Austin: University of Texas Press.

Hawkins, Bruce W. 1981. "Variable Temporal Integration Between Motional Verbs and Locational Prepositions." *Linguistic Notes from La Jolla* 10: 98–127.

————. 1984. *The Semantics of English Spatial Prepositions.* Ph.D. Dissertation. San Diego: University of California.

Herskovits, Annette H. 1982. *Space and the Prepositions in English: Regularities and Irregularities in a Complex Domain.* Ph.D. Dissertation. Stanford, Calif.: Stanford University.

Hofstadter, Douglas R. 1979. *Gödel, Escher, Bach: An Eternal Golden Braid.* New York: Basic Books.

————. 1982. "Metamagical Themas (The Music of Frédéric Chopin: Startling Aural Patterns That Also Startle the Eye)." *Scientific American* 246(4): 16–28.

Hopper, Paul J., and Sandra A. Thompson. 1980. "Transitivity in Grammar and Discourse." *Language* 56: 251–99.

————. 1984. "The Discourse Basis for Lexical Categories in Universal Grammar." *Language* 60: 703–52.

Householder, Fred W., Jr. 1965. "On Some Recent Claims in Phonological Theory." *Journal of Linguistics* 1: 13–34.

————. 1971. *Linguistic Speculations.* Cambridge, Eng.: Cambridge University Press.

Hudson, Richard A. 1976. *Arguments for a Non-transformational Grammar.* Chicago: University of Chicago Press.

————. 1984. *Word Grammar.* Oxford: Basil Blackwell.

Jackendoff, Ray. 1975. "Morphological and Semantic Regularities in the Lexicon." *Language* 51: 639–71.

————. 1977. *X̄ Syntax: A Study of Phrase Structure*. Cambridge, Mass.: MIT Press.

————. 1978. "Grammar as Evidence for Conceptual Structure." In Morris Halle, Joan Bresnan, and George A. Miller, eds., *Linguistic Theory and Psychological Reality*, 201–28. Cambridge, Mass.: MIT Press.

————. 1983. *Semantics and Cognition*. Cambridge, Mass.: MIT Press. Current Studies in Linguistics #8.

Jaeger, Jeri J., and John J. Ohala. 1984. "On the Structure of Phonetic Categories." *Proceedings of the Annual Meeting of the Berkeley Linguistics Society* 10: 15–26.

Keenan, Edward L. 1976. "Towards a Universal Definition of 'Subject'." In Charles Li, ed., *Subject and Topic*, 303–33. New York: Academic Press.

Kempson, Ruth M. 1977. *Semantic Theory*. Cambridge, Eng.: Cambridge University Press.

Keyser, Samuel Jay, and Paul M. Postal. 1976. *Beginning English Grammar*. New York: Harper & Row.

Kirsner, Robert S. 1977. "The Theory." *Columbia University Working Papers in Linguistics* 4: 21–57.

————. 1980. "Meaning, Message, Inference, and the Problem of Units in Linguistics." *Quaderni di Semantica* 1: 307–17.

Kosslyn, Stephen Michael. 1980. *Image and Mind*. Cambridge, Mass.: Harvard University Press.

Kuno, Susumo. 1980. "Functional Syntax." In Edith A. Moravcsik and Jessica R. Wirth, eds., *Syntax and Semantics. Volume 13: Current Approaches to Syntax*, 117–35. New York: Academic Press.

Labov, William. 1981. "Resolving the Neogrammarian Controversy." *Language* 57: 267–308.

Lakoff, George. 1970. *Irregularity in Syntax*. New York: Holt.

————. 1972. "Linguistics and Natural Logic." In Donald Davidson and Gilbert Harman, eds., *Semantics of Natural Language*, 545–665. Dordrecht: Reidel.

————. 1977. "Linguistic Gestalts." *Proceedings of the Annual Meeting of the Chicago Linguistic Society* 13: 236–87.

————. 1982. "Categories: An Essay in Cognitive Linguistics." In *Linguistics in the Morning Calm* (ed. by the Linguistic Society of Korea), 139–93. Seoul: Hanshin.

————. 1984a. "*There*-Constructions: A Case Study in Grammatical Construction Theory and Prototype Theory." Berkeley: University of California, Institute of Human Learning. Berkeley Cognitive Science Report No. 18.

————. 1984b. "Classifiers as a Reflection of Mind: A Cognitive Model Approach to Prototype Theory." Berkeley: University of California, Institute of Human Learning. Berkeley Cognitive Science Report No. 19.

————. 1987. *Women, Fire, and Dangerous Things: What Categories Reveal about the Mind*. Chicago: University of Chicago Press.

Lakoff, George, and Mark Johnson. 1980. *Metaphors We Live By*. Chicago: University of Chicago Press.

Lakoff, George, and Zoltán Kövecses. 1983. "The Cognitive Model of Anger Inherent in American English." Berkeley: University of California, Institute of Human Learning. Berkeley Cognitive Science Report No. 10.

Lakoff, George, and Henry Thompson. 1975. "Dative Questions in Cognitive Grammar." In Robin Grossman, Jim San, and Tim Vance, eds., *Papers from the Parasession on Functionalism*, 337–50. Chicago: Chicago Linguistic Society.

Langacker, Ronald W. 1968. "Observations on French Possessives." *Language* 44: 51–75.

———. 1972. "Possessives in Classical Nahuatl." *International Journal of American Linguistics* 38: 173–86.

———. 1973a. *Language and Its Structure*. Second Edition. New York: Harcourt Brace Jovanovich.

———. 1973b. "Predicate Raising: Some Uto-Aztecan Evidence." In Braj B. Kachru et al., eds., *Issues in Linguistics: Papers in Honor of Henry and Renée Kahane*, 468–91. Urbana: University of Illinois Press.

———. 1975. "Functional Stratigraphy." In Robin Grossman, Jim San, and Tim Vance, eds., *Papers from the Parasession on Functionalism*, 351–97. Chicago: Chicago Linguistic Society.

———. 1976. "Semantic Representations and the Linguistic Relativity Hypothesis." *Foundations of Language* 14: 307–57.

———. 1978. "The Form and Meaning of the English Auxiliary." *Language* 54: 853–82.

———. 1979. "Grammar as Image." *Linguistic Notes from La Jolla* 6: 88–126.

———. 1981a. Review of Talmy Givón, *On Understanding Grammar*. *Language* 57: 436–45.

———. 1981b. "The Nature of Grammatical Valence." *Linguistic Notes from La Jolla* 10: 33–59.

———. 1981c. "The Integration of Grammar and Grammatical Change." *Indian Linguistics* 42: 82–135.

———. 1982a. "Space Grammar, Analysability, and the English Passive." *Language* 58: 22–80.

———. 1982b. "Remarks on English Aspect." In Paul J. Hopper, ed., *Tense-Aspect: Between Semantics & Pragmatics*, 265–304. Amsterdam: John Benjamins.

———. 1984. "Active Zones." *Proceedings of the Annual Meeting of the Berkeley Linguistics Society* 10: 172–88.

———. 1985. "Observations and Speculations on Subjectivity." In John Haiman, ed., *Iconicity in Syntax*, 109–50. Amsterdam: John Benjamins.

Langdon, Margaret. 1971. "Sound Symbolism in Yuman Languages." In Jesse Sawyer, ed., *Studies in American Indian Languages*, 149–73. Berkeley: University of California Press. University of California Publications in Linguistics 65.

Laszlo, Ervin. 1972. *The Systems View of the World*. New York: George Braziller.

Lees, Robert B. 1960. *The Grammar of English Nominalizations*. Bloomington: Indiana University Research Center in Anthropology, Folklore, and Linguistics, Publication 12. *International Journal of American Linguistics*: 26(3), Part II.

Lehmann, W. P. 1973. "A Structural Principle of Language and Its Implications." *Language* 49: 47–66.

Liberman, Mark, and Alan Prince. 1977. "On Stress and Linguistic Rhythm." *Linguistic Inquiry* 8: 249–336.

Lightfoot, David. 1980. "Trace Theory and Explanation." In Edith A. Moravcsik and Jessica R. Wirth, eds., *Syntax and Semantics. Volume 13: Current Approaches to Syntax*, 137–66. New York: Academic Press.

Lindner, Susan. 1981. *A Lexico-Semantic Analysis of English Verb-Particle Constructions with UP and OUT*. Ph.D. Dissertation. San Diego: University of California.

———. 1982. "What Goes Up Doesn't Necessarily Come Down: The Ins and Outs of Opposites." *Proceedings of the Annual Meeting of the Chicago Linguistic Society* 18: 305–23.

Lyons, John. 1968. *Introduction to Theoretical Linguistics*. Cambridge, Eng.: Cambridge University Press.

———. 1977. *Semantics*. Cambridge, Eng.: Cambridge University Press.

McCarthy, John J. 1981. "A Prosodic Theory of Nonconcatenative Morphology." *Linguistic Inquiry* 12: 373–418.

McCawley, James D. 1968. "Concerning the Base Component of a Transformational Grammar." *Foundations of Language* 4: 243–69.

———. 1980. "An Un-Syntax." In Edith A. Moravcsik and Jessica R. Wirth, eds., *Syntax and Semantics. Volume 13: Current Approaches to Syntax*, 167–93. New York: Academic Press.

McNeill, David. 1981. "Action, Thought, and Language." *Cognition* 10: 201–8.

McNeill, David, and Elena Levy. 1982. "Conceptual Representations in Language Activity and Gesture." In R. J. Jarvella and W. Klein, eds., *Speech, Place, and Action*, 271–95. New York: Wiley.

Makkai, Valerie Becker. 1969. "On the Correlation of Morphemes and Lexemes." *Proceedings of the Annual Meeting of the Chicago Linguistic Society* 5: 159–66.

Marantz, Alec. 1982. "Re Reduplication." *Linguistic Inquiry* 13: 435–82.

Marcel, Anthony J. 1983. "Conscious and Unconscious Perception: An Approach to the Relations Between Phenomenal Experience and Perceptual Processes." *Cognitive Psychology* 15: 238–300.

Matthews, P. H. 1981. *Syntax*. Cambridge, Eng.: Cambridge University Press.

Miller, George A., and Philip N. Johnson-Laird. 1976. *Language and Perception*. Cambridge, Mass.: Belknap/Harvard.

Moore, Terence, and Christine Carling. 1982. *Language Understanding: Towards a Post-Chomskyan Linguistics*. New York: St. Martin's Press.

Moravcsik, Edith A., and Jessica R. Wirth, eds. 1980. *Syntax and Semantics. Volume 13: Current Approaches to Syntax*. New York: Academic Press.

Morreall, John. 1979. "Possible Words." *Linguistic Inquiry* 10: 725–27.

Mourelatos, Alexander P. D. 1981. "Events, Processes, and States." In Philip J. Tedeschi and Annie Zaenen, eds., *Syntax and Semantics. Volume 14: Tense and Aspect*, 191–212. New York: Academic Press.

Newmeyer, Frederick J. 1983. *Grammatical Theory: Its Limits and Possibilities*. Chicago: University of Chicago Press.

Norman, Donald A. 1976. *Memory and Attention*. Second Edition. New York: Wiley.

Norris, Evan. 1980. "Organization of Instrumental Prefixes in Eastern Mono." *Journal of California and Great Basin Anthropology, Papers in Linguistics* 2: 25–39.

Oehrle, Richard T. 1977. Review of Georgia M. Green, *Semantics and Syntactic Regularity. Language* 53: 198–208.

Ortony, Andrew, ed. 1979. *Metaphor and Thought*. Cambridge, Eng.: Cambridge University Press.

Palmer, F. R. 1976. *Semantics*. Cambridge, Eng.: Cambridge University Press.

Partee, Barbara. 1973. "The Syntax and Semantics of Quotation." In Stephen R.

Anderson and Paul Kiparsky, eds., *A Festschrift for Morris Halle*, 410–18. New York: Holt.

———. 1975. "Montague Grammar and Transformational Grammar." *Linguistic Inquiry* 6: 203–300.

Perlmutter, David M. 1970. "The Two Verbs *Begin*." In Roderick A. Jacobs and Peter S. Rosenbaum, eds., *Readings in English Transformational Grammar*, 107–19. Waltham, Mass.: Ginn.

———. 1971. *Deep and Surface Structure Constraints in Syntax*. New York: Holt.

———. 1978. "Impersonal Passives and the Unaccusative Hypothesis." *Proceedings of the Annual Meeting of the Berkeley Linguistics Society* 4: 157–89.

———. 1980. "Relational Grammar." In Edith A. Moravcsik and Jessica R. Wirth, eds., *Syntax and Semantics. Volume 13: Current Approaches to Syntax*, 195–229. New York: Academic Press.

Peters, Stanley, ed. 1972. *Goals of Linguistic Theory*. Englewood Cliffs, N.J.: Prentice-Hall.

Postal, Paul M. 1969. "Anaphoric Islands." *Proceedings of the Annual Meeting of the Chicago Linguistic Society* 5: 205–39.

———. 1972. "The Best Theory." In Stanley Peters, ed., *Goals of Linguistic Theory*, 131–70. Englewood Cliffs, N.J.: Prentice-Hall.

———. 1974. *On Raising*. Cambridge, Mass.: MIT Press.

Prince, Alan. 1980. "A Metrical Theory for Estonian Quantity." *Linguistic Inquiry* 11: 511–62.

———. 1983. "Relating to the Grid." *Linguistic Inquiry* 14: 19–100.

Reddy, Michael J. 1979. "The Conduit Metaphor—A Case of Frame Conflict in Our Language about Language." In Andrew Ortony, ed., *Metaphor and Thought*, 284–324. Cambridge, Eng.: Cambridge University Press.

Rhodes, Richard A., and John M. Lawler. 1981. "Athematic Metaphors." *Proceedings of the Annual Meeting of the Chicago Linguistic Society* 17: 318–42.

Robinson, Jane J. 1970. "Dependency Structures and Transformational Rules." *Language* 46: 259–85.

Rosch, Eleanor. 1973. "On the Internal Structure of Perceptual and Semantic Categories." In Timothy E. Moore, ed., *Cognitive Development and the Acquisition of Language*, 111–44. New York: Academic Press.

———. 1975. "Cognitive Representations of Semantic Categories." *Journal of Experimental Psychology: General* 104: 192–233.

———. 1977. "Human Categorization." In Neil Warren, ed., *Studies in Crosscultural Psychology. Volume 1*, 1–49. London: Academic Press.

———. 1978. "Principles of Categorization." In Eleanor Rosch and Barbara B. Lloyd, eds., *Cognition and Categorization*, 27–47. Hillsdale, N.J.: Erlbaum.

Ross, John Robert. 1973. "The Penthouse Principle and the Order of Constituents." In Claudia Corum, T. Cedrick Smith-Stark, and Ann Weiser, eds., *You Take the High Node and I'll Take the Low Node*, 397–422. Chicago: Chicago Linguistic Society.

Rumelhart, David E. 1979. "Some Problems with the Notion of Literal Meaning." In Andrew Ortony, ed., *Metaphor and Thought*, 78–90. Cambridge, Eng.: Cambridge University Press.

Sadock, Jerrold M. 1980. "Noun Incorporation in Greenlandic: A Case of Syntactic Word Formation." *Language* 56: 300–319.

Samuels, M. L. 1972. *Linguistic Evolution*. Cambridge, Eng.: Cambridge University Press. Cambridge Studies in Linguistics 5.

Sanders, Gerald A. 1974a. "The Simplex-Feature Analysis." *Glossa* 8: 141–92.

―――. 1974b. "Precedence Relations in Language." *Foundations of Language* 11: 361–400.

Sapir, Edward. 1925. "Sound Patterns in Language." *Language* 1: 37–51. Reprinted in David G. Mandelbaum, ed., *Selected Writings of Edward Sapir in Language, Culture and Personality*, 33–45. Berkeley: University of California Press, 1963.

Saussure, Ferdinand de. 1916. *Cours de linguistique générale*. Paris: Payot.

Seiler, Hansjakob. 1977. *Cahuilla Grammar*. Banning, Calif.: Malki Museum Press.

Selkirk, Elisabeth O. 1980. "The Role of Prosodic Categories in English Word Stress." *Linguistic Inquiry* 11: 563–605.

Shepard, Roger N. 1978. "The Mental Image." *American Psychologist* 33: 125–37.

Smith, Carlota S. 1983. "A Theory of Aspectual Choice." *Language* 59: 479–501.

Smith, N. V. 1981. "Consistency, Markedness and Language Change: On the Notion 'Consistent Language'." *Journal of Linguistics* 17: 39–54.

Soames, Scott, and David M. Perlmutter. 1979. *Syntactic Argumentation and the Structure of English*. Berkeley: University of California Press.

Stanley, Richard. 1967. "Redundancy Rules in Phonology." *Language* 43: 393–436.

Steele, Susan M., et al. 1981. *An Encyclopedia of AUX: A Study of Cross-linguistic Equivalence*. Cambridge, Mass.: MIT Press.

Stemberger, Joseph Paul. 1981. "Lexical Entries: Evidence from Speech Errors." *Linguistic Notes from La Jolla* 8: 73–88.

Stern, Gustaf. 1931. *Meaning and Change of Meaning*. Göteborg: Elanders Boktryckeri Aktiebolag. Reprinted: Bloomington, Indiana University Press, 1965.

Talmy, Leonard. 1975. "Semantics and Syntax of Motion." In John Kimball, ed., *Syntax and Semantics. Volume 4*, 181–238. New York: Academic Press.

―――. 1977. "Rubber-Sheet Cognition in Language." *Proceedings of the Annual Meeting of the Chicago Linguistic Society* 13: 612–28.

―――. 1978. "Figure and Ground in Complex Sentences." In Joseph H. Greenberg, ed., *Universals of Human Language. Volume 4: Syntax*, 625–49. Stanford, Calif.: Stanford University Press.

―――. 1983. "How Language Structures Space." In Herbert Pick and Linda Acredolo, eds., *Spatial Orientation: Theory, Research, and Application*, 225–82. New York: Plenum Press.

Tesnière, Lucien. 1959. *Éléments de syntaxe structurale*. Paris: Klincksieck.

Tuggy, David. 1980. "¡Ethical Dative and Possessor Omission Sí, Possessor Ascension No!" *Work Papers of the Summer Institute of Linguistics, University of North Dakota* 24: 97–141.

―――. 1981. *The Transitivity-Related Morphology of Tetelcingo Nahuatl: An Exploration in Space Grammar*. Ph.D. Dissertation. San Diego: University of California.

Twaddell, W. Freeman. 1935. *On Defining the Phoneme. Language* Monograph No. 16. Reprinted in Martin Joos, ed., *Readings in Linguistics*. Third Edition, 55–79. New York: American Council of Learned Societies, 1963.

Vandeloise, Claude. 1984. *Description of Space in French*. Ph.D. Dissertation. San Diego: University of California.

van Oosten, Jeanne. 1977. "Subjects and Agenthood in English." *Proceedings of the Annual Meeting of the Chicago Linguistic Society* 13: 459–71.

Vendler, Zeno. 1967. *Linguistics in Philosophy*. Ithaca, N.Y.: Cornell University Press.

Wierzbicka, Anna. 1972. *Semantic Primitives*. Frankfurt: Athenaum Verlag.

————. 1975. "Why 'Kill' Does Not Mean 'Cause to Die': The Semantics of Action Sentences." *Foundations of Language* 13: 491–528.

————. 1985. "Oats and Wheat: The Fallacy of Arbitrariness." In John Haiman, ed., *Iconicity in Syntax*, 311–42. Amsterdam: John Benjamins.

Witkowski, Stanley R., and Cecil H. Brown. 1983. "Marking-Reversals and Cultural Importance." *Language* 59: 569–82.

Wittgenstein, Ludwig. 1953. *Philosophical Investigations*. New York: Macmillan.

Index

Library of Congress Cataloging-in-Publication Data

Langacker, Ronald W.
  Foundations of cognitive grammar.

  Bibliography: v. 1, p.
  Includes index.
  Contents: v. 1. Theoretical prerequisites.
  1. Cognitive grammar.   I. Title.
P165.L36   1987   415   84-51300
ISBN 0-8047-1261-1 (v. 1: alk. paper)